LINCOLN'S DARKEST YEAR

BOOKS BY WILLIAM MARVEL

LINCOLN'S
DARKEST YEAR

❧

The War in 1862

William Marvel

Houghton Mifflin Company
BOSTON • NEW YORK
2008

www.houghtonmifflinbooks.com

Library of Congress Cataloging-in-Publication Data
Marvel, William.
Lincoln's darkest year : the war in 1862 / William Marvel.
p. cm.
Includes bibliographical references and index.
ISBN 978-0-618-85869-9
1. United States — History — Civil War, 1861–1865 — Campaigns. 2. Lincoln, Abraham, 1809–1865—Military leadership. 3. United States — Politics and government — 1861–
1865 — Decision making. I. Title.
E471.M368 2008
973.7 — dc22   2007038416

Book design by Melissa Lotfy

Maps by Catherine Schneider

PRINTED IN THE UNITED STATES OF AMERICA

MP 10 9 8 7 6 5 4 3 2 1

For Ellen,
fortissimo e appassionato

Contents

List of Illustrations and Maps

All illustrations are courtesy of the Library of Congress.

FOLLOWING PAGE 104

Secretary of War Edwin M. Stanton greeting his generals
Searching for the wounded after Fort Donelson
Major General Don Carlos Buell
Major General Nathaniel P. Banks
Union remains on the battlefield of Gaines's Mill
Field hospital at Savage's Station
The retreat from Savage's Station
Major General John Pope
Major General Henry W. Halleck
Lincoln and his cabinet
Old Capitol Prison
Union rally in Washington, August 6, 1862
Longstreet surprising Pope at Second Bull Run
Refugees from Sioux uprising in Minnesota
General Braxton Bragg
Lieutenant General Edmund Kirby Smith

FOLLOWING PAGE 218

Candidates for the Exempt Brigade
Scene, Fifth Avenue
Union troops marching through Middletown, Maryland
Sharpsburg's main street in 1862
Confederate dead in Bloody Lane

Burnside's Bridge
Dead white horse near the edge of the East Woods
Lincoln visiting McClellan in the field
Union troops "monitoring" the election in Baltimore
McClellan's farewell to the army
Ambrose Burnside with his generals
Union troops amid looted property in Fredericksburg
Major General Joseph Hooker
Humphreys's attack on Marye's Heights
Cavalry escorting deserters back to camp
Native Guards on duty in Louisiana

MAPS

All maps by Catherine Schneider

Preface

This is the common story of a war growing completely out of hand and overwhelming the people who started it. As always, opposing factions argued for either peace or continued prosecution, with one group judging the price too great for any potential results and the other reluctant to waste the investment already made. Tragically, victory and peace might have satisfied both parties fairly early, but those opportunities were lost through a closely connected series of blunders, some of which can be traced back to the conscious decisions of Abraham Lincoln. Those executive decisions appear to have been influenced by pressure from Radical Republicans, and in some cases the unfortunate choices contradicted Lincoln's own instincts.

The second half of 1861 had seemed laden with Confederate victories over the Union invaders, but 1862 began with a nearly unbroken string of Union triumphs. Most confrontations in the western theater that winter and spring ended in abject Southern defeat, and occasionally in complete surrender. By the end of April, New Mexico had been rid of Southern intruders; New Orleans had fallen; the Southern legions that had defended Kentucky and Tennessee had been driven into the tier of Gulf States, or conducted north as prisoners. The Atlantic coast bristled with Union bases. In May, Federals swarmed into Baton Rouge — the second Confederate state capital captured within two months — and in northern Mississippi a massive Union army closed in on its main opponent, under General Pierre G. T. Beauregard. In Virginia, despite much-criticized delay, George McClellan's Army of the Potomac lay at Richmond's eastern approaches with a hundred thousand Union soldiers, and forty thousand more stood at Fredericksburg, ready to swoop down on Richmond from the north and west. The Confederate capital could muster barely half as many defenders as the combined Yankee host, and things looked very gloomy for the new nation of slave states.

Then, in a matter of days, it all fell apart. Beginning on May 23, Stonewall Jackson descended on outnumbered Union defenders in the Shenandoah Valley and sent them flying to the far side of the Potomac River. Abraham Lincoln bore primary responsibility for depleting his Valley divisions and appointing incompetent politicians to command them, and at their flight he fell into a panic, scattering his Fredericksburg troops into the Valley in a needless effort to repel Jackson — and in a vain attempt to capture him. That emasculated the overpowering dual movement against Richmond, where on May 31 Confederates pounced on an isolated wing of the Army of the Potomac and delivered an embarrassing, if uncoordinated, blow. Beauregard slipped his army out of beleaguered Corinth, Mississippi, causing weeks of apprehension that he had reinforced Richmond, and that apprehension posed a serious liability for Union arms at the end of June. Believing himself vastly outnumbered by the Confederates who assailed him so ferociously, McClellan retreated from Richmond's door in a weeklong running fight that left his grand army gasping on the banks of the James River, a good twenty-five miles downstream from the chambers of the Confederate Congress.

In forty days the Union juggernaut appeared to have been halted. The battlefield reverses had all come in Virginia, which carried limited strategic importance in the quest to subdue the South, but the Virginia theater encompassed political symbols that far outweighed its military significance. The embattled hundred miles between Washington and Richmond therefore attracted a disproportionate measure of public attention, and that obsession with events in Virginia cost the Union cause dearly in 1862. The repulse of McClellan's promising advance initiated a wave of dejection among the civilian population. The rise of the audacious John Pope, and his bloody disasters at the head of the Army of Virginia that August, had the same depressing effect on Union soldiers. In conjunction with the administration's decision to withdraw McClellan from the James and give most of his army to Pope, Pope's failures also brought the war back to the outskirts of Washington, and then into the loyal states.

The restoration of McClellan to field command in September put much heart back in the army. McClellan brought a more deliberate and methodical approach to warfare, which naturally appealed to the men who would have to do the fighting, but McClellan's soldiers may have admired him equally for his conservative politics: he advocated reunion uncontaminated by any abolitionist agenda, and that seemed to reflect the opinion of most Union troops in the summer of 1862. His success in repelling the Confederates from Maryland does not, however, seem to have restored Northern confidence so abruptly or so completely as retrospective accounts might suggest — as much as it may have dismayed Southern civilians. Their momentary sense of relief aside, many Northern observers gauged the Southern incursions into Maryland and Kentucky that September less as failed invasions than as successful raids that might be repeated any time. It was primarily those who had striven to see the administration adopt a higher ideological purpose than national unity whose spirits brightened in the wake of Antietam, and their optimism arose more from Lincoln's decree on emancipation. Those who awaited improvement in the military situation remained doubtful, and the complication of emancipation infuriated those Unionists who had feared all along that abolitionists were scheming to preempt their cause.

For all the presumed support the president's war enjoyed, recruiters found the Northern population increasingly unwilling to answer federal appeals for troops by the summer of 1862. Partial advance payments on the federal bounty and some local financial inducements attracted a skimming of volunteers, but it was not until bounties began to grow generous that another wave of citizens responded, reflecting an economic condition slightly higher, on average, than those who had previously enlisted. The August militia call introduced the threat of compulsory service, driving communities nationwide to shameless demonstrations disguised as patriotic rallies, where those who wished to avoid the army essentially raised funds for mercenaries to take their places. Only when the money proved sufficiently inviting did enough men start coming forward, but more devastating defeats and the conclusion of the militia draft combined with unpopular political policies like emancipation and arbitrary arrests to dry up that last freshet of volunteers by the end of the year.

Thereafter, Union armies could be replenished by nothing short of general conscription and the astronomical bounties that more comprehensive conscription would eventually wring from a reluctant population. If it were considered a reflection of popular endorsement, recruiting hinted by the beginning of 1863 that the public had lost interest in a war of reunion, and perhaps especially in a war of abolition. Desertion rates suggested similar dissatisfaction within the army.

Letters, diaries, and newspapers from the period have provided most of the popular opinions portrayed in this work. The appearance of newly discovered material in manuscript repositories continues to fuel a renaissance in revisionist history as the words of the people actually living in the period collectively modify or challenge the conclusions of generations of historians who were forced to rely primarily on memoirs and published documents. One of the most glaring differences between contemporary observations and postwar accounts is the degree to which nationalistic or altruistic idealism arises as a factor allegedly impelling Northern volunteers into service. Period manuscripts indicate that at most levels, finances played a significant or even paramount role in the decision to enlist, while memoirs tend to emphasize the motivation of patriotic fervor. Patriotic impulses certainly may have existed alongside more mercenary incentives, but the men who filled the Union army in 1861 and early 1862 consisted in large part of the unemployed, underemployed, or adventurously independent. After recruiting resumed in May of 1862 those populations had been sorely depleted, and most volunteers hesitated until bounties had risen to levels that would be considered exorbitant if translated into modern dollars. Those who would assert that nationalistic or antislavery idealism served as the primary motives for Union soldiers must explain how those sentiments would have infected the poorest classes of society with such disproportionate virulence, compared to the more comfortable.

The presentation of contrary interpretations requires much attention to the contradictory evidence itself, in order to drive the new information home with enough force to crack the armor of established opinion. The volume of offered testimony may therefore occasionally create the impression that no Union soldiers favored emancipation, that none enlisted from pure love of country, and that after a time no one in or out of the army wanted to continue the fight. That was not the case, of course, but the prevalence of those patriotic and altruistic motives may have been overestimated, and perhaps greatly so.

This remains primarily an examination of the Civil War from the Northern perspective, focusing on the Union armies, attitudes and conditions in the North, and Lincoln administration policies. Confederates necessarily surface on campaign and on the battlefield, where they appear primarily through Northern eyes. As in my preceding book, *Mr. Lincoln Goes to War*, comparisons between the U.S. and Confederate presidents, or governments, will be limited to the common context of their circumstances.

Mr. Lincoln does endure a little additional criticism in this volume. The accolades heaped on him as a commander in chief, for instance, usually excuse or rationalize his direct interference in the details of military operations in the spring of 1862, which may have cost the country another three years of war and several hundred thousand lives. The deployment of troops to satisfy the prestige of his political appointees, rather than to address tactical needs, opened the way for a raid that frightened him into sacrificing an unprecedented opportunity to overwhelm Richmond. Showing less nerve than his opposite number in Richmond, Lin-

coln withdrew his country's largest army from the threshold of the enemy's chief city, allowing the foe to instead threaten his own capital — after
first humiliating another entire Union army and demoralizing the Northern public.

As justifiable as it may have been from an administrative perspective,
the decision to remove McClellan also may have caused more harm than
good. The change spawned a debilitating mistrust and antagonism between generals, and while Lincoln certainly bore no direct blame for that,
the politically motivated timing of the order left the army in a half-fin-
ished campaign. That ran counter to the famous maxim against changing
horses in midstream, and the replacement of the cautious McClellan by
the aggressive Burnside set the stage for a disaster more costly than any
that probably would have ensued had McClellan remained in command.
Removing generals fell much more obviously within the prerogative of
the civilian commander in chief than shuffling individual divisions did,
but in this case it initiated another period of defeat and despondency that
would not abate significantly for two-thirds of a year.

Soldiers who otherwise admired Lincoln astutely observed that there
seemed to be a direct correlation between his military and political failures, on the one hand, and his efforts to placate Radical Republicans on
the other. The assignment and reinforcement of John C. Frémont, the
choice of Pope, the mistrust in (and the dismissal of) McClellan, as well
as the withdrawal of McClellan's army from the Peninsula, all reflected
the consideration of radical opinion. So, too, did Lincoln's implementa-
tion of confiscation and his proclamation on slavery — which last decision may have done nearly as much damage to morale within the Union
army as it did to the faltering hope of conciliation.

As the military outlook worsened and the cost in men and money rose,
enthusiasm for coercive reunion diminished and dissatisfaction spread.
The administration addressed the rising outcry with repression, just as
it had in 1861, shutting down newspaper offices and imprisoning critical editors. This time the secretary of war issued his own proclamation,
broadly expanding his authority to curb dissent: anticipating widespread
outrage over even the short-term, state-level conscription of citizens for a
war that had outgrown anyone's expectations, Edwin Stanton personally
declared it a crime to "discourage enlistments." Since almost any comment against Lincoln or his war could be construed as dissuading men
from volunteering, the decree virtually criminalized the expression of political disagreement, and it was largely enforced in that spirit, much to
the detriment of the democratic process. With no legislative legitimacy
beyond vague claims to wartime powers, Stanton invoked that unconstitutional authority in August. Campaigning for the midterm elections had

just begun, and Lincoln's marshals arrested even congressional candidates who rebuked presidential policy too vigorously, effectively muzzling legitimate and growing opposition. The great struggle that was supposedly initiated to preserve government by the people would, it seemed, be waged all the more ruthlessly once it began to look as though too many of the people were turning against it.

PART I

A PROCESSION WINDING AROUND ME

1

Over Them the Swallows Skim

≈⊱ THE MERCURY STOOD at twenty degrees when daylight woke Washington City on the morning of February 5, 1862. A fringe of snow still decorated the perimeters of buildings and byways, but for the first time in many days a brilliant sun climbed over the unfinished dome of the United States Capitol. Under rising temperatures and endless caravans of army wagons, the streets quickly softened from frozen ruts into rivers of mud, and ambitious boys stood by to maintain the foot crossings in the hope of copper tokens tossed by grateful pedestrians.[1]

Inside the Capitol, the nation's leaders needed no sunlight to warm them to their work. That morning, in the upper house, forty-seven U.S. Senators impatiently discussed a few momentous issues of taxation and expenditure before resuming debate on a resolution to expel one of their own members. The topic had dominated Senate business for most of the previous fortnight, and the senior senator from New Hampshire feared that it would consume the entire session, yet still his colleagues rose one by one to belabor points that they or others had already hammered home.[2]

For nearly seventeen years had Jesse Bright occupied a desk on the Democratic side of the aisle. He had known and admired Jefferson Davis of Mississippi, and the previous winter Bright had obliged one of his legal clients with a letter of introduction to Davis in his capacity as President of the Confederate States of America. Thomas B. Lincoln wished to market an unspecified improvement in firearms, and Judge Bright gave him a letter similar to others he had supplied Lincoln in recommendation to U.S. military officials. The letter bore a date of March 1, 1861, six weeks before any hostilities had erupted between North and South, when manufacturers and entrepreneurs across the North were seeking an audience with either Davis or his secretary of war. Even the Republican-dominated Senate Judiciary Committee found nothing in the letter that could warrant expulsion, and recommended defeat of the resolution, but Bright's enemies refused to let mere evidentiary deficiency stand in the way of partisan vengeance. They clung to their accusation of retroactive treason, corroborating it with the damning detail that Bright had actually addressed Davis as "President of the Confederation of States."[3]

On January 10 the chamber had expelled both of Missouri's senators for abandoning their seats to join their state legislature in its struggle against federal authority. There had been little question on that matter: each was removed by a unanimous vote that Bright himself supported. Bright hailed from Indiana, however, and his state remained loyal to the Union. So did Bright, except that he lacked enthusiasm for Abraham Lincoln's war against the South, and there lay the rub.[4]

Bright regarded compromise as the only possible means of restoring the Union, and he supposed that the attempt to conquer the Southern states by military force had only made permanent division more certain. Most Northerners in and out of office had responded to the attack on Fort Sumter with nonpartisan enthusiasm. A vocal minority of Democrats had warned that the war to restore the Union would turn into an abolition crusade, and others had despaired of ever winning the South back by the sword, but they had railed against a tidal wave of intolerant nationalistic fervor. That fervor had already allowed the government to squelch the most effective and rabid newspaper criticism by stopping distribution, seizing equipment, and arresting publishers. Unionist mobs had collaborated in that suppression of free speech during the summer of 1861, destroying the offices of antiwar journals and attacking the editors. Languishing in the bowels of a coastal fort through the winter, Francis Scott Key's own grandson understood how dangerous it had become to utter an unpopular opinion in the Land of the Free.[5]

Now, the party that dominated the United States Senate intended to formalize the concept that meaningful dissent amounted to treason. Resignations and military service had reduced attendance in the Senate chamber from sixty-eight to forty-seven, of whom thirty-four either acknowledged or demonstrated allegiance to the Republican Party, and that should have yielded the two-thirds majority necessary to expel any of the remaining Democrats. Undeterred, therefore, by the discouraging Judiciary Committee report, on January 20 Minnesota Republican Morton Wilkinson produced another letter in which Senator Bright had expressed his opposition to the government's coercive policies. The next day the haughty Charles Sumner, of Massachusetts, remarked that Bright and his fellow Democrats had steadfastly opposed every measure that Sumner had supported in his ten years as a senator. For a moment he stopped there, as though that alone offered sufficient grounds to remove a fellow member, but then he concluded the day's discussion by adding that Bright's former associates were "now all of them engaged in open rebellion." With those words Sumner smeared all dissenting Democrats with the taint of treason, and revealed the ulterior motive behind the resolution.[6]

Through the rest of that week and into the next, Republicans parsed every clause of Bright's letters, insinuating that he had deliberately colluded with men who were plotting to subdue Fort Sumter and denouncing his willingness to acknowledge Jefferson Davis as the president of a competing republic. Timothy Howe, a Republican freshman from Wisconsin, marked Bright as disloyal because "he is not prepared by his legislative action to maintain and uphold this Constitution" — in other words, because he could not be depended upon to vote with the Republican majority on war measures. Pennsylvanian David Wilmot seemed to condemn Bright for his friendship with Davis, the blackest of traitors, and he alleged that similarly diabolical associations had polluted "many gentlemen of the late Democratic party" — as though that organization no longer existed.[7]

If the Democratic Party had not ceased to exist, it had certainly been emasculated. Andrew Johnson of Tennessee exemplified that shift, offering the Senate's foremost example of those War Democrats who had aligned themselves with the Republicans in an overwhelming new pro-Union coalition. Johnson was the only senator who refused to resign when his state seceded, and he reflected the fierce sentiments of a region that knew no neutrality. Taking his cue from Sumner and Wilmot, Johnson enumerated the resignations and expulsions of various senators who had stood for peace, each of whom had since gone South. The implication emerged clearly in the *Congressional Globe,* which editors across the nation would quote: only a traitor would advocate peace.[8]

Bright protested that he had heard so many different accusations since disposing of the original one that he hardly knew what to defend himself against. At one point he tried to explain the innocence of the Davis letter by remarking that he would do the same thing again, under identical circumstances. Quickly recognizing how easily his enemies could twist that statement, he asked the recorder for the *Congressional Globe* to delete it, but Republicans still jumped on it as evidence that he would correspond with the enemy president during active hostilities.[9]

Few stood by him. Most of those who did shared his views, and might find themselves the next targets. The senators from the little slave state of

Delaware, both Democrats, called for their fellow members to come to their senses.

"When a people are mad," warned Willard Saulsbury, "their representatives are seldom wise." He calculated that a third of the Senate's surviving membership also believed — with Bright, and with most of the officers in the army — that war was neither a desirable nor an effective solution to the nation's political difficulties. Would the Senate also vote to expel those other dissenting members? In reminding the chamber of the confused political atmosphere in March of 1861, California's Milton Latham remarked that Bright was no more guilty of treason for writing to Davis than postal officials of the Lincoln administration were for delivering such letters to Confederate recipients, even after the shooting began.[10]

Each senator had made up his mind by that sunny Wednesday of February 5. Three Northern Republicans and an old-line Whig sent by loyal Virginia's rump legislature defended Bright, refusing to join the blatantly partisan ploy. Each of the four felt compelled to read last-minute statements justifying themselves to their constituents. Pennsylvania's Edgar Cowan described himself as "utterly astounded" that so many senators stood ready to pervert the judicial process. John Ten Eyck of New Jersey alluded to friends who had warned him that a vote against expulsion would dig his political grave, and he asked that his epitaph read: "He dared to do what he thought was right." That raised cheers and applause in one section of the gallery, but Vice President Hannibal Hamlin slammed his gavel down and demanded order. Those four apostates joined ten Democrats, mostly from border states and the West Coast, in voting against Bright's removal. Andrew Johnson and one other War Democrat sided with the other thirty Republicans, though, and their two votes tipped the scales. The day's debate ended with one of the most senior members of the U.S. Senate stripped of his office by a bare two-thirds majority — ostensibly because he had betrayed his country, but in reality because he favored peace and lacked the requisite animosity for slavery. This time another quadrant of the gallery erupted in applause, and the gavel sounded again. An Iowa senator rose to introduce a currency bill, but his colleagues refused to hear him; they had accomplished all the work they intended to do that day, and the senators adjourned to the hotels to discuss the effects of their decision.[11]

Some of them wished to end their day early in order to prepare for a grand party that had occupied Mary Lincoln's attention for some weeks. The Lincolns had hosted a few rather plain dinners and public receptions, but Mrs. Lincoln evidently wanted something more memorable as her own inauguration ceremony. The First Lady, whom White House employees had taken to calling the "American Queen," laid out an elaborate feast.

She received her guests in the East Room, where the bodies of two colonels had lain in state within the previous nine months — both of them friends of the president, killed during invasions of Confederate Virginia. Scores of the five hundred invited guests had declined their invitations, at least some of them because they thought it insensitive to enjoy lavish parties during such a war, but hundreds of the most powerful people in the country attended.[12]

The president's wife spared little extravagance, as her own attire illustrated. She wore a white gown cut indiscreetly low in the front, trailing a fathom or two of silk behind her, with so ornate a floral headdress that one unfriendly senator described her as wearing a flowerpot on her head. Solons mingled with generals, admirals, Supreme Court justices, and foreign consuls, at least some of whom still considered President Lincoln a vulgar provincial lacking in either sincerity or statesmanlike qualities. The doorman admitted no one without a personal invitation. His own invitation must have offered some comfort to Brigadier General Charles P. Stone, who had run afoul of some of Washington's more powerful and ruthless politicians. Stone had figured prominently in the city's security since the first days of secession, but that earned him no gratitude among the radicals who intended to ruin him, and he spent the early part of the levee rubbing elbows with the high and mighty of his country for the last time in his life.[13]

John Charles Frémont, the Pathfinder of Western renown, attended the party with his ambitious wife, Jessie. Frémont had been removed from command of Union forces in Missouri three months before, and he lingered in the capital while awaiting a new assignment. He wore a full dress uniform, with the Prussian Cross of Merit dangling from his neck; Jessie had rifled the trunk of a secessionist Missouri cousin to come up with a stunning dress in white and violet tulle. The couple tried to take their leave in the shank of the evening, but Senator Sumner and the president himself hurried out to call them back: Sumner took Mrs. Frémont by the arm, and the president escorted Frémont back into the East Room. It seemed that Frémont had never met Major General George B. McClellan, and McClellan wished to make his acquaintance. Jessie took McClellan's hand in cool courtesy, deeming him the man responsible for her husband's current inactivity.[14]

General McClellan, the thirty-five-year-old commander of the vast Army of the Potomac that sprawled around Washington and northern Virginia, had also assumed control of the rest of the country's armies at the beginning of November, just as Frémont had been relieved in Missouri. The two generals held conflicting political viewpoints: Frémont had been the Republican Party's first candidate for president, back in

1856, and McClellan would carry the standard of the Democratic Party in 1864. Frémont had already embarrassed the administration with a premature proclamation emancipating the slaves of alleged Missouri Confederates, while McClellan had already perturbed the more radical Republicans by his reluctance to interfere with slavery at all.

Those radicals had declared war on conservative generals like McClellan, just as they had combined against Senator Bright. Like most of the soldiers in the army that winter, McClellan had donned a uniform solely to defeat secession, rather than to free slaves, but the radicals could fathom no loyalty that resisted abolition. They had descended with full fury upon General Stone, who had been unfortunate enough to lose a battle and then injudicious enough to observe the federal laws governing the return of fugitive slaves to their masters. At McClellan's headquarters there lay a War Department order for him to arrest General Stone on vague imputations of treason, with no more evidence than hearsay and malicious insinuation. McClellan still hesitated to carry out the order even as he shook Frémont's hand, for he fully understood that Stone had been targeted in place of himself, and perhaps as a means of marking the commanding general for future disposal.[15]

The East Room doubtless hummed with the stunning news of Senator Bright's removal, and with speculation on its implications for others who did not share the radical view of slavery and the war. The revelry and ruminations continued into the wee hours of the morning, and when the last of the guests had gone home some of the dining room staff fell into combat over the remaining refreshments, leaving the rest of the kitchen help stepping over broken bottles and battered skulls.[16]

The success of the cabal against Bright seemed to encourage the radicals to further vigor against Stone, whose persecution began almost the moment Mrs. Lincoln's party ended. A few hours after the White House kitchen fracas, General McClellan's spy chief, Allan Pinkerton, submitted a report of his interview with a refugee from Leesburg, Virginia, who maintained that General Stone was well respected among the Confederate officers in that vicinity. The refugee's babble provided no substantive evidence that Stone harbored any disloyalty to his cause or his country, but it gave an opportunistic new chief of the War Department all he needed to sacrifice one of his generals: when McClellan delivered the report to Secretary of War Edwin M. Stanton a couple of days later, Stanton told him to have Stone cast immediately into Fort Lafayette, where the government confined avowed and suspected secessionists.[17]

Stanton had just taken over the department from Simon Cameron, a machine politician who combined a lack of competence with a tolerance for impropriety. Despite lifelong adherence to the Democratic Party (he had served as attorney general to the hated James Buchanan), Stanton had won Senate confirmation a few weeks before with the full support of the radicals, whom he had met in private to convince them of his conversion.[18]

The Senate radicals were led by the likes of Ben Wade, of Ohio, and Zachariah Chandler, of Michigan, both of whom sat on the newly formed Joint Committee on the Conduct of the War. Wade struck some colleagues as more interested in winning the presidency than the war, and he chaired the committee, which scrutinized military operations from a blatantly partisan perspective reflecting its domination by Radical Republicans. These men had come to loathe the Democrat McClellan: Wade and Chandler had both been told (and now seemed to believe) that McClellan and his coterie held strong proslavery sentiments, and that McClellan refrained from waging aggressive war lest it interfere with that institution.[19]

On the evening of his first official day in office, Stanton invited the entire joint committee to meet with him; their late-night discussion may have inspired Chairman Wade's official inquiry, the next day, about the statutory legitimacy of McClellan's assignment as general in chief. A week into Stanton's tenure Wade sent the three most ardent Republicans on his committee to ply the new secretary with a sheaf of hearsay testimony against General Stone, and the following morning Stanton wrote the initial order for Stone's arrest. The peremptory order that later sent Stone to Fort Lafayette apparently represented Stanton's fulfillment of a venal compact with the radicals, for the secretary was too astute a lawyer to consider the evidence against Stone sufficient for arrest, let alone conviction.[20]

Stanton would exercise a cool, dictatorial demeanor when he came to feel secure in his power, but during the first few weeks after his appointment he devoted much time to ingratiating himself with those whose hostility could harm him as much as their good will might help him. He made an early friend of Charles A. Dana, who managed Horace Greeley's influential *New York Tribune,* and Dana published a flattering piece introducing Stanton as the new head of the War Department. Stanton replied in gushing gratitude, and the two corresponded every few days thereafter, with Stanton characterizing their aims and reasoning as virtually identical. Recalling that the *Tribune* had always demanded aggressive military action from the administration, Stanton lamented the lassitude of the army around Washington. In a letter to Dana dated February 7, Stanton remarked that "we have had no war; we have not even been playing war." He told the *Tribune's* managing editor that the government should have an army of a hundred thousand men sweeping through Kentucky and Tennessee to crush rebellion there.[21]

As it happened, some Union soldiers were playing rather seriously at war in Kentucky and Tennessee while Secretary Stanton courted his newspaper advocate. For nine months the more prominent battlefield confrontations had all gone to the Confederates, who fought defensively on home territory, and that trend had helped weaken public enthusiasm for the struggle. Suddenly the tide seemed to turn. Within days of Stanton's confirmation, a Union division thrashed a couple of Confederate brigades in a fight near a collection of log cabins known as Logan's Crossroads, in southern Kentucky. In the ensuing darkness the Southerners fled south of the Cumberland River and headed toward Nashville, leaving behind their artillery, their wagons, and all their horses, thereby abandoning the right flank of the entire Confederate defensive network across lower Kentucky.

Early in February, near the western end of the Confederate line, a larger Union army from Cairo started up the Tennessee River under Brigadier General Ulysses Grant. This Grant had not done well in life, and he did not enjoy the complete confidence of his professional peers. Major General Henry Halleck, Grant's immediate superior in St. Louis, had been observing the brigadier at a distance for nearly six months when he revealed privately that Grant, though brave enough under fire, seemed not to know how to organize troops for action or how to conduct a campaign. A Regular Army colonel who may have known of Grant in the Mexican War, and who retired to St. Louis while Grant lived there, remarked that Grant owned a long-standing reputation for being "little better than a common gambler and drunkard."[22] He had not entirely shed that reputation, either: a quartermaster whom he arrested at Cairo filed formal charges accusing Grant of becoming "beastly drunk" during a flag-of-truce cruise to Columbus, Kentucky, as well as drinking with Confederate officers there and imbibing heavily in Cairo since.[23]

The previous November, Grant had led an amphibious expedition down the Mississippi to Belmont, Missouri, where his command attacked a small Confederate camp but accomplished little of substance. They captured some ordnance and prisoners, but rebel reinforcements counterattacked and Grant's troops abandoned nearly everything. They fled precipitously back to their boats, leaving behind almost half their wounded and a thousand muskets, complete with ammunition and accoutrements. Grant tried to buff his account of Belmont by exaggerating his trophies and minimizing his losses, and Union veterans of the battle kept looking for something positive about it into the next century, but in fact they and Grant had narrowly averted disaster. The raid has been credited with some arguable advantages of an indirect and intangible nature, but objective contemporary observers must have seen it as a pointless and fairly costly frolic.[24]

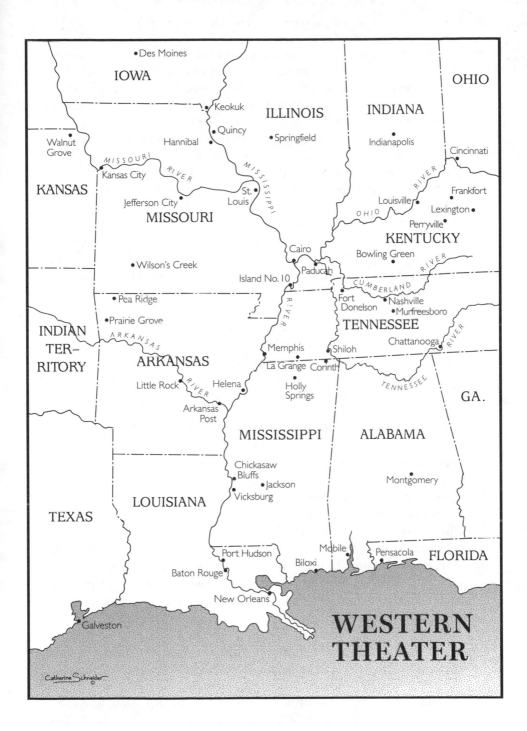

WESTERN
THEATER

This time, several ironclad gunboats of the U.S. Navy accompanied Grant's convoy up the Tennessee. A poorly designed earthwork known as Fort Henry blocked the river just as it crossed into Tennessee, but the gunboats beat the place into submission on February 6, before Grant's army could even surround it. Less than a dozen miles to the east, Fort Donelson guarded the Cumberland River, which ran parallel to the Tennessee. Confederate troops concentrated at Donelson for a more spirited defense while all but two of the gunboats turned back down the river to the Ohio, then up the Cumberland in a roundabout route more than 120 miles long. The other two gunboats steamed upriver all the way across Tennessee to Florence, Alabama, destroying and capturing Southern steamboats on a reconnaissance intended more for psychological effect and propaganda value than for military advantage. During their foray the naval officers found the citizens of Tennessee and northern Alabama at least pretending to harbor warm Union sentiments in those communities where they docked.[25]

Grant had the shorter route: he simply faced his troops about and marched overland to snare the Fort Donelson garrison. In a February 14 attack on the fort, the gunboats fared much worse than they had at Fort Henry, and ultimately Grant had to take Donelson himself. That did not turn out to be especially easy. Knowing that they would be trapped inside the fort, the Confederate garrison hit Grant's lines hard on the morning of February 15, trying to open an escape route to the south; the attack caught his troops by surprise while he was away from his headquarters. The Southerners flung back Grant's right wing, and when he arrived on the scene, half his army was falling back in disorder. He had taken a significant risk in isolating his army on the peninsula between the rivers, and he seemed about to reap the fruits of that recklessness, as though to confirm the doubts about his capacity.

Friendly observers might lionize Grant for rapidly assessing the situation and arranging a counterattack, but his major contribution lay — as it always would — in his failure to panic. Against a more competent opponent there might have been little he could have done to salvage the situation. He called for a charge to "save appearances" after sending a desperate dispatch to the commander of the gunboats. His call for aid from the navy revealed that he feared defeat without some outside help, but the principal help of that sort came, finally, from the Confederate leadership. Brigadier General Gideon Pillow, whose troops had driven Grant from the field at Belmont, inexplicably squandered the initiative. Just as his road to safety lay wide open, and Pillow might have turned on the Yankees to threaten their supply line, he called his men back to their trenches around the fort. Union troops swept back across the roads Pillow had opened, sealing Donelson's fate. The two senior Confederate generals — Pillow and Virginian John B. Floyd, who had served with dubious distinction as James Buchanan's secretary of war — commandeered the only available steamboats; on these they slipped away with some of their troops. Most of the Southern cavalry also avoided the trap by wading through icy marshes, but on February 16 Grant demanded and received the unconditional surrender of Fort Donelson with some twelve thousand prisoners. In four short weeks all Kentucky had been liberated from Confederate grasp, and Tennessee lay ripe for invasion.[26]

While Grant seized the rivers leading into Tennessee, Ambrose Burnside began taking control of the North Carolina coast. The evening after Fort Henry capitulated, Burnside landed an amphibious force on Roanoke Island. The following morning he maneuvered his untried troops through knee-deep water and a murderous fire, finally dispersing the ill-equipped Confederate garrison and capturing nearly three thousand more of the enemy. That gave Burnside a base for operations against North Carolina's sounds: with Grant breaking through to the west and Burnside gnawing away at Confederate territory on the east, it appeared that Virginia might be cut off completely. Those dual incursions cast a somber atmosphere over the Confederate capital, where some began wondering whether independence would be worth a long and devastating struggle.[27]

Northern citizens who had nearly given up hope for Mr. Lincoln's war rejoiced even at the first word of Fort Henry's fall, which had yielded fewer than a hundred prisoners and only limited strategic significance. Charles Eliot Norton, one of the Cambridge literati who had considered the prospect for victory fading fast in December, remarked gleefully on the Tennessee tidings as early as February 9.[28] Commanding a brigade in an isolated corner of Kentucky, Colonel James A. Garfield wrote a friend that he was "beginning to feel encouraged in regard to the war." A Pennsylvania soldier who would die on a Georgia battlefield nineteen months hence told the folks at home that the war was essentially over, and seriously announced that the family might expect him home around the first of April.[29] The complete triumphs at Roanoke and Donelson set bells to ringing throughout the loyal states; ceremonial cannon disgorged robust salutes from the Mason-Dixon Line to the Canadian border, and the bigger towns hosted eerie "illuminations." A young Quaker woman from Delaware who vacillated between instinctive pacifism and nationalist inclinations welcomed an end to "the winter of our discontent."[30]

Southern hopes ebbed as the Union star rose. A Maine woman who had cast her lot with a Southern husband shared the gloom of her Georgia neighbors over the rash of Union successes. From her Shenandoah Valley farm the wife of a Confederate soldier in the Stonewall Brigade reacted venomously to the victories of those "murdering vandals," and while she still hoped for independence she shuddered at the slaughter and sacrifice it would require. South Carolina churches announced two days of fasting and prayer within a single week, while many among those thousands of discouraged Confederate prisoners seemed ready to take the oath of allegiance and resume their former citizenship.[31]

Abraham Lincoln had spent most of the time since his wife's great party worrying over his two younger sons, who had successively fallen victim to the typhoid fever that lurked perennially in Washington's polluted water system. By the time confirmation of Fort Donelson's surrender reached Washington, eleven-year-old Willie Lincoln lay near death, and eight-year-old Tad had grown seriously ill. Until Willie's death, at five o'clock in the afternoon of February 20, Lincoln increasingly ignored all but the most pressing business, refusing even to hear senior senators; only his old friend Orville Browning did the president wish to see, calling for him to bring his wife as well.[32] Edwin Stanton, who had managed to concentrate almost entirely on War Department business despite the commencement of a months-long deathwatch over his own infant son, grasped the opportunity to act on his own from the outset of the president's paternal distraction.[33] He saw the unemployed generals who would have pestered the president for assignments; he appointed additional assistant secretaries of war; he discussed the establishment of loyal governments in occupied Southern states; he dictated a system of censorship for department information, with severe consequences for violations. He troubled the chief executive with few details of even the most irregular events. He never mentioned his planned arrest of so well-known and highly respected a division commander as General Stone, which he originally ordered before Willie even sickened; Lincoln later wrote that he only learned of that surprising development secondhand.[34]

Stanton could not appoint generals on his own authority, though, and three nights before Willie Lincoln's death the secretary came to the White House cabinet room bearing a commission as major general for Ulysses Grant. The president signed it without hesitation, remarking that Westerners, and especially Illinois men like Grant, were a match for Southerners any day. Someone at the table voiced regret at the escape of General Floyd, the former secretary of war, and Stanton remembered that he had last seen Floyd in that very room, when they both still served in Buchanan's cabinet. It had been in December of 1860, on the eve of Floyd's resignation in ostensible indignation over administration policy regarding Fort Sumter. Stanton contended that the two of them had almost come to blows over the Sumter issue, and he alluded to hundreds of thousands of dollars in missing Interior Department funds that had played a more likely role in Floyd's sudden departure. Stanton agreed that it was a pity Floyd had gotten away. "I want to catch and hang him," he said, as though he owned that grim prerogative.[35]

Less than a month of unbroken successes had convinced Stanton that secession was beaten and dying, and in that belief he mirrored the mood of the country. The reports of Union feeling from the naval raid on the upper Tennessee River clearly aided that impression, for no one seemed to consider that the civilians of central Tennessee and northern Alabama might have misrepresented their politics in the presence of landing parties and armed naval vessels. With Lincoln's approval, Stanton took control of all the political prisoners who had been rounded up and imprisoned by William Seward's State Department and ordered them released, if they would take an oath against aiding the nation's enemies. Excusing the administration's arbitrary arrests on the unprecedented strength of the rebellion in the Southern states, Stanton announced that "the insurrection is believed to have culminated and to be declining." Paraphrasing the president's wishes, he promised as much of "a return to the normal course" as the public safety allowed, but he added ominously that his department would have control of future "extraordinary" arrests — by which he referred essentially to those lacking sufficient cause or evidence. General Stone did not benefit from Stanton's wholesale prisoner release: he remained in confinement without charges, and there he would stay for the next six months.[36]

The delirious sense of impending victory prevailed in all quarters except the most prominent theater. The grand Army of the Potomac — the largest and most lavishly supplied of the national armies — seemed unable to accomplish anything. Anxious radicals like Ben Wade had already grown intensely frustrated over McClellan's failure to wield his troops against the enemy, and the president had begun to share that frustration by midwinter. At one point, while McClellan recovered from a vicious bout of typhoid fever, Lincoln even considered taking the field at the head of the army himself, as commander in chief. That impulse died aborning, but in the last week of January Lincoln presented General McClellan with an anomaly that he called President's General War Order No. 1, calling for a general advance of the nation's army and navy against Confederate forces on February 22. In case McClellan entertained any doubt that the order applied to him personally, Lincoln added his President's Special War Order No. 1 four days later, specifically directing him to throw all his disposable troops against the railroad southwest of Manassas Junction.[37]

Lincoln's special order alluded to a plan he had proposed in early December, involving a dual assault on Joe Johnston's army at Manassas Junction. While half the Army of the Potomac assailed the Manassas entrenchments from the front, the other half would steam down the Potomac below the mouth of the Occoquan River and land there, dashing up that stream to the Orange & Alexandria Railroad to sever Johnston's supply line. Lincoln expected that maneuver to either cut Johnston off from Richmond or force him to retreat. McClellan objected: clinging to the classic view of the enemy's capital as the main prize in war, he had already formulated a rudimentary scheme for capturing Richmond by a route much farther downstream. He wished to take most of his army all the way to Chesapeake Bay and then up the Rappahannock to Urbanna, marching overland barely fifty miles to the Confederate capital. He supposed that he could catch Johnston sufficiently off-guard to beat him in that race: if he succeeded, he presumed the war would be over; if he did not, he could simply retreat down to Fort Monroe.[38]

The president acquiesced, and McClellan refined the details of his Urbanna operation. Then came the victories at Fort Henry, Roanoke Island, and Fort Donelson. On February 20 McClellan told Henry Halleck, the overall commander in the western theater, that the Army of the Potomac would move in two weeks, adding that he hoped to be in Richmond soon after Halleck entered Nashville.[39]

Before taking his main army down to the Rappahannock, McClellan conducted a preliminary operation to secure the corridor of the Baltimore & Ohio Railroad, which could be used to threaten Washington from the west. A few days after Lincoln's February 22 deadline McClellan marched all of Nathaniel Banks's division and most of John Sedgwick's (formerly Charles Stone's) to the bank of the Potomac River opposite Harper's Ferry. There he threw a pontoon bridge over the river for his infantry to cross; he had also collected a fleet of canal boats that he planned to use as floats for a sturdier and more permanent bridge to carry provisions and heavy artillery. Once across, he intended to send Banks marching on Winchester while engineers rebuilt the burned railroad bridge and track crews restored the line to the west. The president and his war minister welcomed that preliminary movement as the start of the long-awaited campaign to end the rebellion, but their satisfaction turned to despair and anger when McClellan reported the expedition stymied at Harper's Ferry. Only as he tried to slip them through the lift lock from the Chesapeake & Ohio Canal into the Potomac River did he discover that the canal boats carrying his bridge materials and provisions were too wide by several inches to fit through the locks. On the afternoon of February 27 McClellan told the secretary of war that he would have to "fall back upon the safe and slow

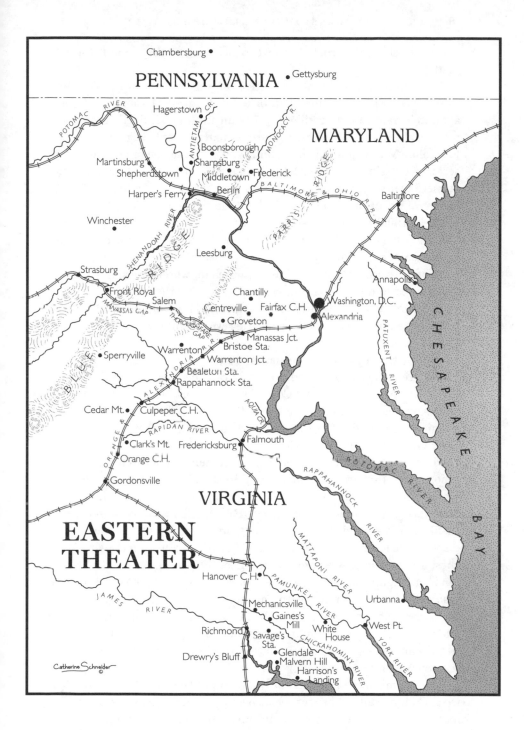

Chambersburg •

PENNSYLVANIA • Gettysburg

Hagerstown

MARYLAND

POTOMAC RIVER

ANTIETAM CR.

Boonsborough
Martinsburg • Sharpsburg
Shepherdstown   Middletown   • Frederick
Harper's Ferry   Berlin

MONOCACY R.

BALTIMORE & OHIO R.R.   • Baltimore

PARRISH RIDGE

Winchester

SHENANDOAH RIVER

RIDGE

Leesburg

Strasburg

Front Royal
Salem   Chantilly
Centreville   Fairfax C.H.   Washington, D.C.
Groveton   Alexandria

MANASSAS GAP

THOROUGHFARE GAP R.R.

Manassas Jct.

Warrenton   Bristoe Sta.
Sperryville •   Warrenton Jct.
Bealeton Sta.
Rappahannock Sta.

BLUE

ALEXANDRIA R.

ORANGE & ALEXANDRIA R.R.

Annapolis •

CHESAPEAKE

PATUXENT RIVER

Cedar Mt. •   Culpeper C.H.
RAPIDAN RIVER

AQUIA CR.

Clark's Mt. •   Fredericksburg   • Falmouth
Orange C.H.

Gordonsville

RAPPAHANNOCK RIVER

POTOMAC RIVER

VIRGINIA

EASTERN
THEATER

MATTAPONI RIVER

BAY

Hanover C.H. •

JAMES RIVER

PAMUNKEY RIVER

Mechanicsville
Gaines's
Mill
Richmond   White
Savage's   House
Drewry's Bluff   Sta.
Glendale
Malvern Hill
Harrison's
Landing

Urbanna •

West Pt. •

YORK RIVER

CHICKAHOMINY RIVER

Catherine Schneider ©

plan" of inching the troops toward Winchester as they rebuilt the railroad.[40]

That evening Mr. Stanton bustled into President Lincoln's office, closed the door behind him, and locked it. He read McClellan's discouraging telegram to the president, pronouncing the heralded commencement of the grand campaign a "damned fizzle." Later, Brigadier General Randolph Marcy entered the room, where he had been summoned to accept a dressing-down in McClellan's stead: Marcy served as the chief of McClellan's staff, apparently because he was also McClellan's father-in-law. With uncharacteristic acerbity the president asked Marcy why McClellan had not measured the width of the boats before spending a million dollars to collect them at the lock, but the general could offer no satisfactory explanation. Lincoln warned that he had come to despair of any accomplishments from McClellan, who increasingly seemed determined to do nothing. Marcy tried to mollify the president with assurances to the contrary, but Lincoln dismissed him rather curtly. Lincoln remained angry two days later, when he revealed his exasperation to Senator Sumner.[41]

Only on the Potomac did the national cause seem to descend into farce. Elsewhere the news continued to corroborate the image of rebellion gasping its last. Nashville, the first Confederate state capital that fell to federal troops, surrendered on February 25 without a shot fired. In mid-February a Union army under Iowa brigadier Samuel Curtis drove the Missouri State Guard out of southern Missouri and into northwestern Arkansas. By virtue of some killing marches that took them out of reach of their provisions, the Missouri State Guard combined with Confederate troops and a brigade of Southern-sympathizing Cherokees and Creeks from the Indian Territory to attack Curtis at Pea Ridge, Arkansas, on March 7, but thanks partly to their hungry and footsore condition Curtis was able to disperse the larger coalition in a two-day battle. By then McClellan's Winchester force had crossed onto what one of the privates called the "sacred mud" of Virginia, and had occupied Martinsburg. A week later Burnside resumed his campaign in North Carolina with the capture of New Bern, the largest city on the sounds, after an ambitious amphibious landing and heavy fighting.[42] Northern newspapers praised such "brilliant operations," announcing "another glorious victory" every few days, and success seemed within reach.[43]

The optimism grew momentarily infectious. Down on the Gulf of Mexico a Connecticut soldier who had begun to regret his enlistment now looked eagerly for an early end to the hostilities. In the mountains of Kentucky a freshly minted brigadier speculated that he might be home by the time the trees leafed out.[44] Even the rank and file of McClellan's twice-defeated army seemed encouraged. By the first of March, William Scott, a shaggy Vermont private whom the president had pardoned from execution for sleeping on guard duty, concluded that "we ar agoing to conkr the rebs bymby." That unlettered rustic reflected the sentiments of many of his comrades. "The end is approaching," wrote Lieutenant Lewis Frederick Cleveland, promising his mother that peace would be restored by the first of June. Another soldier gave the Confederate capital no more than two weeks before the Stars and Stripes reappeared on its buildings.[45]

The new secretary of war grasped at the victories as an opportunity to establish loyal governments in the seceded states. A minority of loyalists in western Virginia had already elected a competing legislature for that state, complete with a substitute governor; Missouri had done the same, after federal troops drove the duly elected officials from office. With the fall of Nashville, Stanton itched to install loyal officers there, and he sent Assistant Secretary of War Thomas Scott to gauge public sentiment. Scott informed his chief on March 3 that it might be feasible to name a military governor for Tennessee by the end of the month, but Stanton did not wait until the end of the day. He immediately chose Andrew Johnson, the fervent Unionist, and persuaded the president to give Johnson a commission as brigadier general to cover the military end of his title. Scott responded the next day that this was the wrong thing to do: Johnson had been too partisan, and would alienate too much of the population, he argued, suggesting a less volatile appointment and a few weeks of patience before assigning a governor. Stanton nevertheless let the controversial appointment stand, and anxiously awaited another chance to impose even nominal federal authority on a fractious province.[46]

Only the appearance of the Confederate gunboat *Virginia* interrupted Edwin Stanton's dream of sweeping rebellion from the country. That heavily armored ram lumbered out of its berth opposite Norfolk, Virginia, on March 8 and attacked the United States fleet in Hampton Roads. In short order the ten-gun ironclad destroyed two wooden warships commanding a total of seventy-four guns, and then it drove the forty-seven-gun *Minnesota* aground, suffering no great damage of its own in the process. An invulnerable craft like that could call an abrupt end to McClellan's amphibious plans, but that evening the general knew nothing of the surprise at Hampton Roads. He had only received Allan Pinkerton's exaggerated report of Confederate forces at Manassas that day, and Washington citizens walking off their dinner saw him gazing reflectively out the window of his home on Lafayette Square, doubtless mulling his odds for success at Urbanna.[47]

The *Monitor*, a clumsy little Union ironclad mounting two big guns on a revolving turret, arrived off Fort Monroe that night. The next day it fought the *Virginia* to a draw, but that news came late to Washington, and for most of the working day on March 9 the White House teemed with nervous officers and officials. Edwin Stanton appeared to be the most nervous of all. Navy secretary Gideon Welles described Stanton as "almost frantic" that day, pacing the floor and predicting that the *Virginia* would come up the Potomac and shell the government out of Washington, or steam up the coast to destroy New York and Boston.[48] The president's personal secretaries corroborated Welles's unflattering depiction, describing the secretary of war as "fearfully stampeded," bursting into the room "very much excited" and stalking back and forth "like a caged lion."[49]

Stanton ordered a squadron of hulks filled with stone for scuttling in the Potomac channel below Washington, to obstruct the Confederate behemoth if it turned that way. General McClellan, meanwhile, appeared concerned mostly that the *Virginia* would disrupt his Urbanna scheme just as he was about to launch it, but the terror subsided as quickly as it had arisen. The *Virginia* steamed back up the Elizabeth River to its moorings; with the *Monitor* waiting nearby, the Confederate ironclad never molested another vessel. By late afternoon Stanton had resumed his desk with his usual proportions of bluster and artifice, and the focus returned to northern Virginia. That night, McClellan crossed the Potomac to investigate an electrifying report from Fairfax Court House: escaping contrabands had slipped into Union lines with tales that Joseph Johnston's Confederate army had pulled out of its entrenched lines around Manassas Junction.[50]

Like most of the information carried by escaped slaves, the Manassas story deserved credence. Apprehending that McClellan would soon attack him — via one of the rivers on his right flank, or by way of the Shenandoah Valley — Johnston had planned his withdrawal in such secrecy that he caught even President Davis by surprise. Union troops crossed the upper Potomac and captured the town of Leesburg on Saturday, March 8, threatening Johnston's left, and the next morning Johnston set his entire army in retreat toward Gordonsville and Fredericksburg. One aggressive New Jersey brigadier lunged forward to seize Fairfax Court House, Centreville, and the railroad stations leading to Manassas Junction. By Monday night curious Yankee soldiers were clambering over Johnston's entire line of earthworks.[51]

Colonel Edward Cross, whose 5th New Hampshire accompanied the vanguard, pronounced those works formidable. By the extent of the camps he judged that Johnston must have had eighty thousand men there, and supposed that he could have withstood an assault by a hundred thousand. Cross, an antiabolition Democrat, may have allowed his admiration for George McClellan to convince him that Johnston had fled because Little Mac had maneuvered him out of the Manassas line.[52]

Republicans, at least, saw it differently. Only a few batteries of dummy artillery remained behind to mark the Confederate line, and to the unsympathetic it seemed obvious that McClellan had allowed Johnston to slip away without a blow. That led to some harsh words on Capitol Hill. Adam Gurowski, a State Department interpreter and vehement advocate of aggressive war, besieged senators with warnings about McClellan's evident incompetence and seeming disloyalty.[53] Senior officers lingering in Washington heard a torrent of abuse about McClellan's lassitude, including Gurowski's public rants about treason: those officers began to suppose that the sun had set on Little Mac's military career, and their suspicions came within an ace of accuracy.[54] Newspaper artists went to work on cartoons lampooning the timid advance of the Army of the Potomac, which their editors displayed beneath headlines mocking the "Full History of the Late Brilliant Achievement of the Grand Army."[55]

To spur McClellan into further action, the president had already issued General War Order No. 2, instructing McClellan precisely how to arrange his army for the field, with his thirteen divisions distributed among four army corps and the four senior generals elevated to lead those corps. To that he added another order giving McClellan until March 18 to begin any change of base to another line of operations. McClellan balked at the formation of corps, complaining that the order impeded his movements just as he was about to start, but that only aggravated the impression of deliberate inactivity. On Tuesday, March 11, the president met with his cabinet for a discussion of McClellan's seemingly aimless floundering, and Attorney General Edward Bates suggested that the president should do away with the position of general in chief altogether. Lincoln should assume the role of commander in chief himself, Bates said, as the Constitution decreed. Lincoln evidently considered that advice during the rest of the day. Through an intermediary he or the secretary of war warned General Marcy that the administration's patience had about run out, and that McClellan had better provide a plan for imminent action against the enemy. Marcy urged his son-in-law to come into the city to talk about it, but McClellan declined, insisting that he was too tired and too busy.[56]

In the evening Lincoln called Stanton back into his office, along with Secretary of State Seward and treasury secretary Salmon P. Chase. The thin, stooping Seward came in first, and before the others arrived Lincoln read him the text of his War Order No. 3, which announced the removal of McClellan as general in chief now that he had taken the field with the Army of the Potomac. It named no successor, instead instructing army and department commanders to report to the secretary of war. Seward, who seemed especially incensed over the fiasco of the canal boats, replied in the hoarse voice of an addicted smoker that the president had acted generously in retaining McClellan in command of that single army. He suggested that Lincoln drop the presidential authority behind the order and instead let it go out in Stanton's name, which he thought would lift Stanton's stock with that part of the public that had grown disgusted with McClellan. Stanton entered the room in the middle of that conversation, but he objected to taking the responsibility for what amounted to McClellan's demotion, fearing that it might be mistaken for a rancorous reaction to the recent canal episode.[57]

The order ultimately went forth over Lincoln's signature. General Marcy read it in the next morning's *National Intelligencer,* and telegraphed the contents to McClellan. Officially accepting the news as an opportunity to demonstrate his selfless devotion to the nation's interests, McClellan sat down to plan the campaign he knew he must undertake immediately if he expected even to remain in command of the Army of the Potomac.[58]

Johnston's new position behind the Rappahannock and Rapidan rivers put him close enough to the Urbanna landing place to frustrate McClellan's cherished plans there. McClellan therefore fell back on an alternative that he had earlier characterized as "a less brilliant movement." Instead of debarking at Urbanna for a quick dash to Richmond, he would begin at Fort Monroe and work all the way up the Peninsula, between the James and York rivers. Within hours of learning that he was no longer general in chief, he arranged with the War Department for troop transports, consulted with the Navy Department for assurances that the *Virginia* could be contained, held a romantic division review beneath a glimmering moon, and convened his first council of war with the four corps commanders Lincoln had named. Meeting until one o'clock in the morning, that council concluded to leave a sufficient force to cover Washington, but they disagreed on how large a force that should be: one said forty thousand, while the rest deemed twenty-five thousand adequate. The balance of the army would repair to Fort Monroe and start for Richmond from there, taking supplies at York River ports. Only if that avenue proved impractical — if the *Virginia* defeated the *Monitor* and barred the way, for instance — the council advocated a direct assault on Johnston's new Rappahannock line, but the Yorktown Peninsula offered the favored route.[59]

The senior corps commander, Irvin McDowell, carried the council's decision to Edwin Stanton for approval. McDowell, a beefy career soldier who had led the first national army to ignominious defeat along the banks of Bull Run eight months before, tasted a second chance for glory with his appointment to corps command and a promotion to major general. The Senate confirmed McDowell's second star the day after he arrived in the city, with a telling preponderance of Radical Republicans favoring his nomination. McClellan's vulnerability left McDowell talking ungenerously about his commander among other officers, and perhaps among government officials as well.[60] In presenting the results of the council of war to the secretary of war, McDowell neither clarified the council's preference for the Peninsula route nor offered details that McClellan apparently expected him to convey, and Stanton telegraphed McClellan that he had no idea how the general intended to proceed. McClellan could only reply that the council had unanimously endorsed the plan "presented to you by Gen. McDowell." President Lincoln finally cut through the confusion with permission for McClellan to move his army to Fort Monroe and begin a new campaign there, "or anywhere between here and there," so long as he moved "at once in pursuit of the enemy by some route."[61]

The first brigade of McClellan's army boarded transports at Alexandria on March 17, steaming off for Fort Monroe sometime after dark that evening, only hours ahead of the president's March 18 deadline. McClellan watched from the wharf as the first brigades departed. He tumbled ingloriously out of the saddle when his horse stepped in a hole, but recovered his dignity and marked the occasion with a round of wine for his generals in the Alexandria collector's office.[62]

That same day, McClellan directed James Shields to cover the Shenandoah Valley, and less than a week later that relatively unknown brigadier sent the famous Stonewall Jackson packing in a fight just up the Valley from Winchester. As good an omen as that may have been for the spring campaign, it overshadowed McClellan's more ambitious but secret maneuver and seemed to illustrate the contrast between fighting generals and strategists. Even without such embarrassing comparisons, the token commencement of McClellan's campaign had come none too soon for the frustrated politicians, and another few days of delay might have ended his career then and there. Radical Republicans in Congress now firmly doubted not only McClellan's ability but his devotion, and that week they applied intense pressure to have him deposed.[63] Edwin Stanton was already casting about for someone willing to take his place, starting with an officer of the old army who had come out of retirement to assume an indistinct staff position. General Ethan Allen Hitchcock, who was approaching his sixty-fourth birthday, declined in horror at the prospect, but Stanton kept browsing for a new champion among some of the army's older and less celebrated generals. The secretary even considered leaping Napoleon Buford, a grizzled Illinois colonel, over every general in the army; Stanton admitted to an Illinois senator that he wanted to simply try one commander after another until he found one who would fight.[64]

In less than three weeks a fleet of contracted steamers transported more than 120,000 men, nearly fifteen thousand horses and mules, 1,150 supply wagons, and forty-four batteries of artillery from the vicinity of Washington to Fort Monroe. Engineer troops arriving in towed canal boats awoke to a vast multitude of their comrades, and to strange sights like the dark little *Monitor.*[65] An itinerant Virginia rebel passing the mouth of the Elizabeth River turned his spyglass on a "for[es]t of masts" in the roadstead around Old Point Comfort, finding it impossible to count them all, and a Michigan lieutenant encamped near Hampton observed that the night sky glowed as far as he could see with the flames of campfires. A New Hampshire boy plunged his bayonet into the dirt, plugged a candle into the socket, and tried to explain to his mother just how "gay" it all seemed.[66] McClellan left Alexandria on April 1 and arrived at Fort Monroe the next day. Two days after that, his advance brigades began the long and bloody march up the Peninsula and exchanged the first shots with Confederate defenders.[67]

No sooner had McClellan left to lead his army against the enemy than Edwin Stanton launched the next phase of his personal campaign against the general. The very evening that McClellan stepped down at Fort Monroe, Stanton sauntered into the president's office, where he found Lincoln in conversation with his old friend Senator Orville Browning. Before those two Kentucky-born Illinois politicians, the secretary produced a letter that he claimed to have just received from "one of the first men of the Nation," whose name he declined to give although he insisted that both his listeners knew the author. He read to them a passage alleging that, sometime in 1860, General McClellan had been inducted into a Southern-leaning fraternity known as the Knights of the Golden Circle by none other than Jefferson Davis himself. The imagined membership of that brotherhood was already becoming the bugbear of Northern war supporters who feared secret legions of traitors waiting to strike a blow for the Confederacy. The letter Stanton read insinuated that McClellan's loyalty lay elsewhere, and that perhaps he worked actively to deliver his army or his country to the enemy. One diligent and perfectly loyal general, Charles Stone, had spent nearly eight weeks in a federal dungeon already on little more evidence than that, imprisoned by Stanton on an implied charge of having sent his troops to deliberate defeat. Stanton professed not to believe the assertion against McClellan, implying that he had merely read the letter to demonstrate the widespread doubt about that general's loyalty, but after the interview he hinted differently. Driving Browning to his lodgings, Stanton admitted that he doubted McClellan would do anything likely to quash secession, and he asked the senator to lobby Lincoln about catapulting that obscure old Illinois colonel, Buford, to command of the army.[68]

On that same carriage ride Stanton revealed his newfound admiration for Irvin McDowell. McDowell had cultivated an ardent following among Radical Republicans: less than one week into the new year the predominately radical Joint Committee on the Conduct of the War had lobbied the president to put him in command of the Army of the Potomac.[69] The radical support may have influenced Stanton's favor for that scheming general, and by extension it may have played a part in the decision to withhold McDowell's corps from McClellan's army.

Trouble next arose over the number of troops that should remain behind to protect Washington. The generals who had opted for the Peninsula campaign had supposed that shifting offensive operations below Richmond would lure the preponderance of Confederate forces that way, and most of those generals — McDowell included — thought that twenty-five thousand men would be enough to keep the capital safe. As he steamed down to Fort Monroe, McClellan calculated that, besides a complement of about eighteen thousand men in the forts around Washington, he had left more than fifty-five thousand men behind. That figure included over thirty-five thousand positioned in the Shenandoah Valley, which seemed too distant for the security of Washington's politicians, and Stanton directed two staff generals to assess the adequacy of that screen. The pair reported on April 2 that too few troops remained within the limits of the city to meet the criteria of the council of war, and that those who were there lacked the training and organization they needed to mount an adequate defense.[70]

Stanton jumped on that conclusion to withhold one of the two corps that had not yet moved to the transports. On April 4, the very day McClellan started up the Peninsula and called for McDowell to join him, army headquarters announced that McDowell's corps of thirty-six thousand would not be coming down. McClellan received that telegram the next evening, as his campaign's first skirmishes wound down, and he implored the president to rescind the order. At the very least, he asked if Lincoln would let him have William B. Franklin's division, headed by the greatest McClellan admirer among the generals in McDowell's corps.

Stanton allowed Franklin to go, but then McClellan promptly asked for George McCall's division of Pennsylvania Reserves, which Stanton withheld. Until Franklin arrived McClellan used a plea of insufficient numbers to excuse himself from seizing Gloucester Point, on the tip of the next peninsula to the north; Confederate batteries there prevented Union transports and gunboats from moving up the York River to supply and support the Army of the Potomac as it struggled up the rain-drenched Peninsula over saturated roads. On April 6 he located his headquarters two and a half miles from the colonial port of Yorktown, which he promised to capture, but he warned that it might be a slow process. He insisted that he needed McDowell's entire corps more than ever.[71]

As early as the next morning, Massachusetts infantry began creeping forward to scout the perimeter of Yorktown, incidentally losing a man here and there. It was still another ten days before McClellan's army fought anything that might have been called a battle, testing Yorktown's defenders in a confrontation between two divisions at Lee's Mill. The day began with bright sun, clear skies, and high hopes, but it ended in repulse, the death of the Vermont private who had expected to "conkr the rebs," and charges that the commander of the Union division came into the fight "too much under the influence of liquor."[72] McClellan's soldiers nevertheless continued to express perfect confidence in him and in ultimate success, assuring the folks at home that Richmond was doomed — perhaps as soon as the Union cordon strangled Yorktown.[73] Partly because of such predictions, citizens of the North also expected great things of McClellan now that he had thrown himself into the fray. Washington citizens looked for the final grand assault on Richmond any day, and with it the end of the war. "The next week . . . ought to settle the question of Union or Disunion," thought a White House visitor. Convinced now that the president would never remove Little Mac once he had committed himself to the campaign, the secretary of war encouraged his demanding general to action with a vision of raising "the shout of victory from the Chesapeake to the Mississippi."[74]

McClellan's repeated appeals for more troops quickly dampened that optimism in administration circles. On April 9 the president sent him a fairly straightforward letter indicating that continued public confidence in McClellan required the general to move decisively and immediately, lest he seem inclined to dawdle away another couple of seasons on the Peninsula as he had before Manassas. Without mentioning the suspicion among radicals that McClellan intended to strip Washington of defenders to lay it open for capture, Lincoln inquired how McClellan could otherwise account for his own failure to provide the capital sufficient security. Assuring McClellan that he remained as supportive of him as ever, the president nonetheless insisted that the general had to either show some fight or suffer the consequences.[75]

Notwithstanding his readiness to sustain McClellan if he would simply get down to work, Lincoln admitted his impatience and dissatisfaction to Senator Browning. Attorney General Bates feared that McClellan's time had about come, and foretold his demise into "acknowledged impotence" if he continued toward the Confederate capital on his present course. The only way Bates believed that McClellan might save himself would be to shift half his army south of the James River, cut Norfolk off, and sweep up toward Richmond through Petersburg. That would allow him to bag all the enemy forces on the Peninsula as well as Joe Johnston's army at Gordonsville, instead of plodding up the Peninsula from Fort Monroe and giving the enemy a chance to evacuate Richmond. Those private observations revealed that Bates also believed, like Lincoln but unlike McClellan, that capturing the enemy's army posed a more worthy objective than occupying his capital. The old solicitor noted the details of his strategy in his journal entry of April 9, exactly three years before another general brought that very plan to a successful conclusion.[76]

While the Army of the Potomac had been shuttling down Chesapeake Bay, Union arms continued to prevail at all other points. In Virginia's Shenandoah Valley, General Shields had delivered Thomas Jonathan Jackson — the celebrated "Stonewall" — that sole defeat of his career on March 23. Way out in New Mexico, Union troops stopped a Confederate invasion at Glorietta Pass five days later, sending the survivors flying back to Texas. By the end of March, six weeks after the capture of Fort Donelson and only ten weeks into a continuous succession of national victories, the main Confederate army in the western theater had withdrawn from Tennessee altogether, falling back into northern Mississippi. Now, to those who knew nothing of his endless complaints about troop deployment, it appeared that McClellan was at last leading the largest Union army of all in an irresistible drive against the enemy's capital.[77]

That indeed seemed like wrapping up a moribund rebellion, and just in the nick of time. The war was costing $1.5 million per day and more; by the end of February contractors were clamoring for payment of nearly $27 million in outstanding requisitions. Soldiers, who could afford it less than most, had to bear much of the treasury deficit in the form of unconscionably tardy paymasters. Chase, the treasury secretary, estimated that the government faced about $45 million in "floating debt" at that time, incurred mainly by the War Department. Like nearly everyone in the government, Chase had expected to see the rebellion crushed within a few months, so he had attempted to pay for the war on a binge of borrowing and the issue of bonds. Early in the winter, dwindling public confidence in the war effort had flooded the subtreasuries with citizens waving their notes for exchange in gold, and late in December Chase suspended all specie payments. Then he turned to Congress to authorize demand notes bearing no interest, to be used as legal tender instead of gold and silver coin. The proposal amounted to printing money on nothing more than the government's promise to pay, as the Confederacy had already begun to do and as the Continental Congress had done — with infamous and disastrous consequences — during the Revolution. That created a furor among confirmed hard-money men (whose ranks had always included Chase, until this crisis), but the question came down to how badly each congressman wished to prosecute the war.[78]

After vigorous wrangling throughout February, the two houses passed the "legal tender" bill at the end of that month, with all the radicals aligned behind it. The new notes, stamped on the reverse in a tint that inspired the nickname "greenbacks," began circulating just as McClellan's army started up the Peninsula. In addition Chase issued millions of dollars in bonds, but the cost of the war only continued to rise.[79]

The army had grown as though without direction or restraint, and that winter and spring it was becoming clear how much waste and inefficiency the blind rush to war had spawned. Perfectly useless company and field-grade officers resigned by the hundreds, or endured summary dismissal. Whole regiments of undisciplined, demoralized, and disgruntled volunteers — like the 53rd New York Infantry, the 7th New York Cavalry, and the 11th New York Fire Zouaves — had to be mustered out of service altogether.[80]

Thanks to the negligent voracity of recruiting officers, the army labored under the burden of boys too young to stand the emotional strain of active duty and men too old or infirm to meet the physical demands. An officer in the 7th Vermont brought his sickly sixteen-year-old brother along with his company, hoping to fill up the company roster and make a man of him, but the boy's constitution could not bear the rigors of camp, let alone the march or battle. The 4th New Hampshire Volunteers left home with boys as young as fourteen and an assortment of men in their fifties, as well as one private who had just passed his sixty-first birthday.[81] Patriotism may have played a part in drawing some of the older, unattached men, while the chance for travel and adventure exerted a significant appeal for their more youthful comrades, but many of those recruits came from the lower working class. "Poor People have to go to the War or starve," wrote a woman in an impoverished corner of New England. A surgeon observed that a majority of the wounded he saw from the spring's deadliest battle represented "generally the humbler walks" of life. To an even greater extent than in the Confederacy, it was primarily the poor who filled the nation's armies.[82]

The most common attraction for such men would have been regular pay and the promises of both bounty money and community support for their families. In some struggling rural regions, aging fathers and stripling sons enlisted together, revising their ages upward or downward to satisfy the military requirements. Sylvanus Bean of Brownfield, Maine, who was already beyond the upper age limit, took his fifteen-year-old son to war; seventeen-year-old George Everest and his fifty-five-year-old father enlisted from Plainfield, New Hampshire, within a week of each other — the son claiming to be eighteen, and the father forty-four. Regimental and brigade surgeons discovered thousands of soldiers who should never have been accepted for service in the first place, and a blizzard of disability discharges buried desks in the War Department.[83]

Jonah Hamilton and Isaac Meader, neighbors in a rocky New Hampshire hill-farm district, obtained two of those discharges. After the deaths of their first wives they had both deeded hardscrabble homesteads to their eldest sons, for whom they had each become resident laborers. Both had recently remarried much younger women, which seemed to infuse them with the last draft of youth even as it gave fresh allure to any promise of regular income. Theirs was the sort of isolated, cash-poor community where houses cost as little as a hundred dollars, and that lent disproportionate appeal to army pay of thirteen dollars a month on top of keep, clothing, a hundred-dollar federal bounty, and municipal allowances for their new wives.[84] Some recruiters had offered advances against bounty, a stipend for room and board until the recruits went into camp, as well as recklessly advertising an unauthorized offer of 160-acre land grants on the assurance of impending congressional approval.[85]

Under such inducements (and a ten-dollar bonus from the wealthiest Republican in his hometown) Hamilton's youngest son had joined the army right after the 1861 harvest. One of Meader's married sons would enlist as soon as the bounties grew a little more attractive.[86] Late in the autumn the patriarchs themselves mustered into the 7th New Hampshire Volunteers as private soldiers, each giving his age as forty-four. In reality those two grandfathers had been born near the end of the eighteenth century, but sleeping on cold ground and standing guard in the rain reminded them of their vintage, and by February they sought the services of medical officers. When the 7th New Hampshire boarded transports for the Deep South on February 13, Hamilton and Meader remained behind with orders to go home. In nine weeks' service to their country they had accomplished essentially nothing, but they had cost their government considerably, besides opening the door to pensions for themselves and their wives.[87] Congress quickly addressed that sort of opportunism by considering a requirement that soldiers complete at least two years of service before expecting the hundred-dollar bounty, but that raised such a howl in the army that the resolution stalled after preliminary discussion.[88]

The winnowing of such chaff had not prevented the army from swelling beyond anyone's expectation. Lincoln's cabinet gasped to learn, just as McClellan's campaign began, that the War Department tallied some seven hundred thousand men presently in uniform. That represented nearly ten times the number of troops Lincoln had first called into service in response to the firing on Fort Sumter (all of whom had since been discharged), and the attorney general saw "reckless extravagance" in the unchecked mobilization. The expenses of his new department weighed heavily on the mind of Edwin Stanton: much of the blame lay with his predecessor, Simon Cameron, who had conducted affairs with greedy abandon, but Stanton feared that he would be blamed for it.[89] On April 3, the day before McClellan started his Peninsula army toward Richmond, the secretary of war called an abrupt halt to the recruiting of volunteers with General Order No. 33. He directed officers on recruiting duty to return immediately to their regiments, selling any public property they used for that purpose. Governors learned that the War Department would pay no more expenses related to recruiting, and half-formed companies were left to disperse, along with the prospective lieutenants and captains who had organized them. The frustration deflated the martial ardor of many an adventurous youth, and disappointment (or relief) sent some impetuous volunteers home for the duration.[90]

A surreptitious newspaper correspondent on the White House staff tried to sell the closing of the recruiting offices as evidence of government satisfaction with the forces that had already taken arms. On the front lines the troops speculated hopefully that it signaled the imminent conclusion of hostilities. Stanton's gesture seemed to promise economy in both men and money: it was as though administration officials hoped to simultaneously instill confidence in the new government currency and cultivate more support for the war by manning the brake lever on the runaway military machine.[91]

Even as Stanton's directive left his desk, Confederate generals in northeastern Mississippi gathered all the forces they could muster to drive Ulysses Grant out of western Tennessee. Albert Sidney Johnston, one of the Confederacy's five full generals, took charge of the whole. Another of those full generals, Pierre G. T. Beauregard, the hero of Fort Sumter and Bull Run, rode along as nominal second-in-command. On the afternoon of April 3 some thirty thousand Southerners swung north out of Corinth toward Grant's Army of the Tennessee, sprawled alongside its namesake river at Pittsburg Landing. More infantry and cavalry converged with them until the Confederate columns approached nearly forty thousand.[92]

The Federals, who could have fielded about the same number, allowed their confidence in the weakness of Southern arms to dissuade them from due vigilance. With astounding negligence Ulysses Grant — having learned nothing from his disaster at Belmont, Missouri, the year before — had once again thrown his army into a vulnerable position on the hostile side of a major river. Taking up his own lodgings miles away from the main encampment, he failed to order any fortifications built and allowed discipline to flag, particularly in the matter of lookouts, and that lapse nearly fixed the doom of his command. With no reconnaissance and lax guards, Grant remained utterly oblivious that so large an enemy force had come so near. Some of his troops had made camp there for three weeks, lounging about their tents, enjoying the beauty of the Southern land-scape, playing baseball, and tantalizing the folks at home with descriptions of peach trees in full bloom by the first week of spring. They had not built the first yard of entrenchments.[93]

Then, on the Sabbath morning of April 6, a solid wall of Confederates "yelling like demons" rolled into and over the Union bivouac around Shiloh meetinghouse, a log chapel the size of a smokehouse.[94] Battalions of surprised Federals fled toward the river at sight of the enemy. Many of those who did fall into line soon threw down their weapons and ran, or took the first opportunity to help a slightly injured man to the rear, but others put up a losing fight that sounded the alarm for their comrades. Deeper into the camp, the stronger spirits in other units shouldered together and waited resolutely for the battle to reach them. That allowed Confederate momentum to overwhelm successive pockets of resistance and consume prisoners by the hundreds. The ferocity of their assail-ants stunned Westerners who had so blithely imagined the rebellion van-quished. Gunfire roared incessantly, and men could not hear themselves talk, let alone understand battlefield commands. The volleys of lead and iron brought down trees on all sides of the harried Yankees, but as they backed toward the Tennessee their shrinking battle lines grew tight and strong, and they delayed the onslaught until the daylight flickered out. By then the Confederates had spent themselves, and an intimidating barrage from two Union gunboats brought the attack to a halt just as Grant's army backed up against the bank of the river in a narrow front buttressed by a dense array of artillery. That Sunday's battle exceeded the scope and sav-agery of any fighting yet seen on the continent, leaving as many men dead and wounded in a single day as had fallen in all the major battles of the war before that date.[95]

At dark the Confederates held most of the Union camps and guns, plus thousands of prisoners, but Johnston had been killed and Beauregard took over. Thousands more terrified Yankees cowered below the river-bank through the night while Grant arranged what was left of his artillery and collected reinforcements. Don Carlos Buell's Army of the Ohio had tossed off knapsacks and made a forced march, arriving that evening on the right bank of the river. In a downpour Buell's fresh brigades crossed on steamboats, sneering at the milling fugitives huddled under the bluffs and pushing them out of the way as they ascended to the battlefield. Some of that mob made for the boats each time they brought reinforcements: only a cordon of guards kept the panicked throng from climbing aboard while the troops unloaded, and after Buell's men debarked, the boats had to hasten away from shore while crewmen staved off the would-be stowaways with billets of firewood. Some of the most frightened skulkers drowned while trying to swim the river.[96]

Buell's leading division commander, William Nelson, found Grant's entire army pressed back against the river in an arc ranging only four hundred yards from the landing. Lovell Rousseau, a brigadier who crossed at dawn, described the same perimeter to the yard. Badly overestimating Confederate strength, both generals believed Grant's men completely whipped and his line ready to collapse. Rousseau assured the secretary of the treasury that Grant's negligence constituted "the most stupendous crime of this age," rather than a mere blunder, and much of Buell's army shared that opinion. Leading his company to Pittsburg Landing that evening, one Ohio captain who would become a Union general learned that the rebels had swarmed right into Grant's camps with no warning and precious little interference; he excoriated Grant for his negligence, characterizing it as "gross and criminal mismanagement."[97]

General Hitchcock, who remembered Grant's bibulous days in St. Louis, informed a friend that everyone in Washington considered Grant "absolutely disgraced and dishonored" after Shiloh: he had fallen into every unforgivable mistake a commander could make, and worse yet (as Hitchcock believed), Grant's personal whereabouts could not be accounted for during several hours of the first day's fight. Hitchcock observed that Grant's dismal performance provoked a review of his one victory at Fort Donelson, where he also seemed to have prevailed more by the gallantry of his men than by his own sound management and good judgment, and upon closer inspection only his demand for unconditional surrender remained to his credit. The principal newspaper chronicler of Shiloh cultivated that dim view of Grant in his own account of the surprise, and with good reason he hinted that Brigadier General William T. Sherman bore some of the responsibility as well. The reporter's appraisal of Grant's unimaginative tactics seemed to corroborate Henry Halleck's poor opinion of Grant's military talents; Halleck so instinctively supposed that Grant would have dug in after a weeks-long occupation that at the first news of the battle he reported a Confederate attack on "our works," as though there had actually been some works. When Halleck arrived at Pittsburg

Landing he found Grant's army in miserable discipline in comparison to Buell's.[98]

At the time, a good many soldiers in the ranks adopted the view that Buell had saved the battle; some Shiloh veterans never forgave Grant, or ever trusted him again. Four weeks later an Iowa enlisted man remarked that "Grant is hated and *despised* by all the men and cursed ever since the 6th of April." At the end of that year, when his field officers solicited three cheers for the general, that same soldier recorded hearing more of his comrades utter groans and oaths than anything complimentary. The veterans' doubts about him infected later recruits as well, and one sergeant who enlisted months after the battle reported holding little confidence in Grant when his regiment was assigned to that general's army.[99]

Alarmed by the "fearful panic" of Grant's troops, the lieutenant colonel commanding an Ohio regiment that arrived at dusk felt his division had come barely in time to forestall absolute disaster. A captain from Indiana who crossed over to Pittsburg Landing in the darkness of April 6 suspected that only the river had restrained Grant's army from a worse stampede than Bull Run; he saw field officers among the demoralized mob, and learned that some of them had beaten their men to the landing. Despite the steady flow of reinforcements, that captain waited for morning in constant anticipation of an order to surrender.[100] In corroboration of that pessimistic atmosphere, another of Buell's officers insisted that only the arrival of the Army of the Ohio had saved Grant from submitting to an unconditional surrender of his own. At least a few in Grant's army wholeheartedly agreed: an Iowan admitted that they would have been "whipt to death" if it hadn't been for Buell, and an Illinois private assured his siblings that the enemy would have captured every man of Grant's army by noon Monday if "Bewel" had not come to the rescue. Union soldiers knew nothing of the decimation and demoralization in their assailants' ranks that Sunday evening; only long afterward, with the benefit of considerable hindsight and a leavening of partisan motive, did they begin to write of that night with much recollected optimism.[101]

With uncommon luck, however, and with Buell's hefty divisions, Grant partially redeemed himself the following day. Buell's troops and Grant's own last fresh division gave him an effective force of forty-five thousand — nearly twice the number Beauregard could find to put into line — and when the sun rose Grant sent that strengthened phalanx straight ahead in a clumsy, disjointed counterattack spearheaded by Buell's men. Remembering how close they had come to complete victory the day before, the exhausted, disorganized, and now heavily outnumbered remnants of the Confederate juggernaut resisted stubbornly at first, and even lashed back,

but the Union reinforcements stopped them cold. By noon the Southerners started to give way. Heavy ranks of blue drove them over the rain-
soaked, corpse-strewn scene of Sunday's fight all the way back to the
Shiloh meetinghouse, whence Beauregard turned the battered remnants
of his army back to Corinth behind a screen of cavalry. Grant permitted
his beaten foe to retire.[102]

Given the tenor of the times, even Beauregard's repulse should not
have saved Ulysses Grant's hide. Everyone but his closest friends and subordinates, like the equally culpable Sherman, seemed to rail against him.
The day after the battle, one of the Iowans who had faced the initial Confederate attack complained that the Union side enjoyed neither generals
nor generalship until Buell arrived; "Grant is played out most decidedly,"
he concluded. General Rousseau declared his early, limited admiration
for Grant "blown to the winds," and he resented what he perceived as
Grant's effort to cast himself as the hero of the battle. In a letter to Grant's
senior senator, a prominent Illinois politician mourned over not only the
poor generalship but the unnecessary sacrifice and the negligent, foolish
confidence revealed by Sunday's surprise.[103]

As though the subject of alcohol brought Grant's name to mind, it
was during a discussion about the alleged drunkenness of another general that Grant's congressman and patron, Elihu Washburne, tried to defend his celebrity constituent on the floor of Congress. Washburne's mail
had included denunciations of Grant's intemperance by outraged citizens
and assurances of his sobriety by one of Grant's staff officers, but the
congressman did not dwell on liquor so much as on competence. Spe-
ciously, perhaps disingenuously, and in the face of his own brother's contradictory opinion, Washburne insisted that there had been no surprise at
Pittsburg Landing, and he claimed the "fullest authority" for that denial.
Washburne suggested that such accusations had come from critics who
hailed from other states, whose troops had (he implied) fought less gal-
lantly than those of Illinois. A week later Senator James Harlan of Iowa
denounced Grant as a reckless incompetent — recounting his near-defeat
at Belmont, his carelessness at Fort Donelson, and his flagrant languor at
Shiloh; Harlan declared that Grant's advocates would "carry on their
skirts the blood of thousands of their slaughtered countrymen."[104]

The colonel of the "Washburne Lead Mine Regiment," from Washburne's
and Grant's own Illinois neighborhood, disabused Washburne of his defensive fantasy, telling him that it would be an understatement to say that
Grant's army was surprised at Pittsburg Landing. "It was worse," wrote
the colonel, who had nearly been swallowed up with all his men; "we were
astonished." He blamed it on the division commanders, of whom he sin-
gled out Grant's favorite, William T. Sherman. Augustus Chetlain, the col-

onel of the 12th Illinois, backhandedly confirmed for Washburne that the army had failed to keep watch: Chetlain initially insisted that there had been no surprise, but then he admitted there had been one — which he, too, attributed to the negligence of division commanders. The editor of the powerful *Chicago Tribune,* Joseph Medill, advised Washburne to stop "whistling against the wind" in defense of his celebrated townsman. Medill concurred that Grant was "played out," and it seemed clear to him that Grant's soldiers were "down on" the general.[105]

A Pennsylvania newspaperman and politician later alleged that a prescient Lincoln rejected his plea to remove Grant at that juncture, remarking that he could not spare the general because "he fights." As dubious as that postwar recollection probably is, the pressure for Grant's replacement grew fairly widespread that spring, and especially among the soldiers camped along the Tennessee River. Grant seemed to recognize as much, and he allowed his staff to alert Congressman Washburne that he would like "extremely well" to be transferred to the Department of the South, on the Carolina coast.[106]

A British immigrant in one of Sherman's Ohio regiments guessed accurately that Shiloh had been "the biggest fight of the new world." The gunfire had almost shredded the forest. Not a single tree seemed to have escaped shot and shell, and nowhere in a two-mile swath through the woods could the eye miss ominous mounds of fresh earth, some of which covered hundreds of dead men. The battle shocked a nation entranced with the image of waning rebellion. Southern determination had at least rebounded from the humiliating defeats of the winter, if it had ever flagged as much as Northerners supposed: the citizens of occupied Tennessee had shown enough defiance to foretell furious resistance in the Deep South.[107]

The Confederates had fought with astounding courage, surging into volleys of canister and musketry that mowed them down like grass before a scythe — in an analogy that more than one Federal employed. Union morale required a mechanical explanation for such valor from the enemy, lest it breed admiration and fear, and thus arose the spontaneous myth that Beauregard had primed his troops for the attack with whiskey.[108] The stubborn assaults had let more blood at Shiloh than most citizens could fathom, with nearly nineteen thousand men listed as killed and wounded and another four thousand missing, many of whom had also died. Grant's army had borne more than half those casualties, and it had been fearfully injured in both body and spirit. Most of the Union losses had fallen on Grant's own Army of the Tennessee, which sacrificed a quarter of its strength, primarily in the first day's fighting. The horror of such extensive slaughter stunned and sickened participants on both sides and citizens of both nations, but the suffering of the wounded evoked worse anguish than the harvest of death. Shot and shell had wrought indiscriminate carnage, maiming beardless boys and greying grandfathers alike; volunteer nurses who flocked to aid the wounded found them "mutilated in every imaginable way." Medical attendants revealed unbearable sadness and dismay as they tried to treat and comfort the human wreckage of the battle.[109]

For weeks thereafter hospital transports plied the Tennessee, Ohio, and Missouri rivers with their staterooms and main decks almost covered by serried cots of wounded men. A contract surgeon on one of those converted steamboats observed that many of the wounded seemed unable to bear up under the pain and helplessness of their condition. One Union officer came out of the fight with a wound in his left arm that the surgeons expected to heal completely, but with a wound in his heart that would not heal at all. An army transport delivered him to a St. Louis hospital, where he lodged comfortably, hired a personal attendant, and sent for his wife. Before she could reach him he sank into a deep depression and gave away all his possessions except his revolver, which he took in his good hand and turned on himself.[110]

2

Demons out of the Earth

For all the bumbling, bloodletting, and sudden evidence of Southern resolution, Shiloh had provided another Union success. Proud headlines again proclaimed glorious victory, however devastating it might have been to the élan of the troops involved and however devoid of tangible results. Western newspapers congratulated Grant's troops for having repelled as many as ninety thousand Southerners on Sunday morning, and such wildly exaggerated estimates of enemy strength failed to dampen Republican editors' confidence in "a speedy winding up of the rebellion."[1]

On the same day that Sidney Johnston attacked Grant's camps, the campaign to open the Mississippi River began with a spectacular artillery duel between Union gunboats and Confederate batteries on Island No. 10, near the watery nexus of Missouri, Kentucky, and Tennessee. Two days after the firing subsided at Pittsburg Landing, seven thousand Confederates evacuated Island No. 10 and meekly surrendered to pursuing Federals just inside the Tennessee state line. Four days after Shiloh, and a hundred miles to the east, a Union division swooped down out of Tennessee to capture Huntsville, Alabama. The town lay on the Memphis & Charleston Railroad, which connected the eastern and western halves of the Confederacy, and on the first day of occupation Union troops secured a hundred miles of that railroad. The Confederates defending Stevenson retreated without firing a shot — "as usual," wrote the Union commander. Possession of the Memphis & Charleston posed an immediate threat to the eastern flank of Beauregard's battered Confederate army at Corinth.[2] A fortnight later United States ships steamed up the Mississippi River, barged past two old forts standing in the way, and after a one-sided battle with a makeshift Confederate fleet continued on to New Orleans; Union officers and their escorts marched brazenly into the Confederacy's largest city and busiest seaport with no more resistance than the imaginative profanity of the indignant citizens.[3] All the while, forts on the North Carolina and Georgia coast were surrendering to Union siege operations, thereby subjecting additional Southern ports to more effective naval blockade and securing staging areas for further incursions into the interior.[4]

The concerted Confederate effort at Shiloh might, therefore, have constituted an aberration, and six weeks after that battle the survivors of a martyred Indiana officer still hoped to see the war end within another month.[5] Certainly, Southern troops had not demonstrated extraordinary mettle or tenacity anywhere else that spring. They had fled New Mexico Territory, abandoning anything that might impede them. The garrison of Fernandina, Florida, decamped on the first rumor of the Federals' approach, evacuating strong fortifications and leaving behind considerable heavy ordnance. Confederates gave up without a fight even at Pensacola, where a year before they had been willing to gamble everything on a battle for Fort Pickens.

From Roanoke Island to Island No. 10 the Confederacy had lost more than thirty thousand troops in just sixty days — about one-tenth of its entire army between the Atlantic and the Rio Grande. By the second week of April the Southern need for reinforcements had grown critical, especially since most of the rest of that army had enlisted for a one-year term that was about to expire, and volunteering had begun to flag. President Davis had already attempted to answer that emergency with a proposal for decidedly un-Confederate legislation giving the central government authority to conscript new soldiers involuntarily from the general population. In addition, he asked to simply extend the one-year enlistment of those already in uniform for another two years. The Confederate Senate addressed Davis's message on March 29 and sent it to committee, but both houses quickly granted the executive appeal after debate in secret session. The bill broke faith with soldiers who had contracted for specified terms, and conflicted sharply with a culture steeped in the doctrine of personal liberty. It also violated the basic principle of states' rights for which the individual states had initially seceded. Some senators fought the conscription law on those grounds, and at least one condemned it as a throwback to European despotism, but only two House members ultimately opposed it. The more passionately independent newspapers and citizens denounced conscription as the death knell of Southern liberty, and prospective conscripts scrambled for exemptions, but the invasion of

their homeland seemed to muffle most Southerners' outrage at the idea of
a central government forcing their friends and neighbors into uniform.[6]

The same week that saw the closing of Northern recruiting offices
therefore also saw the Confederacy begin to vastly accelerate the expan-
sion of its own armies. Davis's call for conscription had been published in
the *Richmond Examiner* late in March, and on April 28 Confederate authorities in Richmond published the draft law in full for distribution to
the army. Three days later — about as long as it would have taken for him
to receive a stray copy of that document — Edwin Stanton felt it necessary to claim that he had only stopped recruiting in order to find out how
many men the states had already supplied in volunteers. As though embarrassed to openly contradict his four-week-old order, Stanton merely
authorized his army commanders to appeal to the governors within their
departments for recruits to fill up the regiments they had already sent to
the field. That yielded only a relative handful of new volunteers, and eighteen days later Stanton caught all the Northern state governors off-guard
by asking how soon they could provide a total of fifty-one new regiments.
Still he hesitated to rescind the official recruiting ban, but he asked each
governor north of the Ohio River and the Mason-Dixon Line to organize
one new regiment immediately. "Do everything in your power to urge enlistments," read the War Department appeal: clearly the secretary of war
saw that he had made a dreadful mistake, though he stubbornly avoided
any admission of it.[7]

There were those who supposed that recruiting would be much more
successful if the government would only transform the war to restore the
Union into a crusade for freedom. Abolitionists of both the active and
passive persuasion had been hoping for as much from the firing of the
first gun, although the concept seemed more spontaneous among Ameri-
cans with the most recent European associations. A few days after Fort
Sumter surrendered, Adam Gurowski — that refugee Polish revolutionary working in the State Department — predicted that slavery would have
to fall and massive armies would have to be mobilized if the nation was to
be reunited. The war had not finished its second week when, way out on
the plains of Minnesota, the sodbusting son of a Swiss immigrant mentioned to relatives that the North lacked any unifying principle: though
he would never deign to fight for it himself, he suggested abolition as a
potential rallying point.[8]

That notion spread as the months passed, and especially within the
Boston sphere, where emancipation had always struck a more fervent
chord. Senator Sumner, the eternal champion of antislavery doctrine,
stood with those who secretly welcomed the Union defeat at Bull Run be-

cause it would prolong the war enough to crush slavery, and before much longer one Regular Army captain with Brahmin ties concluded that meaningful victory could never be won without abolition.[9] A few weeks later one of that captain's fellow Harvard alumni grieved that the administration's hesitation on the subject of slavery threatened any opportunity for "true success." Even among some of the less sophisticated and sympathetic, the idea took root that slavery would have to end if the South was to be wrestled permanently back into the Union. After reading the president's message to Congress in December of 1861, a sergeant from western Massachusetts remarked that Lincoln "don't talk nigger enough . . . Nigger has got to be talked, and thoroughly talked to[o] and I think niggers will come out of this scrape free."[10]

That hardly seemed to reflect the prevailing public opinion, though, and in order to retain both radical and conservative support for the war, the president had played his hand close to the vest, quashing those of his generals who attempted to incorporate emancipation decrees into the management of their military departments. In order to hold Kentucky's good will he had forced Frémont to modify such a proclamation in Missouri in the summer of 1861, but as he prepared his December message for Congress Lincoln confided to Senator Browning his plans for an offer of federal subsidy for gradual, compensated emancipation in the border states. The government could pay five hundred dollars apiece for every slave in Delaware, Maryland, Kentucky, and Missouri without reaching the cost of four months of the war, he calculated, and the program could be carried out over a period of twenty years. Lincoln supposed at the time — and Browning concurred — that the freed slaves should be transported elsewhere for colonization in order to avoid their amalgamation into white society.[11]

He withheld that initiative until after the late-winter military successes, but in March he sent a message to Congress proposing a joint congressional resolution pledging federal aid for any state that might pass an act of compensated emancipation. This time he made no suggestion of colonizing the freedmen. Some border-state newspapers gave it considerable support: the implicit recognition of slave owners' property rights, the acknowledgment that emancipation remained a matter of state jurisdiction, and the emphasis on gradual emancipation made Lincoln's suggestion much more palatable than the immediate and confiscatory federal abolition espoused by most radicals.[12] The antislavery press nevertheless responded to the proposal with great relish, rejoicing at executive attention to any form of abolition, and more moderate organs gave it support as well. The *New York Times* wondered about the pecuniary practicality of buying slaves, but Lincoln responded with a modification of the economic argument he had made to Browning, noting that soon the cost of the war would exceed the cost of paying for every slave on the continent. That brought the *Times* into line.[13]

Charles Sumner called Lincoln's message "an epoch." He told one correspondent that it would win the unqualified allegiance of all the border states, and informed another that "I hope it will commence the end," with no grounds for optimism beyond his own desire. Not one border-state congressman approached Lincoln about it, so the president appealed to his postmaster general, Montgomery Blair. Blair maintained connections in the three largest border states: he had been born and raised in Kentucky, and he had served as a judge in Missouri and as mayor of St. Louis before moving to Maryland to practice law. The president asked him to convene a delegation of border-state representatives for a White House conference, hoping to convince them that this offered a relatively painless and voluntary escape from slavery's inevitable decline.[14] Both houses of Congress passed the resolution on voice votes within five weeks, and Lincoln signed it, but it only proclaimed that the government "ought to" offer financial aid if any slave state should opt for abolition. No border state acted on the tentative offer.[15]

The only abolition victory that spring came in the nation's capital itself. In the first week of the session, back in early December, Congressman John Hutchins of Ohio had introduced a bill designed to end slavery in the District of Columbia. Before Christmas, Senator Henry Wilson of Massachusetts had offered a similar proposal in the upper house, but both bills disappeared into committee. Not until the middle of February, after Senator Bright had been expelled, did the Senate version return with amendments and a recommendation for printing.[16] Senators took up the bill in the middle of March, picking and prodding at it for the rest of the month. It read very much like a resolution that Congressman Abraham Lincoln had tentatively drawn up in January of 1849. Lincoln's plan had called for the gradual emancipation of slaves born within the District from 1850 onward; it had also prohibited the importation of new slaves and provided for federal compensation to owners who opted to free the slaves they already held. The 1849 draft, which Lincoln never formally introduced, had also required a referendum on the question among the District's white male voters.[17]

By the first of April, Republican newspapers were calling for immediate passage of the new bill, and radicals anticipated the demand. Feeling their strength, they argued for immediate and universal District emancipation — contrary, as a Delaware senator reminded them, to the gradual freedom provided in every state that had previously abolished slavery. They also removed the ingredient of voter approval: Senator Lyman

Trumbull contended that District voters had no authority to decide whether his national capital should bear the taint of human bondage. In his 1849 draft Representative Lincoln had reserved the right of slave-holding congressmen to bring personal servants into the capital for the duration of their terms, but the Senate bill contained no such exclusion. Even conservative Republicans balked at the obstinacy of their abolitionist colleagues, but Senator Sumner defended the measure with "unspeakable delight." He spent most of the last afternoon in March counting the virtues of the bill as a debt owed to an enslaved race, reciting a detailed history of the District and tossing in an account of the efforts to free American citizens held in slavery by Algerian pirates.[18]

For the next three days the topic dominated Senate debate just as the expulsion of Bright had, eight weeks before. Thinking about the matter of colonization, which the bill also omitted, Orville Browning tried to manipulate the amount of compensation, which had been reduced from Lincoln's earlier figures of $500 and $400 per slave to $300 apiece. He hoped to raise that number back to $500, but whether that passed or not he wished to reserve everything over $250 for distribution to the slaves themselves, if they would consent to migrate elsewhere. Browning admitted to a preference for mandatory colonization, but in an effort to submit it in time he had scrawled his amendment too quickly to describe a satisfactory colonization process. Freed slaves were barred from many free states, he pointed out, yet they were often required to leave slave states if once liberated, and he described them being driven from place to place like "the wild beasts of the forest." Only expatriation seemed satisfactory. "I do not believe that the races ever can live together in harmony and with mutual advantage," Browning confessed, reflecting the attitude described by his fellow plainsman in the White House, and he hoped the cash incentive would begin the process.[19]

The Senate rejected Browning's amendment as the debate wound down. On the afternoon of April 3 Senate Bill No. 108 passed with a majority of more than two-thirds. After the weekend the House of Representatives took up the bill, where once again all the traditional antagonisms of the slavery fight arose amid less courteous combatants. Abolitionist congressmen sailed into the melee with all their antebellum zealotry, but it was primarily the more moderate Kentucky representatives who took up the sword for the departed Deep South plantation owners. That diluted the rhetoric of the opposition, but the bill's enemies never had a chance. The final battle came on Friday, April 11 — the eve of the war's first anniversary — and it lasted all day. Old John J. Crittenden predicted "much mischief" from the bill's instant transformation of slaves from servitude to freedom, and his fellow Kentuckian Charles Wickliffe doubted the wisdom of allowing Friday afternoon's slaves to become Monday morning's courtroom witnesses; Wickliffe suspected that radicals intended to use such freedmen to "prove" the disloyalty of their former masters. Wickliffe attempted to insert the recognition of officeholders' servants and the hurdle of local referendum, but both amendments died by margins of three and four to one. Even Republicans who sought to make minor changes in the bill found themselves frustrated by a determined majority. William Dunn, a Republican from Indiana, proposed a small reduction in the rather generous salary authorized for the clerk of the commission that would determine the value of freed slaves, only to be ruled out of order when he tried to explain his reasoning.

"If I would utter here some foul abuse of slaveholders," he sneered, "then I suppose I should be perfectly in order."

"Oh, yes," Wickliffe agreed, to the amusement of the chamber, "you would be in order then."

Dunn remarked on an apparent conspiracy to allow no modifications to the bill at all, and he may have been right. His very reasonable housekeeping amendment failed soundly. The dinner hour had already come as the final vote on the original referred bill showed ninety-two supporters and thirty-nine opponents. Thaddeus Stevens, a devoted abolitionist from Pennsylvania, jumped up to invoke the routine parliamentary trick of calling for reconsideration, which he then asked his collaborators to table. They did, thus sealing any attempt to resurrect the issue, and the hungry representatives adjourned at 6:10 PM. An hour later, crowds filled the hotel lobbies on Pennsylvania Avenue, digesting the news with their evening meals.[20]

The Senate had already adjourned for the weekend, and the Speaker of the House failed to send the resolution back to the upper chamber until Monday evening. Senator Browning took it to the White House that very night, where the president received it with some regret. He said he would sign it, but he still preferred the gradual manumission that he had favored in 1849: as passed, the bill would abruptly deprive families of their servants and immediately strip the servants of their owners' protection and support. Furthermore, he told Browning that he would not sign it for another two days. It appeared that Representative Wickliffe had spoken from a personal perspective when he sought exceptions for the slaves of congressmen, for he owned some of his own, and he had asked the president to give him until Wednesday to transport a couple of them outside the District boundaries. Lincoln agreed to postpone the law for that long, as he told Browning in the strictest confidence. Browning faithfully guarded that delicious piece of gossip, so Senator Sumner never knew how close he came to the mark when he accused Lincoln of arbitrarily perpetuating slavery with his mysterious two-day delay.[21]

Brooklyn abolitionist Henry Ward Beecher prodded Lincoln with a telegram on the morning of April 16, asking if that afternoon's edition of his newspaper could report freedom in the District. Such self-righteous souls as Sumner and Beecher might chastise the president for waiting another forty-eight hours to strike the first blow against a centuries-old wrong, but more humble opponents of slavery welcomed the new law with unqualified pleasure. A Quaker weekly in Philadelphia observed that "at least this one blot upon the nation's character has been wiped out by peaceful legislation."[22] The Sixteenth Ward Republican Association of New York City warmly congratulated Lincoln on that first step toward ending the injustice that had brought the war about. A black native of Alexandria, Virginia, who had long since emigrated to Haiti wrote the president directly as soon as he heard of the new law, thanking him personally for signing the bill.[23]

District emancipation gratified some citizens who had not previously numbered themselves with antislavery agitators. From his home on New York City's Gramercy Park, lawyer George Templeton Strong recorded with obvious satisfaction that "the nation has washed its hands of slavery." Recalling that only "damned abolitionists" would have hoped for such a thing a year before, he speculated that "abolitionist" might wear a less pejorative connotation with the passing of another year. Strong may have alluded to his own transformation on the issue: barely a year before, when he had detected implied moral condemnation of slavery in Lincoln's inaugural address, he had complained that "we Northerners object to slavery on grounds of political economics, not of ethics."[24]

In the North, at least, few people had ever doubted that Congress owned the authority to end slavery inside the District of Columbia. That reduced public complaint about District emancipation, which may have led certain advocates of abolition to infer a greater shift in public opinion than circumstances justified.

Unfortunately for Abraham Lincoln, he had just appointed one of those abolition advocates to command the Department of the South. Major General David Hunter was approaching his sixtieth birthday that spring. He had spent all but twenty-two of those years in uniform, but only in the previous year had he achieved significant rank or notoriety, primarily because he had cultivated a belated friendship with Mr. Lincoln. Now he seemed bound to make up for lost time. His department stretched eight hundred miles, from the Florida Keys to the border between the Carolinas, but his effective jurisdiction reached only to the Sea Islands and the coast. Escaped slaves flocked to the camps of his various detachments, and early in May Hunter began collecting the able-bodied men among them at Hilton Head, where he started forming them into companies and regiments for "public service," whether they wished to serve or not. He took that enormous step toward arbitrarily drafting and arming black soldiers with the assent of the secretary of war — the author of the recent recruiting blunder. On May 9, perhaps to lure thousands more fugitives (and potential recruits) out of the interior, Hunter decreed immediate freedom for all slaves within his authority.[25]

General Hunter was the man Lincoln had chosen to relieve Frémont from command in Missouri, where Frémont had issued another emancipation order only to have the president quash it. Hunter must, therefore, have supposed that Lincoln's attitude on the subject had changed, and his misunderstanding may have had its source in Lincoln's proposal for compensated emancipation, as well as in his endorsement of abolition in the District of Columbia.

Lincoln knew nothing about Hunter's controversial pronouncement for a week. The Confederates had evacuated Yorktown in the wee hours of May 4: their army seemed to be on the run, and Lincoln appears to have wanted to be on hand in case McClellan needed direction.[26] He left Washington on Monday evening, May 5, on the revenue steamer *Miami*, taking Edwin Stanton and Salmon P. Chase with him and expecting to return in a day or two. Despite exciting telegrams describing complete victory, McClellan checked his pursuit at Williamsburg the next evening, typically fearing that he faced overwhelming numbers.[27] The final clash that everyone anticipated did not come, though the three top-hatted executives whiled away five days at Hampton Roads, and McClellan never came down to see them. They interviewed generals and commodores, hectoring them to action. They nosed about the shore in tugs and cutters, looking for a place to land troops for the capture of Norfolk. The three of them watched a naval engagement that brought the ironclad *Virginia* into view, and they stood by during the assault on Norfolk, which Chase and Lincoln both thought the generals would never have undertaken without the pressure of executive presence: Chase went right into the city with the troops. Lincoln postponed their return for a few hours on May 11 when he heard that the *Virginia* had been blown up by her crew, but they reached Washington early the next morning.[28]

The purported wording of Hunter's proclamation still took three or four more days to reach the White House through the newspapers. Chase urged the president to let the order stand, allowing Hunter to take the responsibility on the excuse of military necessity. It would gain much support for the administration with little cost, Chase argued, implying as well that if other commanders followed Hunter's example the complication of slavery might be entirely resolved without executive interference. Lincoln replied privately with a single, vehement sentence: "No commanding general shall do such a thing upon *my* responsibility, without consulting me."[29]

By this time Edwin Stanton had grown anxious enough about recruiting the army that he had inquired of the governors how quickly they might raise those fifty-one new regiments. John Andrew, the zealously abolitionist governor of Massachusetts, responded on May 19 that Massachusetts men might not come forward very quickly this time to fight a war of limited goals, but he predicted that if Lincoln would sustain General Hunter "the roads will swarm" with volunteers. That broad hint would have failed to move the president, but it came too late in any case. Lincoln disavowed Hunter's proclamation that same day, reserving to himself alone the authority for such a decree, which he declared that he would exercise only if he felt it crucial to preservation of the government (and Secretary Chase supposed that the time for that contingency lay near). Lincoln also used the occasion to reiterate the offer of compensated emancipation that he had directed primarily at the border states. It was not merely to retain the faith of the border states that he disapproved Hunter's gambit. As far north as Lake Erie, Democratic editors who had otherwise supported the war denounced Hunter's proclamation as illegal, despotic, and a betrayal of the limited goal of reunion articulated since the outset of the fighting.[30]

Governor Andrew's prediction notwithstanding, the annulment of Hunter's proclamation probably had nothing to do with the sudden dearth of willing volunteers. Enrollment had been going slowly since Stanton closed the recruiting offices, and blame might have been cast on an assortment of factors. The very shift in the focus of the war, as illustrated by Hunter's decree, surely dissuaded many a man of conservative political affiliation. Then there was the season of the year, for an agricultural nation turned extremely busy in the spring. The economy had also improved dramatically, thanks largely to the government's insatiable military appetite, and the country no longer teemed with the unemployed tradesmen, operatives, and laborers who had flooded the recruiting offices in 1861. The astonishing brutality of Shiloh had also dampened the ardor of those who might, under other circumstances, have been drawn by the chance for a little adventure; the shocking tales of misery, abuse, and exploitation that discharged or furloughed veterans carried to the home folks dismayed many an eligible neighbor.

Only the occasional, solitary volunteer sought to join the army that spring. Recruiting offices no longer beckoned with bunting and martial music, and only rarely did towns even see the uniformed veteran seeking replacements for vacancies in his regiment. With state recruiting suspended, the Regular Army offered the only avenue for young men overtaken by patriotism or tedium.

Few youths typified the recruit of that period better than Ira Pettit, who lived on his father's farm at the extreme western fringe of New York's Ontario shore. He turned twenty-one on May 12, 1862, when that age still marked a boy's official freedom from parental control, and he greeted adult life with stern resolution. All the following week he continued to plow his father's fields and plant peas, corn, and potatoes, but six days into his majority he formally acknowledged his membership in the local Baptist congregation. Then, after talking with a friend who had come home from his regiment on furlough, Pettit made another momentous decision: a few days later his parents drove him to the county seat, where a sergeant of the 11th U.S. Infantry signed him up for three years in the Regular Army. Soon, the first train Ira Pettit ever rode took him eastward to sights that amazed him, on the first leg of an odyssey from which he would never return. He was the only recruit on the train.[31]

The romantic allure struck deep among young Victorians of all castes, and offered one of the most effective recruiting incentives before the war reached its more brutal stages. A sharpshooter on the front lines before Yorktown could still write home in early May that in fair weather "Picket Duty is of course the Poetry of our life (the matter of killing aside)." Idyllic newspaper engravings of such scenes abetted that illusion, but a taste of even noncombatant service soured the martial ambitions of some youths who should have been most susceptible to that sentimental appeal. One seventeen-year-old boy who had gone to war as the servant of a Massachusetts captain came home that spring when the captain resigned, proclaiming that "home is the best place to be" and disavowing any inclination to return.[32]

Disillusionment — both direct and vicarious — wrought great damage on the appealing classic imagery of soldiering. Newton Colby, a young family man of limited financial prospects, had been hounding Lincoln's cabinet officers for a government sinecure at the outset of the war. In the wake of Fort Sumter he had quickly found adequate government compensation as lieutenant of an infantry company, but after a year he entertained little hope of promotion, so he had resigned and come home to Corning, New York. Finding no occupation sufficiently lucrative in the Tioga Valley, he took advantage of Stanton's resumption of recruiting within a fortnight of his return, rented office space, and began advertising for a company of his own. For long weeks his investment yielded only the most dismal results.[33]

The same lethargy afflicted recruiting nearly everywhere. So seldom did the adventurous impulse inspire men of military age by the middle of May that the governor of New Hampshire, Nathaniel Berry, had experienced much difficulty collecting just a couple of hundred men to fill the gaps in one of his early regiments. On reading the War Department's May 19 appeal he turned to a little independent company of volunteers who garrisoned Fort Constitution, in Portsmouth harbor, signing them up as the nucleus of a new regiment.[34] He named a tentative colonel for that regiment — former state senate president Joseph Gilmore, who immediately began distributing recruiting concessions to prospective captains. Territorial disputes erupted between those captains, however, and Gilmore argued ferociously with Berry for the right to select all his subordinate officers. Within days the would-be colonel quit in a huff, though he played coy for another week or so. Some of the aspiring captains kept soliciting men to sign their informal rolls, but after a month they had collected only a dozen or two unattached teenagers and widowers who had expressed theoretical interest in going to war with them. By the end of June the entire state still had not produced a full company.[35]

Stanton had asked the Northern governors for a regiment apiece on May 21. Like Governor Berry, John Andrew had to look to his harbor forts for ready-made recruits, choosing the six-company battalion that guarded Fort Warren, on Governor's Island. On May 22 he offered to send that battalion to Washington within a few days, promising to recruit four additional companies to complete the desired regiment. The War Department accepted it, but a couple of months would pass before Andrew could forward the first of those companies. Recruiters in Maine had found their task exceedingly difficult even before the butchery at Shiloh, and Governor Israel Washburn likewise had to strip his coastal forts as the only reliable source of immediate volunteers, but that yielded only ten dozen soldiers to allay the concerns of the secretary of war.[36]

Westerners responded no more enthusiastically. Minnesota's governor quickly replied that such a demand would be difficult to meet at that juncture, and indeed he failed to comply. The governor of Wisconsin seemed more optimistic, but he was unable to provide a regiment that season. Neither was the governor of Iowa — where, nearly a month after Stanton issued his call, a college student reported that no one was even talking about enlisting. "The war fever has pretty generally subsided," he concluded.[37]

Congress squandered an opportunity to vastly enhance the inducements for enlistment that spring. For at least the fifth time in a decade, the House of Representatives debated a bill to grant homesteads to settlers on the public land, primarily in the West, and most of the discussion involved additional benefits for the country's soldiers. Imitating the practice of the British crown in colonial times, the government had compensated the soldiers of previous wars with bounty land, and since Lincoln's first call for troops many recruits had supposed that a generous and grateful nation would eventually offer them such an emolument. The original name of the bill heightened that expectation, describing it as a provision not only for homesteads to actual settlers but for cash bounties to soldiers in lieu of bounty lands. When the bill came up for discussion in December of 1861, a few conservatives resisted the idea of bounty land at all, fearing that the recipients would be bilked of the land by speculators, just as earlier veterans had been deprived of their grants at pennies an acre. Some, like Ohio Democrat Clement Vallandigham, also worried that granting land to every soldier would flood the market with such discounted warrants and reduce the value of all the public land. Republican John Covode wanted to withhold any land warrants until after the close of hostilities, lest soldiers find all the prime land taken up by those who declined to serve, but most of his colleagues wanted to see the public lands settled as quickly as possible. The conflict ultimately boiled down to whether soldiers would receive bounty money and land as well, or bounty money alone.[38]

The absence of a majority of Southern representatives removed most of the historic opposition to the homestead bill. Because of uncertainty over the military situation, though, the lower house postponed discussion until February. When they finally took it up again, the military successes of late winter had begun, and in the delirium of apparent victory the representatives retained the provision for cash bounties of thirty dollars to the three-month militia of 1861 and a hundred dollars to those who later volunteered for longer service. On the last day of the month they passed the bill with a margin of nearly seven to one and sent it to the Senate, where it went to a committee that completely transformed it with a flurry of amendments. Not until early May did it reach the floor of the Senate, with none of the bounty provisions. Senator John Carlile, a Virginia loyalist, tried to reinsert a paragraph giving soldiers land in place of more money, but that amendment failed miserably. The bill itself passed on May 6 with only seven slave-state senators and mossback Democrats holding out against it. The House disagreed with the Senate's copious amendments, but no one seemed inclined to scuttle the session's most popular legislation. Within a week committees from either house forged acceptable revisions, and Lincoln signed the bill on May 20.[39]

The act would go into effect on January 1, 1863, allowing each adult male or head of household a quarter-section as large as 160 acres. The only advantage the new law afforded veterans over civilians was the right to file a homestead claim before reaching the age of twenty-one, but that yielded little benefit: nearly all of the soldiers in the army at that point would already be that old if they survived until the end of their terms. The architects of the final version evidently still expected the war to end within the calendar year, which would have given veterans at least an equal opportunity for choice parcels, but most volunteers had signed up in regiments that would not muster out until 1864. While those men were serving out their time, civilian settlers could venture westward to stake out the best land.

Thus perished one of the most promising potential attractions for recruits, even as the secretary of war was growing frantic for men to replenish his army. Mr. Stanton had only begun to comprehend how little martial enthusiasm remained in Northern hearts when Stonewall Jackson delivered the first of several blows that would electrify official Washington over the next hundred days. That crisis struck just when the president and his cabinet wondered whether they might not have to finish the struggle with the armies that had already taken the field.

One of the foremost armies in the field at that moment, so far as White House thinking went, belonged to Irvin McDowell. McDowell was not a drinking man, but as his girth suggested he liked his comforts, and from the fourth week of April he had enjoyed very comfortable headquarters in J. Horace Lacy's home. "Chatham," as Lacy called his Georgian mansion, sat atop a bluff near Falmouth, Virginia, overlooking the Rappahannock River and the city of Fredericksburg.[40] McDowell's first troops had reached the Rappahannock on the morning of April 18, after an all-night march, to find the bridges burning and Confederate infantry scampering up a long slope beyond the city. Those Confederates had come back into town periodically in late April to collect conscripts under the new draft law, but then McDowell crossed the river and took possession of the city. The largest portion of McDowell's corps camped nearby; five or six miles below Fredericksburg lay a few Confederate brigades, but their numbers did not amount to half his own and they offered no serious trouble. McDowell spent a couple of weeks restoring the sabotaged railroad that would carry his supplies to Falmouth from the river landing at Aquia Creek, preparing teams and trains for overland travel meanwhile and trying to stop his troops from stealing all the livestock in the vicinity. While Washington bigwigs pondered what to do with his command, McDowell whiled away the evenings in the various division and brigade headquarters, visiting with subordinates in the commandeered parlors and dining rooms of Fredericksburg's first families. McDowell dropped in continually on one of his more industrious brigadiers, who complained after one late-evening visit that his chief "hangs on terribly."[41]

It was during an afternoon call on that very brigadier, on May 16, that McDowell received a War Department telegram ordering him up to Washington right away. He rode immediately to the landing and steamed up the Potomac for a late-night conference with the president, and the next day the general returned to the Rappahannock with marching orders. Lincoln had decided to build McDowell's corps up to full strength and send him down the line of the Richmond, Fredericksburg & Potomac Railroad toward the Confederate capital, where he would cooperate with the Army of the Potomac. Ten months after his humiliating defeat at Bull Run, McDowell would have the opportunity to redeem his reputation, and with a larger force than he had commanded in the summer of 1861. The prospect so stirred McDowell that he made no effort to keep it a secret, and within twenty-four hours the common soldiers were gossiping about it in letters home.[42]

A few days later, down on the Virginia Peninsula, George McClellan read a copy of that order, and his first thought ran to his right of seniority: when McDowell's troops connected with his own, would he assume command of the whole, by virtue of rank and department boundaries? Lincoln assured him that he would, but the president had told McDowell something a little different: while he expected McDowell to cooperate and obey McClellan's orders once they joined, Lincoln gave McDowell implicit latitude to decline any orders for a movement of his corps that would uncover Washington. Even from a distance of a hundred miles, Lincoln wanted to keep a substantial force between the warring capitals.[43]

While the portly McDowell and the compact McClellan threatened Richmond from the north and east, the president hoped to wield a third army against the city from the west. He had sent General Frémont into the mountains of western Virginia, creating a whole new department to give him a command worthy of his stature and rank — rather than for any strategic necessity; he reinforced that department from the same Army of the Potomac that McClellan had already complained of as too small. Now, as he formulated McDowell's orders, Lincoln asked Frémont about swooping down on the Virginia & Tennessee Railroad west of Lynchburg. By severing that line he could cut the rebel capital off from the western Confederacy and then move against Richmond from that direction.[44]

McClellan still fidgeted before Richmond, which — in his archaic view of war as a chess-like contest for kings and capitals — he considered the goal that would yield complete victory. He supposed that his enemy entertained the same attitude, and would concentrate all his forces to defend the seat of government, so he discounted all the worries over northward thrusts by raiding Confederates, yet he continued to report himself severely outnumbered and wailed for reinforcements. McDowell's movement was meant to answer that wail in a way that Washington politicians would find palatable. The persistent appeals for more men and the repeated warnings of an impending battle against overwhelming numbers had soured much of Washington on Little Mac. "McNapoleon," as the State Department's Gurowski had begun to call him, seemed only to dig, wait, and complain; one of the president's secretaries may have reflected the White House image when he speculated that it would take a new general to put the Army of the Potomac to any use.[45] Even McClellan's original patron at the Treasury Department was losing confidence in him. On May 21 Secretary Chase confided to Horace Greeley that the general was "a dear luxury — fifty days — fifty miles — fifty millions of dollars —" and he recorded his first doubts of McClellan's capacity for battle, "should his army ever fight one."[46]

With the president's suggestion that he could exercise a certain degree of his own discretion even after joining the Army of the Potomac, McDowell wrote to McClellan in a tone more appropriate to an equal than to a subordinate. He spoke not of his corps, but of "the army under my command," and described his instructions to "cooperate with yours." The first person dominated McDowell's entire letter, with not a hint of any plural that included McClellan, and although he acknowledged that he was to cooperate with McClellan he concluded by asking what cooperation he could first expect from McClellan. Clearly McDowell, who had been under McClellan until a few weeks previously, wished to retain as much of his recovered independence as the circumstances would allow.[47]

Before McDowell moved south from Fredericksburg, he had to wait for James Shields to bring his division in from the Shenandoah Valley. That proud and pugnacious Irishman had served in the Illinois legislature with Abraham Lincoln, and had once challenged Lincoln to a duel that nearly came to fruition. During the Mexican War, Shields had been grievously wounded through the chest by a grape shot: his name had grown more famous because of the excruciating treatment he endured, and for his miraculous recovery, than for any military prowess he might have exhibited. He had beaten Stonewall Jackson two months before, however, and that gained him considerable prestige even though he had directed that battle in absentia. Shields pushed his eleven thousand men down the Valley Turnpike from New Market, veered east through Front Royal, and crossed the Blue Ridge at Chester Gap, arriving near Warrenton on May

18 in dire need of shoes for both man and beast. There he remained for nearly three days, while farriers shod as many of the twenty-five hundred horses in his artillery batteries and wagon train as they could. His column left there on the twenty-first and arrived on the Rappahannock the next day, somewhat the worse for wear, but his division brought McDowell's strength to some forty thousand.[48]

The uncertainties of managing army movements at long range so vexed Abraham Lincoln that he champed to visit the front again. On the afternoon of Thursday, May 22, he mounted his horse for a ride through Washington's streets alongside Mrs. Lincoln's carriage, and when they stopped at Senator Browning's residence Lincoln revealed that he planned to slip away to McDowell's headquarters that night. Secretary Stanton telegraphed ahead to have a car ready at Aquia Creek for him and the president, and their boat arrived at the creek landing early Friday morning. Lincoln greeted his old antagonist and friend Shields, whose division he found still lacking footgear, decent clothing, and ammunition, but McDowell cheered the commander in chief with his eagerness to start for Richmond. He could not possibly supply Shields's men in time to leave by Saturday, the general explained, and he did not wish to wait until Monday. That left Sunday, but McDowell said that he knew Lincoln did not like to begin campaigns on Sundays. Apparently the president did entertain such a superstition, or perhaps it was merely a reaction to criticism that Bull Run was lost because it was fought on a Sunday, but he advised McDowell to "make a good ready" on Sunday and step off Monday morning.[49]

In the afternoon, Lincoln and Stanton crossed the river into Fredericksburg, riding out the Telegraph Road past Marye's Heights to Samuel Howison's estate. There, on a hillside a couple of miles south of town, a brigade of four New York regiments sprawled in the most advanced Federal camp. The soldiers dutifully trotted into formation without arms while their brigadier and his civilian guests rode by in review, raising cheers thunderous enough to alarm lookouts for the nearby Confederate force. Then the little celebrity entourage turned back for Fredericksburg. The president and secretary crossed back over the river to take a similarly hasty look at the rest of McDowell's corps, leaving after dark in good humor at the prospect of crushing the enemy between two powerful columns. When he resumed his desk in the White House the following day, Lincoln advised McClellan that McDowell would be coming, asking if McClellan could not assist him by interrupting the roads and railroads that supplied the Confederate force below Fredericksburg. Perhaps McClellan could intercept the lot of them as they retreated: Lincoln would be happy to see Richmond taken, and he fully anticipated that it would be, within a week or so, but he valued the Southern army as a more significant prize.[50]

When it came to the safety of Washington, however, Lincoln reverted anxiously to McClellan's image of a contest for capital cities, and over the following forty-eight hours Stonewall Jackson would exploit that anxiety to great advantage. Even as Lincoln and Stanton cantered before the cheering New Yorkers on Howison's Hill, Jackson flung his howling brigades down on the little Union detachment posted at Front Royal, in the Shenandoah Valley.

Front Royal guarded the Valley side of Manassas Gap, over the Blue Ridge Mountains. It sat astride the Manassas Gap Railroad, from which the Union forces holding the Valley drew their supplies, and Confederate control of the town would isolate those troops. The departure of James Shields's division had seriously depleted the Northern occupation force, leaving Nathaniel Banks at Strasburg with fewer than ten thousand troops. The nearest help of any substance consisted of thirty thousand men under Frémont, a full three days' march away over rugged mountains, and the scent of such vulnerability had brought Jackson crashing down on Banks.

Jackson crushed the little Front Royal garrison the afternoon of May 23, capturing the majority of it. His cavalry chased the survivors northward, toward Winchester, on a road converging with the Valley Turnpike that Banks would have to use to escape from Strasburg. Banks might have been cut off then and there, but long days of forced marches had brought Jackson's men to the end of their tether and he stopped them for the night.[51]

John W. Geary, a new brigadier general assigned to duty with Banks, maintained his headquarters east of the Blue Ridge, at Rectortown. Before the war Geary had served as mayor of San Francisco and territorial governor of Kansas, but wherever he went he soon proved himself a blowhard. Scattered companies of his troops monitored the Blue Ridge passes that evening, and he was the first to report the Front Royal disaster to Washington. In a telegram received at the War Department near 10:00 PM on Friday, May 23, Geary described heavy firing all afternoon from the direction of Strasburg, with the telegraph interrupted somewhere short of Front Royal. "If my position be attacked," he promised, in typically heroic prose, "I will hold to the last extremity." He used similarly soaring rhetoric in a stirring address to his troops, but he fled unashamedly the next day, at the first inaccurate hint of an enemy threat to his position. He left behind so much baggage, with no Confederates close enough to claim it, that

Union soldiers passing the flotsam of his flight a month later still jeered at his empty boasts.[52]

Banks realized his plight belatedly, having doubted the first shocking tales from Front Royal, but on Saturday morning he turned his division back toward Winchester, some twenty-five miles away. Harried by Confederate cavalry at the rear and hurried by reports of Confederate infantry nearing Winchester ahead of them, his troops reached there that evening, footsore and hungry.[53] Early on Sunday morning Jackson fell on them again, outnumbering them by two to one or more, and the fight did not last long. Banks turned north down the pike, toward Martinsburg and the Potomac River: the tail of his column had not cleared the northern edge of town before Jackson's men spilled into the southern outskirts, and the civilians who had borne Union occupation all spring helped the Yankees to hasten their retreat with an occasional round fired from an open window.[54]

At first the retreat promised to turn into a rout. From each street flowed streams of men running wildly for the highway north, flinging their knapsacks and overcoats alongside the road. Civilians black and white joined the exodus, including women on foot with children in tow. Banks and some of his senior officers managed to collar enough fugitive troops to form little squads and companies for resistance, and that helped slow the flight, but it never came to a complete halt until Martinsburg. After a short stop for breath there, the ragged column leaned back into the road for Williamsport, Maryland, thirty-five miles from Winchester, only to find that the Potomac ran too deep with recent rains for any but horsemen to ford it.[55]

Geary's nervous dispatches and the lack of other reliable information left Lincoln and his cabinet at sixes and sevens. By Saturday afternoon they supposed that Banks had already been cut off below Winchester, and Lincoln telegraphed both Frémont and McDowell to go to his aid. Frémont was to march for the Valley with everything he had. Abandoning the best chance that he would see during the entire war for capturing Richmond quickly, the president told McDowell to forget about his advance on Richmond and send half his corps of forty thousand — ten thousand directly overland and ten thousand by way of the Potomac River.[56] From Fort Monroe came a false rumor that "the Rebels are leaving Richmond," and the excitable secretary of war took that as confirmation that the Confederates had stripped their own capital to attack Washington with overwhelming forces.[57] Federal bureaucrats trembled again as they had the previous spring, when apparent threats from front and rear left them isolated from the rest of the country. In Baltimore, Unionist mobs assaulted numerous citizens who revealed satisfaction with the Confederate advance, inspiring perverted reports of another Baltimore riot, and those reports contributed to a paranoid atmosphere that infected citizens of all stations in Washington. One distraught woman rushed from Willard's Hotel to the White House to ask if she ought to flee, and an executive variety of that same terror impelled the president to seize control of every railroad in the United States under military authority.[58]

Edwin Stanton wired frantically for new troops from the Northern governors, and all of his correspondence that weekend reflected the panic in the capital. The War Department had already learned that short-term enlistments produced ineffective soldiers at inordinate cost to the government, but on that Saturday and Sunday the secretary succumbed to the air of urgency and authorized still more emergency militia. He called for the 7th New York to come immediately, as it had in April of 1861, and he yielded to the arguments of governors who had assured him that far more recruits would respond to a call for three months than would enlist for three years. New York and Rhode Island sent ninety-day regiments within a couple of days, while Ohio, Indiana, and Illinois each began recruiting several new ones under the authority of that impulsive decision. A few dozen undergraduates at Dartmouth College and Norwich University formed a company of cavalry, joining a similar group from Brown University for a summer of bloodless, pointless frolic. In what one newspaper characterized as the "Second Uprising of the North," members of uniformed militia companies flocked to their armories. For a day or two recruiters in some cities began doing a fair business in three-month volunteers, but even that short hitch scared away many discriminating applicants, large numbers of whom had mistaken the call for a mere thirty days of service.[59]

Those summer soldiers postured piously, in imitation of the militiamen who had taken arms thirteen months before. "My country calls and I must fight for her," wrote one fastidious Rhode Island schoolteacher, "and if needs be give my life as a sacrifice," but he soon surrendered his rifle and sergeant's stripes for safer duty as the company clerk. "Wont I feel splendid if I come back a tough boy," speculated the dainty captain of one short-term company, "and I am inclined to think I will." Soldiers at the front ridiculed these holiday patriots, whom they satirized as "so rash as to offer their services" for a few weeks; even Senator Wade's son advised his younger brother against following him to war in such a superfluous capacity. Stanton's appeal actually tended to discourage some of the troops in the field when they heard about it: understanding that he had asked for another round of three-year recruits, men who had hoped to finish up the war that summer now assumed it would last at least through another winter.[60]

While Stanton badgered the governors, Banks endured a horrifying night on the edge of the roaring Potomac. His campfires illuminated the Virginia shore as famished, exhausted men heated their first meal in a full day before dropping into their blankets to sleep the sleep of the dead. Teamsters began worrying the wagons over the ford, and behind them the cavalry tried it, while squads of men ferried tediously across in a couple of pontoon boats and a stolen scow. Smaller horses held their heads high in water that ran over their withers. Dragged down by their harness and stumbling trace mates, horses and mules by the dozen drowned, sometimes taking riders, wagons, and all down the river with them. The Potomac fell slowly through the night, and by noon on Monday, May 26, the pitiful remnants of the Valley army lay safe in Maryland. Their "skedaddle," as Union soldiers began calling such abject retreats, had come to an end; Stonewall Jackson molested them no further.[61]

Union armies had known only victory everywhere else in the previous four months: Banks alone had endured defeat, and the comparison left his retreat looking all the more ignominious. Personally, though, Banks earned the applause of his men for preventing a complete rout, and the weary survivors of his flight blamed it all on the secretary of war, whom they held accountable for depleting their army to strengthen McDowell. Knowing little of the pervasive anxiety over Washington that afflicted so many politicians, including the president, most of Banks's men assumed that Stanton had made the decisions by himself. At least one brigadier put his finger on the real problem, though, when he yearned for a unified command in northern Virginia and complained of the political favorites who commanded the competing departments with more jealousy than cooperation. If the Mountain, Shenandoah, and Rappahannock departments were forged into one, that general concluded, no Confederate could have survived there.[62]

Instead, Jackson had been able to thrash Banks the more easily because Frémont and McDowell focused so intently on their own interdependent bailiwicks, and Abraham Lincoln had created such fragmented departments largely to satisfy the dignity of influential politicos who never should have worn major generals' stars in the first place. Political generals were hardly creatures of Lincoln's invention: previous presidents had named scores of them in wartime, and Jefferson Davis had appointed quite a few of his own, but the bumbling of Davis's generals tended to shorten the war, while that of Lincoln's served to prolong it. Lincoln answered this particular crisis by introducing yet another undeserving major general —

Franz Sigel, from west of the Mississippi — and Sigel soon started trying to wrest troops away from the other Valley generals.[63]

With Banks's escape into Maryland and the evident conclusion of Stonewall Jackson's immediate offensive, Secretary Stanton recovered somewhat from his weekend agitation. On Monday he announced that he would accept no more three-month militia — unless, as he confided to one governor, the men would not come forward for the three-year service. Haste was the important thing, he explained, evidently on the belief that a decisive battle could shortly be joined before Richmond. Stanton had already authorized five states to provide ninety-day infantry, though, and twenty-five regiments of short-term soldiers materialized that spring in Illinois, Indiana, Ohio, New York, and Rhode Island.[64] With the sense of urgency abating, most of those troops ended up guarding prisoners of war or key railroad junctions, to the intense disgust of many who had sought a season of travel and excitement in return for their commitment. Some disappointed Ohio militiamen threatened to quit altogether and go home when they were ordered to garrison the prison camp near their state capital.[65]

Those twenty-five thousand ninety-day men did not come as cheaply as they had the previous year, when legions of bored and indigent workmen had leaped at the first opportunity for romantic and remunerative occupation. War production had shrunk the once-teeming ranks of the unemployed dramatically since the previous spring, and volunteers responded much less briskly to army pay of thirteen dollars a month. Only in parts of Illinois were regiments of men still coming forward for serious service without extraordinary inducements, and economics seemed to influence that patriotism as well: wheat had failed in some of those regions the previous summer, while weeks-long steady rains had prevented plowing and doomed much of the next grain crop.[66] With this new requisition for militia more states and local communities found it necessary to provide supplementary income to attract recruits: one town in Rhode Island offered as much as ten dollars a month to any who would come forward, nearly doubling the pay of a private. Even with the inviting opportunity for summer soldiering, most men now required at least as much compensation as they could earn in civilian life before they would step into uniform.[67]

On Sunday, while McDowell's divisions departed Fredericksburg to relieve Banks and entrap Jackson, a nervous President Lincoln had told General McClellan that it was time for him to either attack Richmond or "give up the job" and bring his whole army back to defend Washington. That night Lincoln confessed to Senator Browning his apprehension that

Banks had already been destroyed, but by Monday morning he learned that Banks was safely inside Maryland. By Tuesday the president's fears had subsided along with everyone else's: he instructed Stanton to decline a couple of battalions of three-month men tendered by the governors of Massachusetts and Maine, and to instead insist upon three-year regiments to fill the latest quota. The residual confidence from the successful spring campaigns returned, at least in Washington, as Stanton illustrated when he confided to Governor Andrew that an early conclusion to the war would likely abbreviate the three-year enlistment to a single year. That confidence failed to trickle down to prospective volunteers, though, and except for those short-term militia no state managed to forward a single military unit in response to Stanton's May 21 appeal.[68]

Other than hesitant pursuit by his cavalry, Jackson's army had not followed Banks for more than five miles beyond Winchester. After threatening Harper's Ferry for a couple of days, the Confederate turned up the Valley again to escape the heavy divisions bearing down on him from Frémont's army in the Alleghenies and McDowell's detachments in the Piedmont. Laden with captured arms and supplies, Jackson drove his columns south toward Harrisonburg, narrowly avoiding the enemy's converging forces.

One observer of the military situation accused the country's commander in chief of "great incapacity" for tampering with troop movements that spring. When Lincoln borrowed men from the Richmond operation to chase after Jackson he had acted "like a great jackass," thought John Codman Ropes, a young Boston attorney who would become a careful historian of the conflict. The fateful decision to divert half of McDowell's troops to the Valley — which was indeed Abraham Lincoln's decision, rather than Edwin Stanton's — gave the Confederates at Richmond everything they had hoped for. With that single timid telegram the president threw away his best opportunity to overwhelm the Confederate capital in spite of McClellan's cautious creeping and bring the rebellion to a hasty conclusion: in the spring of 1861 he had decided virtually alone to go to war against secession, and in the spring of 1862 he alone made the unwitting decision that doomed his war to either failure or catastrophic escalation. Placed now in the same position McClellan had earlier occupied, Irvin McDowell mourned that the dispersion of his flanking force dealt the Richmond strategy a "crushing blow." Lincoln seemed to sympathize, but he fell short of the penitence that might have been more appropriate, considering that his obsessive fear for the security of Washington had scuttled the Richmond plan; in his haste to snare Jackson, Lincoln had surrendered the far greater prey. He must have learned no lasting lesson, either, for his chief advisors were still complaining of presidential interference in planned military operations a year later.[69]

McClellan had begun spreading his army around the Confederate capital in a short arc, anticipating McDowell's lumbering approach from his right, and by the time Banks began his race down the Shenandoah Valley, McClellan's army lay within seven miles of downtown Richmond. He had extended his left by sending his Fourth Corps to Seven Pines, beyond the swampy and unpredictable Chickahominy River. In the final days of May he set his engineers and pioneers to work bridging that troublesome stream, and he supported the isolated Fourth Corps with the Third Corps. That put one-third of the Army of the Potomac south of the Chickahominy with only a couple of rickety, makeshift bridges to connect it to the main body.[70]

The Confederate army's Fabian retreat up the Peninsula had suggested to many, North and South, that Joe Johnston would evacuate even Richmond before risking his army in a bloody defense.[71] Without McDowell to worry about, though, Johnston took full advantage of McClellan's precarious position, and on May 31 he slammed into the earthworks shielding the two vulnerable corps south of the Chickahominy. A broad grey battle line rolled into Silas Casey's division, which constituted half the Fourth Corps. Casey threw a regiment out to stiffen his skirmish line, but the Confederate wave engulfed the skirmishers and forced them back on their works. After a severe pounding in which they used up much of their ammunition, Casey's division took headlong flight.[72]

It took a sacrificial counterattack by one-armed Phil Kearny's division to save that portion of McClellan's army from annihilation or capture. The furious Kearny ordered a Rhode Island battery commander to halt Casey's crumbling brigades with a volley of canister, and the Rhode Islander loaded his guns to do so, but in the end he held his fire.[73] The Second Corps crossed the river despite warnings that the bridges would not hold, slogging through knee-deep water and foot-deep mud to take position, finally, between the river and the beleaguered Fourth Corps. Fear gripped some of the reinforcements well behind the firing line: a Second Corps lieutenant watched his major bounding for the rear, ostensibly in chase of his horse, while their regiment advanced. More stayed than ran, though; the fighting continued through a dark, rainy afternoon and into the cold night, but the shaken Union line fell back and held. At the end of the day's contest a bullet struck General Johnston in the shoulder as a stray shard of shell knocked him out of the saddle, and that random mishap prevented him from trying to finish off McClellan's battered

fragment the following day. A less capable subordinate took over, prodding ineffectually at the Yankees on June 1 before drawing back. The
chastised Federals made no counterattack, however, and Little Mac began
to revise his plans with an eye to even greater caution than he had already
exhibited.[74]

Both sides claimed the battle as a triumph. For a couple of days the
Confederates held most of the ground they had taken, considering that
the measure of success, and some of the more refined romantics among
them scorned their opponents as cowards for having hidden behind entrenchments.[75] The Union rank and file who had fended off Johnston's
concentrated attacks considered the fight an unquestionable victory because their isolated divisions had not been destroyed, and when the enemy shrank back toward Richmond the blue columns crept back into the
entrenched positions around Seven Pines. From the treetops they could
still focus telescopes on the Confederate flag flying over the capitol building, and most of them still believed McClellan's persistent promise that
the decisive battle lay only days away.[76] Between the lines, shallow burial
trenches and overlooked bodies of men and horses filled the air with a
putrid stench that worsened with each day, drawing clouds of buzzards
that soared ominously overhead, hinting at the only real beneficiary of the
carnage.[77]

Northern newspapers equivocated somewhat in their assessments of
the battle, but mainly they portrayed McClellan (who had been ill, and
never crossed the river to the fighting) as having worsted the rebels. Rumors contradicted such optimistic journals, particularly regarding the
shameful deportment of Casey's division, which some people recalled as
never having shown much discipline, but the public seemed satisfied that
the Army of the Potomac had at least held its own.[78]

That impression mixed favorably with the news from northern Mississippi. After the battle of Shiloh, Henry Halleck had taken the field himself, combining Buell's Army of the Ohio with Grant's Army of the Tennessee and augmenting them with John Pope's single-corps Army of the
Mississippi. Grant's deadly lapses at Shiloh had given Halleck an excuse
to exile him to the harmless and hopeless post of deputy commander
of that grand army, and with those hundred thousand troops Halleck had
crept southward at least as cautiously as George McClellan. On May 31,
the same day Johnston attacked at Seven Pines, Halleck finally captured
the rail center of Corinth, Mississippi. That opened the way for the capture of Memphis, but Halleck found Corinth as deserted as Manassas
had been in March, and the sudden evacuation of Corinth just prior to
Johnston's ferocious assault suggested ominous implications. It seemed

perfectly feasible that Beauregard's army had hastened to Richmond by rail, joining Johnston to overwhelm McClellan. The possibility initiated apprehensions that lingered for weeks.

"Where can Beauregard be?" asked a Massachusetts lieutenant serving with Banks. "I shouldn't wonder if he turned up unexpectedly, somewhere, and frightened the whole country into another militia fit."[79]

Since McClellan's army was the only one capable of taking the Confederate capital, and thereby lopping the figurative head off the rebellion, all eyes turned on him. Confidence still endured that the Confederacy teetered on its last legs, but a good many of those who had previously believed in McClellan now began to wonder if the young general would be equal to the task. Meanwhile, McClellan's earliest critics accelerated the volume of their abuse in proportion to the growing dissatisfaction. Senator Chandler, whom the secretary of the navy considered "vulgar and reckless," accumulated a considerable audience in the lobby of Willard's Hotel a couple of nights after Seven Pines with a boisterous denunciation of the army commander. Chandler had lately taken to excessive drinking, and with his tongue thus loosened he concluded his philippic with the observation that McClellan was both a liar and a coward. Sam Sturgis, a burly brigadier general who had graduated from West Point alongside McClellan, turned on Chandler, whom he did not know, and instead pronounced the senator a liar, adding that he was a coward as well for publicly maligning someone who was absent at the front. Chandler reportedly bustled out of the hotel without further comment, but similar disapproval permeated the capital.[80]

Whether from the effects of drink or partisan venom, Chandler would soon enough charge McClellan with disloyalty, on top of his more personal condemnations.[81] Congressional hysteria over lurking traitors infected the War Department root and branch. Unguarded expressions of political sentiments could still destroy promising military careers, and officers were expected to demonstrate approbation for their civilian superiors, as well as obedience. Lawrence Williams — a West Point alumnus, a veteran of ten years of continuous service, and a former member of McClellan's staff — found himself in arrest that spring on vague suspicion of "communicating with the enemy" before Yorktown. Williams never learned the source or specifications of the charges: they evidently dissolved for lack of substance, for Major Williams soon resumed leading the 6th U.S. Cavalry against the enemy, but he may have been targeted for his private tirades against abolitionist politicians like Chandler.[82]

McClellan's patriotic devotion did not yet suffer much public scrutiny, but the question of whether he could match the cunning of his opponent grew more acute after Seven Pines (or Fair Oaks, as Yankees began calling the battle, as though to distract from Casey's disgraceful performance at Seven Pines). Less than twenty-four hours after that piece of shell knocked Joe Johnston off his horse, the army defending Richmond went under the control of Robert E. Lee. Lee had not shone brightly among Confederate generals thus far, but his talents became obvious soon after he assumed command.

Doubts also arose about the capacity of the other Union generals operating in Virginia. During an evening chat on June 2, the president told Senator Browning that he feared Stonewall Jackson had given Frémont's army and McDowell's detachment the slip, despite their greater numbers and their earlier departure. In fact, Jackson would toy with those two opponents for another week before turning to deliver each a stunning blow in rear-guard actions; then he disappeared once more into the mountains. Jackson's bold and energetic action impressed grudging admirers within Lincoln's own cabinet and official family, who deemed men like McDowell, Banks, and Frémont vastly inferior in both ability and temerity.[83]

To the disgust of Republicans who saw the pattern in it, McClellan renewed his appeals for reinforcements, citing not only the casualties from Fair Oaks but alarming proportions of sick men stricken (as was McClellan himself) by malarial fevers propagated through Chickahominy mosquitoes; even before Fair Oaks the chief surgeon of the Army of the Potomac had thirty-six hundred sick to deal with, aside from those who lay on hospital ships or had been sent to Northern hospitals. To answer those perpetual appeals, and probably to compensate for depriving him of McDowell's column, Lincoln and Stanton decided to merge the troops at Fort Monroe with McClellan's department, giving him control of another big division. A few days later Lincoln also concluded to send him George McCall's division of Pennsylvania Reserves from Fredericksburg, representing half the remainder of McDowell's corps at that place.[84]

That completed the dissolution of McDowell's once-powerful corps. First William B. Franklin's division had been sent to McClellan, back in April; then Edward Ord's division had gone up the Potomac to meet the retreat of Banks, and Shields had been sent overland to the Shenandoah Valley in a vain effort to catch Jackson. Frémont had appropriated McDowell's cavalry. When McCall moved out for the Peninsula under his new orders only Rufus King's smaller division remained at Fredericksburg, and McDowell's former command lay scattered across the breadth of Confederate Virginia.

While still searching for Stonewall Jackson from his side of the Shenandoah Valley, McDowell bridled when Frémont tried to issue him orders as the "general commanding." McDowell appealed to Washington for redress. Then he started wrangling with his own division commander, Ord, who assumed command as the senior officer when McDowell retired to Washington for an executive conference. The War Department separated the antagonists both bureaucratically and geographically, relieving Ord from his division and promoting James Ricketts to command it, then assigning Frémont and Banks specific portions of the Valley while returning McDowell to Fredericksburg with the old plan of joining McClellan before Richmond. Still, the complications of command in the Valley caused significant concern for the president who had created all those troublesome little departments and contentious major generals. On June 9 their inability to cooperate helped Jackson trounce two separate columns under Frémont and Shields within a few hours of each other, and allowed his escape back to Richmond to confront McClellan, nullifying all the recent reinforcements to the Army of the Potomac.[85]

The terror over Jackson dissipated the instant he left the Valley, and Washington's attention swiftly focused once again on what some military wags were calling the "Army of the Chickahominy." Jackson's disposal of three political generals in barely a fortnight cast McClellan's performance in a much better light. The comparison alone restored some White House faith in him for all his delays, and McDowell, who would clearly be the subordinate officer if he went to Richmond now, tried to convince McClellan that he was happy to be joining him. Not for a moment did McClellan buy that blandishment: he seemed to understand, as others did, that McDowell so fervently wished for his own command that he would pose a threat of rivalry to any superior. Evidently McDowell genuinely did wish to get away from the Valley, though, and he asked for specific orders to march on Richmond, but it was not in the stars.[86] Frémont and Shields both saw ghost divisions of the enemy and said they were prevented from taking their assigned positions because of high water and supply shortages. Banks could not ready his division in time to come down to relieve Shields; Jackson seemed to be gathering significant reinforcements for a new offensive down the Valley, and each general sought to protect his own territory. Then Shields finally did rejoin McDowell near Manassas, but with a division too weary and demoralized to march any farther, let alone fight. For two weeks the excuses followed one after the other.[87]

Still, the president hoped to wind things up in short order with a concerted drive against Richmond, but the slim chances for so clean a conclusion were illustrated by an encounter between two officers on the Mechanicsville Turnpike, six miles north of Richmond. On the drizzly Sunday of June 15 Colonel Thomas Key, a member of McClellan's staff, met Confederate brigadier Howell Cobb on the left bank of the Chickahominy River to discuss prisoner exchanges. They retired to a guard shanty, displacing the picket detail, while Key's escort of dragoons stood nearby. After talking over the exchange issue, Key made an offhand remark about the tragedy of the war and the desirability of peace. Cobb, a former Speaker of the U.S. House of Representatives and secretary of the treasury under Buchanan, replied that peace could be had at any time, if the North simply accepted Southern independence. Key countered with doubt that secession had really been the will of the common people: he supposed it had been imposed on them by the planter class. Cobb failed to rebut that point, but he said that the invasion of the Southern homeland and the resulting slaughter had galvanized the Southern populace with a spirit of resistance. Key asked him to recognize Northern might and determination, but Cobb retorted that the Yankees might take Richmond and every other Southern city, and the fight would go on in the hinterlands. Only by subjugating the entire region and occupying it permanently could Washington exert its will over the Southern states, he insisted.

With that they parted. Riding back to Mechanicsville with his escort and the colonel in charge of that section of the line, Key mulled Cobb's remarks at length before muttering absentmindedly that the senior Confederates "talk as if they would fight."

"Why, who ever doubted it?" asked the colonel.[88]

Despite much testimony of Southern determination a great many had doubted it, in fact — most notably President Lincoln — but the violent confrontations of Shiloh, Fair Oaks, and Jackson's Valley campaign ought to have expunged that doubt. For all of that, McClellan shared his commander in chief's anticipation of ending things in a single overpowering blow. So he said, at least, but he kept calling for reinforcements. Besides the rest of McDowell's corps, he coveted Ambrose Burnside's North Carolina divisions, either as direct reinforcements or as a diversionary expedition into the Carolina interior. During tropical downpours Burnside came up to the sodden Peninsula for a conference on the subject, and then steamed up to Washington for a long interview with Lincoln and the cabinet in which he described the phenomenal transportation difficulties posed by Virginia mud. Burnside carried back the president's assurance of heartfelt support for the beleaguered McClellan, but in return McClellan only asked for still more men. Persuaded (as was President Lincoln) that Beauregard might well have spirited his Mississippi army away from Corinth to save the Confederate capital, McClellan wired Stanton with an eager suggestion to detach a healthy portion of Halleck's army to swell his own ranks.[89]

In the end, the administration chose only one soldier from Halleck's command to reinforce the Union presence in Virginia. That soldier would be John Pope, and the notion of bringing him east entered President Lincoln's mind by the third week of June.

Pope was a career soldier, twenty years out of West Point, who had pressed himself on president-elect Lincoln as an expert on army conditions early in the secession crisis. On the weight of the resulting acquaintance he lobbied loud and long for a general's star from the outset of the war. Complaining that officers junior to him, like McDowell, had been promoted to brigadier in the volunteer service, he had asked for a similar appointment only two months into the conflict: at that time, seniority had seemed very important to him. He had won much credit as commander of the forces that reduced Island No. 10 the previous April, and for that exploit he had been promoted to major general. Afterward he had accompanied Henry Halleck on his creeping operation against Corinth.[90] Pope's greatest qualifications for higher station, however, came by blood and marriage: Abraham Lincoln knew his father as judge of the U.S. District Court for Illinois, and the elder Pope had once supplied Lincoln with a letter of recommendation for federal appointment. Pope's father-in-law represented Ohio in Congress, meanwhile, and enjoyed the acquaintance of both Salmon P. Chase and Edwin Stanton. Unlike most other successful generals, like Grant and Burnside, Pope was also available: after the Confederates evacuated Corinth he had taken leave to visit his family in St. Louis.[91]

By the sultry days of mid-June the president had moved his own family out of the miasmic lowlands along Pennsylvania Avenue to the cooler and more salubrious Soldiers' Home, situated on a wooded knoll north of the city. He occupied a limestone cottage there, rising early on most days and taking a light breakfast before climbing into the saddle for the four-mile ride down the Rock Creek Church Road and Seventh Street to the White House — usually alone. On most mornings he would reach his desk by eight o'clock, two hours before his nominal office hours of ten until four, but on certain days he lingered at the Soldiers' Home until late morning.[92]

June 18 was one of those days. Lincoln had invited Senator Browning out for breakfast, and after the White House carriage picked him up Browning stopped at Willard's for Judge Henry Hilton and the fabulously wealthy retail merchant Alexander T. Stewart, both of whom were visiting from New York City. At the Soldiers' Home their table conversation quickly turned to McClellan. Stewart, an immigrant Orangeman of ruthless business acumen, dismissed Little Mac as incompetent. Lincoln conceded that McClellan's reluctance to attack the enemy at Manassas had disappointed him, that he had disapproved of the change of base to the Peninsula, and that he finally regarded the Peninsula campaign as a blunder. Stewart urged the president to remove McClellan from command of the Army of the Potomac, and he proposed John Pope as a successor. Stewart appears not to have had any connection with Pope, and the general's public reputation was not so illustrious that he would have surfaced as an obvious replacement, leaving the possibility that Lincoln mentioned his name first. He made no comment to Stewart's suggestion, though, and later in the morning they all climbed into the carriage with little Tad Lincoln for the trip to the city.[93]

Pope evidently remained on the president's mind throughout that abbreviated workday, and probably he mentioned his preoccupation to the secretary of war, for Stanton inquired of Pope's whereabouts from his father-in-law, the Ohio congressman, and learned that Pope was visiting in St. Louis. Stanton telegraphed there on June 19, calling Pope to an interview in Washington if his orders allowed for it. Pope asked token permission of Halleck, who objected on the grounds of imminent military action, but Pope ignored him in the face of Stanton's promising call and announced that he was going to Washington.[94]

After sending for Pope, Stanton joined the president for an emergency trip to Alexandria and then, by special train, to Manassas Junction, where McDowell was gathering the remaining divisions of his scattered corps. To the amusement of McDowell's men, many of whom disliked him, the general had endured a nasty accident the day before, and he suffered intensely. He had been reviewing the 1st Rhode Island Cavalry when his horse, Ohio, shied at something, reared, and fell over backward on him, prompting a soldier in James Ricketts's division to solicit three cheers for the horse. McDowell's right leg, arm, and side took the brunt of the fall. A solid bruise discolored him from knee to shoulder, and he would still be limping into early July, but the most dangerous injury came from the pommel of his saddle punching deep into his considerable stomach, knocking the wind out of him and bruising him internally. He had lain senseless for some time, but had recovered enough by the next afternoon for his two superiors to see that he could still exercise command. That appeared to satisfy them, and they remained only a couple of hours.[95]

Two days later Secretary Chase went down to visit McDowell, taking Judge Hilton, the tycoon Stewart, and some other dignitaries. The general still lounged in his dressing gown at midafternoon, managing his division from the back porch of his headquarters at a substantial house along the railroad spur leading to Centreville. There he enjoyed comfortable accommodations, fresh spring water, and an assortment of delicacies gathered by his resourceful staff officers, who included one of the owners of Willard's Hotel. McDowell had recovered enough mobility to offer the guests his right hand and some of the ice cream his quartermaster had produced. He also promised Chase that he would be able to resume the saddle within a few days, lest the treasury chief report back that the commander of McClellan's right wing needed to be relieved.[96]

On Monday evening, June 23, while General Pope's train neared Washington, the president quietly boarded one bound for New York and West Point, on the Hudson River. There, on Tuesday morning, he dropped in on Winfield Scott, who had retired nearly eight months before as commanding general of the U.S. Army, and Lincoln promptly asked the ponderous old strategist what he should do with all the various little armies posted around northern Virginia. Scott replied rather vaguely that Frémont, Banks, and McDowell certainly had enough troops to defend Washington from anything the rebels could throw in their respective directions, adding that the greater part of McDowell's corps could even be sent to McClellan if King's division moved up to Manassas Junction from Fredericksburg; he thought King "entirely out of position" at Fredericksburg, where he was too far from anyone to be of much assistance. Scott expressed confidence that McClellan could conquer Richmond from where he was, and that such a defeat would effectively end the rebellion. If Scott gave Lincoln any advice about consolidating those patchwork departments outside Washington, or suggested a general for the joint command, he made no mention of it in the memorandum he provided on the subject.[97]

The idea of combining those broadcast divisions surely underlay Lincoln's hasty trip up the Hudson, and the logic of it occurred to plenty of military minds that week. Even George McClellan proposed it to the secretary of war in an unusually friendly and diffident telegram wired that Friday.[98]

By then the change had already been made. The president found General Pope in Washington when he returned there, and the two of them evidently spent much of June 25 talking over the consolidation of those forces, with the understanding that Pope would assume the overall command. In Lincoln's absence the secretary of war had already outlined it all for Pope, who later claimed that he resisted the assignment because of strategic difficulties and administrative impediments. The three little armies that were to compose his own lay strewn from the Tidewater to the Alleghenies, while their commanders — Banks, Frémont, and McDowell — all held commissions senior to Pope's. On June 26 the president nevertheless signed an order reducing Banks, Frémont, and McDowell to corps commands in a new Army of Virginia, naming Pope to lead it. To sweeten the pot Lincoln threw in Sam Sturgis's new division, consisting of the troops scattered around Washington City. Pope accepted immediately; his ambitious nature casts doubt on his alleged reluctance to exchange his

Mississippi corps for command of his own grand army. The president gave him the initial job of sweeping down toward Richmond through Charlottesville, on the edge of the Blue Ridge, and cleaning the enemy out of that region, with the ultimate aim of joining McClellan before Richmond.[99]

Frémont, erstwhile Pathfinder of the West, had commanded the Department of Missouri while Pope served as one of his division commanders. He refused to accept the reduced prestige accorded him in the administrative restructuring, and asked to be relieved. That satisfied Pope, who believed Frémont to be naively honest but "foolish," and without the judgment of an adolescent boy. Farther up the chain of command, both Lincoln and Stanton regarded Frémont's pride as unseemly. Stanton observed that neither Banks nor McDowell had used the excuse of seniority as a reason to withdraw their services, and he added that those of the highest rank ought to be the first to recognize their obligation to serve wherever assigned. Lincoln nonetheless relieved him; as willing as the president might be to saddle troops with incompetent generals, they must at least be willing. With his extensive staff and his trademark white slouch hat, Frémont rode for Martinsburg and New York before breakfast on June 28, fading gradually out of the war and, finally, out of history. Franz Sigel took his place.[100]

Since none of his detachments reported enemy activity Pope remained in Washington, lodging at Willard's. He called for Banks and McDowell, who continued to limp from his equestrian accident; the three of them consulted on how best to protect the capital while moving south to cooperate with McClellan against Richmond and the principal army of the Confederacy. As it happened, McClellan was not in a position to cooperate with anyone at that juncture. He had made his initial offensive lunge against Richmond on Wednesday morning, June 25, and since that hour he had hardly drawn a peaceful breath.[101]

3

The Spires of Richmond, Late Beheld

McCLELLAN LAUNCHED HIS June 25 attack right after breakfast. It coincided with — and mirrored — a more aggressive assault that Robert E. Lee had planned on the other side of the Chickahominy. McClellan had left only Fitz John Porter's Fifth Corps north of the Chickahominy, near Mechanicsville. He had gathered his four other corps south of the river for a mighty drive against an entrenched Confederate line near a place called Oak Grove, barely five miles from Richmond's Capitol Square. Lee had arranged precisely the opposite maneuver, leaving two divisions to man the defenses near Oak Grove and moving three others north of the river to attack Porter. He also planned for Stonewall Jackson to arrive with his three divisions from the Shenandoah Valley in time to swing behind Porter and deliver the decisive flank attack, which would presumably separate McClellan from his supply base on the York River and finish Porter's corps, eliminating nearly one-fifth of McClellan's fighting strength.

For his part, McClellan only hoped to "gain a couple of miles toward Richmond" with the movement against Oak Grove, which would have put the city within range of his heavier guns, but some of his troops anticipated victory just over the horizon. In Joseph Hooker's division Sergeant Thomas Leaver, who had seen the worst of the Bull Run stampede, wrote his mother on the eve of the assault that "the end is near at hand."[1] In the morning Leaver's regiment — the 2nd New Hampshire — followed the skirmishers as they plunged toward the enemy line. Leaver's company was armed with breech-loading Sharps rifles, which made it valuable for skirmishing and sharpshooting duties, so he and his messmates always seemed to be in the thick of any fight. So it was with this one. The battle raged for a couple of hours with some success on the Union side before McClellan interrupted it by calling Hooker off. In the afternoon he renewed the advance despite diminished momentum, but desperate counterattacks blunted it here and there, or sent it reeling backward. A New York regiment slung muskets and started building breastworks to hold the new position, only to have their own pickets driven past them in retreat: then the rebels leveled their muskets at the diggers, who fled instantly at sight of the enemy "with their tall hats, and brown coats, looking as if they would like to cut our livers out." By night the lines had shifted only a few hundred yards.[2] It was, Phil Kearny told his wife, "all to no purpose," and scores of men had died on either side, including Sergeant Leaver, whose ambiguous prediction about the end being near at hand had come to pass in a manner he had not intended.[3]

Paralyzed by premature or erroneous reports of massive Confederate reinforcements, including Jackson's Valley army and part of Beauregard's Mississippi army, McClellan refrained from any further aggression of his own. Instead he chastised the secretary of war, and by implication the president, for failing to send him enough men, and telegraphed late into the night for just one more division of infantry, which he somehow reasoned would allow him to "laugh" at Stonewall Jackson. In place of his morning bravado, meanwhile, he offered an unnerving, uncertain promise that the army would not disgrace itself. He imagined that he faced two hundred thousand Southerners, whom he supposed could destroy his army, and his melodramatic assurance that he would die with his men offered precious little comfort to either Edwin Stanton or Abraham Lincoln.[4]

Boldly facing down his own overwhelming enemy at Oak Grove, Lee kept most of his army in position to launch his powerful offensive against Porter the following day. Topographical misunderstandings and ambiguous orders prevented Jackson from coming in on Porter's flank, robbing the day's strategy of any real chance of success, but in the late afternoon the attack began anyway as an overly anxious Confederate division commander sprang impatiently across the Chickahominy above Mechanicsville.[5]

Two Confederate deserters scurried into McClellan's lines below the river that morning, both claiming Massachusetts origins and insisting that they had just been conscripted. They reported widespread dissatisfaction in Lee's army over the mandatory extension of enlistment terms, but Lee's troops showed little disaffection in their actions that day.[6] His infantry hurtled resolutely toward the imposing Union position on the high banks behind Beaver Dam Creek. More Confederates crossed the river on the Mechanicsville Turnpike, pouring past the little shanty where

Colonel Key and General Cobb had theorized about peace and Southern determination. Seven Southern brigades arrayed themselves against the creek, five of them surging ferociously but ineffectively at the enemy line and losing a great many men in the process. Fresh from McDowell's army and fighting their first battle, George McCall's Pennsylvania Reserves held the creek, but they acquitted themselves well in their formidable position. Dark ended the fruitless contest, which gained nothing for Lee except to keep McClellan on the defensive. Just as they were finishing their dinners south of the Chickahominy, Union soldiers of the Second and Sixth Corps trotted out at their generals' behest to celebrate the perceived victory with a formal cheer, but it was the last cheering they would do for a long while.[7]

Overjoyed not to have seen his army crushed, a relieved McClellan backhandedly congratulated himself that he had "completely gained the day — not lost a foot of ground." Within hours he nevertheless abandoned that ground, pulling Porter back beyond Gaines's Mill in the wee hours of June 27 to a plateau protecting his four main bridges over the Chickahominy. That uncovered his Pamunkey River supply base at White House Landing, effectively handing it to Lee, who ignored it for the present. From Washington the president apprised McClellan that General Pope had taken charge there, adding that Pope advised retreating to the White House base, but it was too late for that. Promising that he was leading Lee into a trap, McClellan had already told his wife that he intended to give up his supply line "in order to insure success."[8]

Such confident words suggested that McClellan intended to occupy Lee's main force north of the river with Porter's corps while the bulk of his own army rolled over the Confederate defenses and into Richmond. In fact, by drawing Lee farther away from his own river crossings McClellan had lured him into considerable jeopardy: by full daylight on Friday, Porter sat in an excellent position to hold off double his number (which is about what he faced), freeing McClellan to seize the prize that he valued most. Then the specter of those ghost legions from Beauregard must have paralyzed the commanding general, for while Porter made the fight of his life McClellan failed to do anything at all with his left wing, which contained three-quarters of his army and outnumbered the Confederate defenders on that front by three to one.[9]

In the afternoon Lee again started the attack against Porter without Jackson, but finally the hero of the Shenandoah arrived on Porter's right and pitched into him. Lee flung more than two dozen brigades against a tight battle front nearly two miles wide, bordered by impenetrable swamps on either side. Porter could not be outflanked, and the only hope of defeating him lay in hammering at that solid front until it crumbled, so for more than five hours Lee sent one wave of infantry after another into the serried artillery and rifle fire. The serial assaults passed through torrents of lead and iron before even reaching the foot of the slope where Porter's men stood, grimly waiting. Determined Yankees handily repelled each attack, inflicting deadly vengeance for each, until it seemed that their line could not be broken.

Lee responded to each punishing failure by ordering another advance with his freshest, or least battered, brigades: he betrayed a stubbornness that might have been called foolhardy — and often was, as Ambrose Burnside would discover six months later, after similar persistence at Fredericksburg. The difference lay in luck and a slight change of tactics, for as that Friday's sun threatened to drop beneath the horizon, a couple of Confederate brigades threw themselves at Porter's center without stopping to fire, ignoring their casualties in order to get in among the enemy quickly. That worked, and in the red gloaming of the Peninsula's bloodiest day Porter's line fell apart. Dun-colored waves of riflemen swept over the plateau, engulfing the house that had been Porter's headquarters, where surgeons continued to examine the wounds of field officers even as bullets burst through the plaster and shells exploded overhead. Leaving behind whole batteries of guns and thousands of prisoners, including regiments that surrendered almost to a man, Porter guided the survivors of his corps across the river under cover of last-minute reinforcements from the idle majority of the Army of the Potomac.[10]

Thus ended the third battle of what would come to be known as the Seven Days. Gaines's Mill transformed McClellan's campaign from an offensive into a struggle to save his army from the disaster he foresaw, with no further thought of attacking Richmond. In a midnight dispatch he told Stanton that Porter was "overwhelmed by vastly superior numbers even after I brought my last reserves into action," evidently forgetting that more than seventy thousand of his troops had never gone near the fight, and he blamed everything on the failure to send him enough men. "If I save this army now," he snarled at Stanton, with revealing conditional tones, "I tell you plainly that I owe no thanks to you or any other persons in Washington."[11]

McClellan devoted Saturday to the details of his retreat. He intended to establish a new base on the James River, and while he scouted an escape route Lee's army maneuvered to trap him. Confederates on the Richmond defense line sparred theatrically with the vastly more numerous Yankees who faced them, cowing them into the illusion of overpowering forces on all sides, and eventually McClellan ordered his Richmond line to pull back toward Savage's Station. This was the larger part of the army, which had lain innocuously before Richmond during Porter's fight, and it

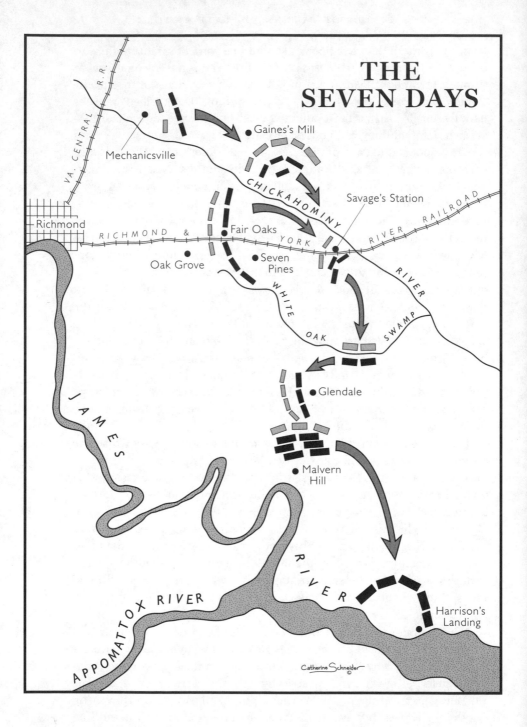

THE SEVEN DAYS

Mechanicsville

Gaines's Mill

CHICKAHOMINY

Savage's Station

Richmond

RICHMOND & Fair Oaks YORK RIVER RAILROAD

Oak Grove Seven Pines

WHITE OAK SWAMP RIVER

Glendale

JAMES

Malvern Hill

Harrison's Landing

APPOMATTOX RIVER RIVER

Catherine Schneider

drew back along the line of the Richmond & York River Railroad. The men of Phil Kearny's division understood that they would be covering the movement, and Kearny had instructed them to take 150 rounds of ammunition apiece, filling their cartridge boxes and then all their pockets, as well. "We . . . intend that the enemy shall have reason to remember Kearny's Div.," remarked a Michigan lieutenant who half expected to die in a desperate rear-guard action: in his journal that day he made his farewell to his family and recorded his wishes for the distribution of his paltry estate.[12]

The wounded from Gaines's Mill had all gone to Savage's Station over bone-shaking corduroy roads, where they joined the sick who had already been moved back there. The luckiest of them were quickly transferred by rail to White House Landing and carried north by steamer for medical treatment. Those who missed the early trains lay about the Savage farm, either in the buildings, in tents, or under the open sky. Teams of surgeons plied their saws all day long June 28, lopping off limbs too mangled for saving amid such demand for their attention. Some thirteen hundred landed there, and half that number could neither rise nor bear further moving. On the news that the army would flee Savage's Station, patients with lesser head injuries or wounds in the upper extremities dragged themselves to their feet and staggered off to the south. Unable to even roll into more comfortable positions, let alone hobble away, those with more serious wounds lay where they were, amid the increasing stench of sun-cooked bodies and amputated fragments. McClellan's medical director called for volunteers to remain with those who could not follow, and hundreds of helpless Union soldiers watched their comrades march away, knowing that the enemy would soon descend upon them.[13]

In order to keep ahead of the overpowering host that he imagined Lee's smaller army to be, McClellan left behind vast acres of supplies. Individual soldiers burned or mutilated all the personal possessions they could not take with them, while officers destroyed their trunks and any of the contents they could not stuff into their saddlebags. Instead of folding his tent and sending it ahead on the retreat, General Heintzelman slept one last night in it and left it vacant for a Southern occupant. Details put the torch to millions of dollars in matériel.[14]

Into the fading daylight of June 29 McClellan's Second and Sixth Corps fended off an understrength Confederate thrust from the direction of Richmond that threatened Savage's Station and their path of retreat. They mowed down their assailants with artillery but then slipped away with their dead unburied, leaving trees across the road in their wake to hamper pursuit.[15] Yankees passing through the station Sunday night and the next morning encountered a scene of apocalyptic proportions: a train of two dozen cars sat burning on the railroad track; mountains of blazing rations boxes and barrels lighted the night sky; the knapsacks of entire regiments lay in tall pyres, snapping and crackling as the flames consumed them. Smoke and the stench of sulfur choked the atmosphere as piles of ammunition took fire. Whiskey gushed from smashed barrelheads, to the intense sorrow of the thirstier passersby, and ground coffee poured knee-deep on the grass. Pieces of coats, pants, and shoes littered the landscape, slashed to rags with knives or chopped to bits with axes. Once the scorching heat of the next morning struck them on the march, most of the men jettisoned their blankets and overcoats, as well, continuing on with nothing but canteens, haversacks, and ammunition.[16] Veterans of the Bull Run disaster recognized all the despair and terror of that inglorious retreat, except for better organization and discipline among the units. Stonewall Jackson's advance swept past the hospital at Savage's Station Monday morning; the rebels kept tramping by "in a continual stream" until nearly nightfall, and whole regiments of stragglers followed them. The patients, surgeons, and nurses around the station could only assume that they were prisoners, but at first no one disturbed them. A volunteer attendant from McClellan's only Minnesota regiment thought their captors treated them "very kindly," and a wounded Vermonter concurred. At least one Georgia surgeon went to work with his enemy counterparts, lopping off arms and legs that accumulated in piles reminiscent of a slaughterhouse.[17]

The huge blue columns turned generally south from Savage's Station, away from the railroad, and that ended their connection with the supply base at White House Landing. The mobs of sick and wounded at White House had already been carted off to Fort Monroe — riding in long, nervous wagon trains or going aboard the transports under the profane direction of tired, desperate officers. On Saturday evening the colonel in charge at the landing had set fire to all the public property there before the last brigade boarded boats and barges to slip away, under tow, behind a screen of gunboats. In the final moments, a New York private took it upon himself to touch off the White House itself: that modest, six-room frame dwelling belonged to Robert E. Lee's eldest son, Colonel George Washington Custis Lee, who had inherited it through his maternal descent from Martha Washington, and bitter Northerners had resented McClellan's efforts to protect the first president's former possession. The conflagration illuminated all the surrounding countryside with an eerie, mournful glow.[18]

The Federal retreat route bisected a boggy, overflowing stream known as White Oak Swamp. The three corps that might have barged into Richmond on Thursday or Friday — the Second, Third, and Sixth — arrayed themselves in front of Savage's Station and backed slowly away before the exuberant Confederates while the Fourth Corps and Fitz John Porter's shaken Fifth Corps made their way over White Oak Bridge. The swamp might have posed a dangerous or even fatal hurdle for the Yankees, considering the dismay and confusion that afflicted the Army of the Potomac from top to bottom, but misunderstandings in the Confederate command abetted the shameless flight of the larger army. It was not until Monday, June 30, that Lee's divided forces caught up with that three-corps rear guard at Glendale, south of White Oak Swamp. Straggling shrank the Federal line fearfully: only eight men fell in with one company of the 2nd New Hampshire. The Yankees also fought without a chief, for General McClellan had reached the James River and boarded a gunboat to confer with the captain of the river flotilla. In his absence Southern infantry nearly cut off the retreat of his men, and hammered them repeatedly with furious assaults by heavy columns. Depending more on cooperation than coordination, five Union division commanders repelled each successive attack, although one of those generals fell into enemy hands and another came close.[19] Some Alabama and South Carolina regiments lost 50 and 60 percent of their battle strength, and in one Southern regiment all ten company commanders went down, including eight killed on the spot. "They fight like tigers," complained a New Jersey colonel.[20] Union artillery belched double loads of canister into the charging Confederates at ranges of barely fifty yards until dusk, when the canister ran out, and then rifles flashed in the night until Lee realized that he had missed another chance.[21]

The Federals crept away in the darkness, forsaking more of their wounded to speed the withdrawal. For the fourth night in a row troops that had spent the daylight fighting lined up to march in the darkness, and a sixteen-year-old Minnesota private observed that his mess had gone without so much as a cup of hot coffee all that time. That night, the Army of the Potomac finally gathered atop Malvern Hill, a broad, open plateau towering above the James River. The air turned unseasonably cool, and fugitives who had discarded their overcoats and blankets slept fitfully. In his dismal bivouac thirteen miles from the center of Richmond, a New York officer who had lain less than six miles away from that goal five nights before realized that midnight would bring the first of July, and he wondered sardonically if he would be in Richmond by the Fourth. The rising sun brightened such spirits, though, for the flat crest of Malvern Hill presented a spectacular panorama: a Massachusetts man estimated that two thousand acres of open ground lay before him, and he guessed that as many as seventy thousand other blue uniforms came within his view. With curiosity and relief, though, he noted the absence of the wagon trains that had encumbered every step of the march to that place.[22]

It was not enough for Robert E. Lee to drive the enemy from before Richmond, or even to thrash him soundly. Ultimate Confederate victory demanded Northern despair, leading to peace and independence, and that required him to essentially destroy the former besiegers: McClellan's army had to be dispersed and captured in detail, or forced to surrender en masse. At Malvern Hill, Lee made his last and most hopeless effort to achieve that end. On that sultry Tuesday afternoon he flung a dozen brigades across a rising plain swept by artillery and musketry. Porter's Fifth Corps and part of the Fourth, neither of which had seen substantial fighting for a few days, held the hill. Behind them stood the rest of the army, showing better confidence with a sense of tactical advantage and the concentration of the two wings.

The Confederate divisions spent most of the day trying to reach their assigned positions: their assault began late, and as the result of miscommunication. Disjointed, piecemeal attacks failed to dislodge the phalanx of blue infantry despite the most valiant sacrifice. Union artillery shredded Lee's brigades, grinding the flower of Southern chivalry into dust. The fighting continued into the evening again, leaving Lee with nearly six thousand casualties while the Yankees suffered barely half as many, and this time he failed even to chase the defenders from the field.[23] The Federals still held their ground at full dark, although they slipped away during the night in such haste that they once again left their dead and wounded on the field, along with some artillery. After what he characterized in dispatches as "a complete victory" (despite the abandonment of his wounded), McClellan had decided to seek safety at Harrison's Landing, several more miles downriver.[24]

McClellan's Peninsula campaign would drag on for another seven weeks in the squalid encampments around Harrison's Landing. He would refresh his troops, reorganize shattered commands, replace livestock and equipment, and restore discipline — coercing cowardly field officers into quitting the army and drumming the most conspicuously timid lieutenants out of camp.[25] For all the preparations, no army McClellan commanded would ever again threaten the enemy capital. From his new headquarters McClellan formulated a grand excuse for his abject flight, blaming his "failure to win" on the enemy's vastly superior numbers and purporting that his retreat had been nothing more than a premeditated change of base from the Pamunkey River to the James. Supposing that no greater battles had ever been fought, he praised his army for the magnificence of its battlefield performances, most of which had been conducted without any direct interference from him.[26]

Lee, who had begun the Seven Days with at least 20 percent fewer men than McClellan, suffered 25 percent higher casualties and ended the fighting with even worse odds against him. He had also failed in his goal of eliminating the Army of the Potomac, but he had struck a mighty blow at the morale of his nation's enemies, in and out of uniform. Some of McClellan's most steadfast troops described complete, enduring exhaustion and a sickness at heart that suggested severe depression.

Within days of the closing engagement, headquarters clerks at Harrison's Landing started processing thick sheaves of resignations. Every battle in every theater reminded a few officers how easy it was to resign their commissions: an Illinois captain whose men noticed him quailing at Fort Donelson submitted his resignation the following morning; Shiloh precipitated a host of resignations; Jackson's campaign in the Shenandoah Valley had nearly cleaned out the shoulder straps in one of Nathaniel Banks's regiments, in which most officers resigned and the rest began thinking about it.[27] Hundreds of officers likewise remembered family and business responsibilities after the Peninsula fighting. Three weeks after his regiment's maiden engagement, a Connecticut lieutenant who had not been in the army six months yet told his wife he would soon seek a furlough, and perhaps resign if he did not get it. After Fair Oaks a Massachusetts lieutenant who prized his promotion from the ranks observed that several of his fellow officers had resigned to go home, and he admitted quite frankly that he might do so himself, or even accept a dishonorable discharge, if necessary, "for it does not seem as if I could live from one days end to the other." That particular officer never resigned, but after the Seven Days many did.[28] "I am trying to get out of the service for every reason," confessed an artillery captain, whose sound health forced him to seek his governor's connivance in having his resignation accepted. Meanwhile, enlisted men slipped away from their companies without benefit of furloughs. Soldiers lucky enough to go home on convalescent leaves began overstaying them, including many who held commissions.[29]

During much of the fighting the Washington government had suffered the horror of having no news from the front. Demonstrating a preference for the anxiety of uncertainty over the panic of rumor, Edwin Stanton tried to keep the country equally ignorant with an arbitrary moratorium on news. Charles Fulton, one of the owners of the *Baltimore American,* tried to wire a dispatch from White House Landing before the evacuation there on Saturday night, but the supervisor of the military telegraph refused to relay it. Fulton's message did gain the attention of the president and secretary of war, however, and they invited the newspaperman for an interview on his way home. They grilled him for everything he knew on Sunday evening, and his reports of no stragglers and very few wounded at White House Landing raised their hopes for McClellan's success. Even as Confederates swarmed into Savage's Station and scooped up all the wounded there, Stanton interpreted Fulton's long-distance observations as evidence that "McClellan will probably be in Richmond within two days."

Mr. Fulton had finally apprised his newspaper of Stanton's information blackout. "The Secretary of War decides that nothing can be telegraphed relative to affairs on the Peninsula," announced the *American*. In a private message he told a New York colleague what he had seen on the Pamunkey and described his meeting with Lincoln and Stanton; that information quickly appeared in New York sheets, crediting the *Baltimore American*. Immediately after Fulton's return to Baltimore soldiers lodged him in Fort McHenry, incommunicado, for allegedly leaking military information.[30]

Once the papers did begin reporting the Seven Days, they provided the same misinformation and unjustified optimism that had typified the loyal press in the first summer of the war. The *Philadelphia Inquirer* described "The Eight Days Battles" as the "greatest Battles ever Fought on This Continent," which was true enough if they were counted as a single engagement, but the headline also asserted that "Our Troops Drive the Enemy." Using fictitious figures that might have come from the deluded McClellan himself, the Albany *Atlas and Argus* explained that his survival had been all the more spectacular, considering that the enemy had fielded 185,000 men to his 95,000.[31]

Fragments of the truth soon crept out, though, as hospital ships started disgorging thousands of talkative victims and soldiers started writing home. A Vermont private who had been forced to leave a boyhood friend bleeding to death at Savage's Station betrayed the deception behind McClellan's claim to have voluntarily changed his base, admitting to his sister that "they drove us back to Harrison's Landing." Clearly there had been no victory, but rather a resounding setback, with another embarrassing skedaddle, and thoughtful citizens feared that McClellan might yet be forced to surrender.[32] Even General Marcy, McClellan's father-in-law and chief of staff, let slip such a possibility in a visit to the White House, infuriating the secretary of war and greatly disturbing the president. At the least, the Seven Days demonstrated the accuracy of Howell Cobb's prediction of furious Southern resistance. The springtime victories no longer meant anything, save in the territory they had gained, although

the hopeful harbored visions of immediate victory if only enough reinforcements could be sent into the field at once.[33]

Such a vision belonged to Abraham Lincoln, who encouraged his beleaguered commander with promises of still more men. He called on
General Hunter to send ten thousand troops to the Peninsula from South
Carolina, and asked Burnside to take all the infantry he could spare from
North Carolina and go to McClellan's aid, scuttling offensive operations
in those two theaters to rebuild the main army. "Try just now to save
the army, material, and *personnel*," the president counseled Little Mac
on July 2, "and I will strengthen it for the offensive again as fast as I can.
The Governors of eighteen States offer me a new levy of 300,000, which I
accept."[34]

Honest Abe betrayed a touch of the disingenuous politician with that dispatch, for the governors' "offer" of a new levy amounted to a sham of his
own orchestration, designed to imply unanimity and diffuse criticism.
Recognizing that executive hysteria had already produced too many false
alarms, including the recent panic over Stonewall Jackson's foray in the
Shenandoah Valley, Lincoln dared not test the public patience so soon
with another call of his own for massive additions to the army. On June
28, as McClellan prepared for his retreat from the Chickahominy River,
the president had sent his secretary of state to New York City bearing
a letter carefully explaining his view of the military situation. That letter, which he obviously intended Seward to present to the various state
governors with suggestions for their own action, virtually adopted George
McClellan's paranoid impression of Confederate dispositions: it supposed
that Robert E. Lee had been heavily reinforced from Beauregard's Mississippi army, and that the great battle of the rebellion still waited to be
fought before Richmond; if only Lincoln could shovel another hundred
thousand men down to McClellan, he felt confident that he could capture
the Confederate capital and "substantially end the war." Lincoln made it
clear, though, that no public appeal for such enlistments could come directly from the White House, warning that it might cause "a general panic
and stampede." The letter did not allude to his more likely concern, as
midterm elections approached, that another unilateral executive demand
for more blood and treasure might fix the wrath of an exasperated public
on his administration.[35]

Subterfuge of that sort called for just such a man as Secretary Seward,
who in years past had impressed some of his Senate colleagues as a "sneak."
Seward went on to confirm that opinion with serial cabinet schemes:
early in Lincoln's presidency the new secretary of state had advised cook-

ing up a war with England to unify public opinion against an external enemy; then, wishing to divert attention from Fort Sumter, he interfered in Navy Department dispositions and deprived the Sumter relief expedition of its most powerful escort. People in and out of the administration thought of Seward when they considered intrigue, as Lincoln did in the closing weeks of 1861, after an overzealous naval commander forcibly removed two Confederate officials from the British steamer *Trent*. Trying to soften the international humiliation of surrendering the prisoners, Lincoln had seriously sought Seward's advice on a wild proposal to dampen relations between Britain and the Confederacy by arresting a fugitive slave visiting in Washington from his new home in Canada, in hopes that the British ambassador would demand the slave's liberation. While the tension with England persisted, a would-be conspirator in St. Louis marked Seward as the man to approach with a plan for weakening the British army by bribing away the impoverished Irishmen who composed half its enlisted men.[36]

Convincing the governors to pretend that they initiated the troop levy would pose little challenge for the calculating Seward. He lodged at the Astor House on lower Broadway, overlooking the phalanx of newspaper offices on Park Row, and to that elegant hotel he called two of his old political cronies, including New York governor Edward Morgan. Andrew Curtin, the governor of Pennsylvania, joined them the next day. Consulting by telegraph with thirteen other Northern governors, three border-state governors, the military governor of Tennessee, and a proxy for the reluctant governor of Kentucky, the four of them drafted a suitable alternative to a presidential proclamation — wording it to appear that the states had petitioned Lincoln to raise more troops, rather than the other way around. They completed the deceptive document within twenty-four hours, and most of the governors replied obligingly. Seward lobbied for 150,000 men in his discourse with the state leaders, rather than the president's original suggestion of 100,000, but so many men could not be had without cost: in the face of certain governors' demands Seward wired the secretary of war late on June 30 for authority to issue recruits an advance payment of one-quarter of the federal hundred-dollar bounty. Edwin Stanton, who usually demanded the most fastidious conduct in matters of pecuniary propriety, instantly authorized the expenditure of that much money from the $9 million remaining in the federal army's recruiting account.[37]

By the morning of July 1 Lincoln had changed his mind again, asking if Seward could not round the request off to 200,000 men. Stanton suggested, however, that Seward go a step further and make it 300,000. That would eat up most of the recruiting fund just to pay the advance bounties, but Stanton reasoned that mass enlistments would produce a lot of wasted manpower, and he advised the largest possible levy. Three hundred thousand would pose no difficulty, Seward replied: none of the governors involved had suggested recruiting fewer than 200,000, and they stood ready to pledge the lives of half a million of their constituents, if Lincoln wished that many.[38]

On the evening of July 1, while the Army of the Potomac slunk away from its position atop Malvern Hill, Seward continued on to Boston to cajole Governor Andrew into the scheme. Putting up at the Parker House, just down Beacon Hill from the Massachusetts State House, Seward met with Andrew the next morning and won his assent to the recruiting appeal, but Andrew still shunned the gubernatorial charade. He refused to append his signature to the fictitious memorial begging Lincoln to raise more men; instead, he gave that game away with a wire to Stanton announcing, "I cordially respond to the President's call for troops." Still intent on preserving the subterfuge, Seward characterized Andrew's reply as "earnest and satisfactory," and suggested that another gallivanting governor's name might be added to the memorial by the consent of his state's senators.[39]

From Boston, Seward intended to go to Cleveland, where he had hailed the Western state governors for another conference, but by then the falsified gubernatorial appeal had already been transcribed and "delivered" to the president, so Seward returned to Washington. Perhaps to avoid casting it in the accurate light of a desperate attempt to salvage McClellan's reverses, scriveners antedated the document to June 28, and by July 2 Lincoln's portion of the farce made newspapers across the country, appearing as a reply to the governors in concurrence with their unanimous opinion. Editors who had been notified earlier in Seward's negotiations announced that the president had called for 200,000 more troops, while those who waited for the actual document found that he had decided on 300,000.[40] Even Governor Morgan, one of Seward's initial conspirators, had to ask which number New York's quota would be based upon. "It was thought safest to mark high enough," Lincoln told him, using the passive voice as though to diminish his own apparent role in the decision. He echoed a recent claim of George McClellan's when he explained to Morgan (and later to the other participating governors) that with 50,000 recruits he could "substantially close the war in two weeks" if only he could have them immediately. A month's delay would cost the existing army 20,000 men from battle and disease, and that would leave him a gain of only 30,000, he wrote, "with the difference between old and new troops still against me." The proclamation called for 300,000, and New York would be required to supply some 60,000 additional men. Governor David Tod, of Ohio (who inadvertently revealed that he had not been approached about the June 28 memorial any earlier than June 30), generously promised to send five new regiments totaling about 5,000 officers and men, but he may have been surprised to learn that Ohio would owe the country nearly 37,000 more of its sons under the latest appeal.[41]

Timed as it was for press distribution on the Saturday before the Fourth of July celebrations, Lincoln's artfully presented appeal sat fresh in each parishioner's mind during Sunday services that inevitably included a touch of patriotic fervor, and Monday morning's holiday editorials tended to characterize the call as a test of each citizen's devotion. "Everywhere our armies are beset by overwhelming numbers," warned an alarmed (and evidently gullible) *Hartford Courant.* "To arms! To arms! Ye brave," heralded the *Cleveland Plain Dealer.* Albany's *Atlas and Argus* observed that it had taken a year for the government to recognize that the rebellion would require ten times as many troops to suppress as originally supposed. "Even yet we underrate it," the *Atlas* predicted, welcoming the latest War Department demand as proof of a national determination that would serve as an antidote against European intervention.[42]

The fear of foreign intervention, particularly from England, still flourished as the summer of 1862 opened. Restrained hostility with the mother country lingered long after the *Trent* affair. For all the boisterous Northern nationalism that had applauded the action, it had come close to igniting a war with England, and a significant proportion of the British population remained antagonistic to the Lincoln government. The very spirit of liberty that had elicited the English commoners' sympathy with the American Revolution inspired admiration for the Southern declaration of independence and antipathy for the seeming hypocrisy of an aggressive, domineering federal government. "When was it that an Englishman did not take the weaker side?" asked one Suffolk Briton who tried to explain his country's attitude to a Wisconsin acquaintance. Not that the British didn't hate slavery worse than the average American, but they doubted that slavery was the real issue, and scorned Northern "brag and bullying." Subjugation of so vast a region seemed perfectly hopeless to him, but the attempt to crush the South had wrought havoc with the textile industries that dominated Lancashire and Manchester, and he supposed that his American friend would better appreciate British patience if he realized what it had cost England to stand idly by.[43]

Lincoln's naval blockade had not entirely closed off the British supply of Southern cotton, but it had sharply curtailed it. Blockade runners failed to bring in enough to meet demand, and by May of 1862 half the looms in England's bigger cotton towns had fallen silent. One-sixth of Lancashire's entire population of 2.5 million depended on that industry, and late in June unemployed operatives gathered at a massive meeting in Blackburn to call for mediation of the American conflict by their government. Support for that option spread to London by the end of the month, and caught the attention of Parliament. By July cotton prices were rising almost daily amid rampant speculation. Spinners and textile manufacturers announced plans to make even further cutbacks in production and to ask higher prices for their finished goods, which only depressed the industry further. The scarcity of raw materials cost each of those producers hundreds of pounds a week: London's principal financial sheet ominously observed that the manufacturers could cut their losses by half if they closed down altogether, and many of them did just that. "Mills are closing in every direction," the son of the American minister noted on the Fourth of July. Confederate successes only promised to prolong the cotton famine, thereby aggravating the British desire to intervene. International braggadocio notwithstanding, the dwindling faction that steadfastly backed Lincoln's struggle for national unity understood that foreign mediation would likely favor Southern independence. Those Unionists viewed an aggressive new mobilization as the best means of assuring Her Majesty's ministers that Washington meant business, and intended to wrap the squabble up in short order.[44]

Such pressures helped instill the latest recruiting drive with an element of desperation not unlike that of a gambler who stakes his home to regain his life savings. Some of the most ardent Unionists muttered, both publicly and privately, that the raising of more men would have gone a long way toward ending the war had it been accomplished two or three months previously, for troops enlisted in April or May would have been moving into the field just in time to meet McClellan's crisis. That criticism carried plenty of merit, and it helped to foster a fresh surge of dissatisfaction with Edwin Stanton, who had instead shut down recruiting three months earlier, sending home plenty of men in the grip of patriotic frenzy just when he should have been capitalizing on such sentiments. Devotion to the Union did not necessarily translate into satisfaction with the Lincoln administration, and at least one New York judge who stood willing to rally men to the flag refused to take part in a demonstration of support for the president — who, the judge's wife noted trenchantly, had precipitated disaster in Virginia through his meddling in military strategy.[45]

The *Chicago Tribune* saddled McClellan with the blame for the recent battlefield defeats, rather than Lincoln, but the editor urged all patriots to come to the rescue, anticipating that most of them would be sent to augment McClellan's army on the James for one last, irresistible blow against treason. Soldiers in the ranks swallowed the widely parroted theme that the war could be won quickly with just one more infusion of fresh troops, especially around Richmond, and they showed keen interest in the raising of regiments at home. Many of them believed that the faster the states met the new levy, the sooner the war would end. In accordance with the president's instructions Ambrose Burnside sent two of his divisions up to the Peninsula from North Carolina, and another two brigades landed there from the South Carolina coast, giving McClellan nearly a quarter of the fifty thousand reinforcements with which he had promised to reverse the fortunes of war. From his temporary camp at Newport News one of Burnside's soldiers — a private who would stop a bullet two months hence — informed his wife and children that he expected to march for Richmond imminently, take that place, and end the war in short order. "Tell everybody that can come to come and help McClellan," the doomed man urged in one letter, asking in the next if any volunteers were enlisting back in Connecticut.[46] A Massachusetts captain with McClellan at Harrison's Landing also shared his general's belief about reinforcements, telling his wife that "I think if they would send along some few thousand fresh troops we might go into Richmond and practically end the war."[47]

Several of the governors described great difficulty in recruiting men for three years of service. Israel Washburn, the only one of the Washburn brothers to have stayed in their native Maine, called it "terribly hard," and William Buckingham of Connecticut doubted that he could provide many such troops on short notice. Their counterparts in Massachusetts, New Jersey, Pennsylvania, loyal Virginia, Kentucky, Indiana, and Iowa all alluded to the same problem when they lobbied for permission to raise some of their troops for shorter terms, ranging from three months to a year. Francis Peirpoint, the putative governor of Virginia's rump Unionist government, insisted that if the rebellion could not be put down in another year it never could be quelled at all: he suggested that the president was discouraging prosecution of the war with his successive recruiting proclamations, each of which seemed to imply that the conflict would be extended for another three years. With his customary equivocation, Stanton accepted some of those appeals for short-term units in the interests of raising troops quickly. Governor Andrew of Massachusetts, who still favored three-month militia, harped especially on the importance of the advance bounty payment, pressuring the government to pay it as soon as each individual company mustered into federal service, rather than waiting until the complete regiment had been organized. Stanton saw to that, too.[48]

Cooperative newspapers gave prominent publicity to the provision for cash advances on bounties, and some tried to stimulate a few enlistments by playing down the potential for danger. "The inducements are much greater than at any previous time," proclaimed the *Plain Dealer.* "The big battles will have been fought, and much of the duty will no doubt consist in holding places already captured, or ferreting out Guerilla parties to let them swing."[49]

Southern volunteers, if they could be so called under the fairly comprehensive conscription of 1862, enjoyed few such benefits. The Confederate bounty consisted of a fifty-dollar payment in depreciated scrip, and the odds of combat fell heavily on the outnumbered rebel army. Despite such incentives for Northern men, few applicants stepped into the new recruiting offices that sprang up all over the country. New York City officials tried to re-create the fervent atmosphere of 1861 with an enormous rally on Union Square, reminiscent of one that had thronged that place a week after the attack on Fort Sumter. Prominent speakers mounted five rostrums around the square, with David Dudley Field, Francis Lieber, and General Frémont among them. Mayor George Opdyke introduced the event as an attempt to "rekindle the half-slumbering patriotism of our countrymen," and a committee published all the speeches for distribution to those who had stood out of earshot, but the patriotic spirit slumbered on. The governor urged President Lincoln to keep Congress in session until it passed a draft law.[50]

Those who considered enlisting often met active discouragement from acquaintances who had already gone into the service. Men who had not been in uniform a year and had seen only one brief campaign described themselves as "all wore out," and felt that they had done their share and more. Veterans of bloodier campaigning declared themselves wholly tired of soldiering; "the next time I enlist I will stay at home," grumbled a disgusted Pennsylvanian. A Massachusetts sergeant in Pope's army persistently cautioned his brothers to resist the mania for military occupation, no matter how generous the financial rewards. "My advice about your enlisting is and always will be not to enlist," the sergeant told his younger brother, "— as long as you have home & friends."[51] That gloomy chorus rose in volume as the threat of conscription prompted more men to consider volunteer options. A Maine corporal beseeched one of his brothers to cease his preliminary talk of enlistment and to hire a substitute if he were drafted, assuring him he would find the soldier's life repugnant. An Illinois soldier whose younger brother threatened to follow him argued against it on several grounds, including the brother's youth and their parents' dependence on his labor.[52] When a Pennsylvania private's teenaged son hinted at joining the army, the father sternly advised him to remain at his mother's table, where he would want to return as soon as he saw what army life was like. An Ohioan promised his little brother to "rest assured that you will most heartily regret it" if he signed up. A New Hampshire corporal serving in the swamps of Louisiana wrote his sister that her husband was "foolish" to think of enlisting, and suggested that he try instead for a job in the Quartermaster Department, or as a teamster, where he would be safer and more comfortable. While most of that advice was aimed at favored friends or relatives, many veterans seemed inclined to offer it indiscriminately, regardless of how they felt about receiving reinforcements.[53]

Newspaper lists of military appointments, promotions, and resignations that appeared alongside reports on the recruiting effort inspired few to cast their lot with the army, top-heavy as those lists were with officers who resigned immediately after the carnage of the Seven Days. One squad of young men did visit Cleveland early in July, seeking nothing more adventurous than three months of service inside the borders of Ohio. An unscrupulous recruiter swore that he could arrange it for them, doubtless counting on the two-dollar federal procurement premium for each of them, but their friends at home all advised them against going into the army, as did a relative of Senator Ben Wade, who was personally acquainted with one of those shrinking volunteers.[54]

Notwithstanding Seward's chicanery with the state governors, the appeal for three hundred thousand men would go down in history and song as "Father Abraham's" call, and two weeks into it supportive editors complained of the people's lethargy in responding. A little New Hampshire weekly soon noted that "the romance of military life has apparently lost its charm," and similar observations appeared spontaneously the breadth of the country. The *Chicago Tribune* conceded that the problem lay mainly in economic conditions: recession had left hundreds of thousands of men without income in 1861, but the army had siphoned most of them out of the labor market and wartime production had absorbed many of those who remained, providing them with better wages than they had ever known. Then, too, the faction that had opposed the war in the first place had gained strength through weariness with the struggle: peace meetings were springing up north of the Ohio, and that disaffection reached soldiers in the field, some of whom were already deserting. Whatever the causes, Cleveland's *Plain Dealer* finally admitted that popular enthusiasm for the war appeared to have all but evaporated.[55]

Everyone seemed to have a scheme for ferreting recruits out of particular occupations and classes. A New England newspaper suggested that store clerks might readily enlist, and let their places be taken by young ladies. The *Plain Dealer* saw great promise in that proposal, which would not only address the need for men but give "many a pale and half consumptive young man" an opportunity for hale and hearty living that might yield both physical and psychological health benefits. The *Chicago Tribune* snidely insinuated that Democrats had not matched Republicans in answering their country's call, and bade them go help their friend McClellan.[56]

Among the wealthy, military service remained an amusing fantasy they might entertain in theory alone, acquiescing to the slightest parental objection or excusing themselves on the pressure of business.[57] Governor Andrew mined the intellectual and commercial elite of Massachusetts to officer his regiments, thereby forging those units with class distinctions as well as the desired political flavor, but many a young Harvard or Yale alumnus who lent his spirit to the war's aims never seriously considered entering the army.[58] A Connecticut major attended the commencement ceremonies at Yale during his last furlough, hoping to persuade some of his alma mater's 1862 crop into the service, but he came away empty-handed. Just before returning to the front, where he would soon be killed, he wondered aloud why educated and gentlemanly young men declined to join the struggle. The major's grieving brother passed that implicit accusation along to those recent Yale graduates who sent condolences, but the posthumous appeal failed to stir most of them, and those classmates who did enlist thereafter chose short-term militia units that seemed destined for garrison duty.[59]

The most painful assessment, and perhaps the most accurate, appeared in an obscure Democratic weekly on the upper Mississippi. Wisconsin had already sent twenty thousand men to the war, noted the Unionist editor of the *Courier* in Prairie du Chien (understating the number of volunteers by several thousand), and the majority of those soldiers had come from the poorest strata of the state's inhabitants. Most of them had left behind needy families in the form of wives and children or impoverished parents, if not both, and the state treasurer was paying out a thousand dollars a day in supplementary support for those destitute families. The pool of such financially distressed volunteers had just about been exhausted, the editor theorized, and it was time for more comfortable citizens to defend the national government that had helped secure their successful station in life. It would save hundreds of thousands of dollars in immediate subsidies to soldiers' families, he argued, and far greater sums in long-term support for the survivors of those who died in the service.

"We have able-bodied men enough among us," the editor contended, with ill-concealed resentment, "— men whose families would not suffer for bread even if their natural protectors should accidentally happen to get shot, or die of fever in camp. It would save the state a vast amount of money if this class would go. Not half the suffering would occur among families if men of property would cheerfully set themselves up as marks for the enemy."[60]

Letters addressed to or by soldiers' desperate wives corroborate such accusations. The rotting of potatoes in the root cellar or cattle breaking into their winter feed raised real fears of starvation, and children had to endure the winter months without hats, or forgo school altogether, until the army found time and money enough to pay the soldiers. Mothers dying of consumption had to choose between feeding their children and buying medicine for themselves, while helpless soldier husbands waited in anguish, unable to obtain leave or to afford the cost of passage home.[61]

The *Boston Journal* made no effort to dispute the circumstances, but offered an entirely different perspective on it. The poor were precisely the people who should fill the armies, claimed that newspaper. They stood to gain the most from preserving the Union (or so ran that editor's argument), because the United States was the only country in which all classes shared the opportunity to advance themselves.[62]

A New Jersey weekly proposed targeting the patriotism of farmers. Innocently supposing that patriotism actually might provide the greatest allure, some cities organized mass public gatherings involving well-known speakers, and in many of the Midwestern states the War Department gave each governor a stipend to hire persuasive orators of the right political stripe. On Sunday night, July 10, three thousand people squeezed into Allyn Hall, in Hartford, to hear Connecticut governor William Buckingham, Senator James Dixon, and a handful of other Nutmeg State notables harangue the crowd for prospective soldiers. Two days later Buckingham assured the secretary of war of great excitement and a favorable spirit among his people, but almost no volunteers stepped forward, so the state instantly switched from patriotic appeals to offers of money. On the fourth day after the disappointing rally at Allyn Hall, the *Hartford Courant,* another steadfastly Republican sheet, ran a bold headline announcing the "Extraordinary Bounty to Volunteers in Connecticut Regiments!" The legislature had authorized the immediate payment of a $2 premium for each man who signed his name to a roll, with an allotment of $6 a month for each married man and $30 more at the end of each year. The state would advance $50 to any man who enlisted before the August 20 deadline for filling the state quota, on top of the $25 advance from the federal government. The *Courant* hinted, broadly, that a single soldier could reap $338 *if the war ended within a year.* Soldiers with families would realize even more within that year: $410, according to the benefits the *Courant* listed, although the newspaper boosted that total to $458 in a miscalculation that only served to amplify the article's persuasive purpose. Even discounting for that exaggeration, a recruit's accumulated pay and allowances held a certain attraction for laborers who had to provide for themselves on about $300 a year, especially when their rations and clothing would theoretically be paid for by the government.[63]

With an abundance of hardscrabble farming operations within its borders, Vermont provided the first new infantry regiment under the July 1 call. The 9th Vermont had been organizing slowly since Stanton's frenetic appeal of late May, but the advance pay and bounties of early July filled the companies out quickly. The completed regiment mustered into federal service at Brattleboro on July 9, starting for Washington on the morning of the fifteenth. It did not hinder recruiting there that the Vermont legislature had already agreed to pay an additional seven dollars per month to the state's soldiers, which most of them dedicated to the support of their families along with varying portions of their army salaries. That relatively small amount of regular income tempted struggling farmers in the declining agricultural economy of the Green Mountains, where almost all the menfolk in some poor families succumbed to the economic pressure and enrolled by squads.[64]

Ira Morse, a close-fisted farmer from Woodbury, had already sent one son and a brother off with the 8th Vermont late the previous winter, and the departing brother had lodged his sickly wife and son with Ira's family. Ira's brother-in-law had also joined the army, leaving his son to board with the Morses, as well, but no sooner did news of Lincoln's three-hundred-thousand-man call reach the northern quarter of the state than that nephew ran off to sign up, refusing to return when Ira traveled to the encampment to collect him. Ira's youngest son, Orlando, swore that he would follow his cousin to war as soon as the haying season ended, dismissing his father's threat to thrash him if he tried it. Before the end of July increased bounty offers led Ira to announce that he, too, intended to enlist when the harvest ended.[65]

A few miles west of Woodbury, the Tillison family would prove even more susceptible to the allure of state subsidies and higher cash bounties. Charles Tillison left his wife, daughters, and one schoolteacher son behind to manage the family farm while he, another son, his nephew, and three of his brothers (including one past fifty) enlisted together. Charles sent almost all his pay home besides the state allotment, earning extra money by washing clothing for his comrades, but for all that additional income the son who stayed at home still considered selling the farm as a losing proposition.[66]

As the editor in Prairie du Chien had pointed out, such indigent populations had already been sorely depleted by the army. The long, grue-some lists of casualties that ran alongside the appeals for troops helped to discourage the vast majority of those who remained; many who har-bored any inclination to take up arms against secession evinced greater reluctance to serve for the moderate emoluments available in early July, however alarming the military situation might be. Forty dollars in fresh greenbacks might attract a trickle of men and boys willing to sign away three years of their lives, particularly in the leaner districts, but most eli-gible men hung back, waiting for a more compelling offer.

The war between Chicago's two principal newspapers helped to illustrate the accidental concurrence that ultimately developed between opposing Northern factions. Joseph Medill's unabashedly Republican *Chicago Tri-bune* supported Lincoln's July 1 levy without reservation. Medill antici-pated that recruits would spring forward spontaneously, however, and in his Fourth of July edition he denounced Jefferson Davis for allegedly commenting that conscription was "absolutely indispensable" to the pres-ervation of Southern independence. "We commend this admission to the consideration of Palmerston, Gregory & Co.," wrote Medill, alluding to prominent British proponents of Confederate recognition. "Is an army that can only be maintained by conscription 'fighting for their rights' and 'never to be conquered'?"

Wilbur Storey, the conservative Democrat who edited the *Chicago Times,* regularly denounced and satirized the Lincoln administration. His vit-riolic editorials would eventually bring him the wartime dissenter's cus-tomary accusation of treasonous sympathy with the enemy, complete with official suppression, but Storey nevertheless advocated an aggressive prosecution of the war and restoration of the Union. Three days after Medill's diatribe against Confederate conscription, Storey returned a sug-gestion that conscription was precisely what the North needed to defeat secession.[67]

The same cry seemed to rise everywhere simultaneously. The *Cincinnati Daily Commercial* lobbied for an immediate draft on July 9. That same day the *Plain Dealer* gently introduced the idea of compulsory service to readers in the Western Reserve, mollifying potential critics with the comfort that Ohio lacked an Enrollment Act, which left her citizens safe for the present.[68] The conservative *New Hampshire Argus and Spectator* acknowledged the sudden popular aversion to military commitment, and hailed mandatory service as a welcome solution. All but the most ra-bidly antiwar papers conceded that conscription seemed necessary, if the army really needed that many men. From his post with the humanitarian

Sanitary Commission at Harrison's Landing, pioneer landscape architect Frederick Law Olmsted urged Senator Preston King to support conscription as the best and fastest means of bringing the war to a close. King need not fear that substantial citizens would be dragooned into military service, Olmsted remarked with drawing-room disdain, for a man's income reflected his value to society, and those with sufficient income would be able to hire less-valuable substitutes to take their places in the ranks.[69]

Inside the steaming chamber of the U.S. Senate, Henry Wilson of Massachusetts rose on July 8 to introduce Senate Bill No. 384, asking permission to have it printed for discussion. He described it simply as an amendment to the Militia Act of 1795, which Lincoln had used as his authority for summoning the seventy-five thousand soldiers who initiated the war. On July 9 Wilson's new bill occupied half the Senate's workday. Ostensibly Senate Bill 384 changed little except the period of time a president might require state militia for federal service, removing the three-month restrictions of the 1795 law and allowing for indefinite mobilizations. Additionally (and more significantly), if individual states failed to meet their militia quotas the federal government would have the option of invoking a draft for the balance. In fact Wilson, a devoted abolitionist, appeared most intent on slipping through a paragraph emancipating any slave — and the entire family of any slave — who "served" the United States government in any capacity, and an accommodating Iowa radical began the day's debate by proposing an amendment making the Militia Act colorblind, thereby subjecting adult males of all races to the risk of compulsory service. Much of that day and the next two, the senators haggled primarily over details affecting the emancipation element.[70]

During the discussion, only a few real questions of military recruiting intruded on the paramount issue of race and freedom. The term "militia" confused one senator, who understood the bill to address specific emergencies, but he finally realized that the government saw no real difference between militia and volunteer units: they both consisted of state troops called into federal service. The conscription portion of the bill would, therefore, logically apply to the entire volunteer army. Because the draft would be imposed only in states that did not meet their quotas, New Hampshire senator John Hale worried whether recruits would be credited against the quotas of the towns where they lived or the towns where they enlisted: since Vermont paid its soldiers an extra seven dollars per month and New Hampshire paid no regular subsidy, Hale feared that Granite State citizens might cross the Connecticut River by the thousands, and newspaper reports from his home state suggested that many of them had already done so. Another member expressed concern over the provision for indefinite service, citing at least one governor who had commented on the impossibility of enlisting volunteers without a specified term. Finally Wilson substituted a new bill limiting federal demands to one hundred thousand militia for nine consecutive months of service, and his colleagues passed that version on July 15 after two hasty bouts of amendments to limit the number of slaves who might benefit from emancipation.[71]

With the congressional session nearing its conclusion the bill went to the House of Representatives the next morning. The congressmen took it up in the middle of that intensely humid summer afternoon. Dense clouds descended over the Capitol building about that time, turning the day as black as night, and gaslights had to be lit for lawmakers to read their documents — including the bill that gave the President of the United States feudal authority to force American citizens into military service. Some may have taken that somber sky as an omen, but most obviously did not. An Indiana Democrat tried vainly to table the militia bill, only to see it passed a few minutes later without further changes and with almost no discussion. President Lincoln went over to the Capitol the next morning and signed it into law in the final hours of the session, assuring himself much more leverage to pry troops out of the states.[72]

Previously, while the federal government had the right to call on the states for militia through presidential proclamation, it had been up to the individual state governors to supply those troops. In most states, all adult males to the age of forty-five theoretically belonged to the militia, and could be required to serve by state authority, but the central government had never enjoyed any power to directly coerce a single man into the ranks. The states' authority to compel service had not been exercised since the War of 1812, and even then dissenters had been able to avoid duty by paying a small fine, even in the face of alien invasion.

For a society that had come to consider conscription the outdated privilege of kings and emperors, and where the danger of invasion remained only theoretical, the North greeted the prospect of a draft with more surprising passivity than the South. The mere rumor of a forthcoming draft law provoked a mob to disrupt a recruiting rally in Detroit, but no such disturbances followed the news of its enactment. Not surprisingly, the greatest applause came from soldiers who had been bearing the brunt of the struggle on behalf of their more comfortable counterparts at home. Most of the men in uniform wanted help fighting the war, so they could wind things up and go home. Occasionally one of them took such pride in his home community that he preferred to see his townsmen come out of their own free will, and soldiers from regions within reach of Confederate depredations that summer — like southern Indiana — rightly supposed that their neighbors would need no prompting to join them.[73] In most cases, though, those soldiers who heard the first rumblings about plans for a draft welcomed the news with vigorous expressions of righteous satisfaction, harboring no tolerance for those who entertained political differences and showing little sympathy with the family obligations of those who declined to serve. Some camps broke into loud cheers at news that the government had decided to draft.[74]

Often the popularity of conscription in the army arose from its very image as a weapon of partisan coercion, since it would likely snare many of those who had most vigorously and consistently opposed the war from the outset, thus forcing them to participate in the fatal folly of their political opposites. "If I had my will," admitted a decidedly undemocratic Indiana captain, "I would draft every man who voted against the Union ticket." Others, who were beginning to feel that they had been sent to war under false pretenses, wanted those who had tricked them to come out and assume the danger with them. Sensing the trend toward emancipation implied by recent congressional legislation, a New Hampshire soldier who resented that change of policy raged in a letter to his wife that "*every* abolishonest should be *compelled* to come out here, and when here to be in the *front rank.*"[75]

Soldiers at the front naturally envied men who continued to enjoy the comforts of civilian life. Hardened by their service, some of those veterans suspected cowardice or a contemptible daintiness among those who had failed to enlist. A Pennsylvanian who had opted for short-term service revealed more than a twinge of jealousy in his complaints about a neighbor's decision to stay home: "I suppose our Patriotic Young Friend Harry McMillen calls out to see you every once and a while," sneered the recruit, in a letter to a young lady; "*O but he is a pretty boy.*" Learning of Senator Wilson's militia bill at Newport News, while waiting to join McClellan, one of Burnside's men could hardly conceal his glee at the notion of certain stay-at-homes having to share the misery of camp and march. Every Union army betrayed a measure of animosity toward those who shunned the crusade, and especially in the cases of those who had wailed loudest in their support for it.[76] Soldiers who had not been home since the previous summer still supposed that Northern towns harbored abundant colonies of idle citizens. A staff officer with General Hooker, on the Peninsula, told his brother that conscription would please him no end, "for there are many loafers round the streets who had much better be facing the enemy than standing on street corners."[77]

"We will make some of those fellows come out who have laid at home sucking their thumb," remarked a Wisconsin officer in the western theater. One Connecticut soldier on the South Carolina coast waxed bitterly sarcastic about his civilian acquaintances. "So," he addressed one of those friends, "Madison has really found out at last that her young men are called upon to do something to save a Gov't & a Union to which they owe their existence, contemptible as it is!" He somehow excused his correspondent's entire family from his blanket condemnation, but as for everyone else he felt content to "let 'em draft." A battle-weary young man in a New Hampshire regiment resented his neighbors' reluctance to enlist, asking his parents in all seriousness what they thought hindered recruiting; instead of wasting money on bounties, he believed the government ought to draft outright, but he had to moderate that opinion when his own father began worrying that he might be among those drafted.[78]

Soldiers' letters frequently lapsed into that sort of hypocrisy — applauding the conscription of strangers and unpopular neighbors while hoping that friends and family would be spared from service — but some veterans addressed the matter more consistently, challenging their friends and relatives to come join a fight that those correspondents may not have supported in the first place. One Pennsylvanian tried to shame his older brother before the family, insisting that he did not care whether the brother died, if he stayed home "like the rest of the cowards" and waited to be drafted; in the end the brother did enlist, and did die. Writing from McClellan's base at Harrison's Landing, an officer from western New York prodded his reluctant law partner with increasing impatience to put his own life on the line, finally demanding boldly, "Why don't you enlist?"[79]

Women and other ineligible citizens at home entertained similar doubts about military-age males who resisted the intoxicating allure of fife and drum, and they often voiced those doubts. Occasionally a man would relent under the pressure of the implied challenge, but that sort of innuendo convinced few of those who could afford to ignore enlistment bounties and family subsidies.[80]

Such frustrations made the draft all the more appealing to war supporters who could neither comprehend nor countenance a different political viewpoint. Joseph Medill, who had so snidely denounced conscription as the imposition of an oppressive Southern government in his Fourth of July issue of the *Chicago Tribune*, warmly embraced Northern conscription by July 15. Observing that no one seemed to be enlisting, he adopted Jefferson Davis's very argument of the draft as crucial to preservation of the Union. That put him on the same side with a lot of his rival Democratic editors, who had already accepted it as more of an odious necessity.[81]

As Wilson's militia bill raced through Congress, its draft clause alarmed a great many citizens who had no wish to join the army. The bill had hardly been introduced before reports started circulating about the mass migration of young men to Canada, and military organizers quickly prepared to use the danger of conscription as an inducement for enlisting. After much publicity the former governor of Ohio and his unsuccessful opponent for that office joined forces with the incumbent governor on the capitol grounds the night of July 15 to address what witnesses believed to be the largest crowd ever gathered in Columbus. With old-fashioned gallery rhetoric they pitched a bipartisan nationalistic spiel founded on the argument that this particular moment — rather than the panic of the previous May, or the previous summer, or April and May of 1861 — represented the critical juncture of the war: enlist now, and the battle was won; lose heart now, and all was lost. Two days later at least one newspaper reported an enthusiastic response to their plea, although any sudden rush of Ohio volunteers might have been ascribed to the news from Kentucky, where two separate Confederate raids drove deep into that state. While politicians inflamed the teeming citizens in Columbus, Confederate cavalry roamed within two easy days' ride of Cincinnati, and a few days later one Southern command crossed the Ohio River.[82]

Once the militia bill became law, public interest in recruiting accelerated dramatically, and patriotic rallies blossomed nationwide. The government had not yet hinted that it would invoke the draft, but there was the matter of that outstanding call for three hundred thousand new troops, and the failure to field those men carried certain inescapable implications. Suddenly the raising of men for the army concerned every healthy male between eighteen and forty-five, regardless of political sympathies, for any community that failed to send the desired proportion of its population in volunteers would see the rest taken forcibly. Tangible evidence of that possibility appeared soon thereafter in the form of enrolling officers who began circulating like lethal census enumerators, taking down names, ages, occupations, and recording "other useful information" about anyone who looked as though he could carry a musket. If a state fell short of presidential troop demands, state officials would have to subdivide the deficit by town and city, drawing the difference from delinquent municipalities.[83]

The War Department would require men only from loyal states east of the territories, but the law applied coast to coast, and it settled an ominous cloud over the land of liberty. From the St. John's River to the Pacific Ocean, fathers and sons who had eaten their breakfasts in something approaching absolute freedom on the morning of July 17 took their dinners that evening as potential conscripts in what many of them considered an imperial army. Soon they became virtual prisoners in their communities, as well: as an afterthought, President Lincoln allowed the secretary of war to deprive such men even of the right to travel outside their home counties without official permission, and virtually forbade them to leave the United States at all. That autocratic edict reached as far as Kansas, where sheriff's posses immediately began arresting trans-Missouri migrants on their way to the Colorado gold fields.[84]

The stunning, unprecedented prohibition caught many a young man away from home. One westering lad visiting relatives in Massachusetts had to obtain a certificate from that commonwealth before he could return to his home in Wisconsin, and for that document he had to swear that he would not try to evade the draft. Provost marshals in Toledo arrested a youth from Louisville who left home to make university arrangements before Stanton disseminated his decree. "A very arbitrary & stringent order —," complained a Massachusetts woman. "New, this, for free born yankees to submit to."[85]

The mere threat of a draft stirred some men to think about military service, but those who despaired of finding civilian employment remained prominent among the would-be recruits. Charles Reed, a young artist from eastern Massachusetts, could find no commercial work at home or in the vicinity of Boston, and in desperation he considered a position as bugler for a new artillery battery. The pay was twenty-one dollars a month: he would get a month's advance pay, a hundred-dollar state bounty in cash, and the twenty-five-dollar advance on his federal bounty. He talked it over with his brother-in-law, who concluded that the risk would be minimal and that Reed would never have to complete the three-year commitment, because with so many Union troops under arms the war was likely to conclude that winter. Besides, an artillery battery would require much longer training than infantry before it went into combat.[86] A significant number of those who joined Reed in considering that option in late July steadfastly declined to simply enlist, instead seeking the aid of influential friends for commissions in the army as a means of improving their lot socially or economically — or both. For many of those petitioners, a commission in the army constituted the last resort, after diplomatic posts or assignment as one of the new revenue collectors.[87]

The public faced a flurry of revolutionary legislation that week. On the same day that he signed the militia bill, Lincoln also took up the new Confiscation Act, which imposed penalties of death, imprisonment, and widespread property confiscation on those who served, aided, or abetted the Confederacy. Although labeled as an effort to punish treason and rebellion, that legislation — like the amendment to the Militia Act —

disguised an ulterior motive to free slaves. The president originally concurred with other conservative Republicans (and presumably Democrats) who found the bill unconstitutional on two major points, including a lack of due process in the determination of guilt. He had intended to veto it, and had composed a lengthy message to explain his objections. Radical Republicans' zeal to satisfy their abolitionist inclinations led Senator Browning to remark, as Congress passed the confiscation bill, that the time had come for Mr. Lincoln to determine whether the radicals would control him or he would control them: the former seemed to be the case, for no confrontation ensued. Both houses passed a joint resolution that only partially allayed Lincoln's fears, but he endorsed the bill while it still contained some of its offensive provisions.[88]

A few days before the congressional session ended, the president formally submitted his draft of a bill to offer compensation for any state that ended slavery statutorily. It represented his idea of the previous winter, and comported with his initial insistence that only the individual states could emancipate their slaves. The border states, where the exchange of cash for divestiture of a moribund institution ought to have been the most attractive, had not responded favorably to Lincoln's earlier overtures. Neither did Congress. That sensible and economical plan for solving the most vexing conflict in the nation's history went directly into the hands of a committee, where it died without further action. Even that tentative movement toward voluntary abolition provoked a panel of Kentucky congressmen to opposition. It also ignited brushfires of resentment among editors and soldiers who read it as an indication of administration movement toward general emancipation.[89] Soldiers in particular fumed over the suspicion that they had been drawn into service on a plea to preserve the Union only to be transformed into unwilling abolitionists. "I came out here to help support the Constitution & Laws of our land," wrote a Granite State sergeant in Burnside's command, "and for *nothing* else." He expressed a sentiment fairly common within the ranks. Another New Hampshireman in the Army of the Potomac bet that any antislavery radicals who entered the service would surely go home as strict Constitution men: "there are no Emancipationists in this army," he assured his parents.[90]

Still thinking of the stiffening tension between himself and the abolition-minded radicals, Lincoln called his cabinet together on the anniversary of Bull Run to discuss how the authority of the confiscation and militia bills might be employed. He proposed three new orders: one allowing military commanders to subsist their commands from the hostile countryside, another permitting the use of contraband blacks as laborers, and a third providing for the colonization of those freed laborers after they were discharged. Stanton remarked that General Hunter had proposed enlisting black recruits in South Carolina to compensate for the thousands of men he had shipped to McClellan, and Stanton endorsed the idea along with both Seward and Chase, but Lincoln rejected it.[91]

The next day, July 22, they reconvened and decided to adopt all the orders except for the colonization scheme. Then the president laid the rough draft of another order on the table. This one, drawing on the precedent of the Confiscation Act, announced that the slaves in any state that remained in rebellion after a certain date would all be declared free. He suggested making this proclamation effective on January 1, adding that he would also renew his effort to have Congress compensate states that abolished slavery gradually, thus providing incentives for Southern states to renounce secession and for border states to relinquish the offending institution. Lincoln had been thinking about general emancipation for some time, in complete contradiction to all his previous statements on the subject, and he had first revealed it to some of his cabinet more than a week before. Stanton and Attorney General Bates greeted the idea warmly, but Seward balked at the effect it might have on cotton-dependent foreign powers. Chase said nothing that Stanton could hear, but that evening Chase recalled offering his "cordial support."[92]

Lincoln's draft proclamation remained a secret of the cabinet. Even relatively conservative men began wondering why he failed to make immediate use of the new powers Congress had granted him. "Why in the name of anarchy and ruin doesn't the President order the draft of one million fighting men at once, and the liberation of every able-bodied Sambo in Southronia?" howled New Yorker George Templeton Strong, who could easily have afforded a substitute. Draft-exempt congressmen friendly to Lincoln pondered the same question, but Lincoln and some of his closest advisors understood that all the recent military setbacks and the poor response to recruiting appeals would leave any such proclamations seeming more indicative of weakness than of strength. New men enlisted too slowly to compensate for the attrition of death, wounds, disease, and desertion, so the army grew smaller rather than larger, and Secretary Seward feared that foreign powers would view that as a distinct decline in Northern will, leading them to intercede on the side of Southern independence.[93]

That concern only aggravated the sense of momentary military impotence, which impelled the secretary of war to conclude the July 22 cabinet meeting with a proposal to draft fifty thousand men immediately under the new Militia Act. Seward suggested doubling that number to the hundred thousand allowed under that law. The president demurred, understandably concerned that any additional levy beyond his July 1 order for three hundred thousand would only further discourage a public that had grown nearly as frustrated by his repeated calls for reinforcements as he was by McClellan's. He authorized Stanton to do anything he could to fill up the old regiments, for that would put new men into the field with far greater speed and efficiency than raising and organizing new regiments. The new Militia Act did include a paragraph allowing men to enlist in the old regiments for a single year, and if Stanton thought he could prompt those enlistments with a draft he was free to do so, as long as any drafted men were subtracted from the required three hundred thousand.[94]

Nothing betrayed the sinking popularity of Lincoln's war so much as the cynical response to the enactment of a draft law. In the shadow of random conscription every governor, town council, and individual citizen suddenly envisioned an army of mercenaries. The majority of those who faced a chance of being drafted chose to solve the shortage in military manpower by convincing someone else to serve in their places, and they seemed willing to devote immense resources to achieve that end. Even those who opposed the war or the administration found that approach attractive, lending the conflict the illusion of greater support than it really enjoyed.[95] Five days after passage of the militia draft, one of the first local drives for volunteers opened with a so-called Union rally in the seat of overwhelmingly Democratic Sussex County, Delaware, where many residents showed as much indecision over which side to serve as they did over whether to serve at all. A similar meeting in Wilmington yielded no immediate recruits, but it produced resolutions that prompted the city council to appropriate a fifty-dollar city bounty for any man who would enlist in a new Delaware regiment: it had already become apparent that the men would not come forth until the money did.[96]

A rally in Cleveland on July 23 adjourned to the open air when more people showed up than the reserved hall could accommodate. Proportionately large crowds attended rural gatherings in the interior of Ohio through the rest of that week, but most came for diversion or to help raise money that might convince others to enlist. The town cannon fired a few salvos to announce a war meeting at Corning, New York's, Concert Hall the next night, attracting twice as many people as the building could seat: two bands and a soprano alternated with speakers, drawing $2,000 in donations for bounties. A similar gathering at the town hall in Burlington, Vermont, defied a soaking rain to adopt long-winded resolutions and raise $2,840. The economic promises made to volunteers there and elsewhere finally started bringing men to the tables, but the cost, unseemliness, and potential corruption of such an avaricious system raised hackles among the strongest supporters of the war. The accelerating generosity of bounties also alarmed the *Cleveland Plain Dealer*, which cautioned against turning the recruiting drive into an auction among competing communities.[97]

As obvious a peril as that might have been, other cities saw no alternative but to at least meet the munificence of neighboring municipalities, and many tried to exceed them. The State of New York initiated a state bounty of $50, and the Tenth Ward of Buffalo matched it. The Buffalo Board of Trade dunned its members more than $8,500 to fund similar inducements citywide, while nearby towns struggled to compete. Clinton, Massachusetts, first voted $75 for each man, to the disgust of a Clinton soldier who wondered why his townsmen raised no such amounts for soldiers who came home disabled. Patriotic promoters at Windsor, Connecticut, accumulated enough contributions at their first rally to meet that town's quota of thirty men with the promise of $150 for everyone who signed up by the August 20 deadline, but before the meeting ended two more citizens found themselves so stirred by the artificial spirit of the meeting (or by the likelihood of escaping conscription) that they respectively enhanced that offer by $25 and $5 per man. Private subscriptions and city allocations for bounties in Philadelphia came to $272,000 by the end of July, not including massive donations from railroad companies headquartered there. A stoutly Democratic sheet in St. Louis, long a loud critic of most administration policies, demanded that the city council appropriate bounties for volunteers.[98]

All but the largest communities responded to their recruiting quotas with some variation on a progressive pattern of initial inattention, belated anxiety, and eventual panic. First the local newspapers reported elaborately orchestrated gatherings in distant cities that appropriated generous sums for the benefit of volunteers or their families. Then, as the deadline for the quota of volunteers neared, those rallies grew closer to home and local men began migrating toward the proffered bounties. That loss of prospective recruits for the home community would finally convince tardy municipal officials to stage their own rallies, which inevitably deteriorated into feverish fundraising exercises.

Lee County, Iowa, faced a quota of some 250 men, and on July 27 the war committee proposed supplementing each volunteer's federal bounty with fifty dollars from local coffers. That and other meetings across the state prompted the editor of the *Waterloo Courier* to make ironic allusion in his August 6 edition to the weeks of idle talk about holding such a meeting in Waterloo, and three days later Waterloo officials came through with a gala Saturday affair. The Waterloo Brass Band and an assortment of speakers left the crowd feeling "patriotic and liberal," allowing solicitors for the recruiting fund to collect fifteen hundred dollars in half an hour. With that purse the committee promised each recruit twenty dollars in cash. No actual volunteers came forth, but a few men pledged to either enlist or pay five dollars a month into the fund.[99]

Committee members soon noticed that many pledges, either of money or of service, went unfulfilled. The moderator of a war meeting in Portage, Wisconsin, alluded publicly to recanting donors who were "prompt to subscribe but dreadfully slow to pay," and Portage's six-page list of pledges included many in the range of two to twenty dollars that were never fulfilled. Only one ten-dollar pledge was redeemed by virtue of enlistment, and that by the subscriber's son rather than by the would-be donor himself. Two pugnacious opponents of the war rebuffed the clerk who dunned them for a contribution. "Nothing," said one of them, when asked how much he would give: "not a damned cent." Editors routinely applauded contributors by publishing everyone's donations, and some retaliated against those who refused by listing them under prominent, accusative headlines.[100]

Previous recruiting had already culled each community's humblest neighborhoods of their most willing young — and not so young — men, and the motley squads still gathered too slowly in the tents at the various encampments. By the end of July, Vermont was still the only state to have sent a new regiment to the front, and no other state had one that would be ready to move in less than a week or two. More than five weeks after the July 1 appeal for three hundred thousand men, therefore, fewer than one thousand fresh troops had taken the field. Interior secretary Caleb Smith no longer believed that the government could rely on voluntary enlistments, observing that "enthusiastic meetings are held, fine speeches are made, and money is liberally subscribed, but the volunteers come in few and far between."[101]

One of those enthusiastic meetings filled the town hall at Claremont, New Hampshire, where the governor and an assortment of local dignitaries beseeched the citizens of Sullivan County to come to their country's aid. A mournful procession of townspeople had filed into that same building exactly six Sundays before to hear solemn eulogies for all the Claremont men who had already died in the war, and the echoes of that lugubrious service seemed to cool the ardor of the governor's listeners, few of whom heeded his plea. Many of New Hampshire's people had not thrown their hearts entirely into the conflict from the very beginning, but similar apathy or disenchantment now appeared to afflict most towns and cities across the country. "We ought to have another patriotic meeting," wailed the principal newspaper in zealously Republican Hartford, late in July.

"The citizens are not as yet sufficiently aroused to the importance of the crisis."[102]

The accuracy of that observation finally sank in at Washington, where Henry Halleck had just taken over as general in chief of the army. On August 3 Halleck delivered the secretary of war a memorandum advising a draft of two hundred thousand militia, in addition to the previous three hundred thousand three-year men.[103]

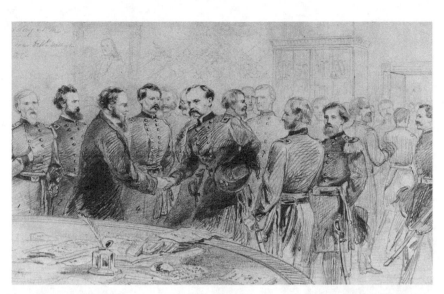

Secretary of War Edwin M. Stanton receives his generals at the War Department. Stanton is shaking hands with Daniel Sickles; between them is George McClellan, and Irvin McDowell is visible over Sickles's left shoulder.

Searching for the wounded after Fort Donelson. *Harper's Weekly*, March 8, 1862.

Major General Don Carlos Buell, whose Army of the Ohio saved Ulysses Grant's Army of the Tennessee from likely defeat at Shiloh.

Major General Nathaniel P. Banks. Although driven out of the Shenandoah Valley by Stonewall Jackson, Banks conducted himself well enough on the retreat to retain the respect of his men. He lost to Jackson again at Cedar Mountain before being reassigned to the Department of the Gulf.

Union remains on the battlefield of Gaines's Mill, still unburied two years later.

Field hospital at Savage's Station. The surgeon in the foreground and the wounded men wearing straw hats belonged to the 16th New York. Most of these men were left behind and captured.

The retreat from Savage's Station, by the light of burning supplies.

Major General John Pope.

Major General Henry W. Halleck.

Artist's rendering of Lincoln as he read the first draft of the Emancipation Proclamation to his cabinet on July 22, 1862. Left to right are Edwin Stanton, Salmon Chase, Lincoln, Gideon Welles, Caleb Smith, William Seward (seated), Montgomery Blair, and Edward Bates.

Old Capitol Prison, which became the home of numerous dissident newspaper editors, political candidates, and other administration critics in the summer of 1862.

Union rally in Washington, August 6, 1862, drawn by Alfred Waud for *Harper's Weekly* of August 23, 1862.

Longstreet's corps bearing down on Pope's surprised left wing at Second Bull Run.

Refugees from Sioux uprising in Minnesota, encamped on the prairie.

General Braxton Bragg, commander of the Confederacy's Western Department and the nominal leader of the Kentucky invasion.

Lieutenant General Edmund Kirby Smith, whose failure to cooperate with Bragg robbed the Kentucky foray of more meaningful achievements.

PART II

SO SHRILL YOUR BUGLES BLOW

4

Torrents of Men

FOR ALL THE UNION successes in the spring of 1862, the greatest chance for an early, meaningful victory was lost through one impulsive decision. The war would be over before historians began hinting at the full consequences of canceling McDowell's march on Richmond, but Lincoln may already have sensed the damage wrought by his amateur experiments in strategy when he appointed Henry Halleck to fill the vacant position of general in chief on July 11. In northern Mississippi, Halleck had shown the same lethargic preference for siege operations that McClellan displayed before Richmond, but Halleck had captured his target city (albeit without capturing its Confederate garrison), and he had commanded in a theater where Union troops had seen far more success than failure. Halleck owed his promotion partly to the influence of John Pope, who had served under him in that department: the president seemed impressed with Pope's opinion, though Postmaster General Blair's personal interactions with Pope led him to the certain conclusion that the general was nothing but a braggart and a liar.[1]

Halleck had met with Ambrose Burnside and Pope as soon as he arrived in Washington, and he made a hasty inaugural visit to the Army of the Potomac, command of which the president and Stanton eagerly wished to give to General Burnside. Burnside had vigorously declined, though, arguing for McClellan as the only man who could handle the army. Burnside, Pope, and Major General Ormsby Mitchel consulted with Halleck at the tea table in Willard's Hotel, and later in private rooms upstairs, concluding that McClellan should have another chance to strike at Richmond while Pope posed his threat from the north. McClellan said he needed twenty thousand more men to make another attempt, and he was to have them out of the troops from the Carolinas that were encamped near Fort Monroe. Then, soon after Halleck returned to Washington, McClellan resumed his old habit of pleading for still more reinforcements, amounting to some fifty thousand men. At that, Halleck had decided to bring McClellan's army back up from the Peninsula's pestilential swamps to northern Virginia, to cooperate with (or possibly to operate under) General Pope. There were those in high places who supposed that Halleck had planned this all along, in collusion with Pope, so Pope could quietly replace the slow and demanding McClellan. Gideon Welles came to believe that the two Western generals were merely fulfilling a conspiracy between Salmon Chase and Edwin Stanton.[2]

Pope had finally joined his army in the field on July 29, after a conference with Halleck and after lobbying, unsuccessfully, for McClellan's removal. McClellan's critics expected much from Pope: the *Philadelphia Inquirer* dedicated its entire front page to a sixteen-inch-tall cut of him astride his battle steed, venturing south to smite the enemy. A flurry of his general orders preceded him, and in sum those directives revealed that the United States would be fighting two different types of war in Virginia. Under the authority of the Confiscation Act, the president had issued a proclamation on July 25 giving secessionists sixty days to desist from rebellion before they forfeited all their property — in addition to his July 22 orders authorizing the military use, consumption, or destruction of private property in the insurgent states. Pope took full and immediate advantage of that authority, announcing that his men would subsist on the surrounding countryside; he threatened to hold civilians responsible for any depredations against U.S. forces in their neighborhoods, and he instructed his various commanders to begin arresting all "disloyal male citizens" within or behind their lines, perhaps partly so their property could be identified for confiscation. Down at Harrison's Landing, George McClellan accentuated his more genteel approach to war (and highlighted his contempt for John Pope's policies) with a general order to his own troops reminding them that they were expected to conduct civilized warfare even in the exercise of the new executive powers. Peaceable inhabitants would not be disturbed, he insisted, and should be protected by guards whenever the demands of duty allowed.[3]

Edwin Stanton seemed to enjoy the exercise of peremptory authority, even to excess, and he did not long ignore the conscription power indirectly accorded him by the Militia Act. While Pope gathered the scattered elements of his new army and McClellan prepared to abandon the Peninsula, Stanton acted on Halleck's advice and Lincoln's license to impose a draft. On August 4 he instructed the adjutant general to distribute an order to twenty-two Northern and border-state governors and to the District of Columbia for three hundred thousand militia to serve for the newly established maximum term of nine months — voluntarily if they would come, but by random selection from the civilian population if they would not.[4]

The United States remained primarily an agrarian nation in the summer of 1862, leaving mid-July through early August an inopportune season to ask farmers to abandon their fields, where hay awaited the blade and crops ripened daily. The regiments at the front had already gobbled up thousands of the footloose laborers who usually signed on for the haying season, and many a harvest crew betrayed more white beards and boys than the customary complement. Those who could find prime hands considered themselves fortunate, and rumors of monthly pay as high as sixty dollars siphoned some of the remaining laborers away to regions where such riches were purportedly available. Women and girls had swarmed into the fields, too, and particularly where a rainy July had delayed the haying. Only where strong antiwar sentiments survived could enough seasonal labor still be had. Farmers struggling more than ever to fill their barns and save their crops had to see extraordinary financial benefits before they could consider removing the best hands from their family workforces.[5]

The communities that still faced deficiencies on their quotas raced to provide those extraordinary financial benefits. As treasury watchdogs noted, the latest levies effectively doubled the cost of the war, and their calculations did not even include the cost of bounties to state and local governments. With Stanton's militia draft came a new round of more desperate recruiting rallies, and (much to the regret of men who had just enlisted for stingier emoluments) bounties began to soar. Some towns held two meetings in a week, and raised phenomenal sums in pledged donations.[6] The chance seemed too inviting for some to pass up: one Vermont man who had resigned a commission the previous year, fearing that he had contracted tuberculosis, ignored the solemn promise he had made to his wife and secured authority to raise another company of infantry. Most citizens lacked his daring, though, and took steps to assure that no shortage of volunteers subjected their communities to a draft. Voters in Middletown, Rhode Island — most of whom were eligible for the draft themselves — originally agreed on $125 for each of the eighteen men the town needed, plus a $20 bonus from the lieutenant governor's pocket. That brought in only three men, so the town meeting hastily reconvened to authorize a bounty of $500 for each volunteer, and town officers offered more cash to coax a railroad contractor into recruiting enough of his Irish laborers to meet the town's obligation.[7]

New Hampshire's towns outbid each other for warm bodies until everyone who could make himself look old enough or young enough for military service considered it. Through a combination of public and private funds the councilmen of Portsmouth, New Hampshire, raised enough to pay $100 to every recruit willing to apply himself to that city's credit. Little Contoocook, New Hampshire, felt constrained to do the same. Barrington, two towns away from Portsmouth, next appropriated $200 for each of the ten recruits it lacked, plus a fund of $1,000 for their wives to draw upon, and at least four resident farmers decided overnight to accept that offer. Then the town of Bristol, in the center of the state, raised its own bounty to $200. Tiny Hampstead voted $300. Those appropriations would send local property taxes skyrocketing, wailed many a thrifty voter, but a Dover boy serving on the coast of South Carolina scoffed at such whining from taxpayers whom he suspected of having approved of the war only so long as they did not have to either pay for it or fight in it.[8]

Individuals contributed to the mercenary mania as well, and sometimes in the same hope of keeping themselves or their sons out of uniform. The treasurer of a textile mill at Laconia, New Hampshire, advertised a $25 bounty to each mill employee who would enlist in one of the state's nine-month regiments, adding the promise of holding his job until his return, but neither the treasurer nor any son of his joined those regiments. Joseph Gilmore, a Concord railroad executive who was destined to be the next governor of New Hampshire, also promised $25 to each of nine men who would fill up the complement of a local company. Gilmore had four sons, but none of them enlisted, then or later (one of Gilmore's nephews did see service in this war, but only in the final days, when Governor Gilmore rescued him from the draft with a commission in the heavy artillery).[9] The financially comfortable clearly provided a smaller proportion of the army's strength: the daughter of one of Gilmore's wealthier employees, Lizzie Corning, kept a meticulous diary of her activities among Concord's largely Republican, prowar upper crust, yet only one of the many young men in her social network appears to have seen military service, as a lieutenant in a nine-month regiment.[10]

Towns in Maine raised some of the most generous early bounties. Some communities posted offers that seemed especially exorbitant, and no more so than to the men who had enlisted for almost nothing during the preceding year. A few soldiers congratulated the state for "doing the fair thing," but John Burrill disagreed. He had been born Down East, but had enlisted in a New Hampshire regiment in the early weeks of the war, seeing the worst of Bull Run, Fair Oaks, and the Seven Days. When his hometown offered each recruit a bounty of $160, two of his brothers jumped for it, and Burrill seemed disgusted that they should be rewarded so liberally for stepping forward so late.[11]

Most troops in the field shared Burrill's exasperation with bounties. Marshall Phillips, a thirty-nine-year-old private in the 5th Maine, reacted with sarcastic fury to the lavish inducements. Phillips had earned a close living as a shoemaker before the war, but he left his wife and children in the summer of 1861 for rewards no more munificent than army pay, the hope of living to collect the federal hundred-dollar bounty, and the Auburn selectmen's vow to support the families of those who marched off to serve their country. Like at least a few other towns, Auburn had failed to live up to its grandiose promises of dependent support, leaving Diana Phillips to supplement her husband's puny salary by begging and borrowing.[12] Private Phillips evidently believed in the war, or at least in the president (he had recently named his youngest son Abraham Lincoln Phillips), but the broken promises soured him. When he learned that his neighbors back in Auburn had voted to pay hundreds of dollars for each man who would volunteer against the community's quota of forty-five recruits, and realized that he would be subsidizing that munificence through increased taxes on his home, he took a seat at Harrison's Landing and composed a lengthy, searing letter for the local newspaper.

The town fathers could no longer pay in promises, Phillips observed, because everyone knew they had reneged on those made to the earliest volunteers. Now, if more worthy citizens were to keep themselves and their precious sons out of the army without incurring the personal expense of hiring a substitute, everyone with any taxable property would have to help pay sizable bounties in advance — including townsmen who had been absent with the army for more than a year already, and lacked the opportunity to vote against that injustice. With a hasty town meeting featuring bands, bunting, and a barrage of insincere rhetoric, the town's leaders would agitate their fellow citizens into a patriotic delirium in which they could hardly refuse the money, while forty-five "poor fellows who are of no account in the world" would probably step forward to risk their lives.[13]

The town of Auburn paid in excess of fourteen thousand dollars for that summer's recruits, and well over two-thirds of the money went to meet the quota of nine-month militia. By war's end Phillips's hometown had spent more than sixty-five thousand dollars on bounties alone, and ballooning property taxes eviscerated the value of the hundred-dollar bounty he took home in 1864.[14]

The men who responded to the lavish assurances of 1862 often encountered the same perfidious public as the volunteers of 1861. Communities that swore to support the new soldiers' families sometimes neglected that responsibility or forgot about it altogether, especially when future draft calls demanded still greater bounties and more extravagant pledges. Before another August came, many of the 1862 recruits would bitterly regret the trust they had placed in their fellow citizens. "They have got us fast," growled an Indiana soldier who had enlisted during the first draft hysteria, "and now they must pay somebody else to come out and save their own hides."[15]

From his extemporized camp desk on the Virginia Peninsula, Private Phillips captured the atmosphere of those patriotic meetings with uncanny accuracy. They spread like a plague after the middle of August, as the deadline neared for meeting municipal quotas. Boston and the surrounding towns held rallies every night, with an occasional torchlight procession of fire companies, tradesmen, home-guard companies, and flocks of recent recruits. The bounty offers were scheduled to expire on August 15. Then they were extended to August 22, after which they were to be discontinued and the draft was supposed to be invoked, and as that day approached the atmosphere in Northern cities and towns turned almost frantic. The hundred-dollar bounty of Portsmouth, New Hampshire, had failed to satisfy the government's demand, and headlines emblazoned with exclamation points heralded another war meeting that would presumably approve a better offer. Many a gambling man brazenly bet that the bounties would be paid for a while longer and go higher still, and those calculating opportunists loitered attentively along the fringes of various communities' rallies until the last possible moment, creating the very type of human auction that more cynical newspaper editors had predicted.[16]

Lucy Larcom, of Beverly, Massachusetts, attended one frenetic gathering at the village green on August 21, where prominent citizens promised the crowd that military service in the mopping-up of Confederate resistance would prove far less dangerous and uncomfortable than it had for earlier volunteers: the massive new armies would bring the fighting to a hasty close, and everyone would come home heroes, with hundreds of dollars in profit. Those who harangued the crowd seemed conspicuously immune to their own pleas, observed Mrs. Larcom, for no one who spoke actually intended to enlist; the only veteran on the rostrum was a discharged Irishman who climbed up to boast about his service in the disaster at Bull Run.[17]

When the bounties reached their peak the occasional recruiter would slip surreptitiously onto the rostrum and wait for some heckler to challenge the speakers to take their own medicine, and sometimes the heckler appeared to work in collusion with the man on the platform. On the same day as the Beverly rally, the city of Hartford held its second "grand war meeting" on the grounds of the state capitol: as a gentleman by the name of Charles Whittlesey was imploring the men of Connecticut to answer their country's call, a voice rose from the throng to say "I'll go if the speaker will." The voice belonged to a man identified by a newspaper reporter as Henry Belden, who clambered up to stand beside the orator. Whittlesey dramatically produced a sheet of paper from his pocket, declaring it to be an enrollment list, and they both signed it. While the audience stared in rapt silence, they raised their hands to utter the oath of allegiance on the spot. The city and state bounty offers had been extended another four days, amounting to as much as $415 for a three-year enlistment, while the offer of city support for families had gone from $6 a month to $16 for all recruits, including the nine-month men. Such largess finally began to convince scores of Hartford men that patriotism might be worth the price. Whittlesey became captain of a nine-month company, as he had evidently intended from the start; he enjoyed a safe and salubrious succession of garrison assignments, but no one named Henry Belden went to war with him. Perhaps Mr. Belden felt that he had rendered sufficient service to his country with his histrionics in the State House yard.[18]

Not all those who addressed the speakers at recruiting rallies shared such sympathy with the cause. Shouts came from the neglected wives of earlier volunteers, critics of administration competence, and opponents of the war's official and clandestine aims. That was to be expected in a nation that treasured freedom of speech, but Edwin Stanton unilaterally abolished that freedom on August 8. Anticipating opposition to his draft order, Stanton appointed a special judge advocate to deal with dissent and issued instructions for local and federal law officers to imprison anyone "who may be engaged, by act, speech, or writing, in discouraging volunteer enlistments, or in any way giving aid and comfort to the enemy, or in any other disloyal practice against the United States." The vague text of the order insured its arbitrary enforcement and invited abuse from partisan federal marshals.[19]

For a year federal agents had been muzzling the more rabid of the government's scolds: men had been jailed and newspapers suppressed in a thinly disguised program to weaken opposition to administration policies. Just prior to Stanton's formal gag order, one newspaper in southeastern Missouri announced the arrest of two citizens charged with using "disloyal language," and named one other local political opponent who might be officially silenced, as well. A critical St. Louis paper characterized Horace Greeley's radical *New York Tribune* as a "pestiferous sheet" and questioned why it failed to merit suppression for far more violent language against the administration than some Democratic presses that had already been shut down.[20]

The imposition of compulsory military service and the hint of impending abolition immediately prodded opposition rhetoric to new levels of volume and ferocity, however, and Stanton's decree presented a specific new public-interest pretext for prohibiting embarrassingly apt political commentary. With renewed vigor, U.S. marshals of predominately Republican pedigree started rounding up malcontents — almost all of them Democrats — on the excuse that their vocal disagreement with presidential policies discouraged men from volunteering. The "disloyal" remarks of this latest crop of state prisoners ranged from justifiable complaints that the military machine disproportionately consumed the poorer classes of society to the rank suspicion that Lincoln's effort to restore the Union disguised a secret agenda for abolishing slavery. Most of the marshals' victims seem to have committed no crime worse than the acerbic expression of opinions that revealed, perhaps, more truth than the administration wished to acknowledge.

In Epping, New Hampshire, an irascible old physician named Nathaniel Batchelder had long resented the excesses of the Lincoln administration. In August of 1861, after a mob of Granite State soldiers attacked the editors of a Democratic Concord newspaper and destroyed their office, Batchelder had led a score of dissenters through town to protest such assaults on freedom of speech. A year later, at an Epping war meeting, Batchelder dared to exercise that freedom himself, with the prediction that death and damnation awaited any who enlisted in the army. Several town officials joined past and present postmasters to file the necessary complaint, and the governor ordered Marshal Jacob Ela to take Batchelder into custody.[21] Ela refused to recognize a writ of habeas corpus issued for Batchelder by the chief justice of the New Hampshire Supreme Court, keeping the doctor locked for weeks at Fort Constitution, in Portsmouth harbor, where his cold, dank cell inflamed his arthritic joints and produced an alarming respiratory congestion. Batchelder offered to post any amount of bond to assure his appearance at a trial, but his captors refused to offer even criminal charges, let alone a trial. "Shall I say that a white man is most as good as a Nigger," Batchelder asked, in a letter to a prominent Democratic legislator, "or shall I say that I live under a free government that has any Constitution at all[?]" After six weeks of uncomfortable confinement Batchelder became something of a martyr to New Hampshire Democrats, and it was that consideration as much as anything that led to his release. He had several conspicuous counterparts in other states, including another well-respected doctor and former Democratic congressman, Edson B. Olds, who was imprisoned in Ohio.[22]

Before he could even begin his duties, one federal enrolling officer in Delaware was arrested on the strength of affidavits "proving" his disloyalty to the government. Charles Bigger, of New Castle County, had reportedly been quite open in revealing his suspicion that President Lincoln was conducting an "abolition war," that the Confederacy carried the greater political rectitude, and that the South could not be defeated. Even if any of those statements had demonstrated active disloyalty, a skeptical prosecutor might have wondered why all the affidavits denouncing the holder of a competitive political office bore the same date, the same handwriting, and identical quotations of Bigger's alleged remarks.[23]

Stanton's dictum quickly led to the arrest of James Caldwell, a Kentuckian who happened to be a brother-in-law to Lincoln's close friend Senator Orville Hickman Browning. That arrest illustrated the damage such autocratic orders might inflict on the Union cause. In a frank conversation with Browning, Caldwell admitted that he hoped the Southern rebellion would succeed, and that Kentucky would become part of the new republic. He had not lifted a finger to aid the rebellion, however, and had no intention of doing so: on an individual basis he continued to exercise the neutrality that his state had maintained through the first five months of the war. That would only change, he noted, if the United States government forced him to choose sides — as it seemed to be determined to do. In that case, he told Browning, he and everything he owned would be at the disposal of the Confederacy.[24]

On August 14 Dennis Mahony, the Irish editor of the *Dubuque Herald*, was arrested by Iowa's U.S. marshal, H. M. Hoxie — a crony of Republican governor Samuel Kirkwood. Mahony resented the heavy burdens the war had placed on his economically disadvantaged countrymen. Another of Kirkwood's friends assessed the effect of Mahony's editorials as "disastrous" to the government cause, and especially in the matter of raising troops. Mahony had been preaching peace for months, asserting that most people wanted peace but refrained from saying so for fear that the weight of official power would fall on those who dared to speak their minds.[25] Marshal Hoxie helped Mahony to prove that very point, but he appears to have done so on extraordinarily premature instructions from the secretary of war. In his report on Mahony, Hoxie admitted arresting him on the authority of Stanton's order of July 26, before the secretary had even imposed a prohibition on "discouraging enlistments." All the affidavits against Mahony were dated August 12 and 13, suggesting that Hoxie had solicited those documents to provide retroactive legitimacy to Stanton's preconceived judgment.[26]

In jail Mahony met David Sheward, his counterpart at the *Constitution and Union*, of Fairfield, Iowa. Sheward had denounced the recruiting bounties as mere bribes offered to suborn citizens to commit treason on behalf of the usurper, "King Abraham." Mahony and Sheward joined the editors of an Illinois newspaper, some Illinois judges, and a few other celebrity dissidents for the long journey to Washington, where Hoxie lodged them in the Old Capitol Prison. Most of them languished there for several months, until they agreed not to file lawsuits against Hoxie and the other federal officers who had violated their civil rights; in his desperation to save his newspaper from mortgage default, even the combative Mahony submitted.[27]

Republican newspapers not only crowed over the administration's latest assault on free speech but published the names of dissident competitors whom they hoped to either intimidate or see imprisoned.[28] Federal officials accommodated much of that partisan vengeance, and prisoners started streaming in from all corners of the country. In New Jersey prominent Democrats were targeted for expressing their opposition to the war; in northeastern Pennsylvania public officials were arrested for advising voters to stay home and vote for peace candidates; in the interior of Wisconsin a man was jailed for telling the audience at a Union rally that few recruits would be forthcoming, and that if he were drafted he would desert to the other side.[29]

Offhand comments like that, or any kind of suspicious activity, inspired numerous other affidavits and arrests in Iowa. A Wayne County Unionist reported to the governor in all seriousness that dissident citizens had descended to such depths of treason that they had actually laughed at their local home-guard company. The superintendent of the draft in Greene County relayed information that large numbers of men seemed to be hunting and fishing in three nearby counties. In Madison County a man named McCarty, who was involved in the organization of home guards, complained to authorities that "Rebel Sympathizers" were hesitating to join their company and had become "very saucy." McCarty accused a local physician of belonging to the "nights [sic] of the Golden Circle," and added that the doctor was raising a company that might be destined for the Confederate army. Other informants nurtured similar hysterical notions about the Knights of the Golden Circle, insisting that the society served as a recruiting conduit for Southern forces or for a popular rising against the government. A man from east-central Ohio spent months in prison after two men claimed he had tried to recruit them as knights.[30]

In Indiana the seeds for a successful Supreme Court challenge to the government's highhanded tactics were sown when the U.S. marshal for Indianapolis first sought permission to arrest Lambden P. Milligan, whose public remarks had turned especially unflattering to Mr. Lincoln's war. No critic of the administration seemed exempt: even William J. Allen, a Peace Democrat newly elected to Congress from southern Illinois, went to jail in that mid-August orgy of repression because of opinions expressed during a political campaign.[31] Allen was actively running for reelection to the congressional seat he had just attained, and many of his fellow prisoners were not released until after the fall elections. Like Marshal Hoxie's victims, the last of them remained in prison until they relinquished even the right to sue their arresting officers for false imprisonment. One prisoner — a discharged officer of the Union army with evident Democratic opinions — found it necessary to essentially apologize for having filed such a suit against an informer whose recklessly malicious allegations had put him behind bars.[32]

The political background of most of the prisoners strongly suggested that their arrests represented political exploitation of Stanton's order. That did not exactly constitute unauthorized abuse of Stanton's instructions, either, since the real purpose of the order appears to have been to intimidate the opposition. Governor Andrew Curtin recognized as much when he advised the release of several well-respected Pennsylvanians, remarking that the arrests alone had accomplished everything the administration desired.[33] Curtin was right, too: the intimidation seemed to work. Citizens who had never feared to express themselves on national issues suddenly balked at the realization that the War Department could simply abolish their First Amendment rights — or, apparently, any other constitutional protection. An officer in Pope's army worried enough about false accusations to warn his own father about remarks made in private, cautioning him that "folks are getting verry Suspicious Now Days." If that revealed paranoia, it flourished with good reason: the malicious tattling of some Ohio busybodies had already brought one distinguished brigade commander before the secretary of war, who grilled him about casual comments the officer had made while on convalescent furlough.[34]

Hundreds, if not thousands, of indignant citizens felt the hand of some sheriff or provost marshal clutching their shoulders that summer, and their arrests chilled the opposition. Doomsayers and detractors fell silent or turned their anger to more private settings, allowing the draft-driven recruiting rallies to continue without interruption. Some courageous editors continued to vilify national policy in the wake of Stanton's dictatorial August 8 pronouncement, but overall dissent abated in tone and frequency at a time when liberty-loving citizens might have been expected to raise their voices in a deafening crescendo.[35]

Those who expressed active disagreement with the government occasionally faced worse consequences than imprisonment, as events in the northeastern corner of Kansas illustrated. That August a group of volunteers in the town of Troy severely beat a citizen whose political observations they resented. Then, a few days later and a few miles away, someone charged the postmaster in the ephemeral settlement of Walnut Grove with discouraging enlistments. Republican newspaper editors in that part of Kansas alleged that Postmaster Grandison R. Wilson had long been known as a "secessionist" — which, in the bitter parlance of the frontier, might have signified nothing more than a vocal lack of support for the war. Certainly Wilson was a Democrat, for Franklin Pierce had first appointed him, and Buchanan renewed the appointment in the waning days of his administration. Perhaps he had made a remark that could conceivably have dissuaded young men from risking their lives in a doubtful cause, although no evidence of it has surfaced. On September 2 a motley posse nonetheless set out from Troy to bring the postmaster to their version of justice. They found him in the shallow, verdant valley of the Wolf River, tending his fields. Like any prudent Kansan beset by armed strangers, Mr. Wilson made for the woods, but his pursuers dropped him with a volley and he soon expired, leaving a postal vacancy to be filled by a loyal Republican.[36]

Political animosity led to the murder of another man in southeastern Missouri a few days later. The victim "was reported not to be very loyal," complained a nearby newspaper, adding that the dead man "had no right to be disloyal to the Government." The paper clearly approved of the killing, adding that certain other individuals would make acceptable targets.[37]

Repression of public comments left family members and friends to make the boldest arguments against military service. Relatives entertained less fear of prosecution in diverting their kin from the conflict, and they enjoyed fair success. Emerging evidence of administration sympathy for emancipation fueled much disapproval among those who might otherwise have been willing to sacrifice their sons and brothers on the altar of national unity, but many an elder objected even to that, alluding to "this unholy war." A New Hampshire woman bridled at her son's suggestion that he would enlist if he could: she remarked that she hoped none of her family would "be guilty of going to this War," which she clearly viewed as an act of aggression. The mother of a fledgling New York lawyer dismissed her son's military maunderings with the observation that black men could either fight for their own freedom or remain forever in slavery. The father of a floundering new Yale graduate chastised his son's abolitionist friends for trying to seduce him into a war that would not have begun without their provocation. Parental advice prevailed in each case, at least to the extent that none of the three sons ever enlisted.[38]

A Harvard undergraduate who considered enlisting that summer encountered vigorous opposition from both his mother and his older brother, who had accepted a commission in a new regiment. Mother and brother both contended that the youth's father, who was away from home on an extended voyage, would insist that his youngest son continue his studies, and time confirmed their opinion. For a few weeks the boy complied, but before his father's return he wore his mother down with persistent pleading until finally she consented, in evident anguish, to him going with his brother's company rather than enlisting among strangers. Except for that reluctant assent, he went to war against the wishes of his entire family, including aunts and uncles.[39]

The arguments of men in uniform again presented nearly as persuasive a deterrent. Soldiers' letters had long described killing marches, miserable living conditions, cruel and unfair treatment by superiors, poor and insufficient food, unpleasant changes in national policy (or, conversely, the failure to change national policy), and the perpetual possibility of fatal diseases, sudden death, or mutilation. A few veterans had always cautioned their home-front compatriots against imitating their gullible mistake, urging them to resist the deceptive temptations of martial glory. It was "a dogs life to live," as one Vermonter told a wavering correspondent back in the Connecticut River Valley, before the bloody spring campaigns began.[40]

With the choreographed "governors'" call for troops, at the beginning of July, those admonitions from the front lines proliferated and increased in intensity. Fresh from the Seven Days fighting, one New Hampshire private ridiculed a friend who pondered enlistment, noting that he could play soldier at home by sleeping on the bare ground without cover through a few nights of rain, and work all night without food or water, with half a bushel of corn strapped to his back. Another veteran of the Seven Days told an inquiring uncle that any man who was not already committed to the army had better stay away from it, and a sergeant serving in the fever-ridden bayous along the lower Mississippi actively solicited a friend back in Vermont to advise their common acquaintances against volunteering, if they should so much as begin talking about it.[41]

Officers who generally clamored for vast, faceless levies to replenish the army would sometimes privately adjure their own friends or relatives to reconsider any inclinations toward military service. A New York captain who had just coaxed enough men into a new company to obtain his commission asked his father to "Tell Henry *not to be fooled into volunteering for if he does he ought to be hung and will be sorry when its too late.*" A lieutenant who had endured the Seven Days beseeched his brother to reconsider his enlistment, assuring him that the bounty would never be worth the risks.[42] Such comments came often enough from the men who had enlisted in 1861, many of whom would have welcomed some help even if they failed to ask their correspondents for it, but earnest warnings against enlistment began flooding back toward home once the army started to fill up with the well-subsidized summer recruits of 1862.[43]

Early letters about ploys for discharge attest that many of the summer's volunteers quickly concluded that they had made bad bargains. The bitter contrition of local men who had just enlisted for sizable bounties soon convinced one woman that "all these $300 men are sick of it."[44] The fear of official retribution and social disapproval confined such impassioned discouragement to personal correspondence, allowing the combination of impending conscription and hefty bounties to draw a trickle of recruits. Once that flow finally began, though, it quickly expanded into a torrent.

New Englanders seemed averse to going to war alone, and nowhere more so than in New Hampshire, where men came to the various regimental rendezvous by platoons. Eighteen members of the Nashua Cornet Band traveled to the state capital on August 7 to enlist in a body. The next evening George Caverly, a farmer with a wife and several children, attended the town meeting that voted sizable bounties and benefits for the town's soldiers, and the morning after that he arranged with three neighbors and relatives to volunteer together. Two days later a train left Portsmouth carrying 132 recruits from that city and other coastal towns. Recruits seemed nearly as gregarious in Vermont, where Joseph Spafford reported his decision in a letter from camp, naming an assortment of common acquaintances who came with him. "So you see," Spafford told his civilian friend, "we are *all* going to war."[45]

Occasionally the sheer volume of recruits impeded the process. George Hitchcock arrived at the camp of the 21st Massachusetts, outside Boston, in the company of a friend. They both wished to volunteer with neighbors who already belonged to that regiment, but so many people filled the camp that no one of any authority paid any attention to their inquiries. After being ignored for two successive days they departed in disgust for the camp of another new regiment, where they were more warmly welcomed, but hometown loyalty convinced them to give the 21st another try. On the afternoon of the third day someone noticed them at last and steered them toward the surgeon, who poked and prodded them uncomfortably before accepting them.[46]

The combined pressures of cash and compulsion exerted a profound effect nearly everywhere. Ohio filled thirty-one regiments of infantry from mid-August through the end of September; Michigan completed nine and Wisconsin eight. Minnesota at least started four new regiments by the end of August. In August and September, Indiana organized twenty-five regiments of infantry, one of cavalry, and four batteries of artillery. By August 10 Chicago had already paid out bounties to 1,040 new soldiers, representing one full regiment from that city alone, and those economic incentives appeared to have created "a perfect mania for enlisting." The next day one Illinois schoolgirl informed a classmate that the last male relative she knew had just joined the army.[47]

Iowa managed to field four regiments in August, including one that completed its organization as early as August 6. That pleased one Iowan on duty in Tennessee, who urged all his friends to enlist at once so Union troops could form a solid line from Washington to the Mississippi and sweep Southern armies into the oceans. Another five Iowa regiments mustered in the following month. Patriotic rallies became a weekly ritual in some corners of the state, and the response proved more than adequate, but widespread opposition to the war produced a scattered geographical pattern to the enlistments. The Phillips family in Van Buren County supplied all three brothers and a pair of cousins, while in Monroe County, twenty-five miles away, Private Jacob Hunter complained of all the disloyal men who stayed at home and heckled the soldiers' families. Yet those who seemed least sympathetic to Abraham Lincoln and his war aims dominated Hunter's company, as though the money alone had lured them.[48]

Needy sodbusters found the bounties difficult to resist, regardless of political persuasion. Gilbert Gulbrandson, a youth from a large and heavily mortgaged Norwegian family along Iowa's Mississippi shore, assumed no patriotic pretensions when he decided to enlist. He simply weighed the loss of his labor against the dent it would make in the debt on their farm: he expected to be able to give his father at least two hundred dollars before he even left the state, and hoped that it would be enough to ease any regrets at his departure. In northeastern Indiana another farmer whose wife disliked their rural existence enlisted right after the harvest, using the bounty and family subsidies as a new source of income while putting his farm on the market for a song. Levi Shell, who had just bought a homestead in Sauk County, Wisconsin, planted wheat and then enlisted, expecting to be home in time to harvest his crop. He expected "a pile from Uncle Sam" by then; with that and the proceeds from the wheat, he thought he could pay off his mortgage.[49]

A middle-aged printer from New Hampshire outlined all his reasons for enlisting in a late nine-month regiment from Massachusetts, but those reasons appeared to include no patriotic impulse. "I had better turn into one of the companies & go with them," he informed his father. "It is the most favorable season of the year, the term is short, the bounty is ample, the draft is almost certain & may come at such a time that the conscripts will be in service during the hot weather & above all we are getting the very *best men* in town. Not a paddy or a nigger is received." Some waited until the last moment to join a nine-month regiment, hoping to shorten their commitment even further for the same attractive bounty. A Maine youth made no effort to hide his image of the nine-month service as a lucrative lark. "I am fairly engaged in 'Uncle Sam's famous Excursion,'" he informed his mother, "where the excursionists receive one hundred & fifty dollars in advance & are clothed & fed during the whole Show." His regiment never lost a man to hostile fire, but his good fortune only illustrated the random consequences of impulsive enlistment: a few weeks earlier a more anxious recruit signed on for three years in a Maine regiment from which more than two hundred men would die in action, and all for a town bounty of only fifty-five dollars.[50]

Money remained short in John Lingle's agrarian community north of Harrisburg, Pennsylvania. Heavy liens burdened many of the farms there, and tax increases to cover the summer bounties only heightened the pressure on struggling families; by late autumn the sheriff had marked a number of homesteads for sale. Lingle's father-in-law, who had secured the prized position as superintendent of the county poorhouse, reacted with surprise and a little dismay when Lingle enlisted in a nine-month regiment. He promised to take in the recruit's wife and provide for her, and adjured his son-in-law to hunt for some lucrative military office. "Make all the Money you Can," he urged. The bounty that evidently lured Lingle into the army failed to rescue his dwindling fortunes: by January the sheriff's shadow had fallen on his own unoccupied farm, and even under her parents' care his wife pleaded for some funds.[51]

Those willing to take the risk could profit from the provision for substitutes, as well, extorting as much as a year's civilian salary from drafted men to serve in their places; the going rate in 1862 ran as high as $300, at a time when a dollar a day represented fair wages for unskilled labor. Some newspaper publishers tried to shame conscripts into accepting their fate, as *Harper's Weekly* did with a cartoon of a New York socialite whose fiancée rejected him because he had chosen not to serve, but efforts to smear the practice largely failed: the militia call of 1862 reestablished that respectable antebellum tradition for those who could afford it. Later, national conscription would eliminate the last hint of opprobrium to hiring a substitute — except, as Grover Cleveland would discover two decades later, in postwar politics. A family man from Youngstown, Ohio, saw the militia draft with its substitute clause as both his economic and social salvation: he doubled his recompense by accepting $225 to enlist as the substitute for a wealthy conscript, and then he raised other recruits to secure a commission.[52]

The chance for such windfalls also attracted threadbare professionals. One lawyer who found business slumping in the summer of 1862 left his wife and children to enlist in the 129th Illinois. He collected a substantial bounty and a county land warrant, which he promptly sold at a discount, but his plan included campaigning for election as a field officer. Evidently no one had explained to him that those positions were usually secured by men with either political influence or scores of volunteers to their credit. When he could finagle no rank at all, the scheming solicitor took refuge in the quartermaster's department, where he managed to reap a sizable if dishonest income by collecting double pay as both a detailed soldier and a civilian clerk; he boarded comfortably in a private home, paying his landlady in provisions filched from quartermaster stores and sharing the substantial civilian salary with his quartermaster, who orchestrated the fraud.[53]

Men who mustered in as officers usually missed out on at least the federal bounty, but the monthly salary of a second lieutenant would have satisfied all but the successful, well-established citizen. A lieutenant from Maine revealed that many officers enjoyed the war for the money they made from it: "a large proportion never lived so well, nor received such pay . . . as they do now," he remarked. "The longer this war continues and the less fighting there is, the better they like it." Enlisted men with enough confidence and connections to hope for promotion hungered for the leap from sergeant to lieutenant, with its sixfold increase in pay, but it was usually only those with gubernatorial connections who could go into uniform with the assurance of becoming line officers. At the outset of hostilities William Bolton, a long-unemployed and admittedly bankrupt machinist from Norristown, Pennsylvania, had enlisted in a ninety-day regiment with the militia company he had formerly commanded, and the men had reelected him captain. With the rest of his regiment Bolton refused a plea to extend his term a few days, instead demanding his discharge on the very eve of First Bull Run. He marched away from that battlefield while the rest of the army marched to the attack, but as soon as he reached home he helped reorganize the regiment for the three-year service and secured the senior captain's commission, which eventually yielded him a promotion to full colonel. Bolton lacked no courage, enduring two wounds during the course of the war, but with his recent venture into indigence he seemed never to consider resignation. He remained in uniform more than four years, only shedding it months after Appomattox, by which time he had accumulated enough money to establish his own business.[54]

The competition for regimental staff positions usually attracted a multitude of opportunists. Sometimes the officers of a regiment chose their chaplain by a preaching competition, in which civilian ministers vied with hopeful privates, but for the most part chaplains and surgeons could solicit direct commissions from the various governors, and frequently those who requested them did so from need. A $200 town bounty clinched one young doctor's decision to enlist during the August recruiting drive; he had obtained a commission as assistant surgeon in a New Hampshire regiment, but considered refusing it until the bounty was paid. The surgeon of the 10th Vermont complained that Congress cut the pay for his grade from $123.81 to $110, but he still knew no other source of such easy money. "I suppose it would be an utter impossibility to [make] any money for practice at home now," he observed.[55] That seemed true for one Iowa physician, whose civilian patients could not or would not pay for his attendance. That summer of 1862 he reluctantly signed on with the 12th Iowa, vowing that when he came home he would no longer treat those patients who ignored his bills — but he was never able to follow through with that threat, for a Mississippi fever killed him within a few months. Another Iowa doctor who carried a great deal of personal debt thought himself fortunate to become surgeon for a regiment in the field after the pay of contract surgeons at the Keokuk hospitals, where he had last worked, was cut to $80 per month. "I should have been dissatisfied had I remained," he told his wife.[56]

Those who did win commissions customarily parted with them reluctantly, and usually only after better financial prospects had surfaced. A lieutenant in the Army of the Mississippi pondered resignation in order to return to his wife, but he decided against it when he considered the pecuniary implications: he wished to support his uncle's suddenly fatherless family, but evidently he knew no other way to earn as much as his army salary. A New Hampshire subaltern who had drawn unfavorable attention for apparent cowardice in two different battles desperately wished to resign after the second and more vicious of those engagements, but he admitted that "for the life of me I do not know what I am to do." Like many who had enlisted in the war's first summer, he remembered rampant unemployment on the civilian front for those without specialized training. Protesting that he lacked the strength to work at farming, he appealed to a fellow officer who had already gone home to find him some kind of employment, "if it is only to light the street lights in the village of Newport."[57]

Yet another lieutenant — a New Yorker who had begun the war with little or no income, no particular skills, and no clear future — seemed perennially preoccupied with the money his wife saved from what he sent her; every other month he forwarded anywhere between $120 and $250 "for a rainy day." He had enjoyed quiet garrison duty from the outset of his service, but the longer the war lasted the more likely was that easy duty to come to an end. He wanted to go home, but he remarked to his wife that "without money we are without friends," and he asked her to investigate opportunities to earn "a comfortable living" in their community. He had heard that there was nothing promising, which she corroborated (despite the dearth of manual laborers). "I ask you," he told her, "will it not be foolish for me to resign as long as I am doing so well?"[58]

In the enlisted ranks, the greatest financial advantages of military service ended with receipt of the initial bounties. That often failed to hold a man's interest long enough, and until a man mustered into federal service he had the option of backing out. For an assortment of reasons many did so: whether their temperaments conflicted with military discipline or they lost confidence in all the guarantees of public compensation and assistance, somewhere between the nationalistic euphoria of the war meeting and the chilling reality of the deadly commitment they changed their minds. When second thoughts caused men to balk, many colonels ordered them drummed out of camp as though under dishonorable discharge, hoping the shame would at least deter others. The colonel of the 25th Iowa denied two of his recruits the right to decline, and when they refused the oath he locked them in the guardhouse on bread and water until they complied. Some of those who finally did submit only wished to avoid being taunted as cowards, which they had come to expect as the price of remaining at home.[59]

An inordinate number of the summer recruits seemed to be married, perhaps because of the economic incentives for soldiers with families. In Massachusetts, a Marblehead tradesman remarked on the town's generosity toward soldiers while noting that everyone seemed to be getting married and going off to war. A recruit in the 37th Massachusetts calculated that married men composed more than half the roster of his regiment. A New Hampshire soldier regretted that so many of his friends had also gotten married before joining the new regiments, reflecting that "this war will make widows enough of them who were married before the war commenced."[60]

Some family men claimed to leave beloved wives only from a compelling sense of duty to their country, and they may well have felt that compulsion, but the sentiment seemed not to strike with irresistible force until the bounties peaked. Volunteers seldom admitted mercenary suasion outright, and veterans almost never did. More often, clues that economics had driven a man into uniform arose indirectly or incidentally in contemporary correspondence, and rarely in postwar reminiscences. A woman in a small New Hampshire town pitied one neighbor for enlisting from "no sence of duty," and another for marrying and enlisting as soon as their town voted a hefty bounty — only to wish immediately that he had not enlisted. A full lifetime after her husband went to war, the nonagenarian widow of an Iowa volunteer revealed the significance of bounties to her family when she admitted that her husband had traveled to a distant town to enlist because it offered more generous inducements than their own community.[61]

Often the recruit's plea of patriotic motive rang perfectly false. During a visit to Boston an unemployed Irishman named Peter Welsh went on a bender that cost him his last penny: he could not even get home to New York, and in desperation he enlisted with a Massachusetts regiment. He confessed the circumstances to his forlorn wife, and assured her that many of his fellow recruits "got in to it in the same way," but not long afterward he adopted a belated tone of righteous nationalism that failed to persuade the woman who knew him best. John Sheahan signed up for the bounty from a strange town, admittedly because he was caught in his state capital without train fare home, but he insisted that he wanted to serve the "cause" in any case; he soon seemed shocked at the vicissitudes and indignities of a soldier's life, urging his brother not to volunteer, but after much complaint on that subject he assured his family that he was not sorry he had enlisted.[62]

At the beginning of the war John Ellis had been working in Paducah, Kentucky, at the mouth of the Tennessee River, but the blockade of the Mississippi had thrown him out of a job. From there he had wandered slowly across Illinois, Indiana, and Ohio, searching in vain for another position. Early in 1862 he secured a few weeks' occupation in Erie, and (as he conceded to his sister) when that ran out he had to join the army as a last resort, but less than a year later he, too, would claim that he had enlisted to "put down the Rebellion." Samuel Thoman, a Pennsylvania farmer with a family and considerable debt, pretended no imperative patriotism. He had enlisted after the 1861 harvest, expecting to be away no more than six or eight months. He filled his letters to his wife with financial instructions that illustrated their poverty, telling her to draw the county relief allotment of $1.66 per week; he advised her to fend off persistent creditors with the reminder that his property could not be attached so long as he served; he informed her how to collect his $100 federal bounty if anything should happen to him. In the end he served only the eight months he had predicted, buying his family a small but steady income with his life.[63]

The "stay" laws that prevented creditors from attaching the property of men in the army offered a convenient haven for perennial debtors, and many volunteers were suspected of having enlisted for the sole purpose of avoiding collection. Wisconsin revoked its stay law to curb such abuses, but that exposed more conscientious volunteers to unfair exploitation through a judicial process they were usually unable to attend.[64]

In central Indiana, farmer William Steele struggled under a heavy mortgage and store accounts. He hoped to reduce those burdens by en-

listing in the summer of 1862, but he left his father and brothers to manage his farm during his absence, and they appropriated most of the crops
and livestock. They paid a portion of his store account from the yield of
his farm, but only after reserving shares for themselves. That left his wife
destitute, and dependent on Steele's perennially tardy army pay. He soon
regretted his decision, and promised never to leave his wife again if he
could just get home, but he lived less than twenty weeks into his enlistment. His estate barely satisfied his creditors.[65]

Edwin Wentworth, an itinerant printer with a history of frequent unemployment, had left his wife and daughter in Maine to seek work in
Massachusetts. He found nothing satisfactory, but then the Militia Act
started wringing local bounty offers out of Bay State communities. His
cash was running out, and he owed money besides, so he informed his
wife that he had decided to enlist under the quota of Springfield, which
would provide a hundred-dollar town bounty and two dollars a week for
his wife and child. The next day he was offered a temporary night job in
Pittsfield — prompting a joyous announcement that there was no longer
any reason for him to enlist — but his health and his eyesight failed quickly
on the somber graveyard shift. Within a month he again considered the
army for economic opportunity, consoling his wife with a promise that
she would no longer want for funds. "Enlisting seems the best thing I can
do," he argued. In a moment of self-congratulation he alluded to the
shame he would have felt had he not answered his country's call, but a
satisfactory job would obviously have outweighed that shame. "In fact,"
Wentworth admitted to his father, "necessity compelled me to enlist, as I
could get no employment." He insinuated little political or philosophical
compulsion; his letters soon deteriorated into denunciations of a war
for which he had no heart, alternating with daydreams about the farm
and the "fresh start in life" that his bounty money would afford him.[66]

So transparent did the economic motive seem that neighbors often
doubted whether men they knew had enlisted from any love of country.
Such barbs struck home among the untold thousands of jobless men who
had enlisted early in the war, at the height of Northern unemployment. "I
wish it distinctly understood," a sensitive Connecticut soldier instructed
his wife, "that whoever says I [went to] war because I was out of work or
that I was from necessity obliged to go falsifies the truth." A young man
from Massachusetts who enlisted under Lincoln's summer call for three
hundred thousand did not even wait for anyone to cast such stones. He
signed the roll of a new company that would convene right after his haying job ended, and asked his father to rest "assured that I have not enlisted because I could not get work," but he indicated that his employer's
need for laborers would end in about three weeks, just as he was to report

for muster. He also failed to mention the substantial bounties he collected.[67]

Federal paymasters and in many cases state agencies (particularly in Iowa, for some reason) withheld those men's bounties unconscionably long. The new volunteers funneled home their advance pay as quickly as they received it, in what was frequently a vain effort to keep their families fed while they waited for the greater share of their expected compensation. Often they fretted helplessly from camp while their wives recounted (or tried to conceal) the deteriorating situation at the home place. A Wisconsin farmer who had hired out the threshing of his wheat so he could enlist for the bounty was still waiting for that bounty well into October, and while he headed down the Mississippi to his doom the threshers badgered his wife for their money. The wife of an Iowa soldier who would not survive his first year of service had to sell her hogs on the hoof and spend what little money her husband sent to replace the grain her cattle broke into and devoured; the gorging threatened to kill one of the cows, and the woman soon worried whether she would have enough food for herself. Private Gulbrandson, the Norwegian who had enlisted as a sacrifice to his family's solvency, complained that his county failed to pay his bounty when he mustered in, as he had been promised.[68]

Municipal officials of dubious integrity sometimes accounted for the delay in delivering bounty money — or now and then for the failure to pay it at all. One middle-aged Vermonter implored his wife to pester a lame-duck selectman for his town bounty, and into December a New York youth begged his family to lobby the local authorities for his. In a Maryland regiment some soldiers reported drawing only a portion of their outstanding bounty as late as January of 1863.[69] Late payments posed an additional difficulty for a lot of men who suddenly discovered that their enlistment windfalls would no longer be adequate even if local governments had paid them punctually. The army did not always provide all of life's necessities, as new troops quickly learned, while legions of swindlers and gougers followed the armies just to separate soldiers from their money.[70]

Big local bounties pleased merchants, whose customers suddenly started paying in cash, but they produced enough paper money and municipal notes to spark instant inflation. Barely a month after her husband joined a New York artillery battery, a new mother complained that local prices had become "*ruinous*," with the doctor charging five dollars to deliver her baby and a few days' groceries taking another five of the twenty dollars that was supposed to last two months. Northeastern Massachusetts greeted cold weather with coal rising to eight dollars a ton, and firewood to eight dollars a cord.[71] An Indiana physician refused medicine to the wife of one recruit unless she paid in advance, although the doctor himself had once owed a substantial debt to the sick woman's husband. A Wisconsin recruit who enlisted before revocation of the stay law counseled his wife not to worry about the money they owed, reminding her that no one could collect a debt against him while he was in the army, but that only diminished the chances of further credit that families needed for continuing expenses. Where stay laws remained operative, potential lenders tended to refuse credit not only to soldiers' families, but to anyone in danger of being drafted.[72] Meanwhile, volunteering aggravated labor shortages and accelerated the price increases, driving firewood and coal still higher by winter.[73]

A second lieutenant drew $104 a month — eight times as much as a private — but freshly commissioned officers often felt the economic pinch. The first complement of company officers in new regiments were customarily elected by the enlisted men, and field officers were chosen by polling the captains of companies, whereupon the state governors would usually issue commissions based on the results of those elections. With no assurances that they would be mustered until their regiments were full, and no pay before that time (or bounties, in most cases), those who expected to wear shoulder straps had to risk a considerable outlay of cash. They needed uniforms and swords, while their recruiting expenses included office rent, advertising, and often loans to their recruits, to assure election loyalty. After local bounties had been paid, prospective officers frequently borrowed from privates (who may have been hoping for future considerations), but those privates sometimes wasted their investments when the recruiters lost the elections and abandoned their companies, sometimes without bothering to repay their creditors.[74]

Even officers with direct appointments, who went on the government payroll right away, recoiled at the expense of supporting themselves while waiting to go into the field with their regiments. "I had no idea that it would cost this much," lamented one surgeon. Once commissioned and mustered, most line officers lived in camp with their men, but surgeons, chaplains, and socialites who preferred to board with families paid unexpectedly high premiums for that luxury. Food and lodging seemed especially high for those in Louisiana. "It is very expensive living here," complained a snobbish Maine lieutenant in the New Orleans garrison, who disdained sharing a tent with the "common farmer sort of officer." Farther up the Mississippi, another surgeon who had hoped to pay his way out of debt soon found his living so expensive that he had to stint his family.[75]

That was a bitter pill for those who had signed up with the idea of enhancing their economic or social positions, and a multitude of such men flocked to the colors with each appeal for troops. The war had begun with two calls for militia and volunteers that absorbed tens of thousands of unemployed and underemployed men. Even those early volunteers who left full-time jobs or marginal subsistence farms often enlisted in the hope of improving on their civilian wages and adding to the comfort of their families, while some of them intended to start businesses with all the money they expected to save.[76] That drain of surplus labor, in combination with military production demands, brought most Northern communities back to full employment, but the seductive bounties of the war's second summer eventually rekindled the martial — or mercenary — spirit. It was probably no coincidence that the only state to provide a three-year infantry regiment during the month after the July 1 call was Vermont, which granted soldiers' families a generous subsidy. Vermont usually kept abreast of its quotas, and often by luring men across the Connecticut River from less liberal New Hampshire.[77]

Philip Arsino, who had also served a short enlistment in 1861, waxed surprisingly frank about his reason for reenlisting in the 10th Vermont. "[I] didn't come out here again to fight," he explained to his mother, "i come out for twenty dollars per month."[78] Few of Arsino's comrades proved so forthright about their motivation at the time, and the passage of years did not improve their candor, but the state's seven-dollar family allotment (which, with Private Arsino's monthly pay, totaled twenty dollars) obviously posed a major consideration for those who poured into Vermont's camps in August and September. Questions and instructions about the "state pay" punctuate most Vermont recruits' early correspondence, the urgency of which occasionally illustrates how desperately they had depended on that money.[79]

The state supplement allowed Vermont towns to satisfy War Department demands with somewhat lower bounties, which otherwise tended to soar in most of the Northeast. One reenlisting Vermont veteran felt rich when he collected a town bounty of $110 for joining a nine-month regiment, but that same month at least two New Hampshire towns offered $200 for a similar enlistment.[80] The absence of state subsidies had already forced many New Hampshire towns to bid higher still, and the more desperate communities assumed additional local expenditures for the care of volunteers' families. That made the army more appealing to heads of households than to bachelors, and inevitably brought more married men into uniform. Stricter local supervision sometimes led to conflict between soldiers and selectmen, though, as town officers disputed the financial need or family relationship of purported dependents.[81]

Wisconsin and Iowa both began paying a five-dollar monthly supplement to families. That helped Iowa to meet its quota, although Wisconsin fell several thousand men short.[82] As late as the third week of August some recruiting advertisements still used the Homestead Act to insinuate that each volunteer would receive 160 acres of land, as though by way of additional bounty, and that deception may have attracted a few aspiring Western immigrants dreaming of an escape from cyclical poverty.[83]

In some regions with chronically depressed local economies it was not even necessary to provide town bounties, salary supplements, or land grants: in those hapless sectors the cash advance of twenty-five dollars on the federal bounty, thirteen dollars advance pay, and two-dollar enlistment premium satisfied the heads of strapped households, who either enlisted or allowed their minor sons to go. Musicians were not expected to meet military age requirements, but each company needed only two musicians, and few rustic youths could play the fife or drum. Financial gain appears to have persuaded innumerable parents to sign permission forms swearing that stripling sons had attained the minimum age of eighteen, and several boys as young as fourteen slipped into the ranks of just one New Hampshire regiment raised that summer. Underage lads outnumbered volunteers who had passed the upper age limit, but fifty-year-old privates were not uncommon.[84]

Albert Merrill, a carpenter of Republican inclinations and modest means from Conway Center, New Hampshire, wished to improve his income and social status with the prestige of a commission in the army.[85] He had been trying to recruit a company since the May appeal, but after five weeks he had found only two adventuresome residents: a destitute widower in his forties and the seventeen-year-old son of one of the poorest farmers in town. The announcement of the July 1 levy, and with it the promise of forty dollars cash in hand, bore fruit for Merrill's recruiting jaunts into Conway's more squalid hill-farm neighborhoods. He convinced four more men to join him between July 1 and July 4; by July 24 he had collected twenty-two, including several more who were younger than eighteen, and all without a penny in municipal contributions or promises. Only two of his recruits lived in the relatively affluent villages, and they would become his noncommissioned officers; Merrill had found all the others on the impoverished fringes of the town, and most of them came from the single poorest district. That little company consisted primarily of footloose laborers or the teenaged sons of struggling farmers, but a couple of the older farmers went with them, including fifty-four-year-old Arthur Burbank, who shaved ten years from his age and accompanied his nephew to the rendezvous, leaving a grown son to try to keep the family farm going. Almost all of them arranged to send their pay to parents or wives.[86] Only in September, after those men had seen their first two battles, did the town of Conway vote to raise a hundred-dollar bounty to meet its quota of nine-month militia. That failed to secure enough men, requiring a second offer of two hundred dollars, and the families of the volunteers who had received no local bounty were assessed a share of that burden.[87]

Perry County, Missouri, seems to have offered no bounty, either, but within a week one officer managed to muster several hundred men into federal service, in addition to a company of mounted men who had thundered into the county seat a few days before to enroll with the state militia. In St. Louis, where the closing of the Mississippi still strangled the steamboat industry, recruiters quickly organized a regiment of men from river towns, with no inducement beyond the federal bounty. A dollar evidently meant much more in Missouri than it did in most of the East, and the new men greeted the paymaster with unusual glee when he announced that he was about to distribute the forty-dollar combination of advance pay, advance federal bounty, and enlistment premium.[88]

Kansans required little cash incentive, either: between the dual threats of Missouri guerrillas to the east and the Plains tribes to the west and south, recruiting proceeded briskly in the country's youngest state. Lighter-than-average rainfall had also brought poor summer crops in some parts of the state, which only augmented the allure of the federal bounties and pay for farmers and their sons. Newspapers exploited the theory that three-year recruits would probably serve no longer than the nine-month militia, reasoning that an army of more than a million men should be able to subjugate the South in less than three seasons, if it could be done at all. Recruiters sometimes carried that suggestion to the level of a promise, and Senator James Lane went a step further. Trying to raise troops for a command of his own, Lane told a crowd of prospective soldiers in Leavenworth that the government intended to crush the rebellion by the first of the year, and he hinted that the men who enlisted with him would never have to leave the state. Those who believed him discovered by spring that Lane's word did not bind the actions of the government (or the actions of Jim Lane, for that matter).[89]

Lane — a man of tremendous political ambition, ruthless character, and doubtful sanity — acted independently of and in direct competition with Governor Charles Robinson, and he did so with the complicity of the secretary of war. Ignoring both the law and the custom that placed recruiting in the governor's hands, Edwin Stanton appointed the radical Lane as his "commissioner for recruiting" in Kansas. Robinson objected, refusing to commission the officers Lane proposed, but Stanton foiled Robinson again by presenting those officers to the president for direct commission. Lane used that patronage to his own advantage, assigning friends and relatives to the four regiments he raised under federal authority. Denying as usual his own initiation of the trouble, Stanton backhandedly chastised Robinson for grousing over the flagrant affront "at a time when all men should be united in their efforts against the enemy." The confrontation between Lane and Robinson created something of a secondary civil war: when a Lawrence newspaper took Robinson's side and exposed the illegality of Lane's recruiting effort, Lane ominously accused the paper of "discouraging enlistments," invoking the phrase that might give him an excuse to close it down with the military forces at his disposal.[90]

By the summer of 1862 most slaves within rumoring distance of Union troops understood that they could usually tag along with a traveling column or congregate at a bivouac without being driven away: one brigade on a routine patrol outside of Memphis came back to camp a couple of days later trailing a caravan of 250 slaves who had slipped away from absent or distracted owners. Federals on the march in Louisiana accumulated similar trains of impetuous emigrants afoot, in pilfered tumbrels, or astride the occasional horse or mule. At Helena, Arkansas, the army set black refugees to work on fortifications, or shipped them up to Cairo by the hundreds.[91]

Eastern armies saw the same. Every night boatloads of contrabands rowed or sailed to Roanoke Island from all over the North Carolina sounds, until one Yankee observed that they had "quite a supply of these varmints here," grinning and gawking while the garrison paraded each evening. As the Army of the Potomac rolled up the Peninsula, driving Confederate arms and authority ahead of it, hopeful slaves had flocked to the perimeter from big riverside plantations. By the middle of June they were coming in by scores daily, often putting themselves in the way as they sought sustenance and employment. They cooked for Union officers, washed clothes for enlisted men, or drove teams for the quartermasters, provoking the soldiers to admiration or annoyance according to their sympathies — and after generations of servitude the slaves' condition seldom elicited a positive impression. "If a person should come out here and see as much of the niggers as we have," claimed a private in Joe Hooker's division, "he would not have so good an opinion of them." Noting that the "feeling against nigars is intensly strong in this army," a corporal in the Irish Brigade explained that black people "are looked upon as the principal cause of this war." Officers frequently displayed similar antipathy, despite backhanded compassion. "I wish they were all at the bottom of the sea," admitted one otherwise generous New York lieutenant who considered himself a sound Republican. "I never did love negroes and now I hate them worse than snakes. That this great country should be destroyed for the sake of these half-brutes is to me a bitter thought. I confess that it's not their fault but for all that they are not worth the trouble and expense of blood and money that this war is costing."[92]

Under the authority of the Militia Act and the Confiscation Act, some generals again proposed filling the country's armies from this host of contrabands. John Phelps, a Vermont brigadier serving under Benjamin Butler in New Orleans, had reported since mid-June on the burgeoning community of runaways around Camp Parapet, north of the city. In July he organized five unarmed companies of them, and counted enough adult black men within his jurisdiction to fill three regiments. Their officers might be promoted from the noncommissioned ranks of the white regiments, he suggested. Transforming them into soldiers would give them employment to support their families and strengthen the Union army, Phelps contended, besides removing the danger of insurrection posed by so many idle, undisciplined fugitives, who had already threatened to turn on the defenseless civilians just a few miles up the Mississippi. Butler, who pegged Phelps for a militant abolitionist, ordered him to desist at least until President Lincoln could review the proposal, and required that the five organized companies should be put to work on the fortifications. Turning righteous and redundantly grandiloquent, Phelps replied that he lacked the ambition to be a slave driver, asking to be relieved from "that darkling sense of bondage and enthrallment . . . like the snake around the muscles and sinews of Laokoon." Then he submitted his resignation.[93]

David Hunter's humiliating executive reverse on his departmental emancipation order seemed not to have quenched his antislavery ardor, and he had forged ahead with plans for a regiment of black South Carolinians without even tentative authority. On the flimsy excuse of old instructions to accept the help of "all loyal persons offering their services in defense of the Union," Hunter retained the hundreds of slaves he had largely pressed into service at gunpoint, dressing them in gaudy red trousers and training them persistently. He freed them from fatigue duty so they could concentrate on close-order drill, which only aggravated the white troops who had to take up the slack under the summer sun. By early August it was time to supply the various companies with officers. The new laws offered better grounds for requesting those commissions, but as much as Stanton may have sympathized with Hunter's scheme he dared not offer that authority in the face of Lincoln's recent disapproval, so he allowed Hunter's request for commissions to languish without reply. Sensing continued resistance, Hunter finally abandoned the experiment and disbanded his conscript regiment.[94]

Senator Lane also exploited the recent legislation to fill out his Kansas brigade, and Lane would not be dissuaded by War Department prohibitions, much less dismayed by a lack of administrative encouragement. One of the Leavenworth dailies advocated the creation of "Zouaves D'Afrique" in Kansas as early as July 26, predicting that the state could supply a couple of regiments, and in his inaugural recruiting speech Lane insinuated that any black man who failed to enlist might find himself forced to do so. A week later a longtime abolitionist in Leavenworth informed a Massachusetts patron that he and his colleagues "have now nearly organized the First Regiment of Colored Kansans — armed uniformed and equipped precisely as other Kansas Regiments." Another Leavenworth paper asked white citizens to drop by the store of Nelson McCracken with donations to support the families of black volunteers, and by the end of the month there were reportedly twenty-one new companies of black volunteers.[95]

On August 23 Stanton notified Lane that he had gone too far: the president had not authorized him to raise black troops, and the War Department would not accept them. Lincoln had already refused an offer to raise two black regiments in Indiana: whether or not the president still harbored his lifelong racial prejudice, he recognized that others did, reiterating his concerns about border states like crucial Kentucky. That prejudice survived in Kansas as much as it did in the slave states. "We advise those interested to keep their black regiment away from the Kansas troops now in the field," warned the *Fort Scott Bulletin*. "We know whereof we speak, when we say that, with one exception, there is not a Kansas regiment from which they would not have as much to fear as from the rebels." That threat failed to deter Lane, either, and he made good on his boast to coerce black volunteers into service. His underlings made at least one raid into Missouri to steal slaves and horses from the loyal and disloyal alike, but, while those jayhawkers herded their captives back to the Kansas training camps, Missouri militia pounced on them and arrested half the raiders. Kansas cavalry came thundering across the border to demand their comrades' release, but Missouri militia backed up the Clay County sheriff's refusal to turn them over. For a time, two loyal states seemed ready to fight each other.[96]

Where the subject of black soldiers arose, it would not fade away. The summer had wrought a drastic change in the thinking of many people, including that of Abraham Lincoln. Salmon Chase, a Free Soil man of old, conceded that it was time to let the South go if universal emancipation did not become one of the war's goals: freeing the slaves would remove the impetus for secession, weakening the Southern will to resist, and it would eliminate the potential for later dispute if reunion could be achieved. Chase furthermore saw that argument wearing down the president's reluctance to offend the border states with emancipation doctrine.

On July 31, only ten days after Lincoln had expressed his continued opposition to arming contrabands as soldiers, Chase wrote Ben Butler that he doubted the president would revoke another proclamation like Hunter's. That letter could not have been long in Butler's hand when he decided to form his own auxiliary force at New Orleans composed of free men of color. Careful as always to skirt complicated legal issues, Butler technically revived the Native Guards, which had been acceptable to polyglot Louisiana's militia organization during the Confederacy's early days, thereby avoiding the inflammatory matter of arming slaves.[97]

On the same day that General Butler announced his order, Mr. Lincoln addressed a letter to Horace Greeley, the editor of the *New York Tribune*. Greeley had objected to Lincoln's lethargy on the subject of emancipation, and Lincoln replied that in his view slavery presented a subordinate issue to the restoration of the Union. He no longer denied his authority to declare slaves free, as he had argued at the outset of the war — in fact he now seemed to presume that he owned that power — but he insisted that he would exercise it only insofar as it was necessary to save the Union. Three days after the president drafted that letter, Edwin Stanton — who enjoyed the same opportunities as Chase to monitor Lincoln's demeanor — stamped the concept of black recruiting with a semblance of White House approval. Despite so recently chastising James Lane for attempting to raise black troops in Kansas, and ignoring General Hunter's plea for his red-legged regiment, the secretary authorized a brigadier in South Carolina to recruit as many as five thousand soldiers from among the contrabands in Hunter's department, and to arm them for defense of the Sea Islands.[98]

Stanton gave that first formal permission during a week of busy correspondence with state officials about stalled regiments, needed arms or equipment, and incomplete draft preparations. Haste trumped every other priority. He waived the requirement for parental consent in the case of minors who wanted to enlist and accepted virtually every offer of troops, whether for special service or regular duty. Even a nine-month artillery battery earned the secretary's nod, although the artillery service required half a year's training. Federal armies were dwindling daily from disease and desertion, while victorious Confederate troops rolled northward on all fronts. Perhaps Stanton himself could not have said whether the decision to field soldiers of African descent reflected a political transformation or an act of military desperation.[99]

The hunger for soldiers inspired efforts across the Atlantic. Late in July, Henry Lord, the United States consul at Manchester, England, reminded the secretary of state that the blockade of Southern ports had caused devastating unemployment in that part of Britain, and he suspected that "many thousands of sturdy men" might cross the ocean for economic opportunity if only they had the money for passage. A steerage berth cost about twenty dollars, and the U.S. Army was paying a twenty-five-dollar advance on bounties, so Mr. Lord wondered if the government could not arrange to cover the fare of migrants who were willing to enlist in the army. He suggested that mustering officers might meet the ships offshore to swear the passengers in before they landed, to minimize defaults.

Secretary Seward received that letter soon after the War Department issued the August 4 call for another three hundred thousand men. He obviously liked the idea, but in deference to Britain's Neutrality Act he opposed the overt exchange of travel expenses for military service. So bountiful a market for recruits demanded some attention, however, and he immediately drafted a letter to all major officials of the American diplomatic corps, requiring them to advertise their country's prosperity in agriculture, industry, and mining as an incentive to "industrious foreigners" of any nationality. They might advise the laboring man or artisan that nowhere else in the world could he find "so liberal a recompense for his services as in the United States," but Seward added that the federal government "had no legal authority to offer any pecuniary inducements" toward such travel. So sly a fellow surely expected his subordinates to read between the lines and find some informal arrangement for covering the transportation expenses of foreign volunteers, and he probably hoped to facilitate the coordination of such a subterfuge when he forwarded Lord's letter and his own Circular No. 19 to Edwin Stanton.[100]

Seward eventually betrayed the real intent of his instructions when he amended them with Circular No. 32, giving priority to male emigrants between the ages of twenty-one and forty, as well as offering the previously objectionable stipend to those who agreed to enlist. That ploy and the extravagant bounties coincided with a new surge in immigration: hundreds of thousands of aliens poured into East Coast ports through the rest of the war, including nearly a quarter of a million Irishmen who landed in 1863 and 1864 alone. Most of the men joined the army.[101] Still, foreign levies came too slowly to satisfy immediate wants. Those demands soared with every new report of aggressive Confederate activity, and Confederate armies grew unusually active with midsummer. Northerners finally began to comprehend the spirit of savage resistance that Howell Cobb had described to Colonel Key in the middle of June. Fair Oaks and the Seven Days proved that the fury of Shiloh had been no flash in the pan. Collectively, those battles signaled an end to the Confederacy's heretofore defensive war.

More insightful Union officers understood, furthermore, that their own army's depredations had gone a long way toward kindling that spirit. Division commander John Sedgwick conceded a few weeks later that "our men . . . think of nothing but marauding and plundering, and the officers are worse than the men." Union soldiers preyed on farmyards and private homes to forage mercilessly and steal whatever struck their fancy — from souvenirs like love letters, personal possessions, and ancient public documents to the furniture, pianos, clocks, and paintings with which they furnished their temporary encampments. Occasionally they even broke into tombs, robbing caskets and desecrating the bodies, or stooped to murder and rape: one particularly brutal band of Union stragglers killed a notoriously loyal Fauquier County planter who challenged them, and then they completely despoiled his estate. The new confiscation laws and the emerging doctrine on emancipation only aggravated Confederate hatred, confirming the perennial predictions of secession's most inflammatory advocates. While Northern citizens avoided enlisting in the army at all costs, hung back to await higher bounties, or gambled on safer service, many Southerners resolved to die to protect their homeland from the abolitionist vandals Lincoln's army had come to represent. More telling still, Southern wives shared that fierce determination: one woman in the Shenandoah Valley let her husband know that she would rather sacrifice him to a Northern bullet than see Lincoln's "ruffian hordes" lay waste to their country.[102]

The confiscation and arrest orders with which John Pope greeted the Army of Virginia merely reflected his government's policy changes. With Radical Republican ascendance, all the earlier guarantees of limited warfare and the protection of private property had gone by the boards, as would Lincoln's pledge not to interfere with slavery. Defeats in the Shenandoah Valley and before Richmond, and the stalled campaign in the West, demanded either that Northern armies give up the conflict or convert it into the war of subjugation that moderate and conservative Unionists had promised it would never become. Pope's bombastic proclamations marked the first formal announcement of a policy of pillage, and that fixed on him the accumulating animosity of his opponents. He had not yet reached his army when that customarily punctilious Southern gentleman, Robert E. Lee, referred to him in an official report as "the miscreant Pope," and many of Pope's own officers thought little better of him. Marsena Patrick, who commanded a brigade in Rufus King's division, thought the new commander's pronouncements the "Orders of a Demagogue."[103] Another brigadier confessed that he had no confidence at all in Pope, "with all his bluster," and a Massachusetts captain thought Pope made about the same impression on his own army as he had on the Confederates, who despised him.[104]

While Pope might provide his immediate target, Lee could not refrain from considering grand strategy. Until taking over the Army of Northern Virginia, eight weeks before, Lee had served as military advisor to President Davis, and he used that personal connection to offer what might otherwise have been considered impertinent proposals about operations in other departments, as well as making suggestions on overall war policy. Early in June, less than ninety-six hours into his command of the army, Lee was urging Davis to reinforce Jackson's little Valley army with troops from the Carolinas and Georgia, so he could strike Maryland and Pennsylvania. Lee anticipated that under such an offensive, Northern leaders would strip the Southern coast of Union forces — precisely as they did a few weeks later, when he launched his own assault on McClellan.[105]

The plan for invading Maryland came to naught just then, but Lee continued to advise aggressive behavior on all fronts. Colonel John Hunt Morgan, a Kentucky Confederate, rode a wide circuit through his home state during nearly all of July with fewer than a thousand cavalry, disrupting and terrifying the Federals there, and Lee gently hinted how productive it might be if that raid were "confirmed" by an invasion of infantry. He supposed that the Army of the Mississippi would make a profound impression on such a mission under its new commander, Braxton Bragg, and Bragg could take along Kirby Smith's smaller army at Knoxville. William Loring and Humphrey Marshall might also cooperate with their smaller commands in southwestern Virginia. The president and secretary of war considered it, and the telegraphs buzzed for a few days, but Morgan returned to his base at Knoxville before a stronger expedition could be organized.[106] Lee had germinated the notion of a coordinated northward push, though, with the goal of taking the war toward — if not into — enemy territory, and by August the idea began to blossom. Whether he was to take part in that offensive or not, Lee first had to "suppress" Pope, as he repeatedly phrased it. With the Army of Virginia hovering so near, that need seemed urgent, and Lee assigned the task to Stonewall Jackson.

5

The Crowd of the Bloody Forms

JACKSON HAD MOVED HIS two battle-thinned divisions up to Gordonsville in the middle of July. Pope made his headquarters at Sperryville, thirty miles or so to the north, with seven divisions and a few loose brigades stretching all the way from Fredericksburg to the Blue Ridge Mountains. The Army of the Potomac remained rooted at Harrison's Landing with eleven infantry divisions, while four more Union divisions awaited orders at the tip of the Peninsula. That combined host outnumbered Lee's seven divisions at Richmond by about two to one, but Lee seemed confident that McClellan could be cowed by any show of force in his front. Lee had been hoping for an opportunity to shuttle Jackson heavy enough reinforcements to pulverize Pope, after which they could return to face McClellan, and he made that gamble at the end of the month. Strengthening Jackson with another big division under Ambrose Powell Hill, he invited Stonewall to strike a rapid blow while the main army held McClellan in check.[1]

Lee disguised the weakening of his army with aggressive action. Trying to prod McClellan to further retreat, Lee made a surprise attack on his supply fleet with an array of artillery that he sent south of the James River, through Petersburg. The guns opened soon after midnight on August 1, sending shells soaring over the river to land among the ships and encampments around Harrison's Landing. Federal guns returned fire, and shells lighted the sky every second or two. The barrage inflicted relatively little damage (some of the sailors slept through it), but it appeared to paralyze McClellan for another week.[2]

In fact, McClellan began loosening his grip on the Peninsula in response to Halleck's orders. Burnside's two divisions at Newport News started boarding transports for Fredericksburg on August 2. McClellan reoccupied Malvern Hill briefly, but then pulled back. Lee hinted to Jackson that the time had come to deal with Pope, especially if the Peninsula forces were heading upriver to his support, and Jackson moved immediately across the Rapidan River toward Culpeper Court House, where Pope had begun concentrating the western elements of his army.[3]

Banks's corps arrived at Culpeper on August 8, as did a division of McDowell's corps under James Ricketts, and Pope ordered Sigel to join them from the Shenandoah Valley. He also called in another division of McDowell's corps, from Falmouth. Pope heard that Jackson intended to draw him on to Gordonsville and fight him there, but he anticipated no real trouble.[4] He arranged his various corps in preparation for a sweeping advance southward toward Richmond with not only the Army of Virginia and Burnside's corps but with most of McClellan's army as well, which he expected to inherit when it arrived from the Peninsula. When he learned that Confederates were coming at him from the Rapidan he mistook it for a reconnaissance and moved Banks ahead to meet it, sending a staff officer after him with oral instructions. As Banks understood those orders, and as his own staff officer copied them down, Banks was to attack the enemy force if he met it. Pope later insisted that he intended Banks only to assume a defensive position and await reinforcements, but the first interpretation — and the only written record of those orders — better matched the aggressive demeanor that Pope had assumed.[5]

Jackson held a significant numerical advantage: he could put more than fifteen thousand men into a fight that day, while Banks commanded fewer than nine thousand in two divisions. Banks led those divisions southward in enervating heat and humidity on the morning of August 9, passing an idle division of McDowell's corps outside of Culpeper, and he collided with Jackson's vanguard eight miles below the town, where Cedar Mountain loomed south of the highway. After an introductory exchange of artillery fire, the opponents stared at each other in silence for about three hours. The broiling sun discouraged unnecessary movement, and after arranging his lines Brigadier General Alpheus Williams invited the field officers of his division to a sumptuous luncheon in the grass. Colonels, majors, and adjutants feasted and sprawled under the shade of a tree, telling stories and laughing as though on a holiday picnic. By dark every one of General Williams's guests would lie dead or badly wounded.[6]

The artillery reopened at midafternoon, and Banks initiated an assault as confidently as a soldier with positive orders and an underestimate of enemy numbers. Most of the killing took place within a single square mile along the Culpeper Road, between two side roads that ran perpendicular to it. Confederate infantry drove back a screen of Union cavalry and settled in, two brigades strong, behind Crittenden Lane. Federal artillery lined up half a mile away, along the road to Mitchell's Station, and dueled for the next couple of hours with Confederate guns. Late in the afternoon Banks threw Christopher Augur's division against Crittenden Lane. Augur maneuvered two of his own brigades through a broad field of mature corn, from which they emerged at the deadly range of three hundred yards into a daunting fire from the front while Southern artillery tore at them from the left, on Cedar Mountain. The long lines advanced in the age-old fashion, plodding ahead into the storm until close enough to deliver their own fire, then trading volleys in the hope that the other side would flinch. A veteran of Bull Run thought Cedar Mountain more furious than that larger engagement, with double the volume of musketry and twice the proportion of casualties. The Confederates shot every mounted Union officer in Henry Prince's brigade from his horse, capturing General Prince himself at the head of his brigade. The commander of the other brigade, John Geary, suffered two wounds, while General Augur and his horse both went down with what looked like fatal injuries.[7]

Meanwhile, Alpheus Williams brought his division up on Augur's right, on the far side of the Culpeper Road. Williams pushed Samuel Crawford's brigade up first, into some woods. Crawford, a doctor by profession, had been the post surgeon of the celebrated little Fort Sumter garrison. Largely on the weight of that notoriety he had obtained a line commission and a volunteer appointment as a brigadier, but his competence remained unproven. Another brigadier from the Old Army knew that Crawford lacked the confidence of his men, and officers within his brigade confirmed as much, but Crawford seemed blessed with the two elements most crucial to success: sheer luck and a tireless capacity for self-promotion. He enjoyed some of that luck as afternoon turned to evening, but he managed to squander it.[8]

Crawford's brigade came out of the woods into a broad, freshly cut wheat field. The woods resumed on the far side of the wheat field, and in that second forest lay the vulnerable left flank of Stonewall Jackson's line, under Thomas Garnett. Two other Confederate brigades, including Jackson's old Stonewall Brigade, were coming up to extend that left flank, but they had not arrived when Crawford rolled across the wheat field with three regiments and struck Garnett just as his first reinforcements arrived, overlapping and crumbling his awkward formation. Crawford impetuously hurled his three regiments obliquely onward into the main Confederate line behind Crittenden Lane, heedless of his own right flank, and he left George Gordon's supporting brigade far behind. The Stonewall Brigade reached the scene just in time to close in behind Crawford, and North Carolinians slammed into his exposed right, slowing his momentum and shearing off some of his three battered regiments. Subjected to crossfire from side and rear, Crawford's brigade disintegrated. Every field officer went down dead or wounded; in one regiment every single officer fell, and the other two brought fewer than a dozen lieutenants out with their men, all in full flight. Half the brigade had been slaughtered or captured.[9]

The 10th Maine, which had been momentarily detached, followed Crawford's brigade into the wheat field alone. The survivors of the other three regiments swept past the Mainers and the better part of four Confederate brigades turned on them, tattering their little line from three sides. In short order they lost well over a third of their men for no perceptible purpose, and their colonel finally pulled them back into the woods.[10]

That left only General Gordon's little brigade on the Union right. Gordon, the only West Pointer in Williams's division, strode into the stubble of the wheat field and slugged it out with those Southern brigades for half an hour while the rest of Banks's shattered corps regrouped. Provost guards in the rear leveled their bayonets at many a strapping fellow who came at them at a dead run, claiming to be "sick" and begging "for Gods sake" to let them by. The commissary of Prince's brigade was just preparing to feed his men from a wagonload of salt beef and a drove of steers when the fugitives swarmed toward him, their hunger forgotten. The commissary's boss butcher absconded with them, and the teamster abandoned his cargo of salt beef.[11]

Gordon's three regiments — the 2nd Massachusetts, 27th Indiana, and 3rd Wisconsin — endured a dreadful pounding. Gordon estimated that he took fewer than fifteen hundred men into action, and he lost nearly a third of them. The bullets flew so thick that he ordered the men to lie down, but the officers remained standing as a courageous example, and they paid dearly for it. The proper Bostonians who led the 2nd Massachusetts suffered the worst: their regiment bore 173 casualties that included the major, six captains, and numerous lieutenants; only eight of the twenty-two officers who entered the fight came out unscathed. As the merciless sun neared the horizon the pressure of four Confederate brigades, all bigger than his, finally forced Gordon to give up the wheat field and slip back through the woods. On the other side of the Culpeper Road the remains of Augur's division followed as more Confederates sprinted down the slope of Cedar Mountain toward them. Many hundreds of the survivors stampeded across Cedar Run in the dusk.[12]

General Pope rode out to meet Banks. As they discussed the situation in the gloaming, Confederate cavalry dashed at their line. Pope, Banks, General Williams, and a flock of staff officers bolted away on horseback, and a cavalryman's runaway horse bowled Banks over, knocking him to the ground hard enough to bruise his hip painfully. A division of McDowell's corps was marching down to relieve Banks just then, and the skirmishers preceding those reinforcements heard the thundering hooves: glimpsing the dim shadows of plunging horses under the bright glow of a full moon, they mistook it for Confederate cavalry and fired into the night. They barely missed their own generals, whose horses had dipped into a gully.[13]

It was, thought most of the officers and men in Banks's two divisions, about time that Pope sent someone to help them: many of them supposed that a little support would have turned the tide at crucial moments in the fighting. They also assumed that plenty of reinforcements had lain idle in their camps, as close as two miles behind the battlefield and no farther away than five miles, for they remembered passing some of McDowell's troops that morning, and McDowell himself had been near enough to dine with Pope since the previous day. The officers of Banks's corps muttered savagely about their boastful new army commander. Their anger sank deep, and it festered.[14]

The shock of the clash at Cedar Mountain stunned those Union soldiers who survived it, producing an epidemic of melancholy that debilitated the remains of Banks's entire corps. A sergeant of the 2nd Massachusetts who customarily wrote long and frequent missives home began to neglect his family correspondents after the battle. In a belated letter to his sister he apologized for not writing, confessing that "since the fight I have not had the heart to. Some how or other I could not," and his letters never resumed their former volume. One of the remaining captains in his regiment seemed similarly downcast as he recounted the many friends who died that sultry summer evening. Banks had lost about a third of his effective force, compared to less than 10 percent casualties on the Confederate side, and thenceforward most of the mail from his corps betrayed evidence of that universal dejection. Recording his long summer's campaign toward the end of that year, a soldier in the 3rd Wisconsin spent five paragraphs describing the anguish he felt after Cedar Mountain.[15]

Gloom afflicted the generals as well. Those who had not been wounded or captured — Crawford, Gordon, and Banks — all struck one staff officer as morose, worn, and discouraged. The normally pompous and self-centered Crawford broke down in tears at the sight of his withered brigade, and Gordon revealed traces of emotion in his official report.[16] The defeat also seemed to dampen John Pope's spirit. Less than a month before, he had scolded the troops of his new army with a preposterous order belittling the concern for "lines of retreat" and "bases of supplies," leading well-trained generals on both sides to ridicule him in turn; one Confederate general predicted that Pope would eat those words, and indeed, on the morning after Cedar Mountain, Pope's bellicose rhetoric turned almost timid. "I will do the best I can," he promised General Halleck, after manufacturing the preliminary excuse that he was heavily outnumbered. Now even the mighty Pope stooped to a consideration of lines of retreat, though he avoided using the word itself: he forewarned Halleck that he would withdraw by way of the Rappahannock River "if forced to retire."[17]

Robert E. Lee intended to force him to retire, if not to obliterate Pope's army. On August 13 Lee investigated a report that McClellan's army had begun boarding transports, presumably to join Pope, and the next day Lee felt satisfied that McClellan did intend to abandon the Peninsula. That required Lee to shift his forces northward from Richmond and thrash Pope before the two commands united to overwhelm him, and he sent Major General James Longstreet to Gordonsville with a big new division composed of more than fifty regiments, augmented by John Bell Hood's smaller division. When Longstreet reached Gordonsville he took command from Jackson, who had withdrawn there from Cedar Mountain two days after the battle, and Lee prepared to follow with as many other troops as he dared pluck from the Richmond garrison.[18]

The tale of McClellan's departure came only a few days prematurely. As it was, some of the troops stripped from the coasts of North and South Carolina were already arriving at Falmouth, fielding rumors that they would soon join Pope. On August 16 the last of the Army of the Potomac marched out of Harrison's Landing, and the next day McClellan and Burnside watched those thousands of veterans tramp across a two-thousand-foot-long pontoon bridge at the mouth of the Chickahominy River, on their way to Fort Monroe and Washington. The romantic McClellan waxed sentimental at the sight, asking Burnside if he had ever seen finer troops. "Oh," he exclaimed, "I want to see those men beside of Pope's." Soon enough he would, and it would require inspired Confederate strategy to defeat the combination.[19]

Lee's suggestion for a collective offensive toward Northern territory posed an example of that sort of strategy, and his idea began coming to life that week. While Lee shuttled his Richmond army toward Gordonsville to attack the Army of Virginia, John Hunt Morgan's Confederate cavalry sliced the railroad at Gallatin, Tennessee, destroying a vital tunnel and disrupting the Union supply line between Louisville and Nashville. At the same time Edmund Kirby Smith led a substantial corps out of Knoxville toward Barboursville, Kentucky, flanking the Federal stronghold at Cumberland Gap, while Braxton Bragg crossed his Chattanooga army to the north side of the Tennessee River with his eye on Nashville and Kentucky. Deep in southwestern Virginia, Humphrey Marshall haggled with William Loring over the return of troops with which he, too, might be able to invade Kentucky. From the Alleghenies of western Virginia, Loring planned his own cavalry raid up the Kanawha River Valley to the Ohio border, hoping to follow it with his infantry. Former vice president John C. Breckinridge had led a division against the Yankees coming up the Mississippi, building a bastion at Port Hudson when he failed to drive them out of Baton Rouge. In central and northern Mississippi, Earl Van Dorn and Sterling Price schemed to operate against much larger Union armies under Ulysses Grant and William Rosecrans. "Our prospects are bright," Bragg told Price on August 12.[20]

Indeed the future did seem bright for Confederate armies that August, despite the overwhelming numbers opposed to them on almost every front. Especially with confiscation orders that foreshadowed abolition, Kentuckians like John Morgan insisted that the Bluegrass would rise up against Union oppression if only an organized Confederate force were sent there to collect them. Several of the cooperating commanders requested thousands of rifles to arm prospective recruits.[21]

Lee intended a northward march of his own, beginning with a rapid movement against John Pope before too many reinforcements reached him. While Lee organized the Army of Northern Virginia into two wings, under Longstreet and Jackson, Pope fidgeted below Culpeper with his three corps and Jesse Reno's two little divisions from Burnside, waiting for McClellan's army before resuming any aggressive movements. That left the Federals stranded between the Rapidan River and the upper Rappahannock; Lee hoped to skirt their left flank, get behind them, and cut them off from their reinforcements on the left bank of the Rappahannock before pouncing on them with everything he had. His infantry and James Ewell Brown Stuart's cavalry rested below the Rapidan on the afternoon of August 19, and Lee expected to hurl them all at the enemy the next morning, but his last long-distance reconnaissance from the summit of Clark's Mountain disclosed that the once-audacious Pope had decided to retreat to the safe side of the Rappahannock.[22]

Pope's retreat showed rare good judgment on his part, but the movement had come off clumsily. Baggage wagons blocked the roads, leaving many of the troops to wait late into the evening of August 18 before beginning a shuffling, halting crawl through the night. The campsites they had to choose the next day fell miserably short of the standards of comfort in their Culpeper bivouacs: even General McDowell located his headquarters in thick, suffocating woods without handy water.[23]

As Pope stumbled back behind the security of the Rappahannock, the first soldiers from the Army of the Potomac started up Chesapeake Bay and the Potomac from Fort Monroe. A division of Fitz John Porter's Fifth Corps disembarked at Aquia Creek on August 20, and the rest landed the next day. By dawn of August 21 a fleet of troop-laden transports trailed out of sight downriver from the creek landing, waiting for a spot to unload their passengers. Meanwhile the Confederate army splashed across the Rapidan at thigh-deep fords on August 20 and moved up to confront Pope's Yankees on the bluffs beyond the Rappahannock.[24]

With Pope's men left safely behind the river, Lee started looking upstream for a way to slip around his right. On August 22 he sent his flamboyant cavalry commander, Stuart, galloping up to Waterloo Bridge to raise havoc in the Union rear. With two thin brigades numbering perhaps fifteen hundred sabers, Stuart swung through Warrenton to Pope's supply line, the Orange & Alexandria Railroad, riding into a drenching rainstorm. As the sodden day turned to blackest night he reached Catlett's Station, a dozen miles behind Pope's headquarters at Rappahannock Station, where he found a dense mass of quartermaster supplies as well as General Pope's own baggage wagon and some of his staff. The prize Stuart really wanted was the railroad bridge over Cedar Run. Could he have destroyed that double-trestle span he would have forced Pope to scramble for provisions, perhaps to the extent of retreating from the Rappahannock toward Washington, where Lee might be able to isolate him for the kill. Rain had soaked the bridge timbers, foiling all efforts to set fire to it, so in desperation the Confederate troopers went looking for axes. The rain-swollen stream and Union marksmen on the opposite bank ultimately drove them from this daunting task, and Stuart fled back the way he had come with a few hundred prisoners, a herd of horses, John Pope's dress coat, and his dispatch book, which revealed Pope's concern for his tactical liabilities.[25]

There would be no more forays over Waterloo Bridge. On the day of Stuart's raid Pope started shifting his own forces one more crossing upriver, hoping to crush a fragment of Lee's army that found itself trapped on the wrong side of the raging Rappahannock, but the movement incidentally lent a little more protection to his only rail line. Pope mistook the trapped rebels for Jackson's entire wing, so he spent most of August 23 arranging his divisions before daring to attack it, and that allowed the single Southern division to escape over a makeshift bridge in the wee hours of August 24. The mildly disappointed Union commander settled in at Warrenton, where Stuart had so recently ridden through, and that evening he joined the epicurean McDowell for dinner at the Warren Green Hotel.[26]

For all its relative lack of success, Stuart's raid showed Lee the way to bait Pope, and he decided to send Stonewall Jackson on a more ambitious expedition. Pope's sideslip to Waterloo Bridge required Jackson to follow a much wider circuit and entailed a tremendous risk, for it divided the

Army of Northern Virginia roughly in half and invited the enemy to destroy Lee in detail, just as he hoped to destroy the Union army. With fourteen brigades in three divisions, Jackson started his march on August 25, following the right bank of the Rappahannock until the river ducked behind the Bull Run Mountains, then fording it and turning north to Orleans and Salem. From there he could follow the Manassas Gap Railroad through Thoroughfare Gap to its junction with the Orange & Alexandria. The route had been chosen to screen Jackson's movements from Union lookouts, but the troops had not been on the road for four hours before one of Nathaniel Banks's staff officers spied them from a signal station and raced back with the news, estimating the force at twenty thousand. Pope assumed it was a diversion into the Shenandoah Valley — which, after all, Lee had earlier pondered as a project for Stonewall.[27]

Still believing himself outnumbered, Pope gladly heeded Halleck's instructions to wait for the rest of McClellan's troops to arrive before taking significant aggressive action. He failed even to act defensively, though, and allowed Jackson to wend his way northward unimpeded, expecting that he would turn west from there, rather than east. A brigadier under Pope remarked to his wife how quiet the last few days had been, wondering if it were not the calm before the storm.[28]

The quartermasters in Pope's army attended carefully to the wants of the generals, supplying luxuries for every bivouac, but the men in the ranks suffered for want of provisions.[29] In Banks's battered and demoralized corps no one saw their baggage wagons after they left Culpeper, which deprived the officers and some men of their blankets, and many of the troops subsisted on green apples and corn pilfered from the roadsides. At Sperryville an Ohio private concluded that Union soldiers had cleaned out the local supply of corn, while army livestock had eaten the last blade of green grass. James Gillette, one of Banks's brigade quartermasters, admitted that the commissaries had virtually abandoned their men and left them starving; Gillette doubled as both commissary and quartermaster in his brigade, bringing up food as well as equipment.[30]

Captain Gillette had previously observed that stragglers from the Army of Virginia would invade occupied homes, including the humble cabins of poor whites, and steal everything edible. He blamed it on the inevitable abuse of Pope's orders for the army to live off the surrounding countryside. So did Marsena Patrick, who led a brigade in Rufus King's division; Patrick thought Pope had given the troops "a general license to pillage, rob & plunder," and it had reduced some of his men to persistent thievery. One of King's New Yorkers confessed that his company feasted regularly on fried pork and mutton, with the occasional treat of a chicken. "Every one who can steals a horse or a mule," he told his wife, "& I have got one of

our boys looking for one for me." For play they incinerated random homes
and businesses, like the White Sulphur Springs resort.[31]

Pope had tried to correct the evil with another general order against
individual foraging, but it appeared to do little good. No sooner did his
army arrive in Warrenton than his hungry horde descended on the farmers in that vicinity, digging up their vegetable gardens, shooting their
cattle as they grazed in the pastures, and emptying their barns and hen-
houses. The army's chief topographer slept his first night there in a house
that had been despoiled by Yankees, who killed all the livestock and "insulted" the old farmer, his wife, and their numerous brood of daughters.
The artist's relative absence of outrage hinted that the "insult" did not far
exceed verbal abuse, but unarmed citizens did not always escape more violent treatment from Union soldiers.[32]

The savage attitude in Pope's command came to the surface on August
25, when a few of his soldiers stopped for refreshment at a house near
Warrenton Junction. A Michigan soldier wandered to the well for water,
and stood about innocently filling his canteen while a New York cavalryman barged into the house, in direct violation of Pope's tardy corrective
order. The patriarch was at home, and he ordered the New Yorker out
of the house, but the cavalryman refused to leave. When the homeowner
tried to push him out the door the intruder lifted his carbine and fired a
bullet through the man's brain, killing him almost instantly while the
horrified family looked on. In his camp less than a mile away, a brigade
commander freshly arrived from McClellan's better-disciplined army
heard of the murder, regretting that he lacked the authority to order a
summary execution himself.[33]

Incidents like that helped to make John Pope the most hated man in
Virginia, and quite a few of those who hated him wore the same uniform.
General Patrick heard the troops at Warrenton damning Pope lustily, and
he suspected that they disliked his senior subordinate, McDowell, nearly
as much. Patrick himself cared little for McDowell, whom he privately
ridiculed as "his Magnificence." Patrick's contempt stemmed as much
from the disorganization in Pope's army as from the uncivilized conduct
he seemed to allow. Pope illustrated that disorganization with a series of
orders, often verbal, that tended to contradict each other: at Warrenton
he issued a sampling of them to Franz Sigel, one of his corps commanders, which provoked a snarling match between them.[34]

Pope also quarreled by telegraph with General Halleck, imagining from
the necessarily terse tone of the telegraph that the general in chief had become dissatisfied with him. Halleck's directions to remain on the defensive until the Army of the Potomac arrived, and his orders to maintain contact with Burnside's headquarters opposite Fredericksburg, had

grown increasingly restrictive as Lee maneuvered against him. The move to Warrenton had broken his connection with the lower fords and the troops from Fredericksburg, and Pope may have worried that Halleck disapproved. He also fretted, as McDowell had the previous spring, over what his status would be when the two armies combined: would he command the whole, despite McClellan's seniority, or would Halleck come out to assume command of the separate armies, as he had before Corinth? Halleck replied somewhat petulantly himself, but he offered no clear answers to any of Pope's more pressing questions.[35]

Back at Falmouth, McClellan also pestered Halleck for clarification of his status. He had arrived there on the morning of the twenty-fourth, joining Burnside at the Lacy mansion, on the bluffs overlooking Fredericksburg. Both he and Burnside lacked any troops, having sent all their available men to Pope, and McClellan shared Pope's concern over who would command whom. He informed Halleck that Pope had marched away without apprising Porter, whose divisions linked him to Fredericksburg, and McClellan hinted broadly that he had his staff there and could move in any direction — including, obviously, to the front. It gave him little comfort that Halleck indicated Pope would command Porter and Reno "for the present," or that Halleck did not care whether McClellan stayed near Aquia Creek or came to Alexandria; his only orders were to direct the landing of his troops. McClellan sat up talking to Burnside until well after midnight that night, inside Burnside's tent in the Lacy yard. In the wee hours he turned disconsolately back to Aquia Creek.[36]

As day dawned on August 26 Pope held nominal control over all or part of six Union corps, including two from McClellan and one from Burnside. McDowell, most of the cavalry, and a division from Porter's corps made for the upper Rappahannock, looking for Longstreet. Reno's Ninth Corps lay on the Orange & Alexandria line. Banks's corps rested between those two points, depleted to about six thousand men who were still badly shaken by the bloodbath at Cedar Mountain — and soured by the perception that Pope had sacrificed them. Sigel remained behind all these at Warrenton, along with two divisions of Heintzelman's Third Corps that had just come in from Alexandria. Porter, who had no idea where Pope was, felt his way up the Rappahannock to Bealeton Station with the rest of his Fifth Corps, reporting to Pope that afternoon. McDowell, Reno, and Banks gave Pope about forty-eight thousand by his own calculation, while the four divisions under Porter and Heintzelman should have added at least twenty-four thousand more. Pope already held a significant advantage in numbers over the Southern army that had divided itself before him, but all day he concentrated intently on the Rappahannock crossings, as though he had forgotten altogether about the big Confederate column wandering loose on his right. Only as the sun set that evening did he even mention it, denying McDowell the last of his troops from Warrenton Junction until he knew what had become of Jackson's flanking column. He had sent a cavalry regiment up the Manassas Gap Railroad, looking for any signs of it.[37]

Just then passed a rare moment on the picket line. A white flag waved from the Confederate side at one of the Rappahannock fords guarded by Marsena Patrick's brigade, and rebel pickets came out with a prisoner wearing the Union uniform, who had recently been captured from Franz Sigel's corps. Southerners did not often give up a captive without an exchange, but upon being taken prisoner this one had evidently revealed a secret that assured instant release: the private was a woman. Such secrets lurked in the army with greater frequency than most soldiers knew. Occasionally a female recruit avoided detection for months or years, slipping through the cursory physical examination despite the habit of stripping most volunteers naked. Influential accomplices sometimes aided materially in the deception, as in a Pennsylvania regiment not far from that scene on the Rappahannock: a corporal in Ricketts's division shared a tent with her captain, whose attentions would eventually gain her a promotion for valor on the battlefield and, soon afterward, a child. A few hundred miles away, a purported niece of General Reno's was masquerading as a cavalryman with a Kentucky regiment. In upstate New York a stocky, sturdy nineteen-year-old girl named Sarah Rosetta Wakeman, who habitually dressed as a man, had just left home after a tiff with her family; she was about to enlist under the name Lyons Wakeman, apparently seeking a promised bounty of $152, an allotment for her mother, and a chance to make her own way in the world.[38]

At the very moment the Confederates handed their distaff prisoner off to General Patrick's pickets, Union guards at Bristoe Station, ten miles behind Pope, learned the whereabouts of Jackson's flanking column. As Tuesday's sun dropped behind the Blue Ridge, a little regiment of Virginia cavalry swept into the station, scooping up or scattering the garrison. Infantry followed, tearing up the tracks, but one train escaped in either direction. Jackson aimed for the bigger prize at Manassas Junction, another five miles toward Alexandria, where supplies had been stacked in massive quantities. He sent some cavalry and two regiments of infantry up the line to take it from the south, where the station fortifications were most vulnerable. Even the warning from the escaped northbound locomotive failed to alarm the station guard, and with no moon Jackson's little force was able to creep within sprinting distance of the depot, easily taking control of the place and sweeping up hundreds of prisoners and horses. Mountains of stores at the depot included fifty thousand pounds of bacon, thousands of barrels of salt pork and flour, and a thousand barrels of corned beef, besides tents, ammunition, and sutlers' delicacies; two miles of railroad cars sat on the side tracks, many of them still loaded. Jackson's lean legions had not seen such bounty since the campaign against Banks in the Shenandoah Valley.[39]

Herman Haupt, the War Department's superintendent of railroads, alerted Washington to the interruption in communications and set about repairing it. Early in the morning he found a brigade of New Jersey troops and put them on the cars for the bridge over Bull Run, which he particularly wanted to save. From there they would have to proceed on foot. At dawn a regiment of New York heavy artillerymen armed as infantry approached Manassas well ahead of the Jerseymen, having marched from Alexandria the day before. They fanned out and inched forward in search of the reputed raiders, but a brigade of Confederate infantry and whole batteries of artillery sent them flying toward the railroad bridge over Bull Run. The New Jersey brigade came next, walking into withering fire from A. P. Hill's division, and their brigadier went down with a fatal wound before the survivors turned and ran. Hill drove them over the Bull Run bridge, where they tried to rally with a couple of fresh Ohio regiments on their way down the railroad, but Hill's men crossed, chased them away, and left the bridge in flames when they withdrew to the other side. That was more damage than Colonel Haupt's construction crews could repair on short notice.[40]

Jackson spent the day at Manassas, distributing the wealth of Union supplies to his quartermasters and commissaries. The men filled their haversacks to overflowing and burned the rest on their second night at the junction. At Bristoe, Richard Ewell faced south with a few Southern brigades in anticipation of the inevitable foray from Pope's army, and that morning Pope did order most of his troops up the railroad, but it was afternoon before any of them came close to Ewell's advance guard. The larger part of the Army of Virginia moved up the Warrenton Turnpike, under McDowell.[41]

While Pope worried about his communications, Lee started north with Longstreet's bigger wing of his army, following Jackson's route behind the Bull Run Mountains. On the morning of the twenty-seventh Pope thought the rebel army was concentrating at White Plains, over those mountains, for a lunge into Maryland; he supposed the Bristoe and Manassas incursion had been nothing more than an ambitious raid meant to embarrass his supply line by burning the bridges. He doubted there would be any attack on him.[42]

Washington also anticipated Confederates coming across the Potomac.

The collapse of the railroad bridge over Bull Run marked the end of Pope's lifeline to Alexandria, and the return of the battered New York, New Jersey, and Ohio regiments brought the last news Washington heard from the direction of Pope's army for days. The president telegraphed everywhere for information, besides begging interviews with anyone who had come near Manassas. General Halleck and the secretary of war could not conceal their alarm, and at the Navy Department Gideon Welles half expected Confederates to come dashing into Washington. Welles ordered a flotilla of gunboats to anchor in the Potomac to protect the capital.[43]

By sunset Heintzelman's troops had driven Ewell back through Bristoe Station toward Manassas Junction, and Pope made his headquarters there that evening. Garrulous prisoners had come in, proudly announcing that it was Jackson, Hill, and Ewell who held Manassas, so Pope rushed to arrange a trap for them all on the morrow. He accurately supposed that Jackson could count on twenty-five thousand men, but by his assessment of Jackson's position he assumed that McDowell and Sigel marshaled nearly forty thousand at Gainesville, on Jackson's right flank, while Heintzelman, Porter, and Banks could put another twenty thousand or more in front of him at Manassas. For extra measure he also ordered Jesse Reno up to Manassas with his eight thousand, assuring Reno that if they moved quickly enough "we shall bag the whole crowd."[44]

As Pope ought to have considered, the game had already flown, and his careful choreography would avail him nothing but the smoldering remains of a million dollars in supplies. Jackson withdrew his wing from Manassas Junction during the night on Wednesday, marching across the battlefield of thirteen months before, crossing the Warrenton Turnpike, and filing down the roadbed of an unfinished railroad that angled from Sudley Springs back toward Gainesville. On Thursday morning his three divisions blended into the woods behind that trackless rail bed, where they lay down to sleep. Pope swung his corps toward what he mistook for Jackson's right flank, while Jackson's veterans napped conveniently close to Pope's own left flank. Worse yet — as only Irvin McDowell seemed to understand — James Longstreet's even bigger wing lurked just over Thoroughfare Gap, at what would soon become the rear of Pope's entire Army of Virginia. On his own initiative McDowell dispatched a division under James B. Ricketts to watch the gap.[45]

Around noon the jaws of Pope's trap closed on nothing but the wreckage of Manassas Junction. Some of the railroad cars were still burning, and a few hungry Yankees cut slabs of roasted beef from the embers, but that was all they could salvage: after a fortnight of sleeping in the open air, one of Reno's regiments found the charred remnants of shelter tents they had requisitioned. From his lair behind the unfinished railroad Jackson watched for an opportunity to lash out at the Yankees and occupy their attention while Lee brought Longstreet's divisions over the mountains to assail them from behind. Such a tactic may have seemed to Pope too bold for serious consideration, leading him to conclude that Jackson had fled precipitously toward Centreville; certainly it required more nerve than John Pope owned for Jackson to match his three divisions against Pope's entire army.[46]

Jackson saw his prey approach just before the dinner hour that Thursday. As the sun sank once more toward the mountains a blue-clad division under Rufus King tramped up the Warrenton Turnpike toward Centreville. Although he was a West Point graduate, King had spent a quarter of a century out of the army before Lincoln made him a brigadier. He suffered from epilepsy, and had fallen into a grand mal seizure just five days before, during a vigorous artillery duel. Since that time he had been complaining of feeling sick, and those around him confirmed that he looked it. He had to face more artillery firing that evening, when, just short of the crossroads hamlet of Groveton, Jackson halted his column with battery fire from the edge of the woods near his hiding place.[47]

King's leading brigade stopped to return the fire, as did the brigade of Wisconsin and Indiana troops that followed, under John Gibbon. Gibbon called up a battery of U.S. Regulars that he had formerly commanded himself, but he also threw the 2nd Wisconsin toward the woods to chase away what he thought was cavalry. Rebel infantry spilled out into the open and a tremendous fight erupted, almost instantly, around the farmhouse of John Brawner. Gibbon sent the 19th Indiana to support his first regiment, and finally he threw his other two Wisconsin regiments into line and called for help from Abner Doubleday, whose brigade came next. Doubleday committed two regiments, as did Marsena Patrick; Patrick found that one of his regiments had simply fled the field, to a man. Jackson arrayed several brigades against the Westerners and pounded them ferociously, but they bore the punishment and returned it in kind, loading and firing as quickly as they could at a range one Wisconsin lad described as only "a few yards." Their bullets leveled two Confederate division commanders — including General Ewell, who was carried to the rear with a wound that would cost him his leg. Muzzle flashes lighted the dusk, turning to sheets of flame in the darkness, and then the firing finally drew to a finish as though through mutual exhaustion. Gibbon, who had begun the fight with about 2,200 men, lost 751 of them in their maiden battle, making it as deadly as Cedar Mountain for the numbers engaged. His men stood their ground until well after midnight, when King decided to pull the isolated division back toward Manassas Junction.[48]

Rufus King was not the only Union general confronting Confederate forces that evening. James Ricketts, whom McDowell had sent to guard Thoroughfare Gap against Longstreet, had not made it to the crest of the pass that afternoon before he met Federal cavalry falling back with the news that Longstreet had already taken possession. Ricketts pushed on and tried to block the road with artillery from below the crest. He managed to hold on until dark, but Longstreet sent men over the mountains by trails that outflanked the four brigades of Federals, and Ricketts retired. A messenger from King warned him of the Confederate presence on the turnpike, so Ricketts marched back to Bristoe Station.[49]

King and Ricketts moved on their own initiative that night because neither of them knew where to find their corps commander. After diverting King to the turnpike, McDowell had gone looking for General Pope, perhaps to remind him about the threat Longstreet posed to their flank and rear. By the time McDowell and his staff reached Manassas Junction it was dark, and they learned there that Pope had gone "to the front," but his idea of where the front lay may have differed from McDowell's. That evening Pope had established himself near Blackburn's Ford, well away from any Confederate forces, while McDowell made his way cross-country over the pitch-black Manassas plain. He lost his way and had to backtrack quite some distance until he stumbled across the Sudley Springs road, which brought him to the home of a man named Pringle. One of McDowell's aides knew the place, and was able to navigate from there, but by then it had grown extremely late. They turned onto the Lewis plantation, which Joe Johnston and General Beauregard had used as their headquarters during the first battle of Bull Run, and there they bivouacked for the night. The absence of tents made for as dismal a camp as most of Pope's troops had been putting up with for weeks. With his entourage McDowell sprawled on the bare ground where, four hundred days before, Confederate soldiers and dignitaries had jubilantly celebrated their victory over him.[50]

Though tactically meaningless, King's savage little encounter at Brawner's farm exerted the desired effect on John Pope. From his headquarters high on the banks of Bull Run he could see the smoke of the engagement as it opened, and later that night he learned the details from one of King's staff officers. Convinced that King had run across the path of Jackson's retreat, Pope turned all his other troops around from Centreville to chase down what he mistook for a desperate enemy in full flight.[51]

Early the next morning Pope sent his topographer, David Hunter Strother, to Fitz John Porter's tent at Bristoe Station, with an order to move his Fifth Corps to Centreville "at early dawn." Porter was still sleeping on his cot when Strother found him at a few minutes after five, but he read the order by candlelight and issued the necessary orders right away.

Then he sat down to write dispatches while Strother ate breakfast with his staff; the topographer remembered Porter asking how to spell "chaos." Porter explained that he had been in touch with Washington, presumably in a roundabout relay by way of the telegraph line he had been running behind him ever since he left Burnside's Falmouth headquarters, and he said everyone in the capital wanted to know where Pope was. Porter's spelling question did not bode well for the assessment he was sending back.[52]

Porter's dispatches that morning carried the same sarcastic flavor as some he had written the day before, when he surmised that Longstreet had popped unchallenged through what Porter called "that enormous gap." He had relayed Pope's Thursday-night report that Jackson had retreated to Centreville, telling Burnside, "You can believe that or not." In his breakfast message on Friday he quipped that Pope had apparently taken Heintzelman's corps and Reno's with him as his personal bodyguard while he knew the fight was raging at Groveton. Burnside cautioned Porter about his indiscreet language but, knowing that the president thirsted for any information from Pope, he passed the messages on to Washington from his Falmouth headquarters. He hesitated to send a couple of the more snide remarks, but his chief of staff convinced him that he had no right to withhold any information Mr. Lincoln could have, and he thought it wholly inappropriate to edit the dispatches, so they went verbatim. Porter would come to rue the tone of those messages, but they reflected a fair and accurate analysis of Pope's bizarre behavior.[53]

The previous night Pope had sent Franz Sigel instructions to make a vigorous attack in the morning. Despite his fairly small corps, Sigel sallied forth against the unfinished railroad with his field batteries blazing. He began near the stone house on the Warrenton Turnpike, at its junction with the Sudley Springs road, which had become the best-known landmark of the 1861 battle of Bull Run. From there Sigel swept diagonally over the hills toward Jackson's line on the rail bed. Back at Centreville, Pope eventually decided he needed more troops below Groveton, where he supposed Jackson was trying to break through and escape. He concocted another order for General Porter that completely contradicted topographer Strother's dawn message, telling him to add King's division of McDowell's corps to his own force and march for Gainesville instead of Centreville — in nearly the opposite direction. He suggested that "the whole force of the enemy" was moving toward Centreville, belatedly acknowledging Longstreet's approach, but he erroneously supposed that Longstreet's portion of Lee's army still lay at least thirty-six hours away. In fact, Union cavalry had spotted Longstreet's leading division marching through Gainesville more than an hour before, and those troops were already deploying against the left flank of the Army of Virginia. Pope seemed to be plucking his estimate of Longstreet's whereabouts out of thin air, and he gave no hint what intelligence might have misled him. Having hopelessly confused and misinformed the leaders of his left wing, whom he imagined to have an open road around Jackson's flank, Pope saddled up and started down the turnpike under another bout of his recurring fantasy that he had snared Stonewall in a hopeless trap. As he cantered toward the rising smoke of Sigel's attack he railed and cursed at little knots of stragglers who sat boiling coffee and cooking stolen provender under the shade of trees beside the road.[54]

General McDowell reappeared that morning at Manassas Junction, wearing the voluminous summer hat that reminded his men of an inverted washbasin, or breadbasket. He located the Weir house, where he had made his headquarters at the outset of the spring campaign, and there he found General Porter. McDowell announced that as the senior officer he was taking command of the whole, but then he took his own troops out of line and turned back toward the Sudley Springs road, where he planned to join Pope. Porter, meanwhile, had found his way to Gainesville blocked by what he thought was Confederate infantry: it was actually skirmishers from Stuart's cavalry, popping away at him with carbines while their comrades dragged brush over the bone-dry roads to simulate the dust cloud of a division. Stuart maintained the ruse long enough for Longstreet to bring up his infantry.[55]

Only Porter's presence off the right flank prevented the reunited Army of Northern Virginia from lunging forward at that moment to engulf Pope's entire army. Jackson faced southeast, engaging Franz Sigel, with Heintzelman and Reno bringing their two corps into action against that front. McDowell's corps wandered about in fragments behind that line: McDowell, traveling with King's division, had gone looking for John Reynolds and his Pennsylvania Reserves, who had joined Sigel in his assault, while Ricketts spent the day coming up to Manassas from Bristoe Station. Four of Longstreet's five divisions hung like an open gate from Jackson's immovable fence, facing due east — into the backs of all Pope's soldiers save Porter's Fifth Corps. Under Pope's vague orders, Porter did not feel authorized to attack, but neither could he continue any farther toward Gainesville, as Pope had ordered, so there he sat, paralyzed by a lack of further instructions — and, apparently, by the belief that he was still under McDowell's orders.

Pope, meanwhile, still expected both McDowell and Porter to fall, unimpeded, on Jackson's right flank and rear, rolling up his line. Pope therefore made no great effort to drive Jackson out of the unfinished railroad grade; he merely dashed one brigade after another against that impromptu breastwork, casually investing the lives of hundreds of men to pin Jackson down for the all-important flank maneuver. It would have been a tactic worthy of Robert E. Lee, had Pope not completely misunderstood his situation.[56]

Under Pope's eye Heintzelman broke up his corps, sending Phil Kearny to the right of the line near Sudley Church and dicing Joe Hooker's fine division into scattered brigades that fought well enough individually, but without much effect. At midafternoon Cuvier Grover's brigade formed for a bayonet charge that broke through two lines of Jackson's troops at the center of his line, but a third line drove them back in a brutal brawl fought with bayonets and musket butts. Soon afterward Reno flung a brigade of his old division in to the left of Grover's attack. In the sweltering heat three regiments under Colonel James Nagle, all veterans of Burnside's victorious North Carolina campaign, shucked their knapsacks and waded in, fixing bayonets for another charge when gunfire failed to clear their way. They punched through, but as they climbed the embankment of the railroad cut and spilled into it Jackson thrust a couple of brigades around their left flank that nearly cut them off. The rifle fire came fast enough to remind the survivors of hailstones, or bees buzzing about their ears. Thirsty Yankees, some of them suffering now from heat exhaustion, fell by scores and surrendered by dozens; those who saw the danger in time turned and sprinted through the woods into a jumble of brigades from two other corps, leaving behind their knapsacks, many of their weapons, and 531 of their dead, wounded, and captured comrades.[57]

The repulse of Nagle's brigade precipitated a flight all along the Union left. Jackson swung his right around perpendicular to the Warrenton Turnpike, flushing thousands of Federals out of the woods, and only by the most strenuous exertions were brigade and division commanders able to patch together a line near the Sudley road. One-armed Kearny met the fugitives and hailed them with his customary battlefield bluster. "Come on and go in again, you sons of bitches," he bellowed, "and I'll make brigadier generals of every one of you." Once he had stopped the panic and formed a line, Kearny put his reins in his teeth, flourished his sword with his right hand, and sailed into the onrushing Confederates with half his division, checking their advance and actually pushing back Jackson's left flank late in the afternoon. With the right of his line now cleared of Union infantry, Jackson shifted other troops to his left and finally stalled Kearny.[58]

For John Pope, who could not give up his delusion of decisive conquest over a helpless opponent, Kearny's last-minute gains seemed to signal the collapse of Jackson's defense. McDowell had left Reynolds and the Pennsylvania Reserves to bolster Sigel's front earlier in the day, and until Ricketts came up from Bristoe, that left him only King's division, which the ailing King had turned over to Brigadier General John Hatch. McDowell and most of that division sat on the Sudley Springs road looking into the setting sun, in line with the tattered corps of Sigel, Heintzelman, and Reno, when Pope decided it was time to chase after Jackson before he slipped away. So certain did the commanding general seem of imminent victory that he infected even the staff of the skeptical McDowell, who turned Hatch westward down the turnpike. Hatch hastened everyone — three brigades of infantry and the 1st New Hampshire Light Artillery — in the hope of turning Jackson's retreat into a rout.[59]

As the head of his column crossed Young's Branch, Hatch thought better of his haste and ordered the 2nd U.S. Sharpshooters out as skirmishers. Their forest-green uniforms spread across the road and they stalked up over the last towering rise before Groveton, thumbing the hammers of their Sharps breech-loading rifles. Just over that hill sat John Bell Hood's division of Southern troops, with James Longstreet's half of the rebel army at their backs. The Confederates opened fire immediately. Hatch brought forward two of the New Hampshire howitzers and filed Abner Doubleday's three-regiment brigade south of the road, marching it up to back the sharpshooters on the skirmish line.[60]

Hatch had no veterans to meet those who bore down on him. Doubleday's brigade had seen its first real engagement only the night before; except for long-range artillery fire, neither the 2nd Sharpshooters nor the New Hampshire artillerymen had ever been in a battle before. The heavy volleys of musketry unnerved the sharpshooters, most of whom ran wide-eyed past the brace of guns, disappearing back down the hill into the gathering darkness. Doubleday lacked the firepower to meet the onslaught, and the Confederates overlapped his little front on both sides. Soon everything came apart and Hatch fell back with his enthusiasm sorely blunted. The captain of the battery ordered one of his guns off before the enemy reached them, but he stayed with the crew of his remaining piece and fired a few more rounds. He ordered one last charge of double canister as a regiment of Mississippians raced toward them; the blast burned the faces of as many of them as it killed, but it also overturned the gun. Rebels swarmed over the upended carriage, swallowing the captain and ten of his gunners. Someone who thought the gun would be too difficult to right grabbed an axe and chopped through the spokes of the wheels, leaving the crippled piece lying in the dust by the side of the road.[61]

Union generals watched the clash at Groveton from the hills to the west: Pope made his headquarters on Buck Hill, behind the stone house, and McDowell joined him there. The last of Hatch's struggle descended into small arms fire that made the distant woods sparkle, reminding one staff officer of fireflies. Despite his professed belief that the affair merely marked another attempt by Jackson to ward off pursuit, Pope pushed no more that night. A message came in from Fitz John Porter revealing that he had never made the expected attack from Gainesville because of a strong intervening force of the enemy. Pope had read John Buford's warning about Confederate reinforcements coming through Gainesville that morning, and he later conceded that he knew those were Longstreet's men, but he refused to take Porter's information as further evidence that Lee's whole army lay before him. Instead he raged over Porter's inaction and threatened to arrest him, but McDowell and some of the other corps commanders dissuaded him. Pope issued no more orders that night, and his generals went to sleep. McDowell rode over to Henry Hill, where his first battle at Bull Run had begun to go wrong. He bedded down on the bare ground again, alongside the ruins of Judith Henry's house and within sight of her thirteen-month-old grave. General Ricketts — whose fieldpieces had killed Mrs. Henry, and who had lost his leg on that very hill — slept nearby.[62]

If Pope had decided to march toward Washington that night, joining forces with the rest of the Army of the Potomac, Robert E. Lee would undoubtedly have been disappointed. He would have succeeded at least momentarily in clearing northern Virginia of Union soldiers, but without serving John Pope the resounding defeat that would have scattered his army to the winds or captured it whole. Pope would have escaped the personal humiliation Lee obviously wished to inflict, and (worse still) his troops would survive intact to swell the overall Union forces.

Pope relieved his opponent of that disappointment. On the morning of August 30 he still believed that the Confederates were retreating before him — or so he later claimed, and John Pope's claims always warranted skepticism. His troops had stood well against Stonewall Jackson for hours before they broke, and Pope seemed to deny that they had broken at all. Then Phil Kearny had made a little headway against Jackson even after that, and Hatch had chased the fugitives into the shank of the evening, only to run into what Pope misinterpreted as Jackson's rear guard. Not many Union generals could say they had bested that Confederate legend: it never occurred to Pope that Jackson had allowed him to keep pummeling his line because it cost Pope far greater casualties, and because he wanted to detain him on the anvil long enough for Longstreet to bring the hammer crashing down. So when the sun rose Pope remained, with most of his army strewn along the Sudley Springs road. He still imagined the Southern army to have taken to its heels during the night, and first reports seemed to confirm as much. Still nervous after Hatch's twilight scrap, General Patrick crept forth from his lodging at John Dogan's house and peered over the rise into Groveton, glimpsing the tail of a Confederate column as it disappeared down the turnpike. Later McDowell and Heintzelman reconnoitered on foot together, and they both concluded that the enemy was leaving the field as quickly as possible. Pope neglected to wonder why they had waited until dawn, instead of escaping under cover of darkness, and no one around him posed that question.[63]

General Porter arrived with his corps that morning, offering his personal report of Longstreet's presence. Pope brushed that information and all other such indications of Confederate might aside, entertaining only the evidence that conformed to his image of a defeated and demoralized enemy. Then he proceeded to inflict this cultivated delusion on the men who served under him: after hesitating for most of the morning he directed McDowell to take command of the "pursuit," giving him Porter's corps, King's division (under Hatch), and Reynolds's Pennsylvania Reserves, with Ricketts and his division to follow.[64]

Porter's infantry tread dutifully into the woods north of Groveton, running into Jackson's still-formidable line, and for the next couple of hours the artillery and skirmishers contended with unusual tenacity for what was supposed to be a rear-guard action. Then John Reynolds discovered a portion of the extended Confederate line that Porter had been complaining about. Advancing toward Groveton on Porter's left, where there should have been no retreating rebels, Reynolds's skirmishers met such stiff resistance that he added a regiment to their line, and then he had to send out another. Finally he grew suspicious about the purported retreat and rode out with a few orderlies to his left, where he detected more of the enemy's skirmishers and a solid rank of cavalry standing perpendicular to the turnpike. Reynolds deduced that those horsemen probably covered a column of Confederate infantry waiting to bear down on him and Porter as soon as their troops swung far enough toward Jackson's front. At that moment the skirmishers fired on him and he reined about, spurring away to the east at a dead gallop while bullets zipped past on all sides, knocking one of his orderlies out of the saddle. Reynolds rode until he encountered McDowell, who told him to wheel his division about and face that new threat, pointing to the ridge near the Chinn house as a sound defensive position.[65]

Knowing nothing of this, Porter aligned his troops for a concentrated assault on Jackson's line. He had three divisions with him, including the borrowed one under Hatch, and he assigned two of them to the attack. Hatch formed on the right, seven ranks deep; ten regiments of Porter's

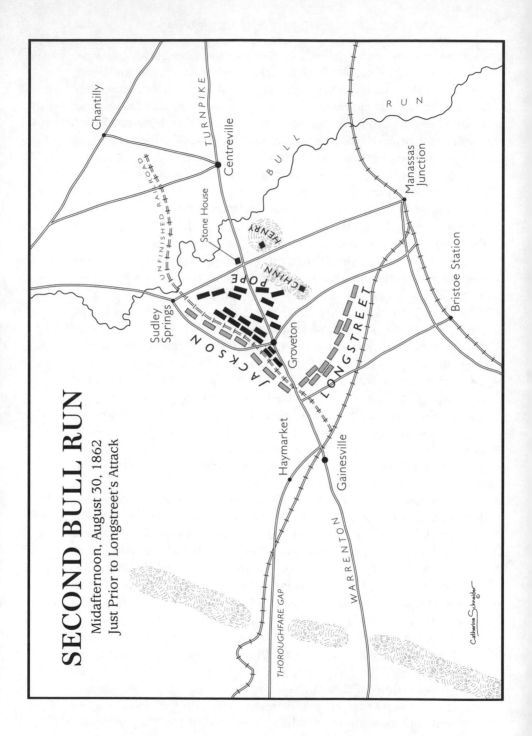

SECOND BULL RUN

Midafternoon, August 30, 1862
Just Prior to Longstreet's Attack

corps joined them on their left. In they went, throwing back Jackson's skirmishers and trotting through a galling crossfire of artillery and musketry. The railroad cut loomed in front of them, ablaze with flaming muzzles, and they stood trading volleys with the entrenched rebels until Southern ammunition ran low. Louisiana soldiers behind a prominent embankment fired their last rounds into the faces of the Yankees teeming below them; some of them gleaned a few more from the cartridge boxes of their dead comrades, and then they started flinging stones at the New Yorkers who tried to scale the outside of the grade. That furious defense kept the blue wave within sight and range of Confederate infantry and artillery up and down the line: showers of lead and iron raked the Union lines from both directions, and finally sapped the strength of the assault. So many dead and wounded Federals sprawled on the ground before the railroad cut that a Louisiana sergeant who glanced over the lip of it could not see a spot of bare ground. Losses among company, regimental, and brigade commanders confused the coordination of movements, and then General Hatch limped off the field with a wound, leaving at least one of his brigadiers unaware that Abner Doubleday had succeeded to the command.[66]

The gunfire reached its peak late in the afternoon. The din of Porter's fight carried all the way to Washington, thirty miles to the east. With no support on his left and no provision for securing any ground he might gain, Porter finally called off the attack, but his three leading brigades came out with angry Confederates at their heels. Those three brigades alone lost two thousand men in little more than half an hour, and hundreds of them were trapped when their comrades bolted for safety.[67]

James Longstreet watched Porter's attack crumble and took that as his cue to spring Lee's own trap. Porter's repulse seemed more like a rout to McDowell, who pulled Reynolds off Chinn Ridge and marched his Pennsylvania Reserves north, across the turnpike, to cover Porter and give him a place to rally his men. Reynolds turned his brigades to the right and started them over the pike one at a time, but the third one had not stepped off before Lee's long-withheld flank attack swept toward them. Four of Longstreet's divisions rolled over the tail of Reynolds's column, and McDowell scurried to find a couple of fresh brigades to post on Bald Hill, hard against the Sudley Springs road and barely a mile from Pope's headquarters on Buck Hill. Those brigades would suffer dreadfully as they tried to stem the Confederate tide, losing an average of 170 men per regiment. Among their dead would be Colonel Fletcher Webster (Daniel Webster's son, commanding the 12th Massachusetts) and Lieutenant Colonel Joseph McLean, who commanded the 88th Pennsylvania. McLean, who had earlier supposed that Stonewall Jackson had "caught a Tartar" when he crossed swords with John Pope, had subsequently grown less sanguine about it. His last two letters home had focused gloomily on what his wife was supposed to do if he should "fall," and on Chinn Ridge he did fall, shot twice through the same leg; an Ohio lieutenant tried to improvise a tourniquet, but McLean bled to death while Confederate infantry sprinted by.[68]

The stand on Chinn Ridge blunted the ferocity of Longstreet's headlong charge and bought some valuable time for the rest of Pope's army. At that moment most of his divisions were backing toward the stone house, where the turnpike crossed the Sudley road. If Longstreet's legions had surged up Bald Hill and across the road to Henry Hill they would have flanked Pope's left and controlled the only road available for his retreat. Pope — or rather McDowell, acting in the absence of much direction from Pope — patched together a defense behind the Sudley road. The commander of the Army of Virginia remained at his position atop Buck Hill until nearly dark, when he decided at last that the enemy really had no intention of retreating after all. Pope — the man who had proclaimed that in the West he had only seen the backs of his enemies — consented that evening to show this new enemy his own back, and he departed for Centreville ahead of the fighting portion of his beaten army.[69]

Much of that army had discarded any idea of fighting. Near Centreville some of William Franklin's fresh Sixth Corps had deployed across the turnpike to check stragglers from the battlefield, but in the dusk what seemed like the better part of Pope's command bore down on that glorified provost detail. There was, said one of Franklin's soldiers, "no stopping them." An Ohio division following Franklin encountered the same stampede, and swung across the road to arrest it. The Ohioans fixed their bayonets and leveled them at their terrified comrades, who simply poured around both ends of the bristling line.[70]

Reno's Ninth Corps covered the retreat. In the twilight he sent a brigade to guard the crest of Henry Hill, choosing the three regiments under Colonel Edward Ferrero, a former dancing master with a weakness for loose women. Ferrero's men sparred with the more numerous Confederates, who appeared to have grown cautious with the coming of darkness and failed to reach for the prize within their grasp. For a time Ferrero's men suspected that General Pope had abandoned them (by then anything seemed possible from that man), but Jesse Reno came from firmer stock. As the fingernail of moon slipped below the horizon this rear guard stole away to the turnpike. Leaving the bridges for the escape of the wagon trains, the infantry waded Bull Run and Cub Run in water that rose to their chests, coming out soaking wet to march into the cool August night.

An easterly wind kicked up to lend a deeper chill, and around midnight it began to rain.[71]

Nearly eight months of occupation by Joe Johnston's Confederate army had left Centreville with an impressive circumference of earthworks. Those works faced the wrong way, but a few hours of shoveling would have reversed them against any pursuing force, so General Lee chose to turn Pope out of his refuge instead of attacking head-on. Sending Jackson around the Yankee's right again, Lee intended to block Pope's route to Washington and bring him to a stand once more. That had to be done quickly, for the damaged, demoralized, and disorganized Army of Virginia that awoke on August 31 might gain strength rapidly, and thereby recover its spirit. At Centreville, in fact, Pope found two more corps from the Army of the Potomac that had come out to meet him, bringing his effective strength back up to what he tallied as sixty-two thousand men.[72]

The reinforcement failed to restore Pope's own bravado. The night before, he had reported to Halleck that the victory over Stonewall Jackson had turned into something that sounded remarkably like defeat. Again he shunned the word "retreat," conceding only that he had been "forced back" here, and had found it prudent to "draw back" there, and he lied outright about both morale and results, insisting that the men still felt good and that he had not lost so much as a single gun or a wagon. In fact the élan of his army had deteriorated abominably, with excellent regiments reduced to company size by the vagabondage of despair. Some commands, like the renowned Pennsylvania Reserves, had drawn nothing to eat for nearly three days, despite all the combat they had withstood in the meantime. Most of the troops had lost all confidence in John Pope as well as a great deal of stomach for the war itself. As for abandoned arms and equipment, on Sunday morning Lee's officers enumerated some 18,500 rifles, more than four full batteries with caissons, and a number of wagons and ambulances among the spoils given up by Pope.[73]

Pope's deteriorating mood did not improve with whatever sleep he managed to steal. On Sunday morning, with a steady rain pattering down outside, he scribbled a note for the telegraph operator that sent shivers up the spines of Henry Halleck and Abraham Lincoln. Despite his claim of good spirits among the troops the night before, Pope promised Halleck in the morning that he would give the enemy "as desperate a fight as I can force our men to stand up to." Then he betrayed the fear he had entertained since the previous evening: that if he fought even a defensive battle against Lee it would end in disaster. "I should like to know," he wrote, "whether you feel secure about Washington should this army be destroyed."[74]

Lincoln, who had gone to bed Saturday night hoping for a grand victory, rode in from the Soldiers' Home Sunday morning to find that despondent telegram. He interrupted his private secretary as he was dressing to announce that "we are whipped again," and to remark disconsolately on Pope's tone. "I don't like that expression," he sighed. "I don't like to hear him admit that his men need holding." The president remained combative, insisting that Pope had to "hurt this enemy before it gets away," but he also seemed to envision the prospect of ultimate defeat. Rambling cryptically on the eventuality that Pope might be driven from Centreville back into the fortified capital, he seemed to ruminate on giving up the war altogether.[75]

In Washington, those who neither heard the cannonading nor learned of the battle from street gossip on Saturday knew of it by Sunday morning. Before they understood the desperation of the situation at Centreville, hundreds of residents and visitors headed out of town on the authority of Edwin Stanton, taking their own carriages, the trains, and public hacks to volunteer as nurses among the wounded. A thousand of them came across the bridges on Saturday night alone. Many of the volunteer nurses seemed to mean well, but a large proportion had obviously come out on a lark: great numbers of them had immediately gotten roaring drunk, and almost none of them had brought any medical supplies or expertise. They soon made incredible nuisances of themselves, impeding the progress of wagons and ambulances on their way to Washington and even hogging the inbound railroad cars when their first night's experience dampened their missionary impulses. Officers at the Washington end of the Potomac bridges finally posted guards to turn them back.[76]

The thousand nurses who slipped through ahead of the guards passed a thousand ambulances lurching back with their fragile cargoes of wounded. Shattered femurs, severed spines, mangled arms, and mutilated faces raised moans and shrieks with every bounce and jar of those stiffly suspended vehicles. The rough ride burst open the delicate coagulation of ruptured arteries, and when the drivers pulled up to the doors of the Washington hospitals they frequently delivered one or more dead men. A fair proportion of those who survived the journey soon died from infection, especially if their wounds opened cavities that doctors of the day lacked the knowledge or drugs to treat. A New York boy came to the hospital at Judiciary Square with a saber cut over his left ear that split open his skull and exposed his brain — a suspicious injury for a man whose regiment had fought no cavalry — and his nurse soon recorded the symptoms of his fatal decline.[77]

General Pope may have sustained no external wound, but in the hour of his mortification he seemed to suffer as much from manic depression as from the slings and arrows of outrageous fortune. Alternating between pessimistic gloom and aggressive enthusiasm throughout August 31, he visualized the annihilation of his army and a vigorous repulse of the enemy within the same dispatches. He sought excuses for his defeat and for every frustration he endured, blaming the quartermaster department for not sending him remounts for the cavalry and an orderly for not guiding him by the hand to a subordinate's headquarters. He viewed the defeat itself as the fault of his corps, division, and brigade commanders; he also accused them of destroying the morale of his troops — whom he had described that very afternoon as "in good heart." On the first of September he turned pugnacious on paper, at least, promising to mount an attack, but then he whined for several pages about the failure of officers from the Army of the Potomac to lend him sufficient support or even obey his orders, concluding that demoralization among those officers demanded that his entire army fall back to the entrenchments surrounding Washington, lest it fall victim to "great disaster."[78]

Pope came closer to the truth when he implied rampant dejection among his troops than when he alluded to their high spirits. "The men are without heart," admitted General Porter in a private note to McClellan, "but will fight when cornered." Phil Kearny, the most combative general in the army, confided to his wife that all the troops had shown the white feather except his own, Hooker's, Reno's, and Gibbon's. "This army ran like sheep," he snarled. "Our men would not fight one bit; it was amusing to watch them." In Alpheus Williams's depleted division a brigade commissary who took a somewhat archaic view of the seasons found September 1 "as dark and gloomy as could be expected of the 1st day of Autumn now upon us."[79]

General Williams had not come from the Army of the Potomac. For his part, he attributed the army's plight and plaints entirely to Pope, who had issued such pompous "after-dinner orders" from "a snug hotel in Washington" before undertaking "the bungling management of his last campaign." Pope, Williams felt sure, did not have "a friend in his command from the smallest drummer boy to the highest general officer." A new lieutenant in one of Williams's regiments corroborated that sentiment. Just arrived from home with a direct commission from his abolitionist governor, Charles Mills of the 2nd Massachusetts discovered to his surprise that his comrades held no bitterness toward the enemy; a brother officer explained that the soldiers on either side were "both in the same boat." Mills told his mother that he heard twice the abuse heaped on Pope ("whom we all hate") as he did for any Confederate, including their leaders.[80]

Many of Pope's reluctant subordinates suspected that he was the one who hesitated to retreat, because it would have brought him back where McClellan waited to resume command in place of the discredited upstart, but Pope's September 1 advice to pull back demonstrated that he no longer dreaded giving up control. In fact, he probably would have welcomed it. It was General in Chief Halleck who cringed at falling back: he wished to hold as much ground as possible, evidently for the sake of public opinion and troop morale rather than for any military advantage Centreville offered. "Don't yield another inch if you can avoid it," he advised Pope late Sunday morning. By Monday, though, the heralds of defeat had begun to reach the defenses of Washington. Stragglers representing nearly every unit in Pope's army began pouring into Alexandria from the Fairfax road, on foot or in wagons driven by teamsters who still whipped their horses as though beset by Southern cavalry. Garrison troops from the forts stopped them and corralled them into provisional companies, herding them by the thousands into the works. This news would have reached army headquarters about the same time as Pope's discouraging assessment of the army's condition, after which Halleck granted permission to retreat successively farther — to Fairfax Court House, or to Annandale, or "if necessary" even to the protection of Alexandria. That permission hung on a double contingency: Pope might retreat if Lee tried to turn his right flank, and if he engaged Lee "without a decisive victory."[81]

By day's end on Monday, both conditions had been met. Stonewall Jackson had led his exhausted corps well north of Centreville, and in the afternoon his lean foot soldiers were swinging down the Little River Turnpike toward the ruins of Germantown, a few miles on the Washington side of Centreville. Union troops already blocked him there, and two divisions piled into Jackson near a tavern stop known as Chantilly. A violent downpour opened soon after the battle did, darkening the evening sky and vying with the roar of the guns. As the daylight flickered out, the opposing troops aimed at the flashes of each other's volleys, blazing away until nine o'clock at night. When the shooting subsided, two of the better Union generals, Isaac Stevens and Phil Kearny, lay dead on the sodden ground. Both sides claimed to have held the field, and one Union general called it a victory, but it fell sufficiently short of a "decisive" victory that Pope felt fully authorized to flee for Alexandria. His troops bent their heads into the sheeting rain and plodded eastward, their shoes sinking into mud a foot deep at every step.[82]

Like nearly ten thousand of the men who had been unfortunate enough to serve under him during the previous month, John Pope had fought his last battle. By the cold, wet morning of September 2 he had surrendered all control over his army and was fairly begging General

Halleck to come out and take over. Reflexively throwing responsibility for his woes on others, he complained that the troops who had joined him from the Peninsula were already demoralized, and he dishonestly focused his assertions of "awful" straggling on McClellan's former divisions, warning that the army would evaporate if something were not done. Lee was pressing him in heavy numbers "and must be stopped in some way," he wailed, but he deemed that beyond the power of the men he disparaged as "these forces under my command." His army would disintegrate if subjected to another confrontation, he feared. When Halleck read that message he appeared to understand that Pope's usefulness had come to an end, and ordered him into the capital's fortified defenses with his entire command. Halleck had put those defenses under the supervision of George McClellan, and he directed Pope to obey any order of McClellan's as though it came from Halleck himself.[83]

In less than a week McClellan's fate had fluctuated from the brink of disgrace, dismissal, and ruin back to the height of distinction. On August 28, within a day of McClellan's return from the Peninsula, Edwin Stanton had made an ominous appeal for information regarding him. The secretary asked Halleck what date he originally ordered McClellan to move the Army of the Potomac up from the James, and whether that order had been obeyed as promptly as the national interest required; he also wanted to know what orders had been issued for the march of Franklin's Sixth Corps to Pope, and whether McClellan had complied with those orders in good season. Without a doubt, Stanton sought grounds for a court-martial or even an executive order for McClellan's dismissal from the service, and he did not wage his campaign alone. The day after submitting his request to Halleck, and before Halleck responded, Stanton dropped in on Salmon Chase. Although Chase had been the staunchest of McClellan's patrons at the outset, he had come to share Stanton's conviction that the young general "ought not to be trusted with the command of an army of the Union." Like John Pope, Stanton and Chase suspected McClellan of deliberately undermining Pope to assure his failure. Together the pair called on Halleck and argued for McClellan's removal, for with Pope's difficulties at Manassas it seemed likely that McClellan might be given another command. Halleck promised an answer to Stanton's questions the following day.[84]

The cabinet cabal forged ahead without waiting to see whether Halleck could provide any evidence for their accusations. Chase met with the attorney general, Edward Bates, a longtime McClellan critic who consented to sign a petition to the president demanding McClellan's removal. Then Chase took it to Gideon Welles, catching him just as he was leaving the Navy Department for the day. Welles concurred with Chase and Stanton in their exasperation with McClellan, but he specifically objected to the accusation of deliberate disloyalty in their petition — which, he noticed, was in Stanton's handwriting. Welles also disliked the business of collecting signatures beforehand; that sort of question should be decided in open discussion, he said, and he refused to sign. In the evening Welles stopped for the latest news at the War Department, where he found Stanton in his office, chatting with the secretary of the interior. The two had evidently been discussing McClellan, with Stanton lobbying for Smith's signature.[85]

By then Halleck had responded to Stanton's inquiries, admitting that he had not been satisfied with the alacrity of either movement, but he included McClellan's excuses for the delays. He noted, for instance, that the withdrawal from the Peninsula was "rapidly carried out" once begun, but that there had been "an unexpected delay in commencing it." That was good enough for Stanton, who regaled Smith and Welles with the document as an indictment of McClellan's crimes. When Smith departed, sufficiently convinced, Stanton dropped his voice melodramatically and questioned Welles about his rebuff to Chase, revealing that Chase had come straightaway to report it. Welles reiterated his argument about a frank exchange of ideas in executive conference, and suggested that the polling of cabinet members ahead of time constituted a discourtesy to the president.[86]

On Monday morning, September 1, Attorney General Bates wrote out a new version of the petition, deleting the insinuation of disloyalty that Welles had criticized and replacing it with the amorphous suspicion that it was not "safe" to retain McClellan in command. Chase hinted that the revision only reflected a pragmatic effort at consensus, for he felt that McClellan had willfully withheld reinforcements and ammunition from Pope, and deserved execution. Stanton, Chase, Smith, and Bates all signed it — Bates at the very bottom, well away from the others, lest he be mistaken for the instigator. William Seward was out of town, and Welles again demurred, though he promised to express his opinion in council. Again Welles chastised Chase for conspiring with Stanton to manipulate the president with preconceived, "ex parte" determinations. Chase admitted that he hoped Lincoln would view the petition as an ultimatum: either the president would summarily dismiss McClellan or the cabinet would "be broken up" after the fashion of parliamentary governments. Lincoln routinely ignored the advice of his cabinet, Chase protested; it took something as drastic as the ministers' memorial to fix his attention. Though disappointed not to have the navy secretary's signature, Chase and Stanton decided that four signatures and one promise of vocal support gave them enough ammunition to confront the president in their cabinet meeting the next day.[87]

Even as Chase plied his arguments, McClellan crossed the Long Bridge into Washington. At army headquarters Halleck informed him that he would be given command of the Washington defenses. For the previous week McClellan had faced the likelihood that he would be shelved outright: in a letter to his wife he pretended to take his latest assignment reluctantly, but he accepted it in the obvious hope of expanding that defensive role. He immediately suggested to Halleck that some competent person ought to ride out to Pope's army "for the purpose of ascertaining the exact condition of affairs," perhaps hoping that he would seem the logical choice, but Halleck sent a staff colonel.[88]

In the afternoon, at Halleck's solicitation, McClellan made his way to Halleck's own residence, where President Lincoln waited to see him with the assurance of privacy. Lincoln went straight to the point, revealing the widespread belief, sparked by snide comments and fanned by Pope's self-serving aspersions, that the reinforcements from the Army of the Potomac were not supporting Pope as diligently as their duty demanded and the country deserved. McClellan, who surely understood the portentous implications of such a charge, said he doubted his soldiers would deny loyal service to Pope, whatever they might think of him as a general or as a man. He agreed nonetheless to telegraph his most intimate subordinate, Fitz John Porter, and ask him to spread the word to all their friends that McClellan only wished them to do their whole duty for Pope, as they would have for him. It was, McClellan wrote, "the last request I have to make of them," as though his new assignment to the city's defenses marked his formal relief from command of the field army. Instead, Lincoln's inquiry on that disturbing point amounted to an examination for possible reinstatement.[89]

At the breakfast hour the following morning, the president appeared with Halleck at the corner of H Street and Twelfth, knocking at the door of McClellan's Washington home. The two were troubled by a report that Halleck's staff colonel had brought back from Fairfax Court House: Pope's army appeared to be just as deeply demoralized as everyone had feared, and was streaming in abject retreat toward Washington with vast clouds of stragglers hovering on all sides. Halleck and the president wished McClellan to gather the troops in as they arrived, organize them, and assign them to appropriate positions in the defenses. Without quite saying it, they were asking him to resume command of everything — the Army of the Potomac as well as the Army of Virginia. The vain and ambitious young general voraciously agreed, doubtless persuading himself that he did so with a convincing air of humility. Halleck issued the order from army headquarters, but the ink had hardly dried before Edwin Stanton learned of it.[90]

The secretary of war therefore entered the cabinet meeting agitated and angry. Welles described Stanton's voice as hushed and quavering when, before the president arrived, he informed his fellow members of McClellan's appointment. Although they may not have comprehended yet that the new assignment would essentially return McClellan to command of the army, the others released a gasp of surprise. Then Lincoln sauntered in and caught the drift of the conversation. At first he tried to soothe them with the technicality that McClellan was merely arranging the defense, but Chase interjected that any good engineer officer could do that; then Stanton objected that the president had essentially promoted McClellan to be second in command of the army, below only Halleck. Lincoln reminded them that McClellan was a good engineer himself, and knew the territory from his many months in charge of it. He might be the wrong man for an offensive campaign, but he could restore the army's morale and organization and defend the city better than anyone else. Montgomery Blair, McClellan's only ally in the cabinet that day, added that no other general could claim more of the troops' confidence than their Little Mac.[91]

It was true that McClellan owned the confidence — and the affection — of the vast majority of his men. That was partly because he went about the business of war deliberately, using heavy ordnance and careful planning to contain and defeat the enemy rather than wasting his men's lives in medieval frontal assaults. McClellan's popularity among the troops also originated in a political affinity that Postmaster General Blair probably understood better than any other cabinet member. McClellan stood for a war to restore the Union, rather than a crusade to snuff out slavery and turn the social order on its head. The soldiers who criticized or mistrusted McClellan tended to be those who harbored a particular aversion to slavery, but they appear to have been significantly outnumbered by the admirers of McClellan, who fought for "the Constitution as it is, and the Union as it was."[92]

Halleck had warned the president that if Pope's army poured into the city as the undisciplined mob that filled the road to Fairfax, Washington was lost. Stanton shared that concern, and had ordered the contents of the Washington arsenal shipped to New York, but Welles doubted that there was any real danger to the capital. Bates remarked that there were plenty of troops available to man the fortifications, and that they would see a wonderful opportunity to strike Lee's army from behind if it made any dash into Maryland. As the cabinet argument continued, the president seemed to collapse, as though in despair, and throw himself on the mercy of his ministers. The decision had caused him enormous anxiety, he explained, because he knew how earnest they were. Lincoln appears not to have been candid enough to confess that he, too, shared Chase's suspicion that McClellan had deliberately foiled Pope, but he begged them to understand his morbid fear for the safety of the national capital; that very day he had issued an order to organize the city's clerks and public-works employees into infantry companies, betraying a desperation worthy of the last ditch. The question of McClellan had caused him such distress, he claimed, that he was willing to resign the presidency — he said he "felt almost ready to hang himself." Chase's observation about the president's disdain for their advice seemed confirmed: the decision had already been made, and the orders had been issued. Despite near-mutiny in the cabinet, there would be no revocation, at least for the present. The conspirators left the meeting in silent defeat.[93]

Riding together, John Pope and Irvin McDowell guided their bedraggled army up the Leesburg Turnpike a few hours later. McClellan had sent instructions ahead to Pope for the distribution of his troops, and the Second, Third, and Sixth Corps had already dropped off to make camp around Alexandria. The somber pair of major generals continued up the pike at the head of a column consisting of McDowell's corps, Porter's, and a division under Darius Couch. As they passed Upton's Hill the unfinished dome of the United States Capitol hove into sight, off to their right, and a little farther on a cluster of mounted men waited by the roadside near Fort Buffalo. Pope's topographer recognized the foremost of the horsemen as General McClellan, but neither Pope nor McDowell gave him the slightest glance as they turned toward a prospective bivouac at Ball's Crossroads. Then someone pointed McClellan out to them, and they trotted over to report themselves for duty.[94]

Pope already knew that McClellan had prevailed, but this was the first inkling of his resurrection for most of those present. Perhaps it was the order of salutes that gave it away: by lifting his fingertips to the brim of his cap first and dropping them only after McClellan reciprocated, Pope would have revealed the change of command, for any soldier instantly recognized such a gesture of subordination. Possibly someone overheard the tone of their conversation, with McClellan dictating and Pope acknowledging. One way or another, it suddenly became clear that McClellan had returned to command the troops, and word spread along the lines. In what must have been John Pope's worst moment of humiliation, cheers suddenly rose from the long, ragged ranks behind him — cheers at the realization that McClellan had superseded him. Here was flattery that George McClellan could not ignore, and he cantered down the road in the direction of the cheering, which only initiated more of it. The news passed from brigade to brigade, from the front of the column to the rear, and into the nearby camps, where men asked what all the fuss meant. Their questions brought answers that sent more volleys of joyous shouts bounding like a fireball across the tops of a burning pine forest, echoing over the hills all the way to Alexandria in a display that remained unforgettable even to the last aged eyewitnesses of that cheering generation. Not again would that army know such elation until it reached a place called Appomattox, which many thousands of those soldiers would never live to see.[95]

6

In Scarlet Maryland

⟨⟩ ROBERT E. LEE HAD TURNED the tide of war in the East as abruptly as George Washington's New Jersey campaign had reversed British fortunes in the winter of 1777, and John Pope's catastrophe marked only the worst of a plague of troubles facing the federal government in the opening days of September. In barely three months the soaring hopes of complete Union triumph had all but collapsed.

The news of a frightening disaster in Kentucky reached the capital on the evening of September 1, while Abraham Lincoln made his anguished decision to turn the entire Washington army back over to George McClellan. Kirby Smith's Confederate army had come crashing over the mountains from Barboursville, materializing like an apparition in the Bluegrass on August 30. While Pope's army abandoned the field at Bull Run, Smith inflicted an even worse proportional defeat at Richmond, Kentucky, a mere twenty miles south of Lexington. With three brigades he fell on a Union division and effectively eliminated it, leaving more than a thousand of the 6,500 or so Federals dead or wounded; he captured most of the rest, including their field commander. Barely a thousand escaped altogether. The 12th Indiana alone lost 781 men, mostly as prisoners. Major General William Nelson hurried to the battlefield in the afternoon and tried to buy time by rallying the remnants — mainly untrained recruits — but they broke within moments and General Nelson went back to Lexington with a bullet in his leg while Southern cavalry rounded up his fugitives. The Ball's Bluff debacle of 1861 paled by comparison, and the fight might have inflicted far more shock nationwide had the public senses not already been dulled by the devastating casualties in

Virginia. The impact fell heavily enough in Kentucky, though. Smith paroled nearly five thousand prisoners, sending them out of the war until Northern prisons disgorged their equivalents in Southern captives; he also picked up nine thousand small arms, nine pieces of artillery, and some much-needed supplies, besides pitching Kentucky into a panic, all at a cost of only 451 Confederate casualties.[1]

Reports from Bowling Green indicated, prematurely, that Simon Bolivar Buckner, the antebellum commander of Kentucky's State Guard, was leading another column of Confederates toward Louisville. The legislature had fled Frankfort to reconvene in Louisville, and one of Lincoln's acquaintances there wired the president on the afternoon of September 1 to warn that the state would be lost entirely if Don Carlos Buell's Army of the Ohio did not come up from Tennessee. The telegram arrived in Washington at 9:15 that night, while Lincoln awaited the demoralized survivors of Pope's army.[2] Smith's success at Richmond also sealed off a large Union division at Cumberland Gap, which soon began to run low on rations when converging Southern columns surrounded it. "Our armies seem to be beaten everywhere," mourned a Regular Army captain who barely escaped that snare.[3]

Confederate cavalry was also running roughshod over western Virginia. On the day of the Confederate victories at Manassas and Richmond, troopers under Albert Jenkins captured the town of Buckhannon, along with five thousand rifles, and then proceeded for the Ohio River, where in a few days they planted the first Confederate flag ever to fly over Buckeye soil. By Tuesday morning, September 2, an informant reported another Southern column marching on Winchester, Virginia, purportedly twenty thousand strong. Halleck sent orders to the Union commander at that place to fall back on Harper's Ferry — which he did, after destroying tons of costly provisions and ammunition. At the same time, down at the Aquia Creek landing, Burnside rushed to evacuate the troops and stores from isolated Falmouth; the colonel he left in command of the rear guard put the torch to a fortune in government materials before taking his leave.[4]

Enemies appeared to be striking everywhere simultaneously. Telegrams reported Texas, Louisiana, and Arkansas Confederates gathering to invade southwestern Missouri, from which one foray was just being driven. Immigrants in the regular wagon trains rolling between Fort Leavenworth and Oregon, who usually worried most about Indians, rattlesnakes, and tarantulas, began posting guards that summer against armed bands of Southern sympathizers even on the Platte River in central Nebraska. Just across the border in Dakota Territory the soldiers at Fort Randall chased hopelessly after Confederate guerrillas who were alleged to infest the Platte country and the upper Missouri, where in late August they were blamed for capturing the regular packet and interrupting all travel on the river. As far up the Platte as Fort Laramie, in Wyoming Territory, a Union general feared that Southern agents had been agitating the Plains tribes against United States authority.[5]

A serious uprising had broken out among Minnesota's Sioux while Pope and Lee danced about the forks of the Rappahannock. Paper currency had enabled traders at the Lower Sioux Agency along the Minnesota River to cheat their illiterate Santee clients far more efficiently than with gold coin, and tempers soared. Rumors hinted that war had left the Great White Father too little gold to keep the promises exchanged for the Santees' Minnesota lands, and then in July the agency failed to pay the tribe's annuity. The agents refused to give the Santee food on credit, and trader Andrew Merrick rebuffed one pleading Sioux with the advice that he and his starving family could eat prairie grass. On August 17 a party of hungry Santee youths killed a settler's cow near Acton, in Meeker County, and when the settler interceded they also killed him, his wife, their adopted daughter, and three visitors. Chief Little Crow tried to convince his people to turn the killers over to the army, but the fear of collective retribution and the accumulated indignities suffered by the Sioux turned the incident into a widespread revolt.[6]

War parties attacked the Lower Agency settlement on August 18, killing six white men including Merrick, whose mouth one of the Sioux stuffed full of grass. Fifty men of the 5th Minnesota marched to the rescue from Fort Ridgely, several miles down the Minnesota River, but more than half of them perished in an ambush at Redwood Ferry. Another company of the 5th Minnesota reinforced Ridgely, and a company of recruits took refuge there on their way to enlist at Fort Snelling. Then other bands attacked Leavenworth, Milford, and Courtland. By August 19 the uprising had spread to Nicollet, Cottonwood, and Murray counties. Eventually the fighting claimed victims in Yellow Medicine County, and Jackson; two dozen or more settlers died at distant Lake Shetek. Some three hundred Sioux struck New Ulm that afternoon, annihilating a refugee party headed there while citizens barricaded the outer streets, staving off several attacks.[7]

The Sioux who attacked New Ulm eventually turned on Fort Ridgely. Soldiers estimated that the Sioux numbered as many as 500, but the garrison, no more than 130 strong, weathered nine days of siege. Whites within a forty-mile radius of the Lower Agency gathered together for protection or gravitated to Fort Ridgely, New Ulm, and Mankato. Citizens of Hutchinson started building their own fort. Some simply abandoned their homesteads for safer climes, paying for their board with daily labor.[8] The entire Sioux nation seemed primed for war against anyone that August: Yankton Sioux from Dakota Territory fell on Pawnees in eastern Nebraska while their Santee cousins terrorized Minnesota as far north as Fort Abercrombie, way down the Red River on the Dakota border. Dakota Territory braced itself, and settlers in Yankton started building a blockhouse in the middle of town. It was, wrote an agitated woman in Anoka, the worst Indian trouble in thirty years, and the Chippewas of the north seemed likely to join the rebellion. President Lincoln's private secretary visited the Chippewa leaders, but returned without reaching any agreement, and for a few days he feared that his party might suffer the fate of the agents along the Minnesota River.[9]

In apparent violation of the cartel on prisoner exchanges, Henry Halleck ordered a paroled Minnesota regiment up from St. Louis to help quell the revolt. Minnesota governor Alexander Ramsey — himself one of those agents who had approved dubious dealings at Sioux trading posts — dispatched the incomplete 6th Minnesota. He sought and obtained the rare permission to call out a mounted regiment of three-month militia, and appealed for a postponement of the militia draft that was scheduled for late in the month, claiming that half the population of the state had fled their homes. Minnesota and Wisconsin recruits found themselves diverted to the Indian war, much to the grief of one Wisconsin teenager who had enlisted to fight rebels, and had always enjoyed good relations with his Chippewa and Ojibway neighbors. The Sioux uprising occupied seven new infantry regiments and part of another for most of the rest of the year, depriving the army of an entire division that might have operated against Confederate armies.[10]

Halleck used paroled prisoners like the Minnesota regiment to neutralize that manpower drain. Whole regiments captured in the Kentucky campaign or by Lee's army came north for active campaigning against the Plains tribes or as supplementary garrison troops around the camps of Southern prisoners, liberating much of the regular guard details for field service. While encamped alongside Confederate prisoners at Chicago and Indianapolis, the paroled men were also expected to continue their training, all of which seemed to conflict with the terms of their paroles, and often they refused on the grounds that violation of their oath could be punishable by execution: understandably, they lobbied to be sent home until exchanged for equivalent Confederate prisoners. Less cohesive contingents of paroled prisoners enjoyed that respite, and the provisions of the cartel allowed for little more, but in its desperation to maintain overwhelming numerical superiority the government clung jealously to the service of every uniformed man.[11]

Reinforcements were on the way: friction between the impending draft and the rising bounties had finally ignited a reasonable facsimile of patriotic fervor among Northern men. Each state clustered new regiments in boisterous camps of instruction like those that had drawn giddy throngs of spectators in 1861, although the new camps included stronger guard details to discourage the escape of bounty jumpers. Washington teemed with fresh, deep-blue uniforms, and Henry Halleck complained that he spent most of his time arranging their disposition. On the last day of August, while the Army of Virginia caught its breath at Centreville, the defenses of Washington included thirty-four regiments of infantry, cavalry, and heavy artillery, amounting probably to fewer than twenty-eight thousand men. Twenty-four of those regiments, perhaps twenty-one thousand men, had left home only a few days before. Some of the infantry carried no ammunition at all, while others had drawn only five rounds apiece. Such shortcomings tormented Halleck and President Lincoln, and helped explain McClellan's reluctance to forward the last divisions of the Army of the Potomac to Pope from Alexandria.[12]

The veterans pouring back into Washington far outnumbered the raw levies, but the futility of their sacrifices had afflicted them with a debilitating gloom. Standing on the ramparts of one of the forts, one veteran in command of a new company watched his former comrades streaming past by the thousands, "in great demoralization." Most blamed it on poor leadership from either Washington bigwigs or the generals they had made. A Michigan soldier joked that without better commanders he would be home in a couple of months, because Stonewall Jackson would probably drive them that far north, while a New York captain ranted bitterly over the butchery that bought undeserving generals the praise of ignorant, insensitive politicians — among whom he evidently included the president. Exhausted soldiers rejoiced in the first days of September at the unfounded rumor that McClellan had been restored to command of all the armies and that Halleck had superseded Edwin Stanton as secretary of war.[13]

An Ohio businessman visiting the capital had promised a report to a Zanesville newspaper editor, but he dared send nothing for publication lest it incite panic. Privately he informed the editor that no one believed there was a general capable of leading the Northern army to victory. As he saw it, Lincoln had restored McClellan to the defense of Washington just to avoid a mutiny of the army. The country was in a shambles, he warned, while Secretary Stanton, their fellow Ohioan, was "a failure & no mistake." The battlefield fumbling and the command shuffling shook the confidence of Union soldiers as far away as the lower Mississippi, where Confederate fortunes shone less brilliantly.[14]

Colonel Orlando Poe, who led a brigade in the lamented Kearny's division, illustrated the frustration felt by thousands of Union soldiers at finding themselves right back in the camps from which they had undertaken their grand campaign, six months and fifty thousand casualties before. "I believe the war is nearly over," Poe confided to his wife on September 4. "I am more desponding now than ever before." The colonel, a West Pointer capable of recognizing the extent of their disaster, expected Lee to strike again, only harder, and he wondered whether McClellan himself would be able to save the country now. A captain deplored the imbeciles at the heads of both army and government, despairing of success. Brigadier General John Sedgwick felt even more certainly that the Union cause was lost: in a letter written the same day as Poe's, Sedgwick seemed to acknowledge that Confederate armies had done everything that should have been necessary to win their country's independence. All that was left, he supposed, was negotiation over where to draw the line between the old nation and the new.[15]

By their absence the enlisted men demonstrated concurrence with those officers. To the dismay of Lincoln and the cabinet, not half the men on the rolls of the Army of Virginia or the Army of the Potomac could be found ready for duty. Officers and men alike had overstayed furloughs, failed to return to their units when separated on the march, or deliberately walked away from their camps or hospitals. The colonel of the 22nd New York had lingered in Washington while Stonewall Jackson battered his regiment at the railroad cut; a private in the 2nd U.S. Sharpshooters "got tired out" on the march, dropping out of the ranks and making his way to Alexandria despite his professed fatigue. Even many of those borne on the rosters as prisoners of war had fallen behind specifically to be captured, so they could go home on parole until they were exchanged. Hundreds of paroled men had sauntered into Washington by Wednesday.[16]

Stoics here and there might grit their teeth and preach grim determination, but the volume of pessimistic correspondence from those first days of September hints that few of the troops falling back on Washington held out much hope for the military situation, at least without much better leadership and an enormous infusion of men and money.[17] The discouragement of the veterans infected the new recruits, who conveyed it to the home front in letters oozing regret at having forsaken family and friends for a cause that appeared to be lost.[18] Those tales of apparently fruitless bloodshed and inept leadership at least contributed to an apparent wave of depression among the women of Union households that September.[19]

Because McClellan had been withdrawn from the Peninsula, it seemed to many civilians that Lee had trounced him, too, leaving Second Bull Run to stand as a second consecutive defeat. George Templeton Strong, who was younger than many privates in the ranks, deplored the military situation from the comfort of his Gramercy Park townhouse. Observing that the eastern army had sought refuge in "its old burrows," where he feared that it might go into early hibernation, Strong echoed Colonel Poe's observation about having lost all the ground gained since spring, after the expenditure of so much blood and treasure. Worse yet, as Strong saw it, Confederate armies threatened Missouri, Cincinnati, and Maryland. Like the secretary of the navy, Strong blamed Edwin Stanton both for orchestrating the battlefield failures and for initiating the ruinous rivalry between the McClellan and Pope factions.[20]

Salmon Chase mentioned to fellow secretary Gideon Welles that week that he feared the country was "ruined," and that "everything was going wrong." His concern emanated from the restoration of McClellan, and perhaps from the attendant implication that Lincoln might shelve his preliminary proclamation on slavery, but there were plenty of men in all stations who thought the war to save the Union had been lost and that it was time to bring the fighting to a negotiated conclusion. Hiram Barney, the Treasury Department's collector of revenue for New York City, came to Washington early in September with reports that "some very reliable men" had lost heart in the war. Barney, himself as ardent an abolitionist as Chase, specifically named Cassius Clay, the erstwhile minister to Russia. Clay had been an outspoken antislavery man in Kentucky when such opinions were worth one's life, and he had clung to the Union like varnish to a mast, but now Barney said Clay was mulling armistice and compromise. Certain that Barney had misunderstood Clay, the president dismissed that characterization out of hand.[21]

Perhaps there had been some misunderstanding, but Lincoln seemed prone to denial at that juncture. Sometime during the crisis of early September he retired to his office and composed a memorandum in which he attributed the war to divine will. "I am almost ready to say this is probably true —" he mused, "that God wills this contest, and wills that it shall not end yet." The document may have been intended as part of a letter, or as the preamble to a proclamation, for Lincoln lacked the diarist's habit, but whatever its literary purpose it suggested a perfectly human rationale against guilt. Although known among his closest friends for an absence of religious fervor, Lincoln had found biblical analogy and allusion effective mechanisms for public address, and now the doctrine of preordination may have yielded him some personal comfort as well as political cover. If the death and destruction of the past seventeen months had arisen from the will of some supernatural power, then Abraham Lincoln need not regret having orchestrated the confrontation that opened the struggle, and his renowned stubbornness bore no responsibility for the decision to persist in it when victory seemed impossible.[22]

The horror and hopelessness caused some officers with the Army of the Potomac to wonder that anyone at home wanted to join them at all — and most men of military age still did not, despite all the bulging new regiments. James Crosby, an aspiring minister just out of Yale, showed little enthusiasm for a conflict that Lincoln ascribed to God's will. Crosby remarked wryly to a classmate that the war did not appear to be progressing very successfully, and that gave him every excuse to indulge his fundamental reluctance to serve. "I shall not volunteer under this call," Crosby concluded. Most of the eligible Northern population evidently felt the same, and many of those who did answer that call left evidence that money exerted considerable influence on their decisions.[23]

Others responded primarily from a delayed sense of duty, and the simultaneous retreats from the James and the Rapidan moved another Yale graduate to come to his country's aid. Edward Wightman, the recipient of both bachelor's and master's degrees, left his job and enlisted as a private at the height of Pope's trials along Bull Run. Wightman had not stepped forward earlier because he thought the army would be able to glean every soldier it needed from the teeming masses of unemployed, but he had not anticipated the conflict lasting long enough to absorb all that surplus labor. Many thousands more new soldiers like Wightman — fifteen times as many as surrounded Washington at the close of August — drilled and dawdled in their regimental rendezvous from Bangor, Maine, to Fort Leavenworth, finding camp life delightful before the onset of regular duty or active campaigning. For some of those recruits, the time was growing short: the stifled dread of departure "for the seat of war" would come in a couple of days, or perhaps a week. Others would wait another month, two months, or more, while unpopular or unlucky officers struggled in vain to complete their companies.[24]

Late in August a Boston merchant named Oliver Peabody felt called to take arms — but only for nine months, and at no rank lower than captain. Establishing his recruiting headquarters in a hotel on the coast of Massachusetts, he aimed primarily for Nantucket sailors, whose custom of leaving home for years at a time might make a nine-month enlistment seem like a little vacation. Recruits came slowly early in September, especially with the news of deadly Union defeats dominating the newspapers, but with the possibility of a draft within the next few weeks Peabody felt no inclination to quit; instead, he lit upon the idea of paying ten dollars a head for squads of men who had agreed to enlist with less successful recruiters. Within a week he presented eighty men healthy enough to pass for soldiers, and claimed his place as their captain. The other companies took weeks longer to complete, and in the scramble for field commissions Peabody seized the second spot of lieutenant colonel, but the regiment still lay in camp outside Boston at the beginning of November.[25]

The delay inherent in recruiting and organizing a new regiment made them all the more appealing to the sensible man who preferred to postpone combat as long as possible. Recruits reasoned that they would be assigned to guard and garrison duty, relieving older troops who would be sent to the front, and many of those in the new units supposed that the war might be over by the time they took the field. A Massachusetts lieutenant recruiting in Cambridge that September for the shrunken ranks of his veteran company groused about the difficulty of persuading men to enlist in an old regiment, accurately supposing that "the cowards dare not Volunteer for them." When a squad of Irish recruits did enroll for the bloodied 9th Massachusetts, they steadfastly refused to leave the depot until they saw the last dollar due on their bounties.[26]

After signing the roll of a prospective company, the would-be soldier usually came home until his company had been filled, which might take a few days or weeks. Once completed, each company repaired to the rendezvous, somewhere within the home state, and remained there until the field officers had been appointed and the entire regiment had been mustered. Customarily that was followed by a furlough of two or three days, during which the new troops went home one last time, in uniform, or received visitors at the camp. Then it was off to a major mobilization center like Washington, Cairo, or (especially after Kirby Smith's Confederates waltzed into Lexington, on September 2) Cincinnati. The host community frequently organized a valedictory salute for the new regiment as it marched from the rendezvous to the rail depot or steamboat landing, with bands blaring and citizens cheering along the way. Most of the men who swarmed to the new regiments had never left their families for any extended period. Even for those who could still doubt or deny the increasingly obvious chance that a departing soldier might never return, the anticipation of lengthy separations tormented husbands and wives at each successive parting.[27]

The Concord rail depot presented an "inexpressibly sad" scene when the 9th New Hampshire entrained for war on August 25; weeping relatives surrounded each soldier as he pulled away from clutching fingers. One of Connecticut's nine-month regiments broke camp below Hartford in a violent downpour, but visitors walked and rode in to say their fare-wells, heedless of the weather. Rain failed to disguise the tears of mothers and wives who leaned from carriages for one more embrace.[28] Cold rain also marred the departure of the 42nd Massachusetts: one private who would fall into enemy hands within six weeks found it excruciating to part from his wife. Friends and relatives descended on the 23rd Wisconsin at Camp Randall, near Madison, as the regiment marched off to Cincinnati, and many of them seemed unable to give their young men up; some of them would not let go of their soldiers until stronger hands tore them away. The family of one Wisconsin recruit who left Baraboo for Camp Randall "could hardly stand it," observed a friend who came along; "it feels as though it is the last time they will see him." An Illinois soldier's wife could not conceal her sadness when she made her final visit to him in the camp at Peoria, and the same sadness struck him as the regiment marched to the depot a week later, when he caught what he supposed might be his last earthly glimpse of her in the crowded street.[29]

Each goodbye seemed worse than the last, as many a husband re-marked after coming back to camp. "I have felt more homesick since I got back to my Regiment than I ever did before," admitted an Ohio colonel late in August, after a brief visit home. "It has a bad effect on a soldier to bask under his own vine and fig for a few days and then be [sent] back to the field again." Now and then even the loneliest husband thought twice before subjecting himself and his family to that final furlough, especially when the cost of round-trip passage home cut so deeply into the bounty for which he gambled his life. An ill-educated Vermonter whose crude missives exuded passion for his wife expressed intense sorrow at not hav-ing seen her before his regiment left for Washington, but in lieu of an em-brace he sent her thirty dollars, much of which he would otherwise have expended on train fare.[30]

More painful, perhaps, than the longing of those who declined the last opportunity to look upon their partners' faces was the disappointment of those whose efforts were foiled by accident. A Wisconsin woman who heard that her husband's regiment was about to muster for service impet-uously harnessed their gelding for the two-day trip to the state capital with a friend, stopping overnight at the home of an acquaintance. Her husband was not with his company when she arrived, but she made the best of the trip and toured the state buildings; at the insane asylum she selected a spot for herself, she said, "for if he gets killed probably I shall go there." When she returned home she discovered that the same impulsive-ness had stricken him, and, ignorant of her plans, he had dashed home during her absence, missing her there as well as on the way back.[31]

Torn from a domestic tenderness they may never have fully appreciated before, rough men crouched over cracker boxes and labored to express sentiments for which they frequently lacked words. "Maria," wrote a musician in a New Hampshire regiment, nine days after he last saw his bride, "I never knew how precious you were to me until the separation came." Encamped with his new artillery battery, Corporal Charles Benton explained to his wife that he, too, never "new" until then how much he loved her.[32]

The women who were left at home may have found it easier to describe their yearning. "You know how I am going to suffer during these years of absence," predicted Corporal Benton's wife, a few weeks into his three-year enlistment — and if he did not know then, he soon learned. "Charlie darling, can't you come home?" she asked, two days later. "Write to me, if you have any pity for me." Lucinda Lewis wept constantly when her husband joined the cavalry at the end of that summer, alluding so poignantly to her tears that he begged her to stop. An impoverished Iowa farm wife managed greater calm: "I have struggled hard to give you up Orlando," she informed the husband she would never see again, consigning him in vain to divine protection. Another Iowa soldier had unwittingly traded his own best chance at marriage for an enlistment bounty, learning by letter only after his departure that the girl he adored reciprocated his affection.[33]

Once Edwin Wentworth had convinced his wife that he had done well, financially, to enlist in the 37th Massachusetts, he set to work easing her fears about his safety. First, he bought a steel vest warranted to stop bullets. Next he consoled her with the rationale that the war could not possibly last much longer. A New Hampshire sergeant tried the same combination, consulting his wife on the purchase of a bulletproof vest that did no more to save him than Wentworth's did; then, just before his regiment left the state, he instructed her to "keep up good spirits, for I shall probably be back in the spring, if not sooner," because everyone said the fighting was nearly over.[34] Seventeen months into the war, that belief in a quick end remained a common delusion among recruits who had not yet encountered the disillusioned veterans at the front. An Iowan who joined the cavalry in early September could not believe the war would last another six months with so many troops turning out; a month later another recruit still expected the war to end that winter, and assured his wife that he would be home by March; a Norwegian lad promised to come home with a lot of money by spring — when, as everyone seemed certain, the war would end.[35]

Men had been volunteering under that misapprehension since the opening guns. Alfred White typified the 1861 recruit: he departed with the 2nd Massachusetts less than six weeks after Fort Sumter, but he admitted to his wife in the summer of 1862 that he never expected to be away from home through a second Fourth of July. Some editors and generals agreed with such optimists: John Hatch thought all the recruits should go into the old regiments because the new ones would be useless for six months, by which time he expected the war to be over.[36] Union soldiers could still see an early end even after Pope's spectacular defeat — some because of the massive army that seemed to be gathering, and some because they saw Southern victory looming.[37]

The impression of impending Confederate victory flourished vigorously before September's first week came to an end. Lee shrank from the imposing Washington defenses toward Leesburg, eyeing the fords of the upper Potomac. Now was the time to liberate Maryland, he informed Jefferson Davis: unless Davis entertained objections (which there would not be sufficient time to communicate), Lee intended to enter that state and, if possible, raid into Pennsylvania to let Northern citizens feel the burden of a hostile army. By Friday morning the White House heard confused rumors that Stonewall Jackson had crossed into Maryland, and when President Lincoln ambled over to the War Department he found the rumors given full credit. The only doubt seemed to arise from the cavalry's failure to pick up any of Jackson's stragglers from the Maryland side, but Lee had issued strict instructions to prevent straggling in a state that he wished to woo for the Confederacy. Jackson had gone a step further by ordering the summary execution of any man who left the ranks without permission.[38]

The invasion of Maryland required Lincoln to select a new field general immediately, in addition to a commander for the Washington defenses: he might abide yielding control of Confederate territory, but it would hardly do to cower inside the forts while a Southern army dined on the bounty of a loyal state. Returning from his Friday-morning visit to the War Department, Lincoln convened his cabinet and circulated the document that John Pope had presented as a report of his tenure at the head of the Army of Virginia. Like most people who operate at arm's length from the truth, Pope found someone else to blame for all his blunders, accusing George McClellan, Fitz John Porter, William Franklin, and one of Porter's division commanders of deliberately undermining his campaign. Lincoln acknowledged Pope's mendacity to the cabinet officers, who all knew that Postmaster General Blair considered Pope a habitual liar, but still they seemed not to question the validity of Pope's allegations. The president knew nothing of Pope's bullheaded refusal to accept the intelligence of Longstreet's early arrival at Bull Run, and he frankly believed the general's excuses, supposing that a few thousand more troops on August 30 would have somehow overcome Pope's psychological deficiencies. Lincoln therefore ordered all the accused generals but McClellan suspended from command pending a court of inquiry. The cabinet officers did recognize Pope's report for an injudicious, partisan provocation, though, and chose to suppress it. Lincoln also seemed to realize the need to suppress Pope, although not in the manner that Robert E. Lee had intended. The president directed Stanton to create a vast new military department encompassing Wisconsin, Minnesota, Iowa, and all the territories between Kansas and Canada, where Pope's pride could be salvaged among soldiers who did not yet hate him and where, perhaps, failure might cost less.[39]

That eliminated Pope as a leader for the field army, if his name had ever occurred to anyone. Next came Ambrose Burnside, the conqueror of the North Carolina sounds. Lincoln summoned Burnside and tried again to persuade him to accept command of the army, but Burnside declined as firmly as he had in July, and on the same grounds: that only McClellan owned the capacity and experience to manage so large a force. Thus, on Saturday morning, September 6, the president collected General Halleck at the War Department and they both repaired to McClellan's house. There Lincoln asked McClellan to take command of the army that went after Lee, and the young general bolted into action. He brought the preponderance of the army north of the Potomac, collected intelligence from upriver, distributed three dozen more new regiments to the various corps, and amalgamated Pope's defunct Army of Virginia into his own Army of the Potomac. He begged the restoration of his suspended generals, arguing that he needed them if he was to move immediately against the enemy, and he asked to have Joe Hooker promoted to the command of McDowell's corps, since McDowell had also been relieved to await a court of inquiry. Lincoln, Stanton, and Halleck gave McClellan everything he asked for.[40]

The next morning John Pope donned civilian clothing and boarded a train for Minnesota, ignored by all but those staff officers who accepted his offer of employment in the West. That evening Little Mac rode out of town with his own staff to lead the army upriver. Gideon Welles encountered him on his way out of the city, and their brief conversation served as the navy secretary's first notice of Lincoln's choice for the field command. The next morning Welles, who also doubted McClellan's fitness for command, must have broached the assignment with the president, but Lincoln disavowed the responsibility: McClellan had been Halleck's choice, said the president, as though unwilling to further offend his disapproving secretary. Lincoln evidently lapsed from his legendary honesty, though, for Halleck insisted under oath that the decision had been Lincoln's alone.

Halleck later told a roomful of demanding congressmen that he had had no idea who would take charge of the field army when he and Lincoln stepped into McClellan's house, adding that he had been surprised when Lincoln turned to McClellan and said, "General, you will take command of the forces in the field."[41]

The pursuit of Lee began with McClellan's departure, on September 7. Burnside took informal command of a wing of the army consisting of his old Ninth Corps, under Reno, and McDowell's old corps, given to Hooker as the First Corps. Burnside's long column passed Lincoln's summer retreat at the Soldiers' Home and headed through choking dust and heat for Leesborough and Goshen, whence he might blunt any drive toward Baltimore; Burnside arrived at Leesborough that Sunday evening, at dinnertime. Edwin Sumner lay at Rockville with his Second Corps and the corps that had belonged to Banks, arrayed to receive any attack by Lee.[42]

Joseph K. F. Mansfield, a white-haired veteran of forty years' service and finally a brigadier general, drew orders the next morning that would ultimately bring him command of Banks's corps. On his way to join McClellan he stopped at the Navy Department to visit his old Connecticut neighbor Secretary Welles, and the two shook hands as Mansfield departed; then he returned inexplicably, and the grizzled pair spoke a little further. Welles wished him success, and they shook hands again. "We may never meet again," remarked the general.[43]

As soon as the army threw its weight on the Maryland side of the river, rumors prompted Lincoln to begin worrying that Braxton Bragg had brought the main body of his Confederate army from Tennessee into the Shenandoah Valley, to join Lee or to attack Washington while Lee occupied McClellan. That rumor arose in Philadelphia and gained a moment's currency in Kentucky, perhaps because of Lincoln's own inquiries on the subject. That evening the normally overcautious McClellan appeased the president's concerns enough to warn the last two corps commanders on the Virginia shore to watch for a raid on Alexandria, but he let it be known that he put little faith in the fear.[44]

Washington remained safe from Lee. He preferred to threaten Pennsylvania, and did so quite effectively without sending a soldier into the state. Jackson's men swarmed into Frederick, Maryland, before lunch on September 6, with a few scattered bands blaring tunes that sounded faintly like "Dixie" and "Maryland, My Maryland." Hundreds of citizens crowded onto the Hagerstown train for Pennsylvania, where Governor Andrew Curtin bellowed for help, and McClellan detailed John Reynolds to organize Curtin's new regiments of volunteers and state militia. Leo Faller, a Carlisle man in Reynolds's Pennsylvania Reserves, deplored his fellow citizens' failure to turn out en masse against the invaders before they tainted home soil, for he feared the Confederates would treat Pennsylvania as harshly as Union soldiers had served Virginia. A bullet had creased Faller's scalp at Bull Run, but he insisted on joining the hunt for Lee.[45]

The rebel troops impressed the people of Frederick primarily with their odor. After nearly a month of relentless campaigning Jackson's men had reduced their clothing to filthy rags and worn themselves down to wiry scarecrows. Many lacked shoes, and the only uniform aspect of their clothing seemed to be the common coating of dust and grime: Lewis Steiner, a local doctor serving with the Sanitary Commission, observed that beneath the dirt the invaders seemed to wear only a slight preponderance of regulation grey over the yellowish "butternut" brown of home-dyed cloth. Most of them lacked knapsacks, the doctor said, and only rarely did he see a toothbrush dangling from a buttonhole. The most surprising feature of the Southern divisions that passed through his town over the next few days was the abundance of black men who accompanied the columns: he estimated them at no fewer than three thousand, dressed in both Confederate uniforms and captured Union clothing, and they carried whole arsenals of firearms and cutlery. A good many of them straddled horses or mules, rode with the artillery or the ambulances, or drove teams. Most of the Confederate transportation appeared to have changed allegiance: hundreds of wagon covers, as well as the carriage cheeks of scores of fieldpieces in the artillery batteries, bore the imprint of U.S. manufacture.[46]

Those redolent Confederates obviously treated the people of Maryland with far greater respect than Yankees had accorded Virginia civilians — better even than some Union soldiers treated the loyal civilians of western Maryland. Federal troops had jailed dissident editors and shut down opposition newspapers across Maryland, including the peace-preaching *Frederick Herald,* which had fallen silent exactly one year before, after denouncing such repression. In contrast, Southern officers placed a guard at the door of the loudly Unionist *Frederick Examiner,* protecting a more virulent critic than Union soldiers would ever have countenanced. Current copies of the *Examiner* provoked an indignant procession of Confederate soldiers to overwhelm that guard and toss the printing equipment into the street, but a provost detail quickly subdued them and forced them to replace everything before escorting them into arrest. That was the only transgression against the populace, save perhaps when officers required the owners of shoe stores to keep their establishments open until their stock had been sold out. Merchants regretfully accepted Confederate notes, correctly supposing that they had little choice in the matter, but some of the soldiers paid in greenbacks or even in gold. Quartermasters gathered up as much forage as they could find in the vicinity, paying for it exclusively in their foreign currency, but that was more than their Yankee counterparts generally did below the Mason-Dixon Line.[47]

Although Dr. Steiner characterized the Confederate occupation as a "reign of terror," he admitted that no citizen was harmed or insulted. He heard a secondhand tale (which may have inspired a legend surrounding a Frederick woman named Barbara Frietchie) of one old woman lurching out of her doorway and serving up a scathing tongue-lashing to Confederate soldiers dragging a United States flag in the dust, but the soldiers suffered her tirade in amused silence.[48]

The Confederates' restraint seemed all the more remarkable in the face of the population's preponderant hostility. Brigadier General Dorsey Pender, a North Carolinian who had recruited for the Confederate army in Baltimore before Fort Sumter, mistakenly supposed that western Marylanders divided evenly between Northern and Southern sentiments. In fact, Unionists of one stripe or another held a firm majority along the edge of the mountains. Colonel Bradley Johnson, a Frederick native who had commanded the 1st Maryland under Stonewall Jackson, tried to revive his disbanded regiment with a long-winded appeal for recruits, but his invitation drew little interest.[49]

Like most of Maryland, Frederick harbored proud and independent citizens who resented the federal government's heel on their necks, but few of them sympathized with secession and fewer still thought it worth fighting for. Perhaps because he had felt the full weight of that heel, John W. Heard, the quondam editor of the defunct *Herald*, sought permission to raise a company for Johnson's prospective new regiment, posting handbills calling for likeminded residents of Frederick County to support the liberation. Mortimer Kilgore, who had already cast his lot with the Confederacy, also used his Maryland roots to attract recruits for a cavalry company headed by a Poolesville native. A handful of adventurers did ride off with different cavalry troops, but would-be foot soldiers found no extant homegrown units to attract them. General Lee had been in Frederick less than a day when he concluded that the countryside would not rise to welcome his army. That conclusion may have eased any qualms about subsisting heavily on local producers.[50]

Loyal citizens of the Old Line State could have found more complaint with the Federal soldiers encamped two days' march southeast of Frederick. The fruitful fields and orchards of Maryland posed enormous temptation to soldiers accustomed to the barren, untended farmland of upper Virginia, and the new regiments showed a particular disregard for Marylanders' private property, making no apparent distinction between a loyal slave state and a seceded state. Some of them cut down peach, apple, and walnut trees to reach the fruit, and others thought nothing of taking chickens "prisoner." Jacob Cox's Kanawha Division of six veteran Ohio regiments reached Leesborough on its first day out from Washington, wading through a sea of bewildered troops looking for their scattered units and inveterate stragglers preying on the orchards and crops along the roadsides. Lieutenant Colonel Rutherford B. Hayes, of the 23rd Ohio, judged his own troops among the best behaved in the army, but when they camped in the stubble of a gleaned cornfield they stooped to raiding some nearby haystacks to soften their beds. Artillerymen and loyal Virginia cavalrymen attached to their brigade finished off those haystacks just as General Reno rode by, and Reno stormed in among them. He addressed them as "damned black sons of bitches," but Hayes shouldered his way through the throng to defend his men and the two officers exchanged some heated words before Reno rode off, highly incensed.[51]

Hayes and the Kanawha Division marched with what he called "Burnside's army," on the right wing. Burnside had also been assigned thousands of brand-new soldiers in clean, dark uniforms, fresh from home, and this introductory march weighed heavily on their tender feet. One contingent of recruits, stragglers, and skulkers spent six hours marching and marking time to cover no more than three miles toward Burnside's camp. Horace Lay, a Connecticut shoemaker, had only left Hartford ten days before when he awoke at Leesborough on Monday morning, and the last letter he would ever write to his wife explained that his heel had grown too blistered and swollen to fit into his boot. A corporal in the 9th New Hampshire whittled a couple of canes to ease the pressure on his tortured feet. The musicians of the same regiment's band had been left behind to pack up the tents, and it took some tall marching to overtake their comrades. They traveled stone-paved turnpikes, and the thin canvas shoes they had been issued gave them little protection against the hard, uneven surface. With their feet too bruised and blistered to go any farther, they sought indoor lodging that night in a store and a sawmill.[52]

Eyewitnesses at Frederick who had seen all of Lee's army calculated that it could not have exceeded sixty-four thousand, while hindsight suggests that it was weaker than that by one-quarter. In his own headquarters tent on a hillside just outside of Rockville, McClellan credited cavalry reports that his enemy numbered one hundred thousand, all safely ensconced on the right bank of the Monocacy River. In McClellan's imagination, or at least in his letters to his wife, that enemy grew by ten thousand a day. Judging his cautious opponent well, Lee took the otherwise enormous risk of dividing his inferior army into four detachments in the presence of the enemy. Jackson's corps was to march over Braddock Heights and South Mountain, turning to cross the Potomac again to interrupt the Baltimore & Ohio Railroad and capture the Union garrisons at Martinsburg and Harper's Ferry. Major General Lafayette McLaws would follow him with two divisions over Braddock Heights as far as Middletown, then veer toward Maryland Heights, which overlooked Harper's Ferry. Another division under John Walker would also cross into Virginia downriver from Harper's Ferry and threaten that vulnerable spot from Loudoun Heights, across the Shenandoah. The rest of the army, consisting of two divisions with Longstreet and one under Daniel Harvey Hill, would follow the National Road toward Boonsborough, where Longstreet would guard the trains while Hill lagged back to defend the passes over South Mountain. The details of that complicated choreography went out on Tuesday, September 9, as Special Orders No. 191.[53]

The hardest marching ended for McClellan's troops once he arranged his infantry in a line perpendicular to the Potomac, covering both Baltimore and Washington. From there he intended to advance by one parallel mountain range and river at a time. First would come Parr's Ridge, running from Damascus to Poolesville, and then the Monocacy River, which flowed just east of Frederick; after that, Braddock Heights marked the Catoctin Mountains, while South Mountain represented the Maryland extension of the Blue Ridge. At each landmark McClellan could be expected to hesitate, and it took him five days to sweep thirty miles forward to Frederick. By then the various fragments of Lee's army had strode confidently away, leaving a rear guard of cavalry.[54]

Burnside's Ninth Corps swung into town first, on the afternoon of September 12, sweeping across the broad meadows of the Monocacy valley in line of battle. The last Confederate horsemen were leaving town when they heard the hoofbeats of Burnside's mounted vanguard on the street behind them, at which they wheeled and charged. Men and women leaned from their windows to cheer the Federals, which only spurred the rebels to strike all the more ferociously before backing away from the stunned Yankees.[55]

A year before, Frederick had been the scene of shameful repression by Union soldiers who foiled a session of the state legislature by arresting every delegate deemed hostile to the Lincoln administration. The affront had offended even strong Unionists, but after a week's occupation by Confederates, Frederick citizens seemed willing to subordinate their state sovereignty to occupiers who would pay in U.S. currency, and for the first time in all their peregrinations against insurgent forces the men in blue found a chance to feel like heroes instead of villains. The people who had greeted the Southern army so coolly gave Union forces a resounding welcome, many of them weeping openly at their deliverance, and one fetching young lady darted into the street to ask General Burnside if she might kiss him. Burnside was only human, and emptied one of his stirrups so she could slip her toe into it and rise up to brush his famous whiskers.[56]

The burly, friendly Burnside seemed to be the man of the hour, enjoying greater affection from some troops than they demonstrated toward McClellan. "Burnside is the most popular general of the day," a fledgling Rhode Island lieutenant apprised his mother, relating how the general's approach could be detected half a mile away by the cheering that followed him on the line of march. The clamor would soar and subside with the intervals between brigades, increasing in volume with each repetition, and then Burnside would come along in his tall, distinctive hat, cantering ahead of his staff on a big bobtailed gelding. Another volleyed greeting would prompt him to lift the hat and wave it, revealing his great, bald dome.[57]

The Ninth Corps settled in that evening on the campsites vacated by Lee's army. Late the next morning McClellan's entourage arrived to a similar reception, with flags flying and handkerchiefs waving. Old men in antiquated uniforms stood and bowed as the head of each brigade passed. Men, women, and children mobbed McClellan as they had Burnside, demanding handshakes and presenting babies for kisses.[58] Then the Twelfth Corps came trudging in, their trousers and shoes still wet from fording the Monocacy. This was Banks's old corps, still led by Alpheus Williams, who had taken over from the injured Banks after Cedar Mountain. McClellan had completely dismantled Pope's Army of Virginia, in which Banks had commanded the Second Corps, but McClellan's Army of the Potomac already had a Second Corps under old Edwin Sumner, so Pope's veterans had to accept a new number. They would also get a new commander: Banks had remained behind to superintend the Washington defenses, and McClellan assigned the white-haired Joseph Mansfield to take over for General Williams. The loss of Banks affected his old corps deeply, said a sergeant in the 27th Indiana.[59]

Company F of the 27th Indiana included Corporal Barton W. Mitchell. Mitchell was past the upper limit of military age, but he had spent two decades coopering in various Indiana settlements, watching his fortunes decline as industrial manufacturing undermined his trade. Then, like a lot of other men in reduced circumstances, he had left his wife and five children in 1861 to go to war. He appears to have held abolitionist views that were rare for a soldier, but the suppression of slavery had provided little motivation for military service when he enlisted. He may have found as much appeal in regular pay, vague promises that his family would be taken care of, and the assurance that he would bring home the wondrous sum of one hundred dollars when the war was finished — which everyone assumed would take less than a year. For the greying corporal and his comrades a year had passed, with no end in sight, but men like Mitchell stuck with it and shunned discharge if the chance came their way, lest they lose that hundred-dollar bounty. Now their home states paid more than that for each recruit, besides the federal bounty.[60]

Corporal Mitchell's regiment had just fallen out in the fields on the edge of Frederick, and he may have been scouting for a tent site when he spotted a packet in the grass that contained three cigars. Wrapped around those cigars was a slip of paper that had been carefully filled with eight paragraphs in a fine hand. It was dated four days before, and headed "Hdqrs. Army of Northern Virginia, Special Orders No. 191." The sheet provided all the details that transformed Lee's bold division of forces into a reckless liability, and the document jumped from company commander to regimental, brigade, division, and corps headquarters, lingering only minutes at each stop. General Williams received it in his tent while savoring the possibility of buying a fresh shirt in the town, and he forwarded it quickly to McClellan with a note explaining that it had been found by a corporal in the 27th Indiana.[61] That anonymous accolade served as Mitchell's only official commendation for his discovery, and after Mitchell's death his sergeant, John Bloss, tried to take credit for finding the envelope.[62]

When the lost order reached McClellan he boiled over with excitement and immediately telegraphed the president. "I have all the plans of the rebels," he boasted at noon, "and will catch them in their own trap if my men are equal to the emergency." Had he moved immediately he might have lived up to that boast, for his men did seem equal to it, but he left most of them idle at Frederick for another seventeen hours.[63]

McClellan's cavalry chief, Alfred Pleasonton, had left town at daybreak on the National Road, groping toward Braddock Heights for the enemy in the last hours before the discovery of Order No. 191. Burnside gave him a division of infantry to support the movement over the heights, and one of his brigades supported Richard Rush's 6th Pennsylvania Cavalry, known as Rush's Lancers for the long pikes they carried. Those lances streamed with billowing red pennants that conjured a "middle ages" atmosphere for one observer. The 9th New York could only have accentuated that image as it marched alongside the lancers in modified Zouave garb reminiscent of vintage European armies. Those knights in blue looked dashing enough on their way to joust with the seedier rebels, but their tilted lances would have fared badly against carbines and revolvers; it was well that infantry came along to do their skirmishing for them, for rebel cavalry put up a stiff fight at the crest, and the echo of horse artillery carried back into Frederick even as Corporal Mitchell grew curious over the packet in the meadow.[64]

Other artillery could be heard to the south, where Lafayette McLaws had begun the assault on Harper's Ferry from Maryland Heights. William Franklin meandered to the rescue of that garrison over gaps to the south, but he still camped east of the Catoctins that night. Meanwhile, Pleasonton pressed on along the National Road. Supported by the division of Burnside's Quaker general from Rhode Island, Isaac Peace Rodman, Pleasonton pushed the enemy cavalry over Braddock Heights and descended sharply into Pleasant Valley. Another fracas began east of Middletown, but the Federals drove the Southerners through town and across Catoctin Creek, nearly a mile on the other side. At that Burnside routed the other three divisions of the Ninth Corps from their camps around Frederick and started them toward Middletown, without the air of urgency that McClellan should have felt over his providential gift. Only that evening did McClellan issue further marching orders to infantry, and he postponed them until daylight of September 14.[65]

As that day's sun rose, the three Confederate columns under Jackson had completely surrounded Harper's Ferry, and they began squeezing their prey. Alerted by Stuart's cavalry of the Yankees' approach, Harvey Hill marched two of his five brigades up the western face of South Mountain from Boonsborough, and when he realized how many roads crossed the mountain there he brought up a third brigade. He had to block two main gaps: Turner's Gap, on the National Road, and Fox's Gap, a mile to the south. Five miles below that lay Crampton's Gap, with Franklin's six brigades bearing down on it; only a couple of Virginia cavalry regiments and some stray Virginia infantry held that pass. Longstreet had continued to Hagerstown with his remaining two divisions, intent on terrorizing Pennsylvania if only by the direction and alacrity of his march, but Hill soon wailed for help and Longstreet turned most of those troops back toward Boonsborough.[66]

One mile east of Turner's Gap lay the crossroads called Bolivar, where two local roads left the National Road: one flanked Turner's Gap on the north and the other to the south, at Fox's Gap. The road to Fox's Gap climbed steeply between rocky pastures and cornfields to the home of a farmer named Wise, right at the crest. Hill had to spread his inadequate force along three miles of the ridge to protect both gaps and their outer flanks from an enemy several times his size.

Back in Frederick, Burnside put Hooker's First Corps on the road at daylight. To Burnside it must have seemed like any other day on the campaign, routinely pursuing the enemy behind a screen of cavalry. If McClellan had revealed to him the contents of Lee's lost order, or indicated any particular need for haste that morning, Burnside made no mention of it and gave no evidence of it. He rode quickly ahead of Hooker's men, who marched steadily but casually, stopping to rest occasionally as army regulations required. Dense clouds of quartermaster and commissary trains drifted behind them, filling the roads and spilling into the surrounding fields.[67]

Ten miles ahead, at South Mountain, Pleasonton tried the passes with cavalry but ran against Hill's Confederates. The Ohio regiments of Cox's Kanawha Division headed the infantry column, and at Pleasonton's behest Cox ordered first one and then the other of his two little brigades over Catoctin Creek toward Bolivar, where he led them up the road to Fox's Gap. Patches of woods alternated with fields as they ascended, but a broad strip of cleared fields adorned their side of the crest, where stone walls ran along the ridge. On the other side of those stone walls lay a rough country road, dense woods full of laurel, and D. H. Hill's Confederates. Cox deployed three regiments, and after an hour or so of feeling their way they met resistance. Samuel Garland's thin North Carolina brigade stretched along the ridge, holding the Yankees back for quite some time with a hail of musketry that winged Lieutenant Colonel Hayes, of the 23rd Ohio. While Hayes started down the mountain, Cox added the weight of his other brigade and drove the Carolinians into the forest just over the ridge, killing General Garland in the process.[68]

Musketry from the woods and artillery near Turner's Gap still punished Cox's infantry, so when Reno rode up and announced that the rest of the Ninth Corps was on the way, Cox drew back and waited for those reinforcements. The next division behind him belonged to Orlando Willcox, who took a wrong turn until Burnside himself galloped after him and called him back to help Cox. Joe Hooker's First Corps had fallen out to eat a leisurely lunch at Catoctin Creek, two miles short of Bolivar, and the Ninth Corps divisions of Sam Sturgis and Isaac Rodman lagged behind Hooker. Two hours passed at Fox's Gap in relative silence as the North Carolinians settled back behind their ready-made stone breastwork along the spine of the mountain.[69]

When Willcox's men finally did lumber up the mountainside toward the Wise farm, they came under fire from a battery near Turner's Gap, a mile or more away to their right. Where the road made a wide curve for the final ascent of Fox's Gap, Willcox posted a section from the 8th Massachusetts Battery to respond to those guns. That battery had been raised under Edwin Stanton's terrified call for short-term volunteers in late May, taking a full month to organize for six months of service. Six months hardly gave artillerymen enough time to learn how to operate their guns, and although this battery had taken part in the last of Pope's campaign it had seen no real action. The gunners unlimbered their pieces and fired three or four rounds before one crew reported its gun disabled; a third piece was coming to replace it when Confederate infantry opened up from the stone wall, sweeping the battery. One man fell dead and four others went down wounded, spilling more blood than those militiamen had bargained for. The cannoneers abandoned their guns and their officers "disappeared," as one of the enlisted men put it. Lieutenant George Evans ordered the caissons to retreat and spurred his own horse down the mountain ahead of them. Lieutenant Charles Griffin sped after him. The color-bearer followed, joining Griffin in reporting the battery "cut to pieces."[70]

That gave Reno pause, and he waited for Sturgis and Rodman before making another lunge for the gap. By then it was late afternoon, and four Union divisions yawned three ranks deep across a front more than a mile wide. The lone brigade of Carolinians, barely a thousand strong, could not even cover the entire front in a single rank. Over at Turner's Gap, Hooker had arrived, and Burnside threw one of his divisions around Hill's left while the other two barged straight up the National Road. Burnside had thus committed his entire wing, and Hill still blocked him with a single division, but on the other side of South Mountain Longstreet was coming.[71]

When Hooker rolled his divisions ahead, Reno did, too, and both corps edged steadily toward the ridge as the sun settled behind it. Advancing south of Fox's Gap, Sturgis's division encountered a few daunting volleys from the stone wall, so Sturgis flung one of his spanking-new infantry regiments at it. Only twenty days from Concord, the 9th New Hampshire lined up, fixed bayonets, and swept forward with a yell, followed by the heavy ranks behind them. From Turner's Gap came some of those long-distance Confederate shells again, plucking a few incidental casualties from the bright blue line, but the vastly outnumbered Carolinians behind the wall sprinted down the other side of the mountain. Right at the gap the Confederates mounted a little counterattack that stalled the assault. Reno rode up to sort it out, and in the gathering dusk a final volley knocked him out of the saddle, but there the fight for Fox's Gap ended. Longstreet's first brigades had arrived to cover the retreat and the battered Confederates filed down the mountain in the darkness, turning toward Sharpsburg and the Potomac River crossings.[72]

On the knoll behind Bolivar, McClellan had joined Burnside to watch the blazing pyrotechnical display as Hooker's battle continued. Longstreet had reinforced Turner's Gap as well — although with a command sorely reduced by recent battles, killing marches, and that final grueling climb up the mountain. In spite of reaching the top weak and winded, his men put up a fierce fight, buying time for the retreat with heavy losses; one company from Appomattox, Virginia, went up the hill that evening with only a dozen men led by a lieutenant, and by firelight that night the lieutenant recorded four of his comrades and neighbors among the dead and wounded.[73]

McClellan's headquarters gathering could also hear the "thug" of artillery from Franklin's fight several miles down the ridge, at Crampton's Gap, where his Sixth Corps labored against similarly light odds. Franklin also faced a brigade of Confederates ensconced behind a stone wall, and he deployed a division to pry them loose. The 5th Maine led the charge, to the chagrin of regimental adjutant George Graffam; taking advantage of his position in the rear rank, Graffam fell gradually behind and finally dropped out altogether. The defenders fired one intimidating volley, but Franklin's men rushed into them and sent them clambering up the mountainside, gaining the pass by nightfall and suffering far fewer casualties than Reno had.[74] Ignoring orders to hold Crampton's Gap to the last man, Georgia brigadier Howell Cobb raced his men down the western slope: that timorous general was the politician who, in their encounter on the Chickahominy three months before, had promised McClellan's staff officer that Southerners would fight to the death. When J.E.B. Stuart rode into the fugitives with some cavalry, Cobb reported the enemy only a furlong behind him. A skeptical Stuart rallied the infantry for a stand, but no Federals came down the mountain that night.[75]

With his way essentially open to attack Lafayette McLaws from behind, Franklin went into camp. Neither did he molest McLaws the next day, so at daylight McLaws turned his attention and his artillery back toward Harper's Ferry. So did John Walker's little division on Loudoun Heights, across the Shenandoah, while Stonewall Jackson assailed the helpless garrison from Schoolhouse Ridge. Not long after breakfast the Union commander sent out a white flag, and within a few hours Jackson's grimy infantry entered the town where many of them had begun their Confederate service. They were, said one Yankee captain who watched the Southerners fraternizing with their new prisoners, "the rustyest looking set I ever saw." Those rusty rebels netted seventy-three pieces of artillery, thirteen thousand rifles with some much-needed ammunition, hundreds of horses and mules, seven tons of horseshoes, seventy-eight tons of hardtack, and forty-six tons of beef on the hoof. They also took 12,500 Union soldiers, including five big new regiments of infantry and one relatively useless regiment of Ohio three-month troops who were due to go home in a few days anyway. The 87th Ohio and the 126th New York each provided more than a thousand captives. The 9th Vermont, the very first of Father Abraham's "three hundred thousand more," surrendered to a man.[76]

Even with Lee and Longstreet in retreat toward Sharpsburg, September 15 counted as a bad day for Union armies. The equivalent of a corps surrendered at Harper's Ferry. On that same day, Major General William Loring announced the Confederate occupation of Charleston, the natural capital of what the United States Congress had already carved out as the future state of West Virginia; Loring even gained some recruits in that largely Union territory, including some from as far away as the Ohio border.[77] Kirby Smith still held the capital of Kentucky and had approached within eight miles of Cincinnati, so terrifying the population there that the governor called out thousands of individual citizens with any firearms they could procure. Braxton Bragg had announced his liberation of Kentucky the day before, and his army was just then enveloping Munfordville, where he would capture some forty-three hundred more Union troops.[78]

One of the potential advantages Lee had anticipated from his incursion into Maryland had been the cultivation of foreign sympathy for Southern self-determination, and his sojourn north of the Potomac did win a measure of international notice. If his Sunday night concluded with the sole hope of saving his army, Monday morning brought him the determination to preserve as much of the psychological and political impact of the campaign as possible. The capture of Harper's Ferry and its garrison would compensate for other lost opportunities and for many dead men, so — once apprised by Jackson of the imminent surrender of that place — Lee abandoned his impulse to hurry across the Potomac and instead started planning to defend the outskirts of Sharpsburg. With only a fragment of his army he presented a brazen front behind Antietam Creek, studding it heavily with artillery.[79]

As spectacular as the fireworks had been at Turner's Gap, Fox's Gap produced the real slaughter: General Garland and his North Carolinians had shown Howell Cobb more of what it meant to hold a position to the last man. Ninth Corps troops went to sleep amid the moaning of the wounded, waking in the morning to find scores of dead lying by the main road and in the lane behind the stone wall.[80] Confederate dead seemed to outnumber their wounded, for the stone wall had protected them against injury to the lower extremities and most of them had been killed by bullets through the head.[81] General Sturgis had ordered a battery up the road the previous evening, but the gunners found their way so littered with dead rebels that Sturgis had put a regiment to work piling the bodies alongside the Old Sharpsburg Road, leaving the impression of stacked cordwood for those who came to gawk. A veteran regiment marching through the gap later that day sat down to take lunch amid the bodies and the burying, but the scene naturally struck the newest troops with the greatest horror, and thousands of wheezing "fresh fish" staggered up that road in time to see the bitter harvest.[82] One young man of academic bent, who had last seen his family at one of those lachrymose depot departures only three weeks before, shuddered to find eighteen corpses heaped on top of each other — all of them, according to another man who witnessed the same sight, the same color as the ground.[83]

All night long the roads back to Middletown had been clogged with caravans of wounded. By morning the churches had been filled — the pews moved aside or outside, and the floors padded with straw — and most private homes housed one or two patients for the inhabitants to tend. Lieutenant Colonel Hayes, of Ohio, lay as still as possible in the home of a merchant while local women gave him all the comforts of home.[84]

A single buckshot wounded Robert Cornwell, of Hayes's regiment, in the upper thigh. He reached Middletown the night of the battle, and a crowded ambulance delivered him to the House of Representatives after a brutal ride of thirty-eight hours. Four weeks later Cornwell went under the knife in a search for the slug, but the surgeon penetrated the peritoneal cavity and the patient died after an agonizing bout of peritonitis.[85]

Enoch Haselton, twenty years old and twenty days a soldier, represented a fair example of the fourteen hundred wounded men Burnside sent back to Middletown. He had spent his entire life in the same impoverished, sparsely settled hill-farm district on the edge of the White Mountains, and he had recently married a girl who lived two farms away. They owned no home of their own, and Enoch may have hoped to provide one with his bounty money when he enlisted that summer. In the bayonet charge of the 9th New Hampshire at Fox's Gap, a shard of one of those long-range shells from Turner's Gap had smashed his right knee before he could fire his first shot. An ambulance deposited him at the Lutheran church, in the center of Middletown, where he joined hundreds of others competing for medical treatment. His wound became infected, and he died seventeen days later. When his young widow sought his back pay and bounty, the army deducted half what he was due to cover the cost of his lost equipment.[86]

While surgeons set to work on the wounded, the rest of McClellan's army turned for the banks of Antietam Creek, where a good many more soldiers would find similar rewards. Lee strung his three lean divisions out west of Sharpsburg, anchoring his left on the hills near the Potomac and his right on Antietam Creek, at the point where it ceased to be readily fordable. Jackson started bringing the rest of the army up to stiffen that skeleton line, leaving a division to supervise the surrender at Harper's Ferry, but when McClellan's leading troops reached the Antietam on the afternoon of September 15 Lee still faced him with nothing more than the battered little force from South Mountain. Lee seemed to invite a death struggle, as though reluctant to face the consequences of his recklessness, but his audacity more likely represented pure bluff, based on his well-placed faith in McClellan's preternatural caution.

Citizens along the road to Sharpsburg reported that the Confederates had shown absolute panic as they passed, and that Lee had publicly acknowledged his army "shockingly whipped." As unlikely as it is that Robert E. Lee ever made any such public admission, the exhausted condition of his men and the perilous position of his army would have flavored his retreat with a measure of trepidation. His abrupt halt behind the creek seemed to belie any desperation, though, and McClellan's hesitancy that afternoon may have reflected a logical apprehension that Lee would not have faced about without substantial reinforcements; certainly George McClellan would not have done so. Hooker, the first corps commander on the scene, generously calculated the Confederate line at thirty thousand men, but McClellan's inflated estimates of the components of Lee's army would have brought it closer to forty thousand. That required more planning and more troops, so the Army of the Potomac spent the rest of the day and evening waltzing into advantageous positions and clogging the narrow roads on the way to the front.[87]

McClellan learned of Lee's halt at midafternoon, during a stop at Boonsborough. He loitered there until about 3:45, then hastened to Keedysville, three miles away, through heavy columns of troops. It was probably not yet five o'clock when he and his staff reined up on a hill half a mile beyond Keedysville to begin examining the enemy position. More than an hour and a half of daylight remained for either reconnaissance or attack. Two of McClellan's divisions had already deployed along the creek in front of Lee, and more were arriving all the time; Burnside came up soon afterward, but darkness fell without any movement toward the creek. By nine in the evening McClellan learned that Harper's Ferry had capitulated, and that seemed to explain Lee's renewed defiance, since it would have freed Jackson to rejoin him. McClellan imagined that he would soon face a re-united Army of Northern Virginia numbering close to a hundred thou-sand men.[88]

Still McClellan hesitated, as though he supposed Lee had already com-pleted his concentration. Ten Union divisions camped within range of Antietam Creek that evening and more lay just behind, but Tuesday dawned without a single Union soldier crossing the stream. Jackson's corps and John Walker's two brigades were then hurrying to Lee's aid, and as the sun rose some of Jackson's troops were fording the Potomac at Boteler's Ford, less than four miles from Sharpsburg. By noon, when McClellan finally made ready to strike a blow, all but three of Lee's nine infantry divi-sions stood ready or had begun falling in with the main army.[89]

Southern artillery barked ferociously until Jackson came up, as a ter-rier might threaten a stray bear. Ordnance dropped inhospitably into the bivouacs of Union soldiers breakfasting beyond the creek. Several rounds landed amid the campfires of Cox's Ohio regiments and Sturgis's division, downstream from the Boonsborough Pike; in the unfortunate 9th New Hampshire, which had experienced so rude an introduction to the war thirty-six hours before, a twelve-pound ball sheared a leg off one recruit and broke the arm of another. Their comrades scattered into the sur-rounding woods, from which their colonel rousted them with an assort-ment of invective, but one of them hid there until the regiment departed; eventually he slipped away to more peaceful latitudes.[90]

New regiments always leaked a trickle of deserters from the day they were mustered, as men decided they could not leave home or that the dangers of a soldier's life conflicted with common sense. The 9th New Hampshire had lost a few disillusioned volunteers on the march from Washington, and another had disappeared into the forest on South Mountain the night of their battlefield initiation: five more privates and three noncommissioned officers would slink away before serious fighting began on their reach of Antietam Creek. Two of the four Averys in Com-pany H fled their regiment forever, while a third dropped out of the col-umn and blew two fingers off his right hand in a desperate gamble for a discharge. Even the captain of their company earned a formal accusation of cowardice at Antietam, which may have helped persuade him to resign a few months later. Many more legs would carry their owners ignomini-ously away from danger within another twenty-four hours, and not all of them would be clad in blue.[91]

As he inspected his lines that morning McClellan found that the Ninth Corps had to be repositioned, and he sent Burnside a sharp note about it. From South Mountain, McClellan's messages had suggested a certain impatience with Burnside, complaining of the promptness and precision of his movements as though preparing a scapegoat against potential failure. Afterward McClellan did offer Burnside as that scapegoat, producing a paper trail to sustain his claim, but at the time McClellan's reprimands only perplexed his old friend, for during the previous ten days the Ninth Corps had marched farther than any other in the army, and had done as much or more of the fighting. Traveling with Burnside, Jacob Cox saw no outward evidence of McClellan's dissatisfaction, but on paper McClellan waxed unreasonably critical, as though he denied Burnside the same excuses he made for his own slow compliance with orders from Washington.[92]

Not until the afternoon of September 16 did McClellan start prodding at the Confederate line, and he failed to push very hard even then. The Confederate army occupied one of those long, low ridges that ripple western Maryland, offering perfect elevations for the defensive use of small arms and artillery against massed infantry assaults. Lee's left flank bent back near the Potomac against high ground called Nicodemus Heights, which he crowned with artillery. From there his line turned south, parallel to and east of the Hagerstown Turnpike, into the dense woodlot near Samuel Poffenberger's farm, following the edge of the hills that sloped generally toward Antietam Creek. Weary Confederates shuffled into position opposite the door of William Roulette's farmhouse, across a sunken road that skirted Henry Piper's farm, and over the Boonsborough Turnpike. South of the Boonsborough Pike the defenders spread out a little thinner for another couple of miles between the outskirts of Sharpsburg and the steep bluffs bordering a tight loop of the Antietam. The grey line petered out near the last practical ford before the creek emptied into the Potomac River.[93]

Three triple-arch stone bridges crossed the creek between the armies. One lay upstream from Phillip Pry's house, where McClellan made his headquarters. Another sat on the Boonsborough Pike, and the third stood downstream from there, on a road that ran past Henry Rohrbach's place. On the afternoon of September 16 McClellan sent most of Joe Hooker's corps over the creek on the upper bridge, but, to the consternation of Marsena Patrick, Hooker directed Abner Doubleday's division to a "very bad ford" just below there. With Confederate pickets pecking away at - them from cornfields on higher ground, the three divisions marched northward, up the creek, and then swung to the west in a search for Lee's left flank. Toward dusk the Pennsylvania Reserves drove back the pickets and began contending for the woods beyond Sam Poffenberger's — the East Woods, as they would come to be known. The enemy fell back a little, but with darkness the firing stopped and Hooker retracted his own lines.[94]

During the night the two divisions of Mansfield's Twelfth Corps marched over the bridge and lay down near the First Corps. Sumner waited with the Second Corps at the edge of the creek with orders to cross before dawn in the morning, but a light rain and the likelihood of a serious fight on the morrow prevented anyone from sleeping very soundly or long. One of Sumner's more sentimental colonels spent the evening hours composing a poem called "The Night before the Battle." A Massachusetts sergeant in the same corps still sat up at 3:00 AM, scribbling a final letter by forbidden firelight in which he revealed how needless the surrender of Harper's Ferry had seemed to some of the troops. "I am growing discouraged," he confessed. "If we are to have traitors in high places shall we ever close the war[?]."[95]

The crossing had given Lee a fair idea of where McClellan would strike, so the Confederate commander spent the night shifting his badly outnumbered troops to meet Hooker's anticipated flank attack. Moving with greater alacrity and with fewer provisions than any Union soldiers seemed able to manage, the two divisions under Lafayette McLaws crossed the Potomac from Maryland Heights into Harper's Ferry on September 16 and marched through the night, arriving in Sharpsburg as the sun rose on September 17. Just as McLaws saw the rooftops of Sharpsburg, firing erupted north of town.[96]

Captain W. H. Humphreys, of the 2nd U.S. Sharpshooters, witnessed the first shot. He awoke before dawn from his dismal bivouac on Joseph Poffenberger's farm, along the Hagerstown Pike, and at the first hint of red on the horizon a call of nature sent him scurrying across the pike. The blare of an alien bugle alarmed him and he rushed back to camp, waking Lieutenant Edwin Hobbs of the 1st New Hampshire Battery, whose guns stood nearby. Hobbs focused his binoculars on Nicodemus Heights, half a mile away, where the dim light seemed to reveal at least a battery of artillery in the act of unlimbering. Hobbs bellowed for his gunners to fall in, and Humphreys loped over to do the same for his riflemen. Within moments a shell came hurtling in among the New Hampshire guns, cutting the throats of two harnessed horses before striking the ground and skipping over the heads of the sharpshooters. The six Granite State howitzers began belching replies, and the bloodiest day of the Civil War had begun.[97]

With that flurry Hooker renewed his attack on Lee's left. He roused his corps, guiding it into a deep ravine and over a prominent ridge, aiming for an elevation on the Hagerstown Pike near a whitewashed Dunker

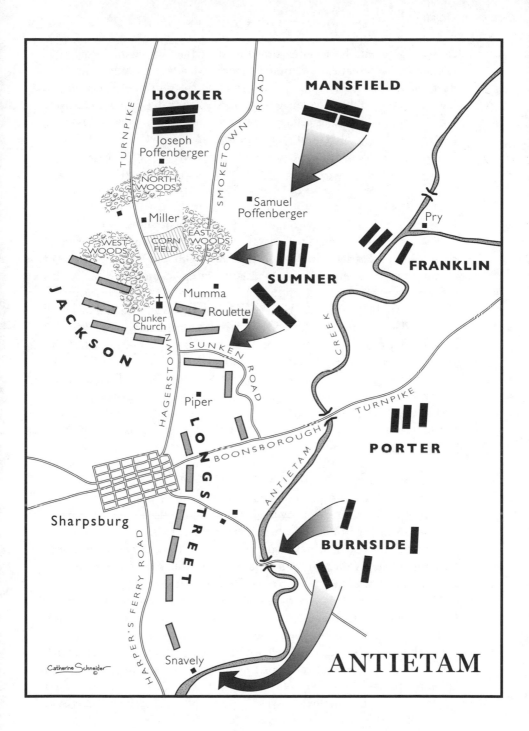

church that would have commanded most of the Confederate lines. The Pennsylvania Reserves, now under George Meade, sailed back into the East Woods and David Miller's cornfield, which connected the woods to the Hagerstown Pike. Hooker sent James Ricketts's division in to Meade's left and flung Abner Doubleday's down the Hagerstown Pike on his right, toward another growth of timber soon to be designated the West Woods. Doubleday's three brigades struck the extreme left of the Confederate position, knocking the supposedly invincible Stonewall Brigade and another Virginia brigade back into the West Woods with embarrassing velocity, but counterattacks stalled Doubleday with thundering volleys of musketry and the artillery on Nicodemus Heights peppered the Union lines.[98]

The ferocity of the engagement gave brave men pause. On the Federal right, General Patrick wryly noted that John Gibbon, a fellow brigadier whom he considered a "despicable toady," hung suspiciously behind his infantry line as it moved down the pike. Patrick observed acerbically that Gibbon halted alongside the battery of Regular artillery he had formerly commanded, adding that during the entire engagement Gibbon was "not seen away from" that battery's position near some large stacks of Mr. Miller's straw. On the opposite end of Hooker's front, Colonel William H. Christian of the 26th New York decamped altogether. Christian commanded Ricketts's second brigade. He had fought in the Mexican War, and one of his subordinates thought he possessed "noble qualities," but he had taken charge of his brigade when it was cut to shreds on Chinn Ridge just nineteen days before and he was evidently unable to bear such carnage again so soon. Confederate artillery rained in so densely that he admitted having a "great horror of these shell," and dismounted to lead his horse forward less conspicuously. Christian finally stopped, and his brigade stopped with him, causing the brigadier behind him to come up and drive it forward again. Then Christian succumbed to his horror and stumbled toward the rear. The next senior colonel took over for him and Christian immediately retired from the war, although he secured a brevet promotion to brigadier general two and a half years later.[99]

The wonder is that more men did not quail that morning. Sheets of bullets ripped through dense vegetation, and shells burst continually. Brigades in different shades of blue and assorted facsimiles of grey surprised each other in the woods and the cornfield, accidentally overlapping each other's fronts and bending a Union or Confederate flank until a regiment could be plucked from somewhere else to brace the line. Colonel Walter Phelps Jr., who had dallied in Washington while his regiment fought at Bull Run, demonstrated at Antietam that it was probably not a lack of courage that had deterred him. Phelps led one of Doubleday's brigades into the Miller cornfield right behind Gibbon's leading regiments, and when rebels spilled around his right flank Phelps calmly detached the 2nd U.S. Sharpshooters to meet them.[100]

The sharpshooter regiment opened a brisk, accurate fire with their breech-loading rifles, but the enemy returned equally hot musketry and the green-clad sharpshooters withered beneath it. Their colonel fell wounded, the adjutant died along with two other lieutenants, and rifle fire disabled most of the rest of the officers. The Confederates concentrated so much musketry on them that Phelps had to throw the rest of his brigade in to support them. When he finally withdrew from the cornfield, most of his wounded remained behind, including fifty-five-year-old Private Joseph W. Everest of the sharpshooters, immobilized by a bullet through his hip.[101]

McClellan had not only taken Hooker's corps from Burnside's wing but had given Hooker command over the reinforcements that were sent to him — including Mansfield's Twelfth Corps, which nominally belonged to Edwin Sumner's wing. Now Hooker sent that corps in, and the white-haired Mansfield led it forward in the close-packed formation he had been taught to favor during the administration of James Monroe. In forty years as a commissioned officer Mansfield had never led so much as a regiment, and his career as commander of a corps did not last half an hour under fire. Alpheus Williams, who had directed the Twelfth Corps until Mansfield's arrival, was chatting with Hooker when he heard that Mansfield had been mortally wounded, so he started deploying both his own division and George Sears Greene's. He pushed Samuel Crawford's brigade toward the East Woods, where tall trees soaked up the sunlight and smothered the underbrush. Crawford's brigade had been heavily reinforced since its ordeal at Cedar Mountain: now it consisted of three wiry veteran regiments and three huge new regiments of nine-month militia, all from Pennsylvania. For men who had not expected to face such action so soon, if ever, the militiamen stood up to it fairly well — at least as long as no one asked them to perform any complicated maneuvers. By the time the Pennsylvanians advanced, Hooker's corps had expended its momentum and was barely holding on, allowing the enemy to turn more firepower on the Twelfth Corps.[102]

In the East Woods, Captain Nehemiah Furbish, of the 10th Maine, found a chance to redeem his reputation. Furbish had fainted ostentatiously during the slaughter at Cedar Mountain, provoking scornful muttering among his men and fellow officers, but in the hailstorm of bullets on September 17 he seemed perfectly reckless, as though attempting to silence the whispers forever. So he did, albeit at the cost of his life. Captain

James Black, of the same regiment, declined a similar opportunity: Black had hidden behind a haystack at Cedar Mountain, and as his company headed for the East Woods he dropped out again with a complaint of illness, disappearing until the fight was over. Antietam would be his last battle, although (like Colonel Christian) he still managed to take home an honorable discharge.[103]

While Crawford assailed the East Woods, General Williams sent George Gordon's brigade straight toward Miller's cornfield, where John Bell Hood's division had stymied all three of Hooker's divisions. As he had at Cedar Mountain, Gordon stood the 2nd Massachusetts, 3rd Wisconsin, and 27th Indiana side by side to shoot it out with an enemy in partial cover, and again Southern muskets riddled those three regiments. In the 27th Indiana, 18 men were killed and 191 wounded, including Corporal Mitchell, who had found Order No. 191; the Wisconsin regiment lost 200. Hood's outgunned, battered Confederates finally fell back, and Gordon sent two regiments through the cornfield into an open pasture alongside the Hagerstown Pike. Hundreds of dead and dying men lay there, and the farther the Yankees advanced the more of those casualties wore grey, lying in windrows just as they had been cut down, with heads or legs off, or bearing the occasional gaping hole of an entire artillery projectile. The Federals had to step carefully to avoid injuring the maimed. The firing lulled as Gordon's men reached the pike, and they used that respite to give water to the grateful wounded of both armies.[104]

With three depleted divisions Stonewall Jackson had fended off five Union divisions for three hours. Both sides had fought themselves out: Mansfield lay dying and Hooker had been carried off with a bullet in his foot, but most Confederate units on that end of the line had spent themselves, and Lee's left flank invited a new assault. A new assault was forming then, too, in the lowland by Antietam Creek, where John Sedgwick's division had just forded the stream. These were the three brigades that Charles Stone had organized and trained the previous autumn, before Edwin Stanton imprisoned him on half-baked suspicion. Sedgwick belonged to Sumner, another white-haired veteran who also favored ancient tactics, so his division came up over the ridge in three closely spaced lines of battle, each one brigade wide, presenting what a Massachusetts officer thought was a "grand sight." Sedgwick aimed straight for the West Woods, passing behind Gordon's brigade and most of the rest of the Twelfth Corps, supposing that this would bring him beyond the Confederate flank and allow him to swing down on it where he could do the most damage. Jackson gathered the remnants of two divisions in the faint hope of staving off this latest attack.[105]

One day earlier, or half an hour earlier, striking that spot would have done a great deal of good, but — just as Sedgwick's three brigades glided within range — up came Lafayette McLaws and his division, with no more than an hour's sleep after an all-night tramp from Harper's Ferry. The Federals reached the Hagerstown Turnpike, climbed the two bullet-splintered post-and-rail fences that still bordered it, and passed into the West Woods. Along with five Georgia regiments borrowed from Lee's right, McLaws slammed into the left flank of all three Union brigades and poured in behind the last of them. From close range J.E.B. Stuart laid into Sedgwick's front with artillery.[106]

Thanks to Sumner's close-packed formation, only Sedgwick's leading brigade could fire without hitting friends. His middle brigade lost more heavily than either of the others, unable to defend itself while taking fire from front and rear. Captain Oliver Wendell Holmes Jr., of the 20th Massachusetts, stood in that middle brigade when a bullet clipped through the back of his coat collar and out the side of his neck, narrowly missing his spine, the carotid artery, and the jugular vein. A big nine-month Pennsylvania regiment from the Twelfth Corps still lingered in the woods to Sedgwick's left: those recruits saw the grey wave coming and bolted away, crashing into Sedgwick's third brigade as they ran, and with that Sedgwick's long, solid lines started dissolving from the southern end. Sumner rode to Sedgwick's rear brigade, gesticulating wildly in the din for the brigadier to face it about and fire into the enemy behind them, but it did no good. In a twinkling Sedgwick went down with three wounds, and his entire division was streaming to the north, along with the remains of the Twelfth Corps.[107]

The 15th Massachusetts, in Sedgwick's front line, suffered the worst. An attached company of sharpshooters brought the 15th to a strength of 582, making a brawny regiment by Army of the Potomac standards in September of 1862: within about twenty minutes of entering the West Woods, 344 of those men had been killed or wounded, and all but a few of the wounded remained behind when their comrades fled, every man for himself. Sergeant Jonathan Stowe, who had sat up at three o'clock that morning writing a dismal letter home, lay in the woods with his right knee shattered. After his division abandoned the spot the shells continued to fly overhead, clipping off limbs that landed among the wounded, and once the shock wore off Stowe's leg began aching fearfully.[108]

So soon after welcoming the aid of Sumner's reinforcements, Alpheus Williams had to help Sumner in turn, flinging three of his least-tattered regiments against the counterattack from McLaws. Those three held until John Walker's division hurried over from Lee's right flank and scattered them back toward the East Woods. "They ran like sheep," thought a North Carolina lieutenant who had just turned seventeen. Williams ordered a five-week-old New York regiment out when the Confederates tried to continue the pursuit, and there the lines stalled. After that the exhausted Southern infantry fell back and let their artillery resume the fight, sending shells screaming over the heads of the terrified New Yorkers. A captain in that regiment, who had sought his position chiefly for the salary and status that it brought, betrayed great relief that he "did not run after all."[109]

A Union flagman watching the artillery duel from the safety of an elevated Sixth Corps signal station found the battle "the prettiest sight I ever beheld — shells flying in all directions, houses burning, musketry cracking & altogether the grandest sight imaginable." Closer by, Sergeant Stowe and Private Everest saw it differently.[110]

Now the action shifted, almost accidentally, to the center of Lee's line. Without Sumner's knowledge or direction, his next division took an entirely different tack. William French, a blustering West Point classmate of Hooker's and Sedgwick's, turned his division to the south, against D. H. Hill. Hill's men occupied the sunken road near Piper's farm, in a conspicuous bend of the Confederate line, and they had piled rails on top of the roadside embankment to add a bit more protection. Against that natural earthwork French hurled his three brigades. Only Nathan Kimball's brigade had any combat experience, and Kimball had been saddled with an ungainly new nine-month regiment; Max Weber's brigade consisted of three older regiments that had never been under fire, while Colonel Dwight Morris commanded three brand-new regiments, including nine-month militia. The new troops had no idea where they were going until they came up the slope and saw gun smoke rising beyond them, and they only seemed to understand they were going into action when a volley caught them from the side, killing a nine-month man and unnerving his comrades. Then they turned toward the rebels in the sunken road, who delivered a furious fire into them.[111]

The untried older regiments led the way, but at fifty yards' distance the first volley dropped many of them in their tracks. Confederates shot down 230 men in French's front-line regiment, the 1st Delaware: many of the survivors bolted for the rear, colliding with supporting troops whom they advised to save themselves. Kimball's brigade pushed on to the same distance and fell back with even greater loss to the brow of the slope, where all of French's men settled into a slugging match with the nine Alabama and North Carolina regiments in the sunken road.[112]

Israel Richardson, another contemporary of French's and his equal in pugnacity, commanded fourteen regiments of experienced Easterners in the last of Sumner's divisions. Coming up on French's left, Richardson threw Thomas Meagher's notorious Irish Brigade at George B. Anderson's brigade in the sunken road. The Irishmen alone outnumbered both of Hill's thin brigades, and they sashayed to point-blank range, where they stood trading volleys with the beleaguered men in the ditch. Hill bellowed for help, and Lee sent his army's last reserve — Richard Anderson's division, which had arrived in the morning with McLaws. That made two Generals Anderson at the sunken road: the first had already left the field with a wound that would kill him, and the second went down within minutes, leaving a rank incompetent to assume command.[113]

When the Irish Brigade had had about all it could stand, and after a reportedly drunken General Meagher had fallen from his horse, Richardson brought up John Caldwell's five regiments. Both brigades broke ranks so Caldwell's men could slide through and take over while Meagher's men stepped to the rear, and they performed this parade-ground maneuver under a close, intense fire. The new brigade edged up within thirty yards of the sunken road, where they could see their opponents clearly whenever the smoke cleared, and a New York colonel could not help but admire the tenacity of the Confederates in the lane. A few weeks later, while recovering from a wound they inflicted on him, he told a New York woman that "their lank, emaciated forms and pale, cadaverous faces made them seem like an army of phantoms."[114]

As the colonel's observation hinted, most of the Southrons had not been eating well. In more than a week most of them had hardly stopped moving long enough to cook a meal, and they had been supplementing their meager rations with green apples and corn from fields like the one that stood in full silk behind the sunken road. A few had foraged well, however. A Pennsylvania artilleryman near the East Woods inspected a dead rebel's haversack that afternoon and found that Maryland had been good to him: the oilcloth satchel contained a can of fat, a few muffins, an ear of corn, a slab of meat, some potatoes, and an apple. Ruminating on his own diet of coffee and hardtack, the gunner supposed that his opponent had enjoyed the more sumptuous fare, if not better fortune.[115]

French's brigades might have shown early success if he had coordinated their assaults, and Richardson had arrived too late to pitch in simultaneously with French, but neither was their more scientific army commander timing his attacks very well that morning. As he claimed four weeks later, McClellan intended to try his might against the Confederate left and then, if that failed, make another effort against Lee's right until something gave way. If that happened, he would throw his reserve into the "center," which he may have calculated as right down the Boonsborough Pike rather than at Hill's little fortress in the sunken road. The First, Twelfth, and Second Corps had all advanced piecemeal, allowing Lee to fend them off successively, and the same was about to happen with Burnside at the lower bridge: when McClellan ordered Sumner's corps in, he also dispatched an order to Burnside to begin his assault on the bridge, promising support if he needed it. That would have been timely if Burnside had been sitting on the right bank of the creek, or if McClellan's engineer had judged the fords well, but neither was the case.[116]

Lee had left responsibility for everything from the Boonsborough road downstream to Brigadier General David Jones, who commanded six brigades from Virginia, South Carolina, and Georgia. In the morning, John Walker's division had also sat astride the lowest usable ford on Antietam Creek, near the Snavely farm. By the time Burnside received his license to attack, Jones had already released one brigade to help repel Sedgwick's division, and Walker's division had departed on a similar mission. Jones tallied only 2,430 men in his entire division that morning. He could not have had many more than 2,000 of them left to cover a front that wound for more than a mile and a half around two doglegs in the creek, while Burnside sat on the other side with 13,000. Jones benefited from the rugged terrain, though, as well as from the tension building between McClellan and Burnside.[117]

The Rohrbach Bridge, as it was known locally, surmounted the creek at the base of a steep bluff, and Jones had positioned four hundred Georgia marksmen from Robert Toombs's brigade along the crest of that bluff. A company or so of other riflemen had spread out along the steep banks of the creek downstream, more as pickets than for serious resistance, and their line fell short of the last easy crossing at Snavely's ford. Aside from the bridge and ford, the creek offered General Jones substantial protection. Thanks apparently to inadequate reconnaissance by McClellan's staff engineer, whom the suddenly critical McClellan had sent to correct the position of Burnside's divisions, Isaac Rodman's flanking division waited in front of a deep, treacherous cattle ford below the first bend in the creek; it was presumably the same engineer who had led Doubleday's division to a "very bad ford" near the Pry house on September 16, when there had been plenty of time to examine the stream and no enemy presence to interfere. McClellan's sudden fussiness appeared to leave Burnside apprehensive of further irritating him, and he left his troops where they were, including Rodman. Confederate artillerymen near the crest of the Boonsborough Pike spied some of Rodman's division between converging slopes, and lobbed shells over the creek at them throughout the morning.[118]

Burnside shared the attack order with Jacob Cox, the nominal corps commander, telling him to order George Crook's Ohio brigade over the bridge. Crook evidently misunderstood his relayed instructions. He reached the creek too far upstream, expecting someone else to make the actual dash over the bridge, but he wheeled a couple of howitzers up to harass Toombs's Georgians and sent one regiment still farther upstream, looking for another ford.[119]

Perceiving Crook's mistake, Burnside next signaled Sam Sturgis to seize the bridge. Sturgis selected the 2nd Maryland and the 6th New Hampshire, which jogged down the bridge road in double ranks with fixed bayonets, but as they came into view the Georgians poured an accurate, punishing fire into them. These men had been roughly handled at Bull Run only nineteen days before, and they instinctively abandoned their mission, scattering for the meager cover of a rail fence that bordered the stream or fleeing altogether. Then, with fresh orders from Burnside to carry the bridge at all costs, Sturgis picked the 51st New York and 51st Pennsylvania for the same chore; a captain in the Pennsylvania regiment marked the receipt of the order at eleven o'clock. This time Sturgis arranged them under the brow of the hill before the bridge, whence they sprang for the short, deadly sprint downhill. Men dropped rapidly, and the fence gate impeded them, but a husky corporal ripped it from its hinges and the Yankees poured through, filing left and right in firing lines facing the opposite bluff. Some took refuge behind a stone wall upstream from the bridge, and Sturgis's other regiments mounted the hill behind them to lay a covering fire into the Georgians. No one tried to cross the bridge itself, as the Georgians could have fired down their throats, but the twin 51sts held their ground on the bank and began picking away at the few hundred riflemen above them.[120]

Rodman, meanwhile, moved one brigade toward his assigned ford. The water flowed too deep at that spot, and the Confederate marksmen on the bluff discouraged a crossing there, so that brigade moved down the serpentine creek behind a screen of skirmishers, looking for low water and shallower embankments. Those ingredients existed only at Snavely's ford, where a single platoon of South Carolinians resisted Burnside's passage with a paltry spatter of musketry. Rodman's New York brigade splashed through first, followed by the 8th and 16th Connecticut and the 4th Rhode Island. Lieutenant Henry Spooner, who had joined the Rhode Islanders through a direct commission less than two weeks before, plunged into water up to his chest. Spooner was only five and a half feet tall, though, and he may have stood aside to give his men the best of the rocky ford, for men of average height found the water less than waist-deep.[121]

The other brigade of the Kanawha Division trailed along as well. That gave Rodman nine regiments, all of them well trained and with some battlefield experience, except the cumbersome 16th Connecticut, which had been with the army only ten days. It took a while to thread four thousand men through the ford, and by the time Rodman started to form his division on the right bank the sun had passed the meridian.[122]

While Rodman organized his flank attack a thousand yards below, Sturgis's two 51sts had whittled Toombs's Georgians down enough to attempt a charge over the bridge. With a sentimental shout of "Remember Reno" those few hundred men leaped to their feet and raced toward the bridge, funneling across as the Georgians rained one final shower of bullets into them. The adjutant of the New York regiment fell dead at the bridge. A captain in the Pennsylvania regiment had been suffering from a severe toothache all morning, but at the entrance to the bridge a bullet smashed into his jaw and removed the offending tooth, along with all the others on that side of his face; he stumbled away while his comrades scrambled up the bluff. Toombs's men, nearly out of ammunition after two hours of incessant firing, spilled out of their makeshift rifle pits and sped away to their next stronghold, behind a stone wall on the slope toward Sharpsburg. A couple of fresh regiments reported to Toombs, who diverted them to meet the first of Rodman's brigades coming up from the ford.[123]

By one o'clock the spearhead regiments, with more of Sturgis's men right behind them, had swept up over the bluff to secure it from counterattack. They need not have worried, for David Jones had too little infantry to even consider aggressive tactics, but he did turn artillery on the bluff once he realized the bridge had fallen, and that stalled the blue lines momentarily. The chaotic bridge crossing completely disorganized the first Union regiments atop the bluff, and intense confusion reigned until the companies reformed, which bought Toombs a little respite.[124]

Crook's brigade joined Sturgis on the bluff, and Cox asked Burnside to send Orlando Willcox's fresh division across to take over for them. Coming from a mile away, Willcox marched one brigade to the right bank and sheltered it beneath the bluff while waiting for the other, but the ammunition wagons rattled over next. Rebel guns had the range on the bridge and bluff, peppering the vicinity, so — with nowhere to hide from the shelling — the ammunition train suddenly turned back against the bridge traffic. A section of the 8th Massachusetts Battery galloped to the summit and unlimbered to reply, but some of that battery's kid-glove officers had already shown a disinclination to die so near the end of their six-month enlistment. Lieutenant Charles Griffin stood the shelling only moments before he turned his horse back down the slope. He negotiated the traffic jam blossoming near the bridge, led his horse into the creek, and took refuge under one of the arches of the bridge. With that example, his two gun crews did not linger long.[125]

Finally Burnside crossed the rest of Willcox's division and the last fragments of the Ninth Corps, except for a few scattered pieces of artillery. The delay in shifting troops, reorganizing units, replenishing ammunition, and arranging lines of battle to renew the assault consumed two hours. By then D. H. Hill had forsaken the sunken road to face the Federals in a stalemate near the Hagerstown Pike, and for two hours the battlefield fell relatively quiet except for the shelling between Burnside and Jones. The hands of most watches approached 3:00 PM before Burnside started his corps toward the thin grey line on the last ridge before Sharpsburg.[126]

The long silence on Burnside's front prompted McClellan to dispatch one of his officers, who came back with word that the Ninth Corps had crossed the creek. Soon thereafter, discouraging news arrived from Sumner, and with a small retinue McClellan rode over the upper bridge to visit his right wing.[127]

Sumner, who had assumed command of all the troops on the right, considered them all too cut up and demoralized to repel any attack. Though he may have overstated the case, the fight had indeed been beaten out of many of those who had borne the battle so far. George Meade counted only seven thousand men in the First Corps out of twelve thousand who had been present for duty, with casualties accounting for only about half the difference: the balance had simply wandered deliberately away from the firing line.[128] Meanwhile, the flood of wounded streaming to the rear tested the courage of those who had not yet seen the field. Stragglers and skulkers thronged the road to Boonsborough, and an officer as far back as Middletown saw "a perfect stream" of armed vagabonds passing all day long, while on the battlefield itself every patch of woods behind the firing lines shielded a population of refugees from the fighting. William Franklin had brought his Sixth Corps to the right wing late in the morning: one of his two divisions had promptly gone in to brace the line while the other stood in ranks just within reach of Confederate guns, and their vigorous shelling had again persuaded Adjutant Graffam of the 5th Maine to find business farther to the rear. When the bombardment subsided Graffam made his way back to his post, but then Franklin began arranging their division for an attack, and as the 5th Maine deployed Graffam and his sergeant major both vanished into the woods behind them.[129]

McClellan and his escort rode up while Sumner and Franklin debated the wisdom of Franklin's attack. With Burnside gathering to push against the feeble Confederate right, a solid diversion at the other end of the line would have been advisable to prevent Lee from shifting his strength, but George McClellan took a conservative view of tactics. He always relished a strong reserve force, and he viewed Franklin's corps as the reserve for the right wing, just as he held Porter's Fifth Corps in reserve at the center. Rather than risk a thrust that might reopen the Hagerstown Pike and allow Lee an avenue back into the heart of Maryland, McClellan decided to keep his right wing idle: Burnside would have to advance without the aid of any diversion. The knot of general and staff officers attracted the attention of Southern gunners, and a shell aimed at them hurtled into the 96th Pennsylvania, taking one man's leg off and clipping the kneecap from another. With that, McClellan turned back to the Pry house.[130]

The hill near Pry's house afforded McClellan's headquarters family a magnificent panorama of Burnside's assault. Willcox's division took the right, nearest the Boonsborough Pike, and Rodman assembled on his left, each of them braced with a brigade from the Kanawha Division. Sturgis's weary division followed in support, giving Burnside eight strong brigades to overwhelm five thin ones. For the first half hour all went well, with Rodman chasing Toombs's men from behind their stone wall, but artillery from other parts of the Confederate line began tearing at the long blue columns. The real trouble, although the Yankees did not yet know it, came when new batteries opened up on the Harper's Ferry road. These were the harbingers of A. P. Hill's division, the last division of Lee's army, which Hill was driving so relentlessly that he left a thick wake of gasping men by the roadside. Rodman's infantry swarmed over one of Hill's batteries, and Willcox neared the summit of the ridge, with the rooftops and steeples of the town just beyond, but that would be the limit of Union success that day.[131]

McClellan could have detected Hill's approach had he used his cavalry for something besides a headquarters guard, but Hill's brigades bore down on Burnside's left flank unseen by any Federal. The same luck that had led McLaws into an awkward new regiment in the West Woods guided Hill's battle line into the left of Rodman's division, where the 16th Connecticut marched. Confederates rolled through tall corn to short range and discharged their muskets in the faces of those astonished rookies, who triggered another panic when their line fell apart. "There was some pretty tall running in the 16th," admitted a private in that regiment, "and I guess that I made myself scarce rather fast." The veteran 4th Rhode Island disintegrated under the same fire, stampeding back through the jumbled ranks of the nervous Connecticut recruits. The officers of the 16th, remarked a captain in a more stable Connecticut regiment, "knew no more about tactics than about hebrew," and some of their confused companies mistook the fleeing Rhode Islanders for charging Confederates, giving them a volley before bounding away.[132]

General Rodman rode in among the two terrified regiments to restore order, only to be shot out of the saddle. A cavalry escort of loyal Virginians attached to the Kanawha Division galloped over to corral the fugitives and rally them, but some of their horses went down before Southern rifles. The flank of Burnside's assault crumbled: an entire brigade scattered back to the bridge, with only one regiment keeping any semblance of a line. That allowed some of Hill's men to slip behind Rodman's portion of the Kanawha Division, just as McLaws had gotten behind Sedgwick; when those Ohioans tried to fall back, some of them ran almost into the arms of Confederate infantry.[133]

Sturgis's two brigades stepped in to prevent Hill from rolling up Burnside's flank, but most of his men had already passed an hour or two of steady firing in the assault on the bridge. The retreat of the ammunition wagons had left them no chance to replenish their supplies, and soon the entire division started running low: the 51st New York and 51st Pennsylvania ran out altogether, and the survivors raided the cartridge boxes of their dead and wounded for a few more rounds, but finally they fixed bayonets and waited.[134]

Willcox, too, found his infantry calling for ammunition. He had reached the edge of the village, the possession of which would have barred Lee's only escape route, and the harried Confederate defenders had drawn back among the yards and orchards around the houses. Unoccupied now along the Hagerstown Pike, D. H. Hill sent a few infantry to harass the northernmost regiments of Willcox's column, training several guns at them from more than half a mile away and fraying their flank. That flank lay along the Boonsborough Pike, within sight of U.S. Regulars from Porter's corps, but McClellan withheld the support he had promised. At the brink of Union victory A. P. Hill convinced his West Point classmate Burnside to bring their other classmate Willcox back with the rest of the corps into a defensive arc around the bridge. With the sun hanging an hour or so above the horizon, the fight on the Union left subsided to skirmish fire.[135]

Except for a belch of musketry here and there, the roar of battle subsided all along the lines as day turned to dusk. When men's ears stopped ringing they began to perceive the agonized groans of the wounded, piercing and plaintive nearer by but rolling like the rumble of distant thunder over the rest of the battlefield. Nearly four thousand men had died that day, and close to twenty thousand had been wounded — some of them horribly and many fatally — but the road to Virginia still lay open to the Army of Northern Virginia. Robert E. Lee did not yet choose to follow it, and as night came many on either side wondered who had won the day.[136]

CANDIDATES FOR THE EXEMPT BRIGADE.—

As though to obscure the personal, political, or philosophical motives that made men reluctant to participate in the war, William Trowbridge's 1862 print *Candidates for the Exempt Brigade* seeks to associate such resistance with cowardice. Few eligible civilians, if any, mutilated themselves to avoid service.

SCENE, FIFTH AVENUE.

He. "Ah! Dearest ADDIE! I've succeeded. I've got a Substitute!"
She. "Have you? What a curious coincidence! And *I* have found one FOR YOU!"

Despite this attempt by *Harper's Weekly* to shame men from hiring substitutes if they were chosen for service, it eventually became the most popular alternative.

Union troops marching through Middletown, Maryland, on September 14, 1862.

Sharpsburg's main street in 1862.

Confederate dead in the sunken road at Antietam (afterward known as Bloody Lane), apparently after most bodies had been removed for burial.

Burnside's Bridge, showing the heights held by Confederate defenders and the retaining wall that shielded Union infantry.

Dead white horse noted by several witnesses near the edge of the East Woods.

Lincoln, at center, visits McClellan in the field, early in October of 1862. McClellan stands sixth from left; the two generals immediately to the right of Lincoln are George Meade and Fitz John Porter.

Union troops "monitoring" the election in Baltimore, November, 1862.

McClellan's farewell to the Army of the Potomac at Warrenton, November 10, 1862.

Ambrose Burnside and some of his generals in the second week of November, 1862. Standing, left to right, are his provost marshal, Marsena Patrick; Edward Ferrero; his chief of staff, John Parke; an unidentified lieutenant; Burnside; John Cochrane; and Samuel Sturgis, who called Senator Zachariah Chandler a liar and a coward. Seated, left to right, are Burnside's chief of artillery, Henry Hunt; Winfield Hancock, Darius Couch, Orlando Willcox, and cavalryman John Buford. Six weeks later Cochrane would go to Lincoln behind Burnside's back and persuade the president to countermand Burnside's marching orders.

Union troops relaxing amid looted property on Caroline Street, Fredericksburg, December 13, 1862.

Major General Joseph Hooker, in a photograph taken months before he assumed command of the Army of the Potomac.

Humphreys's afternoon attack on Marye's Heights, ablaze with artillery and rifle fire.

Cavalry escorting deserters back to headquarters at Falmouth in February of 1863.

The nation's first glimpse of black soldiers on duty: the Native Guards guarding a railroad in the swamps of Louisiana, pictured in *Leslie's Illustrated*, March 7, 1863.

PART III

YEAR THAT TREMBLED
AND REEL'D BENEATH ME

7

Whetting a Sword on a Bible

⚒ THE VETERANS OF ANTIETAM can be forgiven a measure of uncertainty about who prevailed as the battle drew to a close. A century and a half afterward it still seems possible to argue that Lee won a substantial victory if only because of the opportunities he persuaded George McClellan to throw away. After scattering his inferior forces in an audacious gamble, Lee held off an overpowering host long enough to concentrate his troops and find a strong position from which he beat back repeated assaults, and then he calmly held his ground the next day, inviting his much stronger antagonist to fight another round. McClellan declined, and Lee withdrew on the night of September 18, crossing the Potomac over the one precarious ford that stood between him and the entrapment of his country's principal army. Even then he considered swinging back up the Potomac to Williamsport, crossing the river again, and occupying Hagerstown, if only to obscure any impression that he had been subdued.

"We do not boast a victory," wrote one of Lee's personal staff two days after the return to Virginia; "it was not sufficiently decisive for that. The Yankees would have claimed a glorious victory had they been on our side & they no doubt claim it anyhow." Certainly McClellan counted it a "complete" victory, for he had rid Maryland of the invader and had hurt him more than a little in the process.[1] What he had not done, as Abraham Lincoln observed with great disappointment, was prevent Lee's escape and compel his surrender. A less cautious general might have accomplished as much on the afternoon of September 17, or the following morning. McClellan had hesitated to throw his last reserves into Burnside's contest when it hung by a thread, as Lee had done in D. H. Hill's fight for the sunken road. When reinforcements reached McClellan on Thursday morning after an all-night march, he considered them too exhausted to fight — although the equally weary divisions of McLaws and A. P. Hill had fought on Wednesday after their killing marches, saving the day for their commander in both cases. Within the preceding ninety days Lee's army had come to represent the great hope for Southern independence, and its capture should have put an early end to those hopes, perhaps as abruptly as it did in 1865. Had it been possible for the commanders of the two armies along Antietam Creek to exchange personalities, or for the armies to exchange commanders, two-thirds of the people who perished in the Civil War might have died at home, in their beds.

Hundreds died on the ground the night of September 17. More than one weary soldier heard the distinctive cries of particular men whom no one could reach without risking a flurry of bullets, and as the night progressed many of those voices grew weaker, stopping finally altogether.[2] Most of the Union soldiers bivouacked among the dead: a Massachusetts captain counted twenty dead men within a six-yard radius of his sleeping spot. A private in the Kanawha Division, who had left all his accoutrements on the other side of the creek, unwittingly shared a blanket with a dead Georgian on the bluff above what would always thereafter be known as Burnside's Bridge.[3]

A short truce on the day after the battle allowed for the retrieval of some of the wounded and burial of a few of the dead. The work demonstrated how abrupt a transformation overcame good men who had become heartless killers in the tumult of battle. The grey-haired sharpshooter Joseph Everest had lain in Mr. Miller's cornfield as the lines swept back and forth over him on Wednesday, and in passing over him one Confederate had leveled his musket at Everest's head: the Southerner spared him after Everest pleaded that he was a cripple, but the initial impulse to kill a helpless enemy bespoke an inhuman fury that the soldier only conquered with difficulty.[4] A few hours of sleep imbued the combatants of both sides with an overwhelming sympathy, and they treated their wounded opponents with abundant compassion. Lee's destitute infantry rifled the dead for anything valuable and relieved most of them of their shoes, but kindly Confederates served water to Sergeant Jonathan Stowe of the shattered knee and carried him out of the West Woods to a safer location. Henry Ainsworth, who belonged to another company of Stowe's regiment, had fallen in the same vicinity; other rebels found him Thursday morning and tucked him behind a protective limestone outcropping, with a fresh pile of straw to cushion his deathbed.[5] Union stretcher teams, meanwhile, catered with equal tenderness to the most desperately wounded of either army.[6]

The fraternity between the erstwhile enemies profoundly affected a

Union lieutenant from western Virginia, who suddenly recoiled at the bloodshed between men who spoke the same dialect. "I saw our brave and victorious boys carrying water and ministering in every way in their power to the comfort of those who a few minutes before they had met in deadly strife," he explained to his family. "The thought struck me — this is unnatural." Seeking respite from the slaughter, the lieutenant tried to resign soon after the battle.[7]

The sheer devastation of Antietam contributed substantially to a new epidemic of resignations. The men of the 107th New York uttered some snide comments when their colonel promptly departed in the wake of their brutal initiation, while one of their freshly commissioned captains — whose company was criticized for faltering under fire — spent the next six weeks conniving for a safe home-front assignment as a drillmaster or clerk. The particular horror of the battle of September 17 unnerved even stern old soldiers, like Colonel William Lee of the 20th Massachusetts. Lee, a West Point classmate of his distant kinsman Robert E. Lee, had been in the thick of the bloody brawl atop Ball's Bluff in 1861, and had spent months in a Confederate prison afterward. He had fought through Fair Oaks and the Seven Days, where he was injured, but he returned to duty a couple of weeks after his fifty-fifth birthday and a couple of weeks before Antietam, where his brigade lost far more men that day than any other in the Union army. After the fight he ceased giving orders and sat passively, ignoring everyone, and the next morning he mounted his horse and rode away from camp without a word to anyone. One of his captains found him ten miles away that evening, as incoherent as a child who had wandered from home and just turning in to a stable to spend the night.[8]

A Vermont youth who saw the mayhem along the Hagerstown Pike assured his parents that anyone who could have glimpsed the field on the day after the battle would cry for peace instantly. A New Hampshire sergeant who had made the charge against Burnside's Bridge damned no-compromise Republicans up and down as he toured the field; he supposed that if they could see such carnage even they might change their minds, and demand a settlement "in the name of God." The scenes at South Mountain and Sharpsburg horrified the quartermaster of a nine-month Pennsylvania regiment, who thought the politicians who had initiated the war should be "twice damned."[9]

No one found Mr. Everest the day of the cease-fire. The volume of casualties overwhelmed the burial and hospital parties, and the truce concluded with most of the stricken unattended. Not until Friday, the nineteenth, could the rescue resume in earnest, when someone finally carried the old sharpshooter to the shelter of a shed. Wounded were still being found on the third day after the battle.[10] Surgeons at their field stations amputated arms and legs throughout Thursday, Friday, and Saturday: the less seriously injured waited, or climbed into wagons and ambulances bound for Hagerstown. One doctor who had just reached his regiment dressed the wounds of sixty-four soldiers on September 20, after the most urgent amputations had been completed. Local citizens came to the battlefield with wagons and buggies to take some of the injured men into their homes.[11]

Every habitable house and barn became a hospital, but missiles and fire had left some of the houses and many of the barns so damaged that lean-tos and tents provided better protection. The productive Mumma farm, near the Dunker church, had been set ablaze to deprive Federal marksmen of its cover, and other homes had caught fire during the battle. An atmosphere of apocalyptic desolation blighted a landscape that had reflected only natural beauty and pastoral plenty a few days previously. Local farmers' crops had almost all been destroyed, and any that survived went into the maw of the voracious Union army. Trees everywhere bore the scars of shot and shell. Fences had been smashed and scattered. The soil had been haphazardly but thoroughly furrowed by artillery projectiles. Thousands of rifles littered the ground, abandoned by so many dead and wounded men that they lay more common than fence rails; colonels waded among them to re-arm entire regiments with preferred models or uniform calibers, and recruits arriving in the wake of the battle equipped themselves entirely from the debris.[12]

Confederate prisoners elicited abundant comment, particularly among recruits who had never seen their enemies at a speaking distance. A well-educated new private on his way to join the Hawkins Zouaves remarked that only the rebels' dusty homespun uniforms prevented them from making a much better impression than Union soldiers, and especially when compared to the paroled Yankees from Harper's Ferry. "They are naturally more lithe and active than we," he noted. They also struck the Zouave as much more serious in defense of their homeland than the Northern soldiers who had enlisted to stifle their attempt at independence. "There is," he added, "a look of savageness in their eyes not observable in the good natured countenance of our men." The Confederates' month-long pilgrimage had made shoes their greatest want; some of them had come to Maryland, said a Pennsylvanian, with "any old rags on their feet to keep them off the ground." A private in the 36th Massachusetts, which only reached the army after the battle, passed what may have been the same column of prisoners, and he complained that their aroma lingered long after they were gone. "A more dirty, lousy, stinking set of hellcats I never saw in my life," he wrote; ". . . they look more like buzzards than they do like men." A boy in a new regiment from western New York informed his parents that the Southern captives "looked like dogs to me; they looked mean."[13]

Above all, it was the harvest of death that demanded notice. Most descriptions of the dead bodies covering the ground failed to convey the extent of the slaughter, and men of modest vocabularies tended to mimic each other's attempts at more precise portrayals. Commonly they remarked that the dead lay so dense in a certain space — a square rod, an acre, two acres — that one might walk the entire area on them without touching the ground. Numerous witnesses at Antietam maintained that such a feat could have been accomplished for the distance of nearly a mile. Most who made that stunning assertion probably alluded to the sunken road where D. H. Hill's men had met two divisions of Sumner's corps; there one Union general found the dead lying "as thick as autumn leaves." A Union soldier who helped bury those Confederates counted 350 bodies in that short stretch of cart track, which had not yet come to be known as Bloody Lane. Heaps of Alabamians and North Carolinians tumbled over each other, as though they had been stacked — and human hands may indeed have done that work, as their surviving comrades struggled for room to fight. Nearby, where Richard Anderson's division had stood unprotected to support Hill's men, two solid ranks of Southern dead lay in almost the same formation they had assumed in the final moments of life. In the vicinity of the East Woods a whole regiment of Confederates appeared to have perished together with their feet to the firing line: a sauntering general tallied 149 of them stretched out in one distinct rank, with another 70 scattered just behind or ahead of them. One of the Pennsylvania Reserves who had fought there corroborated the general in the plural: the ragged enemy was "just laying in rows as if whole regiments had been mowed down."[14]

Lee's army had hardly vacated Sharpsburg when Alexander Gardner appeared with a wagonload of photographic equipment. By then many of the bodies had already disappeared beneath the sod: few Union soldiers remained in the awkward positions of sudden death, and conspicuous gaps appeared in the sunken road, where the Confederate dead had been said to lie densely and continuously packed. Undaunted, the cameraman erected his tripod and began capturing grim enough images on glass plates, to fascinate or horrify the home front and future generations.[15]

Recruits seemed to provide a disproportionate share of the burial details, and particularly the nine-month men, who were the least accustomed to such grisly duties. These involuntary sextons went about their work in unseemly haste, tossing so little earth over most of the lifeless forms that, as they readily admitted, a light rain would expose the bodies.[16] In some regiments squads banded together to seek messmates, relatives, or neighbors. Roland Bowen, of the decimated 15th Massachusetts, went back into the West Woods looking for Henry Ainsworth, who hailed from Bowen's hometown. After turning over hundreds of corpses he found his chum at last where the enemy had laid him, but the body had been robbed and the shoes were gone; the dead man's pockets had been emptied down to the ambrotype he carried of a special Millbury girl, whose anonymous portrait probably went back into Virginia as the fantasy fiancée of some Southern boy. By such evidence Bowen concluded that his friend had died sometime on September 18, before Lee's army departed. "I don't believe they would take anything from a wounded man," Bowen assured Ainsworth's sister, "especially his shoes." With others from the 15th he dug a broad trench three feet deep. In this they punctiliously spread a bed of hay, then deposited the bodies two deep, applying a topping of hay before piling dirt over the trench. Forty Worcester County men went into the pit, with a board at either end identifying their regiment. To aid future reinterment, some of the diggers recorded how far from either end of the trench their friends lay, and on which tier. The next morning Bowen wrote back to a civilian friend who had been arguing the merits of enlisting against Bowen's attempts to discourage him from it. "I have nothing more to say," wrote the exasperated Bowen. "Enlist if you want to. Come in the 15th so that I can Bury you. I don't know of any body that can do it quicker or with less ceremony."[17]

A romantic, reflective sergeant who had left his New Hampshire home less than a month before watched a similar mass burial of Federal soldiers that Friday. He supposed that decay alone would dissuade most families from retrieving their loved ones' remains, and reflected that no mothers, sisters, daughters, or wives would ever weep over these menfolks' graves at twilight, or cast flowers on them as anniversaries passed. Only "the sighing wind shall be their funeral dirge," he mourned.[18]

As early as Thursday the heat of late summer had begun to cook the corpses. The scent of death rose first at the sunken road, where the killing had been most concentrated, but soon it spread over the whole valley of the lower Antietam. Some of the odor seeped through fissures in the haphazard graves, but most of it radiated from the hundreds of dead horses that dotted the terrain. As beasts they seemed not to deserve the dignity of burial, while their bulk rendered such amenities inconvenient, but the neglect of their remains permeated the environs of Sharpsburg with a stench so nauseating by Sunday that soldiers began to worry that the smell itself carried virulent disease.[19]

One horse near the East Woods attracted particular attention. Of those who recorded it, Alpheus Williams may have seen it first — three of his brigades fought on that ground — and the sight wrung as much emotion from him as any on the field that day. "One beautiful milk-white animal had died in so graceful a position," he recalled, in a letter to his daughter, "that I wished for its photograph. Its legs were doubled under and its arched neck gracefully turned to one side, as if looking at the ball-hole in its side." He found it difficult to believe that the horse was dead, rather than nodding into sleep. One of McClellan's staff officer's evidently saw the same carcass, although he gave it a more rampant aspect in a postwar sketch. Dr. Oliver Wendell Holmes, of Harvard Medical School, found the animal so entrancing that it momentarily distracted him from his preoccupation with a wounded son. The horse — which, after four days in the elements, Holmes considered grey — had reportedly belonged to a Southern colonel who had died in a similarly peaceful manner, as if in a "deep sleep." Apparently his mount had expired slowly, first crumpling in the weakness of blood loss until forced to rest its muzzle on the trampled grass of David Miller's pasture, sternly resisting death until the last with sturdy muscles flexed. General Williams would have an opportunity to fulfill his wish for the creature's likeness, for Mr. Gardner arrived with his photographic wagon the next day and fixed his lens on the animal. Dr. Holmes later saw a print of Gardner's photograph and recognized it as the one he had meditated upon on that gruesome field.[20]

Few of those at home ever considered it, but the wholesale slaughter of horses posed an especially heartrending horror of nineteenth-century warfare for those who loved innocent brutes, and such men abounded. Some generals became famous for their fondness of horses, like Ulysses Grant, who despised gratuitous cruelty despite his readiness to grind men's lives away in bloody offensives. So it was with John Sedgwick, who came upon a Rhode Island artillery lieutenant viciously whipping his confused and exhausted mount one evening early in the Peninsula campaign. With gunners looking on, Sedgwick clamped his knobby fingers around the lieutenant's ear and twisted it painfully, releasing it finally with a promise that he would literally kick the young man out of camp if he ever caught him whipping his horse again.[21]

Army demands weighed heavily enough on horses pressed into service, and men from agricultural regions often pitied the animals that, as one Illinois soldier phrased it, "are forced to enact such a conspicuous part in this Abolition Crusade against the People of the South." Teamsters pushed their mules and horses relentlessly to bring up supplies; "I never saw anything abused as bad as the horses are *(except the men)*," claimed a Vermonter, and the experience of Dr. Holmes corroborated his assessment. Following the path of the army from Frederick to Sharpsburg through Middletown, Boonsborough, and Keedysville, Holmes frequently saw dead horses abandoned on the roadside and left to rot under a hot sun, unless some offended local resident tried to bury them. Like many, the good doctor developed a particular admiration for the army mule. "Sometimes a mule would give out on the road," Holmes observed; "then he was left where he lay, until by-and-by he would think better of it, and get up, when the first public wagon that came along would hitch him on, and restore him to the sphere of duty."[22]

Artillery mounts often had to stay in harness for days at a time, with the leather galling their hide, and during the Seven Days and Pope's Bull Run campaign batteries kept their horses in the traces for a solid week. When Banks fled the Shenandoah Valley before Jackson, numerous helpless, harnessed teams of mules drowned in the haste to cross the surging Potomac. On wet-weather marches teams routinely mired in mud up to their hocks or bellies, and occasionally to their shoulders, and from such depths they seldom emerged: if exhaustion alone failed to kill them, fatigue might compel them to lay their heads down, where they sometimes drowned.[23]

The necessity of such treatment seemed obvious enough, but deliberate cruelty disgusted and infuriated men accustomed to handling their own animals more humanely. An Iowa farmer assigned to duty at Columbus, Kentucky, watched a local man beat an emaciated horse until it fell down; whereupon the Iowan threatened to run the man through with his bayonet: that diverted the Kentuckian briefly, but later the soldier came back to find the horse dead, with its face pummeled to jelly. A Wisconsin soldier at the same post discovered a gully near his camp filled with hundreds of dead horses and mules shot by the Confederates who had evacuated the place, lest they fall into Union hands. Mounts deemed "unserviceable" often found a similar end in some natural depression where the dispatched animals could be more easily covered up or at least hidden from sight. Since such geographic features usually funneled runoff water into streams, their rotting flesh often fouled drinking water; retreating armies sometimes favored the trick of contaminating watercourses and ponds with the bodies of their worn-out horses, to deny drinking water to a pursuing enemy.[24]

A bullet in the brain was the customary reward for any horse that grew weak or lame in government service: cavalrymen, artillerymen, and teamsters lacked the time to care for injured animals, or to allow them to recover their strength. It was cheaper and simpler to shoot them and bring new ones into harness, as the common lands of the national capital testified: dead horses littered the mall surrounding the Smithsonian Institution. Quartermaster advertisements often specified big, strong geldings that stood a minimum of fifteen hands (that is, five feet high at the shoulder): stallions usually gave too much trouble, and mares not only tended to be smaller but might carry foal. Whole squadrons of cavalry remained idle because their horses had given out, and had to endure the indignity of dismounted drill in camp until wholesale purchases of new mounts put them back in the saddle. The army bought horses and mules by the herd; a newspaper correspondent following Grant's army in Tennessee saw droves of them going through the streets of LaGrange at all hours of the day and night. Forage alone for that army required a daily cavalcade of at least a hundred wagons drawn by six-mule teams, driven into the countryside by black muleskinners and brought back laden with corn and fodder.[25]

Their size made them conspicuous on the battlefield. Wounded horses often elicited intense commiseration from men who understood what terror they endured in addition to their pain; for some who witnessed it, the butchery of beasts forced under fire by the whip seemed worse, somehow, than the mutilation of men who had theoretically come to war of their own volition. Solid shot smashed horses' muzzles, or more mercifully took their heads off; shells blew away sleek legs, and left the dying animals gyrating wildly until some compassionate soul turned a pistol on them; bullets and fragments stung them deeply and repeatedly until they succumbed.[26]

Officers who had brought their own mounts usually rode favorites, and the loss of their four-legged friends hurt more than many of those men would normally have revealed. Phil Kearny, the recklessly courageous general who rode like a Plains Indian in battle despite missing half his left arm, unashamedly grieved for a beautiful bay colt killed under him at Fair Oaks. The colt was shot in the flank early in the engagement, but managed to carry Kearny until the fatal bullet struck him in the barrel. Orlando Poe's horse died in the same battle, prompting Poe to write of him as "that good old boy, which was shot dead under me." A week after the battle, in which ten of Poe's men were killed and four dozen wounded, many of them mortally, the colonel confessed to his wife that "I can't help thinking about my poor horse." A Massachusetts adjutant lamented having to abandon his wounded gelding during a minor skirmish on the Rappahannock, explaining to his mother and sisters that "I lost my beautiful, my pet, my almost brother Tommie. I can hardly write it without crying." An Ohio surgeon's horse collapsed while struggling over the mountains of northern Alabama, and the doctor reacted with similar grief when he realized that the animal would not survive: "I could have cried like a child," he confessed. A cavalry officer mourned for his beloved mare, shot through the chest in a routine contest for a mountain gap. A New York lieutenant who rode a massive, eighteen-hand steed throughout the Seven Days developed the same affection for him as for any other comrade who shared every danger of a grueling campaign; anxiety racked the lieutenant when a piece of shell finally lacerated the gelding's fetlock: as minor a wound as that might be considered elsewhere, it required rest and treatment that no mere lieutenant could provide in that theater, and a horse that was even momentarily crippled often had to be destroyed.[27]

Over the course of the war, Congress appropriated $123,864,915 for army horses. At an average cost of less than $120 per animal, that represented more than a million horses purchased for the Union armies alone, not including those impressed and stolen from Southern owners or privately purchased by officers, who were obliged to buy their own. From the first of January, 1864, until the end of the war, the Quartermaster Department bought 193,388 horses just for the cavalry, and of those cavalry mounts 38,277 died at the distribution depots before they were ever saddled for service. In the final eight months of the war, the department purchased 58,818 mules, of which 7,336 died before they were requisitioned. Even worse mortality awaited animals once they reached the armies, where auditors found that livestock was disposed of without any attempt at keeping field returns. The Army of the Potomac alone used up cavalry horses at the rate of 200 per day; the secretary of war estimated, probably conservatively, that 500 horses were destroyed every day throughout the army. That would have translated into three-quarters of a million horses over the course of the war, and it is not clear whether such calculations considered the mules that replaced so many horses on wagon teams.[28]

Tallying the destruction of Confederate horseflesh proved even more difficult, but transportation and other supply problems habitually left the livestock of Southern armies less well nourished than among Federal forces. That could only have worn them out faster, leading to a higher proportion of culling, and it should be safe to suppose that at least two horses or mules died for every soldier who gave his life in the conflict.

Horses and mules were not the only innocents to suffer from the politicians' decision to fight: their war also killed women and children. A young girl was reported killed by a Federal shell in Sharpsburg, and on that same day scores of children and young women died fifty leagues west and north of the battlefield. The Allegheny Arsenal, under the command of an ordnance colonel named John Symington, sat on the hills overlooking the river of the same name, just up Penn Street from downtown Pittsburgh, Pennsylvania; both Symington and the arsenal had gone into service during the War of 1812.[29] The most important part of the arsenal during the summer of 1862 was the laboratory, a big frame building between Butler Street and the Greensburg Pike, where civilian operatives assembled ammunition for the Union army. Some fifteen dozen boys and girls worked there, wrapping rifle cartridges, filling shells with powder, bundling artillery projectiles, or crimping percussion caps. Most of the boys had recently been replaced by girls, whom the foremen considered more "tractable" than adolescent lads — by which the foremen may have meant to say that they were easier to browbeat into faster production. The boys were also inclined to sneak matches into the arsenal, to satisfy newfound tobacco cravings that seldom appealed to girls of that era. A few adult women also worked at the laboratory, in addition to the children and the foremen.[30]

At about two o'clock on the afternoon of September 17, while Ambrose Burnside prepared for the final drive into Sharpsburg, a hundred and fifty miles away, a fatal spark ignited the arsenal. No one ever conclusively explained the cause: someone dropped a shell or knocked one from a bench, speculated many, although no one in the vicinity lived to testify; local rumors held that powder swept into the streets from the laboratory buildings caught fire somehow, just as draymen brought a wagonload of powder from the magazine. The first explosion sent workers in other parts of the arsenal rushing from their stations, but in one long building downhill from the laboratory the managers blocked the doors and shooed the girls back to work. They started back to their benches until a second blast rocked the complex, and then they stampeded for the door again. Once more the foreman refused to let them out, but they scurried away from him toward the windows. The building had been cantilevered over the precipitous hillside, leaving each window a yard higher above the ground than the next, but the three hundred terrified girls leaped anyway, rising with bloody scrapes and injured limbs to run or limp toward their homes down in the valley.[31]

The chief foreman of the works raced to a window at the first explosion, and the second threw him thirty feet, showering him with glass; his daughter was killed in the laboratory. The foreman of Rooms 13 and 14 ran toward the commotion, encountering a mob of shrieking girls too frightened to tell him anything, but as he neared the site he saw a girl completely engulfed in flames. He and another man tried to wrestle her to the ground, but just then the second eruption blew the roof off the engine house, covering them with smoldering debris. The men gave the girl up for lost and fled the grounds.

The sound of the blasts carried into town, where residents with family members at the arsenal doubtless spent their days dreading such an event. No alarm or siren was necessary: within seconds women began spilling out of the houses, already shrieking and sobbing as they flooded up Penn Street toward the buildings they knew would be the source of the explosion. Canister shot and bullets that had rained out of the explosion scattered in a four-hundred-yard perimeter around the wreckage of the building, which had been completely destroyed. The heat prevented anyone from pulling bodies from the rubble for hours afterward, but piles of blackened corpses could be seen through the flames. Other victims were thrown from the building by the force of the explosion. One woman racing up the hill stumbled by the body of her good friend, a Mrs. Shepard: she was burned beyond recognition, but the friend recognized the remnants of her dress. Mrs. Shepard's daughter died, as well. Two girls, Mary Dugan and Mary Donnelly, had escaped too badly burned to survive, and rescuers carried them beneath the shade of a tree, where a doctor tried in vain to ease their suffering for the last agonized hour of their lives.[32]

By evening 63 bodies had been collected, many of them incinerated down to the torsos, and most of the dead could not be identified. Many others remained inside as the sun set. Estimates of the number of employees on duty at the time of the accident ranged from 145 to 175, but no one seemed able to produce a roster or take a count of survivors. The blast came on payday, and many of those who might otherwise have perished had scurried home with their wages, The first day's recovery of bodies sustained early estimates of 75 to 80 killed, but no firm figure of the dead or injured seemed calculable. The names of most of the victims listed in the newspapers revealed Irish ancestry or birth, suggesting that the workforce had been supplied by the lower economic strata in which such perilous jobs were apparently acceptable for pubescent children.[33]

The conflagration at the Allegheny Arsenal earned scant news coverage beside page-long articles on "The Death Struggle of the Rebellion" along Antietam Creek. The army also gave it short shrift. A court of inquiry convened to investigate, and old Colonel Symington took immediate sick leave, retiring the following spring. The next year he died, quietly, at home.[34]

A few months later a similar mishap befell the Confederacy. Most ammunition for the Southern armies came from the old Virginia State Arsenal on Brown's Island, in the James River, opposite the end of Seventh Street in Richmond. The Confederate States Laboratory could not find many male employees, most men having been conscripted or assigned to more strenuous labor. As many as a hundred girls and women between the ages of twelve and sixty filled Department No. 6, which occupied a wooden building a hundred feet long and twenty feet wide. Here, too, the roster of Reilys, Burleys, Dalys, O'Briens, Brannons, Sullivans, and O'Connors betrayed a distinctly Irish flavor. The women specialized in lightweight pistol and breech-loading cartridges, and they worked a six-day week to keep up with demand. On Saturday morning, March 13, 1863, some sixty women stood at their tables along with five boys and the two acting superintendents. Just before noon the roof of the building burst open and the walls collapsed with a surprisingly muffled roar, and the splintered wood all caught fire.

A fire alarm signaled trouble on the island, all of which was devoted to making munitions. As at Pittsburgh, employees from elsewhere in the arsenal came running. Seventh Street swarmed with people from the city — mostly mothers, again — and traffic on the bridge threatened to collapse it until a guard detail pushed everyone back who could not help with the rescue. Only ten workers were found dead at the scene, but most of the badly burned did not survive more than a few hours, especially with the primitive treatment that came with such good intentions. Thinking that it might offer a buffer against the tenderness of their roasted skin, self-appointed nurses swathed victims of third-degree burns in raw cotton, which promptly adhered to the wounds. Some of the girls were burned from head to toe, and others only about the face and eyes. Seven horribly burned victims, one of whom was too severely injured to utter her name, were carried straight up Seventh to General Hospital No. 2, at the corner of Cary Street. Within three days the newspapers announced the deaths of thirty-six women and girls, one boy, and one of the superintendents. Another girl remained missing on March 16. Two dozen other female employees and five boys were still alive that day, but not all were expected to live through the week. Judging from the estimated force on duty, the only occupant of the building who escaped unharmed was the other superintendent.[35]

Another explosion killed a score or so of girls at the Washington Arsenal on June 17, 1864. Sixteen of the victims — again mostly Irish — went to their graves in the Congressional Cemetery in a mile-long procession two days later, with President Lincoln and Edwin Stanton heading the delegation of official mourners. Those who watched the sixteen hearses lumber down Pennsylvania Avenue never forgot it, but the fighting in Virginia overshadowed the news.[36]

With Union armies despoiling the Southern countryside, Confederate citizens may have felt better able to accept such tragedies as sacrifices required in defense of the homeland. As residents of the aggressor nation, Northern citizens may not have found it so easy to justify the immolation of women and children, as much as they might romanticize the butchery of men and boys as the ceremonial laying of lives on the altar of their nation. The cost of the war in men, money, and liberty had already exceeded what many otherwise patriotic citizens considered worth paying to retain the seceded states, and as summer turned to autumn people who shared such sentiments began gathering together to express their weariness with the conflict. They complained of high taxes (especially local taxes, bloated by the cost of bounties), high prices, inflated paper money, and arbitrary arrests, and then in the Midwest they began nominating political candidates whom they hoped might bring the war to a rapid close. Politicians in Ohio and Indiana began fearing an internal civil war among their own constituents.[37]

Calls for peace above the Ohio may have emanated in part from the proximity of Confederate armies in Kentucky. With his variegated assemblage of lightly equipped vagabonds Kirby Smith had captured Lexington, where the Confederacy enjoyed as much popularity as anywhere in Kentucky, and there he had been greeted by tolling church bells and citizens carrying the Stars and Bars. From that town he sent cavalry gallivanting to the outskirts of Louisville and to Frankfort, where a Louisiana regiment raised the Pelican flag over the state capitol on September 3. As usual, federal authorities overreacted to the impending danger in the Bluegrass and started rounding up citizens again on suspicion and flimsy pretenses, which only weakened their popular sympathy all the more. Some of Smith's dirt-encrusted infantry then wandered still farther north, within a few miles of Cincinnati, throwing the community leaders of that city and most of Ohio into apoplexy. Business in Cincinnati shut down altogether.[38]

Governor David Tod called on civilians to mobilize against the foe, and begged for government troops. Response to his appeal hinted that the average citizen shunned military service for reasons other than a fear of fighting. Overwhelming numbers of Ohioans gathered instantly to confront the expected invaders, dressed and armed so provincially that they earned instant renown as "the Squirrel Hunters." They came by the thousands: the little town of Wilmington alone sent 406 men. From all over the Midwest and the old Northwest, swarms of new troops and informal volunteers converged on the Queen City of the West (which a disappointed Wisconsin recruit thought had been transformed into "a kind of dirty looking place" by the ubiquitous use of coal stoves). Grateful citizens feted and treated these saviors at every way station and in Cincinnati itself, plying them with pies, cakes, fruit, and coffee. Don Carlos Buell sat in Nashville with the Army of the Ohio, reluctant to abandon Tennessee, but Louisville quickly assembled a motley garrison of more than 25,000 and Cincinnati accumulated even more volunteers in and out of uniform — either of which force, despite its inexperience, would have easily outnumbered Smith's entire command.[39]

Then Bragg entered Kentucky with, as Union sources overestimated it, 35,000 Confederate soldiers. On September 17 he forced an oversized Union brigade at Munfordville to surrender, taking 4,300 prisoners. A division from Smith's command threatened the 10,000 Federals at Cumberland Gap with a similar fate, and that same evening those Yankees (who had been dreading investment by Bragg or Smith since early July) began a harried hegira northward to the banks of the Ohio. Northern newspapers consoled their public with exaggerated estimates of Confederate losses, but with about 40,000 men between them Bragg and Smith turned central Kentucky into Confederate territory through the entire month of September. In the process they suffered fewer than a thousand casualties, while inflicting 10,000 on the enemy and sending even more than that into headlong flight. By any measure, Bragg and Smith had done at least as well as Lee's army had in Maryland.[40]

While the bigger armies surged north and south on either side of him, William Loring lingered in the Kanawha Valley of western Virginia, driving Union forces toward the Ohio and maintaining his headquarters at Charleston. He enjoyed some success in recruiting, and numbers of armed Unionist citizens surrendered their weapons and offered to take an oath of allegiance to the Confederacy. Loring found that he had to compete with the Virginia State Line — state regiments composed essentially of draft evaders, deserters, and brigands under the incompetent command of a miscreant politician who had disgraced himself in both United States and Confederate service. Rather than assisting Loring, the State Line siphoned strength from his little army, misappropriated horses and provisions that he might have used, and generally soured the populace on Confederate authority. Loring nevertheless held his ground for several weeks, connecting the Maryland and Kentucky incursions geographically to create the impression of a surging Confederate tide. Only after the major armies shrank back east and west of him did he see fit to retreat.[41]

Since late July, Abraham Lincoln had been pondering his proclamation on slavery. He had evidently hoped for a decisive Union victory that would allow him to issue it without lending it the tone of a desperate exercise in bombast, but nowhere had his armies won any decisive contests. Secretary Chase saw little triumph in pushing Lee out of Maryland when he had taken with him all the guns, ammunition, and other equipment he had wrested from Union forces, besides inflicting double his own losses on McClellan and the Harper's Ferry garrison. The navy secretary, Welles, perceived Lee's escape as a distressing loss. Chase supposed that the Maryland campaign had left the Army of Northern Virginia relatively stronger than the Army of the Potomac, and then there was the demoralizing new defeat at Munfordville, Kentucky, on top of the August 30 disaster at Richmond. Even considering Lee's retreat across the Potomac, Confederate forces everywhere between the James River and the Tennessee had driven the Federals back a hundred to two hundred miles. The treasury secretary remained hopeful, but he could not feel confident of ultimate success, and his colleague at the Navy Department found the portents even more foreboding. "A favorable termination of this terrible conflict," Welles observed later that week, "seems more remote with every moment."[42]

Pressure for action on slavery mounted daily from the radicals of Lincoln's party. In mid-August had come Horace Greeley's public demand for an abolition policy to sanctify the Union cause: the president had replied famously that he would free all slaves, no slaves, or selected slaves, as necessary to preserve the Union, but Secretary Chase heard from prominent citizens that emancipation seemed vital to restoration of the Union, and he forwarded their advice along with his own.[43] Senators tested each other for their readiness to demand action — one of them seriously suggesting that Jefferson Davis might preempt Lincoln with his own emancipation declaration, to win European support and cloak his war of independence in a righteous veneer of liberty.[44]

That ludicrous fear aside, timing did seem crucial. As at least one correspondent reminded him, Lincoln could not afford to wait much longer if he were to avoid the dreaded appearance of weakness. In a letter handed to the president by Chase during the September 19 cabinet meeting, Robert Dale Owen noted that Lincoln had issued a proclamation on July 25 warning those in rebellion that the federal government would seize their property under the sixth section of the most recent Confiscation Act: that section specified a sixty-day limit to the warning, and those sixty days would expire on September 23. Owen contended that the failure to make widespread seizures after that date, or to at least mark the passage of the deadline with some significant action, would probably nullify any coercive effect of the July proclamation. Lincoln appears to have given Owen's letter due consideration, and on the second morning after receiving it he rewrote a penultimate draft of his proclamation, incorporating Owen's suggestion to protect loyal slave owners from any economic loss. The president's acute sense of dramatic symbolism also must have left him conscious of the September 23 date implied by his earlier proclamation. McClellan's imperfect victory was the closest the Union had come to a real triumph in months, and with the promise of no other on the horizon it would have to do.[45]

Before noon on Monday, September 22, State Department messengers visited all the cabinet officers with instructions to repair to the White House for a noon meeting with the president. All members heeded the summons, perhaps with stomachs grumbling, but Abe Lincoln was never one to leap directly to his point, and particularly one so momentous as the subject he surprised them with that day. He entered the cabinet room with a copy of Charles Farrar Browne's collection of humorous sketches, all written in dialect under the pseudonym of Artemus Ward, and he annoyed his impatient secretary of war by reading one long passage aloud. All but the humorless Stanton chuckled or smiled when he finished, anticipating some grave announcement, and Lincoln did not disappoint them. He reminded them of their objections and comments when he had proposed a statement on emancipation in July, and said that he had been considering it ever since. He told them that he had made a silent vow during the Maryland campaign to issue the proclamation in return for salvation from the invader. According to Gideon Welles, Lincoln said he promised to announce it "if" God gave the victory to McClellan. Chase recalled it only as a determination to release the document "as soon as" the Confederate army was expelled from Maryland. That time had come, and he told them his decision was final; he merely wished to inform them of it before they read it in the newspapers. He read it aloud to them, accepted a couple of minor corrections, and handed it to Secretary Seward for publication on the morrow — the sixty-day deadline of September 23.[46]

A fellow cabinet member thought that Seward still opposed the proclamation, his antislavery background notwithstanding, but if Seward entertained any reservations he abandoned them once he saw how stiff the wind blew in favor of it. Postmaster General Blair had written down his own objections a few days before, fearing its effect in the border states, in the army, and on the fall elections, but he asked only to have his position statement formally received and filed. His sister greeted the news more harshly the following morning, when she read it in the newspaper. "The President's proclamation took the breath out of me," she wrote. Suspecting that Lincoln had been taken over by the "Phillistines" of Radical Republicanism, she added him to the nation's enemies. With the proclamation, she supposed, "all that could be done to hurt our cause has been done."[47]

Lincoln declared all slaves free in any state that remained in active rebellion after January 1, 1863 — exactly one hundred days after his September 22 announcement, which made such a handy interval that it may have further moved him to act on that date. The restriction to states in rebellion nominally protected the institution in the loyal border states, but everyone understood that slavery could not long survive in the central sliver of an otherwise free nation: Union victory would therefore also assure abolition in the border states. Blair's concern over border-state reaction to that inevitable effect might have been just as valid in some of the Confederacy as well. A loyal Tennessean visiting Senator Orville Browning at his Illinois home the day after the announcement told him that eastern Tennessee was not the only bastion of national loyalty in the

Volunteer State. His own neighborhood in the western part of Tennessee was populated by plenty of secret Unionists, he assured the senator, but he positively dreaded the dampening effect of Lincoln's proclamation.[48]

The observations of Union soldiers in Tennessee corroborated that man's assessment: two months earlier a Wisconsin soldier serving there had noted that most men either had kin in the Confederate army or had been in it themselves, yet they seemed perfectly willing to give up the war if only they could keep their slaves. An Ohio officer had detected a similar feeling in Murfreesboro as early as the previous spring: as rabidly partisan as the populace seemed, and as gleefully as they reacted to Union defeats, they appeared to have given up on independence and merely hoped to save their property. A Nashville lawyer believed the people of Middle Tennessee much less hostile to the Washington government in the summer of 1862, largely as a result of conciliatory policies pursued by generals like Don Carlos Buell.[49]

From Washington City the former editor of the *Nashville Democrat* called Lincoln's proclamation "the crowning act of fanatical folly." This man had championed the Union until his editorials required him to seek a more salubrious latitude, but even in exile he resented the arrogance of abolition by fiat, challenging the right of either the president or Congress to dictate "such a radical change in our social & industrial system." From the perspective of that Southern Unionist, Lincoln had shifted the focus of the war from the suppression of secessionists to the subjugation of the entire South.[50]

An Illinois cavalry captain who had spent the better part of a year in Arkansas offered Senator Browning a similar view of the loyalty that lingered inside the Confederacy, and of the galvanizing effect emancipation might exert on the Southern population. The captain had reached Arkansas before the second and more sweeping of the Confiscation Acts, and the population at that time had seemed almost ready to give up the fight for independence: all the old Whigs and some of the Democrats remained loyal, he averred. Had Union forces secured the state capital, he told Browning, a loyal governor and legislature might have been installed. Instead, the generals ignored Little Rock to seize the valuable cotton at Helena, some of the proceeds of which he firmly believed had gone into officers' pockets, and in the worst spirit of confiscation Union soldiers had pillaged at will among loyal and disloyal citizens alike until they had "made rebels of them all."[51]

Either the president did not recognize the quiet repatriation such men saw in the South or he considered it insufficiently widespread to warrant further cultivation. Only by one argument or the other was it possible to justify the ultimate reversal of his policy toward the rebellious states, by which he alienated any Southerners he had won back by lenience and essentially started over with a goal of military subjugation that did not then seem feasible.

In addition to any divine bargain he may have struck, and a wish to maintain the timeline of his confiscation policy, Lincoln had an immediate practical reason to make the announcement on the day he did. As he read the Artemus Ward sketch to his cabinet members, most of the Northern state governors had already departed their various capitals for Altoona, Pennsylvania, where they intended to convene for a discussion of the conduct of the war. These governors controlled the supply of troops to the nation's armies; it was they who had submitted to the artifice of calling on the president to ask them for more soldiers. Radical Republicans like Zachariah Chandler had been hoping for a revolt among those governors — whom he hoped would extract a demand for more ruthless war under the threat of withholding troops. The New England contingent surely meant to impose such a radical flavor on the convention, and a conservative newspaper reporter suspected them of wanting McClellan's removal in favor of Frémont. If those New England Republicans expected any critical resolutions, though, the emancipation announcement cut the legs from under them. The governors met at Altoona's Logan House right after lunch on September 24, and into the evening they debated what, if anything, to say about the surprise proclamation and the performance of George McClellan. The conference concluded with a vow of continued support and assistance signed by all but the chief magistrates of New Jersey and Maryland, who declined to join in their colleagues' praise of the president's proclamation.[52]

The silent dissent of the two conservative governors represented the mildest of many rebukes. While abolitionist reaction ranged from earnest praise for its noble theme to moderate disappointment with its bland tone, the proclamation elicited a less enthusiastic response from Northern society generally. Telegraphic distribution of the proclamation wrung a sense of betrayal from Democratic newspaper editors who were already upset with the summer's arbitrary arrests and two seasons of military setbacks. The *Courier*, of Prairie du Chien, Wisconsin, deemed the president's action perfectly perfidious. The *Chicago Times*, which had applauded the effort to preserve the Union and had been among the first to propose conscription as a means toward that end, charged Lincoln with an absolute lack of constitutional authority for any such unilateral decision. Supporters tried to legitimize the proclamation by a claim of executive war powers, as they had pleaded during each of Lincoln's earlier unconstitutional actions, but the *Times* pointed out that the Constitution meant nothing if its authority did not prevail in war as well as during peace.[53]

That accusation hit home, for the Republican platform had always included not only a promise not to disturb slavery in the states but an acknowledgment that the national government had no power to do so. Lincoln had explicitly embraced that doctrine in the first moments of his inaugural address, when he reiterated an earlier assertion that "I have no purpose, directly or indirectly, to interfere with the institution of slavery in the States where it exists. I believe I have no lawful right to do so, and I have no inclination to do so." Now he attempted to do what he had specifically insisted he lacked the power to do, and strict constructionists made fair game of that hypocrisy; the contradiction did not escape the Dutch ambassador to the United States, who considered Lincoln either vacillating or sly for openly reneging on his best-known campaign promise. The *Times* accused the president of setting the government itself into rebellion against the very law of the land.[54]

The *Detroit Free Press* clearly disapproved of the proclamation, but the Unionist Democrat who edited that sheet expressed perverse relief at the president's capitulation to radical pressure. Reasoning that Lincoln had tried for a year and a half to fight the war while seeking some means of crushing "the small demon of slavery" — with disastrous results — the editor hoped that now he could devote more attention to "the great demon of disunion."[55]

Samuel Medary, editor of the *Crisis* in Columbus, Ohio, opposed Lincoln's war even though his son served with George Morgan and was at that moment retreating with Morgan over the mountains from Cumberland Gap. To Medary the proclamation represented the nadir of the nation's history. Hated abolitionism, which he and many others credited with spawning the country's devastating war, now ruled the country. Attending a soirée in Salmon P. Chase's home on the evening Medary's editorial appeared, even one of Lincoln's private secretaries seemed sympathetic to that interpretation: Chase and some other officials congratulated each other as "abolitionists," and John Hay cringed at the glee with which they embraced "that horrible name." Medary predicted that the threat of emancipation would "unite the South as one man."[56]

The news met a cool reception in the army, too. An Ohio lieutenant in Buell's army agreed with Medary, anticipating that the next campaign would be the bloodiest yet because Southern troops would fight so fiercely against a war of overt abolition. Soldiers from southern Indiana also seemed vexed by it, for when Buell chased Bragg up to Louisville late in September scores of the 6th Indiana took the opportunity to slip across

the Ohio to their homes, whence they evidently had no intention of returning. Barely 150 men clung to the colors when the regiment marched
after Bragg again, while desertion had similarly weakened the 32nd Indiana and the 5th Kentucky, known as the "Louisville Legion." By October some thirty officers remained absent without leave in the division to
which those regiments belonged. Similar absenteeism afflicted border
regiments in the Army of the Potomac in the wake of the proclamation.
By September 26 the 1st District of Columbia Volunteers had evaporated:
every man not listed as sick, and many who were, had deserted.[57]

Preliminary speculation on general emancipation had initiated some
camp grumbling the previous July, but fewer of the common soldiers
responded to the actual proclamation in September. Vigorous opponents
may have spent their venom on the July rumor, but many of the troops
who had enlisted just before Lincoln's announcement did record the sensation of having been duped. A few days afterward, one bitter New
Hampshire recruit who had reached the Army of the Potomac a week before the Emancipation Proclamation wrote his new bride that "things
look entirely different from what I expected[;] it is hard to tell what we
are fighting for, I can tell you." Another Granite State volunteer observed
that "the soldiers think different of the war than they did when they
inlisted," adding that "if the boys was at home now their wood not 10 of
them enlist again."[58]

That prediction may have been accurate in spirit, if not in proportion.
Recruiting dropped off sharply in late September, as President Lincoln
himself noted before the proclamation was a week old. He may have
hoped for legions of new volunteers from the ranks of abolitionists who
had clamored so boisterously for such a policy; instead, as he pointed out
to his vice president, enlistments had not even kept pace with attrition. At
the end of six days, the armies were weaker than they had been before his
announcement.[59]

In the September summary of his journal a New England farmer gave
theoretical emancipation a timorous reception, ominously scribbling "god
only knows the fuchure," but the wife of a conservative New York Democrat scoffed outright at such "weak threats." A similar assessment of the
proclamation's ineffectuality probably diminished its apparent significance
to many in the army. "I don't know what effect it is going to have on the
war," wrote Walt Whitman's soldier-brother, "but one thing is certain, he
[Lincoln] has got to lick the south before he can free the niggers." One
private suggested that the "old man" had gone far toward winning the war
with his proclamation despite that soldier's own conclusion, a few weeks
previously, that Southerners might abandon the contest if they could only
keep their slaves. This man admitted that he had not enlisted to end slav-

ery, but he accepted the premise that abolition had become a war measure although he seemed unable to articulate why; he expected it to change the way the war was fought, too, but he failed to explain how.[60]

Surprising support also came from soldiers with deep-seated contempt for blacks and abolitionists alike. A Vermont sergeant acknowledged that he hated both, and said the army harbored few abolitionists, but his attachment to the Union persuaded him to embrace emancipation to weaken the South. One confused man still scorned abolition even after accepting emancipation by executive order. "I believe in putting away any institution if by so doing it will help put down the rebellion," he wrote on the New Year's Day deadline, "for I hold that nothing should stand in the way of the Union — niggers, or anything else." In the next sentence, though, this same pragmatist boasted of his comrades murdering contrabands, and five weeks later he rejoiced at the political conversion of an antislavery relative who had come into the army, remarking that "no one can come out here and believe his senses and remain an abolitionist."[61]

Men wearing shoulder straps expressed themselves more particularly about the great document, and the most sophisticated appeared unimpressed by it, or worse. The perennially reflective General Hitchcock, who had lived in slaveholding Missouri, approved of the humanitarian motives behind theoretical abolition but feared that the effort to do right in that regard would lead to unintended injustice and unforeseen consequences. A captain in the Boston-officered 2nd Massachusetts rightly supposed that his family reveled in the decree, but he admitted that it seemed meaningless to him. "Wherever our army has been," he pointed out, "there remain no slaves, and the Proclamation will not free them where we don't go." He saw so little purpose in it that he sincerely asked his mother to solicit one of her abolitionist friends for a written explanation of its potential usefulness as a war measure. Another captain in the equally Brahmin 20th Massachusetts remarked that he and his fellow officers greeted Lincoln's pronouncement with "universal disgust."[62]

Fitz John Porter, commander of McClellan's Fifth Corps, confirmed that revulsion. "The proclamation was ridiculed in the army," Porter revealed to the editor of the *New York World* a week after the document reached the newspapers. It had, he insisted, "caused disgust, discontent, and expressions of disloyalty to the aims of the administration — amounting I have heard, to insubordination." Porter charged that "All such bulletins tend only to prolong the war by rousing the bitter feelings of the south — and causing unity of action among them — while the reverse with us." Two days later Lincoln further aggravated conservatives by suspending habeas corpus nationwide for selected crimes and suspicions, and the Treasury Department clerk who served as chief of the *New York*

Herald's Washington bureau reported that army officers below the rank of brigadier general showed almost universal contempt for the president's course. "The army is dissatisfied and the air is thick with revolution," he informed his newspaper boss, suggesting that the time was ripe for a military coup, if only McClellan were to develop political ambition.[63]

The suspension of habeas corpus on September 24 worried the thoughtful far more than the proclamation of September 22. Many Democrats who supported Lincoln in his war against secession merely snickered at emancipation as a piece of radical folly, but recoiled in horror at his arbitrary abrogation of the Bill of Rights. Pleading with Lincoln to shun the dictator's impulse and return to his constitutional authority, the *Detroit Free Press* echoed the *Chicago Times*, reiterating that the U.S. Constitution meant nothing if it could be rescinded, even in wartime, and especially at the whim of a single executive. "We appeal to him," wrote the Detroit editor, "by that liberty which we believe he loves, not to leave a precedent which a less honest ruler may use to oppress the nation."[64]

Kentuckian Joseph Holt, formerly one of James Buchanan's cabinet officers and now Lincoln's judge advocate general, felt that the time had come for every citizen to subordinate his own interests to victory, whatever the cost: for his part he had swallowed his considerable repugnance for abolition, and his actions as judge advocate suggested that he regarded the suppression of civil liberties as a relatively minor cost. He and others whose blatant loyalty effectively immunized them to most infringements belittled the anxiety over constitutional excesses. "We are for any measure that will put down this rebellion," asserted an Ohio lieutenant, "constitutional or not." As though secession had repealed the Constitution in all the states, he insinuated that it had no power while the rebellion lasted. "Whenever I hear a man commence to quibble about the constitution," he concluded, with unintended irony, "then I begin to doubt his loyalty."[65]

A New York lieutenant who had been in the war from the first seemed perplexed and a bit depressed after publication of the proclamations, complaining to his sister that the "question is getting so mixed up that I'm losing a great deal of interest in it." He reminded her that he and many of his comrades had come into the army "full of hope and confidence," but that now they felt "cast down and discouraged." Colonel Charles Wainwright, the chief of artillery for the First Corps, opined sarcastically on the contradictions within the Emancipation Proclamation itself: he noticed that Lincoln began the document by asserting that the war was being prosecuted to restore the Union, and then he deftly transformed it into a war of abolition. Wainwright confirmed that little was said about it in the army that September, but he deduced that all the officers considered at least the timing of it injudicious, including those who most consistently opposed slavery. A New York adjutant may have recorded the plurality view in his journal: "Will it have much effect . . . ?" he wondered. "I fancy not." Major General William T. Sherman conveyed similar apathy to his brother, Ohio senator John Sherman, supposing that "the President's proclamation can do no good & but little harm."[66]

The presidential proclamations of September 22 and 24 turned the tide for Major Lawrence Williams, of the 6th U.S. Cavalry. Williams had been born in the District of Columbia and graduated from West Point in 1852; he boasted of aristocratic relations in Virginia, but he clove to the Union despite his acquaintances' predictions to the contrary. General McClellan invited Williams to his staff for a time, but his hatred for abolitionists triggered radical doubts of his loyalty, and during the Peninsula campaign someone had ordered him arrested. He never learned who gave that order, or on what grounds, but his revulsion for Edwin Stanton hinted at a logical suspicion. Originally contemptuous of Lincoln, by the summer of 1862 Williams had come to think of him as the only honest man in the administration, and the president's public defection to abolition policy must have demolished the major's last hope for the government. Retiring to New York City without benefit of official permission, Williams drank the autumn and winter away at the New York Club, fulminating against the ruling party in Washington until his prolonged absence brought a formal dismissal.[67]

Other officers repelled by emancipation tried to leave the service honorably, but not always with success. The commander of an Ohio regiment and one of his captains submitted their resignations once the proclamation became effective, citing that policy as their grounds, but they found themselves cashiered as a result. A disaffected Kentucky lieutenant drew the same treatment, with a couple of weeks' imprisonment to boot. The sudden shift in war aims may have fueled much of a new surge of resignations that autumn, although the stated reasons tended to the customary ill health and personal considerations. A Massachusetts lieutenant returning to his regiment after Antietam found eleven other officers under arrest for submitting frivolous requests for discharge, and the most common expression he heard from them was, "If I could only get home the Union might go to H–ll."[68]

The army's officer corps did not, of course, regard the emancipation declaration with unanimous disdain. An aide de camp in Tennessee claimed with exaggerated confidence that the entire Army of the Cumberland endorsed it because it would force white Southerners to stay home and watch their slaves. On court-martial duty in Washington, Brigadier General James Garfield called it "one of the sublimest works of any age." That certainly seemed to be the minority reception, but those who held it seemed perfectly effervescent.[69]

Neither did the enlisted men universally denounce Lincoln's decree. Anticipating it by a couple of weeks, Connecticut recruit Robert Kellogg predicted that slavery would still destroy the country if it were not eradicated, and he regretted the president's hesitation on that issue. Like most with a strong inclination to free the slaves, Kellogg implied a veiled exasperation with McClellan in particular, who represented the stubborn reluctance to complicate the "Union as it was" with any effort toward abolition.[70]

Still, soldiers writing home that September of 1862 seldom evinced Kellogg's eager support for emancipation. Many correspondents accepted the measure, often grudgingly, but for every such letter that survives there is one or two from some bitterly resentful enlisted man who had not gone to war to free the slaves, and who lacked the privilege of resigning from this new crusade. More often, though, men in the ranks failed to note the impending day of jubilee until January approached, but by then the most outspoken of them still seemed dissatisfied with it. Pragmatic privates occasionally hoped the freed slaves could be armed to take over the fighting, but one Pennsylvanian of alleged antislavery principles judged that the "enlisted men are utterly oposed to the Proclamation." He considered it a dangerous digression from the war's original goal besides being badly timed, for by January 1 a new series of military setbacks had left the government looking more feeble than ever. An Iowa private on duty along the Mississippi lamented that his entire company did little but rant about Lincoln and his abolitionist handlers.[71] Mail from every Union army dripped with such bitterness, and the cherished fight to save the flag became "this nigger war," or an "Abolition Crusade." Countless thousands of men felt that way, and they wanted out of it.[72]

Abolitionists were, after all, hated as much as slaveholders by many soldiers and citizens, who assigned them equal blame for inciting sectional differences through antislavery agitation. Men in uniform spurned hometown newspapers that started leaning toward emancipation. It did not go unnoticed that those who had clamored loudest for emancipation at any cost were not well represented in the ranks, and many a soldier who felt used by the radical faction wished every abolitionist in hell, or at least drafted into the front lines. A Connecticut father found it particularly ironic that his son's civilian abolitionist friends tried to persuade his boy to fight in a war that those very people had instigated, and an Iowa farmer whose son had just enlisted could summon no worse epithet than to characterize Mr. Lincoln as "thoroughly Abolitionized." A Pennsylvania captain reprimanded his own brother for daring to stay home after years of espousing radical antislavery doctrine — leaving the fighting and dying to the conservatives who had warned all along of the danger in their provocation of Southern slaveholders. Another conservative Pennsylvanian damned abolitionists and secessionists alike, and in his last letter he seemed to include his own father.[73]

For all the bigoted rhetoric, racial hatred may have influenced the soldiers' hostility to emancipation less than the scent of deception by the very government those troops strove to defend: the issue for many was the feeling that they had been duped into an irrevocable commitment, only to have the rules immediately changed. A man who had joined the army only because he could not find employment guessed that not one in ten of his fellow soldiers would have enlisted, had they but known. Veterans and recruits across the country resorted to dissenting newspapers to vent their outrage at being gulled into fighting for the freedom of "these lazy black niggers," and against the rule of the Constitution, on the pretext of patriotic devotion. "We believe in emancipation," wrote an 1861 volunteer from Maine, "but not in slaying the best men of the country by the hundred thousand to accomplish it." An orderly sergeant in a new three-year regiment dared any man to come out with the army and maintain either his antislavery principles or his nationalistic politics, betting that few would want to hear anything of a "niger proclamation" or even fight a war to preserve the Union.[74]

Some of the most supportive reactions came from soldiers and civilians of the border regions where Montgomery Blair and many others had logically expected the stiffest resistance. The sergeant major of what had just become the 1st West Virginia Cavalry wrote his wife that he favored the proclamation "heart & soul." A Union woman who owned numerous slaves on a Virginia farm confided to a New Jersey colonel that she approved of the proclamation — although she may have had her eye on the provision for compensation to loyal owners, for the colonel noted that most of her slaves had already absconded.[75]

It was Northern territory that provided the most worrisome discontent about the proclamation, including Lincoln's own hometown. John Todd Stuart — the president's political mentor, his first law partner, and Mary Lincoln's first cousin — considered it "most unfortunate" and stood for Congress on an antiadministration platform. Like the suspension of habeas corpus, the proclamation alienated many of those Democrats who had most welcomed the government's other efforts to suppress the rebellion. Even Lincoln's close friend in Washington, Senator Browning, thought the president grew delusional about the political situation, alluding a little later to "the hallucination the President seems to be laboring under" that the war could yet be ended and the rebellion conquered if only Congress would pass his plan of compensated emancipation.[76]

Opposition from kindred political spirits of so many decades' acquaintance illustrated Lincoln's abrupt conversion. Campaign and inaugural promises regarding preservation of the Union had seemed sacred enough to merit the worst war his nation would ever know, but similar promises to leave the future of slavery to the state governments had somehow warranted less faith. The sense of betrayal naturally sank deepest among Democrats who had defended Lincoln from the first against accusations that he waged a war of abolition and subjugation.

Like Lincoln, John Stuart and Orville Browning were Kentucky natives, but both were a little older than the president and both had remained in the Bluegrass into manhood. They more accurately reflected the flavor of Kentucky sentiment, which weighed very heavily against any type of emancipation. In that state the people had managed very well to separate the issues of Union and human bondage, but for many Kentuckians the horror of imminent abolition took precedence over the fear of disunion, and in that state Postmaster General Blair's fear of border backlash ought to have provoked executive anxiety. Kentucky was the keystone of the Union arch, as Lincoln had admitted exactly one year before releasing his proclamation: on September 22, 1861, while explaining his decision to revoke John C. Frémont's own emancipation order in Missouri, Lincoln had written Browning that "I think to lose Kentucky is nearly the same as to lose the whole game." Yet now Lincoln threatened a more general emancipation with more certain and direct effects on his native state, and he did so wittingly, in the face of little-changed public attitudes. Only a few weeks before issuing his proclamation he had learned that his confiscation orders had prompted accusations of abolitionism and an appeal for disunion by a formerly loyal Louisville newspaper. The president had interpreted that editorial as "a declaration of hostility" from all Kentucky's crucial pro-Union Democrats, and the realization had sobered him, yet seven weeks later he had further aggravated that very faction and corroborated the accusation.[77]

With the soldiers' common habit of projecting their own principles universally, two Kentucky cavalrymen pronounced the entire Army of the Ohio demoralized by Lincoln's proclamation: they suspected that most of their comrades would be unwilling to fight another battle if the war no longer amounted to a defense of the Constitution and the old Union. The reports of spontaneous desertions from Kentucky units nevertheless lent such claims an air of truth, and outraged observations on slave-stealing among Northern troops highlighted the validity of Kentucky concern over any form of emancipation, however sincerely it may have been meant to target secessionists alone. Theodore Bell, the Louisville physician who presided over Kentucky's branch of the U.S. Sanitary Commission, described for Joseph Holt a near-riot that took place between city police and soldiers of the 77th Illinois, who had secreted runaway slaves in their camp. The police arrested the fugitives in accordance with both state and federal law, for at least some of those slaves belonged to notoriously loyal citizens, but a squad of armed soldiers under a sergeant tried to liberate the prisoners. An ugly crowd gathered and ultimately persuaded the soldiers to retire, but in Clark County, east of Lexington, another contingent of troops successfully defied a sheriff's posse. Kentucky Home Guards who had thus far defended the government had grown sufficiently incensed at abolitionist Northerners "to abate these outrages with powder and lead," Dr. Bell warned.[78]

Wholesale roundups of Kentucky citizens had wrought nearly as much damage there as the shadow of emancipation, and especially in Louisville, where Brigadier General Jeremiah Boyle wielded federal authority. When Kirby Smith and Braxton Bragg invaded the state, Boyle responded by arresting anyone who uttered a discouraging word, or anyone with a personal enemy vicious enough to bear false witness against him, and news of Boyle's crackdown reached Washington. Joshua Speed, President Lincoln's old Springfield roommate and a firm Unionist, reportedly disapproved of Boyle's heavy-handed administration, and even those who suspected Boyle of harboring good intentions considered him temperamentally unfit for the job. Boyle, an undistinguished Danville lawyer, had surrounded himself with a coterie of apparent opportunists: "Very few old law abiding citizens can approach him," complained a Louisville resident, who added that Boyle's military command betrayed the "poison of insubordination." Apprehension over the delicate political situation in Kentucky brought Boyle a reprimand for his arbitrary arrests from Edwin Stanton, whose customary indifference to the detention of citizens suggested that the reproof may have originated with Lincoln himself. Boyle disingenuously denied having ordered an unusual number of arrests, but Joshua Speed's brother James remarked that "we are rapidly tending towards a military despotism. This is plainly so in Ky."[79]

On the morning that Lincoln sent for his cabinet to read his proclamation to them, Confederate soldiers awoke within sight of his childhood home. Braxton Bragg's tent stood only a few miles from there, and Bragg would pass that spot during the day, while a Confederate cavalry division trailed into nearby Hodgenville that evening and made camp. Women and children poured out of Louisville, and male citizens took up arms in imitation of their Ohio counterparts, but the enemy never ventured closer. Bragg led his army to Bardstown, establishing his headquarters near that town's courthouse square even as Washington newspaper compositors assembled Lincoln's proclamation in type trays. Few residents would have remembered the Lincoln family's sojourn in that vicinity, so not many perceived the irony of the Confederate presence on the day the president issued his most famous order, but most would have comprehended the significance of Bragg's digression from the Louisville road. Don Carlos Buell and the Army of the Ohio followed the Confederate rear guard by a few hours' march, but as Bragg swung east Buell veered to the west, aiming for the Ohio downstream from Louisville. His army had marched fifteen hundred miles since leaving that city the previous winter, one officer caustically observed, with no victory since Shiloh. By September 25 each army had settled in to rest and refit after an exhausting march, but Buell had saved his supply line and Bragg had lost any hope of capturing Louisville and its undependable garrison of untrained levies.[80]

Kirby Smith still lingered at Lexington, where he assembled the scattered commands from southwestern Virginia and the Cincinnati feint. He did not move to join Bragg, nor did Bragg order his presence. That blunder left them to face a Union force twice their combined number in isolation, and gave Buell a chance to concentrate overwhelming forces against one portion of the Confederate army or another. He nearly lost that chance, receiving hand-carried orders on September 29 to turn over command of his army to Major General George Thomas. Thomas himself balked, arguing with army headquarters that Buell was about to launch his various corps against the enemy. Henry Halleck denied having issued that order, and that evening Lincoln suspended it.[81]

Buell's near-removal threw prominent Kentucky civilians into dismay, and it inevitably compromised his position among his subordinates. Brigadier General Jefferson C. Davis introduced another measure of instability to Buell's command when he shot Major General William Nelson to death during a personal argument, even as the order for Buell's replacement circulated. Resuming command amid such electric confusion, Buell assigned Thomas as his second-in-command and arranged his army under three major generals — one of whom had been a mere captain at the beginning of the month, and whose promotion came through administrative error.[82]

It was not enough to secure Louisville and arrest further advances by the two Southern armies: the enemy had to be driven from Kentucky soil as he had been banished from Maryland. As Senator Sherman had pointed out just ten days into the occupation of Lexington, continued Confederate presence in the Bluegrass threatened to win the people over to the Southern cause by means of economic interest and a benevolent occupation that compared favorably to the brigandage of Northern troops.

Sherman also foresaw the danger of Kentuckians' sympathizing with the Confederates over emancipation, which only worsened after Lincoln tipped his hand on that issue.[83]

Buell surprised his opponent by lunging quickly from his base of operations against the invading army: by October 1 Union troops were leaving Louisville on several different roads, some aiming toward Bardstown and some toward Frankfort. To the surprise of one Midwesterner, Kentucky boasted good, hard roads, but those thoroughfares blistered feet and seldom passed good water. Like McClellan's army on the march through Maryland, the reinforced Army of the Ohio moved in long, attenuated columns trailing streams of limping tenderfoots in bright new uniforms who crippled nearly every brigade and dominated some divisions. "There were a good many raw regiments in that army," noted Brigadier General Lovell Rousseau, "who marched badly and fought worse." The fresh troops held no monopoly on straggling, though, and the commander of one veteran Ohio regiment railed about his brigade commander's slack discipline on the march, complaining that he had lost virtually his entire regiment along the roadside.[84]

Bragg had gone to confer with General Smith, leaving Leonidas Polk in charge of the Bardstown forces. Bragg and Smith both hurried to Frankfort to install an erstwhile commissary major as the new governor of the state, and to announce the formal commencement of Confederate authority, holding the ceremony on October 4. Buell's rapid advance convinced Bragg that the Yankees were bound for Frankfort, prompting him to plan a two-pronged attack on the Union column that was approaching the state capital, but General Polk — the same man whose poor judgment had tipped neutral Kentucky into the Union camp, thirteen months before — disregarded Bragg's instructions for his part of the attack. With heavier columns of Federals heading straight for him, Polk withdrew in the direction of Bryantsville, which would take him well south of Lexington and put him on the road to a full retreat toward Cumberland Gap. Detecting a Union diversion toward Franfort, Smith withdrew from the capital, taking the new governor and all his inaugural proclamations with him while Bragg hastened back to his own army. Buell waltzed into Bardstown that same day with the greater part of his forces. Barring a sudden and overwhelming victory on the battlefield, the Confederacy's soaring star had manifestly begun to set in Kentucky. The people had not rallied around their Southern saviors, and evidently would not do so unless the Confederates could first secure the state without their help: each of the corps in Buell's army included Kentucky troops, but there was not a single Bluegrass company in Bragg's army.[85]

Wavering in his conviction about Buell's route, Bragg kept two-thirds of the combined Confederate forces with Smith. Polk, meanwhile, camped at the town of Perryville with just three divisions, each of which fielded about five thousand effective men. Buell followed with seven divisions averaging more than seventy-five hundred men apiece. Two propitiously named streams flowed nearby — Bull Run and Wilson's Creek, each evoking conspicuous Confederate victories — and both those tributaries flowed into Doctor's Creek, on the banks of which Polk positioned his rear guard. The region had seen little rain during the past few weeks, and after a particularly hard march on October 7 most of the Union troops had run out of water, so the moonlight reflections of deep pools in Doctor's Creek drew Buell's leading corps in the wee hours of October 8.[86]

Buell had planned well, disguising his true avenue of advance so adroitly as to isolate a vulnerable but significant portion of Bragg's army. The day ought to have ended in disaster for Polk, had incompetence and miscommunication not afflicted Buell's army worse than it did Bragg's. The day began with an advance by a Union division under Philip Sheridan, who had begun the war as a thirty-year-old second lieutenant in the Regular Army; on the morning of October 8 he had worn the single star of a brigadier general for less than a month. Sheridan moved his division over Doctor's Creek before dawn, shouldering aside a regiment or two of Arkansas Confederates to seize an advantageous height called Peters Hill. His orders dictated holding that position until Buell could bring up all three corps of his thirsty army on each of the three roads leading into Perryville, but Sheridan thought he saw a chance to strike his own telling blow and lunged ahead again, inviting the very engagement Buell had hoped to forestall. His corps commander, Charles Gilbert (the recent captain, unintentionally elevated to major general), ordered Sheridan to pull his command back to Peters Hill.[87]

That morning Bragg had arrived at Perryville and found Polk awaiting an attack instead of initiating one. Bragg resumed command and quickly rearranged his troops to assail the narrow Union front presented by Sheridan's exposed brigades. Lovell Rousseau's division, the leading element of Alexander McCook's corps, came up on Gilbert's left about 10:30 that morning while Bragg realigned his three divisions, and that required Bragg to shift more troops north of town. It was near noon before the first brigades of Thomas Crittenden's corps reached their assigned position, three miles west of Perryville and well to Gilbert's right, and Crittenden's other two divisions trickled in through the afternoon. Buell, who shared George McClellan's penchant for perfect planning, had given up any hope of making an attack that day. As the Federals arrived they thought of little but rest and water; some of McCook's men crept ahead to fill their canteens in the creek, while many others lagged far behind in the stifling heat.[88]

Southern artillery played on both Sheridan and McCook until Bragg finally unleashed his infantry attack, around two o'clock. Even without Crittenden, Gilbert and McCook outnumbered the Confederates two to one (or would have, when and if all their men came up), but even when those new troops who dared to fight came into line they posed as much of a liability as an advantage. Dashing across the creek and up the bluff on the other side, two brigades of Tennessee veterans from Ben Cheatham's division rolled over a ridge straight into James Jackson's division of Midwestern recruits, which all but disintegrated (with at least one regiment preceded in flight by its colonel, who hid first behind a stump and then worked his way to the rear on the plea of a sore back). The remnants of the division eventually scampered back over the bodies of Jackson and both of his brigadiers. Behind those fugitives stood the only other division on the field with McCook — Rousseau's — and his three brigades stepped up to face Bragg's entire assault virtually alone. Gilbert watched Sheridan repel the portion of the Confederate attack that came his way, but he gave Rousseau no help at all as Confederates hammered him persistently in front and threatened to engulf his line, all within a few hundred yards of Gilbert's left flank and in plain sight.[89]

Rousseau held the last line on the Union left. Had his division collapsed, nothing could have stopped Bragg from flanking the overmatched Gilbert and, perhaps, knocking his much stronger opponent back on his heels. Cheatham's initial luck of falling upon Jackson's green division finally brought the same limited results as A. P. Hill's good fortune below Sharpsburg. For the next several hours the bulk of Bragg's Perryville force pounded Rousseau's stubborn, isolated detachment, preempting the assault Buell had envisioned but gaining no advantage except time for a more orderly withdrawal than might otherwise have been necessary.

For much of the afternoon Rousseau's artillery beat back repeated charges, blasting great gaps in the surging grey lines with sweeping volleys of canister. The Confederates kept coming as they had at Shiloh, in disciplined, determined waves that mystified the seasoned Union soldiers and daunted their inexperienced comrades. Their advance brought a baptism of fire for a month-old Wisconsin regiment that lay in the cornfield, under orders to wait until the attack came to point-blank range, but the Southerners tilted toward them so fiercely that they discharged their muskets once and gave way. Two older regiments behind them blunted the charge by rapid, withering volleys and sent the Southerners reeling backward time after time until their ammunition gave out. In exasperation the rebels finally aimed straight for the guns in an irresistible phalanx. Confederates slipped around Rousseau's right flank, unimpeded by Gilbert's stolid line a thousand feet away, and Rousseau closed up his tattered ranks, concentrating his front. Union batteries retired with dozens of horses killed. Rallying his men by galloping about with his hat on the tip of his sword, Rousseau lined up six regiments from his last two brigades, and they, too, fought until the sun sank low and their own ammunition had all been expended. They emptied the cartridge boxes of their dead and wounded comrades to repel one final attack, and three of those regiments fixed bayonets to meet the next column, having fired their last round.[90]

Gilbert, whose actual whereabouts remained a mystery to most of his colleagues on the field, at last responded to McCook's plight by sending a brigade to support Rousseau. That brigade went into the fight late in the afternoon with three regiments, meeting the freshest of Bragg's available troops and falling back in the dusk, an hour later, with more than a third of their numbers killed or wounded. An atmospheric quirk had prevented General Buell from hearing the battle, but by then he had learned of it with "astonishment," and he ordered another of Gilbert's brigades to McCook's aid. That brigade arrived just at dark. Crittenden's corps brushed back the Confederate cavalry that had screened his activities all afternoon, but soon thereafter the firing sputtered out.[91]

As at Antietam, the question of victory seemed uncertain at first. While Bragg had battered McCook severely, he had failed to materially injure Buell. A signal officer who rode with Rousseau considered the battle a draw, and Bragg would surely have liked to claim at least that much, but he seemed to comprehend finally that he had cavorted dangerously close to an army strong enough to crush him. Leaving his dead and most of his wounded at Perryville, he retreated that night toward Harrodsburg to join forces with Kirby Smith. The next morning Buell repulsed a brazen dash by Confederate cavalry and marched into the town, which they found perforated by canister and shells, and nearly every building had been transformed into a hospital. Some fourteen hundred Southern wounded, sick, attendants, and stragglers remained behind for the provost marshal to gather up, representing nearly one-tenth of the troops Bragg had wielded the previous day. Union surgeons, at least one of them blind drunk, seemed to do more harm than good for the wounded of both armies: mortality ran unusually high among those on whom they operated.[92]

For the next two weeks, as frosts burned Kentucky foliage yellow, gold, russet, and crimson, Bragg backpedaled toward the Wilderness Road that would lead him to Cumberland Gap and Tennessee, skirmishing almost daily with his pursuers. His Kentucky campaign had all but ended, as his actions indicated more clearly than his dispatches, and in that denouement the battle of Perryville became a Union victory.[93]

Northern citizens again had cause to feel less certain of that victory. They could not necessarily appreciate Southern disappointment in the failure to beat Buell, capture Louisville, and secure the state with thousands of Kentucky volunteers. Cynics north of the Ohio River would instead remember that the Confederates had feasted mightily in the state and fallen back into their own territory with an enormous advantage in prisoners and captured matériel. Bragg's army remained intact and on the loose, and it appeared he might revisit the Bluegrass any time, just as Lee might cross the Potomac once more.

Preparing to leave Washington on the eve of Perryville, Indiana governor Oliver P. Morton had composed a lengthy letter to Abraham Lincoln warning that the cause might be lost if Northern armies failed to make some material gains within sixty days. He predicted that confidence in paper currency would soon dissolve, perhaps overnight, and bring the machinery of war to a complete halt, while continued survival of the Richmond government would offer British leaders the excuse to grant the recognition he believed they wished to offer. He complained generically of "the cold professional leader, whose heart is not in the cause" and whose career interests depended on continuation of the war: better to rely on the intelligent amateur "whose head is inspired by his heart." "Another three months like the last six and we are lost," Morton emphasized, "lost. We cannot afford to experiment a single day longer with men who have failed continuously for a whole year."[94]

Nearly two weeks after Perryville, Morton reiterated to the president that "distrust and despair are seizing upon the hearts of the people." This time Morton more specifically targeted General Buell, whom he considered ineffective and soft on secessionists. The following day a Louisville acquaintance cautioned Joseph Holt that the danger lay not in Buell's conciliatory deportment but in an overbearing government that arrested citizens and emancipated slaves without constitutional authority. "The fact is, Sir," wrote Holt's informant, "the condition of things in Ky is such that if some change does not take place a storm will arise that will convulse the whole state, & produce a shock that would be felt all over the Union."[95]

Such division and uncertainty in the Northern states only tempered European favor for the Confederacy, which seemed far more galvanized in its own defense than its invaders were in their aggression. The value of the United States dollar had dropped sharply against gold on the Continent, and sympathy for the Southern cause grew on the street as well as in

Parliament. London newspapers watched the war closely, including the business sheets, which paid particular heed to the adventures of Confederate armies in Maryland and Kentucky. By the time Bragg and Buell clashed at Perryville, Londoners remained ignorant of the outcome along Antietam Creek and still believed that Southern forces held Kentucky in a firm grasp. The evening before Perryville (the very day of Governor Morton's prediction about greenbacks and Great Britain) the Chancellor of the Exchequer, William Gladstone, attended a dinner party at which he uttered some remarks sufficiently formal to be taken down by reporters. What he had to say intimated what might have happened if Lee and Bragg had managed to sustain themselves in hostile territory a little while longer.[96]

"There can be no doubt," Gladstone observed over dessert, "that Jefferson Davis has made a nation of the South." British newspapers jumped on the comment, recognizing it as the potential preface to more meaningful action. It was not the official recognition Davis had hoped for, but resounding diplomatic decisions usually required such introductory hints.[97]

8

Our Army Foiled with
Loss Severe

⚔ THE CONFEDERATES WHO INVADED Kentucky had shown
a little less respect for private property than their comrades in Maryland. Given the example of the Confiscation Act, which the U.S. Congress
passed when Confederate troops seemed unable to retaliate in Northern
territory, Lexington retailers might have considered it generous of Kirby
Smith's troops to offer Confederate scrip for goods they took. General
Smith specifically ordered merchants to accept Southern currency, suggesting that some dared to demand gold or greenbacks, but retailers who
withheld their wares generally lost them without any payment. Despite
their conspicuous lack of tents, blankets, or overcoats, though, the rebels
appear to have stolen relatively few compensating comforts. That fall
United States soldiers actually earned as much enmity as Confederates
did among loyal men in Kentucky, and probably more, with the worst behavior coming from those who had just entered the service. One merchant who kept shop opposite an extemporized barracks in Louisville
found soldiers from Buell's army prowling the roof of his building by
day in search of a nighttime entryway, and he complained that "the new
troops seemed to think they had nothing to do but steel." James Speed
condemned the Federals' conduct as "shameful, nay disgraceful." He
thought officers should shoot looters on the spot, but knew that many officers had acted as "mere marauders" themselves. General Rousseau also
advocated resuming summary executions, admitting that Union soldiers
committed many "grievous outrages" in Kentucky, just as they had in
more hostile Alabama.[1]

Still, loyal Kentuckians suffered less than Confederate citizens of any political persuasion. Almost nowhere in the seceded states did Union troops hesitate to ravage the countryside and rob the residents blind. Generals who pursued a conciliatory policy among the Southern population did so at peril of retribution by vengeful Radical Republicans (as the persecution of Charles Stone had advertised), but they also labored against an army of increasingly self-indulgent soldiers who exercised little self-control in their own states, less in the loyal border states, and almost none in the Confederacy. Iowa recruits pilfered vegetables and fowl from their Davenport hosts whenever their appetites demanded it. In Maryland fresh troops aggravated loyal, neutral, and hostile residents equally by filching smaller livestock, corn, fruit, and produce. Once inside the borders of a seceded state Northern soldiers abandoned any semblance of morality on the premise that all citizens presumably supported the Confederate government, and so deserved any misfortune that befell them: any barnyard, orchard, or garden seemed fair game.[2]

Southern soldiers may have learned better behavior from having spent so many months in friendly terrain. Some Confederates did take a heavy toll on their civilian population, like the Virginia State Line regiments that pillaged indiscriminately in western Virginia during the September occupation, but early in the war it was usually local or irregular troops who showed so little discipline.[3] Partly in retaliation for Yankee depredations, regular Confederate troops later turned more predatory in enemy territory, imposing onerous burdens on Northern citizens, and as their desperation increased they leaned more heavily on their own populace.

Union soldiers, however, preyed indiscriminately on Southern civilians from the very outset. Three-month militia and early volunteers inflicted myriad indignities on the residents of even the loyal slave states, including an occasional murder. Ninety-day troops from New Hampshire cavorted so scandalously in Maryland that one of their hometown newspapers published a scathing rebuke, which those summer soldiers punished by sacking the editorial offices on their way home. Their regimental historian attempted to sanitize their conduct a generation later, claiming that the men "almost invariably" paid for what they took, so long as they were "politely treated," and he characterized the protesting youth whom one Granite State sergeant shot to death as "a young Rebel," whose death he recounted as though the murderer had been a passive bystander.[4] A Pennsylvania merchant doing business in occupied Yorktown, Virginia, warned Secretary Seward that recovering Union sentiments in eastern Virginia had suffered immense setbacks from the "unrestrained pillaging" of Yankee soldiers, who stole everything the local farmers grew. Along North Carolina's Outer Banks and on the islands of the sounds, Union occupation forces dined abundantly by killing anything that moved, most of which belonged to inhabitants whose hearts inclined to the Union. Way out in the Flint Hills of Kansas, where almost no one could be mistaken for a secessionist sympathizer, newly mounted Kansas volunteers so victimized the residents of Junction City that the commander at Fort Riley ordered out some Wisconsin infantry to protect the citizens from their own state's troopers.[5]

That perennial failure of discipline worsened perceptibly, though, with the arrival of the new levies. New troops reconnoitering in Maryland or in one of the more loyal sections of northern Virginia made no inquiry into the owner's politics when they emptied a henhouse or slaughtered flocks of sheep, and their officers joked about it. During the Maryland campaign, a captain in a fresh Connecticut regiment described the troops descending on the landscape like a "cloud of locusts."[6] A new lieutenant of New York cavalry stripped a Maryland farmer of all his forage, leaving a receipt that would do him no good before his cattle starved. In northern Mississippi that same lieutenant's brother-in-law had no compunction about instructing his foraging party to clean out the entire plantation of an elderly woman who dared to admit her Confederate leanings. An Iowa captain led a more ambitious foraging expedition from his camp near Helena, Arkansas, with 120 wagons and an escort of eleven hundred cavalry and infantry, returning with the wagons overflowing with corn, yams, and potatoes, as well as a drove of hogs and a flock of chickens. Western soldiers around Helena grew fat on the food they took from surrounding farmers; they "confiscated" whatever they needed or wanted, boasted a rookie from Wisconsin, including "a span of very nice horses."[7]

A Union brigade on a routine patrol from near Memphis dined sumptuously on stolen fruit and melons. Raw Ohio troops sent to garrison threatened Covington, across from Cincinnati, quartered themselves in an empty house that they assumed had been deserted by a rebel Kentuckian, and those who could not fit in the house tore down every single outbuilding for lumber to build shanties. When those troops moved to Tennessee they supplemented their diets with endless quantities of purloined butter, apple butter, honey, and preserves, besides feasting on fresh beef until they grew tired of it.[8] On the second night after they joined Ulysses Grant's army in western Tennessee, a squad of Illinois soldiers strode brazenly into a farmer's yard and slaughtered one of his cattle, taking the quartered carcass back to camp. Citizens often declined to interfere with Yankee thieves out of fear that they might be murdered with impunity, and indeed while many Union officers tried to discourage marauding by their troops, few of them dared to impose the traditional peremptory punishment for such depredations. When a staff officer in the Army of the

Potomac did shoot down a soldier he caught stealing a sheep, it enraged even the field officers in an inexperienced nine-month regiment.[9]

A brigadier with the Army of the Tennessee remarked disgustedly on the thievery and vandalism practiced by so many of the troops raised that summer and autumn. It seemed to him that they "were . . . possessed with the idea that in order to carry on war men must throw aside civilization and become savages." His subordinate officers tried to correct it, but apparently with little effect. "We have had some most heartrending cases," he complained to his wife, "and I do not see how men claiming to be enlightened and educated can do such things." Exaggerated tales of plunder heard from furloughed or discharged veterans may have encouraged the recruits to illicit foraging. Also, as the demand for large bounties implied, the latest recruiting drives had drawn men less accustomed to want than their predecessors, and pampered stomachs made them more susceptible to the temptations of unattended provender. Perhaps they felt the Confiscation Act sanctioned spoil: a disappointed Michigan recruit fumed upon learning that he and his comrades were prohibited from appropriating rebel property, since his recruiting officer had evidently promised otherwise.[10]

Superiors might overlook the theft of food by soldiers for whom they could not assure adequate or regular rations, but unpunished freelance foraging often escalated into wholesale looting and wanton destruction, and sometimes the officers took an active part or even initiated the depredations Edward Hall, a middle-aged New Hampshire soldier serving on the coast of South Carolina, complained in letters to his wife about his rapacious captain, John Wilbur, who was arrested several times for an assortment of misbehavior including absence without leave and misappropriation of government property. According to Hall, the "old scamp" stole from everyone, including the government and his own soldiers. A sympathetic or complicit colonel resigned early in 1862, leaving Wilbur to endure several narrow escapes until he was finally court-martialed and cashiered in May of 1863. Private Hall remarked that there were a lot of other officers in the army just like Wilbur, who looked on a commission as "a license to rob and steal." That was certainly true among quartermaster and commissary officers: a field officer from Indiana characterized two successive brigade commissaries as swindlers, and they seemed to operate under the protection of the brigadier. A Maine corporal commented wryly on an entire family of his neighbors who, through their hometown friendship with Chief Quartermaster Rufus Ingalls, were able to secure positions as brigade quartermasters, wagon master, and quartermaster clerk, from which the four of them worked collaboratively to "plunder uncle Sam."[11]

Western troops may have been the worst foragers, and particularly in backwater regions: one captain saw his loyal Louisiana cavalry ransacking private homes on one operation in their own state, and an expedition in eastern Arkansas proved especially destructive, thanks to some green Iowa regiments. A lieutenant in the two-month-old 24th Iowa found himself under arrest briefly for invading one residence and for ordering the burning of another, while a private in the same regiment participated in a "raid" on a plantation that left every building in ashes.[12] A man in the 30th Iowa recoiled at the deeds of his comrades, who burst into houses occupied only by women, stole everything down to the rings on their fingers, and then burned their homes while they stood helplessly by. New Wisconsin troops — "Prairie Wolves," as one scandalized Midwesterner called them — behaved even more rapaciously. The general leading the expedition, Alvin Hovey, found his troops' rampage unworthy of official mention.[13]

The Yankees at Helena, and particularly Hovey's division, earned a reputation for destructive inclinations. They often exercised a shocking vindictiveness toward innocent civilians on the excuse that the target plantation or community had been the nearest occupied site to the lair of a Confederate marksman. When sharpshooters reportedly fired on a steamboat upriver from Helena there was no attempt to determine guilt: another boat was simply ordered back to destroy the town. A captain of the 29th Wisconsin took his company to a plantation south of Helena, "confiscating" two loads of cotton for private sale to a steamboat captain, and when someone fired on the detail, the captain sent a squad back to burn his victim's home. Colonel Charles Gill arrested that captain, at least for the moment, but on New Year's Eve Gill himself ordered an entire plantation destroyed because someone fired at a picket from that vicinity. Just before Christmas soldiers of William T. Sherman's command disgorged from a steamer below Helena and put the entire town of Friar's Point to the torch while incidentally rounding up horses and burning "rebel property." The practice became widespread thereabouts: an Iowan who embarked on his first campaign later that winter returned to Helena and reported that "we Respected Rebel Property But little & where Ever they Fired on our Boats we landed & Burnt Every thing that would Burn."[14]

In the isolated country of the Mississippi bayous, the people fled ahead of Grant's army, leaving behind civilized luxuries like pianos, coaches, and libraries, which the Yankees promptly demolished. By the time a New England officer reached the Mississippi capitol at Jackson, the central portion of the city had been "pretty much destroyed" by Union troops, although he instinctively supposed that Southern soldiers shared equal blame. Blackened chimneys lined the roads wherever the Federals

marched along the Mississippi River — standing like gravestones for vanished families, observed an Illinois infantryman. The same grim land-
marks adorned Virginia. Marching down the Shenandoah Valley in December, an Ohio officer in a regiment raised that fall detected the earlier
passage of Federal troops by the forlorn chimneys that outnumbered
houses on his route: the sight gratified this man, whose own home never
lay in danger.[15]

Northern Virginia suffered the worst. A Pennsylvania officer passing
through the scenes of John Pope's campaign found everything "laid waste
by the soldier," and the nearer one came to Washington the more thorough had the destruction been. After eighteen months of occupation,
the sliver of Virginia that had been known as the Alexandria Line in 1861
had been reduced to desolation. All signs of agricultural enterprise had
been obliterated in upper Fairfax County: no crops, gardens, orchards,
or fences obstructed the panoramic view of sprawling military encampments. All the grass had been trodden to dust or mud, and the only green
vegetation consisted of surviving trees or bushes. New nine-month men
in particular gaped at the devastation, but later they contributed to it with
ill-disguised enthusiasm. When they needed firewood or lumber to improve the comforts of camp life they simply dismantled any buildings that
happened to be vacant or momentarily unattended; a barn might disappear almost overnight, and a sizable house could be reduced to a chimney
in three or four days through the most casual disassembly. Few white residents remained besides a sprinkling of destitute women and children,
whose survival mystified the soldiers. The picturesque farms, villages, and
hamlets that had dotted Fairfax County when Abraham Lincoln came to
Washington had given way to massive earthen forts linked by intricate
rifle pits, stretching into the distance in either direction like a red-clay
version of China's Great Wall. A New York lieutenant recoiled at the reflection that he bore even a minuscule share of the responsibility for such
destruction; when he thought of it he grew sick at heart, and wished himself a civilian again.[16]

A lot of men in uniform wished they were civilians again, and many
of their uniforms had not yet faded. The new regiments were filled with
volunteers who had either enlisted out of dire economic necessity, like
so many of their predecessors in the army, or who had been drawn by the
deceptive lure of fat bounties. "I believe about half of our Army fight for
the money that is in it," concluded a Pennsylvania captain after a few
months of service, "and not for Patriotism."[17] The latest crop of volunteers
seemed much more needy than their predecessors, and bundles of letters
carried home complaints that soldiering had turned out to be much cost-
lier than anyone had supposed. The rigors of living outdoors demanded

comforts the quartermaster often failed to issue, leaving either the soldier or his family to provide them. Most appetites required regular supplements to the occasionally meager and perennially unappealing army diet, and high-priced delicacies consumed most of each month's pay for many a gourmand who could find no barnyards or kitchens to scavenge. In regions where they faced no competition, sutlers charged a dollar a pound for cheese and as much as a dollar and a half a pound for tobacco, even in the tobacco regions of Kentucky. A soldier whose daily pay amounted to less than forty-three cents often had to pay five cents for a single sheet of paper on which to record the ways everyone cheated him.[18]

Payday, and especially the first payday, soured thousands of gullible patriots who had believed the persuasive speeches at recruiting rallies. Clothing expenses seemed the worst betrayal to many, for everyone who enlisted had been conditioned to count his monthly clothing allowance as part of his pay. Instead, the clothing they had been issued often ate up not only the allowance but most of the base pay as well. Months without pay ended with a disappointing balance for a Maine corporal whose clothing account had exceeded the government allowance after three grueling campaigns. A New Hampshire private fumed over the $27.86 his state charged him for his original uniform, which he had drawn with the explicit understanding that it would be free; the flimsy shoes that he and his fellows had traded off for fifty cents or a dollar a pair appeared on his pay voucher as a deduction of $1.94. A Vermont soldier resented the bogus "gift" of his first uniform through the rest of his service, citing it as the first of many insults that led him to scorn reenlistment. Barracks thieves robbed a middle-aged Wisconsin cavalryman of all his clothing, weapons, and equipment when he was carried to the hospital with a sudden illness, and the paymaster not only dunned him $28 for another outfit but charged him $240 for his lost arms and equipment.[19]

Pay itself came seldom, and always late. Arrearages typically ran between four and six months, with occasional lapses of seven months or more.[20] Generals begged for their men and their quartermasters to be supplied with funds, with little effect. Soldiers thought the government feared they would desert if paid in full. They also believed, correctly, that the treasury let them wait deliberately, paying contractors first. By the end of 1862 Secretary Chase conceded that so many troops had been raised that their pay came due three times faster than he could collect the revenue. They could be paid regularly only by selling bonds at illegally discounted prices or by simply printing more greenbacks, as one reckless congressional amendment proposed. Some troops threatened not to fight again until paid, and others hoped their fellows would support them in a general mutiny: those risking their lives resented being forced to finance a significant portion of the war, without interest, while their families went hungry.[21]

The suspicion or the realization that they had been hoodwinked embittered new soldiers, who suddenly regretted having enlisted. Six weeks into his nine-month enlistment, a Connecticut soldier swore to his wife that "no inducement whatever" could persuade him to repeat his mistake. A newlywed who had just enlisted as a musician in a New Hampshire regiment chided his wife for the patriotic tone of her letters, which he supposed might be extinguished by a month in camp. After only two months in the field, a Massachusetts soldier admitted that he had no heart for the war: he felt certain that his attitude prevailed in his new regiment, and he doubted that one man in fifty would reenlist if they were all discharged on the spot.[22]

John Chipman Gray Jr., a Harvard alumnus newly appointed to a Massachusetts cavalry regiment, no longer supported the president. Gray stood among those enlightened admirers of the Constitution who found the Emancipation Proclamation of September 22 less obnoxious than Lincoln's other proclamation of September 24, curtailing the right of habeas corpus nationwide. In what strict constitutionalists deemed his most heinous misdemeanor yet, Lincoln provided for the indefinite incarceration and trial by military tribunal of "all persons discouraging volunteer enlistments, resisting militia drafts, or guilty of any disloyal practice." By such language Lincoln expanded further on an authority he did not hold in the first place: he implied a presumption of guilt in his backward proposal for military trial of those who were "guilty," and he placed the entire country under a measure of martial law. Lincoln's unconstitutional usurpation undermined the very cause of constitutional liberty for which the soldiers fought, Gray believed, and he felt the administration deserved a rebuke at the polls. His classmate Henry Abbott, a captain in the 20th Massachusetts, shared Gray's contempt for Lincoln's autocratic proclamations, and assured his family the feeling was "universal."[23]

Not all well-educated volunteer officers concurred. One consumptive Yale man in the Third Corps composed a lengthy disquisition in which he went so far as to insist that Lincoln should simply assume dictatorial powers. Rather than signaling an overthrow of the civil administration, he contended, it would actually strengthen civil authority. His reasoning might not have appealed to John Geary, a Pennsylvania brigadier who supported the president's actions despite his fear that "our country is on the verge of anarchy and despotism."[24]

Most of the professional officer corps would have repudiated such notions outright. Dissatisfaction with the war especially infected career soldiers, including generals who fought valiantly for the Union and nursed no grudge against any of Lincoln's objectionable war measures. William Tecumseh Sherman reproached Republicans, including his own brother, for precipitating the war (too soon, he thought) and for underestimating the task, as well as for covering up their underestimate by blaming army commanders. George Meade, a brigadier with more than twenty years' service, who would command the nation's principal army in less than a year, thought the conflict "unnecessary" — and evidently injudicious. The fighting would continue until one side or the other was "brought to its senses" by the cost, he reasoned, yet the South seemed determined to accept material ruin to avoid subjugation. The people of the North, meanwhile, were not allowed to realize the war's cost: the government delayed and disguised it with perilous paper money, deferred taxation through bonds, and avoidance of universal conscription. Meade also implied that the South owned the greater motive for continuing the struggle, while the Northern will to fight would probably already have withered had the public not been deceived by its leadership.[25]

More perceptive citizens did recognize the real cost. Some had dared record their dismay only privately, in pessimistic diary entries, or to neighbors, close friends, and nearby relatives, but that autumn some found it easier to confess their fading support for the war to more casual acquaintances. A Maine man who had spent a few weeks helping out in the Washington hospitals conveyed his change of heart to one of the nurses in his old ward: now that he could fathom the ravages of the conflict, including his own brother's death, he regretted the impetuous rush to arms. The waning months of 1862 also saw an occasional parent revealing disfavor to soldier-sons whose present political sympathies could no longer be detected, like the Connecticut man who tested his son's reaction to the news that everyone at home seemed "worked up" over the endless, pointless fighting.[26]

Mothers and wives often presumed to state the case more boldly. Unwittingly writing to her son the day after his first battle, while he lay severely wounded, a Rhode Island mother vented her absolute disgust with a war that had been diverted to the cause of abolition. She informed him that all their acquaintances heartily condemned the president and their compliant governor, and swore that she never would have given her consent for her son to enlist had she foreseen the administration's trickery. The mother of a Vermont captain hounded her boy to resign his commission, protesting that she could not sacrifice him to "this Unholy War." Another captain from Vermont told his importuning wife that he could not come home as she insisted, regardless of his (or her) dissatisfaction: two fellow officers she reported seeing in town after the Seven Days had simply deserted, he explained, and had been dismissed from the service without back pay. Returning from a sojourn in occupied New Orleans, a Connecticut civilian excoriated his brother for taking a commission in the army, summarizing the Northern political position as "altogether wrong." An Iowa wife simply reminded her husband, a major, that he had told her he could resign whenever he wanted, and she asked whether he did not finally want to — with the unspoken expectation of an explanation if he did not.[27]

Civilians who favored the war acknowledged the existence of antiwar "croakers" at home, but few seemed to resent their neighbors' disagreement. Soldiers showed greater animosity for peacemongers, and especially Western soldiers, perhaps because the Midwest produced the most effective political challengers to the war party. Indiana congressman Daniel Voorhees had originally opposed the war, and although he assented to restoration of the Union he stood as his state's most vocal critic of Abraham Lincoln's despotic policies.[28] Congressman Clement Vallandigham of Ohio had risen from the secession crisis as a critical Union man, opposed only to the chief executive's unconstitutional transgressions, but in his criticism of the government he had come to speak for those who now wished to see the war ended. As the principal representative of the opposition, he labored under all the venom of the Union press and all the power of the administration's political supporters: when prowar editors vilified Peace Democrats as "Copperheads" who cravenly sought to undermine the war effort, they often mentioned Vallandigham by name. To assure his defeat Ohio's Republican legislature gerrymandered his district, while state Republicans initiated streams of lies about Vallandigham and nominated as their champion Robert Schenck, a wounded war hero. Unconditional Unionists yearned for his imprisonment, and during the summer election campaign newspapers of that stripe circulated a false rumor of his arrest on charges of treason.[29]

The Midwest was also the reputed cradle of the Knights of the Golden Circle, which government agents and Republican editors increasingly belabored as an intricate conspiracy devoted to subversive support of the Confederacy. The order began as the scheme of a confidence man selling memberships, but when he finally landed in federal custody he was jailed as a suspected traitor rather than indicted for fraud. Across the country dissident Democrats found themselves accused of recruiting a clandestine army of Knights to rise against the government, and federal marshals imprisoned many of them on whatever testimony their personal and political enemies were willing to supply.[30] Ironically, a very real network of Union committees served as a conduit for such testimony through their own system of secret communications, including symbols indicating that a particular Democrat "must be closely watched," "is suspected of being disloyal," or "must be arrested."[31]

Much of the Democratic opposition to the government arose from such arrests and from the dictatorial, unconstitutional nature of Lincoln's latest proclamations. The arbitrary executive decrees proved for many that Lincoln had, indeed, come to be controlled by the radicals of his party. Hostility to conservative generals like Don Carlos Buell and George McClellan seemed to reflect that Radical Republican influence; sixteen days after the battle of Perryville, Lincoln partially acceded to it, issuing orders for Buell to turn over command of his army to William Rosecrans. The order came by hand, and did not reach Buell until October 30, by which time congressional elections had ended in Pennsylvania, Ohio, and in Buell's home state of Indiana. The Army of the Ohio included no troops from any state east of Pennsylvania, and public support for Buell's tenure ran strongest in the Ohio River valley. The president had deposed him purely for dissatisfaction with his military performance, but he had evidently felt it prudent to wait until the removal could excite no adverse consequences at the polls.[32]

As it was, the administration did poorly enough in elections that came when significant numbers of Midwestern soldiers were beginning to overstay their furloughs or abandon their units, and when many steadfast Unionists doubted Lincoln's capacity to lead.[33] The partisan ploy of legislative redistricting (and Robert Schenck's popularity) sent Vallandigham down to defeat, but only by the votes of the county the legislature had added to his district. Democrats considered Vallandigham's loss "a national calamity," but that was all Ohio Republicans could crow about. In the state's other eighteen congressional districts Democrats took all but four seats, and won the governor's chair.[34]

Democrats also made significant gains in Pennsylvania and Indiana, where Daniel Voorhees was reelected in the Seventh District. Indiana soldiers who shared similar attitudes about most political issues nevertheless reflected the differing reactions to wartime dissent, some viewing any Democratic opposition as treason while others hailed it as the true patriotism of Unionism over abolitionism. "We dont intend to free the nigers," a Hoosier private assured his former teacher; "we will fite for the unity of our country not against it."[35] The elections, one Indiana conservative believed, demonstrated outrage at "the transcendent bad faith of this Administration." Friends of the Lincoln government won all six congressional seats in Iowa's October elections, but even there the most loyal

Republicans admitted that their constituents were growing mortally tired of a war that dragged on interminably with no sign of victory.[36]

George McClellan awaited the same fate as Buell, but like Buell he conducted himself as though he enjoyed the full support of the government. He grew jubilant after the dubious victory at Antietam and hoped to return to the supreme command, even cultivating an advocate at the Altoona governors' conference to demand the removal of both Halleck and Stanton. In that he failed altogether, for the governors only expressed satisfaction with the status quo. John Cochrane, a New York brigadier with powerful political connections, then approached Lincoln directly about appointing McClellan to Halleck's place, suggesting that it ought to be accomplished before the New York elections to gain the trust of Democratic voters. The same general tried to mend things between McClellan and Secretary Chase, but he made no headway in either mission.[37]

McClellan left the enemy unmolested in the days following Antietam, instead focusing on training his new troops, replacing equipment, and replenishing or refitting the army's horses. In late September he maintained that the Army of the Potomac was in no condition to chase Lee or fight him again soon. Still insisting that the Army of Northern Virginia greatly outnumbered him, he announced his intention to hold a defensive position along the line of the Potomac, and started calling once again for reinforcements. Lincoln decided it was time to come visit his general.[38]

The lethargy of McClellan's army troubled the president for political reasons as well as military. Conservatives thought radicals wanted to prolong the fighting until emancipation could be incorporated among the war's goals, but radicals suspected generals like Buell and McClellan of avoiding a decisive confrontation so slavery could be salvaged in a negotiated peace. Major John J. Key, a staff officer at army headquarters, said as much in the wake of the Emancipation Proclamation, and indicated that he would be satisfied with such an outcome himself, if it came to pass. Key had always been a dutiful officer, willing to obey whatever orders came his way, but any expectation that he was entitled to his personal opinions had grown somewhat out of date. His remark passed in the private rooms of Major Levi Turner, the president's chief inquisitor of disloyal behavior, and a report of the conversation soon reached Lincoln's desk. Lincoln wished to make an example of someone to quell the growing dissent among army officers, and merely asked Key if he had made the statement. Key acknowledged that he had, and that was all the president wanted to hear. Ignoring even Major Turner's assurances of Key's loyalty, and rejecting all arguments about the sanctity of personal opinion, Lincoln revoked Key's commission on the spot.[39]

On the evening ride back to the Soldiers' Home, Lincoln hinted to one of his secretaries that he doubted McClellan was guilty of that kind of perfidy, instead interpreting his inaction as a sign of timid uncertainty. Cabinet members feared the popularity of Major Key's observation, and they knew that many in the public saw McClellan's indolence as evidence of his devotion to such a program: Major Key was, after all, the brother of Colonel Thomas Key, of McClellan's own staff. When Lincoln arrived at Harper's Ferry to meet McClellan on October 1 he was still pondering the prevalence of the unfortunate major's forbidden sentiments. Ever friendly with McClellan in person, Lincoln warned the general about his habit of excessive caution, but Major Key's dismissal had earned substantial headlines only a day or two previously, and there should have been no need to elaborate on the consequences the general's caution posed.[40]

The president spent part of each day reviewing troops, beginning with those on Bolivar Heights. McClellan returned to his camp near Sharpsburg that evening, but Lincoln spent the night near Harper's Ferry, at Burnside's headquarters, mingling with lesser generals. At one point he seated himself atop a pile of fence rails for a long chat with Alpheus Williams, who still held temporary command of the Twelfth Corps. Williams found the president refreshingly sincere and unpretentious; he detected a touch of vacillation or indecision, but attributed it to the multitude of alternative policies presented to him, from which he had to choose his own.[41]

After touring Loudoun Heights and Maryland Heights on October 2, Lincoln proceeded to McClellan's headquarters. He discarded McClellan's itinerary for the afternoon, dashing off to see the battlefield: the First Corps stood in line awaiting review by him for five hours, and it was not until well into the evening that the commanding officer gave up and sent his men to a tardy dinner. Late Friday morning, October 3, president and generals reviewed the Ninth Corps near the mouth of Antietam Creek before traveling by ambulance to inspect Franklin's Sixth Corps, the insulted First Corps, and then Porter's Fifth Corps, a couple of miles from the village of Sharpsburg. Officers who held their men in ranks so long under the hot sun frowned bitterly on Lincoln's cursory review, which consisted of galloping past the assembled divisions with hardly a sideways glance, and the soldiers who saw him that day remarked wryly on his dismal appearance.[42] He was dressed like "a farmer," thought a Wisconsin youth, and "looked *worse* than ever," according to a Connecticut captain. A devoutly Republican adjutant from New Hampshire worried that Lincoln seemed "care worn and thin." The tall, sparse frame in the stovepipe hat drew widespread comment, including the irreverent. "Ain't the old bugger lean?" muttered a New York Zouave, as the president sped past amid a cluster of dazzling uniforms. "He wouldn't pay for skinnin'."[43]

Lincoln returned to Washington on Saturday, and McClellan soon forgot his commander in chief's admonition to start pressing the enemy. On Monday the president instructed Halleck to order McClellan across the Potomac to fight Lee or drive him away, but McClellan immediately set about pleading for reinforcements, horses, and supplies. "I cannot persuade him to advance an inch," Halleck grumbled privately. "It puts me out of all patience." McClellan telegraphed almost daily about his preparations for "the advance," but he seemed to be surreptitiously planning for an extensive sojourn in Maryland. He asked the president's permission to meet his wife and child, as though for a visit of a day or two in Washington, but in fact he intended to board them at his new headquarters in Pleasant Valley.[44]

Taking his father-in-law General Marcy with him, McClellan slipped away to fetch his family just as weeks of dry weather brought the Potomac River low enough to allow the passage of Confederate troops almost anywhere. McClellan left Ambrose Burnside in command of the army, donned civilian clothing, and traveled to Philadelphia in a private car provided by the Baltimore & Ohio Railroad. The two of them surprised McClellan's wife Ellen, her mother, and the baby by meeting them on their way south from Connecticut, and after spending the night of October 9 at the Continental Hotel they all boarded the private car for the return trip. In Baltimore someone recognized McClellan and a crowd sent up a cheer, prompting a second lieutenant on his way to join the army to go have a look at his new commanding officer. McClellan was bouncing his daughter on his knee while Ellen sat alongside, looking much prettier than the lieutenant had expected. McClellan's ruddy face disappointed the lieutenant, who found General Marcy's dignified whiskers far more impressive; he observed that "the mother-in-law Mrs. Marcy looked like a mother-in-law."[45]

McClellan returned to an embarrassing crisis, and had to leave the women chatting in his tent while he and General Marcy attended to it. He had hardly departed on his domestic mission when J.E.B. Stuart splashed across the Potomac River with three slim brigades of cavalry and a four-gun battery of horse artillery. Swinging west of Martinsburg and Williamsport, Stuart crossed Maryland near the filament where mountains met piedmont; he galloped straight toward the Pennsylvania line, narrowly missing Jacob Cox's Kanawha Division as it marched back into the Alleghenies. At noon of October 10, while George McClellan's private railroad car rattled toward Baltimore from Philadelphia, Stuart's cavalry trotted through Mercersburg, Pennsylvania, and before McClellan reached his army that night Stuart had captured Chambersburg.[46]

McClellan learned of the raid through Halleck's Washington headquarters, and at 10:00 PM he promised that "every disposition had been made" to cut off Stuart's retreat. The Southern cavalry loitered in Chambersburg through that rainy night. They spent the following morning paroling sick and wounded Union soldiers in the hospital and burning sizable stores of arms, supplies, and equipment, along with railroad buildings and machine shops. Giving the Pennsylvanians a mere taste of the war Virginia civilians had endured for more than a year, foraging parties scoured the countryside for horses, bringing in hundreds of robust specimens. Confederate troopers also corralled a number of citizens, intending to use them as hostages for Virginians who had been arrested under Pope's orders. While Union officers telegraphed frantically for assistance and fumbled to respond, Stuart sped east out of Chambersburg in the direction of Gettysburg, but just short of that town he veered south to Emmitsburg, Maryland. Cutting a wide path around McClellan's army, the rebel horsemen swept east of Frederick and Sugarloaf Mountain, aiming for the Potomac at the mouth of the Monocacy River; after thirty straight hours in the saddle they fended off their only active resistance as they crossed back into Virginia, camping at Leesburg on the night of the twelfth without a single fatality.[47]

As much as Stuart's cavalry needed fresh horses, the greatest achievement of his Chambersburg raid came with the intangible damage inflicted on the morale of Union soldiers and the confidence of the Northern public. The president readily understood those political consequences, and once Stuart's escape had been reported in Washington Lincoln wrote McClellan to remind him that it was time to move after the enemy. In geometric terms he patiently outlined the Army of the Potomac's advantageous position, closer to Richmond than Lee's army, but with frustrating inconsistency he pointed out that if Lee ignored his capital to invade Pennsylvania his line of communications would be at McClellan's mercy: the previous spring and summer Lincoln's paranoia about the safety of Washington had led him to reject that same logic from McClellan. With equal hypocrisy, McClellan now disputed his own former line of reasoning.[48]

Using the recent raid to buttress his claim that the army was unprepared, McClellan blamed Stuart's escape on the lack of sound horses in his cavalry regiments and urged the Quartermaster Department to provide the army with enough horses to remount that arm. Quartermaster General Montgomery Meigs replied to the implicit accusation, noting that he had supplied fifteen hundred horses a week since McClellan resumed command, and the president suggested sarcastically that the enemy would probably not find such leisure to raid north of the Potomac if he were a little better occupied south of it. The telegraphic duel continued for another ten days before a single Union soldier marched south from the Potomac. McClellan cited shortages of clothing and shoes for his men that mystified the quartermaster general, who had already filled the deficiencies, and McClellan probably did not think it expedient to point out that Confederate cavalry had put many of those supplies to the torch. McClellan also continued to call for remounts to replace galled and tired horses. On October 25, after reading McClellan's latest excuses about horses that suffered from sore tongues and general fatigue, Lincoln replied with uncharacteristic acerbity, asking "what the horses of your army have done since the battle of Antietam that fatigue anything."[49]

McClellan was still smarting from that remark the next morning when the vanguard of his grand army shuffled across the Potomac on pontoon bridges at Berlin, Maryland. Twenty days before, Lincoln had ordered him to move while the roads were still passable, fearing the truth of rumors that McClellan meant to go into winter quarters in Maryland. By the time his first troops alighted from the bridge to the Sacred Soil of Virginia stiff winds whipped the heavy rain of the winter's first storm into their faces. Thousands of feet, hooves, and wheels quickly churned the roads into mud, and that night the storm reached gale force, with fierce gusts ripping down tents and baring the chilled soldiers to another soaking. Not until noon the next day did the weather abate, and only to turn colder. Teams slipped far behind their regiments, depriving officers of their tents and bedding that evening, but even those who wrapped themselves in their blankets and spooned unashamedly with their comrades awoke shivering to a white frost, with frozen canteens. For a full week the pontoon bridges rumbled with the step of different divisions; the soldiers slept cold nearly every night, waking stiff, chilled, and weary, while the combination of nighttime freezing, daytime thaws, and heavy traffic transformed highways into thick, red streams. Then, on the morning of November 7, a wet, ponderous snow began to fall.[50]

Troops suffering so intensely from the elements refused to forgo other comforts, disregarding McClellan's orders against freelance foraging. The general himself ignored Henry Halleck's advice and authority to shoot miscreant stragglers on the spot, so his provost marshal was "distressed to death with the plundering & marauding of the Army." Stragglers did not account for most of the thievery, this time: whole companies and regiments participated, with the tacit or explicit approval of their officers. As each division fell out of ranks for the night, the men would simply step to each side of the road as though by signal, dismantling miles of fences without a murmur from anyone who carried a sword, leaving the rails the next morning in the ashes of thousands of campfires.[51] The night of that first snowfall a battery of New Hampshire artillerymen tore down an entire vacant house to fuel a bonfire through the night. Union armies had tread but little on the counties of Loudoun and Warren, where farmers still maintained an abundance of meat on the hoof. "We have a grand time killing and eating their sheep, cattle and poultry," admitted a Massachusetts private who had come into the army solely for the money. Turkeys and hogs had no chance against the swarms of hungry Yankees.[52]

From the east and north came Franz Sigel, gliding down the Orange & Alexandria to Manassas, spreading out from there through Thoroughfare Gap to protect McClellan's left flank. Sigel found little forage in that vicinity, where the armies had preyed so heavily barely two months previously, and it may have been in frustration that his men incinerated the village of Haymarket.[53]

The main body of the army had originally aimed for Culpeper Court House, between the Blue Ridge and the Bull Run mountains, from which McClellan intended to descend on Richmond. It was the route Lincoln preferred, shielding Washington over a shorter road to Richmond than Lee had to follow. That theoretically shorter road and the miserable weather notwithstanding, half of Lee's army reached Culpeper Court House several days ahead of McClellan. Reports of the Confederate movement on Culpeper arrived in Washington the evening of November 3, and the next day McClellan reported his leading infantry still at Upperville, some fifty miles north of Culpeper. On November 5, as though in exasperation over this latest failure, the president issued an order replacing McClellan with Burnside.[54]

Suspecting McClellan of unpatriotic selfishness or even disloyalty, Edwin Stanton feared the general might refuse to obey the order, and he made careful arrangements for the change of command. Stepping into an office adjoining his own, Stanton gave Brigadier General Catharinus Buckingham the orders for McClellan and Burnside, instructing him to first secure Burnside's assent, since he had already refused the command twice. If Burnside declined a third time, Buckingham was to return directly to Washington. Buckingham took a special locomotive down the Orange & Alexandria Railroad and out the Manassas Gap line to Salem, arriving on the afternoon of November 7 in the season's first major snowstorm. He requisitioned a horse and rode some fifteen miles south to Waterloo, where he found Burnside already asleep in the bedroom of a private house. Burnside balked as expected, variously contending that McClellan was more competent than he was and that he owed McClellan too much, personally, to displace him. Buckingham replied that McClellan was to be removed in any case, and that if Burnside did not take the command it would be given to Joe Hooker. That did the trick, for Burnside gravely mistrusted Hooker. Burnside and Buckingham rode the fifteen miles back to Salem, boarded the special locomotive, and steamed up to Rectortown to find McClellan alone in his tent. Herman Haupt and General Patrick, the provost marshal, had been by to report the condition of the railroads and the conduct of the troops, and Haupt had stayed for tea, but he had departed half an hour before. Buckingham knocked on the tent pole to announce himself, entered with Burnside, and after a few moments of idle conversation handed him the orders. McClellan read them and, contrary to Stanton's wild apprehensions, turned to Burnside to acknowledge the exchange of command.[55]

General officers recoiled disgustedly at what they deemed a dangerous and injudicious order founded wholly on politics. The same order relieved Fitz John Porter of his command, with the ominous implication that he would at last have to face trial on John Pope's accusations: after learning of the Democratic gains in New York, an embittered Porter supposed the president had removed McClellan expressly to prevent him from bagging Lee, which might have made Little Mac a viable presidential rival.[56]

In fact, Lincoln had based his decision entirely on McClellan's fatal military shortcomings, but — as with Buell — he had timed it for purely political reasons. Losing the race to Culpeper Court House could have provided a nominal excuse, but such a coincidence was inevitable: so habitually did McClellan procrastinate that his removal at any time would have followed on the heels of some objectionable tardiness. In the cabinet meeting of November 4, before learning about the occupation of Culpeper, Lincoln remarked that he had offered to remove McClellan any time Halleck demanded it, but (as everyone agreed that day) Halleck seemed to lack the moral courage to make the demand. The president therefore wrote out the order himself, choosing November 5 because the New York elections — the last of the season — had concluded the previous evening. As partisan Republican officeholders had warned the White House, their party would be "very hard pressed" in New York because of Democratic victories in the Midwest, and McClellan was the administration's key to conservative support at the polls. General Cochrane had lobbied for McClellan's immediate promotion to general in chief, to ingratiate Unionist Democrats before the election, so if Lincoln were going to fire him altogether he certainly had to wait until after the election; as it happened, he waited less than twenty-four hours.[57]

It was well for his party that Lincoln did wait, for as it was Republicans endured a humiliating defeat in those final fall elections. New Jersey seated a Democratic governor and legislature, while Democrat Horatio Seymour overwhelmed Brigadier General James Wadsworth in the crucial race for governor in New York. The Illinois legislature fell into Democratic hands, as well: William J. Allen was reelected to Congress after having been imprisoned during the August roundup of outspoken administration critics. Lincoln's own congressional district went to his old personal friend and new political enemy, John Todd Stuart. Michigan sustained the administration, but an Ann Arbor law student intimated that news of McClellan's removal would have jeopardized that vote. New England and the extreme Northwest still supported the president, and his party still held a majority in Congress, but a contiguous string of states from the Hudson to the Mississippi had rejected his shift toward autocratic, radical policy. David Dudley Field, a renowned New York lawyer and a firm administration friend, blamed the losses primarily on the arbitrary suspension of habeas corpus, citing some specific and unnecessary instances of it that had proven costly to the party. The government's arrests were condemned by "everybody," he claimed. "There was nobody to pronounce them legal, [and] nobody to consider them expedient, even if they had been legal."[58]

Now Lincoln had alienated much of the army. "The President has committed a great blunder," mourned an angry Indiana major. "Officers & men are much dissatisfied with the removal of this favorite Genl.," admitted a Michigan captain, and a Pennsylvania officer told his mother that the "removal of McClellan has cast a gloom over our army sutch as I have never seen before." Within two weeks of McClellan's exodus the streets of Washington suddenly began teeming with officers absent from their regiments, in numbers that seemed unusual even in a city accustomed to commissioned truants, and the change in command may well have fueled that influx. A New York captain confirmed widespread disapproval among men of all ranks, and the colonel of the 5th New Hampshire thought that when McClellan left he "carried the heart of the Army with him."[59] Even those who considered Burnside at least as competent as McClellan reflected ruefully that McClellan alone held the confidence of the army, and certainly he did command intense devotion from a significant faction. "McClellan's soldiers all have faith in him," a Connecticut captain had recently told his family, and a quartermaster who had served under all the army's generals so far felt that for the Army of the Potomac no one could replace Little Mac.[60]

The discomfited Burnside accorded his friend the farewell gift of a grand review. Most of the army had concentrated at Warrenton, and on the bright, mild morning of November 10 the Second, Fifth, and Sixth Corps drew up on either side of the Warrenton Turnpike to say goodbye to their chief. Many enlisted men seemed initially unaware of the succession, but the emotion displayed that day showed that most understood. A salute of sixteen guns preceded McClellan; then he cantered out into the road alone, between the facing ranks, ahead of Burnside and the staff. The countryside erupted instantly with cheers. Every man saluted as he passed, and many of them wept like children. As he rode past each regiment hundreds of men turned and stared after him, as though stunned. Some regiments broke ranks and thronged him, with at least a few proposing that they march on Washington, but he waved them back into line; a Rhode Island officer had no doubt that he could have led the army into mutiny. He rode slowly, as though trying to scan every face, and more than a few thought they saw tears in his own eyes.[61] At noon McClellan lunched with Porter and his staff. Afterward the First Corps repeated the scenes of the morning, although those troops had known him but ten weeks. Then he met his generals and some old Regulars for a personal goodbye; a few of them demonstrated little more restraint than the rank and file, hinting that the whole army would back him if he refused to step down, but McClellan only told them to support Burnside as they had him. Nothing in his time with the army became him like the leaving of it.[62]

Soldiers seldom achieve unanimity on any subject, and reactions varied from one unit to another, as well as from man to man. A new recruit who had already developed a thorough distaste for the army resented the mile he had to march to see and be seen by the general, whom he did not think worth the shoe leather. Less fawning officers accused their more devoted colleagues of making fools of themselves by muttering treasonously and threatening to resign. "For one I am glad McClellan is removed," wrote a captain in the 32nd Massachusetts, who had grown tired of the general's apparent indecision, and a Pennsylvania private misunderstood that most of the army approved the outcome. The Republican adjutant of a New England regiment promised to tell his sister what he thought of McClellan some day, but he reminded her that another officer had been dismissed for remarking on that general's inactivity.[63]

General Haupt, the railroad man, liked the looks of Burnside and thought he would invigorate the army. A great many men of all ranks esteemed Burnside highly, both personally and professionally, and especially in the Ninth Corps, where his popularity greatly exceeded McClellan's; the Ninth Corps had not participated in the farewell review. The enlisted men found Burnside especially agreeable because he accorded them as much respect as anyone, and showed not a shred of pretension. A Massachusetts private pulling guard duty outside Burnside's headquarters tent saw the general emerge in the middle of the night wearing nothing but a shirt, the tail of which he flipped up to toast his backside by the fire. "He is a jolly bugger," the guard told his parents, "& will joke with a private as quick as an officer."[64]

Burnside's jolly disposition faded when he took over the army. McClellan partisans doubted his capacity, and the fatally modest Burnside concurred. Rumors raced through the upper ranks that he had confessed himself unfit for the job, as did many who found him the most companionable.[65]

The morning after the review, McClellan endured another round of emotional farewells at the Warren Green Hotel. A few hours later a train pulled in from Washington and McClellan boarded it for Trenton, New Jersey, where his orders had inexplicably directed him to await further instructions. Those who saw him off noticed that the same train had brought James Wadsworth, the defeated New York gubernatorial candidate, who was rumored to have been sent to advise Burnside. Wadsworth's impeccably Republican credentials tainted Burnside's ascent with suspicions that the administration intended a political as well as a military changeover: that evening Burnside held a review of his own, afterward greeting his chief commanders in a reception at his tent, and for all the congenial handshakes some of those generals could not have helped wondering if Burnside had gone over to the radicals.[66]

Burnside moved his headquarters up to the Warren Green once McClellan departed. Joe Hooker arrived on November 12 to take over Fitz John Porter's corps, and Porter headed for his court-martial in Washington. Halleck and Quartermaster General Meigs also descended on Warrenton that day, and with General Haupt they convened an all-night conference with Burnside and his corps commanders on how to reach Richmond ahead of the Army of Northern Virginia. No one suggested returning to the Peninsula, although Burnside had advised against leaving there in the first place, for that would have insinuated grievous error on the parts of Lincoln, Stanton, and Halleck. Halleck wanted to press on toward Culpeper, but the Orange & Alexandria lacked the capacity to feed an army of over one hundred thousand, and Virginia's roads deteriorated daily. Burnside therefore proposed dashing down the Rappahannock to Falmouth, crossing the river on pontoon bridges, and proceeding on the line of the Richmond, Fredericksburg & Potomac Railroad. A wagon train of provisions could meet him at Falmouth, after which supplies might come by water, under the protection of navy gunboats, and as the army crossed each navigable river the supply base could shift that much closer to Richmond. As usual, Halleck resisted taking responsibility, but he relayed the proposal to the president, who consented. Lincoln warned, though, that it would fail unless Burnside moved promptly.[67]

While awaiting that answer Burnside grouped the massive army into three grand divisions of two corps each, with the Right Grand Division commanded by Edwin Sumner, the Center Grand Division by Hooker, and the Left Grand Division by William Franklin. Presidential approval reached Warrenton just before noon on November 14, and at daylight the next morning "Bull" Sumner stepped off with a third of the army.[68]

Initial success would depend on bringing the pontoon train down to Aquia Creek by water and carting it overland to Falmouth in good season. In the command conference at the Warren Green either Halleck or Meigs assured Burnside that the pontoons could be in place within three days, and on the evening of November 12 Halleck telegraphed to Washington for Daniel Woodbury, commander of the engineer brigade, to send the pontoons to Aquia. The evening before Sumner's troops started, Burnside had his staff engineer check on the progress of the pontoons, but Sumner was in motion before Burnside learned that the promise of three-day delivery could not be kept. Only three dozen of the pontoons from the upper Potomac had reached Washington, and it required fresh teams and harness to move them south. Woodbury advised Halleck to delay the movement five days, but Halleck refused. He failed to warn Burnside of the trouble, though, or to impart any sense of urgency to Woodbury, who estimated that one train could be started from Washington on Sunday, November 16, or the next morning.[69]

Sumner's troops reached Falmouth November 17, after a three-day march. Rebel cavalry had withdrawn south of the Rappahannock after tearing up the railroad between there and Aquia, but the river ran too deep for infantry and no pontoons had arrived. Woodbury's implied schedule should have brought the first bridge material to Aquia by November 18 or 19, but it went instead to Belle Plain Landing, and no one in Burnside's army knew of its whereabouts. Woodbury telegraphed of repeated delays, and it was not until November 19 that the next train left Washington, again under the supervision of an officer who remained ignorant of its importance. Henry Halleck, the only officer who might have sparked Woodbury to greater haste and invested him with peremptory authority to expedite the pontoons, never told him how crucial they were. That did not deter Halleck from implying that he had done everything he could to hurry the pontoons, though, and he invited Burnside to hold Woodbury responsible for any delay.[70]

Burnside reached Falmouth on November 19 and spent three fretful days watching the river rise. Not until three days after that did General Woodbury and the first pontoons show up, but by then the heights beyond Fredericksburg bristled with Confederate bayonets and artillery. Halleck had also neglected to send the wagon train of bread and other commissary stores, to fill the men's haversacks for that first march south from Fredericksburg. Those dual failures posed serious obstacles, Burnside warned, and he suggested to Halleck that they jeopardized the success of his plan.[71]

Halleck could not have failed to convey this information to the president, as much as he would have disguised his own responsibility for the lapses Burnside cited, and that brought Abraham Lincoln down from Washington on the steamer *Baltimore* for a personal interview with Burnside. The general flatly admitted the dire risk inherent in crossing the river to fight for Fredericksburg now that Longstreet's corps had arrived. The president suggested the eminently sensible option of congregating additional forces under navy protection at Port Royal, downstream, and on the Pamunkey River, nearer Richmond. The two columns could attack in coordination with Burnside's, either trapping Lee in a vise or driving him away from the road to Richmond, which they might then seize. Burnside feared it would take too much time: Halleck had, after all, insinuated that he must assail the enemy soon even if he were to fail. Lincoln reminded Burnside that as commander in chief it was he, rather than Halleck, who held final authority, and he preferred Burnside to wait until he was prepared. When Lincoln posed the Pamunkey plan to Halleck, though, Halleck raised the same objection about insufficient time, so Lincoln abandoned the idea and Halleck resumed pressuring Burnside for immediate action. Halleck injected the administration of the Union army with a conspicuous lack of candor that season: while Lincoln disclaimed any desire for undue haste, Halleck relentlessly prodded Burnside and the commander of the principal army in Tennessee, all the while blaming the president's impatience for his own insistence on speed.[72]

Burnside told those close to him the details of his meeting with Lincoln, so the tale of another army cooperating from the Pamunkey leaked out in garbled form. Nathaniel Banks was gathering a sizable corps in New York for service in the Gulf, but his destination still remained a secret: the rumors raised hopes in the Army of the Potomac that he would have a go at Lee from behind, to the extent of sailing right up the James River at Richmond.[73]

Sumner, whom Burnside trusted as his most loyal and selfless wing commander, shared Burnside's fear of crossing into Fredericksburg in the face of heavy resistance. He suggested building a fieldwork below town for artillery to sweep the plain below the city and enfilade the enemy guns on Marye's Heights, behind the town. With gunboats coming up to add their heavy ordnance they could force the Confederates away without the cost of an infantry assault. That, too, seemed too time-consuming to Burnside in the face of such demand for early results, but he did consider crossing most of the army farther downstream, at Skinker's Neck, to flank

Lee out of his position beyond Fredericksburg. Then the rain, snow, and frosts of early December so softened the primitive roads in that direction that he despaired of moving quickly enough to achieve much surprise. Before Union pioneers could corduroy the roads there, Stonewall Jackson marched in from the Shenandoah Valley and settled some of his corps into intimidating positions on the right bank of Skinker's Neck and Port Royal.[74]

That brought Burnside's attention back to Fredericksburg, which he deemed the least likely spot to cross and, therefore, the spot that would surprise Lee the most. From Stafford Heights, on their side of the river, Union soldiers watched Confederate engineers building gun emplacements on the range of hills behind the city, but with so much of Lee's army downriver Burnside hoped to rush across and intercede before the enemy could concentrate. Had he confined himself to bridging the river on the plain below the city that ploy might have worked, for Lee acknowledged the impossibility of contesting a crossing there, where Union artillery on Stafford Heights dominated the field, but Burnside also wanted to build bridges opposite Fredericksburg itself. There the enemy would find a chance for enough delay to overcome any surprise.[75]

The feint toward Skinker's Neck continued as a diversion, to hold Jackson's troops where they were. Meanwhile, opposing pickets on the narrower reaches of the river chatted idly back and forth. A nine-month New Jersey man who had enlisted to earn a stake for his new family suddenly found himself uncomfortably close to an enemy he may never have expected to see, but in a letter to his pregnant wife he described the rebels as "very gay." A veteran sergeant in the Ninth Corps found the men on the other bank every bit as tired of the war as the Yankees. Behind those Southern sentries, Fredericksburg lay abandoned by most of its inhabitants, wearing the gloomy atmosphere of a medieval city during a plague. When one of the church bells swung into a slow rhythm, a Yankee on the Falmouth side thought it was tolling someone's death.[76]

Hard frosts tortured men sleeping in open shelter tents; a brigadier slept uncomfortably despite a stove in his wall tent. "I almost wish I had resigned," admitted the colonel of the 8th Ohio. "Surely, I have no relish for this winter campaign." The desire for winter quarters nevertheless gave way at many campfires to the sensation that one more strong push might undo the rebellion; as one officer chanted regularly, the coming fight at Fredericksburg promised to decide "the fate of the country." The approach of Lincoln's threatened date for emancipation convinced some that the war must be won by the first of the year or the game would have to be given up, because the South (and perhaps much of the North) would never accept spontaneous abolition. Such reasoning prompted a Pennsylvania captain to think of the final weeks of 1862 as the nation's "Dark hour."[77]

For others, the war seemed lost already. Returning to his regiment after recuperating from his Antietam wound, Captain Oliver Wendell Holmes Jr. wrote that he was convinced the South had effectively won its independence. While he hoped for foreign intervention to save face, he predicted that all the bloodshed and incompetence had prepared the soldiers to give up a hopeless attempt at conquering "a great civilized nation." A New York lieutenant who would not live to see his brother enter the White House confessed a similar conviction that the Union army could never prevail by force of arms. The recent elections also raised the specter of a negotiated settlement for intransigent Unionists, who had been fighting so long against the very concept of compromise.[78]

Further discouraging the soldiers was a growing lack of confidence in Burnside, fueled partly by his own modest admissions and partly by the malicious mutterings of William Franklin and other McClellan naysayers in his Left Grand Division. Their comments seeped through the ranks to infect junior officers and, eventually, the enlisted men. By the time Burnside put his plans into action, the first doubtful appraisals of him were already drifting homeward, supplied primarily by the left wing of the army.[79]

Two hours after midnight on December 11 the generals were awake and moving. Shivering engineers hauled their pontoons down to the broad riverbank and started tying the bridges together. The dull clunking of their hammers carried across the river, but for a time darkness and mist shielded them from Mississippi pickets ensconced in waterfront houses. Up on the bluffs the various corps moved toward the sound under guides from a First Corps brigade that had spent part of the spring encamped on the hills where Lee's army sprawled.[80]

Longstreet's corps occupied the highest of those hills, a mile west of the city. His line ran from a mile above the town to a mile below it, centering on the pillared Marye mansion and the steep rise on which that mansion sat. Longstreet and Lee positioned themselves half a mile south of Marye's Heights, on a hilltop that offered a broad panorama. South of there the hills stood in woods too thick to invite many good artillery vistas, descending nearly to the level of the plain by Hamilton's Crossing of the Richmond, Fredericksburg & Potomac Railroad. From there Stonewall Jackson's corps stretched all the way to Skinker's Neck and Port Royal. Hazel Run cut the Union position in two as it coursed toward the Rappahannock just below the city, and Deep Run posed another impediment to lateral movement on the plain itself. The Richmond Stage Road crossed that plain, running parallel to the railroad until Hamilton's Crossing, where they diverged.

Burnside had hoped his divisions would be tramping across those bridges before breakfast: Sumner on the right, into the city, and Franklin on the left, onto the plain below Hazel Run. The first of the downstream bridges was finished by 9:00 AM, only two hours after work began, and engineers completed the second one two hours later. No such luck attended the construction of the upper bridges, though, and Burnside made his first mistake when he decided to finish them before sending troops over the river. By six o'clock the fog had lifted enough for Confederate pickets to make out the workmen as their bridges dangled eighty feet from the Fredericksburg dock, and a scattering fire drove the engineers back to their own shore. The Federals crept back out for another try, but as they reached the end of the bridge another volley erupted and sent them running again. After several attempts and numerous casualties Burnside's artillery chief, Henry Hunt, tried to blast the marksmen out of their lairs, and three dozen guns pounded the houses on Water Street and Caroline, but when the engineers ventured back out on the bridges the Mississippians opened on them with the same disturbing accuracy. At noon a frustrated Burnside finally directed Hunt to pulverize the buildings, and Hunt did his best. For two hours an ear-splitting barrage destroyed homes all along the river, but when the echoes died away the major in charge of the engineers refused to send his men back out. A collection of volunteers from nearby infantry regiments made the attempt, but from the waterfront rubble came another flurry of musketry that killed a few of them.[81]

The short winter afternoon was half wasted by then, and with it much of the hope for effective surprise. At Hunt's suggestion some three score Michigan and Massachusetts infantry crowded into spare pontoons, poled across the river, and spilled onto the embankment. These few rushed up to the houses and secured the landing, after which more of their comrades came across to pry the Mississippians out of town. Into the dusk they battled street by barricaded street until, at dark, the Mississippi brigade fell back to Longstreet's main line behind town. By then the bridges had been completed, and Union infantry was stacking up on Stafford Heights, waiting to cross.[82]

Most of those columns eventually backed away from the river, either returning to their old camps or bedding down in makeshift bivouacs behind the bluffs. A division from the Second Corps and one brigade of the Ninth Corps occupied the town after dark, cooking over campfires on the edge of the river and sleeping in the light snow that covered the streets. They awoke amid thick fog on Friday morning, December 12, to find the buildings about them pockmarked and battered, with roofs riddled, windows broken, and walls crumbling. The rest of Sumner's grand division started pouring over the bridges as soon as daylight filtered through the morning mist, forming into ranks in the different streets parallel to the river. They stacked arms and fell out to await their next orders, but none came that day, so they began milling around to look at the damage. Scattered bodies still lay on the cobblestones to remind them of the previous day's street fighting, and the structural damage occupied their attention for a time, but when the first soldier ventured inside one of the houses the sack of Fredericksburg began.[83]

At first, of course, it was the food that attracted them. Luxuries like potatoes, sifted flour, butter, honey, sugar, pickles, and preserves tempted hungry men beyond any reasonable powers of resistance. To the addicted the theft of tobacco seemed no worse than foraging for food, and from tobacco it was a small step to wine and whiskey. Next came china, silver plate, and personal wardrobes, as soldiers pulled matronly dresses over their heads, complete with hoops. A night on the frozen streets had highlighted the need for padded bedding, and looters brought bedsteads outside, while the slower of them had to be satisfied with extra bedding and carpets. Colonial-vintage chairs, sofas, and rockers soon lined the streets so the invaders might inspect personal trunks in greater comfort. Flower vases and children's toys lay scattered about. Inside the houses literary dilettantes rifled libraries, dropping uninteresting tomes on the floor or tossing them outside. Soldiers sliced paintings from their frames and rolled them up to ship home as souvenirs. Frustration gripped those who found nothing worth taking, and plundering turned to vandalism. Officers sometimes joined in, as well as ignoring the depredations: a staff major seethed that "their object seems to be to destroy what they can't steal, & to steal all they can." A Massachusetts private confirmed that impression, admitting to his mother that "we stole or distroyed everything in the City." Watches and jewelry vanished quickly, but musical instruments also proved popular, and amateur movers manhandled spinet pianos down front steps for impromptu concerts in the brisk December air. With the aid of some stimulants and a couple of violins, the 1st Minnesota enjoyed a rollicking stag hoedown.[84]

Burnside's provost marshal, General Patrick, tried to curb the looting with little to aid him but the sound of his own voice. He applied his riding crop to one man he caught loading a stolen horse with household possessions, collared a number of officers who had collected some spoil, and roamed the streets all day raging at pillagers as they broke into stores and ransacked homes, but without materially diminishing the rampage. As other divisions crowded into the various blocks, their men sifted the wreckage anew until nothing worthwhile remained. Only the fading of the light and the chill of evening would end the Army of the Potomac's most shameful day.[85]

The city continued to burn here and there from the artillery barrage, and the sight of Yankee soldiers stripping the houses, plainly visible through binoculars, reduced the Confederates' reluctance to fire. Late in the morning a Third Corps division came down the bluffs on the Falmouth side and filled the upper bridges, but so densely had previous units packed into the streets that only the first regiment — nine-month Pennsylvanians — could push ashore. The column halted, backing up across the bridges and up the slope on the other side. The Pennsylvanians' brass band shouldered onto the landing and honked out "Yankee Doodle" for the amusement of their bored brethren, then launched into "Bully for You" just as the dark ribbons of troops climbing up the Falmouth embankment attracted the attention of Southern artillery. One shell exploded in the middle of a big new regiment on one of the bridges, splattering blood and flesh indiscriminately, and that convinced the musicians to adjourn to a safer venue. The rest of the division turned around and climbed back up to Falmouth, out of range.[86]

Union soldiers below Fredericksburg anticipated their marauding comrades in the town. Sixth Corps troops sent to picket the lower bridgeheads the night of December 11 burst onto the isolated plantation of Alfred Bernard and quickly consumed everything edible, including some livestock, before resorting to more senseless destruction. The first Yankees in the house found three Confederates there, taking that as license for pillage. It was as though the entire army had been infected with a deeply malicious spirit.[87]

The First and Sixth Corps flooded onto the plain throughout Friday afternoon, spreading out behind the Richmond Stage Road for more than a mile from Deep Run to below Mansfield Plantation before bending back half a mile to the river. From Stafford Heights the view evoked panoramic European battlefields, but the relatively narrow front forced the fifty thousand men of the First and Sixth Corps to elbow into uncomfortably close quarters under the mouths of Confederate artillery on Marye's Heights. A few of Longstreet's guns below Marye's Heights could not resist so helpless a target, opening a languid fire on Franklin's troops late in the afternoon, but some First Corps batteries wheeled out into the middle of the plain to reply, and soon both sides ceased firing. Cavalry ranging straight across the stage road and the railroad ran into Confederate infantry — indicating that Lee had not been so surprised or overawed by the investment of Fredericksburg as to neglect his right flank.[88]

The sun hung too near the horizon for any attack that day. After arresting the owner of Mansfield, Franklin established his headquarters there and prepared to spend the night. In the evening Burnside came over to adjust the morrow's assault for the loss of surprise, and there they foredoomed their army to defeat. Burnside had slept little the two previous nights, besides driving himself mercilessly since taking over the army: even Franklin seemed concerned about it. Nearing physical and mental exhaustion, Burnside discussed the situation with Franklin and the commanders of the First and Sixth Corps, John Reynolds and William Smith (nicknamed "Baldy," to distinguish him from the plethora of Regular Army Smiths). As Franklin remembered it the next spring, he suggested that he should make a massive daybreak assault against Lee's right with as many as thirty thousand men, and he implied that Burnside agreed. Franklin claimed that to have his troops in position in time he would have to have his orders and two more divisions from Hooker's grand division at hand well before morning.[89]

Burnside left Mansfield by six o'clock. He worked until at least midnight, but it was not until 5:55 AM that his headquarters scriveners completed his vague, ambiguous orders and sent them to the grand division commanders. The orders Franklin received did not explicitly demand the grand assault of the previous evening's discussion, but they could have been interpreted that way. Franklin read his instructions with the dual jaundice of doubt and fear, however: he doubted Burnside's competence, and feared being made a scapegoat for defeat, as Fitz John Porter had been. In the absence of any reference to a change, Franklin might have been expected to interpret Burnside's order as a reflection of their last understanding, or he should have expressed his confusion. He may have been dissuaded from posing a question by the press of time and the presence of James Hardie, a staff brigadier whom Burnside had sent from headquarters as his proxy, for Franklin claimed that Hardie confirmed his conservative approach.[90]

In any case, Franklin's reading of his orders differed substantially from Edwin Sumner's. From his position around Mansfield, Franklin was to prepare all his troops for "a rapid movement down the old Richmond road," sending "a division at least" out to seize Prospect Hill, at Hamilton's Crossing, which marked the right flank of the Army of Northern Virginia. Franklin interpreted that to require one division, aided by the belated and incomplete support of one other. Sumner, meanwhile, was told to assault the heights behind Fredericksburg with "a division or more," and that similar language convinced him to commit five divisions with the support of another. Had he put enough faith in his chief, Franklin could have found justification in his orders for the contemplated all-out assault on

Lee's right. George Meade, his senior division commander, firmly believed that so strong an attack could not have failed, but Meade heard no hint from Franklin that theirs was to be the main assault and he doubted that anyone else on their wing, including Franklin, absorbed that understanding.[91]

Darkness and slick, frozen roads delayed Hardie until well after seven o'clock. The orders he delivered to Franklin called for the attack "at once," and Franklin set Meade's division of Pennsylvania Reserves into motion within the hour. Although Franklin later insisted that his instructions appeared to anticipate only a reconnaissance in force, John Reynolds entertained no such delusion: he ordered Meade to "carry" the low hill beyond Hamilton's Crossing. Meade drew his three brigades up on the stage road, and Reynolds deployed John Gibbon's division on his right. Meade started forward at nine o'clock, but ran into trouble almost immediately. J.E.B. Stuart's cavalry guarded the Confederate right, and one of his guns galloped out on Meade's left flank to begin enfilading the Union formation, causing Meade to haul up short. Meade turned a brigade to face this threat while several Federal batteries swung toward the offending pest.[92]

Noon had approached before that annoying gun could be persuaded to retire, and Meade's Pennsylvanians rolled forward. His attack aimed at a point half a mile north of Hamilton's Crossing: had he proceeded down the stage road to the next intersection, as Burnside appears to have intended, he would have struck Lee's extreme flank, but instead he hit Jackson's infantry head-on. That may have been the result of poor reconnaissance, for Franklin's own map of the battle badly distorted the roads and rail lines, and showed Meade marching directly toward Hamilton's.[93]

By now Lee had reunited his army, and the hills descending to Hamilton's Crossing harbored plenty of Confederate infantry — except in a marshy gap several hundred yards wide on Meade's right. His Pennsylvania Reserves stumbled into that gap, instinctively swinging left and right to widen it, and for a time they managed to rake the Confederate lines with musketry. In the thick sapling growth they could hardly see each other, let alone detect the enemy lines, and they pushed to the crest of the hill, right into a fresh line of Confederates who poured deadly volleys into them. The Pennsylvanians replied in kind, and men fell fast enough to remind another Yankee of autumn leaves dropping from the trees. With a lot more weight they might have driven a wedge into Jackson's line, but Gibbon made little progress on Meade's right and no one at all stood behind him. Meade's momentum waned, and Southern reinforcements came over the ridge to drive him back. His division retired slowly but steadily toward the railroad track, leaving their wounded in the hands of the enemy. The colonel of the 11th Pennsylvania initially counted 236 casualties out of 392 men, and remarked that the Pennsylvania Reserves were "almost annihilated."[94]

While Meade fought his lonely fight four miles away, Burnside stood with Joe Hooker and Sumner on the roof of his headquarters — the home of Alexander Phillips, high on Stafford Heights. In the yard sat "Professor" Thaddeus Lowe's aerial balloon, and telegraph lines had been strung to the Phillips house from both fronts. Burnside anxiously awaited some indication, by eye or wire, that Franklin had persuaded Lee to protect his beleaguered right by weakening his left. Smoke and lingering fog obscured their view of Franklin's front, but at 11:00 AM an encouraging telegram came in from General Hardie, at Mansfield: Meade had advanced into solid lines of infantry, and Reynolds had brought his whole force into line; the enemy appeared to be developing an attack on his left, presumably below Hamilton's Crossing; a Sixth Corps general had been wounded, suggesting (erroneously) that Smith's corps had also been engaged, and a Third Corps division had been put into the fight. Lowe's balloon went up for a look, and the occupants shouted down their sketchy observations.[95]

At noon Hardie reported seeing a column of Confederate infantry traversing the ridge from Lee's left to his right: it consisted of reinforcements from within Stonewall Jackson's corps, who were surmounting the ridge to deal with Meade, but from Hardie's description and from the difficulty Reynolds had encountered it appeared that Lee was heavily reinforcing his right. Burnside concluded that the time had come to launch Sumner's assault on Marye's Heights, and he dispatched Sumner to Chatham, the Lacy mansion overlooking the city, from which he was to direct his part of the battle.[96]

From the western edge of Fredericksburg two parallel roads carried toward Marye's Heights. William Street turned into the Orange Plank Road, climbing the slope north of the Marye mansion, squeezing through a cleft in the ridge, and continuing to the west, toward Chancellorsville and a second-growth forest known locally as the Wilderness. The Telegraph Road followed Hanover Street straight toward the mansion, but just below the summit it turned sharply south; as with many clay thoroughfares in the era of iron tires, its ruts had been cut deep, running several feet below the level of an embankment topped by a stone wall. Longstreet had filled that sunken road with infantry and lined the crest with artillery, besides holding more infantry in reserve behind those guns. He had sent no troops to the right to aid Jackson, contrary to Burnside's evident deduction, and his line remained as strong as ever.

At Sumner's order Darius Couch, commanding the Second Corps, sent

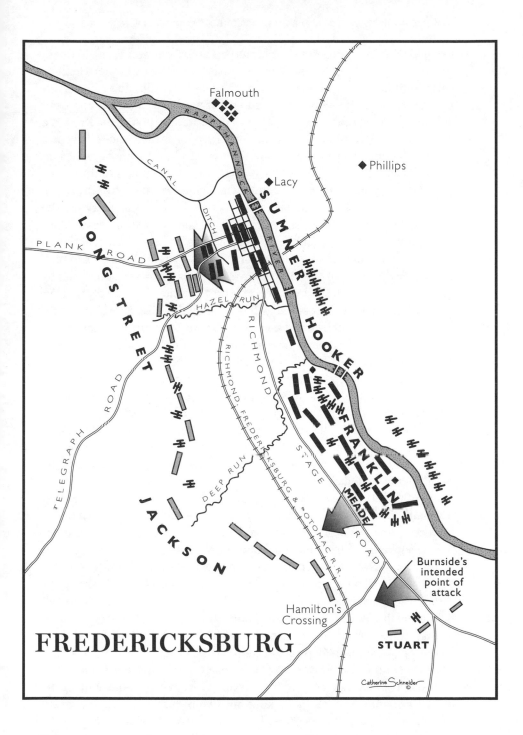

Falmouth

Phillips

Lacy

CANAL

RAPPAHANNOCK

DITCH

SUMNER

RIVER

HOOKER

PLANK LONGSTREET ROAD

HAZEL RUN

TELEGRAPH ROAD

RICHMOND

RICHMOND

RICHMOND, FREDERICKSBURG & POTOMAC R.R.

STAGE ROAD

FRANKLIN

MEADE

Burnside's
intended
point of
attack

JACKSON

DEEP RUN

Hamilton's
Crossing

STUART

FREDERICKSBURG

Catherine Schneider ©

two divisions marching out the plank road and Telegraph Road. William French's division came first, trotting directly toward Marye's Heights, with Southern shells plunging down the length of the blue columns. A millrace bisected the two roads, and one of the bridges over it had been stripped of some of its decking, so that column bunched up badly as the troops hopped across on the framing. Once each of French's brigades cleared the bridges the columns spun left and right into line of battle and rolled forward, preceded by a thick screen of skirmishers. From the moment the long blue lines emerged into the open terrain west of the city, a daunting hail of shell and case shot opened from the artillery on the heights. The nearer the Federals came to the slope the more easily Confederate guns at the extremities of Longstreet's line could fire lengthwise down their ranks. Yankees fell in knots and clusters. Nathan Kimball, whose brigade composed the first wave, had lost a quarter of his men by the time he reached a shallow shelf of land a couple of hundred yards below the sunken road. The stone wall bordering the road now blazed with rifle fire, and the slight depression of that shelf offered Kimball's men their only protection. Down most of them went on their bellies, returning an ineffective fire while rebels picked them off by dozens. Officers fell faster than any, killed by the tradition of standing up to encourage their men: more than half Kimball's regiments lost one or more commanding officers, and Kimball himself collapsed with an ugly leg wound.[97]

Winfield Hancock's division followed a few hundred feet behind Kimball. His brigadiers tried to stir their men with little speeches — or long ones, like that of Thomas Meagher of the Irish Brigade, who seemed to be drunk again as battle neared. By now Confederate artillerists had the range of the streets, and Hancock's divisions suffered much worse than Kimball's. One by one his three brigades surged up the slope with heads bowed against the deadly deluge until they, too, reached the natural depression where Kimball's men had taken refuge. A few brave souls pressed on in their light-blue overcoats, but no one came within a hundred feet of the blazing wall and lived to tell of it. Five of Hancock's regiments went through four commanders apiece as colonels, majors, and captains fell before the firestorm. The 5th New Hampshire took 268 officers and men in that day, of whom 75 remained uninjured by dark. Shellfire bowled men over as they dashed toward the embattled heights. The colonel of the 5th New Hampshire, Edward Cross, fell early in the advance when a shell exploded right in front of him: he described several fragments cutting his head, face, and hand, and knocking out two of his teeth, while a larger shard struck him in the chest and left him lying on the ground.[98]

Others in Cross's regiment insisted that they had been knocked down and dazed by pieces of iron that never broke the skin. Private Rodney

Ramsey told his father that he was laid senseless on the ground by "a piece of shell" that left no appreciable wound, perhaps mistaking the concussive effect of the explosion. When he recovered he retreated to a nearby ditch with another comrade, firing only three rounds toward the heights before a bullet barely grazed his leg and punctured his canteen. After that he and his friend rolled some dead bodies in front of their ditch and lay down to wait for the fighting to end. At dark they made their way back into Fredericksburg, where they found that their regiment had been consolidated into two companies numbering fewer than three dozen men apiece.[99] One of the surviving officers, Lieutenant Sumner Hurd, had fallen out of the advance on a plea of illness. He claimed that a shellburst felled him after he dropped out, preventing him from rejoining the regiment, but he suffered no visible injury and had to endure the sneers of all his comrades; Colonel Cross swore that Hurd would see no promotion in his regiment. After the battle Hurd wrote a cousin that he intended to resign at the first opportunity, even if he was cashiered for the attempt, if only his cousin could find him some means of making a living. The following spring Hurd did submit his resignation, and Cross promptly accepted it.[100]

The obvious ferocity of the engagement below Marye's Heights persuaded a good many men to drop out as their regiments moved toward the edge of town, where the smoke and confusion of the battlefield accommodated further skulking. If nothing else, a man could help a wounded comrade back to the hospitals in the city, and then disappear. Some dispensed with those thin pretensions and fled at a dead run. Enlisted men enjoyed a certain anonymity amid such masses of troops, but officers found it more difficult to avoid detection: despite widespread official assertions about every man doing his duty, most regiments buzzed with the rumors of someone who faltered, and especially when such frailty afflicted someone holding a commission. The commander of the 22nd Massachusetts noted two lieutenants who ducked out of the fighting at Fredericksburg, and he managed to have one of them dismissed in short order. Two days after Fredericksburg a musician in a new regiment observed that his "Capt. Carr proved to be a real coward," adding a couple of weeks later that the captain was pretending to be sick, in hopes of resigning on a claim of ill health — which he did, by the end of January.[101]

So common did the cowardice of officers seem, in fact, that the presumption sometimes inspired unfair accusations, as may have been the case with George Towle, a fifty-two-year-old captain in the 10th New Hampshire. Towle left his company on the way into its first fight, prompting his men to mutter disparagingly and write letters home about it. To those bold enough to ask, Towle admitted that the aspersions hurt his feelings, but he said he had left his post because the major summoned him. Only his honorable service through the rest of the war served to dispel the gossip.[102]

As one astute veteran deduced, the frequency of incompetence or worse among the leaders seemed greater because all the new regiments had come out with fresh complements of untried officers who had to be weeded out all over again; filling up the old regiments would have reduced that problem. Still, the new officers and men showed only a slightly greater propensity to quail than the veterans. As much as the new men might have come reluctantly, or for the more generous emoluments, most of them still represented the heart of their respective communities. Even if they did not feel bound to abide by their deadly contracts, they at least tended to care — and often to care very much — how their comrades and neighbors viewed them.[103]

With more than a thousand of those bright new uniforms filling out the ranks, Oliver Otis Howard's division went in next, to the right of French and Hancock. That extended the Union front to the Orange Plank Road; Longstreet's infantry line stretched that far, too, in such depth and with such abundant artillery that the regiment of North Carolinians holding his left flank on the plank road never fired a shot all day. Howard sent in one brigade by single regiments, and each took a severe drubbing before being driven back within minutes. Under such saturating shellfire Howard's men could do little more than flatten themselves against that slight undulation in the slope. "If I ever dug a hole in the ground with my nose it was that day," remarked a Minnesotan. A Massachusetts man described being almost completely buried in dirt from a shell that landed near him. Bullets whistled uncomfortably close overhead, sometimes arcing low enough to clip knapsacks and blanket rolls or to smash an officer's scabbard.[104]

With the Second Corps completely engaged and starting to give ground in places, Couch turned to the Ninth Corps, under Orlando Willcox. One division of that corps had been diverted between Fredericksburg and Franklin's grand division, leaving two divisions available for the assault, and they each consisted of only two brigades, but all of those brigades had been beefed up by two, three, or four new or nearly new regiments, including a few ungainly nine-month units. Willcox first sent in Sam Sturgis's division, directing it to the left of the Second Corps line. That brought his two brigades into uneven terrain, including a steep railroad cut and a ravine eroded by a branch of Hazel Run, and when it could advance no farther the brigade on the left slid behind the one on the right. This double line approached the southern end of the stone wall at an angle that afforded rebel gunners another opportunity for raking fire. A

Pennsylvania major escaped harm when a shell exploded between him and one of his lieutenants, and the lieutenant got away with only a faceful of gravel, but within their sight one shell nipped a man's arm off and another cut a soldier completely in two, spilling his entrails on the ground. A bullet hit a third man in the mouth, all before they came near enough to fire.[105]

At some cost in casualties a nine-month Rhode Island regiment that had been with the army less than a week tumbled awkwardly into line, suffering from inexperience and insufficient leadership: only one of the three field officers came along, the major having discovered that he was disabled just before the fight. Sturgis's leading brigade stopped at the bank of the branch, a couple of hundred yards from Longstreet's artillery and infantry. There they stood for a time, loading and firing feverishly, but the canister and shell was more than men could bear. A color-bearer in the 21st Massachusetts lost both arms when a shell blew up in front of his flag. A recruit in that regiment saw a dozen men swept away by one projectile, and another round ripped a man's head from his shoulders. Unable to creep any closer, those Yankees also threw themselves to the ground and fired up their ammunition. The entire 35th Massachusetts retired behind a hill on the excuse of low ammunition, leaving the flank of the 11th New Hampshire wide open and eliciting some venomous comment from their abandoned allies. The bullets rained so thick and low that no individual dared to leave the ranks unless he was wounded, but once they were struck men often leaped to their feet and dashed for the rear.[106]

Shortly before Sturgis went in, a frustrated Burnside learned from an aide that Franklin had not yet committed the Sixth Corps. Burnside, who had clearly expected more vigor on the left, sent another aide to Mansfield with orders for Franklin to make an immediate frontal attack on the enemy — characterizing it as a divergence from his morning orders for an assault on the left. The difference between the direction Burnside expected of Franklin's initial attack and Franklin's understanding of those expectations would cost Union soldiers fearfully.[107]

Unlike McClellan, Burnside had estimated enemy strength with fair accuracy; he knew that he would outnumber Lee on one of the two battlefronts. If Franklin had thrown as much force at Jackson's line as Sumner had at Longstreet's, Burnside might reasonably have expected one of the Confederate wings to give way. The great natural strength of Longstreet's line distorted that logic some — but, as Lee had demonstrated at Gaines's Mill less than six months before, a stubborn disregard for casualties could sometimes still overcome modern weaponry and the most intimidating field positions.

The best chance for Union victory lay before Franklin, though, and he committed nowhere near the proportion of his troops that Sumner had.[108] By the time Burnside's latest demand for action reached Franklin's head-quarters, Meade's division was falling back in complete confusion and Gibbon's in only somewhat less disorder. To protect the pontoon bridges, Franklin had kept the entire Sixth Corps, nine brigades strong, lying idle on a plain that the ranked artillery on Stafford Heights might have swept clean of any Confederates. On his extreme left stood Abner Doubleday's four brigades, which had barely thirty men killed all day. Franklin had also been loaned two divisions of the Third Corps, from Hooker's Center Grand Division: of those he pushed only David Birney's to the front — far too late to exploit Meade's breakthrough or to even hold the ground he had gained. Burnside sent another order for an attack with Franklin's "whole force," but Franklin replied that it was too late for another attack. Only when part of the Ninth Corps sidled over to guard the bridges, late in the day, did Franklin finally deploy a couple of divisions from the Sixth Corps: they strode out, exchanged a few savage blasts of musketry, and lay down to have some mud splattered on them by bounding shells, but they suffered little and accomplished less. Firing continued into the darkness, mimicking a torchlight procession as the muzzle flashes rippled down the lines, but in the end Franklin satisfied himself with holding the same ground he had occupied that morning.[109]

Expecting Franklin to obey his orders for aggressive action, Burnside kept pounding at Marye's Heights. A brigade from the Third Corps ap-proached behind Sturgis's division to lend its firepower, while a brigade from the Fifth Corps came to "relieve" Sturgis, although Sturgis's men re-mained pinned until the sun went down: those two brigades collided and fell in together. As the daylight faded a third brigade joined them in a fu-tile assault stymied by the crowding and the volume of Confederate lead and iron. The men took what cover they could and directed sporadic fire toward the southern half of Marye's Heights.[110]

Toward dusk Andrew Humphreys arranged his division of the Fifth Corps for another head-on assault on the heights from between the Tele-graph Road and the plank road. Like Meade's division, which had begun the day's fighting, this one was composed of Pennsylvanians to a man: two brigades of four regiments each, and not one of them had ever been under fire before. The 91st Pennsylvania was a year old, but the other seven had all been raised late the previous summer, and six of those were nine-month regiments. Humphreys formed his first brigade behind an em-bankment at the foot of the slope, just beyond the millrace, in relative safety. When he led it over the crest to the broad, open ground the South-erners in the sunken road opened fire on what looked like a shooting gallery. The Pennsylvanians dashed the two hundred yards or so to the shallower swale where earlier brigades had taken refuge and they, too, lay down and commenced firing. Humphreys and some reckless officers screamed at them to cease fire and fix bayonets for a charge, but so many of them bolted back to the embankment that their brigade commander returned there to rally them, and to bring up the other brigade.[111]

Most of the staff and field officers' horses had been killed or wounded in those first few moments. Taking a courier's mount to replace his wounded animal, Humphreys rode back to the embankment to lead the charge. He waved the officers out in front of their men, urged them to ignore the troops lying in the swale, and told them to run for the stone wall as quickly as they could without stopping to fire, as Lee had done at Gaines's Mill. Calling for a cheer, Humphreys started over the rise with another two thousand men or more. The prone survivors of previous assaults called on them to save themselves from a hopeless folly, and some of them grabbed at the Pennsylvanians' coattails to drag them into the swale. Many complied, but others forged ahead toward the wall, four hundred feet away. The din heightened as Confederates poured increasingly furious fire into those brazen few, and before any of them reached the wall they raised their own rifles to reply. That brief hesitation drained their momentum, and within seconds those who did not fall dead on the ground retreated to the swale, or fled back to the embankment by the millrace. At last Humphreys led the entire division back there.[112]

The repulse of Humphreys did not end the day's slaughter. At sunset, from the lower end of Fredericksburg, George Getty led the last available division of the Ninth Corps (and one of the last two fresh divisions in the city) against the southern end of Marye's Heights. Getty's men had been suffering from the premature explosion of shells fired by their own artillery on the Falmouth side, but the order to move drew no cheers. Like Sturgis's men before them they marched over both manmade and natural impediments as darkness sank upon the field. They, too, descended into the ravine along the branch, taking cover behind some of the undulations in the ground. The fading light diminished the accuracy of Southern fire, but Getty's foremost brigade still lost an average of more than forty men per regiment without influencing the battle at all.[113]

In darkness those men who had spent the day with their faces pressed into the mud of Marye's Heights managed to slip away. They returned to a city crowded with troops and artillery, with piles of knapsacks left by owners who might never retrieve them. The houses all echoed with the cries of wounded, and by lamplight surgeons accumulated heaps of severed limbs in patrician parlors. Here and there a shirking soldier ghoulish enough to ignore the day's bloodshed culled the rubble for valuables, but mental and physical exhaustion overcame nearly everyone.[114]

Major generals slept little. At the Phillips house Burnside's cook served a dinner of canned salmon and peas, in addition to the usual coffee and hardtack. Sumner and Hooker ate with them, as did Hardie, who had returned from Franklin. Franklin himself arrived at nine o'clock that evening, and for the next three hours they discussed the events of that day and the possibilities for the next. Around midnight Burnside rode off with Hardie to inspect the lines, leaving the grand division commanders to rest for the morning's work they all anticipated. Hardie came back when his horse fell on the frozen mud, and by 3:00 AM the generals had all grown fearful of Burnside's safety when he barged in and explained his plans for a grand assault on Marye's Heights at ten o'clock that morning. The less battered divisions of the Ninth Corps would make the attack in company with the division of U.S. Regulars from the Fifth Corps. Burnside intended to lead the charge personally, to make the most of his popularity with his old corps, and Hooker seemed intent on leading the Regulars.[115]

Through one of the Ninth Corps brigade commanders, the generals who had made Saturday's assaults convinced the grand division commanders of the hopelessness of any infantry attack on so strong a position, and it had been further strengthened by new tiers of rifle pits during the night. Before seven o'clock Sunday morning, after less than three hours of sleep, the commanders all arose to prepare for the attack. As soon as Burnside entered the room Sumner proposed a council of war, to which Burnside assented, and Sumner promptly revealed to him the unanimous disapproval of the attack. Bull Sumner had earned his nickname for aggressive battlefield behavior, and cautious advice from such a fighter was more than Burnside could ignore. For the rest of the morning and most of the afternoon they debated alternatives, breaking for dinner and some rest. Sumner spent the recess jotting down a former engineer officer's proposal about building fortified batteries in front of Marye's Heights, to reduce it rather than carry it. He gave the plan to Burnside when they convened again after dinner, but their meeting dragged late into the evening and no sound ideas for offensive operations arose from it.[116]

By sunrise of December 15 fatigue, nausea, and defeat had so weakened and depressed Burnside that he told Sumner he wished to resign, but Sumner urged him to stop thinking such thoughts. Burnside said no more, but left for another look about the lines and did not come back until late afternoon. When he did return he announced that he had decided to abandon Fredericksburg and bring the army back over the river — much to the relief of generals who feared the wholesale destruction of their army.[117]

In the Gulf of Mexico the transports carrying the seasick soldiers of

Nathaniel Banks's expedition stretched between Dry Tortugas and the mouth of the Mississippi, on their way to New Orleans. As conscientiously as Banks had kept the secret from them, his men could not help but guess where they were bound.[118] Their destination had already leaked out at the headquarters of the Army of the Potomac, however, perturbing those who had hoped (despite Burnside's own misgivings) to see Banks try Richmond's back door. A diversion up the James had seemed the obvious use for so strong a force, part of which had fitted out at Fort Monroe.[119] The secretary of the navy himself could not understand why it wasn't done, except that it would have forced Halleck to admit the effectiveness of the Peninsula route, from which he had recalled McClellan; Mr. Welles failed to note that the same admission would have been required of President Lincoln, but Lincoln had conceded as much when he proposed the Pamunkey column, for that had been McClellan's original route. The news that Banks had passed beyond the Atlantic coast quashed rumors to the effect that he had already captured Richmond while Burnside distracted Lee, and the demise of such rumors removed the last glimmer of hope that the dreadful carnage of December 13 had achieved any good.[120]

Truce flags went out on Monday afternoon. Details removed some wounded and buried some of the dead, and individuals searched for comrades, but on Franklin's side of Deep Run, at least, most of the combatants used the pause to relax. Pickets in blue and grey sauntered forward to trade coffee for tobacco, and occasionally for something fermented. They shook hands, chatted about acquaintances living in each other's territory, and then returned to their respective lines to resume their mortal antagonism.[121]

All along the heights, from well above Fredericksburg to Hamilton's Crossing, Confederate soldiers lay their rifles aside for spades, molding Virginia clay into impregnable fortifications. Into the evening Union pickets held the outskirts of the city against their Southern counterparts, making fortresses of the masonry buildings by knocking out a few bricks for loopholes. After dark the retreat began in faint whispers and muffled steps on both fronts, despite a message indicating that General Halleck disapproved of it. Public opinion demanded that they keep the city, Halleck told a messenger from Burnside, even if it meant fighting a losing battle. Halleck addressed Burnside much more vaguely in an official telegram, advising him that he would be sustained in any course he chose, but that merely reflected Halleck's horror of responsibility. Realizing that he could make no further progress with his back against the river, Burnside responded to Halleck's telegraphed discretion rather than to the private pressure, bringing what was left of his army back to safety. Gusty winds from the west helped carry any sounds of the retreat away from the enemy, and by midnight of Monday the last Federals had slipped unmolested over the river. They slept all night in pouring rain, and with Tuesday's sunrise they saw that even the bridges were gone.[122]

In the most lopsided major battle of the eastern theater, the Army of the Potomac had lost nearly thirteen thousand men against perhaps five thousand Confederate casualties. Worse still, it appeared to every Union soldier from the anguished Burnside to the humblest private that it had all been for nothing.[123]

9

The Cold Dirges of the Baffled

══╪ REPLACING GENERAL MCCLELLAN was not the only unpleasant military decision the president avoided until after the elections. The threat to draft men to fill deficiencies in the militia call had been hanging since summer, in hopes that volunteering would accelerate after the harvest and in fear of the trouble a draft might brew. The enrollment of eligible men had, by itself, caused considerable trouble in regions where the draft would fall heavily on specific groups, like the poor Irish coal miners of northeastern Pennsylvania: three successive enrolling officers in Luzerne County retreated from their duties before mobs of irate women, and another female phalanx repulsed a mixed escort of civilians and soldiers who dared to accompany the fourth agent into their neighborhood.[1]

The War Department allowed one postponement after another as governors quibbled over the number of troops they had provided and exacted credit for four nine-month militiamen against every surplus three-year volunteer they raised. Some states had fallen far short of their quotas. In mid-October, Maryland still needed six thousand more men: the central and mountain counties had forwarded plenty, but some wealthier eastern counties had provided only one or two apiece, and in Calvert County not a soul had signed up. No sooner had the last man voted in November than the draft commissioners in delinquent counties prepared to select the names of enrolled men by lot. Troops that now regularly "monitored" the Maryland elections lingered to discourage any violence against draft proceedings, but none surfaced. The Pennsylvania elections had ended early in October, so drafting began there immediately afterward: soldiers had had to use their bayonets to quell at least one disturbance near Pittsburgh, but in that state where Confederate cavalry had recently intruded, more than fourteen regiments of drafted militia submitted to service with little grumbling. Ohio started drafting even before the state elections there, only a couple of weeks after the approach of a Confederate army had thrown the state into a panic, but enough conscripts opted to volunteer to satisfy the quota.[2]

The people of Wisconsin did not submit to compulsory service so meekly as their Eastern counterparts. Several counties showed shortfalls in the hundreds, and the tumblers began turning on November 10. In Ozaukee County a mob carrying banners proclaiming "No Draft" rushed the draft commissioner at the courthouse as he began drawing names, roughing up several court officers and burning all the enrollment lists before ransacking the commissioner's home. New troops had been held back in anticipation of draft resistance, so the state provost marshal commandeered a regiment in Milwaukee and steamed up to quell the riot, but others erupted across the eastern edge of the state. On the same day, in neighboring Washington County, the draft commissioner was driven from his work and fled to Madison, to report to the governor. Another mob put the commissioner from Kewaunee County to flight, and he did not stop until he reached Milwaukee, more than a hundred miles to the south. Armed men showed up at the draft drawing in Brown County as well, and swore they would prevent the army from taking any of them. Stones flew in Sheboygan, injuring one army quartermaster who attended the draft selection. A mob gathered to disrupt the draft in Manitowoc County on November 12, but the commissioner there delayed the drawing.[3]

Newspapers blamed the rioting on "Belgians," but seemed to recognize that their grievance arose more from economics than ethnicity: those who resisted seemed obviously poor, and unable to afford the substitutes or contrived medical exemptions by which the more affluent usually escaped service. "That the draft falls with great severity upon some men it is not disputed," conceded the *Milwaukee Sentinel*, "but that no good can come of resistance, any man with a thimble full of brains can see." More postponements and a military presence allowed the draft to proceed, and Wisconsin eventually conscripted forty-five hundred men, but three in eight never reported and, after a multitude of exemptions, barely a third of those drafted ever saw service.[4]

Every hint of the impending draft sparked worry and plotting among the men who might be drafted and the women who did not want them to go; by autumn most had attempted some means of exemption. Birthright Quakers pleaded health or conscience, or planned to flee if neither succeeded, while bellicose editors sneered at the Quaker revival among those who could not affect "a crick in the back."[5] Physical disability offered the best excuse, and exemption lists included every malady from the obvious loss of a limb to imbecility, insanity, incontinence, "hypertrophy of the head," "drunkness," and leprosy. Vague diagnoses included "constitution impaired," "physically unfit," and the ominous nineteenth-century suspicion of "lung disease." Wisconsin officials refused to exempt newly appointed firemen, superfluous deputy postmasters, and veterans who had been discharged for disability, but local doctors compensated for that stringency with myriad certificates of disability. A Milwaukee physician reviewed exemptions for coughs, rheumatism in various joints, bladder inflammation, "sick headaches," "depression of the breast," "cronical affliction of the Eies," for those certified "deef" or "not stout," and one man with a "rheumatical disease on his left leg."[6]

A Massachusetts woman noted that the draft had also infected many healthy males with mysterious ailments, and that after the state exempted mariners some suspiciously wealthy men had "gone a-fishing for the season." Sudden absence from the home community appealed particularly to enrolled men in the West, where sparse settlement posed a significant challenge to draft enforcement. St. Louis and Leavenworth newspapers detected equivalent ruses west of the Mississippi, where surprising numbers of aunts and uncles who lived in remote locations suddenly required the services of their nephews. Boston society might have looked down on naked subterfuge, so the more innovative young Brahmins combined in an informal insurance pool on the actuarial assumption that their combined resources would cover the cost of enough substitutes to replace any of them who were drafted.[7]

The summer's bloodshed had dissuaded many a would-be soldier, while the death toll and sheer uselessness of Fredericksburg only aggravated that aversion. "I understand that recruiting is played out in N.H.," remarked a veteran of the assaults on Marye's Heights, upon learning that his state could not complete its last nine-month regiment. Common soldiers in the Army of the Potomac certainly shared that increasing horror of the battlefield, as much as they might resent stay-at-homes and draft evaders, and the futility of the debacle on the Rappahannock infuriated soldiers of all ranks: in the days after the retreat they denounced Burnside, Halleck, and Edwin Stanton in a storm of curses. "What a finale to Burnside's grand *advance!*" wrote a Vermont sergeant who had forsaken his Quaker community for the arms of Abraham. "Fifteen thousand as brave men as ever lived, are no more numbered in Lincoln's Invincible Army!"[8]

The sight of so many dead and shattered men had shaken the entire army, including those who had not been engaged. A bitter artillery lieutenant who had watched the action from afar complained to his wife that the lives of Union soldiers were "thrown away like so many dogs," while a Minnesota soldier who had huddled for hours under the brow of Marye's Heights wrote that "I lost a chunk of Patriotism as large as my foot. I would do most anything to get Shut of this most unjust & unGodly uncalled for war." A Massachusetts private whose regiment suffered only two casualties while standing in reserve likewise lost his feeble enthusiasm for the war. The medical director of the Army of the Potomac usually recorded a suicide or two, and sometimes three, in the aftermath of a particularly bloody battle, and especially in the wake of a defeat, but only once did he tally more than three during a single month: of the forty-five suicides reported in that army during its entire four-year existence, seven came in December of 1862. The season evidently had little to do with it, for December seemed an unpopular month for suicide. More likely, depressive men were simply driven beyond hope by the stunning casualties and abject failure, which implied an impossible task that few would survive.[9]

Burnside shouldered complete responsibility for the disaster, but most soldiers initially declined to blame him, recognizing that he had faced great pressure to advance: some supposed that Stanton or Halleck had explicitly ordered him to attack. Still, the army seemed badly demoralized for a fortnight after the defeat.[10] Men who had signed up in the exciting early days of the war saw no end to a conflict they had never expected to last a year, and the escalating carnage raised the prospect of eventual annihilation. The previous year the troops had complained about wasting their time in winter quarters, but this December they champed impatiently for the order to build them. From headquarters tents to picket posts, and from there to families at home, the discouraging opinion spread that the South could never be beaten and would soon achieve full independence — and that belief naturally quelled ardor for the fight. Officers perceived that their men no longer fought with the spirit they had once displayed, blaming much of it on the mercenary attitudes that had brought so many of them into uniform. Subalterns, who knew their men best, recognized that such dismal morale might convince their troops to let themselves be captured, so they could go home on parole. A few enlisted men confirmed privately that they were thinking about that very tactic.[11]

Another blizzard of resignations inundated regimental headquarters right after the battle, falling heaviest in the new three-year regiments. Some nine-month officers suddenly felt too ill to continue in service, and others contemplated resignation, but — particularly in regiments that had not yet been cast into battle — most of them decided to wait out the balance of their time. So obviously did most officers use personal reasons to escape the rigors and horrors of the service that many resignations citing business or family difficulties were met with summary dismissal and dishonorable discharges. A lieutenant in the 20th Maine assumed that officers who cited disagreement with administration policy or a lack of confidence in military leadership were also making excuses to cover their cowardice. One regiment from New Hampshire had mustered in just in time to fight at South Mountain and Antietam, after which the colonel, quartermaster, and four lieutenants all resigned, and that same pattern repeated itself in the weeks after Fredericksburg. Two captains, one of whom had been accused of cowardice at Antietam, turned in their resignations, and so did five more lieutenants — including one who indicated that he would willingly accept a dishonorable discharge if he were not allowed an honorable one.[12]

The epidemic of despair in the Army of the Potomac took root across the country, even where the war had wrought little destruction. Three days after the battle the sutler of a virgin New York regiment near Suffolk, Virginia, detected universal exasperation with the war, apparently as a result of both military mismanagement and the unsavory shift in public policy. Comfortably encamped not far from the site of the country's most infamous slave revolt, those New Yorkers and others near them had apparently absorbed (or confirmed) a view of slaves too dim to admit of emancipation, contributing to an exaggerated anxiety among both officers and men to wash their hands of the conflict.[13]

Racial bigotry may not have motivated the numerous resignations among regimental chaplains, but those camp clerics surely suffered the common dismay over administration bumbling and useless slaughter. Chaplains tended to wear out quickly, perhaps by virtue of their more sensitive dispositions, but attrition accelerated among them in the weeks after Fredericksburg. Six of Maine's twenty-two chaplains asked for discharges in January and early February, and three of thirteen New Hampshire chaplains resigned before the spring campaign began, as did nearly one-fifth of those Massachusetts chaplains on duty at the time of the battle. Despite a pleasant station near Washington, the chaplain of the 2nd Connecticut Heavy Artillery decamped in early January. "We don't miss him much," remarked one of his men; "he was just about as good as none."[14]

The second half of 1862 had not been especially kind to United States arms, and the closing month of the year brought little relief. It seemed, for example, that the promising spring gains in northwestern Arkansas had all been squandered. The military governor of that state charged the department commander, Samuel Curtis, with abandoning a campaign that could have secured the northern half of the state so he could take part in cotton profiteering on the Mississippi River. The governor reminded

Edwin Stanton that the most rabid secessionists had returned quietly to their homes the previous summer to await a resumption of United States authority, but then Curtis's retreat restored Confederate strength in the northwest. Major General Thomas Hindman had resurrected a Southern army there with an eye to operations in Missouri, and early in the autumn a detachment of his troops thrashed a larger Union force sent there by Brigadier General James Blunt.[15]

In November, Blunt entered the Ozarks of northwestern Arkansas and challenged Hindman at Cane Hill, defeating a few lean cavalry brigades, and in the first week of December Hindman started north from the Arkansas River with about ten thousand men to expel the Yankees. Blunt called reinforcements down from Missouri and waited confidently at Cane Hill, less than forty miles from the site of Curtis's supposedly decisive victory at Pea Ridge. During the night of December 6 Hindman slipped around him through an overlooked mountain pass, pouncing on some of Blunt's reinforcements at Prairie Grove late on December 7.[16]

The reinforcements consisted of Francis Herron's two brigades, marching rapidly to join Blunt — as they had been for the four previous days. Hindman attacked them from high ground with infantry and his rather weak artillery; Herron sent a regiment each of Indiana, Illinois, Wisconsin, and Iowa infantry to try to wrest the hill from him, but the Wisconsin and Iowa regiments fell back, leaving more than half their men on the slope of the hill: one community in southeastern Iowa lost six citizens who had enlisted only a hundred days before. With superior artillery Herron held on until late in the afternoon, when Blunt arrived from Cane Hill with the greater part of his troops and more artillery to turn the tide. Darkness ended the battle, and Hindman remained on the field while Blunt fell back to a more defensible position, but early in the morning the Confederates backed quietly away, taking hundreds of rifles but leaving their dead for the foe to bury. Each side lost nearly a thousand in killed and wounded, but those were staggering casualties in that isolated theater. Though rejoicing in their triumph, the surviving Federals might have reflected that they had simply refought the battles of the first year of the war.[17]

Union armies had seen little more progress elsewhere in the Confederacy since the previous spring. Firmly held outposts dotted the Atlantic coast, but the Army of the Potomac had consumed so many detachments from the garrisons there that those bases had launched no serious inland incursions. When Ambrose Burnside moved against Lee he solicited a cooperative blow from John Foster, his friend and former subordinate at New Bern, North Carolina, and while Burnside assailed Fredericksburg, General Foster led the first Union army into the Carolina interior.

Foster aimed first for Goldsborough and then for the state capital at Raleigh. Gathering a column of twelve thousand infantry, cavalry, and artillery (nearly half the infantry consisting of raw nine-month Massachusetts regiments), he strode out of New Bern in thick fog on the frosty morning of December 11, just as Burnside's engineers began bridging the Rappahannock. After two days of slow marching and heavy foraging, Foster approached the Neuse River opposite Kinston, where he encountered Nathan G. Evans, a South Carolina brigadier who had about two thousand men and a history of fighting well against steep odds. Evans stalled the Yankees all day, only retreating when he realized how heavily Foster outnumbered him; some four hundred trapped rebels surrendered, prompting one dainty Bay State lieutenant to recoil at such coarse, unwashed "villains." Foster burned the Neuse River railroad bridge, but he never reached Raleigh or Goldsborough. Simultaneous news of Confederate reinforcements and Burnside's failure persuaded him to scurry back for New Bern as fast as he could move, lighter by six hundred casualties. By December 21 he had reoccupied that quaint little town, and Union forces retained no more Tarheel territory than they controlled at the beginning of summer.[18]

Much energy had been devoted to opening the Mississippi River in the autumn of 1862, to no avail. John McClernand, a former Democratic congressman and a neighbor of Abraham Lincoln, had secured permission in October to raise what the War Department called the Army of the Mississippi. Through November and December he had organized new regiments in Indiana, Illinois, and Iowa and sent them downriver to Memphis, where he wished to inaugurate his campaign, but late in December Ulysses Grant appropriated his troops for an assault on Vicksburg. With his own Army of the Tennessee, Grant intended to strike Vicksburg from the east while his friend William T. Sherman steamed down to a landing just above Vicksburg with McClernand's army and attacked from the north. The very day Sherman embarked, a Confederate raid destroyed Grant's supply base at Holly Springs, forcing him to give up his part of the plan. Unaware of that snag, Sherman boarded another division at Helena, continuing on to the Yazoo River with thirty thousand men in scores of steamboats. He landed them on spongy ground before the bluffs above Vicksburg, losing almost two thousand of them in a hopeless assault on December 29 before drawing back upriver to Milliken's Bend.[19]

Another embarrassing defeat loomed on the Texas coast. From his New Orleans headquarters Nathaniel Banks, who now commanded the Department of the Gulf, had sent three companies of Massachusetts infantry to garrison Galveston. Their nominal mission consisted of protecting citizens on that island and providing a rendezvous where Texas loyalists could enter federal service, but the newly appointed military governor of Texas also badgered Banks for a little Texas soil from which he and his coterie of speculators might begin exercising his authority. The three companies, all freshly arrived nine-month militia, held the post from Christmas until New Year's Day, when Confederate gunboats engaged the four U.S. vessels guarding the harbor. In a rare Confederate naval victory, the *Harriet Lane* fell into Southern hands and the rest of the fleet was scuttled or driven away. Confederate infantry took over from there, pounding the novice militiamen with artillery before closing in to rifle range. A shell tore the legs off one Massachusetts man and a bullet sliced across the abdomen of another, strewing his guts on the sand; with that the Yankee colonel surrendered his detachment. The prisoners — all bounty men who had enlisted under threat of a draft — found themselves treated so well that one of them admitted he would rather spend the remainder of his enlistment in Confederate hands.[20]

With the opening of the New Year, William Rosecrans's Army of the Cumberland (formerly Buell's Army of the Ohio) did manage to repulse an attack by Braxton Bragg's smaller Army of Tennessee. Rosecrans had emerged from Nashville to drive Bragg out of Tennessee, but on December 31 Bragg struck first. He hit Rosecrans along Stone's River, west of Murfreesboro, catching much of Alexander McCook's corps unprepared. Riding toward the commotion, some Union officers encountered McCook's troops in unarmed, wide-eyed flight. The heroes of other battlefields became the cowards of this one, noted a lieutenant. Despite desperate resistance by isolated Federal divisions, most of the first day's fighting went to Bragg. That night, in a cold rain, Rosecrans and his generals took shelter in an old hut and decided to hold their ground rather than retreat. As midnight approached, Union officers shook hands and wished each other a happy New Year, then made verbal disposition of their worldly possessions, just "in case."[21]

After resting through New Year's Day the antagonists grappled again, each side losing more than a quarter of its strength: the size of the armies and their respective casualties matched those at Shiloh. Southern cavalry cut Rosecrans off from his supplies, leaving his men little to eat except their dead horses, but in the end Bragg retreated forty miles toward Tullahoma and Rosecrans proclaimed a victory. Bragg's army escaped without pursuit, but the beleaguered Lincoln expressed heartfelt appreciation for the only noteworthy Union success in months.[22] The bloody fight sorely blunted Southern optimism, but it also produced in Rosecrans's battered army some of the same hints of despair and depression that had surfaced in the Army of the Potomac after Fredericksburg.[23] Reaction to Stone's River among soldiers and civilians in the East, meanwhile, gravitated between wishful credence and a cynical skepticism: the hopeful welcomed it as the turning of the tide, foreshadowing a rapid suppression of the rebellion, but at first some officers saw it as an actual reverse for Rosecrans, or little more than a draw, and it failed to lift their sagging spirits. Such pessimists would have pointed out that Union forces in Tennessee had not yet regained the ground they had held six months before. What was more, the battle had cost Rosecrans heavily, and he kept his army virtually idle for another six months, consuming every scrap of food and forage within a thirty-mile radius. Such inactivity only worked to the Confederacy's advantage.[24]

Lincoln's army seemed able to win a decisive victory only against the most pathetically overmatched enemies, like the Sioux of Minnesota. The more peaceful of them had surrendered to federal authority along the Minnesota River while most of the belligerent holdouts had fled or been captured. Some seventeen hundred "broken-hearted, ragged, dejected" women, children, and old men marched in to Fort Snelling to camp under guard, a dozen to a teepee, until white soldiers decided their fate. Hundreds of Santee men and boys crowded into closer confinement as one witness after another accused anyone who seemed old enough to fire a weapon, and eventually three hundred were selected for execution. Distinguishing between those accused of fighting in pitched battle and those accused of murdering civilians, President Lincoln disapproved the vast majority of the condemnations, but on the morning after Christmas thirty-eight Santee, guilty and innocent alike, marched into daylight from their Mankato prison and mounted a single, square gallows, where they chanted their death song until the executioner's signal cut it short. The contemptuous surgeon of the 10th Minnesota peeled the flesh from two of their bodies for specimen skeletons.[25]

Then came a ragtag Confederate garrison at Arkansas Post, fewer than five thousand strong. Furious that his army had been snatched from under him, John McClernand steamed down from Memphis and claimed Sherman's troops at Milliken's Bend, as well as those he had collected at Helena. He put all thirty thousand men back aboard a cloud of riverboats and turned upstream without orders from anyone, veering into the Arkansas River. Through the sheer impulsiveness of his action he surprised the three little brigades at Arkansas Post, for no one in either army expected so grand a flotilla to be diverted to so insignificant a purpose. Arkansas Confederates were not well equipped — a prisoner who had just returned to Helena from Little Rock found the garrison there wearing a variety of threadbare civilian dress. They generally lacked good arms as well, but from their fortifications at Arkansas Post the Southerners poured a hot fire into McClernand's kidnapped army and held their own for two days. Eventually an accident threw the victory to the Yankees when unauthorized white flags rose from different wings of a dismounted Texas cavalry regiment: that persuaded enough Confederates to cease fire until the enemy swarmed in close, forcing a real surrender. With his six-fold superiority in numbers McClernand should have been able to take the place anyway, as strategically useless as it proved to be, but it cost more than a thousand men to accomplish the stunt.[26]

Most of the Helena troops eventually returned there, much to their chagrin. Considering how little their presence in that town contributed to their cause, they had good reason for complaint. Bad water and swamp-bred fevers posed greater dangers than most battlefields, and illness quickly reduced any unit stationed there. Few who served at Helena avoided some serious malady of a bilious, intestinal, or febrile nature. After a few weeks a quarter of one new regiment had been consigned to the sick list, and a dozen men had already died. "I suppose you have danced the tune arkansaw traveler lots of times," an Iowa soldier suggested to his fiancée, "but the next time you hear them playing it tell the fiddles to stop for he is dead and Buried just below Helena."[27]

Disease followed the big rivers with particular virulence, filling hospitals and cemeteries from Cincinnati to New Orleans; many of the troops found it convenient to replenish their canteens over the side, in the same water that served as the steamboats' sewers. The deadly danger of drinking from the rivers was borne out by troops confined for long periods aboard transports, which carried insufficient drinking water for so many passengers. Thirty-eight men died in less than a fortnight on one boat. Cooped up on the *Stephen Decatur* at Young's Point, opposite the Yazoo, an ailing Iowa veteran of the Arkansas Post fight described most of his regiment as sick, including fifty men from his own company. "We all dread the boats more than anything else," remarked an Iowa captain, adding that his new regiment could field but 250 rifles when it disembarked at the same place.[28] The 23rd Wisconsin had been in service barely five months, but one company averaged only thirty men a day at roll call after three weeks aboard the *J. A. Dickey*, which disgorged its passengers at Young's Point with every man staggering from weakness. Over the next month in that miasmal bivouac, fever carried off daily victims from the 23rd, killing even that rarest of officers — a chaplain whom the men admired; by war's end that regiment lost seven times as many men to disease as to bullets. The descent from hale health to the brink of death did not take long, observed one recruit, and letters from the camps above Vicksburg adopted a tone of discernible despair.[29]

General Banks found his army on the lower Mississippi similarly afflicted. Mosquitoes had tormented unaccustomed Federals since the capture of New Orleans, and Banks's delicate nine-month men suffered especially: some of them spent months in the hospital, or returned repeatedly to the surgeon's care until they were discharged or died. The camps in his department produced a monotonous procession of increasingly casual funerals by the end of winter, and the short-term regiments seldom mustered half their original roster by the time Banks put them into action. The 16th New Hampshire never faced hostile fire during its brief term, but more than a quarter of the men in that regiment perished before they reached home: within a year of their arrival in Louisiana, three in every ten of them were dead.[30]

Smallpox broke out in several Union armies right after Fredericksburg, adding its customary panic to the usual misery and mortality of military life. At the same time it erupted in little epidemics in communities from the mid-Atlantic to the prairie, as sick soldiers made their way between camp and home. That only heightened the anxiety of homesick men who had borne as much as they thought they were able.[31]

The mere congregation of men in dense camps offered dangerous opportunities for infectious disease, and illness often tithed regiments before they ever left their home states. Except for troops who enjoyed enclosed barracks and cooked rations, like much of the New Bern garrison, it was the men who kept moving without benefit of steamboats or railroads, marching from camp to camp or on active campaign, who seemed to thrive best. Grouse as they might about fatigue and inconvenience, the most active soldiers reported far better health and far fewer deaths among their companions, boasting of gaining anywhere from ten to forty pounds on hardtack, salt pork, and all they could glean from the countryside.[32]

The Army of the Potomac enjoyed little activity through December and most of January, although Burnside wished otherwise. The Virginia winters never inflicted such staggering mortality as the bayous of the Mississippi, but severe cold made it miserable enough for those who had to serve there. By the middle of autumn the fluctuation between daytime heat and nighttime cold had initiated plagues of upper respiratory infections that left a third of whole regiments "barking round" with seemingly innocuous coughs that would nevertheless kill some of them. November rains followed by frigid nights brought chills and ague, and with December the mercury fell far enough to freeze men's shoes and toes. New regiments shed scores of discharged invalids suffering with everything from hernias and hepatitis to typhoid and tuberculosis, and not a few of them died on the journey home. By Christmas something symptomatic of meningitis forced one young Pennsylvania private to supervise the construction of a coffin for his older, married brother, whom he had shamed into enlisting the previous summer.[33]

The most pervasive disease in Burnside's army after the battle of Fredericksburg may have been the psychological malaise that infected ranks high and low. Two young career officers hinted at the toll taken by serial defeats on bloody fields, one confessing to his sister that he could not bear to think of Fredericksburg and the other warning his wife that he could stand no more strain: "I *must* have peace of mind and complete mental quiet," he wrote after the battle, beseeching her to keep his desperation confidential.[34]

Fredericksburg and its aftermath had also saddled Abraham Lincoln with the greatest distress of his political life. A few days after the battle a caucus of radical senators worsened the president's anguish over the lost battle with a determination to oust Secretary Seward from the State Department. Angered at Seward's relatively conservative influence, they concluded that nothing would satisfy them save his resignation. Getting wind of this latest cabal, Seward volunteered to go, as did his son the assistant secretary, presenting their resignations to Lincoln on December 17. The president called his old friend Browning in and confided to him that he supposed the senators actually wanted Lincoln to step down, or at least aside. "I am sometimes half disposed to gratify them," he admitted, but Browning urged him to resist that impulse with the argument that Lincoln's downfall would be the country's: to surrender the reins would be to give up the fight. Harking back to his July advice on controlling the radicals, Browning told the president that he should have "crushed" them the previous summer, apparently meaning that he should have defied their demands on confiscation and emancipation. Now, Browning said, he must defy their demands for Seward's head.

"We are now on the brink of destruction," the president lamented. "It appears to me the Almighty is against us, and I can hardly see a ray of hope."

"Be firm," Browning told him, "and we will yet save the country."[35]

A delegation of Republican senators headed by Charles Sumner and Ben Wade paraded to the White House on the evening of December 18 and delivered their demand. Lincoln took the matter up with the cabinet the next morning, expressing his willingness to face the senators down, and that evening the senators returned to discuss the absent Seward with Lincoln and the cabinet. Sumner, the quintessential Massachusetts abolitionist, seemed especially offended at the revelation that Seward considered the radical brand of abolitionism to be as responsible for the war as the defenders of Southern slavery. The meeting broke up in less hostile tones than had begun it, but perhaps only because the radicals thought they had convinced their audience.[36]

The president continued to agonize over the dispute, groping for a solution that would not alienate the senators: the only cabinet member he wished to replace was the ineffectual Caleb Smith, of the Interior Department, for whose job he was considering Senator Browning. Salmon P. Chase, whom Browning suspected of having set the radical senators on Seward in the first place, may have sensed the president's reluctance to meet the demand, and on the morning of December 20 he appeared in Lincoln's office with the apparent intention of forcing his hand. Welles and Stanton had already arrived, and a roaring fire crackled in the fireplace when the secretary of the treasury announced that he had prepared his own resignation. To Chase's manifest dismay, the beleaguered president brightened immediately. "Where is it?" he asked, and when Chase reached into his coat pocket for it Lincoln thrust out his long arm and said, "Let me have it." After a moment's pause Chase handed it to him, and the big fingers tore eagerly into the envelope. "This cuts the Gordian knot," Lincoln declared after reading the letter, revealing such glee that Chase twisted uncomfortably in his chair. Probably supposing that the president had decided to clean out the cabinet and start fresh, Stanton melodramatically added that he was willing to tender his resignation, as well. "I don't want yours," Lincoln blurted, dismissively. "This is all I want." With that he sent everyone from the room. Chase left with the accurate impression that he had inadvertently delivered Lincoln from his dilemma; as he surmised, Lincoln deftly mollified all factions by rejecting both resignations.[37]

Settling the political confrontation in Washington failed to banish the universal dejection of late December. The dark days of early winter coincided with what may have been the darkest days of the Republic. The pall cast by the Fredericksburg fiasco reached all the way to the lower Mississippi, where a New Hampshire sergeant who knew victims of the fight admitted that the news discouraged him more than anything thus far. Across the North, too, spirits drooped as the extent of the disaster emerged. Disbelieving initial optimistic dispatches, a Connecticut woman remarked sarcastically that the rebellion had long since been reported quashed, only to grow stronger since. "Oh, how many widows and orphans are now in this land," pined the wife of a middle-aged Wisconsin soldier, on hearing exaggerated estimates of thirty thousand casualties at Fredericksburg; the figure seemed improbable, she knew, but she reasoned that the first news usually carried the rosiest accounts.[38] Indignation, noted a Wall Street lawyer, "is fast growing revolutionary." The battle, the antagonism between generals and War Department, and news of

the cabinet crisis all tended toward an impression of government collapse. "Unless something occurs very soon to brighten up affairs," scribbled a Washington officeholder, "I shall begin to look upon our whole Nation as on its way to destruction."[39]

Hoping to redeem his resounding defeat across the Rappahannock before
the morale of the army and the public deteriorated any further, Burnside
waited less than a fortnight after his withdrawal from Fredericksburg to
issue orders for a flanking maneuver. Halleck was also pushing him again
for some kind of activity, but a rare spell of relatively fair weather seemed
to invite another offensive: warm, dry days filled the last week of December and the first half of January. The plan called for a mixed column of
cavalry, infantry, and artillery to march up the Rappahannock as a diversion while the greater part of the army crossed elsewhere, but the diversionary force had no sooner jolted into motion than the generals of
Burnside's left wing began working to sabotage his plans. William Franklin, who admittedly expected any campaign of Burnside's to end in disaster, took the unheard-of step of permitting a pair of brigadiers to visit
Washington on the eve of a general movement. The two called on the
president to intervene against the plan, and any cachet that remained
to Burnside as commander of the army evaporated when Lincoln succumbed to that insubordinate intrigue. The president instructed his army
commander to sit tight for the present, and Burnside instantly called the
operation off, but he hurried to Washington to see what had happened.[40]
    Burnside spent two days in the capital, lodging at Willard's. Fitz John
Porter was staying there during his court-martial, and between stops at
the White House Burnside testified sympathetically for the defendant.
For the president and general in chief he outlined his intended movement, asking for approval, but Halleck demurred and Lincoln left the
question unanswered. Burnside learned that a conspiracy of generals had
undermined his maneuver, so he naturally suggested that it was time
for those men to be removed or for him to step aside and let another
man take the helm. As though unaware (or unwilling to admit) how badly
he had damaged Burnside's effectiveness, the president brushed aside
the notion and sent him back to his post, where everyone soon knew that
he had been undone by the connivance of defiant subordinates. In their
zeal the two conspirators had evidently revealed the details of Burnside's
plans while they were in Washington, and that information had reportedly leaked into the hands of Southern sympathizers, so Burnside had to
start from scratch on a new scheme.[41]
    It still seemed advisable to move against Lee, for Union intelligence
suggested that Braxton Bragg's vigorous attacks at Stone's River reflected

heavy reinforcements from Lee's army. Taking the initiative would also re-kindle morale, but reconnaissance and planning for a completely new operation consumed the autumn-like weeks of early January. Burnside reviewed the army one corps at a time, and then in larger increments; he perhaps perceived the rebounding confidence and affection of many of his enlisted men, but he seemed unable to detect or admit their fears about the uncooperative generals, which doomed their own hopes for suc-cess.[42] He finally issued the orders for his next offensive on the last of those bright, crisp days: while the Eleventh and Twelfth Corps moved down to fill the void, most of the army was to march upstream and cross beyond Lee's left flank on pontoon bridges. Once again General Franklin and his left-wing hecklers condemned the campaign as hopeless before it even began. In the Center Grand Division, Hooker was said to disparage the movement as well, although he would direct the army over the same route with much greater confidence a hundred days later. Sumner's Right Grand Division produced openly critical officers, too — mostly in the Sec-ond Corps, where cheering had come weak and thin during Burnside's re-view on January 17; some catcalls and groaning could even be heard from those divisions as the order for the advance filtered down to the men in the ranks. It was rumored that New York's Tammany Regiment actually hooted Burnside as he rode past, and a captain from Boston wondered if a portion of the army might not refuse to march.[43]

Nevertheless, it all began auspiciously enough on the morning of Janu-ary 20. Even in Franklin's wing, officers delivered stirring orations about marching over the river again to avenge Fredericksburg, and men lifted their hats to cheer the news. The colonel of a nine-month Pennsylvania regiment reined up in front of his regiment to make such a speech, only to have his horse rear up and throw him to the ground before he uttered a word, but no one interpreted that as an omen; spirits seemed to have re-vived. Just before noon the sky clouded over and a chill wind blew in from the northeast, threatening rain or snow to those who knew nature's signs, but it was still dry when dark fell. By evening some troops had reached Kelly's Ford, camping wherever they could. A fortunate few appropriated sheds, shanties, or houses for quarters, but a Sixth Corps regiment had to camp in a pine thicket so dense that one man swore a bird could not pene-trate it. They had hardly rolled into their blankets when a drizzle started in and the wind picked up. The drizzle thickened into a steady rain and then into a torrent, driven almost horizontally by gale-force gusts. Water ran under every tent, soaking the backs of weary men, while wind-driven rain blew through every opening to drench blankets and clothing.[44]

The rain continued all night and the next day, turning occasionally to snow, with the howling gale still driving it. Back near Falmouth the Ninth

Corps had remained in its old quarters, where one soldier awoke to "the worst storm that I ever knew in my life." It appeared to him that everything was working against them, not least of all when reveille blew at four o'clock in the morning, and orders circulated to follow the army upriver. "Never dreaded to turn out as now," admitted a Massachusetts field officer.[45]

Drums beat along the Rappahannock at 5:00 AM, and men who had slept little or not at all staggered shivering into line with their clothing completely soaked; some ignored the call, hiding in whatever shelter they had found. The torrent foiled any hope of breakfast fires, and men wrung out their blankets and shelter halves as well as they could before strapping those sodden burdens to their knapsacks and lurching into hopeless motion. They soon churned the mud a foot deep, and then knee deep. Ambrose Burnside rode away from his tent that morning without a wink of sleep, and fatigue may have prolonged his hope that the rain would stop. Finally he learned how far behind the pontoons had fallen, with each boat inching along under the power of double teams of horses and 150 men up to their knees in red mud, and he called off the entire operation. The leading gun in one light artillery battery had made less than four miles that entire day, while the rest of the guns, caissons, forge, and battery wagon stretched out for two miles behind. Officers and men who already hovered on the verge of prostration lost no time when the word to halt echoed down the line: they fell out where they were and tried to find some cover. The driest firewood available stood on the stump, and innovative pioneers felled some of it, nursing the green wood into roaring bonfires that defied the tempest.[46]

The downpour persisted through another night and into Thursday morning, but the troops had come out with three days' rations and January 22 was the last of those three days, so the miles-long column had to start slogging back toward Falmouth. Mired horses strained under relentless whips to drag wagons, pontoons, caissons, and artillery pieces out of the liquefied Virginia soil. Eight spans of horses could not move a wagon half full of corn. Dozens of men waded into the soup and took hold of ropes to aid each conveyance, but one artillery piece refused to budge with seventeen horses and a score of men hitched to the trail; loaded caissons with thirty-two horses still needed fifty or a hundred men at the ropes to make any progress. Teams that had been exposed in harness without feed throughout the storm drooped from utter exhaustion until they could move no more and lay choking in the mud, too weak to lift their heads. When a horse collapsed the driver would abandon him to die, or recover, as fate dictated. For all the misery the soldiers endured, chilled to the bone and caked in mud from head to toe, they voiced more sympathy for the horses on that march than they ever had before; one infantry-man counted two hundred of them dead on the side of the road, including nineteen concentrated within two hundred yards.[47]

Whole regiments went to work building corduroy roads for the wheeled vehicles while the infantry all but dispersed to find more solid ground. Two-thirds of the troops straggled along behind their comrades in the main body, and for that matter the main body no longer really existed. The rain tapered later in the morning, but mist hung in the air and no sun shone to dry the mud until near sunset. For two days Confederates on the far shore taunted the Yankees with offers to send over a few regiments to pull them out of the mud — or, with more savage insinuation, to help them bring up their pontoons, so they could get across the river again. By Friday one set of pranksters had hung a sign on the Confederate side of the river proclaiming "Burnside stuck in the mud," and rebels gathered along the riverbank to bellow that observation. While their opponents struggled, Southerners alternated such amusement with playing ball and shoveling languidly on a new series of earthworks.[48]

A profound exasperation and gloom overcame wet, half-frozen men with miles of mud to navigate before they could hope for a warm fire or a hot meal. Mutinous language echoed across Stafford and Fauquier coun-ties. Artillerymen straining at guns buried to their hubs tossed their ropes away in disgust and challenged passing infantry to desert with them: if the foot soldiers would throw down their rifles they would spike the guns, they said, and every man of them would head for home. The provost mar-shal would find that many who uttered such statements meant it, too: a Vermont sergeant reported the desertion of a score of artillerymen from one battery that accompanied his division, and a few Confederate pickets yelled across the river that if the Yankees would desert en masse they would do the same.[49]

Most of the troops had reached their old camps by Saturday afternoon. The slowest stragglers plodded in on Sunday, and a heartless officer here and there filed court-martial charges against sick men for failing to keep up. After them came company-size herds of bedraggled deserters under the bayonets of special detachments sent to collect them on the roads leading to the rear. General orders again discouraged commissioned of-ficers from seeking their customary alternative of resignation at such a juncture, and some of them had been dishonorably discharged in front of their regiments for so much as submitting the request, so instead they sought furloughs in droves.[50]

That evening General Burnside returned to Falmouth from his last mad dash to Washington. The president had finally acceded to his re-peated argument that either he or a host of backbiting generals would have to be removed, and in his pocket Burnside carried an order elevating Joseph Hooker to command of the army.[51]

Burnside's last brief expedition in command of the Army of the Potomac would go down in history as the Mud March, renowned above all the hundreds of other marches in the notorious mud of the American South. It ended with the army more demoralized, perhaps, than it had been after the two Bull Run battles, and despairing troops cherished rumors that McClellan was coming back to take over. His partisans insisted that the enlisted men no longer held any confidence in Burnside, and no one could dispute the widespread skepticism, but plenty of others lamented Burnside's removal, considering him merely the victim of demeaning and uncooperative subordinates, contradictory orders from Washington, and other circumstances beyond his control.[52]

Among Washington officials, Edwin Stanton had already become the favorite target of public outrage. "Unless Stanton be speedily shelved," thought New York diarist George Templeton Strong soon after Fredericksburg, "something will burst somewhere." Burnside had restored partial confidence in the secretary of war when he took full blame for Fredericksburg in a public letter, but the dissatisfaction and doubt lingered. One theory in the ranks held that politicians (and presumably Stanton in particular) had deliberately foiled Burnside in the matter of the pontoons, if not otherwise, in order to keep the war alive. A Massachusetts soldier conveyed a common impression when he assessed the country's political leaders as nothing but "a pack of imbeciles cowards traitors ruffians & scoundrels whose object is the almighty God-damned dollar," for whom the war turned a tidy profit. Fully half the government's military expenditures, he charged, disappeared into the pockets of swindling contractors and the kickbacks they paid to crooked politicians. An Illinois soldier used nearly the same phrasing to describe peculating generals, whose conniving natures, chronic drinking, and licentious diversions were imitated by far too many junior officers.[53] A promising officer from New Jersey, too young to vote but thoroughly educated in letters and life, reserved the same animosity for all government contractors and their political accomplices. "Patriotism now a days only reaches half way down the pocket," he sneered.[54]

There was nothing new about the notion of mercenary interest driving the war: civilians and soldiers alike had suspected as much quite early, and newspapers had been broadcasting those suspicions since at least the previous summer. Midway through 1862 an unfriendly newspaper editor had pointed out that the Lincoln administration had long since exceeded the profligate spending of Buchanan's, adding that the Republican Congress had overseen a level of corruption never tolerated until the departure of the Southern representatives. That winter, though, the cynical conviction pervaded not only the Army of the Potomac but all Union armies that the war amounted to a grand conspiracy between power-hungry congressmen and greedy contractors to defraud the government, with the collusion of army officers who were lining their own pockets.[55]

A captain in the Regular Army commented on the greed of his brother officers, as well as all politicians. Belief in the corruption of speculators in shoulder straps took an especially firm hold on soldiers serving in the Deep South, and not without justification. In Florida, Union officers alerted relatives to speculative opportunities posed by planters facing confiscation. Quartermaster fraud flourished in Tennessee, where headquarters hangers-on profiteered from the occupation. Illicit cotton speculation seemed particularly unrestrained on the rivers below Memphis, where officers of all ranks dealt in cotton stolen by others or by themselves. New regiments hardly disembarked at Mississippi port towns before company officers started rousing their men for nighttime raids on plantations, where they appropriated wagonloads of cotton (or bought it at ruinous, gunpoint prices) for sale to northbound steamboat captains. Those who lacked the time or troops for such ventures, like staff officers, called on kin to come down and reap the profits.[56]

Almost everyone wanted part of that cotton trade, including General Grant's father, whose opportunism later brought Grant significant political embarrassment. Samuel Curtis, commanding the department west of the Mississippi, was widely believed to be making a fortune in cotton speculation. The military governor of Arkansas had accused Curtis of squandering his military advantage in northwestern Arkansas precisely because so much cotton lay at Helena, begging for buyers and shippers, and he had alleged that Curtis's subordinate, General Hovey, went a step further by trading contraband slaves for cotton. At least one government official at Cairo kidnapped contraband employees and literally sold them back down the river into slavery, for cash or cotton.[57]

For all their scrutiny and criticism of financial management in the Buchanan administration, Republican apologists dismissed the rampant corruption as unavoidable, but few of the soldiers bought that argument. By February of 1863 the provost marshal at Keokuk, Iowa, reported that troops coming back up the Mississippi exhibited "an almost universal feeling of intense bitterness from the conviction that they have been, and are, used principally for the benefit of cotton speculators, officers, and outsiders." Such observations suggest that their disgust sank even deeper than their surviving letters indicate, for it was generally understood that derogatory comments about military and civilian superiors constituted serious violations of military regulations, as well as risking arrest and indefinite detention in federal dungeons. Those who did dare to send their complaints home often cautioned their correspondents to keep the letters confidential, but some shrank from any comment at all, perhaps fearing accidental discovery or clandestine examination of the mail. A month into Burnside's tenure a New York artilleryman had warned his wife that "free speech has played out here, as it has all over the United States," and the increasing volume of dissent had not improved tolerance within the high command. An air of such repression hovered over the army that a Harvard-educated captain seemed to believe a tale that President Lincoln intended to dismiss some officers who had ridiculed his jokes. Lest he invite similar punishment, the captain lapsed into satirical commendation of the president's "military genius."[58]

A disgusted Vermont private conveyed a common belief when he marked the president for "a partey man and nothing else."[59] Contempt for Lincoln and his war revealed itself most obviously through the number of soldiers who left their posts without permission. Desertion rates soared in the Army of the Potomac, partly because it had suffered the heaviest losses and the worst campaign conditions, but also because it was easier to walk away from that army than from any other in the field. Men assigned to other border regions, like Kentucky, slipped to the rear with some frequency, but in order to reach his home from the Carolinas, Tennessee, or the Mississippi theater, a soldier had to either desert to the enemy or traverse hundreds of miles without being caught by rear-guard units or murdered by guerrillas. The logical route from the most distant stations would have been by sea or river, but travel restrictions and cost deterred most deserters. Desertion rates might have climbed nearly as high in other armies had escape been as easy (though one veteran Ohio company deep in Tennessee lost four deserters within the first few weeks of 1863), but the stream of men who successfully absconded from the Potomac army exaggerated the demoralization in that theater.[60] By the end of Burnside's Mud March, one Pennsylvania regiment alone was draining away deserters at the rate of ten to twenty-five a day. On the day Hooker took command of the army a cavalry officer remarked that "desertion is the order of the day," and he attributed that phenomenon mainly to the frequent changes in commanders. Burnside had twice failed, for whatever reasons, and most of the men had never put much faith in Hooker: McClellan alone could command the confidence of the troops, he assured his doubting family.[61]

By the fifth week of 1863 the problem had become epidemic. "Men are deserting by the hundreds," confessed a Second Corps captain on the first of February, after a cavalry patrol brought in four hundred absentees snared in the rear of the army: some of them had been building a raft to float across the Potomac near Aquia Creek. That same week a company of Wisconsin veterans made a sweep of the roads leading away from their camp, coming back with a dozen surly prisoners. A Vermont sergeant in the Sixth Corps observed that it was not unusual for captains to call out their companies in the morning and find half their men missing. Courts-martial usually returned the miscreants to the ranks with loss of pay and extra duty, but occasionally the punishment included the humiliation of shaved heads, the stripping of buttons from uniforms, and drumming out of camp between details of guards with fixed bayonets. Often that ritual merely marked the beginning of a long term at hard labor, and sometimes with the medieval punishment of a brand on the cheek.[62]

Orders read at dress parade pleaded with the troops to keep faith with their cause and their leaders, to little avail. Most men knew someone who had deserted, and, ominously, their comrades now often deemed them justified in their flight; sympathetic officers occasionally abetted the truants by reporting them on muster rolls as hospital patients, allowing them to collect their pay until they could be induced to return. It was the three-year men who most frequently took leg bail, fearing that they would never survive their long enlistment at the rate of attrition prevalent since Antietam. Nine-month militiamen hardly blamed them, but rarely joined them. "I don't think it would pay to dessert for nine months," reasoned a short-term man from Connecticut, but he could find little fault with deserters from the three-year regiments. "I tell you if I was in it for three years I would have a strong desire to get away."[63]

That desire to get away prevailed, and it inspired some innovative methods. Escape through hospital confinement proved more popular and more successful than simply walking away from camp. If a sick or wounded man made it to one of the sprawling Washington hospitals he only needed a suit of civilian clothing and train fare to make his way home with little risk of interference. With a convalescent furlough and the friendship of a local physician, he could simply stay home and feign continued ill health or stiffness from his wound. Others took routine furloughs, traveling directly home from their regiments, and sought medical extensions that were generally denied, but months would pass before anyone came looking for them, and sometimes no one came looking at all. Company and regimental commanders sent regular lists of deserters to local newspapers to shame them into coming back, or to encourage neighbors to turn them in for the standard thirty-dollar reward, but they might evade detection for years by migrating to other communities and melting into the attenuated labor pool under assumed names. The government's war had lost so much stock in the public eye by the late winter of 1863 that family members and friends often harbored deserters at home, or found distant places for them to live.[64]

The abuse of furloughs made them a rare privilege, at least for enlisted men. Usually no more than one or two men from a company were allowed to leave, and often the next furloughs were withheld until the previous recipients had returned. A soldier from upstate New York regretted surrendering his furlough to a comrade whose mother had died, for on his return trip the bereaved soldier "got on the wrong train," which took him to Canada instead of Washington. If men failed to return, their colonels would often stop all subsequent furloughs: a sudden moratorium on leaves of absence in the 96th Pennsylvania may have initiated the spontaneous mutiny in that regiment on February 18, and it did lead to the resignation of at least one lieutenant, the following day.[65]

Schemes for getting out of the service could grow quite complicated and devious. Besides the additional pay and prestige, one of the principal attractions of a commission was the theoretical ability to resign at will, at least when no general orders prohibited it. After surviving the Seven Days, one Indiana lad sought his father's state-house influence for a commission as lieutenant specifically so he could resign, and when his father indignantly refused he tried for months to get out of the army on the excuses of a hernia, diarrhea, and bad eyesight until a harried surgeon relented and sent him home. In February, when the War Department finally authorized the enlistment of black troops under white officers, hordes of privates and noncommissioned officers applied for appointments, and a good many of those applicants privately admitted seeking their commissions for the sole purpose of resigning them and going home.[66]

Clearly the dissatisfaction was not confined to the Army of the Potomac. When other troops saw an opportunity to desert they often did so, and sometimes with near-unanimity: at least two Illinois regiments dissolved from desertion during the winter. Nearly 40 percent of the enlisted men in the 109th Illinois wandered away from their posts below Memphis, and the remainder burst into open mutiny. When ordered out to defend their Holly Springs supply base from a massive raid, the regiment refused to leave camp, instead drawing into a defiant circle and preparing to surrender to the first Confederates who came their way. Thereafter, members of the 109th leaked steadily into the interior to be paroled by the enemy. Eventually the remnants were brought back to Memphis under guard, refusing to give up their weapons until Grant agreed to disband their regiment altogether. The 128th Illinois, which never numbered more than 860 men, lost over 700 of them to desertion before it, too, was disbanded, with a handful of survivors transferred to a veteran regiment.[67]

Grant blamed the epidemic dissatisfaction in those regiments on incompetent officers, but the sheer extent of desertion and the opinions of other observers contradicted his explanation. In late November of 1862, only two months after the Emancipation Proclamation, Confederate officers reported hundreds of Union deserters wandering through middle Tennessee, looking for someone who could parole them. Two months later the provost marshal at St. Louis warned that "desertion in the armies of the West is assuming fearful proportions," although he naively doubted that those men were deserting to the enemy. A couple of weeks after that the Union general in command of Columbus, Kentucky, warned Grant that rampant desertion there resulted from the "present excitement and political intrigues of the State of Illinois," adding that Illinois troops had better be kept as far away from their home state as possible to reduce the temptation for flight.[68]

That general's reference to "present excitement and political intrigues" acknowledged the growing popular antagonism toward Lincoln's war measures, illustrated as it was by the autumn elections that brought so many antiadministration Democrats into power in Illinois and elsewhere. As New Year's Day approached, and with it Lincoln's threatened emancipation of Southern slaves, soldiers who had enlisted solely to preserve the antebellum Union grew increasingly angry over what they viewed as a breach of contract. Even those who entertained no thought of abandoning their duty fulminated against the government, the president, and the abolitionists who had influenced him. Even Union generals would complain that their troops fought with less enthusiasm than their enemies, and some attributed that to the absence of a unified purpose: while the Confederates struggled for the independence of their homeland, Northern aims had become confused and adulterated. "The most serious question discussed among the soldiers now," reported a captain in the 24th Michigan, "is 'What are we fighting for?'"[69]

Captain Jacob Haas, of Pennsylvania, summarized the conservative Unionist's image of abolitionists in a letter to his civilian brother. Denouncing the brother for promoting fervent antislavery views and demanding hasty action from the troops in the field, Haas declared himself "utterly disgusted" with Lincoln's proclamation — and apparently with his brother as well.[70] Those dissidents who sensed a measure of sympathy and security on the home front, like the soldiers from Illinois, found it a little easier to make the leap to disobedience, mutiny, or desertion.

The end of the year brought joyous celebrations in the contraband camps: in Baton Rouge hundreds of men, women, and children cavorted in a dance without music, as rhythm keepers stamped their feet and slapped their thighs. Such spectacles amused the troops, and endeared a few of them to the revelers, but most Union soldiers evinced little sympathy for slaves except when they discovered some who had been severely abused. All but the most insightful Northerner troops mistook the adverse effects of the slaves' oppressed condition for racial traits, and as a result they often dreaded the day of jubilee.[71] One enlisted man who accepted emancipation as a means of suppressing the rebellion nonetheless insisted that "a negro is none to good to be held as a slave." He despised abolitionists, and rejoiced when his brother recanted his antislavery principles after coming south with a new regiment.[72]

The passage of January 1 did not end the hostility toward emancipation, or the activism against it. As the month progressed, opposition newspapers hammered at the potential economic competition freed slaves would present to the working classes, and that argument found a receptive audience among the countless white laborers whose straitened situations had led them to enlist for financial incentives. That, and the feeling that the government would spend millions to free the slaves while leaving the soldiers unpaid for endless months, bred seething resentment that aggravated the prevailing prejudice. "I came out for my Cuntrey," a Massachusetts soldier fumed, months after the New Year's deadline, "not to fight for the damed nigers."[73]

Northern opponents had anticipated that the proclamation might be repealed, especially since it had seemed to convince Confederates to fight to the last ditch, and an occasional Southern Unionist hoped to reduce it to a negotiating point. When John McClernand arrived in Memphis in the final days of 1862, he received a Southerner "of the first respectability" just back from Grenada, Mississippi. This man had allegedly spoken with erstwhile McClernand friends who had gained high rank in the Confederate Army of Mississippi, and they seemed willing to talk peace so long as Lincoln abided by his earlier promise to leave slavery untouched. Whatever weight that thirdhand communication from unauthorized spokesmen may have deserved (and the president did want to hear any further overtures), it reached the White House too late. On January 8 Lincoln replied that, once having issued his proclamation, he could not retract it.[74]

Those who might have been pleased with emancipation still found cause to complain about the war they supported, and in the first month of 1863 the devaluation of the national currency provided a common grievance. Through various sources the federal treasury was taking in about a million dollars a day, but that fell far short of accumulating expenses. By the first of the year the government already owed about $60 million in back pay to the army and navy, while barely one-fifth of that amount could be raised against the obligation. Congressmen introduced a resolution calling for prompt payment of the troops, acknowledging that their country owed it to them, but they proposed to cover the debt with $50 million in worthless currency, printed without specie or revenue to sustain it. The president doubled that figure to $100 million, and within days the value of paper currency dropped by a quarter. That devaluation alarmed investors and amateur economists to whom the "bloated degraded currency" posed as frightening a danger as any external enemy, but the inevitable inflation weighed heaviest on the struggling families of the very soldiers the resolution pretended to benefit. The condition of those families prompted letters from home filled with enough anti-administration vitriol to shock soldiers who remained devoted to the president. "Your language indicated that your sympathies and feelings are with the Rebels," an Ohio soldier cautioned his sister, while a Michigan sergeant in New Orleans claimed that every Union soldier in the South supported the war "although half of you at home are turning out to be Rebells."[75]

East and west, Union soldiers from private to general fell into despondency over the perpetual replacement of commanding generals, repeated defeats, costly but indecisive battles, continuing congressional wrangling over freedom and freedmen, the financial panic, the revelation of a December cabinet crisis, and "the going-to-hell-tending of every thing." An abusively critical newspaper editor concluded that the country had "fallen upon evil times," and a good many men in and out of uniform concurred. "This is the winter of our discontent," wrote a government telegraph operator at the southwest pass of the Mississippi Delta, who writhed at every fragment of bad news that clacked in over his wire. "Every thing looks dark now," confessed a family man who would give his arm for the cause, "and I am afraid this once happy land will have to be divided."[76] A cynical Maine officer commenting on "this causeless war" implied some hope for reunion, but only in the distant future and at enormous sacrifice in life: he doubted that many of the country's soldiers would live to see that day. Soldiers who had been with the army less than six months had already seen all the military service they wanted to, whether or not they had heard the sound of hostile fire, and political differences only magnified the misery, ennui, and exasperation. A seasoned Vermont soldier announced on Christmas Day that he was going home when his term was up, "and then the Union can go to the Devil for all I care."[77]

Significant proportions of those who composed the Union armies from one end of the country to the other had given up any hope that their arms would prevail, and men had begun admitting to their friends and families that they thought it was time to compromise — and to give up altogether, if the Confederacy refused to do so. "For my part I am sick and discouraged," admitted a Maine cavalryman who resented the shift in war aims; it was, he thought, time to either offer a compromise or let the South go, and he was hardly alone. "If this is the way the war is to be carried on," complained a Vermont sergeant, "I think the sooner we are divided the better."[78]

The winter's dejection weakened the will of many who, though they had come out with the purest motives, wished to waste neither their time nor their lives in a fruitless crusade. To thousands of soldiers who had exhausted themselves in national service, the war was "about played out."[79]

Contending pickets saluted each other across the Rappahannock and often fell into friendly chat, concluding that theirs was not a personal struggle. They sometimes rowed across the river to visit with their opposites, or shuttled miniature ferryboats on ropes, trading tobacco and coffee or the occasional bottle of spirits. Georgians who still resented the blanket extension of their one-year enlistment the previous spring suggested to disillusioned nine-month Connecticut militiamen that each could return to their respective capital cities and hang the chief representatives of their governments: after that they would meet again at the river to shake hands, before going home.[80]

As any private could comprehend, the military impasse dampened volunteering considerably, especially when munificent bounties petered out in the face of diminishing draft quotas: it was the fear of being drafted that fueled patriotic rallies and bounties, and both withered away as each community met its quota. The last regiments of the 1862 crop languished incomplete after the debacle at Fredericksburg, and only political maneuvering by their ambitious would-be officers postponed their consolidation with emaciated old regiments. The altruistic motive of emancipation had failed to attract any new surge of white volunteers, while the recruiting of black regiments had begun too late and proceeded too slowly to augment the existing armies. The previous May, Governor John Andrew of Massachusetts had urged Lincoln toward abolition and the raising of black troops, promising that if he did so "the roads would swarm, if need be, with multitudes whom New England would pour out to obey your call." Andrew's conditions had been met in full by the end of that year, but a Pennsylvania officer wondered sarcastically when those multitudes of reinforcements might be coming.[81]

Few believed that the war could be won by the troops already in the field, for many of their terms would be running out by the time the roads dried. The War Department had accepted some 31,000 two-year men in the first weeks of the conflict, almost all of them from New York, and thirty-eight regiments of them would begin going home by the middle of May. Eleven states and the gestating territory of West Virginia had raised more than 88,000 nine-month troops, and they were due for discharge during the course of the summer.[82]

The departure of the two-year men would represent a more significant drain in experience than in numbers, while the loss of the short-term militia would cripple the armies but little by comparison. Everyone estimated them at 300,000 strong, since Edwin Stanton had demanded that many, but most of the quota had been satisfied by applying a surplus of three-year recruits at a four-to-one ratio. The nine-month men served mainly in Virginia, North Carolina, and in the Banks expedition to Louisiana. Of the ninety-two regiments, three dozen never lost a man to combat and half the rest reported fewer than a score of men killed in action: three-quarters of the 1,377 militiamen who were killed fell in the three dozen regiments assigned to the Army of the Potomac. Another 4,649 perished from disease — more than half of them from the twenty-one regiments sent to Louisiana.[83]

The accomplishments of the so-called drafted militia remained relatively inglorious, consisting primarily of guard duty that freed more experienced troops for the field: the veterans would not miss them when their time was up. Edward Cross, the pugnacious colonel of the 5th New Hampshire, reported that the incessant grumbling of the nine-month men made them especially unpopular. In Baton Rouge a Massachusetts lieutenant gauged them "poor stuff" after a season of service alongside them. "They think only of getting home again," he reported, "and have a terrible fear if there is any danger of a fight. Our 3 years men despise them." The abuse that met all recruits dogged these short-term men throughout their service. A Maine cavalryman greeted them as "poor trash," and an Indiana major considered their contribution "little better than nothing."[84] Generals seeking volunteers for dangerous operations or additional field service found few among the militia. Despite courageous failures like the dusk assault on Marye's Heights, nine-month regiments earned a reputation for unreliability under fire as well as for an inability to keep up on the march or bear rough camp conditions. Veteran commanders often relegated them to the most demeaning fatigue duty.[85]

The militiamen felt that scorn long after discharge. At veterans' gatherings the survivors of three-year regiments (many of whom had served less than nine months themselves) would greet strangers with the question of whether they had been real soldiers or mere "nine-months' men." A veteran of the 4th Massachusetts Militia subtitled his wartime memoirs "the Adventures of that despised object . . . 'A Nine Months Man.'" During their service they endured journalistic humiliation as unpatriotic "9 month beauties" and the heckling of three-year men who called them "the Picknic party." Seasoned troops cast relentless jibes about the militia bounties, and a nine-month Vermont lieutenant supposed that nothing less than their annihilation on the battlefield would satisfy such tormentors, as though their hefty bounties had deprived them of the right to survive.[86] As their terms drew toward an end the militia soldiers recognized the antagonism of the three-year men for the envy that doubtless underlay it, and reacted to it with better humor. Some of them felt considerable pity for those volunteers with another year or two left to serve, and especially when those desperate unfortunates offered enticing fees for discharged militiamen to stay behind as their substitutes.[87]

Militia regiments did field a conspicuously larger share of dandies than their predecessors. The ninety-eight men in one company of the 44th Massachusetts included eight lawyers, two physicians, four "literateurs," two engineers, and an assortment of other professionals, merchants, and skilled artisans. Sixteen graduates or undergraduates of Harvard University enlisted in the company, against only five farmers and a single shoemaker — impoverished shoemakers having composed the plurality of early three-year regiments from Massachusetts. Cape Elizabeth, Maine, reflected a less glaring but nonetheless prominent disparity in the relative wealth of recruits in the volunteer and militia service: in the summer of 1862 two dozen mostly poor residents joined a three-year regiment before the bounties soared out of control, while thirty-seven predominately comfortable citizens signed up with the 25th Maine for generous incentives and nine months of ultimately safe, soft duty. The pool of willing poor had been sorely depleted by the time recruiting began for the nine-month regiments, leaving their more comfortable and demanding neighbors to compete for bounties that rose to meet their requirements.[88]

Nine-month men also seemed more dependent upon tailored uniforms, home-cooked food, and comfortable lodging than their compeers, and more prone to raucous complaint when they were issued any but the most palatable fare.[89] They made early and frequent calculations of the dates they thought they were supposed to be released: starting from the day they first enrolled in their companies, they kept close track of their remaining time, and the inevitable discrepancy between their own count and the War Department's calculations brewed a surliness that ignited into occasional mutiny.[90]

North Carolina provided the duty that militia recruits seemed to expect: reasonably good weather, clean and comfortable living conditions, little active campaigning, and comparative safety. "If anyone wants to join the army," advised a member of the New Bern garrison, "this is the place."

A dozen Massachusetts and Pennsylvania regiments spent most of their nine-month terms at New Bern, and only four of them ever came within close range of an armed enemy, losing a grand total of thirty-four killed. Nothing could be guaranteed, and an epidemic or a falling tree could send a soldier to his grave as quickly as anywhere else; the wife of a nine-month man might answer a summons to the express office of her local rail station to find her husband's coffin on the platform. Nearly three hundred nine-month men died in North Carolina hospitals during the winter and spring, but mortality of less than 3 percent fell far below the average in Union regiments. Death came so infrequently to soldiers in New Bern that in February of 1863 whole regiments still turned out for a single funeral, complete with an honor guard, drummers tapping a mournful rhythm, and a private hearse to carry away the casket.[91]

The most arduous duty at New Bern consisted of provost details, which some militia guards enlivened by arbitrarily searching the persons of attractive women, and detaining them if they objected. For many in the garrison, the most time-consuming chore consisted of finding sufficient entertainment. Perennially fair skies usually suggested regular sports, and one youth from Springfield, Massachusetts, told the folks at home that all he and his comrades did was play ball and pitch quoits. A lieutenant from the patrician 44th Massachusetts organized a regimental dramatics association, which alleviated winter boredom with a grand masquerade ball; in March the same troupe presented an opera written by one of the members, using one of the regimental barracks as a theater.[92]

The very mention of barracks would have amused most field soldiers, but the troops at New Bern enjoyed the luxury of carefully engineered winter quarters, dormitory housing with real walls and a solid roof, or lodgings in private homes. Their later regimental histories (which represented some of the costliest productions in that genre) contain token sketches of soldiers camped before shelter tents, but the abundant photographs depict men airing their blankets in the open windows of brick or frame houses. As winter approached, officers often appropriated private residences to quarter their troops on the excuse that the owners had "insulted" Union soldiers; that happened to a pair of sisters who expressed their political sentiments from their New Bern balcony, only to find a Massachusetts company suddenly lodged throughout their home. Aggravated as it was by the petty abuses of pampered garrison soldiers, the oppressive nature of martial law excited further indignation, resulting in still more of those comfort-hungry troops camping out in the parlors and bedrooms of proud Carolinians.[93]

Generals harangued the nine-month men on the subject of reenlistment, promising more of the same easy duty in that salubrious climate, but few of the militiamen deigned to extend their abbreviated terms; their own officers doubted that the men would agree to remain on duty as much as a few extra days or a week, even in the face of an imminent national emergency, and events confirmed those doubts. In most cases their service had lasted just long enough to satisfy their thirst for adventure or their limited martial aspirations, and to convince them that the army was no place for a civilized, liberty-loving citizen. Reenlistment eventually entailed bounties higher than those paid in 1862, but militiamen who succumbed to that mercenary appeal usually chose safer service in the navy, heavy artillery, or other short-term units.[94]

The bounties of 1862 had siphoned off the last stratum of men who would risk military service for such deceptively generous compensation. That left the government only three options: continue the war with the army in the field, regardless of the steady attrition; make peace even if it meant disunion; or resort to an effective form of compulsory service.

Military demands precluded the first option: the failures of a Union army that already outnumbered its enemy by two to one seemed to demand a steady supply of fresh recruits, if not a sizable increase in the army.[95] Political obstinacy precluded a negotiated peace, for a majority of Republicans and War Democrats still appeared unwilling to abandon the enormous commitment they had already made in blood and treasure. Congress therefore began considering outright compulsion as early as January 28, when Senator Henry Wilson again introduced a bill "for the encouragement of reënlistments, and for enrolling and drafting the militia, and for other purposes." The Senate consigned the bill to Wilson's own Committee on Military Affairs, and (apparently with the secret collaboration of Edwin Stanton) Wilson refined it into an amended version that he resubmitted early on February 4, along with a flurry of additional amendments that consumed the rest of the day's deliberations in acrimonious debate.[96]

The principal difference between the new bill and the Militia Act of 1862 appeared to be that the president could call out state troops for up to two years of federal service, rather than for the current maximum of nine months. More significantly, though, it also required the enrollment of all able-bodied male citizens between the ages of eighteen and forty-five under regulations devised by the president himself, and it made those men automatically subject to the harsh strictures of military law from the moment their names were drawn. That deprived the individual states of any control, giving the federal government — and specifically the president — an extraordinary power over common citizens that had been previously unknown in the United States. The Richmond government had enacted a similar draft, but the Southern draft had, itself, been touted as evidence of

Confederate tyranny. Privately, even Secretary Seward considered conscription incompatible with the cause.[97]

Senator John Carlile, of Virginia, raised the first cry against the wholesale surrender of state authority to the chief executive. The bill might be appropriate if the people of the United States belonged to their government, he said, but it was his belief that the reverse was true. If the people felt too little interest in the government they owned to fight a war to preserve it, he doubted the government had the authority to force them to do so. William Richardson, a Douglas Democrat who had recently replaced Orville Browning as the junior senator from Illinois, objected that Wilson's bill would "confer upon the President of the United States more power than belongs to any despot in Europe or anywhere else." Implied in his argument was the suggestion that a just war would attract sufficient volunteers, and that an unjust war deserved none. "Under the operation of this bill," said Richardson, "the President of the United States has the absolute power to take every man into the service who may differ with him in political sentiment and political views. He is to make the regulations; he is to make the law." Richardson charged that the president, secretary of war, and the Republican Congress had already interfered too much in military affairs, insinuating that Wilson's bill only worsened the damage. Under it the president might draft exclusively Democrats, he argued, or Republicans, and partisan state officials could then arrange to have only the politically reliable regiments given an opportunity to vote, as was already reported to have happened in Republican-dominated Iowa.[98]

The Senate wrangled over federal prerogatives most of the next day before returning the bill to Wilson's committee for revision. In the middle of February it reappeared in printed form as the Conscription Law, taking up an entire day and evening of business. Senators who otherwise seemed to favor the bill began offering amendments to include a host of draft exemptions for specific persons and occupations — beginning with their own. They ultimately decided against the blatant selfishness of exempting themselves, but only after one member calculated that all but three or four of them had already reached the upper age limit of forty-five: Brigadier General Jim Lane, the senior member from Kansas, impishly proposed raising the draft age to fifty, but anguished cries of "Oh, no" filled the chamber, and he withdrew the motion. A number of senators wanted to raise the minimum age from eighteen to twenty or twenty-one, however. It was unfair to take young men from their schools and colleges before they had graduated, ran the reasoning, and in support of the motion John Sherman absurdly contended that the cold climate somehow caused Northern boys to mature more slowly. Except for General Lane, most senators wished to increase the lower age limit for one sympathetic reason or another, but it was Edgar Cowan of Pennsylvania who may have hit upon the foremost consideration for that change: young men under twenty-one, he reminded his fellows, would provide the main source of substitutes.[99]

The substitute represented the main hope for a drafted man who wished to avoid service. Militia laws had usually permitted members to send others on active duty in their places, and the Regular Army had discharged soldiers who hired substitutes, as Edgar Allan Poe did in 1829. To this alternative the congressmen added a commutation provision, by which a conscript could pay a flat fee to be excused from that particular draft call. That, too, represented a holdover from the antebellum state militia tradition, although the new legislation first proposed raising the token payments of previous wars to $250 at a time when laborers earned only a dollar a day; the House of Representatives would raise that amount to $300, thereby compounding the impression that the clause was meant to favor the wealthy. Theoretically the cost of substitutes would be limited by a fixed-price alternative for onetime exemption, but the commutation fee illustrated better than anything the elitist attitude that the wealthy should have an option in case substitutes were not available. As the general secretary of the U.S. Sanitary Commission had opined to a New York senator, a man's value to the nation was reflected by his fortune, and a wealthy man could easily afford to compete with government bounties by hiring someone to serve in his place: such a man would find it simpler still to avoid negotiating with brokers or prospective replacements, and just leave the cash with a federal agent.[100]

Pacifist principles attracted too little sympathy among the congressmen to warrant any exemption, even for recognized Quakers and Shakers. A motion exempting religious dissidents under their state militia laws failed because too many senators feared that hostile legislatures in New Jersey, Indiana, or elsewhere might exempt their entire state populations on the pretense of conscientious objection. Any drafted citizen who was opposed to war on principle could pay the commutation fee, reasoned the senators, none of whom seemed to realize that scrupulous pacifists might consider such a payment tantamount to indirect support for war.[101]

After that long day's work the bill went to the House, where Representative Abram Olin of New York reported it in the final week of February and tried to rush it through in spite of its acknowledged flaws. "I do not expect to see any captious opposition to this measure," he warned — smearing would-be critics before they could utter a word. He nevertheless found plenty of opposition to provisions that threatened alarming civil liberties violations, and the lower house wrestled with the question until nearly midnight. Philadelphian Charles Biddle challenged the establishment of deputy provost marshals in every congressional district, who would have the authority to report on "treasonable practices" and arrest citizens whom they considered guilty. Recounting episodes of editors arrested for publishing unflattering characterizations of political figures, and law-abiding citizens abducted by federal marshals, Biddle reminded the House that the protections of civil law had been "swept away by the fiat of executive power" the previous summer, when the will of the president became the supreme law of the land, backed by military might. He conjured the specter of popular revolt over such authoritarian rule, and he may have been speaking of Representative William Allen, of Illinois, or Edwin Olds, of Ohio, when he alluded to the inhabitants of federal dungeons whom the people had elected to prominent offices. Allen sat within earshot, waiting to deliver a hopeless but blisteringly sarcastic speech on conscription, economic policy, and the majority party's apparent contempt for the Constitution.[102]

Opposition (the "captious" nature of which depended on the listener's political perspective) came from such celebrated dissidents as the outgoing Clement Vallandigham and the reelected Daniel Voorhees. War Democrats like Hendrick Wright, of Pennsylvania, also assailed the unprecedented powers given to the deputy provost marshals, and Ohio representative Chilton White railed against the military power the bill gave the sitting president over every citizen, effectively turning the nation into "one vast military camp." Advocates of the bill obdurately resisted those arguments, demonstrating a disregard for constitutional guarantees best illustrated by John Bingham, of Ohio. After exaggerating the alleged remarks of a dissenting citizen from his state, Bingham told his colleagues in all seriousness that anyone who would utter such a statement should be hanged without trial, and the bill's presumed supporters greeted that statement with applause. Bingham's constituents had heard enough of such talk, and had voted him out of office; the president would console him with an appointment to the Judge Advocate General's Department — where he could (and did) more effectively exercise his disdain for due process.[103]

Outnumbered Democrats filibustered for concessions. Olin's parliamentary chicanery actually contributed to slight modifications in the bill, as some Republicans sided with indignant Union and Democratic congressmen against the blind rush to passage, but no one ever doubted the bill's ultimate success. On March 2, two days before the end of the session, it went back to the upper house for approval and the following day the president signed it. Within days constituents started harrying congressional Republicans with applications for appointment as deputy provost marshals, and within a fortnight those new deputies began arresting political dissenters for the alleged expression of divergent opinions.[104]

Notwithstanding their varied opinions on the prospects for victory, the wisdom of their leaders, or the advisability of administration policy, most of those in uniform shared similar opinions on dissenters and the draft. Almost all soldiers took the administration side of the conscription debate, if not all for the same reasons. Republicans in the ranks deemed the new law crucial to avert Southern independence, but nine-month men with little personal commitment to the war also applauded the decision to force others into uniform — just as those three-season veterans were heading home, temporarily immune to the new law. "I can sit in my easy chair and laugh at the rest of them when they are going," admitted a Vermonter who would resume civilian life that summer. A militiaman who had delayed his enlistment to collect the largest possible bounty in August complained in March that draftees would be able to buy their way out of service for three hundred dollars, although he rejected a similar amount to act as a substitute for another unfortunate who had signed on for three years. A two-year man in a New York regiment thought of some particular armchair strategists he hoped to see at the front before he headed home.[105]

There remained that hypocritical discrimination over who might and might not be drafted, as revealed by a Maine musician who chuckled that the draft was "going to take some of the fellows out," but with another moment's thought he asked his sister "how old is Father I think he would be exempt."[106] Whether they had enlisted from patriotic impulse, pecuniary distress, or to avoid the draft, most soldiers had grown to regard healthy male civilians (at least those to whom they bore no personal relation) with a contempt grounded at least partly in envy. Reflection on the comfort of young men at home grievously amplified the misery of standing guard duty in the rain and cold, and inspired calculations on the increased odds of stopping a bullet. Overlooking the possibility of political disagreement with the war, or denying that the right to dissent existed, many of those in uniform assumed that only cowardice would prevent a man from enlisting. To the delight of their embattled brothers and beaux, some girls snubbed the "home watchers," as a New Hampshire corporal called them, spurning their invitations to dance despite an embarrassing surplus of women at benefit balls.[107]

One woman reportedly refused to live with her husband after he deserted, but she represented a rare specimen of patriot. More often, wives welcomed or even lured their errant husbands homeward, while greying bachelors and widowers found themselves in surprising demand from young women on the lookout for dancing partners or opportunities for flirtation. The wife of one dutiful soldier confessed that she held just as much regard for those who refused to leave their families as she did for those who (like her husband) left everyone behind to serve what she considered a pointless cause and a perfidious administration. She boasted that her brothers would surely refuse to be drafted, and wished she were a man long enough to defy it herself.[108]

Tales of fierce civilian antagonism to the draft caused more mature soldiers to worry so about insurrection at home that some assured their families they would come home if a revolt erupted. Most of their comrades characterized any critics or opponents as treasonous Copperheads, though, daring them to resist the draft and predicting bayonets and canister for any who interfered. Some troops immediately mobilized impromptu forays against draft opponents: soldiers camped near Keokuk, Iowa, ransacked the Keokuk *Constitution* as soon as that newspaper denounced conscription.[109]

"Draft and make them come," wrote a Pennsylvania officer embittered by the failure of abolitionists to answer the call. "A man can learn to load and shoot in 1 week and 3 weeks is enough to learn him to go ahead. He will learn to retreat himself."[110]

From the very passage of the bill the commutation fee drew the most abuse from both political extremes. Indiana's governor, Oliver P. Morton, ridiculed the provision in a letter to Stanton, both for the animosity it would generate and for the loophole it offered the well-funded antiwar associations he imagined to exist in the Midwest. In Columbus, Ohio, Samuel Medary summarized the new law in the *Crisis* under the heading "$300 or your life," and three days later a hundred or more soldiers from Camp Chase descended on his newspaper armed with pistols, sabers, and, apparently, John Bingham's aversion to the First Amendment; they demolished his office, but Medary remained undaunted and Democratic newspapers took up his cry, using commutation to symbolize the class differences that filled the army with poor men.[111]

It was not the details of the Conscription Law that disturbed most opponents so much as the unique shift in governmental power represented by the law itself. More than any previous action taken in pursuit of the war, the draft law strengthened the power of the central government with authority it had stripped from the states, fulfilling the fears of nervous states' rights Unionists who had long accused Republicans of pitting the federal government against the states as much as against secession. That and emancipation, the war's most widely suspected ulterior motive, became the primary issues in New England's spring elections, which followed on the heels of the congressional session.

New Hampshire Democrats stood the best chance in New England of toppling Republican rule, and by hammering on the administration's usurpation of state prerogatives they nearly did so. Democrats held a majority of the popular sympathy in the state, if not a majority in the legislature, and they saw their fight as one between conservatism and "abolitionism of the Massachusetts school," labeling the incumbents as "Republico-Abolitionists."[112] Cagier state politicians understood that the only way Republican Joseph Gilmore could win the governor's chair would be to prevent a majority vote by encouraging a third-party candidate and throwing the election into the Republican-dominated legislature. Some of Gilmore's own advisors warned him that such a scheme would only advertise his weakness, but ambition triumphed over pride. Colonel Walter Harriman, an antebellum Democrat who commanded a regiment in the Army of the Potomac, cooperated by accepting a tardy, sacrificial nomination on a Union platform.[113] The 2nd New Hampshire, from the Republican southern counties, came home on furlough to assure a few hundred extra votes. Despite strenuous efforts by its officers, the 5th New Hampshire, with a preponderance of Democrats from the northern counties, remained at the front, as did the 14th New Hampshire, which had cast a straw-poll majority of 119 for the Democratic candidate.[114] Republican town officials trod their outlying districts with unusual persistence to persuade wavering constituents, thereby advertising their fear of "a close rub" to insightful observers. Gilmore dispensed free passes for travel on his railroad for promised votes, and received some thinly disguised requests for petty bribes.[115]

Republican and "Union" Party speakers, including prominent army officers, actively branded New Hampshire's Democratic candidates as "vile, unpatriotic, and in league with traitors," and soldiers with the temerity to support the opposition ticket felt the fury of partisan vengeance: the War Department obligingly cashiered a lieutenant of the 4th New Hampshire for merely distributing Democratic literature.[116] For all the Republicans' coercion, artifice, palm greasing, and mudslinging, however, they nearly lost everything. Even the devoutly Unionist father of a New Hampshire major made a special effort to reach the polls so he could vote against "that rascal Gilmore."[117] Democratic nominee Ira Eastman won a sizable plurality but fell five hundred votes short of a majority, leaving the election to the New Hampshire General Court, where the dominant Republicans quickly seated Gilmore. One of the state's three congressional radicals lost his seat to a Democrat, and the other two Republican incumbents clung to office by margins of only 150 and 350 votes, respectively. Seven of the ten counties stood with the opposition.[118]

A few Lincoln men saw the results of the New Hampshire elections as a

ray of hope, but the actual voting there left faithful New England looking a little less true. Congratulate themselves as they might on winning
three out of four statewide races, Granite State Republicans had not attracted a majority: they had prevailed largely through partisan manipulation, much as their Ohio brethren had in the lone triumph over Vallandigham. New York's town elections, meanwhile, all seemed to be
going to Democrats. Anyone who read the returns could see the trend,
and might deduce that antiadministration Democrats would only gain
strength if the president should exercise his newfound power to conscript
soldiers — which, the reasoning ran, he must do if he wished to continue
the war.[119]

Talk of peace and compromise filtered across the country. The fighting
men tended to bristle at that apparent reproach to their cause, or to the
implied futility of their sacrifices, yet many of those same soldiers shared
the dark foreboding of the war's most dedicated detractors. They howled
at the incompetence of the president and secretary of war, scorned the
dishonesty and dissipation of Congress and the generals, and grieved over
the loss of favorite generals like the deposed McClellan and the ruined
Fitz John Porter, whom a biased court-martial had finally cashiered.[120]

The war promised only debt, death, disease, and misery. More Union
soldiers succumbed to disease in February of 1863 than in any other
month of the war. Patients died by platoons in bayou hospitals along the
Mississippi; in Virginia whole regiments suffered from colds that deteriorated into pneumonia, consumption, or the mysterious meningitis. One
of the autumn regiments from Wisconsin was losing men daily by March,
and the chaplain who had ministered so tenderly to those victims finally
joined them in their soggy cemetery upriver from Vicksburg, causing a
pessimistic Sauk County lad to prepare his mother for his own demise,
just in case.[121]

Men whose families wanted food and clothing had not been paid in as
much as seven months. In many cases their wives had not received the
promised support from their towns and states, and they thoroughly resented the supplies and provisions lavished on contrabands by the Quartermaster Department. So poor was the family of an older private in one
of Hiram Berdan's U.S. Sharpshooter regiments that he had to decide
whether to have someone back home shoot his dog, on which town selectmen had imposed a tax to help pay for enlistment bounties; he would hate
to see the dog killed, he told his cash-strapped wife, but she would have to
do as she thought best.[122]

Few Union soldiers or Northern citizens had the opportunity to study a
map depicting Union progress in the valleys of the Mississippi and Tennessee, but if they had they might have reflected how quickly Confeder-

ates had recovered much of that territory in 1862. A Massachusetts soldier who had served under Nathaniel Banks since 1861 could not help noticing, as the war neared its third spring, that the Army of the Potomac occupied nearly the same positions it had held a year before, after casualties in the tens of thousands and hundreds of millions of dollars in expenses. Troops in South Carolina had spent nearly a year and a half on the coast without penetrating the interior, and Fort Sumter remained firmly in Confederate hands. A Southern artilleryman rejoiced that "the star of the confederacy never shone brighter than it does now," while subscribers to Northern newspapers saw little to encourage hope.[123]

Confederates, and particularly Confederates on horseback, humiliated the Federals at every turn. At three o'clock on the pitch-black, rainy morning of March 9, Captain John S. Mosby led twenty-nine Virginia cavalrymen into Fairfax Court House, ten miles behind Union lines. Thanks to residents and spies he knew exactly where to find the local commander, and he personally climbed the stairs of a narrow brick Federal home to shake Brigadier General Edwin Stoughton out of a sound sleep and declare him a prisoner. The general, whose brigade of nine-month Vermonters lay all around his boudoir, departed meekly enough for enemy lines with several staff officers, thirty of his men, and fifty-eight prime horses. Eight days later, with forty-two men in light-blue Union overcoats, Mosby dealt Vermont pride another blow near Dranesville. Riding up to a Union picket post as though they were the relief guards, Mosby's men gathered in Major William Wells of the 1st Vermont Cavalry, four of his officers, and more than two dozen troopers, with all their arms and mounts. "It appears to me we are advancing backwards very fast," remarked a disgusted Yankee lieutenant.[124]

Officers shed their commissions in flocks, going home as fast as they could find other employment that paid as well as the War Department. Privates, corporals, and sergeants continued to desert, albeit in somewhat smaller numbers than during the depths of winter, while others secretly planned to abscond if denied the furloughs their officers so often enjoyed. "There aint one of them from the Colonels on down to the drummer boy that wouldnt go home to morrow if he could only get away," a Regular Army captain complained of the volunteers. "Nobody wants to stay here and you can't get some of them down here by all the threats and orders you can give."[125] The scandalous indulgence of furloughs to commissioned officers caught the attention of army headquarters in early March, when the consolidated reports of the U.S. Army showed just under ten thousand officers absent from their commands. President Lincoln thought as much as half the army was absent at any given moment, in large measure because of the desertion of enlisted men. Under the incidental authority of the Conscription Act he announced an amnesty on March 10, calling all deserters back to their commands by the first of April, but men in the ranks reported no sudden influx of returning penitents.[126] Nine-month soldiers in all but the most salubrious assignments refused to consider repeated appeals to reenlist, and scoffed at suggestions that their terms could be extended by legislative action. Men who were stuck in uniform for three years swore that neither they nor their comrades would ever reenlist if they could be discharged on the spot — the Union be damned.[127]

Citizens who scorned the radical image of victory still harbored hope for a reunited country. One middle-aged man in western Connecticut who had embraced the war in 1861 had long since repented as the winter of 1863 ended: along with thousands of soldiers, he concluded that fighting would never resolve what he called a "great family Quarrel." The tremendous cost of the war would lead the Republican administration to give it up and let the South go, he feared, unless Democrats took control and negotiated for reunion through conciliation. "We are now standing amid the new made graves of 200,000 northern men," he reminded a neighbor who favored war to the finish: crepe and mourning darkened every town, and bankruptcy threatened the entire nation. How, he wondered, could anyone call it treason to seek peace in the face of such devastation? A Michigan law student concurred. "'The Union as it was' is the only safe, practical ground for loyal men to occupy," he argued. "We must learn to be respectful and tolerant of the opinions of others, if we want to enjoy the fruits of wisdom and the blessings of free government." He softened his terms to avoid offending the damsel he prized, but what the aspiring attorney tried to convey was that the means used to win the war would only destroy the very liberties that the former Union had represented.[128]

Those opinions had been firm enough in February. March brought enormous new encumbrances on the taxpayer, with congressional authorization for another $950 million in bonds, treasury notes, and unsecured currency, on top of more than a billion and a quarter in earlier war-related appropriations.[129] Then came the Conscription Act, which spawned its own objectionable form of involuntary servitude as well as a national force of political police. That dropped the final straw on a burden of undemocratic impositions many citizens were already unwilling to bear.

"The time to quit has arrived," declared an outspoken Iowa newspaper editor, who found the rebellion stronger than ever after nearly two years of bloodshed. Constitutional Unionists of his persuasion resented Lincoln's ventures into radical reform, which lent an atmosphere of fraud to his war for the Union, and they blamed his dismissal of McClellan for the more spectacular military defeats and the subsequent demoralization of the army. The extraordinary measures the president employed to compensate for those predicted blunders simply infuriated his critics. Civilian observers warned the president of a "malignant hatred" of the administration and its war; few turned as bitterly on the president as those who had accorded him the greatest credence, only to feel betrayed.[130]

"I am perfectly disgusted with this administration," complained a student at Pennsylvania College, at the crossroads town of Gettysburg. "I once thought that Lincoln was a perfectly honest man[;] now I believe he is one of the greatest hypocrites and rogues in the country. If he does not take care he will never go to Illinois again with his head."[131]

Epilogue

UNCONDITIONAL UNIONISTS — or no-compromise Unionists, as they might more accurately have been called — responded to the surge of antidraft, antiwar, antiadministration sentiment with the creation of secret societies much like those of their Copperhead chimera. In imitation of the imagined rituals of the Knights of the Golden Circle (the phantom legions of which they excoriated as sneaking cowards for their secrecy), those Unionists gathered into a network of clandestine societies known collectively as the Union League, or the Loyal League. Joseph Medill, editor of the *Chicago Tribune*, threw much of his own energy into creation of the organization; he seemed almost apologetic about the league's secrecy, but exempted it from the condemnation he accorded KGC secrecy on the grounds that the league was "strictly patriotic." In Indiana, Governor Oliver Morton encouraged the creation of such societies across the state by provoking the same paranoia that had persuaded Abraham Lincoln to imprison the Maryland legislature in 1861, claiming that the Democratic majority in Indianapolis "would attempt to wrest the Government from the constituted authorities and revolutionize." The secret Unionist brotherhoods swept the Midwest, eventually reaching the East, and by March of 1863 local chapters were petitioning the president to remove federal employees who had hired men suspected of disagreement with administration policy.[1]

Local Union Leagues served not only as partisan watchdogs but as organizational vehicles for more patriotic rallies, where speakers harangued crowds with the rhetoric of the recruiting frenzy, although usually without either the intention or the result of drawing men to enlist. Friendly newspapers reported massive gatherings in Cincinnati and Indianapolis, where the faithful disseminated their side of the election debate long after the election had ended.[2] Some Union Leagues arose in the East that shared no apparent connection to the leagues of the Midwestern cantons. The Union League Club of New York reflected its predecessor in Philadelphia when it adopted an aristocratic air, restricting membership more by privilege than by secrecy. A few dozen prominent businessmen and socialites convened late that winter to establish the club. They accumulated an original membership of several hundred wealthy Unionists tired of the Democratic palaver they encountered at the New York Club, where at least one field-grade deserter from the Regular Army maintained membership. Their main purpose appeared to be to provide themselves with a watering hole where only the most loyal comments might be heard, although they held one great rally of their own at Cooper Union in the second week of March. The members paid dues of twenty-five dollars per year, renting a dismal old mansion for their clubhouse. From that headquarters they published pamphlets explaining their uncompromising support for a war in which they would never have to fight, meanwhile snorting at the city's more pedestrian Union Leagues when those lesser organizations held plebeian public rallies for the flag and the president.[3]

The administration greatly needed such propaganda by early March. President Lincoln's early promises to maintain the social order had long since evaporated into emancipation, turning tens of thousands of loyal Union citizens and soldiers against him. National conscription had not hurt him much with the army, but the very notion offended a sizable share of the public, and the "$300 swindle" of the commutation clause infuriated many of his warmest supporters. Then, as spring spread across the land, the first dreaded harbingers of racial equality emerged in the form of black men wearing blue uniforms.

Outside Boston, Colonel Robert Gould Shaw, lately a captain in the 2nd Massachusetts, drilled scores of recruits for the 54th Massachusetts Colored Infantry. "They are not the best class of nigs," he commented to his father (who might have found the phrase jarring), although they were all freemen who had either never known slavery or had escaped it long before. A couple of weeks' drill and the arrival of some literate recruits improved Shaw's image of his new troops, with many of whom he would die only four months hence. In the South, regiments of freedmen had been training for months. David Hunter's defiant experiment in South Carolina persisted amid widespread doubt that it could ever succeed. "As to being made soldiers," predicted a Harvard-educated officer, "they are more harm than good." Similar skepticism prevailed in Louisiana, where the polyglot Native Guards had been resurrected for Union service from a state militia organization. A staff officer with Nathaniel Banks found that the presence of black troops only impaired the efficiency of the white regiments, so many of which had come freshly into the army: the white soldiers grew as lazy and demanding of the Native Guards as so many overseers, forcing them to perform all the fatigue labor and violently assaulting them in their camps for occasional entertainment.[4]

The new black regiments offered broad opportunity for men in the ranks to obtain commissions, and for junior officers to win promotion, but ambition sometimes failed to trump racial disdain: a soldier from Iowa who yearned for shoulder straps conceded that he would rather remain a private in his white regiment than become an officer in a black one, while a New York lieutenant ridiculed the suggestion of seeking command of black troops: "How would you like to see me at the head of a regiment of big 'niggers,'" he asked his sister; "I think I should try to get them killed off as fast as possible." The son of Lincoln's minister to England laughed at a family proposal that he take command of such a regiment, observing that he had no desire to "become a 'nigger driver' in my old age," although he accepted just such a commission two years later.[5]

Some of the enlisted men who applied for those commissions only wanted an opportunity to resign. Meanwhile, men who already held commissions, and valued them for the prestige and income they provided, started to think of quitting as they watched their government begin to arm the slaves it had just declared free. "I am sick and tired of this Nigger War," wrote an older lieutenant, by way of introducing the dissatisfaction that would soon lead to his own resignation.[6]

Second Lieutenant John Mooney had tried to resign soon after the battle of Fredericksburg, but he had been rebuffed on the authority of a general order forbidding all such requests for honorable discharge. He made no reference to issues of health, although tuberculosis would kill him in less than four years. He cited no particular reason for wishing to go home, leaving his superiors to wonder if he had lost his nerve or whether some family hardship, political objection, or discouragement with his country's leadership had prompted him to quit the service. When his first request for honorable discharge came back disapproved he submitted another, early in February, asking to be released under either honorable or dishonorable circumstances. That extraordinary demand made its way up the chain of command while Mooney's regiment lay at Newport News. Mooney's letter finally reached the hands of Major General John Dix, who read it with astonishment and drew up a general order of his own, immediately discharging the lieutenant "because the military service is disgraced by his connection with it." Like all such orders, this one was published for distribution throughout the department and read to the troops at dress parade. Early in March the chastised veteran started home from Fort Monroe, by way of Washington.[7]

Lieutenant Mooney suffered from no lack of courage. As a sergeant he had fought at South Mountain and Antietam with such valor that he was promoted to a vacancy left by a more timid officer.[8] He may have found it easier to accept ignominious dismissal because he had enlisted under an assumed name, claiming that he had been forced into the Confederate army in 1861 while working in Georgia, but neither his assertion of forced enrollment nor his tale of escape survives close scrutiny. Evidently he wished to obscure some other, more compromising activity — desertion from Union States forces, for instance. Whatever the motive behind his alias and his sudden resignation, Mooney stopped in Washington long enough to secure a job as clerk at Willard's Hotel, and there he remained through the rest of the war.[9]

In the first half of March, Washington's hotels held many an army officer on his way home, on his way back to the front, or lounging on furlough. Some passed through on regimental business, looking for deserters who had been reported at home. On the eleventh of March alone, the 8th Michigan provided its major, chaplain, and senior captain to the crush of idle officers in the capital city: the three of them passed through together, having had better luck than Lieutenant Mooney in the matter of resignations. Edward Cross, the colonel of the 5th New Hampshire, also lingered at the National Hotel. Damp weather had brought him up lame as he returned to his regiment from convalescent leave. The colonel had suffered three wounds in as many battles, and Pennsylvania Avenue offered a convenient spot from which to decide whether to resign or seek a brigadier's star. The chances of promotion seemed at least fair, for the president had appointed a host of dunderheads and scoundrels of late, as Cross and other senior officers noted. "What has become of the act of Congress requiring aspiring generals to have distinguished themselves on the field?" wondered a New York colonel of artillery, while Cross rested at the National. "Mr. Lincoln would have hard work to designate the place and time in which some of his candidates won their laurels." Cross himself observed that Lincoln had reappointed one brigadier who had been court-martialed for drunkenness and attempted rape, and another whom the Senate had rejected for incompetence.[10]

With his numerous scars, commendations, and experience, Cross would have had good reason to anticipate success had he not been so outspoken a Democrat, but while in Washington he learned that the Republican "fanatiks" of his state's congressional delegation were well versed on his political viewpoints — including his aversion to abolitionists and his conviction that brigadiers could not be confirmed unless they subscribed to "the malice of Niggerism." He swallowed his antipathy for abolitionists long enough to have Senator John P. Hale escort him to the White House on March 11 for an interview with Lincoln. The president listened attentively to a slightly exaggerated version of the colonel's credentials and promised him the commission, but then Lincoln scrawled a message to the secretary of war that fell conspicuously short of an actual appointment, instead merely noting that Cross had appealed for promotion on the merits of his record. Stanton evidently felt no obligation to take the matter any further, helping to confirm Cross's suspicions of political favoritism. Sixteen weeks later Cross died leading his brigade into battle, still wearing a colonel's eagles.[11]

While Cross communed with his commander in chief, his best friend back in their New Hampshire hometown, Henry Kent, struggled in vain to complete his own regiment of infantry for the nine-month service. Six months of earnest effort had brought only three partial companies into the camp of the nominal 17th New Hampshire. While Kent strove to gather enough companies to confirm his commission, the 2nd New Hampshire had come home to augment the Republican vote and, incidentally, to enjoy a little respite from camp and battlefield. The depleted ranks of that seasoned regiment caused the secretary of war to leer enviously at Kent's stalled fragment as a potential reinforcement, but the recruits of the 17th balked at such a sacrifice of their organizational identity — and perhaps at the prospect of immediate assignment to the front ranks.[12]

For twelve long, delicious weeks the veterans of the 2nd New Hampshire enjoyed the labor and leisure of home: they embarked on evening sleigh rides with their neighbors or sweethearts, adapting the use of their buffalo robes accordingly; they cut firewood; they tapped sugar maples in the sweetest season of the New England year, forgetting momentarily about the mud and misery of Virginia or the chicanery and corruption of Washington. For some the respite proved too tantalizing, and convinced them to throw off the military yoke permanently. Dozens of them finagled discharges or resigned during the furlough, and no fewer than thirty-four men, representing more than half of an average company, either failed to return from the furlough or slipped away at each transfer point on the journey back to Washington. Contrary to the provost marshal general's postwar representation of desertion as "a crime of foreign rather than native birth," native-born New Englanders composed the vast majority of those deserters.[13]

Henry Kent's regiment was the only military unit under organization in New Hampshire during the first three months of 1863, and no new men had enrolled in it since before Christmas. Other states found recruiting equally difficult, or nearly so. The volunteer army — even a mercenary volunteer army — seemed dead. Passage of the Conscription Act attracted no new disciples to defend an increasingly centralized federal authority, and it may have alienated many of those who had already enlisted: their motives doubtless varied, but more than a quarter of the recruits in the 17th New Hampshire deserted after the enactment of a law so odious to independent Yankees. War weariness clearly afflicted the civilian population as badly as it did the soldiers, but with another sweeping exercise in coercion the federal government had found a way to continue its war even in the face of popular reluctance, at least for the duration of one more Congress.[14]

NOTES

BIBLIOGRAPHY

SOURCES AND
ACKNOWLEDGMENTS

INDEX

Notes

AAS: American Antiquarian Society
ALP: Abraham Lincoln Papers, Library of Congress
BGSU: Bowling Green State University
BPL: Boston Public Library
CCHS: Cumberland County Historical Society, Carlisle, Pa.
CG: U.S. Congress, *Congressional Globe*
CHS: Connecticut Historical Society
CinHS: Cincinnati Historical Society
CL: Clements Library, University of Michigan
CWL: Basler, *The Collected Works of Abraham Lincoln*
CWP: Sears, *The Civil War Papers of George B. McClellan*
DC: Dartmouth College
DU: Duke University
IHS: Indiana Historical Society
ISL: Indiana State Library
ISU: Iowa State University Archives
IWA: Iowa Women's Archives, University of Iowa Libraries
KSHS: Kansas State Historical Society
LC: Library of Congress (Manuscripts Division, unless otherwise specified)
MEHS: Maine Historical Society
MHS: Massachusetts Historical Society
MNHS: Minnesota Historical Society
NA: National Archives
ND: Notre Dame University
NH Archives: New Hampshire Division of Records Management and Archives
NHHS: New Hampshire Historical Society
NHSL: New Hampshire State Library
OHS: Ohio Historical Society
OR: War of the Rebellion: A Compilation of the Official Records of the Union and Confederate Armies (all citations from Series 1 unless otherwise noted)
OR Atlas: Atlas to Accompany the Official Records of the Union and Confederate Armies
PEM: Peabody Essex Museum
PPL: Providence Public Library

RIHS: Rhode Island Historical Society
RJCCW: Report of the Joint Committee on the Conduct of the War
SHC: University of North Carolina, Southern Historical Collection
SHSI-DM: State Historical Society of Iowa, Des Moines
SHSI-IC: State Historical Society of Iowa, Iowa City
SHSM: State Historical Society of Missouri
SHSN: State Historical Society of Nebraska
SHSW: State Historical Society of Wisconsin
SM: Sheldon Museum
TSLA: Tennessee State Library and Archives
UIA: University of Iowa Libraries
UNH: University of New Hampshire
UR: University of Rochester
USAMHI: U.S. Army Military History Institute
UVM: University of Vermont
VPISU: Virginia Polytechnic Institute and State University
VTHS: Vermont Historical Society
WRHS: Western Reserve Historical Society

1. Over Them the Swallows Skim

1. Taft Diary, January 29–February 5, 1862, LC.
2. *CG*, 37th Cong., 2nd sess., part 1, 564, 642–44.
3. Ibid., 89, 287, 391–93, 395. See numerous Northern offers of military goods and services in February and March of 1861, on Reel 1 of Letters Received by the Confederate Secretary of War (M-437), NA.
4. *CG*, 37th Cong., 2nd sess., part 1, 126.
5. See Marvel, *Mr. Lincoln Goes to War,* 185–87, 197–98.
6. *CG*, 37th Cong., 2nd sess., part 1, 391–93, 419.
7. Ibid., 431–35, 447–54, 470–77, 559–64.
8. Ibid., 585–89.
9. Ibid., 391, 591; Pease and Randall, *Browning Diary,* 1:529.
10. *CG*, 37th Cong., 2nd sess., part 1, 393, 539, 541, and part 4, 37–42.
11. *CG*, 37th Cong., 2nd sess., part 1, 644–55.
12. Burlingame, *With Lincoln,* 66, 67, 68; French, *Witness,* 384; Jessie Benton Frémont manuscript, quoted in Nevins, *Frémont,* 552.
13. Burlingame, *With Lincoln,* 216, n. 21; *Washington Star,* February 6, 1862; Nordholt, "The Civil War Letters of the Dutch Ambassador," 361, 364; Laas, *Wartime Washington,* 102.
14. Jessie Benton Frémont manuscript, quoted in Nevins, *Frémont,* 552–53; Herr and Spence, *Letters of Jessie Benton Frémont,* 311–12.
15. *RJCCW*, 2:502, 504; Beale, *Bates Diary,* 229.
16. Pease and Randall, *Browning Diary,* 1:529; Burlingame, *With Lincoln,* 68.
17. Pinkerton to McClellan, February 6, 1862, Reel 16, McClellan Papers, LC; *RJCCW*, 2:502–4.
18. Pease and Randall, *Browning Diary,* 1:524; "Trumbull Correspondence," 103; Salmon P. Chase to William Pitt Fessenden, January 15, 1862, with Fessenden's endorsement, Reel 1, Stanton Papers, LC. The Chase letter is quoted in the transcribed statement of Francis Fessenden.
19. Joshua Giddings to George Julian, January 28, 1862, Book 4, Giddings-Julian Papers, LC; J. H. Jordan to Henry Wilson, December 23, 1861, Reel 3, Wade Papers, LC; William Doubleday to Chandler from New York, December 6, 1861, Reel 1, Chandler Papers, LC.

20. *RJCCW,* 1:75, 76, 78, and 2:502.

21. Stanton to Dana, January 24 and February 1, 1862, quoted in Dana, *Recollections,* 4–6; Stanton to Dana, February 7, 1862, Box 1, Lincoln Papers, Yale.

22. Henry W. Halleck to Ethan Allen Hitchcock, April 18, 1862, and Hitchcock to "Dear Cox," undated (but spring, 1862), Hitchcock Papers, LC.

23. Statement of charges by William J. Kountz, January 26, 1862, Reel 2, Stanton Papers, LC; *OR,* 7:552.

24. *OR,* 3:271, 310; Seaton, "The Battle of Belmont," 314–18. For a detailed (and somewhat more positive) treatment of the little battle, see Hughes, *Battle of Belmont.*

25. *OR,* 7:79–81, 103–4, 124–25, 153–56.

26. Ibid., 159–60, 166, 618, and Series 2, 3:281–82. For the most positive accounts of Grant's performance that day see Wallace, "The Capture of Fort Donelson," 421–23, and Grant's *Memoirs,* 1:304–8.

27. Ibid., 9:75–79; Seagrave Diary, February 7 and 8, 1862, USAMHI; Daniel Mead to "Dear Sister," February 14, 1862, USAMHI; Gangewer Diary, February 11, 1862, USAMHI; Sally Grattan to Alexander Brown, February 11, 1862, Brown Papers, DU.

28. Norton and Howe, *Letters of Charles Eliot Norton,* 1:246, 251.

29. Williams, *Wild Life of the Army,* 70; Truxall, *Respects to All,* 67–68.

30. Rundell, "Despotism of Traitors," 338; Hancock, "The Civil War Diaries of Anna M. Ferris," 234.

31. Carter, *Burge Diary,* 123; Martha Read to Thomas Read, February 16, 1862, Read Family Correspondence, ND; Grimball Diary, February 27, 1862, SHC; William W. Henry to Mary Jane Henry, February 23, 1862, Henry Family Papers, VTHS.

32. Burlingame, *With Lincoln,* 70–71; Pease and Randall, *Browning Diary,* 1:530; Taft Diary, February 20 and 24, 1862, LC; Palmer, *Selected Letters,* 2:101; Browning to Isaac Arnold, November 25, 1872, transcript in the James G. Randall Papers, LC.

33. Stanton to "My dear Sister," March 24, 1862, Stanton Papers, OHS.

34. George W. Morgan to "My Dear Governor," February 20, 1862, Medary Papers, OHS; *OR,* Series 3, 1:964; Joseph Holt to Stanton, February 27, 1862, and undated "Order Respecting Newspaper Reporters," Reel 2, Stanton Papers, LC; *CWL,* 7:285.

35. Burlingame, *With Lincoln,* 69–70.

36. *OR,* Series 2, 2:221–23. For confidence derived from the loyalty reported on the Florence naval raid, see Burlingame, *With Lincoln,* 71, and Hammond, *Diary,* 103.

37. Pease and Randall, *Browning Diary,* 1:523; *OR,* 5:41.

38. *CWL,* 5:34–35; *OR,* 5:42–45.

39. *OR,* 5:46 and 7:641.

40. Ibid., 5:48–49, 726–30.

41. Burlingame, *With Lincoln,* 72–73, 217–18.

42. *OR,* 7:424–25, 8:58–62 and 191–92, 9:197–99; Simpson Diary, March 4–7, 1862, USAMHI.

43. *New York Tribune,* February 13, 1862; *Cleveland Plain Dealer,* March 19, 20, 21, 24, 1862; Francis Sturtevant to "My Dear Mother," March 4, 1862, UVM.

44. Albert A. Andrews to "Dear Brother and Sister," March 9, 1862, CHS; Williams, *Wild Life,* 74.

45. William Scott to "Dear cuson," March 1, 1862, VHS; Lewis F. Cleveland to "Dear Mother," March 2, 1862, USAMHI; Tom Bamber to "Friend Jackson," March 11, 1862, Jackson Papers, SHSW.

46. Scott to Stanton, March 3 and 4, 1862, with Johnson's commissions, Reel 2, Stanton Papers, LC.

47. *OR,* 5:736–38; Taft Diary, March 8, 1862, LC.

48. *OR,* 51(1):548–49; Beale, *Welles Diary,* 1:62–63.

49. Burlingame and Ettlinger, *Inside Lincoln's White House,* 35; Burlingame, *With Lincoln,* 74–75.

50. *CWP*, 199–200; Burlingame and Ettlinger, *Inside Lincoln's White House*, 35.

51. Cutrer, *Longstreet's Aide*, 78–79, 81; *OR*, 51(2):487–88, and 5:526–28, 537, 549.

52. Holden, Ross, and Slomba, *Stand Firm*, 103–4.

53. French, *Witness*, 391; Gurowski to Zachariah Chandler, March 8, 1862, Reel 1, Chandler Papers, and to Benjamin Wade, March 13 or 14, 1862, Reel 4, Wade Papers, both in LC.

54. Sparks, *Inside Lincoln's Army*, 50–51, 59.

55. *Cleveland Plain Dealer*, March 18, 1862.

56. *CWL*, 5:149–51; *OR*, 5:739; Beale, *Bates Diary*, 239; *CWP*, 201–2.

57. Burlingame and Ettlinger, *Inside Lincoln's White House*, 36; *CWL*, 5:151. Seward's personal appearance is described by Henry Adams in *Education*, 104.

58. *CWP*, 206, 207; *OR*, 5:54.

59. *OR*, 5:45, 55–56; *CWP*, 206; Heintzelman Diary, March 12, 1862, Reel 1, Heintzelman Papers, LC.

60. *OR*, 51(1):551; Sparks, *Inside Lincoln's Army*, 53; Niven, *Chase Papers*, 1:332.

61. *OR*, 5:750; *CWP*, 207; *CWL*, 5:157–58.

62. Heintzelman Diary, March 18, 1862, Reel 1, Heintzelman Papers, LC.

63. *OR*, 11(3):10; Beale, *Bates Diary*, 241.

64. Croffut, *Fifty Years*, 438–39; Hitchcock to Stanton, May 13 and 26, 1862, Hitchcock Papers, LC; Pease and Randall, *Browning Diary*, 1:533, 539.

65. *OR*, 5:46; "Warren" [Thomas W. Beddoe] to Harriet Beddoe, April 1, 1862, CHS.

66. Scarborough, *Ruffin Diary*, 2:269–70; Sears, *Country Cause, & Leader*, 214; George W. Moran to "Dear Mother," April 10, 1862, NHHS.

67. *OR*, 11(1):6, 9, 285, 298–99.

68. Pease and Randall, *Browning Diary*, 1:538–39.

69. Ibid., 539; Niven, *Chase Papers*, 1:322.

70. *OR*, 5:56, 61, and 11(3):62.

71. *OR*, 11(3):65–66, 68, 71, 74, 86, 90.

72. George Moran to "Dear Mother," April 10, 1862, NHHS; Dan Mason to Harriet Clark, April 24, 1862, and H. L. Suydam to Justin Morrill, April 23, 1862, William Farrar Smith Papers, both in VTHS.

73. George Redlon to "Dear Father," April 13, 1862, MEHS; Sears, *Country, Cause & Leader*, 220; Weld, *War Diary*, 98; Alden Buttrick to "My Dear Cousin Lucy," May 1, 1862, Brimblecom Family Papers, Yale.

74. Laas, *Wartime Washington*, 125–26; French, *Witness*, 392–93; *OR*, 11(3):79.

75. *CWL*, 5:184–85.

76. Pease and Randall, *Browning Diary*, 1:540; Beale, *Bates Diary*, 248–49.

77. *OR*, 12(1):335–37; 9:534–45; 10(2):367–71.

78. Niven, *Chase Papers*, 1:312, 3:112–14, 126–27, 141, 183; George Redlon to "Dear Father," April 13, 1862, MEHS.

79. *CG*, 37th Cong., 2nd sess., part 1, 679–95, 787–804, and part 2, 994; Burlingame, *Dispatches*, 68.

80. Dyer, *Compendium*, 1375, 1409, 1424; *OR*, Series 3, 1:671, 675.

81. Jackson Parker to "Dear Father & Mother," April 12 and June 1, 1862, VTHS; Hutchinson, "History of the Fourth New Hampshire," Roster, 134, 158, 182, 187, 190, 197, 199, 201, Laconia Public Library.

82. Arvilla Thompson to "Dear Children," January 7, 1862, Aldrich-Thompson Family Papers, NHHS; Josyph, *Wounded River*, 48. "Poor men almost invariably make up our armies," wrote Confederate Major General Thomas Hindman late in 1862: see *OR*, 22(1):145.

83. James Brown to "Dear Brother," April 13, 1864, MEHS; Snyder, "They Lay Where They Fell," 154; *OR*, Series 3, 1:721–22.

84. Seventh U.S. Census (M-432), Reel 429, 19–20, Eighth U.S. Census (M-653), Reel 667, 934, and Ninth U.S. Census (M-593), Reel 837, 274, RG 29, NA.

85. *Daily American,* August 9 and 10, 1861; *CG,* 37th Cong., 2nd sess., part 1, 135.

86. Ayling, *Register,* 310, 490; *Daily Chronicle,* November 15, 1861; Eben Meader pension application, certificate No. 274244, RG 15, NA.

87. Ayling, *Register,* 373, 383; Lucy Hamilton widow's pension application 436291 and Hannah Meader widow's pension certificate 247503, RG 15, NA.

88. *CG,* 37th Cong., 2nd sess., part 1, 118–19, 146; Isaac Webb to "Dear Father," February 18, 1862, MEHS. The resolution eventually succeeded.

89. Beale, *Bates Diary,* 239.

90. *OR,* Series 3, 2, 2–3; Augusta Kidder to Olivia Brown, May 18, 1862, Brown Papers, SHSW.

91. Burlingame, *Dispatches,* 70; George M. Redlon to "Dear Father," April 13, 1862, MEHS.

92. Welker, *Keystone Rebel,* 83; *OR,* 10, 385–86.

93. Throne, *Boyd Diary,* 42; Amos Currier to "Dear Bro Stoddard," March 26, 1862, Currier Papers, SHSI-IC; Throne, "Civil War Letters of Abner Dunham," 310.

94. Welker, *Keystone Rebel,* 84. Shiloh meetinghouse is described in a letter fragment, John D. Pugh to an unidentified correspondent in the spring of 1862 (Achilles Pugh Papers, Earlham). Notwithstanding the size of a modern reconstruction, Pugh — a Quaker who examined the building during a stint as a volunteer nurse soon after the battle — characterized it as "a small log church not quite as large as our smoke house."

95. *OR,* 10:100–105, 386–87, 395; Welker, *Keystone Rebel,* 84–85; Magee Diary, DU, April 6, 1862; William R. Stimson to "Dear Wife and little Children," April 10, 1862, and St. John Diary, April 6, 1862, both in LC; Henry Huffer to "Dear wife and children," April 13, 1862, USAMHI. See Daniel, *Shiloh,* on the battle.

96. *OR,* 10: 386–87; Andrew F. Davis to "Dear Brother," April 21, 1862, USAMHI; Niven, *Chase Papers,* 3:168; Samuel M. Buford to "Dear Charlie," April 21, 1862, Buford Papers, LC.

97. Niven, *Chase Papers,* 3:168, 172–74; Emerson Opdycke to "My dear Father," May 25, 1862, Reel 1, Opdycke Papers, OHS. Through either exaggeration or orthographic error, Nelson wrote that Grant's perimeter covered only "5" acres: a semicircle with a radius of four hundred yards would exceed fifty acres.

98. Williams, *Wild Life of the Army,* 82; Hitchcock to "Dear Cox," undated, and Halleck to Hitchcock, April 18, 1862, Hitchcock Papers, LC; *Cincinnati Gazette,* April 14, 1862; *OR,* 10:98. Halleck's background sniping at Grant has been attributed to jealousy over Grant's potential as a rival (Catton, *Grant Moves South,* 186–88), but see also Marszalek, *Commander of All Lincoln's Armies.*

99. Throne, *Boyd Diary,* 47, 94; Shannon, *Andrus Letters,* 28.

100. Anderson, *Letters and Journals,* 143; Andrew Davis to Sarah Davis, April 17, 1862, Davis Papers, UIA; Andrew Davis to "Dear Brother," April 21, 1862, USAMHI.

101. Samuel Buford to "Dear Charlie," April 21, 1862, Buford Papers, LC; William R. Stimson to "Dear Wife and little Children," April 10, 1862, LC; Jacob Behm to "Dear Brother & Sister," April 27, 1862, USAMHI.

102. Alexander Varian to "Dear Brother," April 10, 1862, WRHS; Williams, *Wild Life of the Army,* 82–83; Truxall, *Respects to All,* 71; Magee Diary, DU, April 7, 1862; Taylor, *Reluctant Rebel,* 36; OR, 10:387.

103. *Burlington Hawk-Eye,* April 18, 1862; Niven, *Chase Papers,* 3:174; Gustave Koerner to Lyman Trumbull, April 24, 1862, LC. In *The War for the Union* (2:84), Allan Nevins mistook Koerner's scrawled signature for that of General John M. Palmer.

104. N. G. Speer to Washburne, April 17, 1862, W. R. Rowley to Washburne, April 19, 1862, and C. C. Washburn to Washburne, April 17, 1862, Washburne Papers, LC; *CG,* 37th

Cong., 2nd sess., part 3, 1931–32, 2036–37. Unlike his two politically active brothers, Elihu Washburne spelled his last name with an *e*.

105. J. E. Smith to Washburne, May 16, 1862, A. L. Chetlain to Washburne, May 24, 1862, and Joseph Medill to Washburne, May 24, 1862, Washburne Papers, LC.

106. McClure, *Lincoln and Men of War-Times,* 195–96; W. R. Rowley to Washburne, May 24, 1862, Washburne Papers, LC.

107. Edgar Pearce to "Dear Folks at Home," April 10, 1862, Gilder Lehrman Collection, New-York Historical Society; George Thomas to "Dear Minerva," April 27, 1862, Thomas Family Correspondence, ND; William J. Palmer to Robert Henry Lamborn, April 1, 1862, Palmer Letters, Yale.

108. Andrew Davis to Sarah Davis, April 17, 1862, Davis Papers, UIA; John St. John to "Dear Father," April 14, 1862, St. John Papers, LC.

109. *OR,* 10(1):107–8, 112; Alison Diary, April 9, 1862, SHC; Perry Journal, April 19, 1862, SHC; Harwell, *Kate,* 14–18.

110. Josyph, *Wounded River,* 48–49; Mary Jane Vaughn Clark to "Dear Sister," May 9, 1862, SHSM.

2. Demons out of the Earth

1. *Cleveland Plain Dealer,* April 9, 1862; *Waterloo Courier,* April 16, 1862; *Daily Evening Courier,* April 21, 1862; *Northern Advocate,* May 13, 1862.

2. Bargus Diary, April 6, 1862, USAMHI; William H. Collins to "Dear Wife," April 10, 1862, SHSI-IC; *OR,* 8:89, 132–33, 10(1):641–42.

3. De Have Norton to "Dear Father," May 3, 1862, Norton Letters, SHSW; *OR,* 6:133–34.

4. Henry M. Vanderbilt to Loren Jesse Ames, May 6, 1862, Ames Papers, UR; Daniel Reed Larned to "My Dear Sister," April "22" [25], 1862, LC; *OR,* 9:281–84.

5. Elizabeth Hammond to "Dear Sister," May 18, 1862, Huffer Letters, USAMHI.

6. Escott, *North Carolina Yeoman,* 321–22; *OR,* Series 4, 1:1095; "Proceedings of the First Confederate Congress," 26–35, 130; Chesnut, *Diary,* 212, 222; Wadley Diary, April 20, 1862, SHC. For some Southern attitudes toward conscription see, for instance, Rable, *Confederate Republic,* 139–41.

7. "Proceedings of the First Confederate Congress," 26; *OR,* Series 4, 1:1095, and Series 3, 2:44–49, 61.

8. Gurowski, *Diary, 1861–1862,* 33–35; Bowen, *A Frontier Family,* 181.

9. Palmer, *Selected Letters,* 2:74; John W. Ames to "My dear Mother," June 21 and 28, 1863, USAMHI.

10. Norton and Howe, *Norton Letters,* 1:246; Blight, *This Cruel War,* 64.

11. Pease and Randall, *Browning Diary,* 1:512.

12. *CWL,* 5:144–46, 152–53; newspapers quoted in Moore, *Rebellion Record,* 4: Documents, 237–39.

13. *Friend,* March 22, 1862; Burlingame, *With Lincoln,* 73.

14. Palmer, *Selected Letters,* 2:104, 105; Burlingame, *With Lincoln,* 73–74.

15. *CG,* 37th Cong., 2nd sess., part 2, 1634.

16. *CG,* 37th Cong., 2nd sess., part 1, 16, 36, 89, 153, 785.

17. *CG,* 37th Cong., 2nd sess., part 2, 1011, 1299–1303, 1319, 1333–39, 1350–60, 1375–80; *CWL,* 2:20–22.

18. *Hartford Courant,* April 1, 1862; *CG,* 37th Cong., 2nd sess., part 2, 1446–50, 1516–17, 1524.

19. *CG,* 37th Cong., 2nd sess., part 2, 1467–79, 1490–1504, 1520.

20. *CG,* 37th Cong., 2nd sess., part 2, 1564, 1634–38, 1645–48; Taft Diary, April 11, 1862, LC.

21. Pease and Randall, *Browning Diary*, 1:541; Palmer, *Selected Letters*, 109.

22. Beecher to Lincoln, April 16, Reel 34, ALP; *Friend's Intelligencer*, April 26, 1862.

23. H. C. Parke to Lincoln, May 6, 1862, and John B. Hepburn to Lincoln, May 7, 1862, ALP.

24. Nevins and Thomas, *Strong Diary*, 3:106, 216, 217.

25. *OR*, Series 3, 2:42, 57, 59-60.

26. *OR*, 11(1):399-401; Burlingame, *With Lincoln*, 77.

27. *OR*, 11(1):448-49; Beale, *Bates Diary*, 255, 256.

28. Niven, *Chase Papers*, 1:336-44; Pease and Randall, *Browning Diary*, 1:545.

29. Niven, *Chase Papers*, 1:344; *CWL*, 5:219.

30. *OR*, Series 3, 2:42-43, 45, 174; *Cleveland Plain Dealer*, May 28 and 31, 1862.

31. Ray, *Diary of a Dead Man*, 33-38. Pettit died at the Andersonville, Georgia, prison camp in 1864.

32. William W. Winthrop to "Dear Family," May 3, 1862, Winthrop-Weston Family Papers, Yale; Crosby Diary, April 9, 1862, Yale.

33. Hughes, *Colby Papers*, 7, 126-30.

34. *OR*, Series 3, 2:61-62; Ayling, *Register*, 986-88.

35. Gilmore to Berry, May 31, 1862, and to Chester Stevens, June 7 and 9, 1862, Executive Correspondence, NH Archives; Recruiting Stations Records, Adjutant General's Records, NH Archives.

36. *OR*, Series 3, 2:61-68, 76; Sawyer, *Godfrey Letters*, 5.

37. *OR*, Series 3, 2:61, 64; Thomas Blanchard to Sarah Walker, June 15, 1862, ND.

38. *CG*, 37th Cong., 2nd sess., part 1, 133-35, 136, 139.

39. *CG*, 37th Cong., 2nd sess., part 3, 1035-36, 1347, 1915-16, 1951, 2061, 2147-48, 2263.

40. Willard Diary, April 22, 1862, LC; *RJCCW*, 3:436.

41. Mathew Hopkins to Albert Fletcher, April 27, 1862, SM; *OR*, 12(3):135, 170, 196, 885-6; Sparks, *Inside Lincoln's Army*, 73-79.

42. Sparks, *Inside Lincoln's Army*, 79; *OR*, 12(3):196; Ransom Towle to "Dear Sister" May 18, 1862, VTHS.

43. *OR*, 11(1):28-29, 11(3):184; *CWL*, 5:219.

44. *OR*, 12(1):10.

45. *OR*, 11(1):26-27; Gurowski, *Diary, 1861-1862*, 210-12; Burlingame, *With Lincoln*, 78.

46. Niven, *Chase Papers*, 3:203.

47. *OR*, 12(3):214.

48. Ibid., 160, 161, 202, 207-8, 213-14; 309; *RJCCW*, 3:428.

49. Pease and Randall, *Browning Diary*, 1:546; *OR*, 12(3):214; *RJCCW*, 3:428.

50. Sparks, *Inside Lincoln's Army*, 75, 82; *OR*, 11(1):30, 12(3):219, and 51(1):75; Niven, *Chase Papers*, 1:345.

51. *OR*, 12(1):555-8, 702-3.

52. Blair, *A Politician Goes to War*, ix; *OR*, 12(3):215, 224; *Wood County Independent*, July 9, 1862.

53. Eby, *Virginia Yankee*, 39-41; Duncan, *Blue-Eyed Child*, 204; Raab, *With the 3rd Wisconsin*, 68.

54. Duncan, *Blue-Eyed Child*, 203-4; Eby, *Virginia Yankee*, 42; Quaife, *Cannon's Mouth*, 79-82.

55. Marshall Barrus to "Dear Brother and Sister," June 13, 1862, Barrus Family Papers, UNH; Eby, *Virginia Yankee*, 42-45; Quaife, *Cannon's Mouth*, 82-84.

56. Niven, *Chase Papers*, 1:345; *OR*, 12(3):219, 228; *RJCCW*, 1:684.

57. John Wool to P. H. Watson, May 24, 1862, Reel 3, Stanton Papers, LC; *OR*, Series 3, 2:68.

58. *Baltimore American,* May 26, 1862; Burlingame, *With Lincoln,* 78–79.

59. *OR,* Series 3, 2:68–72; Ayling, *Register,* 1089–95; *Cleveland Plain Dealer,* May 27, 1862.

60. Phelon Diary, May 27, 1862, RIHS; Virgil Taylor to "Dear Maggie," June 1, 1862, Bunt Family Papers, WRHS; James F. Wade to "Dear Mother," June 7, 1862, Reel 4, Wade Papers, LC; W. Hazen Noyes to "Dear Mother," May 25, 1862, USAMHI.

61. Quaife, *Cannon's Mouth,* 83–87; Eby, *Virginia Yankee,* 45. The first recorded notice of "skedaddle" appears to have been in the *New York Tribune* of August 10, 1861, which defined it as "a phrase the Union boys up here apply to the good use seceshers make of their legs in time of danger." By the spring of 1862 those Union boys were using it to describe their own retreats.

62. Quaife, *Cannon's Mouth,* 75, 87, 90; Duncan, *Blue-Eyed Child,* 204.

63. *OR,* 12(3):320, 395.

64. *OR,* Series 3, 2:76–77, 94; Dyer, *Compendium,* 1076–77, 1140, 1535–36, 1408–22, 1431–32, 1635.

65. *Cleveland Plain Dealer,* May 31, 1862; Virgil Taylor to "Dear Maggie," May 29, 1862, Bunt Family Papers, WRHS.

66. L. Eastebrook to B. F. Burnside, September 17, 1861, Burnside Papers, RIHS; *Chicago Tribune,* April 18, 1862; *Hartford Courant,* April 26, 1862; Catherine M. Snedeker to Catherine E. L. Snedeker, May 14, 1862, IWA; Dyer, *Compendium,* 1074–75.

67. Sarah E. Fales to Edmund Fales, May 4, 1862, Fales Family Papers, RIHS.

68. *CWL,* 5:235–36; Pease and Randall, *Browning Diary,* 1:547; *OR,* Series 3, 2:85.

69. *War Letters, 1862–1865,* 47; *OR,* 12(3):219, 220; Croffut, *Fifty Years,* 447. McClellan has been much criticized for his performance before Richmond, and with good reason, but his numerical advantage over Johnston was roughly the same as that enjoyed by Grant over Lee two years later. Grant nevertheless consumed nearly ten months accomplishing what McClellan was apparently expected to do within a season or so. The additional pressure of McDowell on Johnston's left would have been almost impossible to resist, as Lee clearly recognized when Pope began preparing a similar advance with a similar force.

70. *CWP,* 273–75; *OR,* 12(1):142–44, 668–69, 812; Holden, Ross, and Slomba, *Stand Firm,* 24–25.

71. Luther Lawrence to "Dear Brother," May 25, 1862, North Yarmouth Historical Society.

72. Robertson, *McAllister Letters,* 167; William Henry Croop to "Dear Father," June 17, 1862, USAMHI.

73. Robertson, *McAllister Letters,* 167–68; Kearny to Cortlandt Parker, "Just after Fair Oaks," Kearny Papers, LC; Walter Bartlett to "Dear Sister," June 21, 1862, Bartlett Family Papers, UR.

74. Howe, *Touched with Fire,* 47–50; Holden, Ross, and Slomba, *Stand Firm,* 27–34; *OR,* 12(1):933–35, 992–93. As was often the case with runaway officers, Major James Madison DeWitt of the 71st Pennsylvania was honorably discharged seven weeks later (Acken, *Inside the Army of the Potomac,* 88, 448, n. 32).

75. Cutrer, *Longstreet's Aide,* 87–88; Hassler, *One of Lee's Best Men,* 152.

76. Scott, *Fallen Leaves,* 129; Robertson, *McAllister Letters,* 168; Coco, *Ball's Bluff to Gettysburg,* 99.

77. Lewis F. Cleveland to "Dear Louise," June 21, 1862, and to "Dear Mother," June 24, 1862, USAMHI.

78. Lomax, *Washington Diary,* 198; Laas, *Wartime Washington,* 153–54.

79. Nevins and Thomas, *Strong Diary,* 3:229; Duncan, *Blue-Eyed Child,* 210.

80. Beale, *Bates Diary,* 260; Beale, *Welles Diary,* 2:633.

81. See Chandler to Lyman Trumbull, September 10, 1862, Reel 13, Trumbull Papers, LC, and Chandler to P. W. Watson, September 10, 1862, Reel 4, Stanton Papers, LC.

82. Heitman, *Historical Register*, 1:1047; *Cleveland Plain Dealer*, May 22, 1862; Nevins and Thomas, *Strong Diary*, 3:243; *OR*, 11(1):436, 692.

83. Pease and Randall, *Browning Diary*, 1:548; Beale, *Bates Diary*, 261; Burlingame, *With Lincoln*, 81.

84. Palmer, *Sumner Letters*, 2:118; *OR*, 11(1):200–201, and 11(3):207; *CWL*, 5:255.

85. *OR*, 12(3):336, 347, 349, 354, 355,

86. *OR*, 11(3):220–21, and 12(3):391; *CWP*, 293; Sparks, *Inside Lincoln's Army*, 46, 53.

87. B. F. Craig to "Dear Col.," June 15, 1862, Hunt Papers, LC; *OR*, 12(3):379–81, 391–93, 405, 410, 417.

88. Thomas Key to Edwin Stanton, June 16, 1862, Reel 3, Stanton Papers, LC; *OR*, 11(1):1057–60.

89. Daniel Reed Larned to "My Dear Sister," June 16, 1862, LC; Burnside to McClellan, June 13, 1862, Reel 25, McClellan Papers, LC; *CWP*, 295.

90. Pope to Lincoln, January 27, 1861, ALP; *CWL*, 4:411.

91. *CWL*, 2:53–54; Niven, *Chase Papers*, 1:69 and 2:459; *OR*, 17(2):17.

92. Burlingame, *With Lincoln*, 81, and *At Lincoln's Side*, 109.

93. Pease and Randall, *Browning Diary*, 1:552.

94. *OR*, 17(2):17–18, 20.

95. Sparks, *Inside Lincoln's Army*, 97; Eby, *Virginia Yankee*, 65; Willard Diary, June 19, 1862, LC; John Viles to "Frank," June 18, 1862, USAMHI.

96. *OR*, 51(1):79; Niven, *Chase Papers*, 2:220–21; Willard Diary, June 16 and 21, 1862, LC.

97. Niven, *Chase Papers*, 3:221; Winfield Scott memorandum, June 24, 1862, ALP.

98. *OR*, 11(3):264–65.

99. *OR*, 12(3):435; Pope, "The Second Battle of Bull Run," 449–50.

100. *OR*, 12(3):437–38, 444; Eby, *Virginia Yankee*, 63, 65.

101. Eby, *Virginia Yankee*, 64–65.

3. The Spires of Richmond, Late Beheld

1. *CWP*, 307; Leaver to "My Dear Mother," June 24, 1862, NHHS.

2. *OR*, 11(2):108–10, 121, 173–75; John Stevens to "Dear Brother & Sister," June 26, 1862, NHHS; Haynes, *Minor War History*, 58; Sears, *On Campaign*, 29–31.

3. Philip Kearny to Agnes Kearny, June 26, 1862, Kearny Papers, LC; Ayling, *Register*, 64.

4. *OR*, 11(3):252–54; *CWP*, 309–10.

5. Jackson was long criticized for his failure to attack Porter on June 26, until A. Wilson Greene deduced that Jackson had strictly complied with orders composed under a misapprehension of geography. Lee had anticipated that Jackson's march would, by itself, force Porter to retreat, and that there would be no need for Jackson to attack (Greene, *Whatever You Resolve to Be*, 46, 48). Jackson's recent biographer adopted Greene's argument, as well (Robertson, *Stonewall Jackson*, 472–73).

6. Ransom Towle to "Dear Friends," June 26, 1862, VTHS.

7. *OR*, 11(2):384–87, 834–36; Judd Diary, June 26, 1862, KSHS; Wolf, "Taylor Diary," 140.

8. *OR*, 11(3):259; *CWP*, 315, 317.

9. The most careful, insightful, and engaging study of McClellan's performance during the campaign is Sears, *To the Gates of Richmond*.

10. *OR*, 11(2):223–26, 491–93, 553–56, 562–64; Tilton Diary, June 27, 1862, MHS; Robertson, *McAllister Letters*, 186.

11. *CWP*, 322–23.

12. Sears, *On Campaign*, 34; Sears, *Country, Cause & Leader*, 256.

13. Judd Diary, June 27–28, 1862, KSHS; Heffelfinger Diary, June 27–29, 1862, USAMHI; *OR*, 11(1):190–91, and (2):556, 627. Stonewall Jackson estimated capturing 3,000 Union patients and medical staff at Savage's Station; his brother-in-law, Major General Daniel Harvey Hill, only counted 1,100, but McClellan's medical director implied that fewer than 650 were taken. In the Union ranks, soldiers heard of 400 to 500 sick and wounded captured, with 50 attendants (Coco, *Ball's Bluff to Gettysburg*, 106).

14. Heintzelman Diary, June 28, 1862, and journal, same date, Reels 1 and 7, Heintzelman Papers, LC; William Candler to "My dear Brother," July 7, 1862, Candler Papers, VPISU.

15. Cooledge Diary, June 29, 1862, VTHS; Walter Hurd to "Dear Mother," "28/62" [but early July, 1862], SM; John F. Cook to "Friend Olin," July 18, 1862, VTHS; Keiser Diary, June 28–29, 1862, USAMHI.

16. J. C. McMichael to Elizabeth Rooke, July 5, 1862, LC; Sears, *On Campaign*, 34–35; Coco, *Ball's Bluff to Gettysburg*, 106; Rosenblatt and Rosenblatt, *Hard Marching*, 38.

17. Wolf, "Taylor Diary," 141; Cooledge Diary, June 30 through July 3, 1862, VTHS.

18. Benjamin Ashenfelter to "Father Churchman," July 7, 1862, USAMHI; *OR*, 11(2):330–31, 333; Edwin Stanton to McClellan and McClellan's reply, both June 7, 1862, Reel 3, Stanton Papers, LC.

19. *OR*, 11(1):65; John Burrill to "Dear Parents," July 5, 1862, USAMHI; Hassler, *One of Lee's Best Men*, 161; Philip Kearny to Agnes Kearny, July 9, 1862, Kearny Papers, LC.

20. Cutrer, *Longstreet's Aide*, 95; Robertson, *McAllister Letters*, 187.

21. Charles E. Goddard to Catharine Smith, July 6, 1862, MNHS; Sears, *Country, Cause & Leader*, 260.

22. Sears, *On Campaign*, 35; Coco, *Ball's Bluff to Gettysburg*, 108.

23. *OR*, 11(2):496, 629; Haynes, *Minor War History*, 59.

24. *OR*, 11(2):629, and (1):70; Heintzelman Diary, July 1, 1862, Heintzelman Papers, LC.

25. Scott, *Fallen Leaves*, 136; John Burrill to "Dear Parents," August 8, 1862, USAMHI.

26. *OR*, 11(3):282, 287–88.

27. John D. St. John to "Dear Parents," March 26, 1862, LC; Solomon Hamrick to A. D. Hamrick, June 28, 1862, IHS.

28. Andrew Knox to "My dear wife," June 18, 1862, USAMHI; Blight, *This Cruel War*, 152, 174–75.

29. Samuel Partridge to Francis Macomber, July 6 and 25, 1862, and Partridge's disapproved resignation of August 9, 1862, Macomber Papers, UR; Walter Bartlett to "Dear Sister," July 7 and August 14, 1862, Bartlett Family Papers, UR; Elijah Cavins to "Dear Father," July 18, 1862, Cavins Papers, IHS.

30. *Atlas and Argus*, July 7, 1862; *OR*, 11(3):274–75, and Series 2, 4:108–9. It is not clear whether Stanton arrested Fulton for revealing the military situation or for announcing that Stanton had arbitrarily banned such reporting; neither is it obvious why Stanton blocked Fulton's erroneously positive information in the first place.

31. *Inquirer*, July 7 and 8, 1862; *Atlas and Argus*, July 4, 1862. On June 20 McClellan had more than 127,000 men present, with 115,000 present for duty; Lee never fielded as many as 95,000.

32. Elijah Brown to "Dear Sister Frankey," July 14, 1862, Brown Letters, VTHS; Nevins and Thomas, *Strong Diary*, 3:236–37.

33. Pease and Randall, *Browning Diary*, 1:559; French, *Witness*, 400–401.

34. *OR*, 11(3):290, 322, 9:407, and 11(1):71; Ford, *A Cycle of Adams Letters*, 1:164–65.

35. *OR*, Series 3, 2:179–80.

36. Benjamin Wade to Caroline Wade, October 25, 1861, Wade Papers, LC; *CWL*, 5:83; John Mechan to Seward, February 9, 1862, Reel 68, Seward Papers, UR.

37. *OR*, Series 3, 2:181–82, 186.

38. Ibid., 186–87.

39. Ibid., 186–87, 198–99.

40. Ibid., 180–88; *Cleveland Plain Dealer, Atlas and Argus,* and *Chicago Tribune,* all July 2, 1862.

41. *OR,* Series 3, 2:188, 196, 199–201, 203, and Series 1, 12(3):281; *CWL,* 5:304.

42. *Hartford Courant,* July 4, 1862; *Cleveland Plain Dealer,* July 5, 1862; *Atlas and Argus,* July 3, 1862.

43. *Blackburn Standard,* December 4, 1861 and April 23, 1862, quoted in Ellison, *Support for Secession,* 38–39, 136; J. Loder [?] to Henry Churchyard, May 20, 1862, SHSW.

44. *Blackburn Standard,* July 2, 1862, quoted in Ellison, *Support for Secession,* 136; *Commercial Daily List,* July 1, 3, and 10, 1862; Ford, *A Cycle of Adams Letters,* 1:164. Mary Ellison provides a detailed examination of this issue, dismantling the myth that British factory operatives supported Lincoln's war as a crusade against slavery.

45. *The Constitution,* July 8, 1862; Nevins and Thomas, *Strong Diary,* 3:237; Hammond, *Diary,* 158–59.

46. *Chicago Tribune,* July 4 and 6, 1862; Gustavus Soule to "Cousin Hattie," July 21, 1862, USAMHI; John C. Holwell to "Dear Wife," July 14 and 27, 1862, CHS.

47. Josiah C. Fuller to "My dear Wife," July 13, 1862, Fuller Papers, MHS.

48. *OR,* Series 3, 2:199, 201–6, 212, 219, 232.

49. *Citizen and Telegraph,* July 17, 1862; *Cleveland Plain Dealer,* July 7, 1862.

50. *OR,* Series 4, 1:1096; *Proceedings at the Mass Meeting,* 19–20; *OR,* Series 3, 2:223.

51. Ruel Clark to "Dear Mother," May 13, 1862, and Thomas Caldwell to "Dear Brother," July 27, 1862, both at USAMHI; Henry Comey to "Dear Brother," July 28, 1862, Comey Papers, AAS.

52. James Brown to "Brother Tom," September 4, 1862, MEHS; Dan Bennett to Edwin Bennett, October 29, 1862, Bennett Family Papers, SHSI-DM.

53. Samuel Thoman to "Dear Wife and Son," September 19, 1861, USAMHI; Martin Shrenk to Kate and Eli Shrenk, November 24, 1862, CinHS; Daniel Veasey Durgin to "Dear Sis," August 22, 1862, NHHS.

54. "Hal" to "My dear Sister," July 7, 1862, Reel 4, Wade Papers, LC; *Atlas and Argus,* July 7, 1862.

55. *New Hampshire Argus and Spectator,* July 11, 1862; *The Constitution,* July 22, 1862; *Chicago Tribune,* July 9 and 15, 1862; "Margaretta" to Leander Harris, August 10, 1862, UNH; Solomon Hamrich to his father, June 17, 25, 28, and July 27, 1862, IHS; *Cleveland Plain Dealer,* July 10, 1862.

56. *Cleveland Plain Dealer,* July 14, 1862; *Chicago Tribune,* July 6, 1862.

57. M. M. Macomber to Francis Macomber, July 21, 1862, Macomber Papers, UR; Richard Cary Morse Sr. to Richard Cary Morse Jr., July 21 and 23, 1862, Morse Papers, CL.

58. See Miller, "Brahmin Janissaries," on Governor Andrew's elitist appointment policies, and Adams, *Education,* 129, for the ease with which a privileged son could be dissuaded from enlisting.

59. J. P. Blake to Richard Cary Morse Jr., August 16, 1862, and James M. Crosby to Morse, September 5, 1862, Morse Papers, CL.

60. *Prairie du Chien Courier,* July 24, 1862.

61. Albert Rake to "Dear Lucy," April 15, 1862, USAMHI; Agnes Allen to Amasa Allen, November 12, 1862, SHSI-DM; Benjamin Morse to "Dear Rosina," July 4 and September 18, 1862, VTHS.

62. *Boston Journal,* August 13, 1862.

63. *The Constitution,* July 22, 1862; *OR,* Series 3, 2:213, 221; *Hartford Courant,* July 9, 10, 11, and 14, 1862.

64. *OR* Series 3, 2:95, 105, 226–27;

65. Benjamin F. Morse to "Dear Rosina," July 4 and 7, 1862, and John Orlando Morse to Franklin Morse, July 20 and 27 and August 22, 1862, all in Gale-Morse Family Papers, VTHS.

66. Theodore Tillison to Dudley Tillison, December 28, 1862, and May 24, 1863, and Charles Tillison to Dudley Tillison, February 27, April 13, and May 31, 1863, VTHS; Peck, *Revised Roster*, 49, 494, 674.

67. *Chicago Tribune*, July 4, 1862; *Chicago Times*, July 7, 1862.

68. *Cincinnati Daily Commercial*, July 9, 1862; *Cleveland Plain Dealer*, July 9, 1862.

69. *New Hampshire Argus and Spectator*, July 11, 1862; Olmsted to King, July 9, 1862, ALP.

70. *CG*, 37th Cong., 2nd sess., part 4, 3178, 3197–3207, 3227–37, 3249–54.

71. Ibid., 3207–8, 3252, 3254, 3289, 3320–22, 3337–38; *National Eagle*, July 17, 1862. James W. Geary convincingly argues (in *We Need Men*, 22–29) that the emancipation clause served as Wilson's main motivation for sponsoring the bill.

72. *CG*, 37th Cong., 2nd sess., part 4, 3397–98, 3403; Pease and Randall, *Browning Diary*, 1:560; Burlingame, *With Lincoln*, 85.

73. *Detroit Free Press*, July 17, 18, and 20, 1862; Marshall Phillips to "Dear Wife," July 25, 1862, MEHS; Jacob S. Kiester to "Dear Father," July 27, 1862, USAMHI; McCutchan, *"Dearest Lizzie,"* 215.

74. George F. Hall to "Dear Father," August 9, 1862, UIA; George Smith to "Dear Mother," August 9, 1862, Smith Papers, MHS.

75. Elijah Cavins to "Dear Ann," October 25, 1862, IHS; George Upton to "My Dear Sarah," July 17, 1862, NHHS.

76. George C. Fisher to "Miss Emma," August 23, 1862, Suter Papers, USAMHI; George Smith to "Dear Mother," July 11, 1862, Smith Papers, MHS; Charles Cady to "Dear Parents," August 17, 1862, UIA.

77. William Candler to "My dear Brother," July 15, 1862, VPISU.

78. Blegen, *Heg Letters*, 108; Samuel B. Shepard to "Friend Thomas," July 30, 1862, CHS; John Burrill to "Dear Parents," July 26, August 8 and 12, 1862, USAMHI.

79. Henry Heisler to "Dear Sister," August 10 and December 20, 1862, LC; Samuel Partridge to Francis Macomber, July 25 and August 9, 1862, UR.

80. William A. Russell to "Dear Col," November 16, 1862, UI; Jane Thompson to William Thompson, September 13, 1862, SHSI-DM; E. D. Apthorp to Richard Cary Morse Jr., August 9, 1862, and Richard Cary Morse Sr. to same, August 13, 1862, CL.

81. *Chicago Tribune*, July 15 and 16, 1862; *Crisis*, July 30, 1862.

82. *Cleveland Plain Dealer*, July 15, 16, and 17, 1862; *OR*, 16(1):768–69, 813–15.

83. *OR*, Series 3, 2:280–82

84. *OR*, Series 3, 2:290, 370; *The Kansas Chief*, August 14, 1862.

85. Certificate, dated August 21, 1862, Hanscom Papers, SHSW; G. D. Prentice to Levi Turner, [August] 11, [1862], Case 153, Turner-Baker Case Files (M-797), NA; Carolyn White Diary, August 9, 1862, AAS.

86. Charles W. Reed to "Dear Sister," with Samuel Tilton's endorsement, July 25, 1862, LC.

87. H. M. Ridenhower to Lyman Trumbull, July 19, 1862, Trumbull Papers, LC; William G. Purnell to J. A. J. Creswell, July 18, 1862, and John P. Bennett to Cresswell, July 25, 1862, Cresswell Papers, LC.

88. Pease and Randall, *Browning Diary*, 1:558, 560; *CG*, 37th Cong., 2nd sess., part 4, 3379–83, 3400; *CWL*, 5:328–31; *OR*, Series 3, 2:275–77.

89. *CWL*, 5:324–35; *Cleveland Plain Dealer*, July 15 and 22, 1862.

90. George Upton to "My Dear Sarah," July 17, 1862, NHHS; John Burrill to "Dear Parents," July 18, 1862, USAMHI.

91. Niven, *Chase Papers*, 1:348–49.

92. Ibid., 350–51; Beale, *Welles Diary*, 1:70–71; memorandum, July 22, 1862, Reel 3, Stanton Papers, LC.

93. Nevins and Thomas, *Strong Diary*, 3:244; Pease and Randall, *Browning Diary*, 1:561–62.

94. Niven, *Chase Papers*, 1:352; *CWL*, 5:338; *OR*, Series 3, 2:280.

95. *Tri-Weekly Missouri Republican*, July 24, 1862.

96. *Peninsula News and Advertiser*, July 18 and August 1, 1862; *Delaware Journal*, July 29, 1862.

97. *Cleveland Plain Dealer*, July 22, 24, and 26, 1862; John Kehrwecker to "Dear Brother," July 29, 1862, BGSU; *Corning Democrat*, July 31, 1862, quoted in Hughes, *Colby Papers*, 128–29; *Burlington Free Press*, July 28, 29, and 31, 1862.

98. *Buffalo Courier*, August 21, 1862; *Atlas and Argus*, July 25, 26, and August 1, 1862; Edward Klein to "Dear Brother," July 24, 1862, BPL; *Hartford Courant*, July 28, 1862; *Missouri Republican*, July 24, 1862.

99. *Daily Gate City*, July 29, 1862; *Waterloo Courier*, August 6 and 13, 1862.

100. Minutes of War Meeting, Clark Papers, SHSW; *Daily Gate City*, August 21, 1862.

101. *OR*, Series 3, 3:204; Smith to Edwin Stanton, July 29, 1862, Reel 3, Stanton Papers, LC.

102. *National Eagle*, July 3 and August 7, 1862; *Hartford Courant*, July 28, 1862.

103. Halleck to Stanton, August 3, 1862, Reel 3, Stanton Papers, LC.

4. Torrents of Men

1. Beale, *Welles Diary*, 1:104–5, 116, 126. As early as 1866 William Swinton blamed "the war council at Washington" for allowing Jackson's Valley raid to foil McDowell's advance, although he offered no direct criticism of the president, whose assassination remained so fresh in the public mind (*Campaigns*, 125–26).

2. *RJCCW*, 1:638–39, 650; Edgar F. Brown to "Hannah Dearest," July 27, 1862, LC; *CWP*, 372, 376; *OR*, 12(1):80–81; Beale, *Welles Diary*, 1:105, 108. Brown, a New York lawyer staying at Willard's, saw the four generals in conclave and concocted a fantastic story for his wife, in which he dropped in on President Lincoln at the Soldiers' Home and discussed the high command with him. For the first attempt to give the command to Burnside, see Marvel, *Burnside*, 99–100 and 440, n. 6.

3. Eby, *Virginia Yankee*, 70–71; Niven, *Chase* Papers, 1:350–53; *Philadelphia Inquirer*, July 26, 1862; *OR*, 12(2):50–52, and 11(3):362–64; *CWL*, 5:341.

4. *OR*, Series 3, 2:291–92.

5. Clement A. Boughton to "Friends at Home," August 3, 1862, CL; *Northern Advocate*, July 29, 1862; Myron Rice Wood to "My dear home," July 30, 1862, MHS; Sanborn Diary, July 19 and 31, 1862, NHHS; Sewall S. Farwell to "Dear Brother," August 6, 1862, SHSI-IC.

6. *Atlas and Argus*, August 5, 1862; Edson Cheever to "Dear Uncle," October 12, 1862, Marvel Collection; Carolyn White Diary, AAS, August 9 and 12, 1862.

7. William Wirt Henry to Mary Jane Henry, January 22 and August 13, 1862, VTHS; Sarah Fales to Edmund Fales, August 6 and 13, 1862, RIHS.

8. *Daily Chronicle*, August 8 and 9, 1862; Sanborn Diary, August 7, 1862, NHHS; Caverly Diary, August 9–12, 1862, NHHS; Emily Harris to Leander Harris, August 16, 1862, UNH; Edward F. Hall to "Dear Susan," September 16, 1862, NHHS.

9. *Daily Chronicle*, August 9, 1862; *Farmer's Cabinet*, November 18, 1864.

10. Miss Corning mentioned a distant cousin who died of disease in the army, but most of her military-age gentleman friends remained civilians. Lizzie Corning Diary, January 17, March 4–10, 1863, NHHS.

11. Gustavus Soule to "Cousin Hattie," July 21, 1862, and John Burrill to "Dear Parents," August 8, 1862, both at USAMHI.

12. Marshall Phillips to "Dear Wife," November 23, 1861, and June 25, 1862, MEHS; John Gilbert to "Dear Sir," February 4, 1862, NHHS. Cincinnati, the largest city west of the Alleghenies, reduced its initial allowance for soldiers' families in the fall of 1861, and similar retrenchments elsewhere in Ohio may have prompted the state to start taxing specifically for the relief of soldiers' dependents in 1862 (Holliday, "Relief for Soldiers' Families," 98–99, 103).

13. Marshall Phillips to "Dear Wife," October 3, 1861, and July 25, 1862, and Phillips to unidentified correspondent, undated (but August, 1862), MEHS.

14. *Report of the Adjutant General of the State of Maine*, 38–61.

15. Woodworth, *Musick of the Mocking Birds*, 117; Thomas H. Brown to "Dear wife," October 23, 1862, VTHS; John Peirce to his wife, January 3 and June 23, 1864, PEM.

16. *Cleveland Plain Dealer*, August 1 and 15, 1862; *Daily Chronicle*, August 19, 1862; Woodwell Diary, August 20–29, 1862, LC; James B. Law to "Dear Sister," November 19, 1862, CHS; *Atlas and Argus*, August 28, 1862.

17. Lucy Larcom Diary, August 21, 1862, Addison Collection, MHS.

18. *Hartford Courant*, August 22, 1862. A Hartford man named Emerson Belden did enlist in another regiment two days later, but he seems to have had no connection to Whittlesey.

19. *OR*, Series 3, 2:321–22.

20. *Weekly Perryville Union*, August 2, 1862; *Tri-Weekly Missouri Republican*, July 26, 1862.

21. Affidavit of Gardiner Durgin et al., August 27, 1862, Nathaniel Berry to Ela, August 28, 1862, and Ela to Levi Turner, August 30, 1862, Case 200, Reel 8, Turner-Baker Case Files (M-797), NA.

22. *Daily Chronicle*, September 22 and October 9, 1862; Batchelder to John H. George, September 17, 1862, NHHS; *Crisis*, August 20, 1862.

23. Affidavits of Timothy Palmatory, John Ochiltree, and others, August 16, 1862, Case 1659, Reel 48, Turner-Baker Case Files (M-797), NA.

24. Pease and Randall, *Browning Diary*, 1:569.

25. *Dubuque Daily Times*, August 17, 1862; *Daily Gate City*, July 31, August 15, 1862; Kirkwood to Edwin Stanton, October 3, 1862, Kirkwood Papers, UIA; C. C. Flint to Kirkwood, August 14, 1862, Disloyal Sentiments File, SHSI-DM.

26. Hoxie to Stanton, August 22, 1862, and the affidavits of F. J. Herron, Frank Robinson, and H. A. Wiltse, Case 413, Reel 14, Turner-Baker Case Files (M-797), NA.

27. *Daily Gate City*, August 15 and 27, 1862; *Fairfield Ledger*, July 31, 1862; *OR*, Series 2, 5:117–18; Mahony to Charles Mason, October 4, 1862, SHSI-DM.

28. *Daily Gate City*, August 18, 1862.

29. A. Q. Keasbey to Levi Turner, August 14, 1862, Case 600, Reel 19; A. Ricketts to Turner, August 20, 1862, Case 385, Reel 13; and J. Jay Buck affidavit, Case 201, Reel 8, all in Turner-Baker Case Files (M-797), NA.

30. J. Wilkins Moore to N. B. Baker, August 12, 1862, H. M. Bowman to Samuel Kirkwood, undated, Dan Mills to Kirkwood, August 29, 1862, B. McCarty to "Dear Sir," August 27, 1862, and George Rose affidavit, all in Disloyal Sentiments File, Adjutant General Correspondence, SHSI-DM; Calvin Hess and T. Simpson affidavits and A. C. Sands to Turner, Case 154, Reel 6, Turner-Baker Case Files (M-797), NA.

31. D. G. Rose to Edwin Stanton, August 16, 1862, Case 389, Reel 13, Turner-Baker Case Files (M-797), NA; *Chicago Tribune*, August 18, 1862.

32. Nicholas Roth affidavit, Case 202, Reel 8, Turner-Baker Case Files (M-797), NA.

33. Curtin to Levi Turner, September 2, 1862, Case 385, Reel 13, Turner-Baker Case Files (M-797), NA.

34. Solomon Hamrick to A. D. Hamrick, undated (but late summer, 1862), IHS; Orlando Poe to "My dear Wife," August 2, 1862, LC.

35. Mark Neely amassed records reflecting some fourteen thousand arrests during the war before he abandoned the task as impossible to complete; he characterized the August crackdown as the "low tide for liberty," acknowledging that it represented the heaviest incidence of repression (*Fate of Liberty*, 234).

36. *The Kansas Chief*, September 4, 1862, and March 13, 1863; *Kansas State Journal*, September 11, 1862; Records of Appointments of Postmasters, Reel 40, Doniphan County, Kansas, M-841, NA.

37. *Weekly Perryville Union*, September 13, 1862.

38. Arvilla Thompson to "Dear Children," January 7, 1862, Aldrich-Thompson Family Papers, NHHS; M. M. Macomber to "My Dear son Francis," July 21, 1862, Macomber Papers, UR; Richard Cary Morse Sr. to Richard Cary Morse Jr., August 13, 1862, CL.

39. Samuel Storrow to "My dear Father," October 12, 1862, MHS.

40. Stephen Brockway to "Friend Allard," March 2, 1862, USAMHI.

41. Charles Jewett to "Dear Brother & Sister," July 18, 1862, NHHS; Walter Hurd to "Uncle P — ," July 10, 1862, SM; Rollin Green to "My friend King," July 12, 1862, VTHS.

42. James W. Davidson to "Friend Bill," July 13, 1862, BGSU; Hughes, *Colby Papers*, 135; Andrew Knox to "My dear wife," August 21, 1862, USAMHI.

43. See James Gillette to "Dear Mother," September 8, 1862, LC; William Drake to "Dear Cousin," September 29, 1862, CHS; Abram Rowell to "Dear Wife," November 18, 1862, UVM; T. J. Lindsay to "Absent Uncle," January 19, 1863, Leeds Historical Society; David Nichol to "Dear Father & Home," March 10, 1863, USAMHI; George E. Parker to "My Dear sister Eliza," February 18, 1864, VTHS.

44. Emily Harris to Leander Harris, September 28, 1862, UNH.

45. John Bailey Diary, August 7–9, 1862, and Caverly Diary, August 8–12, both in NHHS; *Daily Chronicle*, August 14, 1862; Joseph Spafford to Homer White, August 24, 1862, Spafford Letters, VTHS.

46. Watson, *Ashby to Andersonville*, 2–3.

47. *Chicago Tribune*, August 10, 1862; Bell Beach to Catherine Snedecker, August 11, 1862, IWA.

48. Charles Cady to "Dear Parents," August 17, 1862, UIA; Jennie Scott to Asahel Mann, September 29, 1862, Mann Family Papers, UIA; Fatherson, "Pioneer Pieces," IWA; Jacob Hunter to Maria Hunter, November 7, 1862, and January 29, 1863, SHSI-DM.

49. Gulbrandson to "Dear Parents, Brothers and Sisters," August 20, 1862, USAMHI; Henry Robinson to "Dear Wife and Family," January 2, 1863, IHS; Levi Shell to "Dear Brother," January 5, 1863, and to "Dear Mother," January 26, 1863, SHSW.

50. Nathan G. Gould to "Father," undated (but late September or early October, 1862), NHHS; Robert E. Miller to "Dear Parents," CL; John M. Jackson to "My Dear Mother," October 27, 1862, ND; Silliker, *Rebel Yell*, 25.

51. Henry Brown to John Lingle, December 16, 1862, Mary Lingle to same, January 5, 1863, and John Lingle to Mary, January 25, 1863, USAMHI.

52. *Harper's Weekly*, August 30, 1862; Delina Hopper to "Dear Sister" (late 1862), Hopper Papers, WRHS.

53. Bohrnstedt, *While Father Is Away*, 18, 19, 96, 98.

54. *Portland Daily Press*, March 6, 1863; Blight, *This Cruel War*, 33, 40, 43; Fred Lyman to "Dear Brother and Sister," December 8, 1861, VPISU; Sauers, *Bolton Journal*, 7–8, 13–14, 24, 27, 270.

55. Frank C. Morse to "Dearest Ellen," August 25 and 26, 1862, MHS; Child, *Letters*, 17; Joseph Rutherford to "My Dear Wife," January 23, 1863, UVM.

56. Myron Underwood to "My Dear Wife," September 14, 1862, and to "Dear Wife," February 8, 1863, UIA; Throne, "An Iowa Doctor in Blue," 99–100, 139.

57. William H. Collins to "Dear Wife," May 3, 1862, SHSI-IC; Sumner Hurd to Ira M. Barton, January 27 and February 10, 1863, DC.

58. Skipper and Taylor, *Handful of Providence*, 6, 19, 189, 191, 201, 209.

59. Adoniram Withrow to Libertatia Withrow, September 15, 1862, SHSI-IC; William Russell to "Dear Col," November 16, 1862, UIA.

60. Lewis R. Caswell to "Dear Brother," October "14" [1862], PEM; Edwin Wentworth to "Dear Carrie," September 16, 1862, LC; Calvin Burbank to "Dear Cousins," October 28, 1862, DC. The date of the original Caswell letter has been inaccurately corrected to October 19, while Silber and Sievens (*Yankee Correspondence*, 145–46) mistakenly date it 1863; Caswell's reference to the departure of the 10th Massachusetts Battery "to day" confirms a date of October 14, 1862.

61. Pratt Diary, UIA, August 22–25, 1862; Dunlap, *Culver Letters*, 3; Emily Harris to Leander Harris, August 24, September 28, and October 12, 1862, UNH; "The Patchwork Quilt," Parsons Collection, IWA. Leander Harris seemed overpowered by a sense of obligation to serve in 1861, but he indicated that it was the generous bounties that persuaded him to reenlist in 1864, over his wife's fervent opposition.

62. Kohl, *Irish Green*, 6, 17, 73–75; John Sheahan to "Dear Father," August 29, 1862, to "Dear father and Mother," September 18, 1862, and to "Dear father and Sister Mary," September 22, 1862, MEHS. Sheahan's protestations of patriotic devotion seem much more sincere than Welsh's.

63. John C. Ellis to "Dear Sister," May 23, 1862, and to "Dear Nephew" (early 1863), USAMHI; Samuel Thoman to "Dear Wife and Son," September 19, 1861, and to "Dear Wife," October 19 and November 30, 1861, and April 13, 1862, USAMHI.

64. *Prairie du Chien Courier,* January 22, 1863; Elijah Cavins to "Dear Father," October 9, 1862, IHS.

65. Olive Steele to William Steele, September 14 and October 8, 1862, Ebenezer Steele to William Steele, November 16, 1862, William Steele to "Dear Wife," November 17, 1862, and his estate inventory, IHS.

66. Edwin Wentworth to Caroline Wentworth, July 20 and 21, September 4, and October 9, 1862, and to Robert Wentworth, September 17 and November 10, 1862, LC.

67. William A. Willoughby to "Dear Wif," August, 1862, AAS, quoted in Silber and Sievens, *Yankee Correspondence*, 68–69; Myron Wood to "My dear home," July 30, 1862, and Chauncey Wood to "Mr. Wood," November 1, 1865, both in Wood Letters, MHS.

68. Jacob Hunter to Maria Hunter, November 4 and 13, 1862, SHSI-DM; Thomas Sterns to "Dear Wife," October 6 and 10, 1862, UIA; Agnes Allen to Orlando Allen, September 7, 1862, and Orlando to Agnes, September 12, 1862, SHSI-DM; Gilbert Gulbrandson to "Dear Parents," September 2, 1862, USAMHI. Hunter, Sterns, and Allen all died of disease in 1863.

69. Thomas H. Brown to "Dear Wife," October 23, 1862, and to "Horace," September 25 and December 21, 1862, VTHS; Marcellus Darling to "Dear parents, brothers, sisters, friends," December 6, 1862, UIA; Henry Flegeal to "Dear brother and Sister," January 18, 1863, USAMHI.

70. Alonzo Jack to "Dear Parents," September 26, 1862, SHSW; Burgess, *Uncommon Soldier,* 21; Peter Abbott to "Friends at Home," October 11, 1862, VTHS.

71. Kent Diary, October 28, 1862, NHHS; Cora Benton to Oliver Benton, October 1, 1862, ND; Lewis R. Caswell to "Dear Brother," October 14, 1862, PEM.

72. David Werking to "Dear Wife," March 4, 1863, IHS; Allen Church to "My Dear wife," August 23, 1862, SHSW; Butterworth Diary, August 5, 1862, Earlham.

73. Larimer, *Love and Valor,* 112; Skipper and Taylor, *Handful of Providence,* 172.

74. Harrison Randall to "Dear father mother," September 7, 1862, ND; Burgess, *Uncommon Soldier,* 21, 22.

75. Myron Underwood to "My Dear Wife," September 14, 1862, UIA; Sawyer, *Godfrey Letters,* 12; Throne, "Thrall Letters," 139.

76. On the economic motivation of early volunteers see, for instance, George Sargent to "Dear Mother," June 13 and "June" [July] 5, 1862, John O. Stevens to "Dear Father," July

24, 1862, and George Upton to "My Dear Sarah," December 2, 1862, all in NHHS; Lewis Cleveland to "Dear Mother," June 24, 1862, USAMHI; Skipper and Taylor, *Handful of Providence*, 6, 19, 65–66; Blight, *This Cruel War*, 33, 40, 43, and Marvel, *Mr. Lincoln Goes to War*, 49–62, 167–70.

77. *National Eagle*, July 17, 1862; Snyder, "They Lay Where They Fell," 154.

78. Arsino to "Dear Mother," January 7, 1863, VTHS.

79. Peter Abbott to "Friends at Home," September 23, 1862, and Esther Thayer to Willard Thayer, January 23, 1863, both in VTHS; Joel Glover to "Dear Wife," November 22, 1862, and Richard Irwin to "Dear Mother & Sister," December 8, 1862, both at UVM; O. Sanford to "Dear Father," January 13, 1863, SM; Harrison Varney to "Absent One," March 12, 1863, DC.

80. Joseph Spafford to "Dear Sister," October 24, 1862, VTHS; Town Clerk's Records, 5:691–99, Conway Town Hall; Emily Thompson to "Dear Brother & Sister," September 26, 1862, Aldrich-Thompson Family Papers, NHHS.

81. Ransom Sargent to "Dear Maria," January 8, 1863, DC. The reference of Silber and Sievens (*Yankee Correspondence*, 133) to a New Hampshire law requiring towns to pay twelve dollars a month to the families of enlisted men appears to be mistaken, but individual towns did often pay such stipends.

82. John Frederick to "Dear Wife," January 5, 1863, SHSI-IC; "The Patchwork Quilt," Parsons Collection, IWA; Charles Branich to "Dear Mother," January 12, 1863, MNHS; *OR*, Series 3, 2:867.

83. *Peninsula News and Advertiser*, August, 1862; *Buffalo Courier*, August 21, 1862.

84. Andrew J. Stone to "Medical Director," undated, NHHS; George W. Morton discharge certificate, 9th New Hampshire Collection, NHHS; Samuel A. Richards gravestone, Westlawn Cemetery, Goffstown, N. H. Richards, who was born May 12, 1812, enlisted in August of 1862.

85. Joel Eastman to Nathaniel Berry, July 24, 1862, Executive Correspondence, NH Archives.

86. Albany-Conway folder, Recruiting Stations Records, and allotment receipts, 9th New Hampshire Enlistment Records, Adjutant General's Records, NH Archives. Arthur Burbank was later rejected.

87. Town Clerk Records, 5:691–99, Conway Town Hall.

88. *Weekly Perryville Union*, August 2, 9, and 16, 1862; Henry Carroll to "Dear Father," August 31 and September 1, 1862, USAMHI.

89. *Kansas State Journal*, July 31, 1862; *Kansas Chief*, August 7, 1862, and March 12, 1863; *Fort Scott Bulletin*, July 26 and August 16, 1862; *Daily Times*, August 5 and 6, 1862.

90. *OR*, Series 3, 2:411, 431, 444, 479, 959; *Kansas State Journal*, August 14, 1862.

91. Alfred Foreman to "Dear hunkel and hant" September 5, 1862, ISU; Sawyer, *Godfrey Letters*, 20; Jonathan Rickett to Peter Mowrer, September 1, 1862, Miller Collection, UIA.

92. Hosea Towne to "Dear Friends" June 5, 1862, NHHS; John Burrill to "Dear Parents," September 15, 1862 and January 1, 1863, USAMHI; Kohl, *Irish Green*, 62; Lewis Cleveland to "Dear Louise," June 15, 1862, USAMHI.

93. *OR*, 15:486–90, and Series 3, 2:276, 281; Butler, *Private and Official Correspondence*, 2:125, 142–46.

94. *OR*, Series 3, 2:57, 197, 292, 346; Ford, *A Cycle of Adams Letters*, 1:169, 174.

95. *Daily Times*, July 26, 1862; *Leavenworth Daily Conservative*, August 6, 27, and 28, 1862; George H. Hoyt to George L. Stearns, August 13, 1862, Stearns Papers, KSHS.

96. *OR*, Series 3, 2:445; *New York Times*, August 6, 1862; *Fort Scott Bulletin*, July 26, 1862; *OR*, 13:618–19.

97. Niven, *Chase Papers*, 3:235–36; *OR*, Series 3, 2:436–38.

98. *New York Tribune*, August 20, 1862; *OR*, Series 3, 2:433, and Series 1, 14:377.

99. *OR*, Series 3, 2:431–32, 434, 440–41, 445, 446, 455, 456.

100. Ibid., 2:358–59.

101. Balace, *Recrutements en Belgique*, 2, 5.

102. Ford, *A Cycle of Adams Letters*, 1:165, 175; *OR*, 11(3):331 and 12(1):47–53; *Correspondence of John Sedgwick*, 2:80; James Gillette to "Dear Mother," July 31, 1862, LC; Martha Read to Thomas Read, August 7, 1862, ND. For Union admissions of illicit foraging and casual thievery see, for examples, Mushkat, *A Citizen-Soldier's Civil War*, 71; Clement Boughton to "Dear Mother," June 22, 1862, CL; Washington Roebling to John Roebling, April 9, 1862, Rutgers; Lewis Cleveland to "Dear Louise," May 7, 1862, USAMHI; Joshua Breyfogle to "Dear Mary," August 3, 1862, DC; Jared W. Davis to Samuel Bell, August 23, 1862, Bell Papers, NHHS; Horace Currier to Edwin Currier, December 19, 1861, SHSW. For a complaint of rape, see B. E. Harrison's letter of July 28, 1862, Letters Received by the Secretary of War, RG 107, NA, quoted in Lowry, *The Story the Soldiers Wouldn't Tell*, 36. One Union soldier was hanged for the murder of a Virginia woman as early as August 2, 1861 (Ayling, *Register*, 72).

103. *OR*, 11(2):936; Sparks, *Inside Lincoln's Army*, 108.

104. John P. Hatch to "Dear Father," August 2, 1862, LC; Duncan, *Blue-Eyed Child*, 224–25.

105. Freeman, *Lee's Dispatches*, 5–6; *OR*, 11(3):575.

106. Freeman, *Lee's Dispatches*, 38–40; *OR*, 16(1):766–70, 16(2):737, 745, and 12(3):921–22.

5. The Crowd of the Bloody Forms

1. *OR*, 12(3):917–19.

2. *OR*, 11(1):76 and (2):941–42; Benjamin Ashenfelter to "Father Churchman," August 3, 1862, USAMHI; Daly, *Aboard the USS Monitor*, 199, 203. See Greene, *Civil War Petersburg*, 98–99, on Lee's ambitions for interrupting McClellan's riverborne supply line with a more effective bombardment than ultimately ensued.

3. Daniel Reed Larned to "My Dear Sister," August 3, 1862, and to Mrs. Ambrose Burnside, August 8, 1862, LC; *OR*, 11(2):951, 963–64, as 12(3):923, 925–26.

4. *OR*, 12(3):547–50; Eby, *Virginia Yankee*, 75.

5. See Robert Krick's comprehensive *Stonewall Jackson at Cedar Mountain*, 43, on the disputed order.

6. Quaife, *Cannon's Mouth*, 99–101.

7. *OR*, 12(2):158–59; James Gillette to "Dear Parents," August 12, 1862, LC.

8. John P. Hatch to "Dear Father," August 13, 1862, LC; Jordan, *Gould Journals*, 157. For a sketch of Crawford see Marvel, "A Thorn in the Flesh."

9. *OR*, 12(2):146–47, 151–52, 215, 220, 223; Quaife, *Cannon's Mouth*, 100–101.

10. Jordan, *Gould Journals*, 168.

11. *OR*, 12(2):807–8; John C. Ellis to "Dear Sister," August 15, 1862, USAMHI; James Gillette to "Dear Parents," August 12, 1862, LC.

12. *OR*, 12(2):137, 808; Duncan, *Blue-Eyed Child of Fortune*, 228–30; Henry Comey to "Dear Father," August 11, and to "Dear Sister," August 20, 1862, AAS.

13. Eby, *Virginia Yankee*, 77–78; Quaife, *Cannon's Mouth*, 102–3.

14. Duncan, *Blue-Eyed Child of Fortune*, 232; Henry Comey to "Dear Sister," August 20, 1862, AAS; John P. Hatch to "Dear Father," August 13, 1862, LC; Jesse Reno to Ambrose Burnside, August 16, 1862, Stuart Collection, LC; Quaife, *Cannon's Mouth*, 101–2; Willard Diary, August 8–9, 1862, LC.

15. Henry Comey to "Dear Sister," August 20, 1862, AAS; Duncan, *Blue-Eyed Child of Fortune*, 228–35; James Gillette to "Dear Parents," August 12, 1862, and to "Dear Father," August 27, 1862, LC; Raab, *With the 3rd Wisconsin*, 75–76.

16. Eby, *Virginia Yankee*, 79; Jordan, *Gould Journals*, 171; *OR*, 12(2):808.

17. Hassler, *One of Lee's Best Men*, 167; *OR*, 12(3):474, and (2):132.

18. Dowdey and Manarin, *Wartime Papers*, 251–55; *OR*, 12(3):928–29.

19. George E. Bates to "Dear Cousin Albert," August 11, 1862, USAMHI; Daniel Reed Larned to "My Dear Sister," August 18, 1862, LC.

20. *OR*, 12(2):756–57, 12(3):927, 15:76–81, 16(1):857, 16(2):759, 761, 763, and 17(2):662–66, 675–77.

21. *OR*, 16(2):763, 765, 876.

22. *OR*, 12(2):728–29. John Hennessy's *Return to Bull Run* is by far the best account of this entire campaign.

23. Cheney Diary, UNH, August 19, 1862; Eby, *Virginia Yankee*, 84; Sparks, *Inside Lincoln's Army*, 124–25; Willard Diary, August 19, 1862, LC.

24. *OR*, 12(3):613; unidentified Confederate diary quoted in Moore, *Rebellion Record*, 12:660.

25. *OR*, 12(2):730–32; Trout, *Pen and Saber*, 93; Eby, *Virginia Yankee*, 86.

26. Eby, *Virginia Yankee*, 87; *OR*, 12(2):705–7; Willard Diary, August 24, 1862, LC.

27. *OR*, 12(2):66–67, 650, and 12(3):653, 654–55; Eby, *Virginia Yankee*, 88–89.

28. Orlando Poe to "My dear," August 25, 1862, LC.

29. Joseph Willard's Diary (LC) describes finding comforts like ice and ice cream for General McDowell.

30. Coco, *Blood and Fire*, 11; Duncan, *Blue-Eyed Child*, 237; Anthony Ross to "Dear Wife," August 8, 1862, USAMHI; James Gillette to "Dear Father," August 27, 1862, LC.

31. Gillette to "Dear Mother," July 31, 1862, LC; Sparks, *Inside Lincoln's Army*, 120, 127; Frederick Ranger to "My Darling Wife," August 14, 1862, USAMHI; Washington Roebling to "Dear Father," August 24, 1862, Rutgers.

32. *OR*, 12(3):573; Coco, *Blood and Fire*, 13; Eby, *Virginia Yankee*, 87.

33. Hodge, *Mayo Letters*, 216; Orlando Poe to "My dear," August 25, 1862, LC.

34. Sparks, *Inside Lincoln's Army*, 128–29. Hennessy describes the confrontation between Sigel and Pope in *Return to Bull Run*, 104–5.

35. *OR*, 12(2):65–66, and 12(3):666.

36. *OR*, 12(3):645–46; Daniel Reed Larned to "My Dear Sister," August 25, 1862, LC.

37. *OR*, 12(2):347–48, 350–52, 465, and 12(3):675. August 10 returns for the divisions of Kearny, Hooker, Morell, and Sykes showed 27,171 officers and men present for duty; see *OR*, 11(3):367.

38. Sparks, *Inside Lincoln's Army*, 130; Elijah Cavins to "Dear Ann," January 19, 1863, IHS; George Marden to unidentified correspondent, April 16, 1863, DC; Daniel Reed Larned Journal, May 14, 1863, LC; Burgess, *Uncommon Soldier*, 10, 18, 20–22.

39. *OR*, 12(2):643–44, 650–51, 720–21, 747–48, and 12(3):679.

40. *OR*, 12(2):402–4, 539–44, 670, 680.

41. *OR*, 12(2):70, 71, 334, 644, 651, 655–56, 670.

42. *OR*, 12(2):335, 564, and 12(3):684; Eby, *Virginia Yankee*, 89.

43. *CWL*, 5:397–400; Beale, *Welles Diary*, 1:93.

44. *OR*, 12(3):704; Eby, *Virginia Yankee*, 89–90.

45. *OR*, 12(1):127, 137–41, and 12(2):383–84, 670.

46. *OR*, 12(2):37; Priest, *Wren Diary*, 52; Sauers, *Bolton Journal*, 75.

47. *OR*, 12(1):212–13, 255; Eby, *Virginia Yankee*, 86. One soldier claimed that he saw King in another seizure just before the clash at Brawner's farm, but his failure to tell the story for thirty years casts doubt on his credibility. See the *National Tribune* of July 14, 1892, quoted in Gaff, *Brave Men's Tears*, 66–67.

48. *OR*, 12(1):213–14, 12(2):378, 645; Reid-Green, *Letters Home*, 33; Sparks, *Inside Lincoln's Army*, 131; Holford Diary, September 4, 1862, LC.

49. *OR*, 12(2):384, 564.

50. *OR*, 12(2):337; Willard Diary, August 28, 1862, LC.

51. *OR*, 12(1):206, and 12(2):37; Eby, *Virginia Yankee*, 91.

52. Eby, *Virginia Yankee*, 91–92; *OR*, 12(2):Supplement: 846.

53. *OR*, 12(3):732–33 and 12(2), Supplement:1002.

54. *OR*, 12(2):265–66, and 12(2), Supplement:902, 1046, and 12(3):730; Eby, *Virginia Yankee*, 92.

55. Willard Diary, August 29, 1862, LC; Trezigulny Diary, August 29, 1862, USAMHI; Charles R. Johnson to "Dear Nellie," September 11, 1862, USAMHI; *OR*, 12(2), Supplement:902, and 12(2):736.

56. *OR*, 12(2):39. Pope clung to his mistaken interpretation long after events had proven him wrong.

57. *OR*, 12(2):411–13, 439, 545; George Smith to "Dear Mother," September 10, 1862, Calvin Smith Papers, MHS; Priest, *Wren Diary*, 53–54; George Upton to "My Dear Wife," September 3, 1862, NHHS; Hosea Towne to "Dear Friends," September 6, 1862, NHHS.

58. Priest, *Wren Diary*, 54; *OR*, 12(2):413, 416, 671.

59. *OR*, 12(2):40, 339, 367, and 12(2), Supplement:832–33, 951; Willard Diary, August 29, 1862.

60. *OR*, 12(2):367, 565.

61. *Portsmouth Journal of Literature and Politics*, September 13, 1862; *OR*, 12(2):367, 370, 565, 623; Cheney Diary, August 29, 1862, UNH; *Report of the Adjutant General of the State of New-Hampshire*, 2:914. The gun was recaptured a year later (*Daily Chronicle*, September 18, 1863).

62. *OR*, 12(2):41, 339, 384, and 12(2), Supplement:840–41, 849, 85; Eby, *Virginia Yankee*, 93–94; Willard Diary, August 29, 1862, LC.

63. *OR*, 12(2):41, 340; Sparks, *Inside Lincoln's Army*, 133–34; Willard Diary, August 30, 1862, LC.

64. *OR*, 12(2):361.

65. *OR*, 12(2):340, 394, 472, 473–74, 481.

66. *OR*, 12(2):368, 471, 668–69; anonymous letter of September 6, 1862, quoted in Moore, *Rebellion Record*, 5:403; Cutrer and Parrish, *Brothers in Gray*, 120; Sparks, *Inside Lincoln's Army*, 135.

67. Lomax, *Leaves from an Old Washington Diary*, 210; *OR*, 12(2):254, 257, 472–73.

68. *OR*, 12(2):255, 340–42, 384, 394–95, 565–66; Eby, *Virginia Yankee*, 95–96; Joseph A. McLean to "Dear Wife," August 14 and 22, 1862, and W. J. Runnels to Mrs. Joseph A. McLean, October 3, 1862, USAMHI.

69. Thomas and Silverman, *A Rising Star*, 46; *OR*, 12(2):43, 341–42; Eby, *Virginia Yankee*, 96–97.

70. Keiser Diary, August 30, 1862, and Schweitzer Diary, same date, both at USAMHI.

71. *OR*, 12(2):43; Sauers, *Bolton Journal*, 76–77; Loving, *Whitman Letters*, 62–63; Priest, *Wren Diary*, 58; Sears, *On Campaign*, 89; Rosenblatt and Rosenblatt, *Hard Marching*, 42. On Ferrero's predilection for feminine companionship see Ransom Sargent to Maria Sargent, June 22, 1863, DC.

72. *OR*, 12(2):44, 647; Eby, *Virginia Yankee*, 98.

73. *OR*, 12(2):78–79, 80, 565, 566, 647; *Diary of General S. M. Jackson*, 44; J. Trezigulny Diary, August 30, 1862, USAMHI.

74. *OR*, 12(2):80, and 12(3):768.

75. Burlingame and Ettlinger, *Inside Lincoln's White House*, 37–38. As recorded by John Hay, perhaps inexactly, Lincoln's ambiguous comment was, "If this be not so, if we are really whipped and to be whipped we may as well stop fighting."

76. Blackburn, *With the Wandering Regiment*, 41; Eby, *Virginia Yankee*, 98; Burlingame and Ettlinger, *Inside Lincoln's White House*, 37; *OR*, 12(3):775–76.

77. Maycock Diary, August 30, 1862, USAMHI; James A. Wiley to "Dear Sister," September 5, 1862, with the endorsement of nurse J. H. Fowle, USAMHI.

78. *OR*, 12(2):81–83. Hennessy alludes to Pope's depression (*Return to Bull Run*, 444), and the symptoms seem obvious enough to support a clinical diagnosis.

79. *OR*, 12(3):768; Phil Kearny to "Dearest Love," August 30, 1862, LC, and Styple, *Letters from the Peninsula*, 166–67; James Gillette to "Dr Parents," September 1, 1862, LC.

80. Quaife, *Cannon's Mouth*, 110–11; Coco, *Blood and Fire*, 19.

81. Weld, *War Diary and Letters*, 136; OR, 12(2):79, and 12(3):785, 788; Nevins, *Diary of Battle*, 90.

82. *OR*, 12(2):84, 418, 647, and 12(3):785–86; Priest, *Wren Diary*, 59; Loving, *Whitman Letters*, 63; Sauers, *Bolton Journal*, 77; Keiser Diary, September 1, 1862, USAMHI.

83. *Diary of General S. M. Jackson*, 44; *OR*, 12(3):796–97.

84. *OR*, 12(3):706; Niven, *Chase Papers*, 1:366.

85. Niven, *Chase Papers*, 1:366–67; Beale, *Welles Diary*, 1:93–95, 100.

86. *OR*, 12(3):739–41; Beale, *Welles Diary*, 1:95–98.

87. Undated petition filed with 1862 documents, Reel 4, Stanton Papers, LC; Niven, *Chase Papers*, 1:367–69; Beale, *Welles Diary*, 1:100–4.

88. *Letter of the Secretary of War*, 182–83; *CWP*, 428.

89. *Letter of the Secretary of War*, 183.

90. Beale, *Welles Diary*, 1:111; *Letter of the Secretary of War*, 183–84; *CWP*, 428; *OR*, 12(3):807.

91. Niven, *Chase Papers*, 1:368; Beale, *Welles Dairy*, 1:104–5.

92. Among the commanders of the Army of the Potomac, McClellan and George Meade probably enjoyed the most popularity with their soldiers, and both disliked the tactical offensive; McDowell, Pope, Burnside, and Hooker preferred it, but were less well liked. Robert E. Lee's mania for the offensive, meanwhile, seemed to work the opposite effect among his men. See McWhiney and Jamieson, *Attack and Die*, for a varied discussion on the topic. "The Constitution as it is . . ." was the favorite slogan of conservative Democrats.

93. *CWL*, 5:486; *OR*, 12(3):802, 807; Beale, *Welles Diary*, 1:105; Burlingame and Ettlinger, *Inside Lincoln's White House*, 37, 38; Niven, *Chase Papers*, 1:369. Sears vividly details this episode of late August and early September in *George B. McClellan*, 254–61.

94. *Letter of the Secretary of War*, 184; Willard Diary, September 2, 1862, LC; Eby, *Virginia Yankee*, 99–100.

95. Weld, *War Diary and Letters*, 136; Avery Cain to "Dear Father," September 4, 1862, VHS; Holden, Ross, and Slomba, *Stand Firm*, 120. Jacob Cox, a brigadier traveling with Hatch's division, credited the Pope-hating General Hatch for initiating the demonstration by announcing McClellan's return and calling for three cheers (Cox, *Military Reminiscences*, 1:244–45).

6. In Scarlet Maryland

1. *OR*, 16(1):909, 915, 933–34, 936, and 16(2):467; Smith and Cooper, *Union Woman*, 28–29; W. P. Hill to "Dear Father," September 18, 1862, Hill-Hudelson Family Papers, Earlham.

2. Cuthbert Bullitt to Lincoln, September 1, 1862, ALP; *OR*, 16(2):465.

3. *OR*, 16(1):990; John Henry Knight to "My Darling Sue," September 5, 1862, SHSW.

4. *OR*, 12(2):758–60, 772, 12(3):799–801, and 19(2):196–97.

5. *OR*, 13:591–93, 596, 601–3; Timothy Stevens to "Dear Sister," November 22, 1862, Robinson Family Papers, Rokeby Museum Collection, SM; Louisa Cook Walters to "My Dear Mother & sisters," June 11, 1862, and Lambert A. Martin to "Friends at Home," August 24, 1862, both at Yale.

6. *Chicago Tribune*, August 24, 1862; *Executive Documents, 37th Cong., 3rd sess.*, 2:204; testimony of George W. Crooks, and Rebecca MacAlmond Diary, August 18, 1862, Dakota Conflict, MNHS.

7. *Chicago Tribune,* August 24 and 27, 1862; Testimony of George W. Crooks, Dakota Conflict, MNHS; *Executive Documents, 37th Cong., 3rd sess.,* 2:205–6, 212.

8. *Executive Documents, 37th Cong., 3rd sess.,* 2:207–8, 210; Rebecca MacAlmond Diary, August 19–23, 1862, and Electa Currier to "Dear Brother Henry," September 12, 1862, both in Dakota Conflict, MNHS.

9. *Kansas Chief,* September 4, 1862; Mary Crowell to "Dear friend," September 14, 1862, Dakota Conflict, MNHS; *Dakotian,* September 22–23, 1862; Burlingame, *With Lincoln,* 88.

10. *OR,* 13:595–97, 599; "A Badger Boy in Blue," 80.

11. *OR,* Series 2, 4:499, 542, 600, 619–20, 644–45; Bable Shirrell to Madison Carlton, October 31, 1862, IHS.

12. Friedrich P. Keppelman to "Dear Parents," September 2, 1862, USAMHI; *OR,* 12(3):691, 725, 767, 782.

13. Acken, *Inside the Army of the Potomac,* 104; Hodge, *Mayo Letters,* 217; *War Letters of William Thompson Lusk,* 189; Scott, *Fallen Leaves,* 140.

14. E. Ball to John T. Shyrock, September 5, 1862, WRHS; Langsdorf, "Trego Letters" 308.

15. Poe to "My dear Wife," September 4, 1862, LC; *War Letters of William Thompson Lusk,* 189; *Correspondence of John Sedgwick,* 2:80.

16. Beale, *Welles Diary,* 1:117; Walter Phelps to "Dear E.," September 4 and 7, 1862, USAMHI; Hastings, *Letters from a Sharpshooter,* 146; Maycock Diary, September 3, 1862, USAMHI.

17. Loving, *Whitman Letters,* 64; Holden, Ross, and Slomba, *Stand Firm,* 119–20. Evidence of optimism at this juncture can be found, although the most unequivocal example may be that of Regis de Trobriand, whose original letters have undergone both a postwar transcription and subsequent translation, either of which might have introduced subtle modifications of the tenor (Styple, *Our Noble Blood,* 71–72).

18. See, for example, Hodge, *Mayo Letters,* 217; Benjamin F. Robb to "Dear Sir," September 9, 1862, USAMHI; Ransom Sargent to "Dear Maria," September 28, 1862, DC; John Henry Knight to "My Darling Sue," September 5 and 26, 1862, SHSW.

19. Hammond, *Diary,* 170–71; Mahon, *Winchester Divided,* 58; Jones Diary, September, 1862, Earlham; Laas, *Wartime Washington,* 185; Emily Harris to Leander Harris, August 31, September 7, and September 16, 1862, UNH.

20. Nevins and Thomas, *Strong Diary,* 3:252; Beale, *Welles Diary,* 1:108.

21. Beale, *Welles Diary,* 1:112, 117.

22. *CWL,* 5:403–4, dates the memorandum as early as September 2, and no later than September 22. Lincoln used similar language in a letter to Albert G. Hodge of Kentucky on April 4, 1864 (*CWL* 7:282). On Lincoln's relative lack of religious devotion see Orville Hickman Browning to Isaac Arnold, November 25, 1872, Randall Papers, LC.

23. Hammond, *Diary,* 170; James M. Crosby to Richard Cary Morse Jr., September 5, 1862, CL.

24. Longacre, *Antietam to Fort Fisher,* 25. On the languor and temptations of camp life see, for instance, Franklin Foster to "Dear Sister," July 13, 1862, NHHS, and Gavin, *Infantryman Pettit,* 5–6.

25. Peabody to "My Darling Wife," September 10, 1862, Peabody Papers, MHS.

26. Edwin Wentworth to "Dear Carrie," July 20, 1862, LC; Bright, *This Cruel War,* 181, 183–84.

27. Stockwell Diary, September 1–7, 1862, WRHS; William Kemper to "Dear Brother," October 8, 1862, SHSI-DM; Pratt Diary, August 22 and 25, 1862, UIA.

28. Robinson Diary, August 25, 1862, DC; Gwillem Diary, October 2, 1862, CHS.

29. Hodgkins Diary, November 21, 1862, Yale; Levi Shell to "Brother Daniel," September 19, 1862, SHSW; "Abbie" to "My very dear Sister," August [31], 1862, Savage Family Papers, UVM; Stockwell Diary, September 26 and October 4, 1862, WRHS.

30. Ellsworth Phelps to "My Dear Wife," October 30, 1862, CHS; Mushkat, *A Citizen-Soldier's Civil War,* 79; Jacob Hunter to "Dear Wife," September 24, 1862, SHSI-DM; Tabor Parcher to "Dear Sarah," "September" [August] 31, 1862, UVM.

31. "Cousin Mag" to "Cousin Will," September 23, 1862, Kynett Family Papers, SHSI-DM.

32. Ransom Sargent to "Dear Maria," September 21, 1862, DC; Charles Benton to "Dear Cora," October 20, 1862, ND.

33. Cora Benton to Charles Benton, October 5 and 7, 1862, ND; Thomas Jefferson Lewis to "My Dear Wife," September 21, 1862, SHSI-DM; Agnes Allen to Amasa Orlando Allen, undated, SHSI-DM; Thomas Coffman to "Dearest Girl," September 25, 1862, SHSI-IC.

34. Edwin Wentworth to "My dear Wife," September 25, 1862; John Henry Jenks to unnamed recipient, October 3, 1862, UNH.

35. Thomas Jefferson Lewis to "Dear Wife," September 13, 1862, and James Sudduth to "Dear Martha," October 23, 1862, both SHSI-DM; Gilbert Gulbrandson to "Dear Parents, Brothers and Sisters," August 20, 1862, USAMHI.

36. Alfred Metcalf White to "Ever Dear Wife," July 4, 1862, MHS; *Kansas Chief,* August 7, 1862; John P. Hatch to "Dear Father," August 2, 1862, LC.

37. George Chapin to Ella Chapin, October 14, 1862, USAMHI; Solomon Hamrick to A. D. Hamrick, November 10, 1862, IHS.

38. *OR,* 1(2):590–94; Burlingame and Ettlinger, *Inside Lincoln's White House,* 38; Beale, *Welles Diary,* 1:110; Jackson Letterbook, 60, cited in Freeman, *Lee's Lieutenants,* 2:149.

39. Beale, *Welles Diary,* 1:109–10, 116, 126; Niven, *Chase Papers,* 1:370; *OR,* 13:617, 618.

40. *RJCCW,* 1:451, 453–54, 650; *OR,* 19(2):189–97; *CWP,* 436–37; *CWL,* 5:407.

41. Eby, *Virginia Yankee,* 102; Beale, *Welles Diary,* 1:114–16; *RJCCW,* 1:451, 453.

42. *CWP,* 436; Williams, *Hayes Diary,* 2:346; Hawes Diary, September 7, 1862, MHS; Brun, "Palace Guard View," 21, 23; *OR,* 19(1):416, and 19(2):213. Burnside's wing command was made official on September 14 [*OR,* 19(2):290].

43. *OR,* 19(2):214; Beale, *Welles Diary,* 1:140.

44. *OR,* 16(2):495–97, 500, and 19(2):202, 207; *CWL,* 5:408–10.

45. *OR,* 19(2):203, 204; Leo Faller to "Dear Parents," September 8, 1862, USAMHI.

46. Steiner, *Report,* 8–9, 19–21.

47. *Frederick Herald,* September 3, 1861; Steiner, *Report,* 10–11; Tower, *Lee's Adjutant,* 43.

48. Steiner, *Report,* 11, 18.

49. Hassler, *One of Lee's Best Men,* 172; *Richmond Examiner,* September 18, 1862; Trout, *With Pen and Saber,* 97.

50. Steiner, *Report,* 13, 16–17. See, for instance, Compiled Service Records of John Hartigan and Otis Johnson, 1st Maryland Cavalry (M321, Reel 3), John W. Heard, 2nd Maryland Battalion (M321, Reel 19), RG 109, NA; *OR,* 19(2):596.

51. Holford Diary, September 9, 1862, LC; James Lathe Letters, September 3 and 8, 1862, DC; Williams, *Hayes Diary and Letters,* 2:346–48.

52. Gavin, *Infantryman Pettit,* 8; Horace Lay to "Dear Wife," September 8, 1862, CHS; James Lathe Letters, September 13, 1862, DC; John Bailey Diary, September 8–12, 1862, NHHS.

53. Steiner, *Report,* 19; Eby, *Virginia Yankee,* 102–3; *CWP,* 441, 442, 445; *OR,* 19(2):281, 603–4.

54. Eby, *Virginia Yankee,* 103.

55. Williams, *Hayes Diary and Letters,* 2:352; James Munnerlyn to "My dear sister," October 9, 1862, SHC.

56. Williams, *Hayes Diary and Letters,* 2:352; Daniel Reed Larned to "Dear Sister," October 3, 1862, LC; *OR,* 19(2):285.

57. Henry Spooner to "Dear Mother," September 14, 1862, RIHS.

58. Wilcox Diary, September 12, 1862, NHHS; Eby, *Virginia Yankee*, 105; Frank Kelley to "My Dear Parents," September 22, 1862, USAMHI.

59. Quaife, *Cannon's Mouth*, 121; Solomon Hamrick to A. D. Hamrick, September 10, 1862, IHS.

60. Seventh Census (M432), Reel 152, p. 127, and Eighth Census (M653), Reel 291, p. 28, RG 29, NA; John Bloss to Mitchell (circa 1867), Menuet Collection. Mitchell left no written evidence of his motives for enlisting, but his situation mirrored that of many other middle-aged soldiers who did. See, for instance, Charles Mumford to Clarissa Mumford, August 23 and December 24, 1862, SHSW. Two of Sergeant Mumford's adult sons enlisted, as did Mitchell's son Charles.

61. Quaife, *Cannon's Mouth*, 121; Bloss to Mitchell (circa 1867), and certificate of Silas and Theodore Colgrove, March 19, 1867, Menuet Collection; Williams to McClellan, September 13, 1862, Reel 31, McClellan Papers, LC.

62. Bloss, "Antietam and the Lost Dispatch," 84. The best account of the lost order is in Sears, *Controversies and Commanders*, 109–30; Sears (*Landscape Turned Red*) is also the definitive source on the entire Antietam campaign.

63. *OR*, 19(2):281.

64. *OR*, 19(1):209, 416, 449–50, and 19(2):282; Eby, *Virginia Yankee*, 103; Blackburn, *With the Wandering Regiment*, 42.

65. *OR*, 19(1):209, 374, 417; Scott, *Forgotten Valor*, 365; Priest, *New Bern to Fredericksburg*, 64; Wilcox and John Bailey Diaries, September 13, 1862, NHHS.

66. *OR*, 19(1):374–75; 817–18, 839, 1019; John Turner to "My Dear Family," September 18, 1862, CCHS.

67. Sparks, *Inside Lincoln's Army*, 143.

68. *OR*, 19(1):458–59, 1040–41; Williams, *Hayes Diary and Letters*, 2:355–57.

69. *OR*, 19(1):428, 443, 450; Sparks, *Inside Lincoln's Army*, 143.

70. *OR*, 19(1):428, 433–34, 1041; Hawes Diary, September 14, 1862, MHS.

71. *OR*, 19(1):267, 460, 1041–42; Sparks, *Inside Lincoln's Army*, 143–44.

72. Wilcox and John Bailey Diaries, September 14, 1862, NHHS; Eby, *Virginia Yankee*, 106–7; Blackburn, *With the Wandering Regiment*, 42.

73. *OR*, 19(1):839, 19(2):289; Harvey Diary, September 14, 1862, Appomattox Court House National Historic Park.

74. Eby, *Virginia Yankee*, 107; Keiser Diary, September 14, 1862, USAMHI; Smith Bailey Diary, September 14, 1862, DC; *OR*, 19(1):375, 870.

75. *OR* 19(1):818–19, 870, 19(2):289; Trout, *Pen and Saber*, 100.

76. *OR*, 19(1):549, 855–56, 960–61; Valentine Barney to "Dear Wife," September 22, 1862, VTHS.

77. *OR*, 19(1):1071–72; Muster Roll of Otey's Battery, July and August, 1864, Compiled Service Record of Channing M. Smith (M-324), Reel 236, NA.

78. Ira Conine to "Jennie," September 12, 1862, BGSU; *OR*, 16(2):513, 514, 825, 830, and 16(1):967, 971.

79. Tower, *Lee's Adjutant*, 44; *OR*, 51(2):618–19, 19(1):951, and 19(2):608–10; Sparks, *Inside Lincoln's Army*, 145–46.

80. Henry White Diary, September 14 (and 15), 1862, AAS; John Bailey Diary, September 14 and 15, 1862, NHHS; Loving, *Whitman Letters*, 67.

81. Henry Spooner to "My Dear Father," September 20, 1862, RIHS; Priest, *New Bern to Fredericksburg*, 68.

82. Eby, *Virginia Yankee*, 107; Masonheimer Diary, September 15, 1862, and Frank Kelley to "My Dear Parents," September 22, 1862, both at USAMHI.

83. Furst Diary, September 15, 1862, USAMHI; Robinson Diary, September 15, 1862, and James Lathe Letters, September 20, 1862, both in DC.

84. Furst Diary, September 14, 1862, USAMHI; Samuel Partridge to Francis Macomber, September 25, 1862, UR; Williams, *Hayes Diary and Letters*, 2:354.

85. Robert Cornwell to "Dear friends at home," September 20, 1862, to "Dear Brothers & Sisters" October 3, 1862, and J. E. Hewitt to "Mrs. Cornwell," October 13, 1862, all USAMHI.

86. *OR*, 19(1):184–88; Recruiting Stations Records, Albany-Conway folder, Adjutant General's Records, NH Archives; *Daily Chronicle*, October 2, 1862; muster-out roll, Enoch Haselton Service Record, RG 94, NA.

87. Stowe Diary, September 15, 1862, USAMHI; *OR*, 19(2):294–95, 19(1):67, 217; Sparks, *Inside Lincoln's Army*, 146.

88. *CWP*, 465; Eby, *Virginia Yankee*, 108; *OR*, 19(2):296–97, 19(1):67.

89. *OR*, 19(1):915, 955; Cutrer and Parrish, *Brothers in Gray*, 121–22; Schiller, *Captain's War*, 18. The Second, Ninth, and Twelfth Corps and parts of the First and Fifth Corps slept near the creek that night.

90. Schweitzer Diary, September 16, 1862, USAMHI; John Bailey and Wilcox Diaries, September 16, 1862, NHHS; Marvel, *Race of the Soil*, 464.

91. Marvel, *Race of the Soil*, 438, 439, 445, 469–70, 477, 487, 488; William Webster to Alex. Watson, October 20, 1862 (Correspondence and Orders), and notice of proceedings against Captain Charles W. Edgerly, John E. Mason Memorandum Book, October 17, 1862, both in 9th N.H. Collection, NHHS. Lee's army also suffered from a debilitating number of stragglers during and after the Maryland campaign (*OR*, 19(2):592–93, 626–27); the traditional explanation has held that many Confederates refused to cross the Potomac because principle limited them to defending their homeland, and that argument may have merit, but the carnage at Second Bull Run and Antietam surely discouraged the bravest men.

92. *OR*, 19(1):55, 19(2):314, and 51(1):836–38. See Marvel, *Burnside*, 125–31, on McClellan's alleged vexation. Jacob Cox initially liked McClellan, who treated him "very cordially" (Cox to Lorenzo Thomas, November 4, 1862, Oberlin), but later he scorned him for trying to revise history. In the margins of Cox's copy of *McClellan's Own Story* are corrections and comments suggesting a belief that McClellan concocted his dissatisfaction with Burnside only after the fact, to excuse his own shortcomings and to injure someone against whom he had developed a grudge (Cox Papers, Oberlin). I am indebted to Stephen Sears for sharing his notes on Cox's revealing marginal observations.

93. *OR*, 19(1):839, 889; *OR Atlas*, Plate 28, Map 2.

94. Sparks, *Inside Lincoln's Army*, 146–47; *OR* 19(1):55, 217–18, 275; *Diary of General S. M. Jackson*, 47.

95. Quaife, *Cannon's Mouth*, 124–25; Samuel Sexton to unidentified recipient (salutation clipped from letter), October 23, 1862, and Franklin Sawyer to Sexton, November 26, 1862, OHS; Jonathan Stowe to unnamed recipient, September 17, 1862, USAMHI.

96. *OR*, 19(1):857; Schiller, *Captain's War*, 18.

97. W. H. Humphreys to John M. Gould, March 9 and 23, 1894, and S. S. Piper to Gould, February 16 and 22, 1894, all in Collection of Antietam Papers, DC; Cheney Diary, September 17, 1862, UNH; *OR*, 19(1):218.

98. *OR*, 19(1):269–70; *Diary of General S. M. Jackson*, 47; Henry Comey to "Dear Friends," September 18, 1862, AAS.

99. Sparks, *Inside Lincoln's Army*, 143, 147–48; *OR*, 19(1):171, 224, 246; W. B. Holstead to John M. Gould, March 9, 1893, Enoch Jones to Gould, February 28, 1893, and George W. Watson to Gould, April 22, 1893, all in Collection of Antietam Papers, DC; Hunt, *Brevet Brigadier Generals*, 110.

100. Cutrer and Parrish, *Brothers in Gray*, 122–23; *OR*, 19(1):224, 248; Phelps to "Dear E.," September 7 and 28, 1862, USAMHI.

101. *OR*, 19(1):189, 202, 233; White, *White Diary*, 18, 37–38; Walter W. Smith to "Dear

Parents Brothers and Sisters," September 15, 18, and 20, 1862, DU, quoted in Marshall, *War of the People,* 104–6; Snyder, "They Lay Where They Fell," 156–57.

102. *OR,* 19(1):217, 475, 484; Quaife, *Cannon's Mouth,* 126; Jordan, *Gould Journals,* 194.

103. Jordan, *Gould Journals,* 169, 171, 195, 203, 222.

104. *OR,* 19(1):198, 494–95; Duncan, *Blue-Eyed Child,* 240–41; Colgrove, "Lost Order," 603; David Nichol to "Dear Sister," September 27, 1862, USAMHI.

105. Quaife, *Cannon's Mouth,* 128; Duncan, *Blue-Eyed Child,* 241; *OR,* 19(1):275, 305.

106. *OR,* 19(1):275, 305–6, 820, 858; Edward Walker to George Knight, October 5, 1862, quoted in Moe, *Last Full Measure,* 180–81.

107. *OR,* 19(1):275–76, 306, 492, 858; Quaife, *Cannon's Mouth,* 128; Howe, *Touched with Fire,* 64–65.

108. *OR,* 19(1):192, 313; Coco, *Ball's Bluff to Gettysburg,* 121, 127; Stowe Diary, September 17 and 19, 1862, USAMHI.

109. Quaife, *Cannon's Mouth,* 128–29; Duncan, *Blue-Eyed Child,* 241; *OR,* 19(1):198; 496, 914–15; Schiller, *Captain's War,* 18; Hughes, *Colby Papers,* 153–55.

110. Furst Diary, September 17, 1862, USAMHI.

111. *OR,* 19(1):323–24; *War Letters, 1862–1865,* 11; Masonheimer Diary, September 17, 1862, USAMHI.

112. Sears, *Dunn Browne,* 9; *OR,* 19(1):323–24, 327, 337, 1037, 1047.

113. *OR,* 19(1):277–78, 1023–24. George T. Anderson, another Confederate brigadier, escaped unharmed.

114. *OR,* 19(1):277–78; Hammond, *Diary,* 190. For Meagher's alleged intoxication see Eby, *Virginia Yankee,* 113, and Jacob Cox's marginal notations in his copy of *McClellan's Own Story* (595), Oberlin.

115. David Nichol to "Dear Sister," September 27, 1862, USAMHI.

116. *OR,* 19(1):30, and 51(1):842, 844. On the timing of the order see Marvel, *Burnside,* 135, 445 (n. 13).

117. *OR,* 19(1):885–86, 909, 914.

118. Henry Spooner to "My Dear Father," September 20, 1862, RIHS. See Marvel, *Burnside,* 137–38, and Marvel, "More Than Water under Burnside's Bridge," on the creek's effectiveness as a military obstacle.

119. *OR,* 19(11):419, 471–72.

120. *OR,* 19(1):444; Priest, *Wren Diary,* 71; Sauers, *Bolton Journal,* 86; Loving, *Whitman Letters,* 67.

121. *OR,* 19(1):452–53, 889; Spooner to "My Dear Father," September 20 and October 11–12, 1862, RIHS.

122. Belden Diary, September 19, 1862, and Horace Lay to "Dear Wife," September 8, 1862, CHS.

123. Loving, *Whitman Letters,* 67–68; Elijah Couillard to "Dear Parents," October 19, 1862, MHS; Sauers, *Bolton Journal,* 86; *OR,* 19(1):451, 890–91.

124. Henry White Diary, September 17, 1862, AAS; Watson, *Ashby to Andersonville,* 21–22; *OR,* 19(1):425, 886, 891.

125. *OR,* 19(1):420, 425, 434; Hawes Diary, September 17, 1862, MHS. Lieutenant Griffin was quietly mustered out three days later.

126. Blackburn, *With the Wandering Regiment,* 43; *OR,* 19(1):420, 425.

127. Strother, "Personal Recollections," 284.

128. *RJCCW,* 1:626–27; Meade, *Life and Letters,* 1:317–18; *OR,* 19(1):191.

129. Nevins, *A Diary of Battle,* 100–101; Smith Bailey Diary, September 17, 1862, DC.

130. *Letter of the Secretary of War,* 207–8; *RJCCW,* 1:626–27; Keiser Diary, September 17, 1862, USAMHI.

131. Strother, "Personal Recollections," 284; Schweitzer Diary, September 17, 1862, USAMHI.

132. Belden Diary, September 17, 1862, and William Drake to "Dear Cousin," September 29, 1862, both CHS; Charles Coit to unidentified recipients, September 18 and October 4, 1862, Yale.

133. Charles Coit to unidentified recipient, October 4, 1862, Yale; James Abraham to "Dear Friends," September 20, 1862, and Schweitzer Diary, September 17, 1862, both USAMHI.

134. Loving, *Whitman Letters*, 68; Priest, *Wren Diary*, 73; *OR*, 19(1):448–49.

135. *OR*, 19(1):431, 1024–25; Priest, *Wren Diary*, 73.

136. Watson, *Ashby to Andersonville*, 22–23; Eby, *Virginia Yankee*, 112; Tower, *Taylor Letters*, 44.

7. Whetting a Sword on a Bible

1. *OR*, 19(2):330, 626–27; Tower, *Taylor Letters*, 44.

2. Watson, *Ashby to Andersonville*, 23; Masonheimer Diary, September 18, 1862, USAMHI.

3. Duncan, *Blue-Eyed Child*, 241; Schweitzer Diary, September 17, 1862, USAMHI.

4. Duncan, *Blue-Eyed Child*, 241; Keiser Diary, September 18, 1862, USAMHI; Snyder, "They Lay Where They Fell," 157.

5. Charles Goddard to Catharine Smith, September 19, 1862, Orrin Smith Papers, MNHS; Stowe Diary, September 18, 1862, USAMHI; Coco, *Ball's Bluff to Gettysburg*, 127.

6. Strother, "Personal Recollections," 285–86; Holden, Ross, and Slomba, *Stand Firm*, 121.

7. James Abraham to "Dear Friends," September 23 and October 19, 1862, USAMHI.

8. Hughes, *Colby Papers*, 154–55, 180, 182, 184, 185; Scott, *Fallen Leaves*, 143.

9. Walter Hurd to "Dear Parents," October 1, 1862, SM; George Upton to "My Dear Sarah," September 29, 1862, NHHS; John Turner to "My Dear Family," September 18, 1862, CCHS.

10. Snyder, "They Lay Where They Fell," 156; Horace Currier to Edwin Currier, October 10, 1862, SHSW.

11. Maycock Diary, September 18, 1862, and Stowe Diary, September 20, 1862, both USAMHI; Child, *Letters*, 33; Charles Goddard to Catharine Smith, September 19, 1862, Orrin Smith Papers, MNHS.

12. Eby, *Virginia Yankee*, 113–14; Sears, *Dunn Browne*, 11; Samuel Sexton to Mrs. Sexton, September 21, 1862, OHS; Elijah Cavins to "Dear Ann," October 1, 1862, IHS; Holden, Ross, and Slomba, *Stand Firm*, 121; Longacre, *Antietam to Fort Fisher*, 39.

13. Longacre, *Antietam to Fort Fisher*, 37; Truxall, *Respects to All*, 31; Walter A. Chapman to "Dear Parents," September 21, 1862, Yale; Marcellus Darling to "Dear Parents," October 5, 1862, UIA.

14. *War Letters, 1862–1865*, 11; Quaife, *Cannon's Mouth*, 130; Sears, *Dunn Browne*, 10; Eby, *Virginia Yankee*, 114; Holden, Ross, and Slomba, *Stand Firm*, 121; Truxall, *Respects to All*, 31.

15. For a fascinating study of Gardner's Antietam photographs see Frassanito, *Antietam*.

16. Longacre, *Antietam to Fort Fisher*, 39; Masonheimer Diary, September 19, 1862, USAMHI; Eby, *Virginia Yankee*, 113.

17. Coco, *Ball's Bluff to Gettysburg*, 122, 127–29.

18. Robinson Diary, September 19, 1862, DC.

19. Keiser Diary, September 18, 1862, USAMHI; Charles Goddard to Catharine Smith, September 28, 1862, Orrin Smith Papers, MNHS; Sears, *Dunn Browne*, 11.

20. Quaife, *Cannon's Mouth*, 130; Strother, "Personal Recollections," 288; Holmes, "My Hunt After 'The Captain,'" 748, and "Doings of the Sunbeam," 11; Jordan, *Gould Jour-*

nals, 198. William Frassanito located the site of the photograph (*Antietam,* 122–25), and speculates that Louisiana colonel Henry Strong may have been the horse's rider.

21. David Patterson to unidentified correspondent, June 13, 1862, RIHS.

22. Shannon, *Andrus Letters,* 43; John Wallace to "Dear Sister Em," November 10, 1862, VTHS; Holmes, "My Hunt After 'The Captain,'" 745.

23. Gilbert Reynolds to "Dear Wife," August 24, 1862, UR; Quaife, *Cannon's Mouth,* 86; James Gillette to "Dear Mother," January 29, 1863, LC.

24. Jacob Hunter to "Dear Wife," December 25, 1862, SHSI-DM; Clement Boughton to "Friends at Home," June 5, 1862, CL; *OR,* 12(2):403.

25. Special Order, November 16, 1862, 9th New Hampshire Collection, NHHS; Jackson and O'Donnell, *Back Home in Oneida,* 56; *Burlington Free Press,* July 21, 1862; Merritt Stone to unidentified correspondent, October 18, 1862, VTHS; Sylvanus Cadwallader to "Dear Carrie," November 13, 1862, LC.

26. James Moffatt to "Miss Huffer," April 28, 1862, Huffer Letters, USAMHI; Eby, *Virginia Yankee,* 92–93.

27. Kearny to "My Dear Parker," "Just After Fair Oaks," LC; Poe to "My dear Wife," June 1 and 7, 1862, LC; Blight, *This Cruel War,* 264; Henry Seys to "Dear Hattie," October 2, 1863, CL; Albert Huntington to "Dear sister Sue," undated, and Samuel Partridge to Francis Macomber, undated, both UR.

28. *OR,* Series 3, 3:1041, 4:1212, and 5:220–21, 253–56. The army bought horses as low as $96 apiece in 1861; the price rose to $144 apiece by the middle of 1864, and $185 by June 30, 1865, or $118.04 during an average month.

29. Eby, *Virginia Yankee,* 114; Returns from U.S. Military Posts, 1800–1916 (M-617), Reel 21, Allegheny Arsenal, October, 1861, NA; Heitman, *Historical Register,* 1:146–47.

30. *Philadelphia Inquirer,* September 18 and 19, 1862; "Sister Annie" to "My dear brother," September 21, 1862, Nichol Papers, USAMHI.

31. *Philadelphia Inquirer,* September 18 and 19, 1862; "Sister Annie" to "My dear brother," September 21, 1862, Nichol Papers, USAMHI.

32. *Philadelphia Inquirer,* September 18 and 19, 1862.

33. *Philadelphia Inquirer,* September 18 and 19, 1862; "Sister Annie" to "My dear brother," September 21, 1862, Nichol Papers, USAMHI.

34. *Philadelphia Inquirer,* September 19, 1862; Special Order 288, October 10, 1862, initiating Allegheny Arsenal Court of Inquiry, RG 153, NA; Heitman, *Historical Register,* 1:146–47.

35. *Richmond Examiner,* March 14, 1863; *Richmond Whig,* March 14 and 16, 1863.

36. Benjamin French to Henry French, June 19, 1864, NHHS; French, *Witness,* 513.

37. *Dayton Empire,* September 5, 1862; Solomon Hamrick to A. D. Hamrick, October 18, 1862, IHS; Niven, *Chase Papers,* 3:240–41, 287.

38. Smith and Cooper, *Union Woman,* 29–31; *OR,* 16(1):933, 939, 16(2):519, 520; Niven, *Chase Papers,* 3:262–63.

39. *OR,* 16(2):476, 482, 500, 507; Butterworth Diary, September 4, 1862, Earlham; Levi Shell to "Friends at Home," September 17, 1862, SHSW; Ira Conine to "Jennie" September 12, 1862, BGSU. The governor of Ohio later issued thousands of "Squirrel Hunter" discharges — for example, that of Thomas J. Adams, CL.

40. *OR,* 16(1):982, 991, 1090, 16(2):501–2; Charles Medary to "Dear Father," July 2, 1862, OHS; *Brooklyn Daily Eagle,* September 19, 1862.

41. *OR,* 19(2):611, 627–28, 635, 656, 661.

42. Niven, *Chase Papers,* 3:275, 277–78; Beale, *Welles Diary,* 1:140, 145.

43. *New York Tribune,* August 13 and 20, 1862; *CWL,* 5:388–89; Niven, *Chase Papers,* 3:250–51, 261.

44. Jacob Howard to Lyman Trumbull, August 16, 1862, Trumbull Papers, LC.

45. Niven, *Chase Papers,* 3:254–55, 276–77; Robert Dale Owen to Lincoln, September

17, 1862, ALP; Burlingame and Ettlinger, *Inside Lincoln's White House,* 40. In his September 17 letter Owen inadvertently calculated the sixty-day limit as September 25.

46. Niven, *Chase Papers,* 1:393–95; Beale, *Welles Diary,* 1:142–43.

47. Niven, *Chase Papers,* 1:395; Beale, *Welles Diary,* 1:143; Laas, *Wartime Washington,* 186.

48. Pease and Randall, *Browning Diary,* 1:574. Lincoln later mentioned having allowed "a one hundred days fair notice" of his intentions regarding emancipation (*CWL,* 6:48–49).

49. Clement Boughton to "Friends at Home," July 21, 1862, CL; George Landrum to "Dear Amanda," March 28, 1862, WRHS; *OR,* 16(1):497.

50. W. R. Henley to John J. Crittenden, October 3, 1862, Reel 14, Crittenden Papers, LC.

51. Pease and Randall, *Browning Diary,* 1:578.

52. Chandler to Lyman Trumbull, September 10, 1862, Trumbull Papers, LC; *New York Herald,* September 25, 1862; *Atlas and Argus,* September 26, 1862; *OR,* Series 3, 2:582–84.

53. *Prairie du Chien Courier,* October 2, 1862; *Chicago Times,* September 23, 1862.

54. *CWL,* 4:263; Nordholt, "Civil War Letters," 364. See Guelzo, *Lincoln's Emancipation Proclamation,* 157–61, for some civilian reaction.

55. *Detroit Free Press,* September 26, 1862.

56. *Crisis,* September 24, 1862; Burlingame and Ettlinger, *Inside Lincoln's White House,* 41.

57. Alexander Varian to "Dear Sister," October 5, 1862, WRHS; *OR,* 19(2):435.

58. Ransom Sargent to "Dear Maria," September 28, 1862, DC; William Combs to Eliza Combs, November 23, 1862, ND.

59. *CWL,* 5:444.

60. Sanborn Diary, September 30, 1862, NHHS; Hammond, *Diary,* 177; Loving, *Whitman Letters,* 71; Clement Boughton to "Mother Brothers & Sister," September 28 and October 26, 1862, and to "Friends at Home," March 26, 1863, CL.

61. George Oscar French to "Friends at Home," January 17, 1863, and to "Father," September 11, 1864, VTHS; John Burrill to "Dear Parents," January 1 and February 6, 1863, USAMHI.

62. Hitchcock to "Dear Mrs. Mann," October 5, 1862, LC; Duncan, *Blue-Eyed Child,* 245; Scott, *Fallen Leaves,* 161.

63. Unidentified correspondent [Porter] to Manton Marble, September 30–October 3, 1862, Marble Papers, LC; L. A. Whiteley to James G. Bennett, September 24, 1862, LC.

64. *Detroit Free Press,* September 28, 1862.

65. Joseph Holt to Bellamy Storer, September 24, 1862, CinHS; George Landrum to "Dear Amanda," February 6, 1863, WRHS.

66. Lewis Cleveland to "Dear Louise," October 5, 1862, USAMHI; Nevins, *Diary of Battle,* 108–9; Sears, *On Campaign,* 138; Simpson and Berlin, *Sherman's Civil War,* 312.

67. Heitman, *Historical Register,* 1:1041; Nevins and Thomas, *Strong Diary,* 3:137–38, 190, 195, 243, 286; *CWP,* 98; *Cleveland Plain Dealer,* May 22, 1862; Returns of the 6th U.S. Cavalry, September, 1862 through March, 1863 (M-744), Reel 61, RG 94, NA.

68. George Benson Fox to "My Dear Father," January 21, 1863, CinHS; Flavius Bellamy to "Dear Brother," October 26, 1862, ISL; *Crisis,* November 19, 1862; Blight, *This Cruel War,* 187.

69. George Landrum to "Dear Amanda," February 6, 1863, WRHS; Williams, *Wild Life of the Army,* 207.

70. Robert Kellogg to Silas Root Kellogg and Lucy Church Hale Kellogg, September 10, 1862, CHS.

71. Thomas Cheney to Luther Cheney, January 10, "1862" [1863], UNH; William

Willoughby to "My Dear Wife," January 22, 1863, AAS, quoted in Silber and Sievens, *Yankee Correspondence*, 97; John Ellis to "Dear Nephew," undated, USAMHI; Jacob Hunter to Mary, January 29, 1863, SHSI-DM.

72. John Harpin Riggs to "Dear Father," January 2, 1863, New Haven Colony Historical Society; Skipper and Taylor, *Handful of Providence*, 185; Shannon, *Andrus Letters*, 43. See also Mitchell, *Civil War Soldiers*, 126–31. James McPherson calculated (*Cause and Comrades*, 117–18) that three in ten Union soldiers supported emancipation in the first eighteen months of the war, and "many more were eventually converted to it." The ratio among original, unrevised sources for the same period in this study ran to only one in four, including some very equivocal support. Laudatory comments on emancipation from before 1863 seem more common in diaries and letters that the veterans themselves were able to revise in later years (see, for instance, Norton, *Army Letters*, 43, and Watson, *Ashby to Andersonville*, 25), which may explain the proportional discrepancy between McPherson's analysis and the results of this smaller sampling. I have thus far surveyed too few sources dating after 1862 to characterize later opinions, but McPherson's report of increasing support seems neither invalid nor illogical.

73. William Stevens to "Dear Sister," September 7, 1862, SM; George Geer to "Dear Wife," August 3, 1862, Mariners' Museum; George Upton to "My Dear Sarah," July 17, 1862, NHHS; Longacre, *Antietam to Fort Fisher*, 44–45; Richard Cary Morse Sr. to Richard Cary Morse Jr., August 13, 1862, CL; Henry Kynett and R. E. Kynett to "Dear Son," November 9, 1862, SHSI-DM; Jacob Haas to "My Dear Bro.," December 18, 1862, USAMHI; Jacob Kiester to "Sir," August 31, 1862, USAMHI. Mitchell, *Civil War Soldiers*, 14–15, offers more evidence of antagonism for abolition; although he cautions against exaggerating that antagonism, his treatment seems compatible with the thrust of this paragraph.

74. John Ellis to "Dear Nephew," undated, USAMHI; *New Hampshire Patriot*, February 4, 1863; *Crisis*, December 31, 1862; *Prairie du Chien Courier*, January 22 and February 5, 1863; *Portland Advertiser*, March 6, 1863; Solomon Dodge to "Dear sister Eliza," January 17, 1863, NHHS.

75. Henry Johnson to "Dear Clara," January 14, 1863, CL; Robertson, *McAllister Letters*, 212.

76. Pease and Randall, *Browning Diaries*, 1:585, 591.

77. *CWL*, 4:532; Niven, *Chase Papers*, 1:357.

78. E. T. Bainbridge to Joseph Holt, October 28, 1862, and Bell to Holt, October 20, 1862, Holt Papers, LC.

79. E. T. Bainbridge to Joseph Holt, October 22, 1862 (two letters), LC; *OR*, 16(2):519; James Speed to Joseph Holt, November 8, 1862, LC.

80. *OR*, 16(2):546, 859, 864, 876; William Steele to Olive Steele, September 19 and 25, 1862, IHS; John Henry Knight to "My Darling Sue," September 26, 1862, SHSW.

81. Davis and Swentor, *Bluegrass Confederate*, 151; *OR*, 16(2):554–55.

82. *OR*, 16(1):557–58.

83. Niven, *Chase Papers*, 3:263.

84. *OR*, 16(1):350, 16(2):564–65, 575; Robert Hanna to "Dear Wife," October 10, 1862, IHS; Anderson, *Letters and Journals*, 161.

85. *OR*, 16(1):1091, 1094–95, 16(2):876, 905; Davis and Swentor, *Bluegrass Confederate*, 152–53.

86. Kaiser, "Carr Letters," 268–69; *OR*, 16(1):1024.

87. *OR*, 16(1):239, 356, 1072. Gilbert characterized the difference between Sheridan's orders and his actions as a "misunderstanding," but it was a type of misunderstanding to which Sheridan became particularly prone. See Gilbert, "On the Field of Perryville," 53.

88. *OR*, 16(1):69, 90, 358, 527. The most recent and most thorough study of this battle is Noe, *Perryville*.

89. Walker Diary, October 8, 1862, USAMHI; George Landrum to "Dear Amanda," October 12, 1862, WRHS; *OR*, 16(1):344–46, 1046, 1062, 1072.

90. *OR*, 16(1):1046; George Landrum to "Dear Amanda," October 12, 1862, WRHS; Kaiser, "Carr Letters," 268–69; Alexander Varian to "Dear Father," October 15, 1862, WRHS.

91. *OR*, 16(1):94–95, 97, 98, 1023, 1035, 1075–76, 1079–81.

92. George Landrum to "Dear Amanda," October 12, 1862, WRHS; Sturges Diary, October 10, 1862, USAMHI; Marion Ward to "Home," "September" [October] 21, 1862, WRHS; Andrew Davis to "My dear Wife," October 16, 1862, UIA; Henry H. Seys to "My dear Wife," October 15, 1862, CL; Barnes, *Medical and Surgical History*, 2:255.

93. Henry H. Seys to "Dear Wife," October 27, 1862, CL; George Hodges to "Dear Wife," October 20, 1862, WRHS.

94. Newspaper clipping of Morton to Lincoln, October 7, 1862, Morton Papers, ISL.

95. *OR*, 16(2):634; E. T. Bainbridge to Holt, October 22, 1862, LC.

96. J. A. Fischer to William Lehmann, August 7, 1862, Lehmann Family Papers, SHSW.

97. *Commercial Daily List*, October 9, 1862.

8. Our Army Foiled with Loss Severe

1. Smith and Cooper, *A Union Woman*, 31–33; E. T. Bainbridge to Joseph Holt, October 22, 1862, and James Speed to Holt, November 8, 1862, LC; *OR*, 16(1):348–50. In his legendary memoir, Tennessee Confederate Sam Watkins claimed (*"Co. Aytch,"* 81) that while standing picket in Perryville the night before the battle, he joined his Yankee counterpart in raiding an unoccupied local home for dainty edibles; as implausible as the story is, it may reflect a credible disdain for residents of a state that had failed to support their "liberators."

2. G. L. Wakefield to "Dear Friends," December 4, 1861, More Collection, UIA; Sewell Tilton to "Dear Brother & Sister," October 7, 1862, NHHS; Clement Boughton to "Dear Mother," June 22, 1862, CL.

3. *OR*, 19(2):628.

4. *New York Times*, August 11, 1861; Abbott, *First New Hampshire*, 137–38, 162.

5. Edward Darlington to William Seward, October 17, 1862, ALP; Alfred Holcomb to "Dear Father and mother," February 13, 1862, USAMHI; Clement Boughton to "Friends," April 30, 1862, CL.

6. George Dudley to "Brother Elias," January 14, 1863, MHS; William Moore to "Sister Lizzie," October 20, 1862, NHHS; Sewell Tilton to "Dear Brother & Sister," October 7, 1862, NHHS; Sears, *Dunn Browne*, 5.

7. Albert Huntington to "Dear Mother," January 28, 1863, and Horace Hooker to Susan Hooker, November "31st," 1862, UR; Larimer, *Love and Valor*, 66; John Barney to "all at Home," December 26, 1862, SHSW.

8. Alfred Foreman to "Dear hunkel and hant," September 5, 1862, Sisson Family Letters, ISU; Marion D. Ward to "Dear Aunt," September 5, 1862, and to "Home Friends," January 31, 1863, WRHS; John D. Pugh to "Dear Sister," September 26, 1862, Achilles Pugh Papers, Earlham.

9. Christopher Keller to "Dear Carrie," November 9, 1862, CL; Sylvanus Cadwallader to "Dear Carrie," November 13, 1862, LC; Philo Buckingham to "My Dear Wife," January 4, 1863, AAS.

10. James Denver to "My Dear wife," November 29, 1862, USAMHI; William Augustus Smith to "Dear Father," September 26, 1862, Smith Brothers Papers, CL.

11. Edward F. Hall to "Dear Susan," December 7, 1862, and May 26, 1863, NHHS; Elijah Cavins to "Dear Ann," October 20 and 25, 1862, and to "Dear Riley," October 25, 1862, IHS; James Brown to "Dear Brother," April 13, 1864, MEHS.

12. Sawyer, *Godfrey Letters*, 19; William Rigby to "Dear Folks at Home," November 23, 1862, UIA; Amasa Allen to Agnes Allen, November "18," 1862, SHSI-DM.

13. Thomas Coffman to "Dear Girl," November 22, 1862, SHSI-IC; *Crisis*, January 7, 1863; *OR*, 13:358–60.

14. Thomas Hughes to "My Dear Wife," December 21, 1862, CL; John Barney to "all at Home," January 2, 1863, SHSW; Thomas Sterns to "Dear Wife," January 1, 1863, UIA; Levi Shell to "Dear Brother," January 5, 1863, SHSW; Woodworth, *Musick of the Mocking Birds*, 13; Newton Scott to Hannah Cone, April 9, 1863, Proudfoot Collection.

15. Horace Hooker to Susan Hooker, February 26, 1863, UR; Sewell Tilton to "Dear Bro & Sister," July 28, 1863, NHHS; Christopher Keller to "Dear Carrie," January 12, 1863, CL; Davidson, *Hartley Letters*, 20.

16. Benjamin Ashenfelter to "Dear Mother," November 12, 1862; Isaac Morrow to "Dear Brother," August 18, 1862; Hall Diary, October 6 and November 4, 1862; Charles Riley to "Dear Sir," November 14, 1862; Orrin William Bennett to "Friend Sam," October 31, 1862; Lewis Cleveland to "Dear Louise," November 21, 1862; all in USAMHI.

17. Jacob Haas to Frederick Haas, December 18, 1862, USAMHI.

18. Peter Abbott to "Friends at Home," October 11, 1862, VTHS; Alonzo Jack to "Dear Parents," September 26, 1862, SHSW; Peter Faulk to "Dear Sister," December 26, 1862, BGSU.

19. James Brown to "Dear Friends at Home," December 30, 1862, MEHS; Hosea Towne to "Dear Friends," December 5, 1862, NHHS; William Stow to "Dear Parents," December 10, 1863, UVM; Charles Mumford to "Dear Wife," December 13, 1862, and February 1, 1863, SHSW.

20. For a sampling of complaints about slow pay see: George Redlon to "Dear Father," April 13, 1862, MEHS; George Chapin to Ella Chapin, October 14, 1862, IHS; "One who wants his pay" to James G. Bennett, October 22, 1862, LC; George Randall to "Dear Joey," October 31, 1862, PPL; William Russell to "Dear Col," November 16, 1862, UIA; Daniel Faust to "Dear mother," March 14, 1863, USAMHI; Francis Boland to "Dear Sir," December 2, 1862, USAMHI; Lewis Cleveland to "Dear Louise," December 2, 1862, USAMHI; William Thompson to Jane Thompson, December 22, 1862, SHSI-DM; William Pressley to "Dear Father," December 23, 1862, USAMHI; Adoniram Withrow to Libertatia, January 3, 1863, SHSI-IC; Levi Shell to "Dear Brother," January 5, 1863, SHSW; Solomon Hamrick to "Brother Charley," January 16, 1863, IHS; Elijah Cavins to "Dear Ann," January 18, 1863, IHS; D. W. Perkins to George Wheeler, January 23, 1863, DC; M. P. Wheeler to Gideon W. Allen, March 10, 1863, SHSW; George Rowell to "Dear Parents," March 18, "1862" [1863], NHHS; Marion D. Ward to "Home Friends," March 21, 1863, WRHS; Larimer, *Love and Valor*, 126, 132; Woodworth, *Musick of the Mocking Birds*, 117.

21. *OR*, 22(2):91, 115; David Nichol to "Dear Father & Home," November 26, 1862, USAMHI; Niven, *Chase Papers*, 3:358, 362, 367; David Leigh to Herman Drumgold, November 17, 1862, DC; James Brown to "Dear Friends," October 11, 1862, MEHS.

22. Ellsworth Phelps to "My Dear Wife," October 30, 1862, CHS; Ransom Sargent to "Dear Maria," September 28, 1862, DC; Edwin Wentworth to "Dear Father," November 10, 1862, LC.

23. *War Letters, 1862–1865*, 6, 13; *CWL*, 5:436–37; Scott, *Fallen Leaves*, 161.

24. Composition dated October, 1862, Harvey Bloom Papers, Yale; Blair, *A Politician Goes to War*, 56.

25. Simpson and Berlin, *Sherman's Civil War*, 311–12; Meade, *Life and Letters*, 1:322.

26. Sanborn Diary, November 30, 1862, NHHS; Ira Getchell to Ellen Forbes, November 23, 1862, MEHS; Robert Wentworth to Caroline Wentworth, December 25, 1862, Edwin Wentworth Papers, LC; John Riggs to "Dear Father," December 12, 1862, New Haven Colony Historical Society.

27. "Your Mother" to James Remington, December 14, 1862, RIHS; Henrietta Parker to Charles Parker, December 25, 1862, and January 8, 11, and 13, 1863, UVM; Orville Bixby to "My Owne dear Frances," December 10, 1862, UVM; Andrew Knox to "My dear

wife," November 18, 1862, USAMHI; Jane Thompson to William Thompson, November 28, 1862, SHSI-DM.

28. Nathaniel Harris to Amasa Tracy, November 24, 1862, UVM; William Mann to "Dear Father," August 17, 1862, UIA; Solomon Hamrick to A. D. Hamrick, November 10, 1862, IHS.

29. *Ohio Statesman,* May 9, 1862; *Dayton Journal,* September 5 and 10, 1862; *Civilian and Telegraph,* July 31, 1862; *New York Herald,* August 5, 1862. On Vallandigham see Klement, *The Limits of Dissent.*

30. *Daily Democrat,* September 2, 1861; *Chicago Tribune,* August 26, 1862; Calvin Hess affidavit, August 14, 1862, Case 154, Reel 6, and George Bickley to William Seward, August 14, 1863, Case 1649, Reel 48, Turner-Baker Case Files (M-797), NA.

31. "CGSUC Ind. North" to Joseph K. English, September 26, 1862, and cryptographic alphabet, Henry K. English Papers, ISL.

32. *OR,* 16(2):641–42, 654.

33. James Adams to "Dear Father," December 1 and 7, 1862; Elijah Cavins to "Dear Father," July 18, 1862; Solomon Hamrick to A. D. Hamrick, June 25 and October 19, 1862; all in IHS.

34. *Ohio State Journal,* October 16, 1862; *Crisis,* October 22, 1862; A. T. Goodman to Alexander Long, October 28, 1862, Long Papers, CinHS.

35. Burlingame, *With Lincoln,* 89; Solomon Hamrick to A. D. Hamrick, October 18 and 19, November 10, 1862, IHS; Allen J. Sherrill to Madison Homer Carlton, November 11, 1862, IHS.

36. Thomas Dudley to John Crittenden, December 1, 1862, Crittenden Papers, LC; Francis Springer to Hawkins Taylor, October 19, 1862, ALP.

37. *CWP,* 473; Cochrane to Lincoln, October 26, 1862, ALP; Niven, *Chase Papers,* 1:415–16.

38. *CWP,* 479, 482–83.

39. *CWL,* 5:442–43; Key to Lincoln, September 27, 1862, ALP. Two months later Lincoln essentially acknowledged the injustice he had done Major Key while contending that political considerations prevented him from correcting it (*CWL,* 5:508–9).

40. Burlingame and Ettlinger, *Inside Lincoln's White House,* 41; Niven, *Chase Papers,* 3:304; Beale, *Welles Diary,* 1:176–77; *CWL,* 5:460.

41. *CWL,* 7:548; Quaife, *From the Cannon's Mouth,* 136.

42. *CWL,* 7:549; Sparks, *Inside Lincoln's Army,* 155–56; Nevins, *Diary of Battle,* 109–10; Cheney Diary, October 2 and 3, 1862, UNH; Lewis Cleveland to "Dear Louise," October 5, 1862, USAMHI.

43. Holford Diary, October 3, 1862, LC; Charles Coit to "Dear All," October 4, 1862, Yale; George Chandler to "dear Kate," October 3, 1862, NHHS; Longacre, *Antietam to Fort Fisher,* 48.

44. *OR,* 19(1):72, 19(2):387, 394; Halleck to "My dear Wife," October 7, 1862, CL; *CWL,* 5:452.

45. Daniel Reed Larned to "My Dear Sister," October 12, 1862, LC; J. W. Garrett to McClellan, October 8, 1862, Reel 33, McClellan Papers, LC; Mary Ellen Marcy to Mary Shipman, October 15, 1862, CHS; *War Letters, 1862–1865,* 1. Though previously suspected (see Marvel, *Burnside,* 154), McClellan's absence on October 9 and 10 was not confirmed until 1996, when Stephen Sears found the corroborative letter to Mary Shipman.

46. Sparks, *Inside Lincoln's Army,* 161; *OR,* 19(2):52.

47. *OR,* 19(2):52–54, 59–81; Robert Shortelle to unidentified recipient, October 14, 1862, Shortelle Family Papers, LC; Holford Diary, October 15, 1862, LC.

48. *CWL,* 5:460–61.

49. *OR,* 19(2):417, 421, 422–24, 465, 485, 490–91, 496; James Shortelle to Robert Shortelle, October 14, 1862, LC.

50. Watson, *Ashby to Andersonville*, 31, 36–40; Sparks, *Inside Lincoln's Army*, 168; Priest, *New Bern to Fredericksburg*, 82; Sears, *Country, Cause & Leader*, 283–84; Colburn Diary, October 26–November 8, 1862, USAMHI; *OR*, 19(2):523; Willand Diary, November 8, 1862, NHSL; Hawes Diary, November 5–7, 1862, MHS; Willard Templeton to "Dear Brother," November 8, 1862, NHSL.

51. *OR*, 19(2):394–95; Sparks, *Inside Lincoln's Army*, 171; Watson, *Ashby to Andersonville*, 40; Sears, *Country, Cause & Leader*, 284; William Teall to "My darling Wife," November 17, 1862, TSLA.

52. Cheney Diary, November 7, 1862, UNH; Edward Wentworth to "My dear Wife," November 8, 1862, LC; Acken, *Inside the Army of the Potomac*, 157; Silliker, *The Rebel Yell*, 49.

53. *OR*, 19(2):534; Hall Diary, November 7, 1862, USAMHI.

54. *OR*, 19(1):152, 19(2):541, 542, 545.

55. *Chicago Tribune*, September 6, 1875 (page misdated September 5); Herman Haupt to "My Dear Sis," November 9, 1862, LC; Sparks, *Inside Lincoln's Army*, 172.

56. Meade, *Life and Letters*, 1:325; Nevins, *Diary of Battle*, 124; Porter to Manton Marble, November 9, 1862, Marble Papers, LC.

57. Beale, *Welles Diary*, 1:179–80; Henry B. Stanton to John G. Nicolay, October 17, 1862, and John Cochrane to Lincoln, October 26, 1862, both in ALP.

58. Mattie Blanchard to Caleb Blanchard, November 9, 1862, CHS; John Cochrane to Lincoln, November 5, 1862, ALP; Gideon Allen to Annie Cox, November 24, 1862, SHSW; Field to Lincoln, November 8, 1862, ALP.

59. Elijah Cavins to "Dear Ann," November 9, 1862, IHS; William Speed to "My dear Sister," November 13, 1862, CL; Benjamin Ashenfelter to "Dear Mother," November 12, 1862, USAMHI; Walter Gardiner to "My Dear Friend," November 25, 1862, PPL; Lewis Cleveland to "Dear Mother," November 10, 1862, USAMHI; Holden, Ross, and Slomba, *Stand Firm*, 53.

60. Charles Coit to "Dear All," October 4, 1862, Yale; James Gillette to "Dear Mother," September 8, 1862, LC.

61. Masonheimer Diary, November 10, 1862, USAMHI; William Moore to "Father," November 18, 1862, NHHS; Holden, Ross, and Slomba, *Stand Firm*, 53; Acken, *Inside the Army of the Potomac*, 164; Henry Young to "Dear Mother," November 10, 1862, USAMHI; Lewis Cleveland to "Dear Mother," November 10, 1862, USAMHI; Keiser Diary, November 10, 1862, USAMHI.

62. Acken, *Inside the Army of the Potomac*, 164–65; Nevins, *A Diary of Battle*, 125; Leib Diary, November 10, 1862, USAMHI; John D. Wilkins to "My Dearly beloved wife," November 11, 1862, CL.

63. Edwin Wentworth to "Dear Father," November 10, 1862, LC; Josiah Fuller to "My dear Wife," November 13, 1862, MHS; Isaac Morrow to "Dear Brother," November 26, 1862, USAMHI; George Chandler to "dear Kate," October 3, 1862, NHHS.

64. Haupt to "Dearest," November 15, 1862, LC; Blair, *A Politician Goes to War*, 69; Henry Marsh to "Dear Father," November 25, 1862, ISL; James Remington to "Dear Father," November 17, 1862, RIHS; Walter Chapman to "Dear Parents," October 19, 1862, Yale.

65. Meade, *Life and Letters*, 1:325; Quaife, *From the Cannon's Mouth*, 151.

66. Sparks, *Inside Lincoln's Army*, 175.

67. Nevins, *A Diary of Battle*, 126; Sparks, *Inside Lincoln's Army*, 175; Haupt to "Dearest," November 15, 1862, LC; *OR*, 21:83–84.

68. *OR*, 21:84.

69. *RJCCW*, 663–65, 671; *OR*, 21:84–85.

70. *OR*, 85–87, 792; *RJCCW*, 664–65.

71. *OR*, 21:86, 102–4; David Lovell to "Sister Hattie," November 22, 1862, USAMHI.

72. Daniel Larned to "My Dear Sister," November 27, 1862, LC; *CWL*, 5:514–15; Sparks, *Inside Lincoln's Army*, 182–83; *OR*, 20(2):117–18.

73. Sparks, *Inside Lincoln's Army*, 182–83; Notes on the Battle of Fredericksburg, Larned Papers, LC; Lewis Cleveland to "Dear Mother," December 10, 1862, USAMHI.

74. Sumner to Burnside, November 23, 1862, Box 3, Burnside Papers, RG 94, NA; *OR*, 21:87, 551–52, 1133; Coburn Diary, December 1–7, 1862, USAMHI; Orlando Poe to "My dear Wife," December 6, 1862, LC.

75. George Rowell to "Dear parents," December 3, 1862, NHHS; *RJCCW*, 652; *OR*, 21:87–88, 551–52.

76. *RJCCW*, 652; Charles R. Johnson to "Dear Nellie," November 29, 1862, USAMHI; George Upton to "My Dear Sarah," December 2, 1862, NHHS; Benjamin Ashenfelter to "My Dear Wife," December 10, 1862, USAMHI.

77. Orlando Poe to "My dear Wife," November 24 and December 9, 1862, LC; Franklin Sawyer to Samuel Sexton, November 26, 1862, OHS; Benjamin Ashenfelter to "Dear Mother," November 12, 1862, USAMHI.

78. Howe, *Touched with Fire*, 73; Lewis Cleveland to "Dear Mother," November 10, 1862, USAMHI; Hugh Henry to "Dear Sarah," November 7, 1862, UVM; Blight, *This Cruel War*, 189.

79. Orville Bixby to "My Owne dear Frances," December 10, 1862, UVM; Henry Rogers Smith to "Dear Father," December 10, 1862, AAS; George H. Legate to "Dear Sister," December 27, 1862, USAMHI.

80. Sparks, *Inside Lincoln's Army*, 187.

81. *OR*, 21:168, 173–74, 179, 182–83, 191; Josiah Fuller to "My dear Wife," December 11, 1862, MHS; Charles Coit to "Dear All," December 14, 1862, Yale; Oscar Robinson to "Dear Mother," December 14, 1862, DC.

82. *OR*, 21:282–83; Notes on the Battle of Fredericksburg, Larned Papers, LC. A thirteen-year-old drummer boy allegedly accompanied the Michigan landing party (*Portland Daily Press*, December 30, 1862).

83. Holford Diary, December 11, 1862, LC; Longacre, *Antietam to Fort Fisher*, 87; Wolf, "Taylor Diary," 236; Masonheimer Diary, December 12, 1862, USAMHI; Henry White Diary, December 12, 1862, AAS.

84. Wolf, "Taylor Diary," 236; undated letter fragment, Charles E. Chase Papers, UVM; Henry White Diary, December 12, 1862, AAS; Charles Goddard to "Dear Mother," December 16, 1862, MNHS; Charles D. Chase to Charles Chase, January 11, 1862, NHHS; Robinson Diary, December 12–13, 1862, DC; John Godfrey to "Bro Horace," December 14, 1862, NHHS; Coco, *Ball's Bluff to Gettysburg*, 142.

85. Sparks, *Inside Lincoln's Army*, 189; Henry White Diary, December 12, 1862, AAS.

86. Wolf, "Taylor Diary," 236; *OR*, 21:393; Isaac Morrow to "Dear Brother," December 21, 1862, USAMHI; Charles Chase to "Dear Mother," February 3, 1863, UVM.

87. Whitmore Diary, December 11, 1862, MHS.

88. Nevins, *Diary of Battle*, 138; *OR*, 21:108–9, 465, 467, 1121; Holford Diary, December 12, 1862, LC; Cheney Diary, December 12, 1862, UNH.

89. Nevins, *Diary of Battle*, 138–39; Franklin, *Reply*, 6.

90. Franklin, *Reply*, 6; *OR*, 21:109–10; *RJCCW*, 1:709–10.

91. *OR*, 21:71; Meade, *Life and Letters*, 1:360, 365–66.

92. Hardie to Burnside, March 12, 1863, Box 6, Burnside Papers, RG 94, NA; *OR*, 21:454, 511; Nevins, *Diary of Battle*, 139, 141.

93. Compare the map tipped into Franklin's *Reply* with *OR Atlas*, plates 33, map 1, and plate 39, maps 2, 3.

94. Benjamin Ashenfelter to "Father Churchman," December 23, 1862, USAMHI; Heffelfinger Diary, December 13, 1862, USAMHI; Truxall, *Respects to All*, 35; Holford

Diary, December 13, 1862, LC; George Legate to "Dear Sister," December 27, 1862, USAMHI; Meade, *Life and Letters*, 1:340; *Diary of General S. M. Jackson*, 61.

95. *RJCCW*, 1:667; Herman Haupt to "Dearest," December 13, 1862, LC; William Teall to "My darling Wife," December 13, 1862, TSLA; *OR*, 21:91, and Series 3, 3:294.

96. William Teall to "My darling Wife," December 13, 1862, TSLA; *OR*, 21:91, 286–87.

97. *OR*, 21:227, 290, 291–92, 294; Masonheimer Diary, December 30, 1862, USAMHI.

98. *OR*, 21:129–30, 227; Holden, Ross, and Slomba, *Stand Firm*, 56–57; Kohl, *Irish Green*, 43.

99. Ramsey to "Dear Father," December 24, 1862, NHHS.

100. Hurd to "Dear Coz," January 27 and February 10, 1863, Barton Papers, DC; Ayling, *Register*, 243.

101. Longacre, *Antietam to Fort Fisher*, 91; Masonheimer Diary, December 13, 1862, USAMHI; Holden, Ross, and Slomba, *Stand Firm*, 60; Tilton Diary, December 15, 1862, MHS; Ransom Sargent to "Dear Maria," December 15, 1862, and January 1, 1863, DC; Ayling, *Register*, 563. For instance, compare Brigadier General Hiram Berry's December 14 report (*OR*, 21:375) that the conduct of the 101st New York "together with all its officers, was unexceptionable," to Theodore Dodge's December 20 observation that the lieutenant colonel of the 101st had just been dismissed for cowardice (Sears, *On Campaign*, 121).

102. James S. Howes to "My Dear Wife," January 11, 1863, NHHS; Ayling, *Register*, 549.

103. Sears, *On Campaign*, 121. For battlefield behavior in general see Hess, *The Union Soldier in Battle*.

104. *OR*, 21:263; Pearce, *Chambers Diary*, 75; Scott, *Fallen Leaves*, 148–49; Mathew Marvin to "Dear Brother," December 24, 1862, MNHS; Coco, *From Ball's Bluff to Gettysburg*, 142.

105. *OR*, 21:311, 316, 319–20, 325–26; Priest, *From New Bern to Fredericksburg*, 95–96.

106. *OR*, 21:320, 327, 328–29; Loving, *Whitman Letters*, 76; Watson, *Ashby to Andersonville*, 49; Willard Templeton to "Dear Brother," December 15, 1862, NHSL; Henry White Diary, December 13, 1862, AAS.

107. *OR*, 21:93–94, 128; Franklin, *Reply*, 23–24; *RJCCW*, 1:656.

108. Of the twenty-five brigades at his disposal (not counting Burns's division of the Ninth Corps), Franklin threw only six into his assault, using another six, and eventually nine more, to repel the counterattack; Sumner, meanwhile, attacked with nineteen of the twenty-two brigades he controlled (again, not counting Burns).

109. *OR*, 21:92–94, 451; John Stevens to "Dear Parents," December 22, 1862, NHHS; Whitmore Diary, December 13, 1862, MHS; William Stevens to "My dear Sister," December 22, 1862, SM; Sylvanus Nye to "Dear Brother," December 17, 1862, VTHS; Charles Johnson to "Dear Nellie," "Dec. 1862," USAMHI.

110. *OR*, 21:397, 404–5; 408–9, 410; Acken, *Inside the Army of the Potomac*, 182–85.

111. *OR*, 21:430–31; Thomas French to "My dear Mother," December 19, 1862, quoted in Alexander, *126th Pennsylvania*, 128–29.

112. *OR*, 21:433–34. See Carol Reardon's essay on this attack, "The Forlorn Hope," in Gallagher, *The Fredericksburg Campaign*, 80–112.

113. *OR*, 21:133, 332–33; Longacre, *Antietam to Fort Fisher*, 89–90; Belden Diary, December 13, 1862, CHS.

114. Sears, *Dunn Browne*, 50; S. W. North to "Dear Brother," quoted in Alexander, *126th Pennsylvania*, 130–31; Longacre, *Antietam to Fort Fisher*, 90–91.

115. William Teall to "My darling Wife," December 13, 1862, TSLA; John Crocker to "My Dear Hattie," December 13, 1862, Cornell; John Godfrey to "Bro Horace," December 14, 1862, NHHS.

116. William Teall to "My darling Wife," December 13, and 14, 1862, TSLA; Longacre, *Antietam to Fredericksburg,* 91; Blackburn, *With the Wandering Regiment,* 48; Sparks, *Inside Lincoln's Army,* 190; Sumner to Burnside, December 14, 1862, Hay Collection, LC.

117. William Teall to "My darling Wife," December 15, 1862, TSLA; Sparks, *Inside Lincoln's Army,* 190.

118. Hammond Diary, December 11–18, 1862, USAMHI; Charles Herbert to "Dear Parents," November 30, 1862, and to "Dear Parents & Sister," December 31, 1862, NHHS; Samuel Bartlett to "Dear Sister," December 21, 1862, CHS; Andrew Farnum to "Dear folks at home," December 23, 1862, NHHS.

119. Notes on the Battle of Fredericksburg, Larned Papers, LC; Nevins and Thomas, *Strong Diary,* 3:280.

120. Beale, *Welles Diary,* 1:192; Willard Templeton to "Dear Brother," December 16, 1862, NHSL.

121. *Diary of General S. M. Jackson,* 65; Whitmore Diary, December 15, 1862, MHS; Charles Johnson to "Dear Nellie," "Dec. 1862," USAMHI; Cheney Diary, December 15, 1862, UNH.

122. Henry Beecham to "Dear Mother," December 19, 1862, SHSW; Wilcox Diary, December 15, 1862, NHHS; Holford Diary, December 15, 1862, LC; Nevins, *Diary of Battle,* 146; Sears, *Country, Cause & Leader,* 298–99; William Goddard to Burnside, December 16, 1862, Box 3, Burnside Papers, RG 94, NA.

123. *OR,* 21:142, 562, 572.

9. The Cold Dirges of the Baffled

1. *Luzerne Union,* October 1, 1862, and *Pittston Gazette,* October 2, 1862, quoted in Palladino, *Another Civil War,* 100–101.

2. *Civilian and Telegraph,* October 16, 1862; Henry Burnham to "Dear Sister Lora," November 30, 1862, VTHS; "Sister Annie" to "My dear brother," September 21, 1862, Nichol Papers, USAMHI; Norman Ball Journal, October 25, 1862, CHS; *OR,* Series 3, 2:650, 3:760.

3. *Prairie du Chien Courier,* October 30, 1862; *Milwaukee Sentinel,* November 12, 13, 17, 18, 19, and 21, 1862; Thomas Sterns to "Dear Wife," October 28, 1862, UIA.

4. *Milwaukee Sentinel,* November 17, 1862; *OR,* Series 3, 2:867. Figures taken from the report of Adjutant General Augustus Gaylord, quoted in Klement, *Wisconsin and the Civil War,* 38.

5. Loretta Howe to George Howe, August 28, 1862, SM; David Marshall to Oliver P. Morton, August 13, 1862, Butterworth Diary, August 27, 1862, Albertson Journal, September 4, 1862, and John Harvey to "Dear Mother," August 3, 1862, all at Earlham; *Kansas Chief,* September 11, 1862.

6. Second District Draft Exemptions, 1862, RIHS; Exemption Applications and Certificates of Disability, Dane County Draft Records, SHSW; assorted certificates and correspondence, Favill Papers, SHSW.

7. Lucy Larcom Diary, Addison Collection, August 21, 1862, MHS; "Henry" to "Dear Lal," September 23, 1862, Summers Papers, SHSI-DM; *Daily Times,* July 30, 1862; Samuel Storrow to "My dear Father," October 12, 1862, MHS.

8. George Upton to "My Dear Wife," January 15, 1863, NHHS; William Patterson to "Dear Mother," December 24, 1862, USAMHI; Sears, *Country, Cause & Leader,* 299; William Stevens to "My dear Sister," December 22, 1862, SM.

9. Walter Hurd to "Dear Parents," February 7, 1863, SM; Andrew Knox to "My dear wife," December 18, 1862, USAMHI; Mathew Marvin to "Dear Brother," December 24, 1862, MNHS; Edwin Wentworth to "My dear Carrie," January 5, 1863, LC. Suicide statistics from Barnes, *Medical and Surgical History,* 1:34–35, 178–79, 328–29, 494–95.

10. *War Letters, 1862–1865,* 51; John S. Willey to "My Dear Wife," December 19, 1862,

USAMHI; Charles Benton to "Dear Wife," December 20, 1862, ND; John Godfrey to "Bro Horace," December 14, 1862, NHHS; John P. Hatch to "Dear Father," February 19, 1862, LC.

11. Thomas Cheney to David Gilchrist, January 2, 1863, UNH; Blight, *This Cruel War*, 189, 205; Plumb, "Letters," 69; Sparks, *Inside Lincoln's Army*, 192–93, 199; James Bromley to "Dear brother and sister," December 25, 1862, VTHS; Thomas Brown to O. G. Morrison, December 30, 1862, VTHS; Ransom Sargent to "Dear Maria," December 19, 1862, DC; Robert Wentworth to Caroline Wentworth, December 25, 1862, and Edwin Wentworth to "My dear Wife," December 22, 1862, January 2 and 5, 1863, LC; Jacob Haas to "My Dear Bro.," December 18, 1862, USAMHI. In "Morale, Maneuver, and Mud" (Gallagher, *The Fredericksburg Campaign*, 171–227) A. Wilson Greene offers evidence that the demoralization persisted only briefly after Fredericksburg, and that morale was recovering by the beginning of January. The correspondence and diaries cited above tend to corroborate that argument, for — except for perennial complainers like Brigadier General Marsena Patrick and Private Edwin Wentworth — the worst of the discouragement is recorded before the end of December.

12. *Portland Daily Press*, December 29, 1862, and March 6, 1863; Sarah Fales to Edmund Fales, December 18, 1862, RIHS; Sears, *Country, Cause & Leader*, 304; Ayling, *Register*, 475, 476, 481, 484, 491, 493, 495, 498, 499, 502, 986; G.O. No. 16, service record of Lt. John Mooney, 9th N.H.V., RG 94, NA.

13. J. Harvey Polley to "Dear Wife," December 16, 1862, CL; Skipper and Taylor, *Handful of Providence*, 185, 189.

14. *Report of the Adjutant General of the State of Maine*, 1052–1142; Ayling, *Register*, 32, 262, 594; Higginson, *Massachusetts in the Army and Navy*, 2:393–95; George Henry Bates to "Dear Parents," January 21, 1863, CL.

15. Report of John S. Phelps, October 20, 1862, Reel 4, Stanton Papers, LC; *OR*, 13:286–301.

16. *OR*, 22(1):43–59, 71–73, 138–41; Tilley, *Federals on the Frontier*, 57.

17. *OR*, 22(1):73–76, 105, 140–44; Charles Chapman Diary, December 3–7, 1862, ISU; Tilley, *Federals on the Frontier*, 59; Fatherson Memoir, UIA; Edward Davis to "Dear Mother," January 4, 1863, UIA; John Gere to "Dear Mother," December 12, 1862, USAMHI; Thomas Lewis to "My Dear Wife," December 10, 1862, SHSI-DM.

18. *OR*, 18:54–58, 60, 112–14; Charles Woodwell Diary, December 11–21, 1862, LC; Marcotte, *Private Osborne*, 103–5; James Cartwright to "My dear Mother," December 23, 1862, Nelson Chapin to "My Dear Son," February 20, 1863, and William E. Dunn to "Dear Sister," January 8, 1863, all in USAMHI; Edwin Burbank to "Dear Mother," December 25, 1862, CL.

19. Edwin Stanton to McClernand, October 21, 1862, Reel 4, Stanton Papers, LC; *OR*, 17(1):477, 605–10, 625; Thomas Blanchard to Sarah Blanchard, December 21, 1862, ND; Adoniram Withrow to Libertatia Withrow, January 3, 1863, SHSI-IC; Larimer, *Love and Valor*, 89–91.

20. *OR*, 15:199–220; John A. Hodgkins Diary, January 1–3, 1863, Yale.

21. George Landrum to "Dear Obed," January 7, 1863, and to "Dear Minnie," January, 1863, WRHS.

22. "James" to "Dear Sister," January 13, 1863, Civil War Soldiers' Letters, DC; Anderson, *Letters and Journals*, 167; William Carson to "Dear Parents," January 7, 1863, USAMHI; *OR*, 20(1):186.

23. Younger, *Inside the Confederate Government*, 36, 42; Wiggins, *Gorgas Journals*, 55–56; John S. Walker to "Dear Wife," January 5, 1863, USAMHI.

24. Oakley Smith to "Dear Father," January 11, 1863, USAMHI; Nevins and Thomas, *Strong Diary*, 3:286–87; Sparks, *Inside Lincoln's Army*, 199; Lewis Cleveland to "Dear Louise," January 9, 1863, USAMHI; David Werking to "Dear Wife," February 20 and March 4, 1863, IHS.

25. John Huftelen to Jane Huftelen, October 16, 1862, Dakota Conflict, MNHS; "A Badger Boy in Blue," 99; *Chicago Tribune,* January 1, 1863; *CWL,* 5:493, 550–51; *Dakotian,* January 27, 1863; Joseph Hazen to Sarah Jane Warren, December 28, 1862, and Samuel Sheardown to "Dear Brother & Sister," January 2, 1863, Dakota Conflict, MNHS. At least one Sioux, named Chakadan, who had not killed anyone and had actually saved lives, was among those hanged (Sarah Wakefield to Abraham Lincoln, March 23, 1863, ALP).

26. *OR,* 17(1):700–709, 716–19, 780, 782, 783, 791; Asahel Mann to Jennie Scott, November 26, 1862, UIA; Larimer, *Love and Valor,* 101–5; Julius Wood to "Dear Parents & Sister," January 12, 1863, WRHS.

27. Langsdorf, "Trego Letters," 309; Thomas Blanchard to Sarah Blanchard, December 4, 1862, ND; Adoniram Withrow to Libertatia Withrow, December 19, 1862, and Thomas Coffman to "My Dear Girl," November 8, 1862, SHSI-IC.

28. Gilbert Robie to "My Dear Wife," February 18, 1863, DC; Charles Turner to "Dear Parents," March 31, 1863, WRHS; Philip West to "Dear huncul and Aunt," April 24, 1863, ISU; Howe, *Passages,* 123; Woodworth, *Musick of the Mocking Birds,* 26–28; Jim Giauque to "Folks at Home," January 23, 1863, UIA; Larimer, *Love and Valor,* 114.

29. Levi Shell to "Brother Daniel," September 19, 1862, to "Dear Brother," February 7, 1863, and to "Dear Mother," March 3, 1863, SHSW; Cyrus Stockwell to "Dear Parents," March 14, 1863, WRHS.

30. Stephen Spaulding to James Peck, July 8, 1863, VTHS; David Hill Diary, January 7, 26, and 29, and February 13 and 18, 1863, DC; Anonymous Diary, January 30–March 16, May 16–18, June 10–16, 1863, NHHS; Albert Austin to "Dear Mother," March 3, 1863, NHHS; Gregg Diary, March 29 and April 7, 1863, DC. See Marvel, "Back from the Gates of Hell," on the extraordinary mortality in the 16th New Hampshire.

31. Larimer, *Love and Valor,* 77–78, 122; Sallie Stafford to "Dear Cousin," March 22, 1863, Oblinger Letters, SHSN; Houston, *Keep Up Good Courage,* 87; Charles Spire to "Dear Wife," "september" [December] 16, 1862, USAMHI.

32. Charles J. Branich to "Dear Mother," January 12, 1863, MNHS. For testimony of weight gained by active troops, see Joel Glover to "Dear Wife," January 22 and February 14, 1863, UVM; Tabor Parcher to "Dear Sarah," April 3, 1864, UVM; Joseph Cross to "Dear Wife & Children," October 2 and 27, 1862, AAS; Ransom Sargent to "Dear Maria," October 12, 1862, DC; T. J. Lindsay to Abial Bishop, January 19, 1863, Leeds Historical Society; Thomas Brown to "my wife," February 30, 1863, VTHS; Jane Thompson to William Thompson, October 30, 1862, SHSI-DM; Charles A. Turner to "Dear Brother," November 3, 1862, WRHS; John Barney to "all at Home," December 26, 1862, SHSW; Christopher Keller to "Dear Carrie," January 18, 1863, CL; Jones, "Bent Letters," 27; Davidson, *Hartley Letters,* 21–22.

33. Alonzo Pierce to "Dear Mother," October 23, 1862, NHHS; Masonheimer Diary, November 20, 1862, USAMHI; Keiser Diary, December 6, 1862, USAMHI; Solomon Dodge to "Dear sister Eliza," January 17, 1863, NHHS; Henry Heisler to "Dear Sister," August 10 and December 22, 1862, LC.

34. Emory Upton to "My dear sister Louese," December 23, 1862, USAMHI; Orlando Poe to "My dear Wife," December 14, 1862, LC.

35. Pease and Randall, *Browning Diary,* 1:596–600; Beale, *Welles Diary,* 1:194.

36. Pease and Randall, *Browning Diary,* 1:601; Beale, *Welles Diary,* 1:194–95; Beale, *Bates Diary,* 269–70.

37. Pease and Randall, *Browning Diaries,* 1:593, 595–96, 604; Beale, *Welles Diary,* 1:201–2; Niven, *Chase Papers,* 3:340–41; *CWL,* 6:12–13.

38. Claude Goings to Mary Goings, January 20, 1863, DC; Libbie Bassett to "Dear Sister," December 14, 1862, WRHS; Clarissa Mumford to "Dear Husband," December 22, 1862, SHSW.

39. Nevins and Thomas, *Strong Diary,* 3:281; French, *Witness,* 415.

40. *OR*, 21:894–901; Sears, *Country, Cause & Leader*, 301, 304; Franklin to Orville Babcock, December 24, 1862, Newberry Library.

41. Daniel Larned to "My Dear Uncle," January 1, 1863, LC; Burnside to Porter, December 30, 1862, Dispatch Book, Burnside Papers, RIHS; *RJCCW*, 1:717–18.

42. Taft Diary, January 5, 1863, LC; Rodgers Diary, January 6, 1863, USAMHI; David Beem to "My dear Wife," January 18, 1863, IHS; Sears, *Country, Cause & Leader*, 304–5.

43. Nevins, *Diary of Battle*, 157–58; Raymond, "Extracts," 421; Edward H. Wade to "Dear Nell," January 18, 1863, CL; Scott, *Fallen Leaves*, 162–63, 164.

44. George Hawk to "Dear Father," January 25, 1863, USAMHI; Lyman Williams to "Dear Sister," January 29, 1863, VTHS; Coburn Diary, January 20, 1863, USAMHI; Raymond, "Extracts," 421; Miles Diary, January 20, 1863, VTHS; Smith Bailey Diary, January 21, 1863, DC; Cheney Diary, January 21, 1863, UNH.

45. Keiser Diary, January 21, 1863, and Rodgers Diary, January 21, 1863, USAMHI; Ransom Sargent to "Dear Maria," January 21, 1863, DC; Hawkes Diary, January 21, 1863, USAMHI.

46. Daniel Larned to "My Dear Sister," January 20, 1863, LC; George Hawk to "Dear Father," January 25, 1863, USAMHI; John D. Cooper to "My dear Daughter," January 25, 1863, DC; Lyman Holford Diary, January 21, 1863, LC; Marshall Phillips to "Dear Wife," January 26, 1863, MEHS; Raymond, "Extracts," 421; Cheney Diary, January 21, 1863, UNH; Smith Bailey Diary, January 21, 1863, DC.

47. Baily and Coburn Diaries, January 22, 1863, USAMHI; Holford Diary, January 22, 1863, LC; George Rowell to "Dear Parents," January 24, 1863, NHHS; Levi Huber to Peter Filbert, January 30, 1863, 96th Pennsylvania Collection, USAMHI; James Gillette to "Dear Mother," January 29, 1863, LC; George Hawk to "Dear Father," January 25, 1863, USAMHI; Frederick Godfrey to "Dear Sophia," January 29, 1863, Park-McCullough House, quoted in Marshall, *War of the People*, 132–33; Edwin Wentworth to "My dear Wife," January 25, 1863, LC.

48. Robertson, *McAllister Letters*, 261; Edwin Wentworth to "My dear Wife," January 25, 1863, LC; Sparks, *Inside Lincoln's Army*, 206; Sears, *Country, Cause & Leader*, 307–8; Theodore Barton to "dear sister," January 25, 1863, VTHS; Susan Hooker to "My darling," undated, UR; Smith Bailey Diary, January 24, 1863, DC; John Baily Diary, January 24, 1863, USAMHI.

49. Smith Bailey Diary, January 21 and 30, 1863, DC; Sparks, *Inside Lincoln's Army*, 206–7; Edwin Wentworth to "My dear Wife," January 25, 1863, LC; Frederick Godfrey to "Dear Sophia," January 29, 1863, Park-McCullough House, quoted in Marshall, *War of the People*, 132–33.

50. Coburn Diary, January 24, 1863, USAMHI; Whitmore Diary, January 28, 1863, MHS; Britton and Reed, *Hartwell Letters*, 45; Baily Diary, January 25, 1863, USAMHI; Nevins, *Diary of Battle*, 160; Scott, *Fallen Leaves*, 162; Sparks, *Inside Lincoln's Army*, 207.

51. Daniel Larned to Mary Burnside, January 28, 1863, LC.

52. Nevins, *Diary of Battle*, 160; George Hawk to "Dear Father," January 25, 1863, USAMHI; Sears, *Country, Cause & Leader*, 308; Robertson, *McAllister Letters*, 261–62; Charles Coit to "Dear All," January 30, 1863, Yale; *Portland Daily Press*, March 6, 1863.

53. Nevins and Thomas, *Strong Diary*, 3:281; Walter Chapman to "Dear Brother," December 24, 1862, Yale; Christopher Keller to "Dear Carrie," January 18, 1863, CL; Theodore Sage to "Dear Sister," March 27, 1863, USAMHI; Eben Roberts to "Kind Cousin," April 16, 1863, Eben Calderwood Letters, MEHS; William Christie to "Dear Father," February 16, 1863, MNHS; Thomas Orwig to Eli Slifer, March 14, 1863, USAMHI; William Cheney to "Dear Uncle," February, 1863, Savage Family Papers, UVM.

54. Edward Burd Grubb to "Henry," October 26, 1862, CL.

55. *Atlas and Argus*, July 2, 1862; A. B. Schaeffer to Richard Yates, September 8, 1862,

Illinois State Library (now Abraham Lincoln Presidential Library), quoted in Hesseltine, *Lincoln and the War Governors,* 253; Blight, *This Cruel War,* 189; Edwin Wentworth to "Dear Father," November 10, 1862, LC; Orville Bixby to "My Owne dear Frances," December 10, 1862, UVM; Calvin Burbank to "Dear Cousin," December 29, 2862, DC; Edward Hall to "Dear Susan," January 8, 1863, NHHS; John Parris Sheahan to "My Dear Father," January 29, 1862, MEHS; Lucius Wood to "Dear Ones at Home," January 20, 1863, WRHS; Hiram Barton to Mary Barton, February 22, 1863, VTHS; *Portland Daily Press,* March 6, 1863; Claude Goings to Mary Goings, March 25, 1863, NHHS.

56. John D. Wilkins to "My Dearly beloved wife," March 29, 1863, CL; Horace Hooker to Susan Hooker, December 5 and 24, 1862, UR; Charles Dana to Edwin Stanton, September 8, 1863, Reel 5, Stanton Papers, LC; John Barney to "all at Home," January 2, 1863, SHSW.

57. *New York Tribune,* September 19, 1872; Joseph Kohout to "Dear Father and Mother and Sister," March 4, 1863, UIA; Phelps's unsigned report, October 20, 1862, Reel 4, and Edwin Stanton statement of March 26, 1864, Reel 7, Stanton Papers, LC.

58. *Hartford Courant,* January 28, 1863; *OR,* 22(2):106; Marshall Phillips to "Dear Wife," June 2, 1863, MEHS; Charles Benton to Cora Benton, December 8, 1862, ND; Scott, *Fallen Leaves,* 168.

59. William Stow to "Dear Father & Mother," February 23, 1863, UVM.

60. Nathan Hiatt to "Respected Sister," January 5 1863, ISL; Arthur D. Simpson to "Dear Parents," February 19, 1863, CL.

61. George Oscar French to "Friends at Home," January 23, 1863, VTHS; Ford, *Adams Letters,* 1:241.

62. James Gillette to "Dear Mother," January 29, 1863, LC; Scott, *Fallen Leaves,* 168; Holford Diary, January 30 and February 21, 1863, LC; Frederick Godfrey to "Dear Sophia," January 29, 1863, Park-McCullough House, quoted in Marshall, *War of the People,* 132–33; Keiser Diary, March 23, 1863, USAMHI; Charles Caley to "Dear Juliaette," April 4, 1863, ND.

63. James S. Howes to "My Dear Wife," February 2, 1863, NHHS; Holford Diary, January 30, 1863, LC; Francis Boland to "Dear Sir," December 2, 1862, Brislin Letters, USAMHI; James Law to "Dear Sister Agnes," March 18, 1863, CHS.

64. Griffin Stedman to "Sir," January 14, April 13, 1863, CHS; James Adams to "Dear Father," December 7, 1862, IHS; Elijah Cavins to "Dear Father," July 18, 1862, IHS; *Daily Chronicle,* March 9, 1865; Hastings, *Letters from a Sharpshooter,* 166–67, 170, 172.

65. Jackson and O'Donnell, *Back Home in Oneida,* 64; John Fernsler Diary, February 12, 19, and 25, 1863, 96th Pennsylvania Collection, USAMHI; Keiser Diary, February 19, 1863, USAMHI.

66. Eben Calderwood to "Dear Wife," April 15, 1863, MEHS; Origen Luther to James H. Luther, July 20, September 13, October 12, and October 29, 1862, ISL; Charles Benton to Cora Benton, February 24, 1863, ND.

67. *OR,* 17(1):515, 17(2):590–91, 23(2):65, 24(1):68; Dyer, *Compendium,* 1093, 1100.

68. *OR,* 17(2):590, 20(2):428, 22(2):77, and 23(2):65.

69. John Buck to Albert Fletcher, October 21 and December 30, 1862, SM; William Barrus to "Dear Brother," May 10, 1863, UNH; Eben Roberts to "Kind Cousin," April 16, 1863, Calderwood Letters, MEHS; Richard Irwin to "Dear Mother & Sister," May 30, 1863, UVM; *Correspondence of John Sedgwick,* 2:80; William Speed to "My dear Sister," December 29, 1862, CL.

70. Haas to "My Dear Bro.," January 3, 1863, USAMHI. In her study of Civil War desertion, Ella Lonn may have inadvertently hinted at Union troops' disaffection with Lincoln's proclamation when she noted the relative infrequency of Union soldiers surrendering to the enemy "until late in 1862" (*Desertion,* 198).

71. Frank Sterns to "Dear Parents," December 30, 1862, and January 15, 1863, CL;

Frank Daniels to Frederick Pratt, January 1, 1863, AAS; George Henry Bates to "Dear Parents," March 6, 1863, CL; Larimer, *Love and Valor,* 73–74; John Riggs to "Dear Father," January 2, 1863, New Haven Colony Historical Society.

72. John Burrill to "Dear Parents," January 1 and February 6, 1863, USAMHI.

73. *New Hampshire Patriot,* January 28, 1863; Marion Ward to "Home Friends," March 21, 1863, WRHS; Claude Goings to Mary Goings, January 20, 1863, DC; William Barrus to "Dear Brother," May 10, 1863, UNH.

74. Henry French to Benjamin French, November 9, 1862, NHHS; McClernand to Lincoln, December 29, 1862, ALP; *CWL,* 6:48–49.

75. Niven, *Chase Papers,* 3:357–59; *CG,* 37th Cong., 3rd sess., part 1, 199–200, 381; Joseph Medill to Lyman Trumbull, January 28, 1863, Trumbull Papers, LC; Martin Shrenk to "Dear Kate," February 4 and March 10, 1863, CinHS; William Henry Shaw to "Sister Emma," March 14, 1863, CL.

76. Franklin Sawyer to Samuel Sexton, February 20, 1863, OHS; Milton Bassett to "Dear Julia," December 31, 1862, CHS; Edward Hall to "My dear Susan and Eddie," January 1, 1863, NHHS.

77. Frederick Speed to "My dear Sister," January 27, 1863, CL; Levi Shell to "Dear Brother," February 7, 1863, SHSW; Joseph Cross to "Dear Wife and Children," January 4, 1863, AAS; James Bromley to "Dear brother and sister," December 25, 1862, VTHS.

78. Calvin Burbank to "Dear Cousin," December 29, 1862, DC; Augustus Paddock to "My Dear Cousin Mary," March 6, 1863, UVM; Peter Faulk to "Dear Sister," December 26, 1862, BGSU; John Sheahan to "My Dear Father," January 29, 1863, MEHS; Frederick Godfrey to "Dear Sophia," January 29, 1863, Park-McCullough House, quoted in Marshall, *War of the People,* 132–33; M. P. Wheeler to "Friend Allen," March 10, 1863, SHSW; John Frederick to "Dear Wife," January 9, 1863, SHSI-IC.

79. Truxall, *Respects to All,* 36; Frank Daniels to Frederick Pratt, January 1, 1863, AAS; Smith Bailey Diary, January 30, 1863, DC; Hadley Diary, February 1, 1863, NHHS; George Howe to "Dear Sister," February 19, 1863, SM.

80. O. Sanford to "Dear Mother," undated, SM; Mathew Hopkins to Albert Fletcher, January 13, 1863, SM; George Bradley to "Dear Friends at Home," February 20, 1863, Yale.

81. Kent Diary, August 30, 1862, NHHS; A. D. Searles to E. G. Searles, December 25, 1862, BGSU; George Upton to "My Dear Wife," January 15, 1863, NHHS; *OR,* Series 3, 2:45; Jacob Haas to "My Dear Bro.," December 18, 1862, USAMHI.

82. *OR,* Series 3, 2:291, 3:751. The War Department appeared not to count the 16th West Virginia among the nine-month regiments (ibid., 3:782).

83. Mortality tabulations are taken from the pertinent regimental sketches in Dyer, *Compendium.*

84. Holden, Ross, and Slomba, *Stand Firm,* 126; H. F. Morse to "Dear Sis," Morse Papers, MHS; George Spinney to "Dear Sister," November 19, 1862, BPL; Elijah Cavins to "Dear Ann," January 25, 1863, IHS.

85. Stanton Diary, June 14, 1863, AAS; Charles Troup Diary, July 7, 1863, MHS; Elijah Cavins to "Dear Ann," October 1, 1862, and May 6, 1863, IHS; Levi Leland to "Dear Brother Willard," January 2, 1863, VTHS; Dan Mason to Harriet Clark, May 7, "1862" [1863], VTHS; Almon Sanborn to "Dear Brother and Sister," December 19, 1862, MEHS; John Bumstead to Timothy Loomis, November 4, 1862, CHS; Edwin Metcalf to "Dear Alf," October 24, 1862, USAMHI.

86. Mann, *History of the Forty-Fifth,* 304; Stevens, *History of the Fiftieth,* 191; Dargan, *My Experience,* title page; Joseph Spafford to "Dear Sister," April 19, 1863, VTHS; John Burrill to "Dear Parents," September 15, 1862, USAMHI.

87. James Law to "Dear Sister," November 19, 1862, and to "Dear Sister Agnes," March 18, 1863, CHS.

88. Haines, *Letters from the Forty-fourth*, 23; Ledman, *A Maine Town Responds*, 122–23.

89. George Troup Diary, August 7, 17, 21, and 27, 1862, MHS; William Burbank to "Dr. Mother," December 7, 1862, CL; Richard Irwin to "Dear Mother & Sister," March 21, 1863, UVM; Eben Calderwood to "Dear Wife," November 13, 1862, MEHS.

90. Joel Glover to "Dear Wife," January 22–23, 1863, UVM; Abram Rowell to "Dear Adaline," January 30, 1863, UVM; Roswell Farnham to "My Dear Wife," May 24, 1863, VTHS; Benjamin Appleby to "Lavinia," undated, USAMHI; "William" to Wealthy Field, January 24, 1863, VTHS; Harrison Varney to "Absent One," June 6, 1863, DC; Mark Waterman to "Dear Wife and Children," June 10, 1863, MEHS; *OR*, 26(1):14.

91. Frank Daniels to Frederick Pratt, May 29, 1863, AAS; Frederick Twiss to "Dear Mother," April 5, 1863, and David Grime to Orilla Twiss, April 28, 1863, NHHS; Olive Cheney to "Dear Children," June 7, 1863, VTHS; Philo Buckingham to "My Dear Wife," February 6, 1863, AAS; Woodwell Diary, February 5, 1863, LC.

92. Frank Daniels to "Dear Friend Fred," March 19, 1863, AAS; Ora Harvey to unidentified correspondent, April 1, 1863, ND; handbills for the ball and "Il Recruto," Cartwright Family Correspondence, USAMHI.

93. Oliver Peabody to Frank Peabody, February 19, 1863, MHS. For examples of a well-illustrated, expensive regimental history see Mann, *History of the Forty-Fifth*.

94. Frank Daniels to "Friend Fred," May 29, 1863, AAS; Roswell Farnham to "Dear Mary," June 29, 1863, VTHS; Leonard Valentine to "Dear Father and Mother," June 3, 1863, MEHS; W. H. Hammond to "dear Wife," October 29, [1862], Cary Library; T. J. Lindsay to "Absent Uncle," January 19, 1863, Leeds Historical Society. See also Marvel, "Back from the Gates of Hell," 115–17.

95. On December 31, 1862, the Union army numbered 868,591, with 664,163 present for duty (*OR*, Series 3, 2:957) and Confederate forces 449,439, with only 304,015 present for duty (*OR*, Series 4, 2:278).

96. *CG*, 37th Cong., 3rd sess., part 1, 558, 705–16 ; Beale, *Welles Diary*, 1:396–97.

97. *Chicago Tribune*, July 4, 1862; Pease and Randall, *Browning Diary*, 1:618.

98. *CG*, 37th Cong., 3rd sess., part 1, 706, 708–9.

99. *CG*, 37th Cong., 3rd sess., part 1, 728–39, 816, and part 2, 960, 976, 978, 983, 990–91, 1002.

100. James House to "General," March 30, 1829, quoted in Allen, *Israfel*, 192–93; *CG*, 37th Cong., 3rd sess., part 2, 981–84, 1202; Frederick Law Olmsted to Preston King, July 9, 1862, ALP.

101. *CG*, 37th Cong., 3rd sess., part 2, 995.

102. *CG*, 37th Cong., 3rd sess., part 2, 1213–16, 1235, 1404–5.

103. *CG*, 37th Cong., 3rd sess., part 2, 1218–19, 1224, 1226–27, 1229. The dissident remark Bingham embellished was the common argument that Democrats should stay home and vote before (or instead of) enlisting, for which uttered opinion many Democrats were arrested on charges of discouraging enlistments. See, for instance, A. Ricketts to L. C. Turner, August 9, 1862, Case 385, Reel 13, Turner-Baker Case Files (M-797), NA.

104. *CG*, 37th Cong., 3rd sess., part 2, 1454; *OR*, Series 3, 3:93. See, for instance, Benjamin Cory and Peter Chane to Ben Wade, March 10, 1863, Robert Sherrard to Wade, March 11, 1863, and numerous other applications dated March 10 and 11, 1863, Wade Papers, LC; assorted reports in Union Provost Marshal's File (M-416), particularly reel 15, NA. Geary (*We Need Men*, 57–61) recounts House debate on Senate Bill No. 511, including Abram Olin's duplicitous manipulation of the process.

105. Messent and Courtney, *Hopkins Letters*, 221; Thomas Blanchard to Sarah Blanchard, March 7, 1863, ND; Lewis Cleveland to "Dear Louise," March 2, 1863, USAMHI; Charles E. Parker to "My dear Father & Mother," March 22, 1863, UVM; "Historickal Crotchets," 185–86; Elijah Cavins to "Dear Ann," April 9, 1863, IHS; Richard Irwin to

"Dear Sister," January 11, 1863, UVM; James Law to "Dear Sister Agnes," March 4 and 18, 1863, CHS; Theodore Barton to Mary Barton, February 25, 1863, VTHS.

106. William B. Adams to "Sister Dora," March 7, 1863, MEHS. Daniel Brown relished the draft of "copper heads" but frantically advised his brother to avoid it: Brown to "Dear Brother," July 28, 1863, MEHS.

107. Griest Diary, January 14 and 15, 1863, USAMHI; Elisha Kempton to "Dear Folks at Home!" April 23, 1863, NHHS; Blight, *This Cruel War,* 214.

108. Elijah Cavins to "Dear Father," July 18, 1862, IHS; Augusta Kidder to "My Dearest Ollie," March 8, 1863, SHS; Emily Harris to Leander Harris, February 20, July 13, and July 26, 1863, UNH.

109. Charles Mumford to Clarissa Mumford, March 15, 1863, SHSW; Charles Benton to Cora Benton, March 15, 1863, ND; Horace Hobart to "Dear Brother," March 2, 1863, IHS; Lassen, *Dear Sarah,* 85; Harris and Niflot, *Dear Sister,* 73; *Daily Gate City,* February 20 and 25, 1863.

110. Jacob Haas to "My Dear Bro.," May 12, 1863, USAMHI.

111. *Eastern Argus,* March 3, 1863; Morton to Stanton, March 6, 1863, Stanton Papers, LC; *Crisis,* March 4, 1863; *Dayton Empire,* March 14, 1863; *Ohio State Journal,* March 7, 1863.

112. *Union-Democrat,* February 24, 1863; *New Hampshire Patriot,* March 4, 1863; John George to John Crittenden, January 7, 1863, and S. G. Clarke to Crittenden, February 5, 1863, Crittenden Papers, LC.

113. B. M. Colby to Gilmore, December 13, 1862, Joseph Gilman to Gilmore, January 22, 1863, NHHS.

114. Hadley Diary, February 28, 1863, NHHS; Child, *Letters,* 108; Houston, *Keep Up Good Courage,* 78.

115. Emily Harris to Leander Harris, March 8, 1863, UNH; G. W. Bentley to Gilmore, December 31, 1862, John Garfield and James Eastman to same, January 26, 1863, NHHS.

116. Ayling, *Register,* 169; George Towle to "Dear B.," April 3, 1863, Brewster Letters, NHHS.

117. H. Philbrick to John George, March 2, 1863, NHHS; Julia Leeds to Samuel Duncan, March 11, 1863, DC.

118. Baron Stow to Joseph Gilmore, March 11, 1863, NHHS; *Daily Chronicle,* March 12 and 13, 1863.

119. Edward Davis to "Sallie," April 16, 1863, UIA; Chapin Diary, March 11, 1863, RIHS; Taft Diary, March 5, 1863, LC.

120. *Dubuque Herald,* February 13 and 22, 1863; *Fairfield Ledger,* February 5, 1863; *Bugle,* February 18, 1863, quoted in Wubben, *Civil War Iowa,* 96; James Giauque to Alfred Giauque, March 15, 1863, UIA; Edward Davis to "Sallie," March 22, 1863, UIA; Robert Hanna to "My Dear Wife," January 29, 1863, IHS; Jacob Cox to A. F. Perry, February 9, 1863, Oberlin; Robert Moyle to "Dear Father & Mother," February 15, 1863, UIA; James Johnston to William Pinkerton, February 6, 1863, WRHS; James Gillette to "Dear Mother," January 29, 1863, LC; William Smith to "Dear Parents & Sisters," March 12, 1863, CL; Charles Herbert to "Dear Parents, April 21, 1863, NHHS; William Stow to "Dear Father & Mother," February 23, 1863, UVM.

121. Barnes, *Medical and Surgical History,* 1:296–301; Gregg Diary, March 29, 1863, DC; Cyrus Stockwell to "Dear Parents," March 14, 1863, WRHS; George Howe to "Dear Sister," March 18, 1863, SM; Levi Shell to "Dear Brother," February 7, 1863, and to "Dear Mother," March 3, 1863, SHSW; Harrison Varney to "Dear Catty," March 5, 1863, and to "Absent One," March 12, 1863, DC.

122. Orra Bailey to unidentified recipient, March 25, 1863, CHS; Thomas Sterns to "My dear Wife," April 3, 1863, UIA; George Rowell to "Dear Parents," March 18, "1862" [1863], NHHS; Marion Ward to "Home Friends," March 21, 1863, WRHS; Isaac Morrow

to "Dear Brother," February 18, 1863, USAMHI; Daniel Faust to "Dear Mother," March 14, 1863, USAMHI.

123. Hazen Noyes to "My Dear Mother," March 13, 1863, USAMHI; W. A. Campbell to "Dear Sister," April 13, 1863, MEHS; Magee Diary, February 24, 1863, Duke; Taft Diary, March 6, 1863, LC.

124. OR, 25(1):43–44, 65–66, 1121–22; Moore, Rebellion Record, 6:443–44; Charles Cummings to "Dear Wife," March 9, 1863, VTHS; Joseph Boynton to "Dear brother," March 12, 1863, Lorentio King to "My dear Aunt," March 20, 1863, Augustus Paddock to "Dear Father," March 18, 1863, and William Wells to "Bro Charles," March 17, 1863, all at UVM; Albert Huntington to "Dear Sister Sue," March 10, 1863, UR.

125. George Thomas to Minerva Thomas, March 19 and 26, 1863, ND; Skipper and Taylor, Handful of Providence, 189, 191; Blackburn, With the Wandering Regiment, 51; Edwin Wentworth to "My dear Wife," March 15, 1863, LC; John D. Wilkins to "My Dearly beloved wife," March 20, 1863, CL.

126. OR, 25(2):123; Pease and Randall, Browning Diaries, 1:594–95; CWL, 6:132–33.

127. Frank Sterns to "Dear Parents," undated, CL; Joel Glover to "Dear Wife," March 20, 1863, UVM; Richard Irwin to "Dear Mother & Sister," March 21, 1863, UVM; Levi Shell to "Dear Brother," February 7, 1863, SHSW.

128. S. H. Norton to A. P. Plante, February 21, 1863, CHS; Gideon Allen to Annie Cox, February 10, 1863, SHSW.

129. Report of the Secretary of the Treasury, 44–47.

130. Democratic Clarion, March 18, 1863, quoted in Wubben, Civil War Iowa, 96; State Register, February 27 and March 12, 1863; James White to Abraham Lincoln, April 2, 1863, LC.

131. Adam Fair to Jacob Lowenberg, March 12, 1863, Fair Letters, SHSI-IC.

Epilogue

1. Medill to Lincoln, May 15, 1863, ALP; Calvin Fletcher Diary, January 2, 5, and 11, 1863, IHS, quoted in Klement, Dark Lanterns, 47; Resolutions of the Springfield Union League, March 17, 1863, ALP.

2. Medill to Lincoln, May 15, 1863, ALP; Larimer, Love and Valor, 129.

3. Nevins, Strong Diary, 3:286, 306–7, 312; New York Tribune, March 3, 1863; Hammond, Diary, 223.

4. Duncan, Blue-Eyed Child, 300–308; Ford, Adams Letters, 1:171; Eby, Virginia Yankee, 154.

5. Albert Ritter to "Dear Cousin Helen," February 1, 1863, Chandler Family Papers, UR; Lewis Cleveland to "Dear Louise," February 6, 1863, USAMHI; Ford, Adams Letters, 1:171.

6. Charles Benton to Cora Benton, February 24, 1863, ND; Skipper and Taylor, A Handful of Providence, 185, 189.

7. Mooney to J. H. Taylor, February 5, 1863, and G.O. No. 16, John Mooney military file, RG 94, NA.

8. Muster rolls of Company A and Company B, 9th N.H.V., John Mooney military file, RG 94, NA.

9. "Lt. John Mooney," sketch, 9th N.H. Collection, NHHS; John M. Merrill Family headstone, Green Grove Cemetery, Ashland, N.H. Census and Confederate service records contradict Mooney's story, while the purported details of his conscription and desertion to Union lines suffer from fatal anachronisms.

10. Robertson, McAllister Letters, 267, 271; Blackburn, With the Wandering Regiment, 51; Holden, Ross, and Slomba, Stand Firm, 60, 133–34, 136–37; Nevins, Diary of Battle, 171.

11. Holden, Ross, and Slomba, *Stand Firm*, 136–37; *CWL*, 6:133.

12. George Upton to "My Dear Wife," January 15, 1863, and Kent Diary, April 16, 1863, NHHS.

13. Hadley Diary, March 4–May 25, 1863, NHHS; Ayling, *Register*, 29–96; *OR*, Series 3, 5:668.

14. Ayling, *Register*, 794–800.

Bibliography

Manuscript Sources

American Antiquarian Society, Worcester, Mass.
    Philo Beecher Buckingham Letters
    Comey Family Papers
    Joseph Cross Letters
    Frederick Sumner Pratt Letters
    Henry Rogers Smith Letters
    William Stanton Diary
    Carolyn Barrett White Diary
    Henry White Diary
    William A. Willoughby Letters
Appomattox Court House National Historic Park, Appomattox, Va.
    Edward B. Harvey Diary
Boston Public Library, Boston, Mass.
    Edward Klein Letters
    George A. Spinney Letters
Bowling Green State University, Bowling Green, Ohio
    Askew Family Correspondence
    Ira B. Conine Correspondence
    James William Davidson Papers
    Peter Faulk Papers
    Kehrwecker Family Papers
    William H. Perigo Papers
    Rachel Stanton/Searles Papers
Cary Library, Houlton, Maine
    W. H. Hammond Letter
Cincinnati Historical Society, Cincinnati, Ohio
    George Benson Fox Letters

Alexander Long Papers
Martin Shrenk Letters
Connecticut Historical Society, Hartford
Albert A. Andrews Letter
Orra B. Bailey Letters
Norman Ball Journal
Milton H. Bassett Papers
Elizur B. Belden Diary
Caleb Blanchard Letters
Civil War Letters
Albert A. Andrew Letter
Perkins Bartholomew Letter
Samuel Bartlett Letter
Harriet Beddoe Letter
Charles A. Boyle Letters
John W. Bumstead Letter
William H. Drake Letter
John C. Holwell Letter
Horace Lay Letter
Ellsworth N. Phelps Letter
Alfred B. Talcott Letter
George W. Webster Letter
Reese B. Gwillem Diary
John C. Holwell Letters
Robert Hale Kellogg Collection
George Kies Letters
James B. Law Letters
S. H. Norton Letters
Samuel B. Shepard Letters
Charles E. Sherman Collection
Griffin A. Stedman Letters
Welling Collection: Horace Greeley Letter
Conway Town Hall, Center Conway, N.H.
Town Clerk's Records
Cornell University, Ithaca, N.Y.
John S. Crocker Letters
Cumberland County Historical Society, Carlisle, Pa.
John Turner Letters
Dartmouth College, Hanover, N.H.
Smith G. Bailey Diary
Ira M. Barton Papers
Elmer Bragg Letters
Joshua D. Breyfogle Papers
Calvin Burbank Letters
Civil War Soldiers' Letters
Collection of Papers Relating to the Battle of Antietam

Royal Cook and A. M. Gillett Letters
John D. Cooper Letters
Samuel Duncan Letters
Claude Goings Letters
Hiram Gregg Diary
David W. Hill Diary
James W. Lathe Letters
David Leigh Letters
Henry S. Muchmore Diary
Henry Clay Newell Correspondence
Gilbert Robie Letters
Oscar D. Robinson Papers
Ransom F. Sargent Papers
Lewis Simonds Diary
Harrison W. Varney Letters
George Wheeler and D. W. Perkins Letters
Duke University, Durham, N.C.
Alexander Brown Papers
John Euclid Magee Diary
Walter W. Smith Papers
Earlham College, Richmond, Ind.
Oliver Albertson Journal
Clarkson Butterworth Diary
John Harvey Letters
Hill-Hudelson Family Papers
Margaret Jones Diary
David Marshall Collection
Achilles Pugh Papers
Illinois State Library (manuscripts now in Abraham Lincoln Presidential Library),
    Springfield
Richard Yates Papers
Indiana Historical Society, Indianapolis
James A. Adams Letters
David E. Beem Papers
Madison Homer Carlton Letters
Elijah H. C. Cavins Papers
Chapin Family Papers
Solomon S. Hamrick Letters
Robert Barlow Hanna Papers
Horace Hobart Letters
Julietta Starbuck Letters
William Steele Letters
David Werking Letters
Worthington B. Williams Papers
Indiana State Library, Indianapolis
Flavius Bellamy Papers

Henry K. English Papers
Nathan Hiatt Letter
James H. Luther Collection
Henry C. Marsh Letter
Oliver P. Morton Papers
Iowa State University Archives, Ames
Charles W. Chapman Diary
Robert and Mary Ann Sisson Letters: Alfred Foreman and Philip West
Kansas State Historical Society, Topeka
Judd Family Diaries: John Judd Diary
George L. and Mary E. Stearns Papers
Laconia Public Library, Laconia, N.H.
John G. Hutchinson, "History of the Fourth New Hampshire Volunteers"
Leeds Historical Society, Leeds, Maine
T. J. Lindsay Letter
Library of Congress, Washington, D.C.
James G. Bennett Papers
Edgar F. Brown Letter
William G. Brownlow Papers
Charles Buford Papers
Sylvanus Cadwallader Papers
Zachariah Chandler Papers
John A. J. Cresswell Papers
John J. Crittenden Papers
Charles A. Dana Papers
William Franklin Draper Papers
Joshua R. Giddings and George W. Julian Papers
James J. Gillette Papers
John P. Hatch Papers
Lewis M. Haupt Family Papers
Samuel P. Heintzelman Papers
Henry Heisler Papers
Ethan Allen Hitchcock Papers
Lyman C. Holford Diary
Joseph Holt Papers
George Washington Julian Papers
Philip Kearny Papers
Daniel Reed Larned Papers
Abraham Lincoln Papers
George B. McClellan Papers
J. C. McMichael Letter
Manton Marble Papers
Orlando M. Poe Papers
James G. Randall Papers
Charles W. Reed Collection
Bela T. St. John Papers

Shortelle Family Papers
Edwin M. Stanton Papers
George Hay Stuart Collection
William R. Stimson Letters
Horatio Nelson Taft Diary
Lyman Trumbull Papers
Benjamin F. Wade Papers
Elihu Washburne Papers
Edwin Oberlin Wentworth Papers
Willard Family Letters: Joseph Willard Diary
Charles H. Woodwell Diary
Maine Historical Society, Portland
William Bryant Adams Papers
Henry Black Letter
Daniel Webster Brown Correspondence
James Brown Letters
Eben S. Calderwood Letters
W. A. Campbell Letter
John O. Crommett Letter
Ira Getchell Letter
Marshall Phillips Correspondence
George M. Redlon Letters
Allen R. Sanborn Letter
John Parris Sheahan Correspondence
Leonard Valentine Correspondence
Mark P. Waterman Letters
Isaac Webb Letter
Mariners' Museum, Newport News, Va.
George S. Geer Letters
William Marvel, private collection, South Conway, N.H.
Edson Cheever Letters (transcripts)
Massachusetts Historical Society, Boston
D. D. Addison Collection: Lucy Larcom Diary
Elijah Couillard Letters
George Dudley Papers
Everett-Peabody Papers
Josiah C. Fuller Papers
William Clark Hawes Diary
James Miller Diary
Frank C. Morse Papers
James Albert Osborne Diary
Oliver Peabody Papers
Calvin Smith Papers
Samuel Storrow Papers
William S. Tilton Diary
Troup Family Papers

Alfred Metcalf White Letters
George Arms Whitmore Diary
Myron Rice Wood Letters
Robert Mitchell Menuet Collection, Orlean, Va.
Barton W. Mitchell Papers
Minnesota Historical Society, St. Paul
Charles J. Branich Collection
Christie Family Letters
Dakota Conflict of 1862
Mathew Marvin Papers
Orrin F. Smith Papers: Charles E. Goddard Letters
Cyrus Stone Papers
National Archives, Washington, D.C.
Record Group 15, Records of the Pension Office
Pension Applications and Certificates
Record Group 28, Records of the Postmaster General
Record of Appointments of Postmasters, 1832–Sept. 30, 1971 (M-841)
Record Group 29, Bureau of the Census
Seventh Census of the United States (M-432)
Eighth Census of the United States (M-653)
Ninth Census of the United States (M-593)
Record Group 94, Records of the Adjutant General
Ambrose E. Burnside Papers, Entry 159
Case Files of Investigations by Levi C. Turner and L. C. Baker (M-797)
Individual Service Records
Returns from Regular Army Cavalry Regiments, 1833–1916 (M-744)
Returns from U.S. Military Posts, 1800–1916 (M-617)
Record Group 107, Office of the Secretary of War
Letters Received by the Secretary of War (M-22)
Record Group 109, War Department Collection of Confederate Records
Letters Received by the Confederate Secretary of War (M-437)
Compiled Service Records of Confederate Soldiers Who Served in Organizations from the State of Maryland (M-321)
Compiled Service Records of Confederate Soldiers Who Served in Organizations from the State of Virginia (M-324)
Record Group 110, Provost Marshal General's Bureau
Union Provost Marshals' Files (M-416)
Record Group 153, Records of the Judge Advocate General
Case Files of General Courts Martial, Courts of Inquiry, and Military Commissions
Allegheny Arsenal Court of Inquiry
Newberry Library, Chicago, Ill.
Orville E. Babcock Papers
New Hampshire Division of Records Management and Archives, Concord
Adjutant General's Records

Executive Correspondence
Miscellaneous Military Records
New Hampshire Historical Society, Concord
Aldrich-Thompson Family Papers
Albert T. Austin Letter
Anonymous Diary, 16th N.H.V.
John Batchelder Bailey Diary
Bell Family Papers
Charles Gilman Brewster Letters
Orrin Brownson Papers
Samuel Burnham Letters
George H. Caverly Diary
George H. Chandler Papers
Lizzie M. Corning Diary
Cram Family Papers: Daniel Veasey Durgin Letters
Julian Dodge Letters
Samuel Dodge Letters
Elisha Douglas Letters
Andrew Farnum Letters
John Harrison Foye Letters
Franklin H. Foster Letter
Benjamin B. French and Henry F. French Correspondence
John H. George Correspondence
John S. Godfrey Papers
Nathan G. Gould Letters
Solomon Grannis Diary
Sylvester Erwin Hadley Diary
Edward F. Hall Letters
Charles H. Herbert Letters
James S. Howes Letters
Christopher Hoyt Letters
Elisha M. Kempton Papers
Richard Peabody Kent Diary
Thomas B. Leaver Papers
William Adams Moore Correspondence
George W. Moran Letter
9th New Hampshire Regimental Collection
Alonzo F. Pierce Letters
Rodney H. Ramsey Letters
George H. P. Rowell Letters
Cyrus King Sanborn Papers
Ezra Sanborn Diaries
Albert B. Stearns Letters
John O. Stevens Letters
Andrew J. Stone Papers

    Sewell D. Tilton Papers
    Hosea Towne Letters
    Frederick Waite Twiss Papers
    George Upton Letters
    John E. Wilcox Diary
New Hampshire State Library, Concord
    Willard J. Templeton Letters
    Herbert J. Willand Diary
New Haven Colony Historical Society, New Haven, Conn.
    John H. Riggs Letters
New-York Historical Society: Gilder Lehrman Collection
    Pearce Family Correspondence
North Yarmouth Historical Society, North Yarmouth, Maine
    Luther Lawrence Letter
Notre Dame University, Notre Dame, Ind.
    Benton-Beach Family Correspondence: Charles and Cora Benton Letters
    Blanchard-Walker Letters
    Charles C. Caley Letters
    William Combs Letters
    Ora Harvey Letter
    John M. Jackson Letters
    Miller Family Correspondence
    Harrison E. Randall Letters
    Read Family Correspondence
    Thomas Family Correspondence
Oberlin College, Oberlin, Ohio
    Jacob Dolson Cox Papers
Ohio Historical Society, Columbus
    Samuel Medary Papers
    Emerson Opdycke Papers
    Edwin M. Stanton Papers, 1862–1867
Park-McCullough House, North Bennington, Vt.
    Frederick Godfrey Papers
Peabody Essex Museum, Salem, Mass.
    Lewis R. Caswell Letters
William Scott Proudfoot, private collection, Santa Cruz, Calif.
    Newton Scott Letters
Providence Public Library, Providence, R.I.
    Walter E. Gardiner Letters
    George Randall Letters
Rhode Island Historical Society, Providence
    Ambrose E. Burnside Papers
    William W. Chapin Diary
    Draft Exemptions, Second District
    Edmund Fales Family Papers
    Daniel A. Handy Letters

David B. Patterson Letter
Benjamin R. Phelon Family Papers
James H. Remington Papers
Henry J. Spooner Letters
Rutgers University, New Brunswick, N.J.
Roebling Family Papers
Sheldon Museum, Middlebury, Vt.
Albert Fletcher Correspondence
Howe-Wolcott Collection: George and Lorette Howe Correspondence
Walter J. Hurd Letters
Rokeby Museum Collection: Robinson Family Papers
Sanford Family Collection
State Historical Society of Iowa
Des Moines
Adjutant General's Correspondence: Disloyal Sentiments File
Amasa Orlando Allen Papers
William R. Barnes Letters
Bennett Family Papers
Henry Bobinhouse Letters
Jacob Hunter Papers
William R. Kemper Letters
Kynett Family Papers
Thomas Jefferson Lewis Papers
Charles Mason Papers
James William Sudduth Letters
Laurel Summers Papers
William and Jane Thompson Letters
David West Papers
Iowa City
Sewall S. Farwell Collection
William H. Collins Letters
Thomas Coffman Papers
Amos Noyes Currier Letters
George DeHart Letters
Adam Fair Letters
John M. Frederick Letters
Adoniram Judson Withrow Letters
State Historical Society of Missouri, Columbia
Western Historical Manuscript Collection: Mary Jane Vaughn Clark Letter
State Historical Society of Nebraska, Lincoln
Uriah Oblinger Family Letters
State Historical Society of Wisconsin, Madison
Gideon Winan Allen Letters
John J. Barney Papers
Henry J. Beecham Letters
Allen Church Letter

Henry Churchyard Letter
John T. Clark Papers
Newton H. Culver Papers
Horace Currier Letters
Dane County Draft Records
John Favill Letters
W. S. Hanscom Papers
Olivia Brown Hazelton Papers
Alonzo Gilbert Jack Letters
Henry W. Jackson Letters
John Henry Knight Letters
Lehmann Family Papers
Charles N. Mumford Letters
De Have Norton Letters
Levi Shell Letters
Tennessee State Library and Archives, Nashville
William W. Teall Letters
University of Iowa Libraries, Iowa City
Bean Family Papers
William Combs Letters
Marcellus W. Darling Papers
Andrew F. Davis Papers
Edward E. Davis Letters
Giauque Family Papers
George F. Hall Papers
Iowa Women's Archives
Catherine Snedecker Hill Collection
Ellen Mowrer Miller Papers
Florinda Wakefield More Collection
Mary Jane Parsons Collection
Ruth Fatherson Taylor Collection: Editha Phillips Fatherson Memoir
Samuel J. Kirkwood Papers
Joseph Kohout Papers
Mann Family Papers
Martin Mericle Papers
John W. Pratt Diary
William Titus Rigby Papers
Russell Family Papers
Sterns Family Papers
Myron Underwood Papers
J. L. Wilson Papers
University of Michigan, Ann Arbor
Clements Library
Thomas J. Adams Discharge Certificate
George Henry Bates Letters
Clement Abner Boughton Papers

Edward Burd Grubb Letter
Henry W. Halleck Letters
Thomas Hughes Letters
Henry Johnson Papers
Christopher Keller Letters
Robert E. Miller Letters
Richard Cary Morse Letters
J. Harvey Polley Letters
Arthur D. Simpson Letters
Henry H. Seys Letters
William Henry Shaw Letters
Smith Brothers Papers
William and Frederick Speed Letters
Frank H. Sterns Letters
Edward H. Wade Letters
John Darrah Wilkins Letters
University of New Hampshire, Durham
Barrus Family Papers
Thomas Carleton Cheney Papers
Leander Harris Letters
Charles E. Jewett Letters
University of North Carolina, Chapel Hill
Southern Historical Collection
Joseph Dill Alison Diary
Meta Morris Grimball Diary
James Munnerlyn Papers
Benjamin Franklin Perry Papers
Sarah Wadley Diary
University of Rochester, Rochester, N.Y.
Loren Jesse Ames Papers
Elisha Bartlett Family Papers
Lyman Chandler Family Papers
Eastwood-Bigelow Family Papers
Huntington-Hooker Papers
Francis Allen Macomber Papers
Gilbert H. Reynolds Papers
William Henry Seward Papers
University of Vermont, Burlington
Orville Bixby Letters
Charles E. Chace Papers
Joel Glover Letters
Henry Family Papers
Richard Irwin Letters
Lorentio King Papers
Augustus Paddock Papers
Tabor H. Parcher Letters

Charles E. Parker Papers
Cyrus Pringle Collection
Abram Rowell Letters
Joseph C. Rutherford Papers
Savage Family Papers
Luther and Erastus Scott Letters
Bradford F. Sparrow Letters
William Stow Letters
Francis C. Sturtevant Letter
Amasa Tracy Papers
William Wells Papers
U.S. Army Military History Institute, Carlisle, Pa.
Walter Phelps Jr. Papers
Civil War Miscellaneous Collection
    Henry W. Gangewer Diary
    Alfred Holcomb Letters
    Daniel Merritt Mead Letters
    Albert Rake Letters
    Frederick Ranger Letters
    John Viles Letters
    Henry H. Young Letters
Civil War Times Illustrated Collection
    James Abraham Letters
    Benjamin F. Appleby Letters
    George Bargus Diary
    Jacob Behm Letters
    John Burrill Letters
    Caldwell Family Correspondence
    William J. Carson Letter
    Cartwright Family Correspondence
    Nelson Chapin Letters
    Ruel S. Clark Letters
    Robert S. Coburn Diary
    William Henry Croop Letters
    Francis C. Davis Diary
    Andrew F. Davis Letter
    William E. Dunn Letters
    Feargus Elliott Letters
    John W. Ford Letters
    John Nelson Gere Letter
    George W. W. Hawk Letters
    Jacob Heffelfinger Diary
    Friedrich P. Keppelman Letters
    Jacob S. Kiester Letters
    Thomas G. Orwig Letters
    Benjamin F. Robb Letters

Anthony Ross Letters
Edward E. Schweitzer Papers
William Seagrave Diary
Jonathan Stowe Papers
Eben P. Sturges Papers
Harrisburg Civil War Round Table Collection
John W. Ames Papers
Benjamin F. Ashenfelter Letters
John H. Baily Diary
Augustus Barr Letters
Orrin William Brackett Letters
John Brislin Letters
Henry Carroll Papers
Camp Curtin Letter ("Smith" to "Friend Black")
Robert B. Cornwell Letters
James W. Denver Letters
Ellis-Marshall Family Letters
John and Leo Faller Letters
Daniel Faust Letters
Flegeal Family Papers
Luther C. Furst Diary
Alva Griest Diary
Gilbert Gulbrandson Letters
Jacob W. Haas Papers
William C. Hall Diary
John A. Hammond Diary
George P. Hawkes Diary
Henry Franklin Huffer Letters
Charles R. Johnson Letters
Henry Keiser Diary
Frank Kelley Letter
Andrew Knox Letters
George H. Legate Letter
Henry Leib Diary
John Lingle Letters
David Lovell Letters
Lewis Masonheimer Diary
John Maycock Diary
Joseph A. McLean Letters
Edwin Metcalf Letter
Isaac and Joseph Morrow Letters
David Nichol Papers
96th Pennsylvania Volunteers Collection
W. Hazen Noyes Letters
William Patterson Letters
John F. Plimpton Letter

      William Presley Letters
      Charles Riley Letters
      Robert W. Rodgers Diary
      Theodore Sage Letters
      A. W. Simpson Diary
      Skelly Family Letters
      Oakley H. Smith Letters
      Gustavus Soule Letters
      Charles W. Spire Letters
      John Suter Papers
      Samuel Thoman Letters
      J. Frank Trezigulny Diary
      Emory Upton Papers
      John S. Walker Letters
      James A. Wiley Letters
      John S. Willey Letters
   Wendell Lang Jr. Collection
      Stephen H. Brockway Letter
   William Marvel Collection
      George E. Bates Letter
      Lewis Frederick Cleveland Letters
Vermont Historical Society, Barre
   Peter M. Abbott Letters
   Philip Arsino Letters
   Valentine G. Barney Papers
   Barton Family Letters
   David Bent Letters
   Boardman and Miles Family Papers
   James W. Bromley Papers
   Elijah S. Brown Letters
   Thomas H. Brown Letters
   Henry P. Burnham Letters
   Avery B. Cain Letters
   Calvert-Parker Letters
   Cheney-Watts Collection
   John F. Cook Letter
   Daniel F. Cooledge Diary
   Charles Cummings Papers
   Roswell Farnham Correspondence
   Wealthy Field Letters
   George Oscar French Letters
   Gale-Morse Family Letters
   Rollin M. Green Papers
   Edwin C. Hall Papers
   William Wirt Henry Family Papers
   William Hogan Letters

James Hope Papers
Alfred Horton Keith Letters
Levi P. Leland Letters
Dan Mason Letters
Lorenzo Miles Diary
Sylvanus Nye Papers
Jackson V. Parker Letters
William Scott Letter
William Farrar Smith Papers
Joseph Spafford Letters
Stephen Spaulding Letter
W. B. Spoor Letter
James F. Stoddard Letters
Merritt H. Stone Letters
Esther M. Thayer Correspondence
Dudley Tillison Letters
Ransom W. Towle Letters
John S. T. Wallace Letters
Daniel S. White Letters
William White Letters
Lyman Williams Papers
John Wilmot Letters
Virginia Polytechnic Institute and State University, Blacksburg
William Latham Candler Papers
Fred Lyman Letter
Western Reserve Historical Society, Cleveland, Ohio
Bassett Family Papers
Alexander Bunt Family Papers
George W. Hodges Letters
Daniel D. Hopper Papers
George W. Landrum Letters
Chauncey Mead Papers
Pinkerton Family Papers
John T. Shyrock Papers
Cyrus H. Stockwell Papers
Charles Albert Turner Papers
Alexander Varian Letters
Marion D. Ward Letters
E. G. Wood Papers
Yale University, New Haven, Conn.
Beineke Library
Brimblecom Family Papers
William Coates Letters
Edward T. Crosby Diary
John A. Hodgkins Diary
Abraham Lincoln Papers

Lambert A. Martin Diary and Letters
William J. Palmer Letters
Louisa Cook Walters Letters
Sterling Library
    Bradley Family Papers
    Harvey H. Bloom Papers
    Walter A. Chapman Papers
    Charles M. Coit Papers
    Winthrop-Weston Family Papers

Published Works

Abbott, Stephen G. *The First Regiment New Hampshire Volunteers in the Great Rebellion.* Keene, N.H.: Sentinel Printing Co., 1890.

Acken, J. Gregory, ed. *Inside the Army of the Potomac: The Civil War Experience of Captain Francis Adams Donaldson.* Mechanicsburg, Pa.: Stackpole Books, 1998.

Adams, Henry. *The Education of Henry Adams: An Autobiography.* 1918. Reprint, with an introduction by D. W. Brogan, Boston: Houghton Mifflin, 1961.

Alexander, Ted, ed. *The 126th Pennsylvania.* Shippensburg, Pa.: Beidel Printing, 1984.

Allen, Hervey. *Israfel: The Life and Times of Edgar Allan Poe.* New York: Farrar and Rinehart, 1934.

Anderson, Isabel, ed. *The Letters and Journals of General Nicholas Longworth Anderson: Harvard, Civil War, Washington, 1854–1892.* New York: Fleming H. Revell Co., [1942].

Atlas to Accompany the Official Records of the Union and Confederate Armies. Washington, D.C.: Government Printing Office, 1891–1895.

Ayling, Augustus D., comp. *Revised Register of the Soldiers and Sailors of New Hampshire in the War of the Rebellion, 1861–1866.* Concord, N.H.: Ira C. Evans, 1895.

"A Badger Boy in Blue: The Letters of Chauncey H. Cooke." *Wisconsin Magazine of History* 4, no. 1 (September, 1920), 75–100.

Balace, Francis. *Recrutements en Belgique Pour Les Troupes Fédérales, 1864–1865.* Brussels: Center for American Studies, 1970.

Barnes, Joseph K. *The Medical and Surgical History of the War of the Rebellion (1861–65).* 15 vols. 1870. Reprint, Wilmington, N.C.: Broadfoot Publishing, 1990.

Basler, Roy P., ed. *The Collected Works of Abraham Lincoln.* 8 vols. New Brunswick, N.J.: Rutgers University Press, 1953.

Beale, Howard K., ed. *The Diary of Edward Bates.* Washington, D.C.: Government Printing Office, 1933.

———, ed. *The Diary of Gideon Welles, Secretary of the Navy under Lincoln and Johnson.* 3 vols. New York: W. W. Norton and Company, 1960.

Becker, Carl M., and Ritchie Thomas, eds. *Hearth and Knapsack: The Ladley Letters, 1857–1880.* Athens: Ohio University Press, 1988.

Blackburn, George M., ed. *With the Wandering Regiment: The Diary of Captain Ralph Ely of the Eighth Michigan Infantry.* Mount Pleasant: Central Michigan University Press, 1965.

Blair, William Alan, ed. *A Politician Goes to War: The Civil War Letters of John White Geary.* University Park: Pennsylvania State University Press, 1995.

Blegen, Theodore C., ed. *The Civil War Letters of Colonel Hans Christian Heg.* Northfield, Minn.: Norwegian-American Historical Association, 1936.

Blight, David W., ed. *When This Cruel War Is Over: The Civil War Letters of Charles Harvey Brewster.* Amherst: University of Massachusetts Press, 1992.

Bloss, John M. "Antietam and the Lost Dispatch," *War Talks in Kansas.* Kansas City, Mo.: Military Order of the Loyal Legion of the United States, 1906.

Bohrnstedt, Jennifer Cain, ed. *While Father Is Away: The Civil War Letters of William H. Bradbury.* Lexington: University Press of Kentucky, 2003.

Bowen, Ralph H., ed. *A Frontier Family in Minnesota: Letters of Theodore and Sophie Bost, 1851-1920.* Minneapolis: University of Minnesota Press, 1981.

Britton, Anne Hartwell, and Thomas J. Reed, eds. *To My Beloved Wife and Children: The Letters and Diaries of Orderly Sergeant John F. L. Hartwell.* Madison, N.J.: Fairleigh Dickinson University Press, 1997.

Brun, Christian. "A Palace Guard View of Lincoln." *Soundings* 3, no. 1 (May, 1971), 19–39.

Burgess, Lauren Cook, ed. *An Uncommon Soldier: The Civil War Letters of Sarah Rosetta Wakeman, alias Private Lyons Wakeman, 153rd Regiment, New York State Volunteers.* Pasadena, Md.: Minerva Center, 1994.

Burlingame, Michael, ed. *At Lincoln's Side: John Hay's Civil War Correspondence and Selected Writings.* Carbondale: Southern Illinois University Press, 2000.

———, ed. *Dispatches from Lincoln's White House: The Anonymous Civil War Journalism of Presidential Secretary William O. Stoddard.* Lincoln: University of Nebraska Press, 2001.

———, ed. *With Lincoln in the White House: Letters, Memoranda, and Other Writings of John G. Nicolay, 1860-65.* Carbondale and Edwardsville: Southern Illinois University Press, 2000.

Burlingame, Michael, and John R. Turner Ettlinger, eds. *Inside Lincoln's White House: The Complete Civil War Diary of John Hay.* Carbondale: Southern Illinois University Press, 1997.

Butler, Benjamin F. *Private and Official Correspondence of General Benjamin F. Butler during the Period of the Civil War.* 5 vols. N.p.: privately published, 1917.

Carter, Christine Jacobson, ed. *The Diary of Dolly Lunt Burge, 1848-1879.* Athens: University of Georgia Press, 1997.

Catton, Bruce: *Grant Moves South.* Boston: Little, Brown & Co., 1960.

Chesnut, Mary Boykin. *A Diary from Dixie.* Boston: Houghton Mifflin, 1949.

Child, William. *Letters from a Civil War Surgeon: The Letters of Dr. William Child of the Fifth New Hampshire Volunteers.* Solon, Me.: Polar Bear & Co., 2001.

Coco, Gregory A., ed. *From Ball's Bluff to Gettysburg: The Civil War Letters of Private Roland E. Bowen, 15th Massachusetts Infantry, 1861-1864.* Gettysburg, Pa.: Thomas Publications, 1994.

——, ed. *Through Blood and Fire: The Civil War Letters of Major Charles J. Mills, 1862–1865.* Gettysburg, Pa.: Privately printed, 1982.

Colgrove, Silas. "The Finding of Lee's Lost Order." In *Battles and Leaders of the Civil War,* edited by Robert U. Johnson and Clarence C. Buel, vol. 2, 603. New York: Century, 1884–88.

Correspondence of John Sedgwick, Major-General. 2 vols. New York: C. and E. B. Stoeckel, 1902–1903.

Cox, Jacob D. *Military Reminiscences of the Civil War.* 2 vols. New York: Charles Scribner's Sons, 1900.

Croffut, W. A., ed. *Fifty Years in Camp and Field: Diary of Major-General Ethan Allen Hitchcock, U.S.A.* New York: Putnam's Sons, 1909.

Cutrer, Thomas W., ed. *Longstreet's Aide: The Civil War Letters of Major Thomas J. Goree.* Charlottesville: University of Virginia Press, 1995.

Cutrer, Thomas W., and T. Michael Parrish, eds. *Brothers in Gray: The Civil War Letters of the Pierson Family.* Baton Rouge: Louisiana State University Press, 1997.

Daly, Robert W., ed. *Aboard the USS Monitor, 1862: The Letters of Acting Paymaster William Frederick Keeler.* Annapolis, Md.: Naval Institute Press, 1964.

Dana, Charles A. *Recollections of the Civil War: With the Leaders at Washington and in the Field in the Sixties.* 1898. Reprint, with an introduction by Charles E. Rankin, Lincoln: University of Nebraska Press, 1996.

Daniel, Larry J. *Shiloh: The Battle That Changed the Civil War.* New York: Simon & Schuster, 1997.

Dargan, James F. *My Experience in Service; or, A Nine Months Man.* Los Angeles: California State University, 1974.

Davidson, James J., ed. *The Civil War Letters of the Late 1st Lieut. James J. Hartley, 122nd Ohio Infantry Regiment.* Jefferson, N.C.: McFarland & Co., [1998].

Davis, William C., and Meredith L. Swentor, eds. *Bluegrass Confederate: The Headquarters Diary of Edward O. Guerrant.* Baton Rouge: Louisiana University Press, 1999.

Diary of General S. M. Jackson for the Year 1862. [Apollo, Pa.: Privately published, 1925].

Dowdey, Clifford, and Louis H. Manarin, eds. *The Wartime Papers of R. E. Lee.* New York: Virginia Civil War Commission, 1961.

Duncan, Russell, ed. *Blue-Eyed Child of Fortune: The Civil War Letters of Colonel Robert Gould Shaw.* Athens: University of Georgia Press, 1992.

Dunlap, Leslie W., ed. *Your Affectionate Husband, J. F. Culver: Letters Written during the Civil War.* Iowa City: Friends of the University of Iowa Libraries, 1978.

Dyer, Frederick H. *A Compendium of the War of the Rebellion.* 1908. Reprint, with an introduction by Lee A. Wallace Jr., Dayton, Ohio: Morningside Press, 1978.

Eby, Cecil B. Jr., ed. *A Virginia Yankee in the Civil War: The Diaries of David Hunter Strother.* Chapel Hill: University of North Carolina Press, 1961.

Elder, Donald C. III, ed. *A Damned Iowa Greyhound: The Civil War Letters of William Henry Harrison Clayton.* Iowa City: University of Iowa Press, 1998.

Ellison, Mary. *Support for Secession: Lancashire and the American Civil War*. Chicago: University of Chicago Press, 1972.

Escott, Paul D., ed. *North Carolina Yeoman: The Diary of Basil Armstrong Thomasson, 1853–1862*. Athens: University of Georgia Press, 1996.

Executive Documents Printed by Order of the House of Representatives, during the Third Session of the Thirty-seventh Congress, 1862–63. 12 vols. Washington, D.C.: Government Printing Office, 1863.

Ford, William Chauncey, ed. *A Cycle of Adams Letters*. 2 vols. London: Constable, 1921.

Franklin, William B. *A Reply of Maj.-Gen. William B. Franklin to the Report of the Joint Committee of Congress of the Conduct of the War, Submitted to the Public on the 6th of April, 1863*. New York: D. Van Nostrand, 1863.

Frassanito, William A. *Antietam: The Photographic Legacy of America's Bloodiest Day*. New York: Charles Scribner's Sons, 1978.

Freeman, Douglas Southall, ed. *Lee's Dispatches: Unpublished Letters of General Robert E. Lee, C.S.A., to Jefferson Davis and the War Department of the Confederate States of America 1862–1865*. 1957. Reprint, with additional dispatches and foreword by Grady McWhiney, Baton Rouge: Louisiana State University Press, 1994.

———. *Lee's Lieutenants: A Study in Command*. 3 vols. New York: Charles Scribner's Sons, 1942–44.

French, Benjamin Brown. *Witness to the Young Republic: A Yankee's Journals, 1828–1870*. Hanover, N.H.: University Press of New England, 1989.

Gaff, Alan D. *Brave Men's Tears: The Iron Brigade at Brawner Farm*. Dayton, Ohio: Morningside, 1985.

Gallagher, Gary W., ed. *The Fredericksburg Campaign: Decision on the Rappahannock*. Chapel Hill: University of North Carolina Press, 1995.

Gavin, William Gilfillan, ed. *Infantryman Pettit: The Civil War Letters of Corporal Frederick Pettit*. New York: Avon Books, 1991.

Geary, James W. *We Need Men: The Union Draft in the Civil War*. DeKalb: Northern Illinois University Press, 1991.

Gilbert, Charles C. "On the Field of Perryville." In *Battles and Leaders of the Civil War*, edited by Robert U. Johnson and Clarence C. Buel, vol. 3, 52–59. New York: Century, 1884–88.

Grant, U. S. *Personal Memoirs of* ———. 2 vols. New York: Charles L. Webster, 1885.

Greene, A. Wilson. *Civil War Petersburg: Confederate City in the Crucible of War*. Charlottesville: University of Virginia Press, 2006.

———. *Whatever You Resolve to Be: Essays on Stonewall Jackson*. Baltimore, Md.: Butternut and Blue, 1992.

Guelzo, Allen C. *Lincoln's Emancipation Proclamation: The End of Slavery in America*. New York: Simon & Schuster, 2004.

Gurowski, Adam. *Diary, from March 4, 1861, to November 12, 1862*. Boston: Lee and Shepard, 1862.

———. *Diary, from November 18, 1862, to October 18, 1863*. New York: Carleton, 1864.

[Haines, Zenas T.]. *Letters from the Forty-fourth Regiment, M.V.M., A Record of the Experience of a Nine Months' Regiment in the Department of North Carolina in 1862-3, By "Corporal."* Boston: Herald Job Office, 1863.

Hammond, Harold Earl, ed. *Diary of a Union Lady, 1861-1865.* 1962. Reprint, with an introduction by Jean V. Berlin, Lincoln: University of Nebraska Press, 2000.

Hancock, Harold B., ed. "The Civil War Diaries of Anna M. Ferris." *Delaware History* 9, no. 3 (April, 1861), 221-64.

Harris, Robert F., and John Niflot, eds. *Dear Sister: The Civil War Letters of the Brothers Gould.* Westport, Conn.: Praeger, 1998.

Harwell, Richard Barksdale, ed. *Kate: The Journal of a Confederate Nurse.* 1959. Reprint, Baton Rouge: Louisiana State University Press, 1987.

Hassler, William W. *One of Lee's Best Men: The Civil War Letters of General William Dorsey Pender.* 1965. Reprint, with a foreword by Brian Wills, Chapel Hill: University of North Carolina Press, 1999.

Hastings, William H., ed. *Letters from a Sharpshooter: The Civil War Letters of Private William B. Greene, Co. G, 2nd United States Sharpshooters (Berdan's), Army of the Potomac, 1861-1865.* Belleville, Wis.: Historic Publications, 1993.

Haynes, Martin A. *A Minor War History Compiled from a Soldier Boy's Letters to "The Girl I Left Behind Me," 1861-1864.* Lakeport, N.H.: privately published, 1916.

Heitman, Francis B. *Historical Register and Dictionary of the United States Army, from its Organization, September 29, 1789, to March 2, 1903.* 2 vols. Washington, D.C.: Government Printing Office, 1903.

Hennessy, John. *The First Battle of Manassas: An End to Innocence.* Lynchburg, Va.: H. E. Howard, 1989.

Herr, Pamela, and Mary Lee Spence, eds. *The Letters of Jessie Benton Frémont.* Urbana and Chicago: University of Illinois Press, 1993.

Hess, Earl J. *The Union Soldier in Battle: Enduring the Ordeal of Combat.* Lawrence: University Press of Kansas, 1997.

Hesseltine, William B. *Lincoln and the War Governors.* New York: Alfred A. Knopf, 1948.

Higginson, Thomas Wentworth. *Massachusetts in the Army and Navy during the War of 1861-65.* 2 vols. Boston: Wright and Potter, 1895.

"Historickal Crotchets." *New York History* 82, no. 2 (spring, 2001), 183-86.

Hodge, Robert W., ed. *The Civil War Letters of Perry Mayo.* East Lansing: Michigan State University, 1967.

Holden, Walter, William E. Ross, and Elizabeth Slomba, eds. *Stand Firm and Fire Low: The Civil War Writings of Colonel Edward E. Cross.* Hanover, N.H.: University Press of New England, 2003.

Holliday, Joseph E. "Relief for Soldiers' Families in Ohio during the Civil War." *Ohio History* 71, no. 2 (July, 1962), 97-112.

Holmes, Oliver Wendell. "Doings of the Sunbeam." *Atlantic Monthly* 12, no. 69 (July, 1863), 1-15.

———. "My Hunt After 'The Captain.'" *Atlantic Monthly* 10, no. 62 (December, 1862), 738-64.

Horrocks, James. *My Dear Parents: The Civil War As Seen by an English Union Soldier.* New York: Harcourt Brace Jovanovich, 1982.

Houston, Alan Fraser, ed. *Keep Up Good Courage: A Yankee Family and the Civil War.* Portsmouth, N.H.: Peter Randall, 2006.

Howe, Henry Warren. *Passages from the Life of ——, Consisting of Diary and Letters Written during the Civil War, 1861–1865.* Lowell, Mass.: Courier-Citizen Co., 1899.

Howe, Mark De Wolfe, ed. *Touched with Fire: Civil War Letters and Diary of Oliver Wendell Holmes, Jr. 1861–1864.* New York: Da Capo Press, 1969.

Hughes, Nathaniel C., Jr. *The Battle of Belmont: Grant Strikes South.* Chapel Hill: University of North Carolina Press, 1991.

Hughes, William E., ed. *The Civil War Papers of Lt. Colonel Newton T. Colby, New York Infantry.* Jefferson, N.C.: McFarland & Co., 2003.

Hunt, Roger D., and Jack R. Brown. *Brevet Brigadier Generals in Blue.* Gaithersburg, Md.: Olde Soldier Books, 1990.

Jackson, Harry F., and Thomas F. O'Donnell, eds. *Back Home in Oneida: Hermon Clarke and His Letters.* Syracuse, N.Y.: Syracuse University Press, 1965.

Jones, Bruce E. "The Letters of Lauren Elmer Bent." Master's Thesis, Keene State College. 1976.

Jordan, William B., Jr., ed. *The Civil War Journals of John Mead Gould.* Baltimore, Md.: Butternut and Blue, 1997.

Josyph, Peter, ed. *The Wounded River: The Civil War Letters of John Vance Lauderdale, M.D.* East Lansing: Michigan State University Press, 1993.

Kaiser, Leo M., ed. "Civil War Letters of Charles W. Carr of the 21st Wisconsin Volunteers." *Wisconsin Magazine of History* 43, no. 4 (summer, 1960), 264–72.

Kent, Charles N. *History of the Seventeenth Regiment, New Hampshire Volunteer Infantry, 1862–1863.* Concord, N.H.: Veterans Association, 1898.

Klement, Frank L. *Dark Lanterns: Secret Political Societies, Conspiracies, and Treason Trials in the Civil War.* Baton Rouge: Louisiana State University Press, 1984.

——. *The Limits of Dissent: Clement L. Vallandigham and the Civil War.* Lexington: University of Kentucky Press, 1970.

——. *Wisconsin and the Civil War.* Madison: State Historical Society of Wisconsin, 1963.

Kohl, Lawrence Frederick, ed. *Irish Green and Union Blue: The Civil War Letters of Peter Welsh.* New York: Fordham University Press, 1986.

Krick, Robert K. *Stonewall Jackson at Cedar Mountain.* Chapel Hill: University of North Carolina Press, 1990.

Laas, Virginia Jean, ed. *Wartime Washington: The Civil War Letters of Elizabeth Blair Lee.* Urbana: University of Illinois Press, 1991.

Langsdorf, Edgar, ed. "The Letters of Joseph H. Trego, 1857–1864, Linn County Pioneer." *Kansas Historical Quarterly* 19, no. 3 (August, 1951), 287–309.

Larimer, Charles F., ed. *Love and Valor: The Intimate Civil War Letters between Captain Jacob and Emeline Ritner.* Western Springs, Ill.: Sigourney Press, 2000.

Lassen, Coralou Peel, ed. *Dear Sarah: Letters Home from a Soldier of the Iron Brigade.* Bloomington: Indiana University Press, 1999.

Ledman, Paul J. *A Maine Town Responds: Cape Elizabeth and South Portland in the Civil War.* Cape Elizabeth, Maine: Next Steps Publishing, [2003].

Letter of the Secretary of War, Transmitting Report on the Organization of the Army of the Potomac, and of Its Campaigns in Virginia and Maryland, Under the Command of George B. McClellan, from July 26, 1861, to November 7, 1862. Washington, D.C.: Government Printing Office, 1864.

Lomax, Elizabeth Lindsay. *Leaves from an Old Washington Diary.* [New York]: Books, Inc., 1943.

Longacre, Edward G., ed. *From Antietam to Fort Fisher: The Civil War Letters of Edward King Wightman, 1862–1865.* Rutherford, N.J.: Fairleigh Dickinson University Press, 1985.

Lonn, Ella. *Desertion during the Civil War,* 1928. Reprint, Gloucester, Mass.: Peter Smith, 1966.

Loving, Jerome M., ed. *Civil War Letters of George Washington Whitman.* Durham, N.C.: Duke University Press, 1975.

Lowry, Thomas P. *The Story the Soldiers Wouldn't Tell: Sex in the Civil War.* Mechanicsburg, Pa.: Stackpole Books, 1994.

McClure, A[lexander] K. *Abraham Lincoln and Men of War-Times.* 1892. Reprint, with an introduction by James A. Rawley. Lincoln: University of Nebraska Press, 1996.

McCutchan, Kenneth P., ed. *"Dearest Lizzie": The Civil War as Seen Through the Eyes of Lieutenant Colonel James Maynard Shankin.* Evansville, Ind.: Friends of Willard Library Press, 1988.

McPherson, James M. *For Cause and Comrades: Why Men Fought in the Civil War.* New York: Oxford University Press, 1997.

McWhiney, Grady, and Perry Jamieson. *Attack and Die: Civil War Military Tactics and the Southern Heritage.* Tuscaloosa: University of Alabama Press, 1982.

Mahon, Michael G., ed. *Winchester Divided: The Civil War Diaries of Julia Chase and Laura Lee.* Mechanicsburg, Pa.: Stackpole Books, 2002.

Mann, Albert W. *History of the Forty-Fifth Regiment Massachusetts Volunteer Militia.* Boston: privately published, 1908.

Marcotte, Frank B., ed. *Private Osborne: Massachusetts 23rd Volunteers.* Gretna, La.: Pelican Publishing, 2002.

Marshall, Jeffrey D., ed. *A War of the People: Vermont Civil War Letters.* Hanover, N.H.: University Press of New England, 1999.

Marszalek, John F. *Commander of All Lincoln's Armies: A Life of General Henry W. Halleck.* Cambridge, Mass.: Belknap Press, 2004.

Marvel, William. "A Thorn in the Flesh." *Civil War Times Illustrated* 41, no. 3 (June 2002), 42–49, 60–62.

———. "Back from the Gates of Hell: The Deadly Campaign of the Drafted Militia." *Historical New Hampshire* 44, no. 3 (fall, 1989), 105–19.

———. *Burnside.* Chapel Hill: University of North Carolina Press, 1991.

———. *Mr. Lincoln Goes to War.* Boston, Mass.: Houghton Mifflin, 2006.

———. "More Than Water under Burnside's Bridge." *America's Civil War* 18, no. 6 (January, 2006), 46–50, 52.

———. *Race of the Soil: The Ninth New Hampshire Regiment in the Civil War.* Wilmington, N.C.: Broadfoot Publishing, 1988.

Meade, George. *The Life and Letters of George Gordon Meade, Major-General United States Army.* 2 vols. New York: Charles Scribner's Sons, 1913.

Messent, Peter, and Steve Courtney, eds. *The Civil War Letters of Joseph Hopkins Twichell: A Chaplain's Story.* Athens: University of Georgia Press, 2006.

Miller, Richard C. F. "Brahmin Janissaries: John A. Andrew Mobilizes Massachusetts Upper Class for the Civil War." *New England Quarterly* 75, no. 2 (June, 2002), 204–34.

Mitchell, Reid. *Civil War Soldiers.* New York: Viking, 1988.

Moe, Richard. *The Last Full Measure: The Life and Death of the First Minnesota Volunteers.* New York: Avon Books, 1993.

Moore, Frank, ed. *The Rebellion Record, a Diary of Events with Documents, Narratives, Illustrative Incidents, Poetry, etc.* 12 vols., 1861–69. Reprint, New York: Arno Press, 1977.

Mushkat, Jerome, ed. *A Citizen-Soldier's Civil War: The Letters of Brevet Major General Alvin C. Voris.* DeKalb: Northern Illinois University Press, 2002.

Neely, Mark E., Jr. *The Fate of Liberty: Abraham Lincoln and Civil Liberties.* New York: Oxford University Press, 1991.

Nevins, Allan, and Milton Halsey Thomas, eds. *The Diary of George Templeton Strong.* 4 vols. New York: Macmillan Company, 1952.

Nevins, Allan, ed. *A Diary of Battle: The Personal Journals of Colonel Charles S. Wainwright, 1861–1865.* New York: Harcourt, Brace, & World, [1962].

———. *Frémont: Pathmarker of the West.* New York: D. Appleton-Century Company, 1939.

———. *The War for the Union.* 4 vols. New York: Charles Scribner's Sons, 1959–71.

Niven, John, ed. *The Salmon P. Chase Papers.* 5 vols. Kent, Ohio: Kent State University Press, 1993–98.

Noe, Kenneth W. *Perryville: This Grand Havoc of Battle.* Lexington: University Press of Kentucky, 2001.

Nordholt, J. W. Schulte. "The Civil War Letters of the Dutch Ambassador." *Journal of the Illinois State Historical Society* 54, no. 4 (winter, 1961), 341–73.

Norton, Oliver Willcox. *Army Letters, 1861–1865.* Chicago: Privately printed, 1903.

Norton, Sara, and M. A. DeWolfe Howe, eds. *Letters of Charles Eliot Norton.* 2 vols. Boston, Mass.: Houghton Mifflin Company, 1913.

Oeffinger, John C., ed. *A Soldier's General: The Civil War Letters of Major General Lafayette McLaws.* Chapel Hill: University of North Carolina Press, 2002.

Palladino, Grace. *Another Civil War: Labor, Capital, and the State in the Anthracite Regions of Pennsylvania, 1840–68.* Urbana: University of Illinois Press, 1990.

Palmer, Beverly Wilson, ed. *The Selected Letters of Charles Sumner.* 2 vols. Boston, Mass.: Northeastern University Press, 1990.

Pearce, T. H., ed. *Diary of Captain Henry A. Chambers.* Wendell, N.C.: Broadfoot's Bookmark, 1983.

Pease, Theodore Calvin, and James G. Randall, eds. *The Diary of Orville Hickman Browning*. 2 vols. Springfield: Illinois State Historical Library, 1925 and 1933.

Peck, Theodore, comp. *Revised Roster of Vermont Volunteers and List of Vermonters Who Served in the Army and Navy of the United States during the War of the Rebellion, 1861–66*. Montpelier, Vt.: Watchman Publishing, 1892.

Plumb, R. G., ed. "Letters of a Fifth Wisconsin Volunteer." *Wisconsin Magazine of History* 3, no. 1 (September, 1919), 52–83.

Pope, John. "The Second Battle of Bull Run." In *Battles and Leaders of the Civil War*, edited by Robert U. Johnson and Clarence C. Buel, vol. 2, 449–94. New York: Century Co., 1884–88.

Priest, John Michael, ed. *From New Bern to Fredericksburg: Captain James Wren's Diary*. Shippensburg, Pa.: White Mane, 1990.

Proceedings at the Mass Meeting of Loyal Citizens on Union Square, New-York, 15th Day of July, 1862, Under the Auspices of the Chamber of Commerce of the State of New-York, The Union Defence Committee of the State of New-York, the Common Council of the City of New-York, and Other Committees of Loyal Citizens. New York: George F. Nesbitt & Co., 1862.

"Proceedings of the First Confederate Congress: First Session Completed, Second Session in Part." *Southern Historical Society Papers* 45 (1925), 4–286.

Quaife, Milo M., ed. *From the Cannon's Mouth: The Civil War Letters of General Alpheus S. Williams*. Detroit, Mich.: Wayne State University Press, 1959.

Raab, Steven S., ed. *With the 3rd Wisconsin Badgers: The Living Experience of the Civil War through the Journals of Van R. Willard*. Mechanicsburg, Pa.: Stackpole Books, 1999.

Rable, George C. *The Confederate Republic: A Revolution against Politics*. Chapel Hill: University of North Carolina Press, 1994.

Ray, J[ean] P. *The Diary of a Dead Man*. [Conshohocken, Pa.]: Acorn Press, 1979.

Raymond, Henry W., ed. "Extracts from the Journal of Henry J. Raymond." *Scribner's Monthly* 19 (January, 1880), 419–24.

Reid-Green, Marcia, ed. *Letters Home: Henry Matrau of the Iron Brigade*. Lincoln: University of Nebraska Press, 1993.

Report of the Adjutant General of the State of Maine for the Years 1864 and 1865. Augusta, Maine: Stevens and Sayward, 1866.

Report of the Adjutant General of the State of New-Hampshire for the Year Ending June 1, 1866. 2 vols. Concord, N.H.: George E. Jenks, 1866.

Report of the Joint Committee on the Conduct of the War. 3 vols. Washington, D.C.: Government Printing Office, 1863.

Report of the Secretary of the Treasury on the State of the Finances, for the Year Ending June 30, 1863. Washington, D.C.: Government Printing Office, 1863.

Robertson, James I., Jr., ed. *The Civil War Letters of General Robert McAllister*. 1965. Reprint, Baton Rouge: Louisiana State University Press, 1998.

———. *Stonewall Jackson: The Man, the Soldier, the Legend*. New York: Macmillan Publishing, 1997.

Rosenblatt, Emil, and Ruth Rosenblatt, eds. *Hard Marching Every Day: The Civil*

War Letters of Private Wilbur Fisk, 1861–1865. Lawrence: University Press of Kansas, 1992.

Rundell, Walter, Jr., ed. "'Despotism of Traitors': The Rebellious South through New York Eyes." *New York History* 45, no. 4 (October, 1964), 331–67.

Sauers, Richard A., ed. *The Civil War Journal of Colonel William J. Bolton, 51st Pennsylvania: April 20, 1861–August 2, 1865.* Conshohocken, Pa.: Combined Publishing, 2000.

[Sawyer, Candace, comp.]. *Civil War Letters of Captain John Franklin Godfrey.* Portland, Maine: [Candace Sawyer], 1993.

Scarborough, William Kauffman, ed. *The Diary of Edmund Ruffin.* 3 vols. Baton Rouge: Louisiana State University Press, 1972–89.

Schiller, Herbert M., ed. *A Captain's War: The Letters and Diaries of William H. S. Burgwyn, 1861–1865.* Shippensburg, Pa.: White Mane, 1994.

Scott, Robert Garth, ed. *Fallen Leaves: The Civil War Letters of Major Henry Livermore Abbott.* Kent, Ohio: Kent State University Press, 1991.

———, ed. *Forgotten Valor: The Memoirs, Journals, and Civil War Letters of Orlando B. Willcox.* Kent, Ohio: Kent State University Press, 1999.

Sears, Stephen W. *Controversies and Commanders: Dispatches from the Army of the Potomac.* Boston: Houghton Mifflin, 1999.

———, ed. *For Country, Cause & Leader: The Civil War Journal of Charles B. Haydon.* New York: Ticknor and Fields, 1993.

———. *George B. McClellan: The Young Napoleon.* New York: Ticknor and Fields, 1988.

———. *Landscape Turned Red.* New York: Ticknor and Fields, 1983.

———, ed. *Mr. Dunn Browne's Experiences in the Army: The Civil War Letters of Samuel W. Fiske.* New York: Fordham University Press, 1998.

———, ed. *On Campaign with the Army of the Potomac: The Civil War Journal of Theodore Ayrault Dodge.* New York: Cooper Square Press, 2001.

———, ed. *The Civil War Papers of George B. McClellan.* New York: Ticknor and Fields, 1989.

———. *To the Gates of Richmond: The Peninsula Campaign.* New York: Ticknor and Fields, 1992.

Seaton, John. "The Battle of Belmont." In *War Talks in Kansas,* 1906. Reprint, Wilmington, N.C.: Broadfoot Publishing, 1992, 306–19.

Shannon, Fred Albert, ed. *The Civil War Letters of Sergeant Onley Andrus.* Urbana: University of Illinois Press, 1947.

———. *The Organization and Administration of the Union Army, 1861–1865.* 2 vols. 1928. Reprint, Gloucester, Mass.: Peter Smith, 1965.

Silber, Nina, and Mary Beth Sievens, eds. *Yankee Correspondence: Civil War Letters between New England Soldiers and the Home Front.* Charlottesville: University Press of Virginia, 1996.

Silliker, Ruth L., ed. *The Rebel Yell and the Yankee Hurrah: The Civil War Journal of a Maine Volunteer.* Camden, Maine: Down East Books, 1985.

Simpson, Brooks D., and Jean V. Berlin, eds. *Sherman's Civil War: Selected Correspondence of William T. Sherman, 1860–1865.* Chapel Hill: University of North Carolina Press, 1999.

Skipper, Marti, and Jane Taylor, eds. *A Handful of Providence: The Civil War Letters of Lt. Richard Goldthwaite, New York Volunteers, and Ellen Goldthwaite.* Jefferson, N.C.: McFarland & Co., 2004.

Smith, John David, and William Cooper Jr., eds. *A Union Woman in Civil War Kentucky: The Diary of Frances Peter.* Lexington: University Press of Kentucky, 2000.

Snyder, Charles M. "They Lay Where They Fell: The Everests, Father and Son." *Vermont History* 32, no. 3 (July, 1964), 154–62.

Sparks, David S., ed. *Inside Lincoln's Army: The Diary of Marsena Rudolph Patrick, Provost Marshal General, Army of the Potomac.* New York: Thomas Yoseloff, 1964.

Steiner, Lewis H. *Report of Lewis H. Steiner, M.D., Inspector of the Sanitary Commission, Containing a Diary Kept during the Rebel Occupation of Frederick, Md.* New York: Anson D. F. Randolph, 1862.

Stevens, William B. *History of the Fiftieth Regiment of Massachusetts Volunteer Militia in the Late War of the Rebellion.* Boston: Stillings Press, 1891.

[Strother, David Hunter]. "Personal Recollections of the War." *Harper's New Monthly Magazine* 36, no. 213 (February, 1868), 273–91.

Styple, William B., ed. *Letters from the Peninsula: The Civil War Letters of General Philip Kearny.* Kearny, N.J.: Belle Grove Publishing Co., 1988.

———, ed. *Our Noble Blood: The Civil War Letters of Régis de Trobriand, Major-General U.S.V.* Kearny, N.J.: Belle Grove Publishing Co., 1997.

Swinton, William. *Campaigns of the Army of the Potomac.* New York: Charles B. Richardson, 1866.

Taylor, F. Jay, ed. *Reluctant Rebel: The Secret Diary of Robert Patrick, 1861–1865.* 1959. Reprint, Baton Rouge: Louisiana State University Press, 1987.

Terrell, W. H. H. *Indiana in the War of the Rebellion: Report of the Adjutant General.* N.p.: Indiana Historical Society, 1960.

Thomas, Samuel N., Jr., and Jason H. Silverman, eds. *A Rising Star of Promise: The Civil War Odyssey of David Jackson Logan, 17th South Carolina Volunteers, 1861–1864.* Campbell, Calif.: Savas Publishing Co., 1998.

Throne, Mildred, ed. "An Iowa Doctor in Blue: The Letters of Seneca B. Thrall, 1862–1864." *Iowa Journal of History* 58, no. 2 (April, 1960), 97–188.

———, ed. "Civil War Letters of Abner Dunham, 12th Iowa Infantry." *Iowa Journal of History* 53, no. 4 (October, 1955), 303–40.

———, ed. *The Civil War Diary of Cyrus F. Boyd, Fifteenth Iowa Infantry, 1861–1863.* Millwood, N.Y.: Kraus Reprint Co., 1977.

Tilley, Nannie M., ed. *Federals on the Frontier: The Diary of Benjamin F. McIntyre, 1862–1864.* Austin: University of Texas Press, 1963.

Tower, R. Lockwood, ed. *Lee's Adjutant: The Wartime Letters of Colonel Walter Herron Taylor, 1862–1865.* Columbia: University of South Carolina Press, 1995.

Trout, Robert J., ed. *With Pen and Saber: The Letters and Diaries of J.E.B. Stuart's Staff Officers.* Mechanicsburg, Pa.: Stackpole Books, 1995.

"Trumbull Correspondence." *Mississippi Valley Historical Review* 1, no. 1 (June, 1914), 101–8.

Truxall, Aida Craig, ed. *Respects to All: Letters of Two Pennsylvania Boys in the War of the Rebellion*. Pittsburgh, Pa.: University of Pittsburgh Press, 1962.

U.S. Congress. *Congressional Globe*. 37th Congress.

U.S. Congress. House. *Loyalty of Clerks and Other Persons Employed by the Government*. 37th Cong., 2nd sess. H. Report 16.

Wallace, Lew. "The Capture of Fort Donelson." In *Battles and Leaders of the Civil War*, edited by Robert U. Johnson and Clarence C. Buel, vol. 1, 398–428. New York: Century Co., 1884–88.

War Letters of William Thompson Lusk, Captain, Assistant Adjutant General, United States Volunteers, 1861-1863. New York: privately printed, 1911.

War Letters, 1862-1865, of John Chipman Gray and John Codman Ropes. Cambridge: Massachusetts Historical Society, 1927.

War of the Rebellion: A Compilation of the Official Records of the Union and Confederate Armies. 128 vols. Washington, D.C.: Government Printing Office, 1880–1901.

Watkins, Sam R. *"Co. Aytch" Maury Grays First Tennessee Regiment; or, A Side Show of the Big Show*. 1882. Reprint, Wilmington, N.C.: Broadfoot Publishing Co., 1987.

Watson, Ronald, ed. *From Ashby to Andersonville: The Civil War Diary and Reminiscences of George A. Hitchcock, Private, Company A, 21st Massachusetts Regiment, August 1862-January 1865*. Campbell, Calif.: Savas Publishing, 1997.

Weld, Stephen M. *War Diary and Letters of Stephen Minot Weld, 1861-1865*. Boston: Massachusetts Historical Society, 1979.

Welker, David A., ed. *A Keystone Rebel: The Civil War Diary of Joseph Garey, Hudson's Battery, Mississippi Volunteers*. Gettysburg, Pa.: Thomas Publications, 1996.

White, Russell C., ed. *The Civil War Diary of Wyman S. White, First Sergeant of Company F, 2nd United States Sharpshooter Regiment, 1861-1865*. Baltimore, Md.: Butternut and Blue, 1993.

Wiggins, Sarah Woolfolk, ed. *The Journals of Josiah Gorgas, 1857-1878*. Tuscaloosa: University of Alabama Press, 1995.

Williams, Charles Richard, ed. *Diary and Letters of Rutherford Birchard Hayes, Nineteenth President of the United States*. 5 vols. Columbus: Ohio State Archaeological and Historical Society, 1914–26.

Williams, Frederick D. *The Wild Life of the Army: Civil War Letters of James A. Garfield*. East Lansing: Michigan State University Press, 1964.

Wolf, Hazel C., ed. "Campaigning with the First Minnesota: The Diary of Isaac Lyman Taylor." *Minnesota History* 25 (1944), 11–39, 117–52, 224–57, 342–61.

Woodworth, Steven E., ed. *The Musick of the Mocking Birds, the Roar of the Cannon: The Civil War Diary and Letters of William Winters*. Lincoln: University of Nebraska Press, 1998.

Wubben, Hubert H. *Civil War Iowa and the Copperhead Movement*. Ames: Iowa State University Press, 1980.

Younger, Edward, ed. *Inside the Confederate Government: The Diary of Robert Garlick Hill Kean*. Baton Rouge: Louisiana University Press, 1973.

Newspapers

Atlas and Argus, Albany, N.Y.

Baltimore American

Blackburn (Lancashire, Eng.) *Standard*

Boston Journal

Brooklyn (N.Y.) *Daily Eagle*

Buffalo (N.Y.) *Courier*

Bugle, Council Bluffs, Iowa

Burlington (Vt.) *Free Press*

Burlington (Iowa) *Hawk-Eye*

Chicago Times

Chicago Tribune

Cincinnati Daily Commercial

Cincinnati Gazette

Civilian and Telegraph, Cumberland, Md.

Cleveland (Ohio) *Plain Dealer*

Commercial Daily List, London

Constitution and Union, Fairfield, Iowa

Corning (N.Y.) *Journal*

Constitution and Farmers' and Mechanics' Advertiser, Woodbury, N.J.

Crisis, Columbus, Ohio

Daily American, Manchester, N.H.

Daily Chronicle, Portsmouth, N.H.

Daily Democrat, Louisville, Ky.

Daily Evening Courier, Madison, Ind.

Daily Gate City, Keokuk, Iowa

Daily Times, Leavenworth, Kans.

Dakotian, Yankton, Dakota Territory

Dayton (Ohio) *Empire*

Dayton (Ohio) *Journal*

Delaware Journal, Wilmington

Democratic Clarion, Bloomfield, Iowa

Detroit (Mich.) *Free Press*

Dubuque (Iowa) *Daily Times*

Dubuque (Iowa) *Herald*

Eastern Argus, Portland, Maine

Fairfield (Iowa) *Ledger*

Farmer's Cabinet, Amherst, N.H.

Fort Scott (Kans.) *Bulletin*

Frederick (Md.) *Herald*

Friend, Philadelphia

Friend's Intelligencer, Philadelphia

Harper's Weekly

Hartford (Conn.) *Courant*

Kansas Chief, White Cloud

Kansas State Journal, Lawrence

Leavenworth (Kans.) *Daily Conservative*
Luzerne (Pa.) *Union*
Milwaukee (Wis.) *Sentinel*
Missouri Republican, St. Louis
National Eagle, Claremont, N.H.
New Hampshire Argus and Spectator, Newport
New Hampshire Patriot, Concord
New York Herald
New York Times
New York Tribune
Northern Advocate, Claremont, N.H.
Ohio State Journal, Columbus
Ohio Statesman, Columbus
Peninsula News and Advertiser, Milford, Del.
Philadelphia Inquirer
Pittston (Pa.) *Gazette*
Portland (Maine) *Advertiser*
Portland (Maine) *Daily Press*
Portsmouth (N.H.) *Journal of Literature and Politics*
Prairie du Chien (Wis.) *Courier*
Richmond (Va.) *Examiner*
Richmond (Va.) *Whig*
State Register, Springfield, Ill.
Tri-Weekly Missouri Republican, St. Louis
Union-Democrat, Manchester, N.H.
Washington Star
Waterloo (Iowa) *Courier*
Weekly Perryville (Mo.) *Union*
Wood County (Ohio) *Independent*

Miscellaneous

Headstone inscriptions, Westlawn Cemetery, Goffstown, N.H.
Headstone Inscriptions, Green Grove Cemetery, Ashland, N.H.

Sources and Acknowledgments

In accordance with my increasingly obsessive habit, the information and interpretations in this book are drawn almost entirely from contemporary, primary documents, excluding most ex post facto recollections. Many historians still put great faith in memoirs, or accept hearsay testimony of a certain vintage, but it seems improbable that such sources could yield an accurate reflection of the spirit of any vanished age. Even the published papers of participants may suffer the distortion of revision by an author whose opinions have inevitably changed: diaries or letters that were "transcribed" for publication by veterans or their loved ones are often no more trustworthy than reminiscences. The careful scholar will rely primarily on original papers or on published versions prepared by conscientious editors who had no stake in public reaction to the content. The problems of bias and motivation mar those contemporary observations, as well, but they are often easier to recognize than clandestine or unconscious distortions resulting from personal or political changes of heart.

For those who prefer not to spend their time in the somber vaults that house the original letters of people who lived during the Civil War, there are numerous published collections of letters that offer accurate overviews of those primary sources. Perhaps foremost among such anthologies is Jeffrey Marshall's *A War of the People: Vermont Civil War Letters,* in which judicious selection and diligent editing provide a clear picture of the broad range of contemporary observation and opinion. Nina Silber and Mary Beth Sievens, editors of *Yankee Correspondence: Civil War Letters between New England Soldiers and the Home Front,* arrange manuscripts from across the region to illustrate common perspectives on social, military, and political aspects of the war; their misreading of handwritten dates occasionally leads to anachronistic interpretations, but their collection yields salient social factors that have escaped many historians.

In pursuing this project I have incurred debts to a legion of curators and research assistants. These include Sarah Hartwell of Dartmouth's Rauner Library; Bill Copeley and David Smolen of the New Hampshire Historical Society; Nick Noyes, Bill Barry, and Jamie Kingman Rice of the Maine Historical Society; Paul Carnahan and Marjorie Strong of the Vermont Historical Society; Jeff Marshall and Prudence Doherty of the University of Vermont; Jane Albers of the Henry Sheldon Museum in Middlebury, Vermont; Bill Ross of the University of New Hampshire; Eric Frazier of the Boston Public Library's Special Collections Department; Phil Weimerskirch of the Providence Public Library; Karen Eberhart at the Rhode Island Historical Society; Kathryn James at Yale's Beineke Library and Cynthia Ostroff at the Sterling Library, also at Yale; Mary Huth at the University of Rochester; Dick Sommers, David Keough, and Art Bergeron of the U.S. Army Military History Institute; John Haas of the Ohio Historical Society; Thomas Hamm at Earlham College; George Rugg at Notre Dame; and Lin Fredericksen of the Kansas State Historical Society.

An assortment of knowledgeable and accommodating staff members, most of whom I know only by sight or by first name, assisted me at the Massachusetts Historical Society, Dickinson College, the Cumberland County Historical Society of Carlisle, Pennsylvania, Cleveland's Western Reserve Historical Society, the Cincinnati Historical Society, the Indiana Historical Society, the Indiana State Library, the Clements Library at the University of Michigan, the State Historical Society of Wisconsin, the State Historical Society of Iowa (at both Iowa City and Des Moines), the University of Iowa (Special Collections and the Iowa Women's Archives), the Library of Congress, the Virginia Historical Society, the Southern Historical Collection at the University of North Carolina, and Duke University.

Others came cordially to my rescue by mail, or by modern equivalents thereof, when circumstances prevented me from coming to them. Among those were Irene Axelrod of the Peabody Essex Museum, James Campbell of the New Haven Colony Historical Society, Melissa Gottwald and Tanya Zanish-Belcher of Iowa State University, and Steve Nielsen at the Minnesota Historical Society.

I am extremely grateful to both Jeff Wieand of Concord, Massachusetts, and Will Greene of Petersburg, Virginia. Each read different drafts of the manuscript, pointing out technical errors, stylistic lapses, and instances of lopsided presentation. In forwarding a new viewpoint an author must decide how much of the conventional wisdom to reiterate before launching into the differing interpretation, and these two well-informed readers helped immensely in the search for that balance.

Several colleagues habitually supply me with tips and share generously of their own discoveries, with Stephen Sears and George Rable most prominent among the number. Mike Pride alerted me to an intriguing and pertinent civilian diary that had not yet found its way into a manuscript repository, while George Cleveland allowed me the use of his great-uncle's wartime letters. Rob Menuet invited me to his Virginia home to peruse the private correspondence of his own ancestor, Barton Mitchell, who found Robert E. Lee's lost order in a Maryland meadow.

As usual, the historian's family carries a heavy share of the burden involved in producing a book. Excepting only a cat named Allegheny Johnson, all denizens of this house have graciously acceded to persistent appeals for silence and solitude in which I might try to assemble a cumbersome mass of research material. This is particularly true of Ellen Schwindt, whose musical compositions require — and sometimes compete for — that same silence and solitude.

Index

Numbers in italics refer to illustrations and maps.